A HISTORY OF WESTERN AMERICAN LITERATURE

EDITED BY

SUSAN KOLLIN

Montana State University

CAMBRIDGE
UNIVERSITY PRESS

CAMBRIDGE
UNIVERSITY PRESS

32 Avenue of the Americas, New York, NY 10013-2473, USA

Cambridge University Press is part of the University of Cambridge.

It furthers the University's mission by disseminating knowledge in the pursuit of education, learning, and research at the highest international levels of excellence.

www.cambridge.org
Information on this title: www.cambridge.org/9781107083851

First published 2015

Printed in the United States of America by Sheridan Books, Inc.

A catalog record for this publication is available from the British Library.

Library of Congress Cataloging in Publication Data
A history of western American literature / edited by Susan Kollin, Montana State University.
pages   cm
Includes bibliographical references and index.
ISBN 978-1-107-08385-1 (hardback)
1. American literature – West (U.S.) – History and criticism.
2. West (U.S.) – In literature.   I. Kollin, Susan, editor.
PS271.H57   2015
810.9'3278–dc23   2015016876

ISBN 978-1-107-08385-1 Hardback

Contents

Notes on Contributors　　　　　　　　　　　　　　　　　*page* ix
Acknowledgments　　　　　　　　　　　　　　　　　　　　xv

Introduction: Historicizing the American Literary West　　　1
Susan Kollin

PART I　HOMELANDS

1　Indigenous Memories and Western American
　　Literary History　　　　　　　　　　　　　　　　　15
　　Susan Bernardin

2　The Recovery Project and the Role of History in
　　Chicano/a Literary Studies　　　　　　　　　　　　31
　　José F. Aranda Jr.

PART II　MAKING A REGION

3　Domestic Frontiers: Settler Narratives by European
　　American Women Writers　　　　　　　　　　　　　49
　　Nicole Tonkovich

4　Labor and the Land: Narratives of Trading, Mining,
　　and Ranching　　　　　　　　　　　　　　　　　　65
　　Nathaniel Lewis

5　Nature Writing and the American West　　　　　　　82
　　Sarah Jaquette Ray

6　Tall Tales and Short Stories　　　　　　　　　　　　98
　　Nicolas S. Witschi

7 The Popular Western   111
  Daniel Worden

PART III   GEOGRAPHIES OF THE LITERARY WEST

 8 Literature of the Great Plains: Nature, Culture,
   and Community   129
   Susan Naramore Maher

 9 Southwest Literary Borderlands   145
   Audrey Goodman

10 Imagining the Rocky Mountain Region   162
   Nancy S. Cook

11 Writing the Pacific Northwest   177
   Stephanie LeMenager

12 The Far North: Literatures of Alaska and Canada   192
   Ernestine Hayes

13 The Problem of the Critical in Global Wests   205
   Krista Comer

PART IV   THE TWENTIETH CENTURY AND BEYOND:
LITERARY MOVEMENTS AND CRITICAL PERSPECTIVES

14 Early Cinematic Westerns   225
   Christine Bold

15 The Environmental Novel of the American West   242
   Dana Phillips

16 Hard-Boiled Fiction and Noir Narratives   256
   Lee Clark Mitchell

17 The Beats and the American West   270
   Robert Bennett

18 Contested Wests: Indigenous Americans and the
   Literature of Sovereignty   282
   John Gamber

19 Asian American Writers and the Making of
   the Western U.S. Landscape   298
   Jane Hseu

20 African American Literature: Recasting Region through Race   314
    Jonathan Munby

21 Hollywood Westerns: 1930s to the Present   331
    Andrew Patrick Nelson

22 Urban New Wests   345
    Stephen Tatum

23 Queer Frontiers: Gender and Sexuality in the American West   362
    David Agruss

24 Postwestern Literature and Criticism   374
    Neil Campbell

Selected Bibliography   389
Index   397

Notes on Contributors

DAVID AGRUSS is lecturer in Barrett, the Honors College, at Arizona State University. He was trained in comparative literature – with a focus on British, French, and Russian literatures – and works primarily on nineteenth-century British literature and culture, and occasionally on twentieth- and twenty-first-century popular American literature and culture. His research focuses on nineteenth-century British gender, sexuality, colonialism, empire, science studies, and popular culture. He has published articles on Victorian vivisection and South Seas adventure fiction and is completing a book on boys' public school fiction, colonial adventure fiction, and island-stranding fiction.

JOSÉ F. ARANDA Jr. is an Associate Professor of Chicano/a and American Literature. He is the author of *When We Arrive: A New Literary History of Mexican America*. He has also written articles on early U.S. criticism, nineteenth-century Mexican American literature, and the future of Chicano/a Studies. Most recently, he has undertaken an investigation of the relationship between modernity and Mexican American writings, entitled *The Places of Modernity in Early Mexican American Literature, 1848–1960*.

ROBERT BENNETT is Associate Professor of English at Montana State University and coeditor with Christopher Schaberg of *Deconstructing Brad Pitt*. His analysis of the suburban American West, "Tract Homes on the Range," appeared recently in *Western American Literature*, and he is currently writing a cultural history of lithium.

SUSAN BERNARDIN is Professor of English and Chair of Women's and Gender Studies at SUNY Oneonta. A coauthor of *Trading Gazes: Euro-American Photographers and Native North Americans, 1880–1940*, she also facilitated a new edition of *In the Land of the Grasshopper Song* in collaboration with Terry Supahan and André

Cramblit. She has published articles on foundational and contemporary Native writers, including Gertrude Bonnin, Mourning Dove, Sherman Alexie, Eric Gansworth, Gerald Vizenor, and Louis Owens. She served as Guest Editor of the 2014 special issue of *Western American Literature*, entitled *Indigenous Wests: Literary and Visual Aesthetics*. She is a two-time recipient of Western Literature Association's Don D. Walker Award for best published essay in Western American Literary Studies.

CHRISTINE BOLD is Professor of English at the University of Guelph. She is author and editor of six books and many essays on popular culture, cultural memory, and the New Deal. *Choice* named her most recent book, *The Frontier Club: Popular Westerns and Cultural Power, 1880–1924*, an "Outstanding Academic Title" of 2013; it also won the 2014 Thomas J. Lyon Book Award and the 2014 Robert K. Martin Book Prize.

NEIL CAMPBELL is Professor of American Studies at the University of Derby, United Kingdom. He has published widely in American Studies. His major research project is an interdisciplinary trilogy of books on the contemporary American West: *The Cultures of the American New West*, *The Rhizomatic West*, and *Post-Westerns*. He edits the book series Place, Memory, Affect with Rowman Littlefield International and is currently working on a new book, *Affective Critical Regionality*.

KRISTA COMER is Associate Professor of English at Rice University and Associate Director of Rice's Center for the Study of Women, Gender, and Sexuality. Her work has long been concerned with placing questions of feminism as liberation philosophy at the center of U.S. Western literary and cultural theory. She is author of *Landscapes of the New West: Gender and Geography in Contemporary Women's Writing* and *Surfer Girls in the New World Order*, as well as many essays. Her current work, *The Feminist States of Critical Regionalism*, considers storytelling in the present through sources in contemporary literature, film, and feminist theory as well as in the public humanities. In 2003, she served as President of the Western Literature Association.

NANCY S. COOK is Professor of English at the University of Montana, Missoula, where she teaches courses in western American studies, literature and environment, and American culture. She has published articles on U.S. ranching cultures, water policy, Montana writers, social class, and place. Her work has appeared in books and journals in the United States, the United Kingdom, and Spain. She is past President of the Western Literature Association. When not teaching, she manages a ranch near Clyde Park, Montana.

JOHN GAMBER is Assistant Professor in the Department of English and Comparative Literature and the Center for the Study of Ethnicity and Race at Columbia University. His book *Positive Pollutions and Cultural Toxins* examines the role of waste and contamination in contemporary U.S. literature by authors of color. He has numerous publications on Native American literature by authors such as Sherman Alexie, Louise Erdrich, Gerald Vizenor, Craig Womack, and Stephen Graham Jones, among others, in edited collections and journals including *PMLA* and *MELUS*. His current project examines alternative constructions of Native American nationhood in literature.

AUDREY GOODMAN is Professor of English at Georgia State University. She is the author of *Translating Southwestern Landscapes* and *Lost Homelands: Ruin and Reconstruction in the Twentieth-Century Southwest* as well as a contributor to *Postwestern Cultures: Literature, Theory, Space* and the *Blackwell Companion to the Literature and Culture of the American West*.

ERNESTINE HAYES (Tlingit) is Assistant Professor at University of Alaska Southeast. Her first book, *Blonde Indian: An Alaska Native Memoir*, received the American Book Award and was a finalist for the PEN Nonfiction Award. Her essays, short stories, and poetry have been published in *Studies in American Indian Literature*, *Huffington Post*, *Alaska Quarterly Review*, *Tipton Review*, *Poetry in Place*, and other forums. She makes her home in Juneau.

JANE HSEU is Assistant Professor of English at Dominican University in River Forest, Illinois. She specializes in Asian American and Latino/a literature and the politics of language. Her essay "Teaching Race and Space through Asian American and Latino Performance Poetry: I Was Born with Two Tongues' *Broken Speak* and Sonido Ink(quieto)'s *Chicano, Illnoize*" appeared in *Asian American Literature: Discourses and Pedagogies*. She is currently working on a project on Asian Americans and mental illness.

SUSAN KOLLIN is Professor of English at Montana State University, where she was also named a College of Letters and Science Distinguished Professor for 2011–14. Her recent publications have addressed the Western in fiction and film, environmental humanities, and transnational American literature. Her essays have appeared in *American Literary History, Contemporary Literature, Modern Fiction Studies,* and *Studies in American Fiction.* She is the editor of *Postwestern Cultures: Literature, Theory, Space* and author of *Nature's State: Imagining Alaska as the Last Frontier* and *Captivating Westerns: The Middle East in the American West.*

STEPHANIE LEMENAGER is Barbara and Carlisle Moore Professor of English and Environmental Studies at the University of Oregon. She is author of *Living Oil: Petroleum Culture in the American Century, Manifest and Other Destinies,* and coeditor of *Environmental Criticism for the Twenty-First Century* as well as the forthcoming *Teaching Climate Change in the Humanities.* She is a founding Editor of *Resilience: A Journal of the Environmental Humanities.*

NATHANIEL LEWIS teaches English and directs the Environmental Studies Program at St. Michael's College in Vermont. In addition to numerous articles on American literature, he is the author of *Unsettling the Literary West* and coeditor (with William Handley) of *True West: Authenticity and the American West.*

SUSAN NARAMORE MAHER has published widely on the literature of the American and Canadian West and is author of *Deep Map Country: Literary Cartography of the Great Plains.* A past President of the Western Literature Association and the Willa Cather Foundation, she is currently Dean of the College of Liberal Arts at the University of Minnesota Duluth.

LEE CLARK MITCHELL teaches American literature and film at Princeton University, where he is Holmes Professor of Belles-Lettres. His recent essays have focused on Cormac McCarthy, the Coen Brothers, Henry James, and noir fiction. His books include *Witnesses to a Vanishing America: The Nineteenth-Century Response, Determined Fictions: American Literary Naturalism, The Photograph and the American Indian,* and *Westerns: Making the Man in Fiction and Film.* Currently, he is completing a study of close reading in modernist American novels.

JONATHAN MUNBY is Senior Lecturer (Associate Professor) in the Lancaster Institute for the Contemporary Arts (LICA), Lancaster University, United Kingdom, and Alumnus Fellow of the W. E. B. Du Bois Institute at the Hutchins Center for African and African American Research, Harvard University. He has published widely on African

American literature, film, and music. His most recent book is *Under a Bad Sign: Criminal Self-Representation in African American Popular Culture.*

ANDREW PATRICK NELSON is Assistant Professor of Film History and Critical Studies at Montana State University. He is author of *Still in the Saddle: The Hollywood Western, 1969–1980*, editor of *Contemporary Westerns: Film and Television since 1990*, and coeditor of *ReFocus: The Films of Delmer Daves.*

DANA PHILLIPS is an Associate Professor of English at Towson University in Maryland and a Senior Research Associate at Rhodes University in Grahamstown, South Africa. He is the author of *The Truth of Ecology: Nature, Culture, and Literature in America.* Currently, his work focuses on material ecocriticism, the environmental humanities, environmental novels, and narratives of collapse and climate change.

SARAH JAQUETTE RAY is Assistant Professor of Environmental Studies at Humboldt State University in Arcata, California, where she also leads the Environmental Studies Program. Her first book, *The Ecological Other: Environmental Exclusion in American Culture,* focuses on how dominant environmental discourses distinguish between people who are ecologically good and ecologically "other," through discourses of the body and disgust. She is working on several edited volumes: *Critical Norths: Space, Nature, Theory*; *Disability Studies and the Environmental Humanities: An Anthology*; and *Latin@ Environmentalisms: Literary Theories and Cultural Histories.*

STEPHEN TATUM is Professor of English at the University of Utah. He is the author of *In the Remington Moment* and coeditor (with Melody Graulich) of *Reading The Virginian in the New West.* Among his recent article publications is (with Nathaniel Lewis) "Tumbling Dice: The Problem of Las Vegas" in *A Companion to the Literature and Culture of the American West.* He is also a past President of the Western Literature Association.

NICOLE TONKOVICH is Professor of Literature at University of California, San Diego. Her research focuses on nineteenth-century women's literature and culture. Her most recent projects include *The Allotment Plot: Alice C. Fletcher, E. Jane Gay, and Nez Perce Survivance* and an edition of an antipolygamy novel, *Elder Northfield's Home.* She is former Editor of *Legacy: A Journal of American Women Writers.*

NICOLAS S. WITSCHI is Professor of English at Western Michigan University. He is the author of *Traces of Gold: California's Natural Resources and the Claim to Realism in Western American Literature*; of a Western Writers Series monograph, *Alonzo "Old Block" Delano;* and of articles and essays on Mary Austin, John Muir, Sinclair Lewis, Henry James, Raymond Chandler, and Mary Hallock Foote. A past Co-president of the Western Literature Association, he is also the editor of *A Companion to the Literature and Culture of the American West* and the coeditor with Melody Graulich of *Dirty Words in Deadwood: Literature and the Postwestern.*

DANIEL WORDEN is Associate Professor in the Department of English at the University of New Mexico. He is author of *Masculine Style: The American West and Literary Modernism,* which received the Thomas J. Lyon Book Award in Western American Literary and Cultural Studies. He is also the editor of *The Comics of Joe Sacco: Journalism in a Visual World* and the coeditor of *Oil Culture.*

Acknowledgments

The task of editing a volume on the literary history of the American West is a major undertaking that involves many people. I wish to thank the contributors for their time, hard work, and insightful suggestions in making this collection possible. I also would like to thank Ray Ryan for inviting me to edit this volume and Caitlin Gallagher, Vincent Rajan, and Susan Thornton for guiding me through the production process at Cambridge University Press.

Thanks to Montana State University's Office of the Vice President for Research and Economic Development for granting me a Scholarship and Creativity Award as well as the American Studies Program at MSU for providing me with a graduate research assistant in spring 2015. For her work in proofreading and formatting many of the essays in this collection, I thank Tonya Robinson. I also wish to thank Dan Flory, David Agruss, and Robert Bennett for reading sections of the volume at various stages of its development; Susan Bernardin, Nancy Cook, Audrey Goodman, and Stephen Tatum for their suggestions and feedback on my ideas for this volume; as well as Alexandra Flory and Michaela Kollin for their ongoing support of my work. Finally, Christine Bold thanks the Social Sciences and Humanities Research Council of Canada for funding, Rachel Hunt for research assistance, and Monique Mojica (Guna and Rappahannock) and Michelle St. John (Wampanoag) for serving as Research Consultants.

Introduction
Historicizing the American Literary West
Susan Kollin

The project of historicizing the American literary West and the production of regions themselves has been enormously and productively complicated by recent scholarly developments. With diaspora studies, borderlands scholarship, comparative Indigenous approaches, Pacific Rim studies, transnational feminisms, settler colonial theory, and critical regionalism opening up important new archives, literary historians are developing more complex methods and nuanced accounts of the American West.[1] Likewise, as cultural and literary production associated with the West circulates transnationally and unevenly under the pressures of globalization, many of these regional texts accrue new audiences as well as diverse and often contested meanings. In her memoirs *Funny in Farsi* and *Laughing without an Accent,* for instance, Firoozeh Dumas takes on the genre of the popular western, noting changes in its reception across literary history and geographical contexts in ways that highlight the challenges facing regional studies. Describing her coming of age in California in the late 1970s and 1980s as the child of Iranian immigrants, the author often focuses on her father's life in recounting her experiences of cultural dislocation, regional identity, and the struggle for national belonging. At one point, Dumas recalls his childhood in Iran, noting how much her father loved watching movies. "Had it been up to him, he would have happily spent his entire childhood in front of the big screen, dreaming his life away," she writes.[2] "His favorites were the American westerns, where the good guys always won."[3]

Looking back on her California childhood, the author mostly remembers the kindness she received from her neighbors, but at one point tells of drastic changes that occurred after the Iranian Revolution. "It all started in 1979," Dumas writes. "It seemed like on Monday, everyone was asking us if our carpets really do fly. Then on Friday, those same people were putting 'I Play Cowboys and Iranians' bumper stickers on their cars."[4] While her father may have aligned himself with the good guys featured in the westerns he enjoyed in Iran, the subject position he claimed for himself would be challenged by responses to international events unfolding in the late 1970s. U.S. orientalist discourse, which often portrayed Iranians as intriguing exotic Others hailing from the land of Persia, dramatically shifted in the wake of the Iranian Revolution and the American hostage crisis. Her father's beloved westerns were now deployed against him in the United States, their meanings reconceptualized as he and other Americans of the Iranian diaspora found themselves placed on the side of savagery, as the enemy to be defeated by the Anglo cowboy who introduces progress, freedom, and civilization to the global frontier.

The project of casting groups perceived to be national threats into the predetermined role of "bad guys" has served as an ongoing ritual shaping and informing settler colonial understandings of the American West. Jodi A. Byrd notes, for instance, how the Indian as "the original enemy combatant" has often served an important role in popular and political discourse where it circulates globally as the primary means by which the United States defines groups perceived as dangerous to American interests and national security.[5] In her study *The Transit of Empire: Indigenous Critiques of Colonialism*, Byrd addresses the practice in broader terms, tracing how the figure of the Indian and the idea of Indianness are often the foundation upon which "the U.S. empire orients and replicates itself by transforming those to be colonized into 'Indians' through continual reiterations of pioneer logics, whether in the Pacific, the Caribbean, or the Middle East."[6] The act of depicting enemies as Indians provides a justification for U.S. power and creates the "conditions of possibility" for a seemingly exceptional America simultaneously to enact and to mask its imperial designs.[7]

These accounts of the contested meanings of the western and westernness as well as of Indians and Indianness open up important lines of inquiry for the project of writing a literary history of the American West and for understanding the emergence of regions themselves. Building on insights articulated by Dumas and Byrd, scholars may recognize how ideas often associated with the popular western and western American literature in general – including stories about heroes and villains, frontier violence and land claims, as well as battles between savagery and civilization – are rarely bound by or restricted to local issues or national concerns. It is interesting to note, for instance, that even during an era when the popularity of the genre ebbs and flows, the western has come to serve a critical function in U.S. discourses that circulate inside and outside the country. The deployment of the western after 9/11, for instance, drew renewed attention to the global dimensions of regional culture and how the iconography and rhetoric of the West have often been used to speak to developments beyond regional and national boundaries.[8] Scholars of the American West have increasingly engaged transnational and comparative frameworks in their literary histories, foregrounding how cultural production carries significance across diverse spaces. David Rio develops this line of thinking, noting the manner in which western American literature has never been a "literature of regional interest only" while foregrounding the crucial "theoretical and practical aspects of interpreting the literature as part of a global phenomenon."[9] As he explains, "the international dimension of the West is not only related to the traditional power of western mythology to engage the imagination of non-American audiences, but also to the sheer origins of the West as an international borderland."[10]

Just as Iranians and Iranian Americans saw the western deployed against them as a morality tale that placed them in the role of the enemy, so Arabs and Arab Americans have experienced a similar shifting history and set of concerns in their position as the new national threat after 9/11. The Jordanian American author Laila Halaby takes on this history in her novel *Once in a Promised Land* (2007). Reexamining notions of the West as an exceptional space in an exceptionalist nation, her story centers on the experiences of an Arab couple living in Arizona and the terror they face in being considered national security threats after 9/11. The characters are familiar with the western and how it has been used to define and restrict various populations in and outside the United States. At first the husband, Jassim, jokes about being placed under surveillance by a vigilant security guard who mistakes western movies for reality and who now "thinks she's Clint Eastwood."[11] Once pulled toward an America that promised "Disneyland and hamburgers, Hollywood and the Marlboro Man," the couple becomes increasingly unsettled, their new status summed up quite well by a sticker on a teenager's skateboard that reads "Terrorist Hunting License."[12] As a real estate agent who sells others access to the American Dream, the wife, Salwa, no longer finds herself at home in the West, shut out of the "promised land" as the U.S. war on terror leads to their increased sense of dislocation and alienation.

Randa Jarrar, who grew up in Kuwait and then moved to the United States after the first Gulf War, takes up similar ideas in her novel of the American West, *A Map of Home* (2008). When her father is relocated to Texas, the main character, Nidali, confesses her fears about the region and its inhabitants, anxieties that may be traced historically to global circulations of the western in U.S. political discourse across places such as the

Middle East. At one point, she expresses concerns for her father's safety, how she is "afraid of Texas, afraid of the cowboys that would lasso him away from us," while at another point, her father wonders whether he should buy "some cattle," a "gun," and a "cowboy hat" in order to fit in to his new home better.[13] After settling in Texas, Nidali also notes uncanny similarities between the Middle East and the American West. While cowboys inspire fear, the landscape appears familiar to her. Upon her arrival at the family's home in Texas, she considers the "short dirt" road to her new house as akin to "desert" streets in the Middle East; these roads are "cut out of rock, like in Palestine."[14] Arriving in the United States, she is surprised that no one asks about weapons of mass destruction and that she is able to avoid undergoing a full body search at the airport. On the other hand, the savagery/civilization binary underpinning the western starts to take on new meanings for her. The character notes that many streets in Texas are lined with "cans of Lone Star," which she discovers is not "the soda they drink here," even though "some people could drink it like water."[15] She is also disappointed by the apparent barbarity of Americans, especially in terms of bodily hygiene. "There was no bidet. This came as a shock," she says. "How did Americans wipe their asses?"[16]

Perhaps it is no surprise that at a time when U.S. borders constitute sites of deep anxiety and are being shored up in the name of national security, writers in the West as well as scholars of the region are increasingly addressing broader geographical frameworks and a more diverse set of archives. This move entails connecting stories of the American West to global contexts, extending postcolonial criticism to literary histories of the region, placing previously marginalized groups at the center of this work, and questioning what counts as the beginnings and the ends of regions themselves. In his recent book *How to Read the American West: A Field Guide*, William Wyckoff addresses many of these issues, reminding us of the ways geographers have long argued that landscapes are never merely local; rather, "every place is connected to and defined by other places." He takes care to examine how western American landscapes are always linked "to the world beyond" and thus require the use of greater scales of assessment and frames of study.[17] Hsuan Hsu likewise notes the ways regions themselves are called into being through larger geopolitical pressures and concerns taking place in other spaces or across national and global contexts. In this way, regions carry certain obligations. As Hsu explains, the region is frequently meant to embody "familiarity, loyalty, and authentic experience," while representing a past that is perennially threatened by the forces of globalization.[18]

In their introduction to a recent volume of the *European Journal of American Studies*, Florian Freitag and Kirsten A. Sandrock also call attention to broader frameworks that are reshaping regional studies and literary histories. "Border(land) studies, New Southern studies, and Postwestern studies exemplify the shifting scholarly landscape in the field of regionalism towards more border-crossing, processual, pluralistic, and rhizomatic concepts of regions."[19] They posit a practice of "transnational regionalism" that "reads, and re-reads, regional texts from new perspectives while also adding new, previously marginalized texts to the debate"; such an approach to the writing of regional literary histories "enriches and diversifies the imaginary reservoir of a given region, destabilizing and deterritorializing received myths about and unified concepts of North American regions without necessarily doing away with the concept of region as such."[20]

Walter Mignolo's observations about the colonial matrix and recent realignments in hemispheric politics are useful to note in the context of transnational regionalisms and western American literary history. As he points out, the twenty-first century has been marked by historical shifts in the global economy and world politics toward the East in an act of what he calls "de-westernization." Mignolo examines developments in the seventeenth century when European cartographers used their vantage point to divide the planet into two hemispheres. In the nineteenth century, the United States appropriated the Western Hemisphere for its own geopolitical purposes, declaring U.S. claims across the continent and thus upending Europe's power. This was a critical development for the nation in a global setting. As he reminds us, "up to that point, the idea of the 'Western hemisphere' referred to European colonies in the New World/America. From that moment onward Western Hemisphere named and defined 'America' from a US perspective and management: the US became equivalent to America."[21] Theodore Roosevelt, a crucial figure in casting the American West as a significant terrain for U.S. interests, went further by proclaiming that Europe would remain out of "American" soils and that the United States would now serve as the "guardian" and "putative manager" of the hemisphere.[22] As Mignolo explains, since that time the "rhetoric of salvation changed," as the nation's foreign policy began positioning the United States as the agent of "world order and world freedom."[23] In adopting a "vision of its own imperial design molded in the name of liberty," the United States ultimately obscured its participation in the colonial matrix by framing its imperial discourse as "civilization, progress, and development."[24]

The logic of the colonial matrix addressed by Mignolo deeply informs the historical emergence of the western itself, with its central conflict embodied in the struggle between the forces of savagery and civilization along an ever-shifting colonial frontier. While the genre is often framed as a uniquely American form, various scholars have pointed out that the western is actually not a homegrown genre, but in fact developed out of a global history of settler colonialism. The western thus shares much in common with narrative traditions found in other cultures, where the tale may be known as the colonial adventure story, the Outback narrative, or the *plaasroman* (African farm novel).[25] In narratives that wage battles between savagery and civilization and that pre- or coexist alongside the western, however, there is often tremendous ambivalence about the modernizing project, just as there has always been resistance to the cultural and political enterprises upholding the colonial matrix.[26] Mignolo points to recent projects of de-westernization and other long-standing efforts to "decolonize subjectivities that have been captured and enslaved by the rhetoric of salvation and the illusion of happiness and well-being in the name of modernity."[27]

This collection of critical essays on the literary history of the American West places regional production in comparative and global contexts while also addressing the diverse cultural traditions and critical perspectives composing this body of work. In adopting a more extensive scope of study and frame of reference, critics are able to take up the challenge offered by Christine Bold in her recent analysis of the "frontier club" and American cultural power. Bold's work shows how an elite group of eastern Anglo-Saxon males in the late nineteenth and early twentieth centuries played a crucial role in defining the region in narrow ways that served to enhance and uphold their own racial and class interests. The literary and regional visions they produced and promoted worked alongside legislation they helped enact, all of which shaped the development of the American West for their own purposes. In doing so, members of the "frontier club" successfully marginalized other voices, interests, and understandings of the region, such that today scholars are still grappling with the consequences of these exclusionary practices.[28] Bold's study encourages critics to ask questions about how we narrate the "beginnings" in our literary histories of the region and to attend to how our frames of study may unwittingly work to exclude or marginalize key players from the past and the present.

In many ways, this work also connects with observations offered in Amy Hamilton and Tom Hillard's edited volume *Before the West Was West*, which asks important questions about how we determine the starting points – the ways regions such as the American West come into being as such. The editors note, for instance, that while "the intersections of geography and culture have been foregrounded in attempts to reconsider region – and the West in particular – issues related to temporality have been in the background."[29] In his foreword to the volume, Michael P. Branch also argues that in focusing their primary attention on "the 'where' of the West in the trans-Mississippi region," literary historians have often restricted their work to a narrow "temporal framework" that ultimately "ignores important elements of its ideological roots, which were struck in soils east of the Mississippi, south of the Rio Grande, and long before the dawn of the nineteenth century."[30] As he explains, "there is tremendous value in asking when was the West, for it is only within the fluid context of cultural and environmental change that the dynamic literary geography of the region can be fully figured."[31] Hamilton and Hillard further point out that by questioning the starting point of the West, literary historians may also succeed in diversifying their object of study by destabilizing the idea that "there is a singular western story."[32]

In an effort to narrate more inclusive stories about the region, *A History of Western American Literature* opens with the section "Homelands," which complicates how critics determine what constitutes the beginning moments of the literary West and how the space has accrued a regional identity. In her essay, Susan Bernardin examines literary and cultural production before the West was understood or defined as such, at a time when the terrain was a homeland to numerous and distinct Indigenous populations and a space that would only later become the site of many nations' colonial desires. In his chapter, José F. Aranda Jr. contributes to a similar critical project that complicates historical beginnings by tracing "the Recovery Project" of Hispanic literatures in the United States, which locates and examines published work written between the colonial period and the 1960s. Ultimately, the project has helped recast literary histories of the region by offering more extensive visions of the western American past that are not centered on Anglo origins.

The process through which a landscape becomes a region is the subject of a number of essays in the second part of the collection. This section, "Making a Region," begins with Nicole Tonkovich's discussion of gender, race, and national imperatives embodied in the domestic frontiers shaped by European American women writers in settler colonial communities. The section continues with Nathaniel Lewis's treatment of nineteenth-century tales of labor that involve trading, mining, and ranching and that may be read for the intellectual work they performed in transforming the space into an American terrain. Next, Sarah Jaquette Ray's essay about how western nature writing in general and the nature essay in particular historically served U.S. expansionist interests by recording, describing, and organizing landscapes so that these spaces could be better understood, claimed, and managed for the national mission. In addition, Nicolas S. Witschi focuses on the development of a distinct regional voice and tradition of humor in the "local color" writing of the nineteenth century, while Daniel Worden addresses the emergence of the literary western, its relation to other traditions of popular writing including the detective story, its malleability as a cultural form that is able to address a number of ideological positions, and finally its persistence in the twenty-first century in a wide range of global culture.

The third part of the collection is titled "Geographies of the Literary West." Susan Naramore Maher's essay in this section excavates the buried histories of dispossession, violence, and thwarted dreams in Great Plains literature, while Audrey Goodman's essay examines the complex intermingling of Indigenous, Latino/a, and Anglo cultures in the literary borderlands of the Southwest. Nancy S. Cook addresses conflicted understandings of the Rocky Mountain West, as numerous populations struggle over the place-based meanings of this diverse terrain, while Stephanie LeMenager attends to the different outcomes that result in offering social and cultural definitions of the Pacific Northwest or in choosing ecological ways of explaining regional development. In her essay, Ernestine Hayes examines the important forms of knowledge that emerge when literary critics remap the Far North of Canada and the United States from Indigenous rather than settler colonial perspectives. Finally Krista Comer extends discussions of regional literary production to incorporate global concerns. She notes that while the U.S. West has always had an international dimension, critics must proceed with caution in using transnational perspectives in their histories of regional cultural production, lest they unwittingly replicate the expansionist claims and acquisitionist efforts of their literary and political predecessors.

The final section of the volume is titled "The Twentieth Century and Beyond: Literary Movements and Critical Perspectives." In her chapter on early cinematic westerns, Christine Bold restores to memory Indigenous presences and absences and foregrounds how evidence of Native performances in these films is often "hidden in plain sight," left undetected by audiences and critics who are trained to overlook Indigenous contributions to the early history of cinema.

In his essay, Dana Phillips examines western American literature and the concept of "environing," a term he borrows and extends from Timothy Luke to address the ways environments are never static or inert entities, but function in an interactive manner with the human populations who historically engage and produce them in turn. Lee Clark Mitchell's chapter examines the tradition of hardboiled or noir fiction in the American West as a body of writing typically set in urban spaces that displaces romantic notions of the region as a wilderness or that celebrates it as an unspoiled terrain. Robert Bennett also reframes critical discussions about the region in his essay on Beat writers. Rather than focusing on the Beats as a tradition or generation, he redirects our discussions to ideas about geography and movement, specifically to the diasporic mobility of Beat authors, whose travels internationally shaped the concerns and themes of their writings about the region.

John Gamber's essay likewise examines ideas about temporality and place. His discussion of Native American writers and the literature of sovereignty points out how Indigenous writers counter erasure and reconfigure literary history by imagining new futures for Native peoples. Meanwhile, Jane Hseu restores to memory the literary production of Asian America, examining how popular understandings of the region and stereotypes about race have often marginalized Asian Americans and their contributions to the West in general and the development of the region's literature in particular. Jonathan Munby likewise notes how a focus on the frontier myth has necessarily excluded African Americans from literary histories of the region. His argument shifts critical attention to how black writers productively worked both with and against this rhetoric in narrating African American experiences across rural and urban Wests.

Andrew Patrick Nelson contributes to discussions of western cinema by focusing on Hollywood film production after the 1930s, tracing the development of the genre across a time when it reached tremendous heights of popularity. While fewer westerns are being produced today, Nelson points out that the genre is gaining new attention as a prestige art form that is now able to garner important awards and gain greater respectability and presence in the industry. Next, Stephen Tatum takes up the challenges of historicizing urban spaces by looking at the emergence of the New West and by using critical regional studies that attend to postmodern developments and the globalizing world system, both of which are rapidly reshaping the region's economies, identities, and narratives. Meanwhile, David Agruss redirects popular accounts of the region's literary history, using queer theory and close readings of the literary and cinematic productions of *Brokeback Mountain* as a means of challenging the heteronormativity that has typically defined the West. Finally, Neil Campbell examines the emergence of new narrative possibilities for the region that are offered by what might be called the post-western, a broad term describing developments in literary, cinematic, and critical texts that disrupt Frederick Jackson Turner's "creation myth" about American national identity.

During an era of rapid global change ranging from climate and other environmental transformations to increased flows of culture, capital, and labor, scholars of the U.S. West are extending and complicating their conceptualizations and historical understandings of the region. New literary scholarship is attending to the ways the places and histories of the West often exceed the confines of the region yet is also proceeding with some caution, adopting greater frames of study while being careful not to engage in colonizing practices, or what Mignolo might call projects of "re-westernization."[33] As this collection seeks to demonstrate, the field of western American literary and cultural production remains a vibrant area of inquiry, as regional, national, and global scholarship along with critical studies of race, gender, and sexuality continue to complicate our literary histories as well as our spatial and cultural understandings of this diverse body of literature.

Notes

1 For examples of this work, see Ella Habiba Shohat and Evelyn Azeeza Alsultany, eds., *Between the Middle East and the Americas: The Cultural Politics of Diaspora* (Ann Arbor: University of Michigan Press, 2013); Gloria Anzaldúa, *Borderlands/La Frontera: The New Mestiza* (San Francisco: Aunt Lute Press, 1987); Chadwick Allen, *Trans-Indigenous: Methodologies for Global Native Literary Studies* (Minneapolis: University of Minnesota Press, 2012); Lisa Lowe, *Immigrant Acts: On Asian American Cultural Politics* (Durham, NC: Duke University Press, 1996); Sonia Saldívar-Hull, *Feminism on the Border: Chicana Politics and Culture* (Berkeley: University of California Press, 2000); and Neil Campbell, *The Rhizomatic West: Representing the American West in a Transnational, Global, Media Age* (Lincoln: University of Nebraska Press, 2008).
2 Firoozeh Dumas, *Funny in Farsi: A Memoir Growing up Iranian in America* (New York: Villard, 2003), 88.
3 Ibid., 89.
4 Firoozeh Dumas, *Laughing without an Accent: Adventures of a Global Citizen* (New York: Random House, 2009), 161.
5 Jodi A. Byrd, *The Transit of Empire: Indigenous Critiques of Colonialism* (Minneapolis: University of Minnesota Press, 2011), xviii.

6 Ibid., xiii.

7 Ibid., xvii.

8 I discuss these issues in my essay "Introduction: Postwestern Studies: Dead or Alive," in *Postwestern Cultures: Literature, Theory, Space,* ed. Susan Kollin (Lincoln: University of Nebraska Press, 2007), xi–xix, and in greater length in my book, *Captivating Westerns: The Middle East in the American West* (Lincoln: University of Nebraska Press, 2015).

9 David Rio, "The American Literary West in an International Context: An Introduction," in *Exploring the American Literary West: International Perspectives,* ed. David Rio, Amaia Ibarraran, José Miguel Santamaría, and Maria Felisa López (Bilbao: Argitalpen Zerbitzua, 2006), 13, 15; Melody Graulich likewise addresses issues of globalizing western American literature in "'Ain't the World Small, Though!': Constructing an International West," in *Exploring the American Literary West,* 39–53; for this discussion, also see the collection *The Western in the Global South,* ed. MaryEllen Higgins, Rita Keresztesi, and Dayna Oscherwitz (New York: Routledge, 2015).

10 Rio, 15.

11 Laila Halaby, *Once in a Promised Land* (Boston: Beacon Press, 2007), 28.

12 Ibid., 49, 231.

13 Randa Jarrar, *A Map of Home* (New York: Penguin, 2008), 203, 246.

14 Ibid., 215.

15 Ibid., 246, 215, 228.

16 Ibid., 216.

17 William Wyckoff, *How to Read the American West: A Field Guide* (Seattle: University of Washington Press, 2014), 7.

18 Hsuan L. Hsu, "Literature and Regional Production," *American Literary History* 17, no. 1 (2005): 36.

19 Florian Freitag and Kirsten A. Sandrock, "Introduction: Transnational Approaches to North American Regionalism," *European Journal of American Studies* 9, no. 3 (2014): 2, http://ejas.revus.org/10402 (accessed February 24, 2015).

20 Ibid., 5.

21 Walter Mignolo, "Decolonial Reflections on Hemispheric Partitions: The 'Western Hemisphere' in the Colonial Horizon of Modernity and the Irreversible Historical Shift to the 'Eastern Hemisphere,'" *FIAR: Forum for Inter-America Research: The Journal of the International Association for Inter-American Studies* 7, no. 3 (November 2014): 45, http://interamericaonline.org/volume-7-3/Mignolo/ (accessed January 29, 2015).

22 Ibid.

23 Ibid.

24 Ibid., 46.

25 See John G. Cawelti, *The Six-Gun Mystique Sequel* (Bowling Green, OH: Popular Press, 1999), 25; Tom Lynch, "'Nothing but Land': Women's Narratives, Gardens, and the Settler-Colonial Imaginary in the US West and the Australian Outback," *Western American Literature* 48, no. 4 (Winter

2014): 374–99; J. M. Coetzee, "Farm Novel and 'Plaasroman' in South Africa," *English in Africa* 13, no. 2 (October 1986): 1–19; and Troy Blacklaws, "John Wayne in Sophiatown: The Wild West Motif in Apartheid Prose," *English in Africa* 41 (May 2014): 127–42.

26 For more on this ambivalence, see Stephen Tatum, "The Problem of the Popular in the New Western History," in *The New Western History: The Territory Ahead*, ed. Forrest G. Robinson (Tucson: University of Arizona Press, 1998), 153–90.

27 Mignolo, 53.

28 Christine Bold, *The Frontier Club: Popular Westerns and Cultural Power, 1880–1920* (Oxford: Oxford University Press, 2013).

29 Amy T. Hamilton and Tom J. Hillard, "Introduction: Reconsidering the 'When' of the West," in *Before the West Was West: Critical Essays on Pre-1800 Literature of the American Frontiers*, ed. Amy T. Hamilton and Tom J. Hillard (Lincoln: University of Nebraska Press, 2014), 1

30 Branch, "Foreword," *Before the West Was West*, x.

31 Ibid., ix.

32 Hamilton and Hillard, "Introduction," 2.

33 For a discussion of global change and the writing of history, see Libby Robin, Sverker Sörlin, and Paul Worde, "Introduction: Documenting Global Change," in *The Future of Nature: Documents of Global Change*, ed. Libby Robin, Sverker Sörlin, and Paul Worde (New Haven, CT: Yale University Press, 2013), 1–14; for more on "re-westernization," see Mignolo, 47.

PART I

Homelands

CHAPTER I

Indigenous Memories and Western American Literary History

Susan Bernardin

Indian Country

In a series of paintings instigated by the Columbus Quincentenary, Jaune Quick-to-See Smith (Confederated Salish and Kootenai) repeatedly reframes the map of the lower forty-eight United States through shifting, startling perspectives. One pair of paintings, entitled *Tribal Map* and *Tribal Map II*, replaces state names with the names of Indigenous nations in current "recognized" locations.[1] The swath of states empty of Indigenous names, as well as the numerous names spilling across the borders of Oklahoma, invoke histories of forced removals and new homelands. At the same time, drips of paint that bleed the boundaries between states gesture toward the violent materiality of how those states were formed. Enlarging the frame to encompass hemispheric Indigenous presence, Smith includes text equations that compress histories of both continuance and containment: "Canada 2,250 reserves"; "American Indians Mexico 23.5 million"; "American Indians South America 20.4 million." The names and numbers assert the hemispheric persistence of Indigenous peoples within geopolitical boundaries not of their own making. The dense narrative landscape of two other map paintings, *Indian Map* and *Indian Country Today*, papers the United States with newspaper clippings and photographs, illustrating the diversity and complexity of Indigenous experiences in the Americas.

Just as many state names are also Indigenous words, constant reminders of a history hidden in plain sight, Smith's maps also notably reference landmarks of Indian Country: In *Memory Map*, boldly colored petroglyphs move across and beyond the frames of the United States. In doing so, they visualize the foundational premise of Native studies: that everywhere is Indian Country. With these multiple invocations to remember, Smith also recognizes the continuing communicative power of Indigenous languages and expressive forms that mark specific, ongoing relationships to land, relationships that map political, spiritual, storied geographies. One of these paintings resides in the nation's capital at the Smithsonian American Art Museum. In the artist's statement that accompanies *State Painting*, Smith directs viewers on how to read her visual text of resistance and remembering: "I can't say strongly enough that my maps are about stolen lands, our very heritage, our cultures, our worldview, our being.... Every map is a political map and tells a story – that we are alive everywhere across this nation."[2]

In their play on the familiar and less familiar, on the recognizable map and the often unrecognized but tenacious presence of Indigenous peoples in and across borders, Smith's map paintings reach to the very heart of the history of western American literature. Her map series serves as a mnemonic device – of histories, communities, and territories that rarely have visibility on the national stage. That staging of Indigenous memory anchors Native literature, epitomized by Deborah Miranda's poem, "Indian Cartography." In the poem, the speaker's father "opens a map of California / traces mountain ranges, rivers, county borders / like family bloodlines."[3] Tracing removals and disappearances – the Santa Ynez River dammed to create Lake Cachuma; the "salmon coming back / to a river that wasn't there" – Miranda (Ohlone-Costanoan Esselen) animates family memories of central California land, home, and territory submerged under Lake Cachuma. Miranda's poem and Smith's map paintings remind us that categorizations of state and region are uneasy placeholders: marking occupied territories, routes of exile and forced displacements, embattled and surrounded homelands. Consider, for example, the term "Indian Country," which connotes both an imagined and a physical geography, a shifting, shifty transhistorical term wielded by treaty signatories, by settler and Native peoples. Jessica L. Horton highlights its freighted etymologies: "The term 'Indian Country' was part of a settler narrative that identified sovereign territory occupied and governed by Indians across North America. Formal treaties adopted the expression to identify the territory colonized, negotiated, and allotted in federal trust." The idea of Indian Country called forth "warfare (at home and abroad) and adventure and exploration. Subsequently, the term has been reclaimed by Native people and interpreted 'as a place that gathers Native North Americans together, wherever – on any reservation, at any pow wow or Native conference, in any Indian bar or Native centre, at any Native ceremony, feast, or community event.'"[4]

Smith's and Miranda's articulations of Indian Country communicate a crucial task of Indigenous studies. In *Transit of Empire*, Jodi Byrd

(Chickasaw) details that for her, Indigenous critical theory challenges "settler, native, and arrivant ... [to] reconceptualize space and history to make visible what imperialism and its resultant settler colonialisms and diasporas have sought to obscure. Within the continental United States, it means imagining an entirely different map and understanding of territory and space: a map constituted by over 565 sovereign indigenous nations, with their own borders and boundaries, that transgress what has been naturalized as contiguous territory divided into 48 states."[5] What if we privilege "an entirely different map and understanding of territory and space" in our considerations of another elusive "place": the American West? What if we approach the history of western American literature, whether understood through a chronological narrative, or a developmental arc, instead through Native histories, methodologies, memories? What alternate relationships, genealogies, and maps become more visible? What new frameworks and questions emerge?

Moving West(s)

It is now commonplace in western American historiography to denote the shifting terrains and borderlines of "Wests" in the national imagination. In western American literary studies, those vantage points unsettle temporal and spatial settings in the nineteenth-century West to consider when the East was West, or as Amy Hamilton and Tom Hillard's volume shows, *Before the West Was West*. In *Firsting and Lasting*, Jean O'Brien (White Earth Ojibwe) scrutinizes the nineteenth-century archive of southern New England local histories whose recitations of the "last Indian" in their communities erased the continuing presence of Native peoples in and around those very communities. Those town histories codified a narrative that remains virtually undiminished in that region, even as milestone anthologies such as *Dawnland Voices: An Anthology of Indigenous Writing from New England* document long genealogies of writing histories in and across Indigenous nations. Yet as O'Brien underscores, "much of the narrative construct about Indians in New England can be found in local histories elsewhere."[6]

The willful, wishful imposition of vanishing on American Indians extended across the country to Miranda's home state with the exuberant media coverage of "Ishi": the "last wild man" who walked into the town of Oroville in 1911 after decades of living in hiding. "Ishi" was not his name; he refused to reveal it during the nearly five years he lived at the University of California Anthropology Museum in San Francisco. Shortly after being relocated to the Bay Area from his homelands in northwestern California, Ishi narrated an hours-long story to the anthropologist Alfred Kroeber and the linguist T. T. Waterman, the "Wood Ducks" story that centered him within a storied intellectual tradition. During his tenure in San Francisco, the 1915 Panama-Pacific International Exposition show-cased James Earl Fraser's monumental, and monumentally popular *End of the Trail* sculpture. The Anishinaabe writer Gerald Vizenor has repeatedly turned to Ishi in his own work: In his play *Ishi and the Wood Ducks*, in essays and fiction, he has forged an active relationship with an intellec-tual predecessor at the University of California. For years, Vizenor led a public fight at Berkeley to rename a university building in recognition of Ishi's contributions as the first Native UC employee. After being rebuffed, Vizenor wrote to the UC chancellor in 1992: "the very institutions and the foundational wealth of this state are based on stolen land and the murder of tribal people."[7] With his advocacy, Vizenor repeatedly called attention to state-sanctioned genocidal practices aimed at exterminating Indigenous peoples in northern California: "Ishi had endured the hate crimes of min-ers, racial terrorists, bounty hunters, and government scalpers in northern California.... California natives barely survived the gold rush and colonial missions. Only about fifty thousand natives, or one in five of the original estimated population a century earlier, were alive in the state at the turn of the twentieth century. Ishi was one of those survivors."[8]

In remembering Ishi, and in reframing him as survivor, intellectual antecedent, and storier, Gerald Vizenor affirms both the power and the potentiality of intergenerational Indigenous memory. More specifically, Vizenor's vital engagement with Ishi's *continuing* intellectual and creative legacy models interactive relationships between present and past enacted by Native activists, writers, artists, and intellectuals. As Deborah Doxtator (Mohawk) once noted, "Indian writers and artists are constantly mix-ing and juxtaposing the past with the present, because, from their view-points, it is the connections rather than the divisions that are important."[9] For example, the scholars Daniel Justice, Craig Womack, and Margaret Noodin have delineated literary histories of Cherokee, Muscogee, and Anishinaabe nations, respectively, that are grounded in tribally specific knowledge, methodologies, and aesthetic influences. Other vital projects in Native literary studies identify relationships among oral, written, and visual languages, and affiliations that cross time, tribal citizenship, and home territories. Some of these projects are well known, such as those tracing the contemporary relevance and revitalization of Native cosmo-logical narratives in works by Silko (*Ceremony*) or Momaday (*House Made of Dawn*). Or, scholarship that continues to reshape the map of Native, U.S., and borderlands literary history, such as James Cox's *The Red Land to the South*, which addresses the transnational narrative treatment of Indigenous Mexico in the work of lesser-recognized Native writers from the mid-twentieth century such as Todd Downing (Choctaw), whom Cox deems "one of the most prolific and neglected American Indian novelists of the twentieth century."[10] Or in Robert Dale Parker's literary recovery project, *Changing Is Not Vanishing*, a 2011 collection that gathers poetry – most of it previously unknown to scholars – by eighty-two Native writers from the nineteenth and early twentieth centuries. Like the collaborative efforts of Siobhan Senier and the team of Indigenous leaders, educators, and writers who curated *Dawnland Voices*, Parker's archival work underscores the unsung role of local, small-circulation, and ephemeral print venues in the formation of Native writing histories.

If we extend the reach of Native aesthetics to encompass visual arts, mixed-genre, and performative works, other relationships between present and past, between traditional and contemporary, come into focus. Consider, for example, the reanimation of mounds and earthworks in contemporary poetry by Allison Hedge Coke (*Blood Run*) and in collaborative theatrical performance by LeAnne Howe and Monique Mojica (*Sideshow Freaks and Circus Injuns*). Or Michael Nicoll Yahgulanaas's dramatic reimagination of iconic Haida formline in his wall murals and comic books, a style he has termed "Haida Manga." Diego Romero (Cochiti) fuses U.S. comic book, Greek, and Pueblo design aesthetics in ceramics that visualize scenes of Pueblo resistance to Spanish occupation during the Pueblo Revolt in 1680. Such scenes enact Yahgulanaas's assertion that "innovation is our tradition" while instigating curiosity about a history largely unknown for those whose origin story resides firmly on its East Coast.[11] These few examples suggest that from the Southwest to the Northern Pacific, Native writers and artists both animate and activate intergenerational memory. In doing so, they align aesthetic innovations with living histories of Indigenous survival and sovereignty. Unlike the translated oral narratives typically placed at the beginning of standard U.S. literary history anthologies, these stories and expressive media refuse to stay "put," to keep tethered to their implicit place at *the beginning* of a progressivist narrative. In insisting on futurity rather than vanishing, they center alternate maps and origin stories of homeland, memory, and resistance.

In California, the region famously dubbed "west of the West" by Theodore Roosevelt, the state's literary origin story was first supplied by a Cherokee in exile. Decades before Ishi's terminal removal from Lassen Mountain foothills to the Bay Area, John Rollin Ridge worked as an editor and writer in the very region where Ishi's family and community had been slaughtered. Ridge had been in long flight from the agonizing conflict among Cherokee citizens that erupted in the wake of his family's signing of the unsanctioned Treaty of New Echota (1835) that led to the forced Cherokee diaspora to Indian Territory. The foundational novel he published in the first years of statehood, *The Life and Adventures of Joaquin Murieta: The Celebrated California Bandit* (1854), refracts his experiences of loss and exile through the rise, resistance, and defeat of a Sonoran immigrant folk hero/outlaw. Opening episodes in which Murieta is forced to witness the rape of his wife, the lynching of his brother, and the forcible dispossession of his home by "American miners" legitimate his turn toward retaliatory violence. Through frequent ironic asides, the narrator counterpoints Murieta's subsequent robbing, raiding, and killing sprees with descriptions of a pervasive settler cultural climate defined by harassment, robbery, and lynching, which he at one point wryly equates with "civilization."[12] Occupying the symbolic role usually reserved for Indians after military defeat, Joaquin Murieta embodies a contained romance of heroic resistance that Ridge refused to ascribe to Native peoples in northern California. With its founding statement about the status of California Indians – the 1850 "Act for the Government and Protection of Indians" – the state constitution legitimated the wholesale murder, kidnapping, and sale of Native peoples for slave labor. As the first editor of the *Sacramento Bee*, and of papers in Marysville and Grass Valley, Ridge called out the genocidal practices endemic to the region. In a 1857 editorial in the *Sacramento Bee*, Ridge asserts, "A great many Indians here have been shot down in cold blood by these white savages, and the inhuman practice of kidnapping is now going on with the steadiness of a regular system."[13] Yet Ridge's role in bearing witness to atrocities in the early years of California statehood was fraught: In other editorials he participates in the era's patronizing dismissal of California Indians, the kind nationally disseminated by Mark Twain's best-selling narrative *Roughing It*.

Ridge's father, John Ridge, had helped launch the Cherokee Nation's bilingual newspaper, *Cherokee Phoenix*, first published in New Echota (Georgia) in 1828. Decades later, the writer and editor Alexander Posey ran the *Indian Journal* and published his *Fus Fixico* letters: slyly humored, trenchant Creek English satirical commentaries on Indian Territory and Muscogee (Creek) politics. In taking control of the means of Indigenous representation, Posey, like those first Cherokee newspaper editors, underscored the role of Indian newspapers and journals in serving as vital sites of mobilization, networking, and resistance. At the same time, we can discern how Native intellectuals and activists tried to intervene in prevailing discourses about American Indians through the "white noise" of newspaper articles about, not by American Indians. Cari Carpenter has sifted through the racialized and gendered mockery of Sarah Winnemucca's performances and public lectures in the American West she found in "hundreds of newspaper articles about [her] between 1864 and her death in 1891."[14] Carpenter tracks how despite such mockery, "creating and controlling news coverage was key to [Winnemucca's] political strategy."[15] In doing so, she widens the lens for understanding an activist-writer whose self-narrative, *Life Among the Piutes* (1883), is widely recognized as a foundational text of Native, U.S., and western American literary history, and which, like Ridge's novel, has tended to serve as representative shorthand for Native experience in the nineteenth-century West. Akin to the satire wielded by Posey in Indian Territory periodicals, Winnemucca "mobilized a humor that was in turn biting, self-deprecating, and regionally specific."[16] Alongside tracing these networks of Indigenous interventions in the public record are Phillip Round's current efforts to identify postreservation networks of epistolary community building and intertribal activism across territories.

Indigenous Mnemonics

The Cree curator Gerald McMaster observes that "Native heritage is marked with memories of events that newcomers seldom remember and Indians never forget."[17] In his November 2014 op-ed for the *New York Times*, "Remember the Sand Creek Massacre," the historian Ned Blackhawk (Western Shoshone) makes visible both the specific massacre on November 29, 1864, of hundreds of Cheyenne and Arapahoes, and affiliated crimes of ethnic cleansing – Navajo Long Walk; the Bear River massacre – perpetrated during the Civil War. In this preeminent national, even international forum, Blackhawk challenges the continued national amnesia over its history of violent dispossession and murder of Native peoples as well as its inability to recognize the survival of Native peoples "amid continuing cycles of colonialism."[18] Equal parts condemnation and commemoration, Blackhawk's editorial also acknowledges the work of descendants and allies who marked the 150th anniversary of the massacre in November 2014 with its annual memorial run from Sand Creek to Denver. It also echoes the Acoma poet Simon Ortiz's plea, demand, and invocation to "Remember Sand Creek," the message at the heart of what he calls his "book-length poem," *From Sand Creek*.[19] Through paired poems that move across geographies of present and past, and personal and collective remembrance, Ortiz answers the opening question of his preface: "how to deal with history." Absent any national reckoning, any Truth and Reconciliation Commission, Ortiz balances grief with healing in his epigraph poem: "This America / has been a burden / of steel and mad / death, / but, look now, / there are flowers / ... rising / from Sand Creek."[20] Across the West, annual memorial rides and runs enact similar renewal ceremonies: from South Dakota to Minnesota, the Wokiksuye (memorial) Ride activates the memory of the December 26, 1862, mass hanging of thirty-eight Dakota men by executive order of President Lincoln in Mankato. From Nebraska to Montana, Northern Cheyenne descendants and relations commemorate those ancestors who escaped imprisonment in Fort Robinson in 1878, in flight for their homelands. Most were shot or recaptured by U.S. soldiers. Moving through territories of memory, descendants and tribal members remember and in doing so reconfirm a living, interactive relationship with homelands. In *Violence over the Land: Indians and Empires in the Early American West*, Blackhawk states that "the significance of the Bear River Massacre [January 1863] to Shoshone peoples and its absence from discussions of U.S. history illustrate the often extreme disconnects between Indians and non-Indians in contemporary America. Unknown to most while painful to others, Bear River can offer opportunities for bridging such divides."[21]

More than a century before Blackhawk's expressed hope to "bridge divides" by remembering Sand Creek and Bear River, S. Alice Callahan (Muscogee) wrote her novel *Wynema: A Child of the Forest* (1891) to intervene in the public remembrance of Wounded Knee. Writing in the massacre's immediate wake, Callahan recasts prevailing "public opinion" that demonizes Lakotas, privileging instead both Indian Territory editorials and survivor accounts of the massacre. In a move that anticipates contemporary remembrances of such atrocities, Callahan's narrator confronts an imagined audience:

> "But," you ask, my reader, "did not the white people undergo any privations? Did not the United States army lose two brave commanders and a number of privates?" Oh yes. So the papers tell us; but I am not relating the brave (?) deeds of the white soldier. They are already flashed over the world by electricity; great writers have burned the midnight oil telling their story to the world. It is not my province to show how brave it was for ... *civilized* soldiers to slaughter indiscriminately, Indian women and children. Doubtless it was brave, for so public opinion tells us, and it cannot err.[22]

Establishing a different memory from that of newspaper and official accounts, Callahan anticipates the ongoing challenges of wresting control over historiography and popular memory that Blackhawk's editorial confronts.

Blackhawk's public history lesson was instigated by the recognition that for most of his readers, Bear River and Sand Creek remain stubbornly off the map of national memory. When non-Natives do recognize a figure from Native history, such as Sacajawea, her own story "remains unknown to most." When Diane Glancy (Cherokee) read the journals of Lewis and Clark, she observed that Sacajawea barely registers as a presence: "it was like she wasn't there at all … I want[ed] her side of the expedition."[23] Glancy's novel *Stone Heart* commemorates the two hundredth anniversary of the Lewis and Clark Expedition by imagining Sacajawea's experiences as a young mother, struggling with an abusive husband amid traumas of exile and separation. Glancy enacted her own route of remembrance by retracing the journey by car. That imagined movement appears in the fictional passages she ascribes to Sacajawea in the novel's experimental multivoiced form and that she juxtaposes with Lewis and Clark's terse journal entries. The imperative to remember what non-Indians will not is conjoined with a writer's restorative impulse, akin to Vizenor's efforts to wrest Ishi from the terminal narratives too often assigned to him.

The relationship Glancy forges with Sacajawea underscores the importance of recognizing intergenerational models of Native women's writing in the West. Callahan's novel also maps out a relationship between women's personal sovereignty and Native sovereignty of territory. Novels such as *Elsie's Business* by Frances Washburn (Lakota) and *The Round House* by Louise Erdrich (Turtle Mountain Ojibwe), set in South and North Dakota, respectively, show how unprosecuted acts of sexual violence against Native women in the West sustain an ongoing history of intergenerational settler colonization and Indigenous trauma. Like her literary descendants, Sarah Winnemucca wrote at the fraught nexus of naming trauma and imagining a future, of grieving seemingly incalculable losses and asserting Native women's sovereignty over their bodies and lands. Her 1883 narrative, *Life Among the Piutes: Their Wrongs and Claims*, bears agonizing witness to crimes of settler sexual terrorism against girls and women in Paiute homelands. The apocalyptic urgency of her text is underscored by her observation "My people have been so unhappy for a long time they wish now to *disincrease*, instead of multiply. The mothers are afraid to have more children, for fear they shall have daughters, who are not safe even in their mother's presence."[24] The first words of Gertrude Bonnin's serial fictionalized memoir, published in the *Atlantic* in 1900, are "a wigwam," an assertion of both the preciousness and precariousness of home.[25] Her first chapter narrates forced displacement and family members' violent deaths at the hands of U.S. military. This early work, widely anthologized and taught, as *Life Among the Piutes* has, overshadowed the lesser-known but extensive record of Bonnin's varied writing activism: the collaborative Sun Dance Opera, poems and essays for the *Society of American Indians* quarterly journal, controversial articles on Indian Country in the 1920s.

Several generations before Bonnin's delineation of her "mother-hunger" amid punitive boarding school rituals, Jane Johnston Schoolcraft (Bamewawagezhikaquay) crafted a bilingual poem, "On Leaving My Children Jane and John at School, in the Atlantic States, and Preparing to Return to the Interior." The poem hinges sorrow at physical separation from her children with an insistent refrain of belonging to Ojibwe homelands: "To my home I shall return / That is the way I am, my being / My land // My land / To my home I shall return / I begin to make my way home /Ahh but I am sad."[26] Calling her "our literary Sky Woman" in her poem "In Search of Jane's Grave," Heid Erdrich (Turtle Mountain Ojibwe) recognizes Schoolcraft as a formative literary ancestor.[27] Her body of work, including English translations of Ojibwe narratives and songs, served as unattributed source material for her husband, the pre-eminent ethnologist Henry Rowe Schoolcraft, as well as for his friend Longfellow, in composing the iconic "Song of Hiawatha." Robert Dale Parker's edited collection of Jane Schoolcraft's writings, including those he found housed with her husband's papers in the Library of Congress, has reframed nineteenth-century Native women's and U.S. literary production. Together, Erdrich's restorative poetics, alongside Parker's recuperative archival research, animate alternate origin stories of Native and U.S. literary histories.

In her novel *Cogewea: The Half-Blood: A Depiction of the Great Montana Cattle Range* (1927), Christine Quintasket (or Mourning Dove) indigenizes the formulaic western romance to highlight what Winnemucca had decried a few generations earlier to a national audience: the interrelationship of settler land seizure and sexual violence against Native women. In *Mark My Words*, Mishuana Goeman examines how "mapping, both as a metaphor and as the physical mapping of lands and bodies ... supports and naturalizes race, gender, heteronormativity, and colonial power relations." Surveying the long reach of mapping and its gendered violences, she shows how, "yet, in the end, it was the power of the word and marking of Native place passed on through stories that refuted settler power."[28]

In *Cogewea*, the grandmother of the eponymous heroine harnesses that "power of word" and "marking of Native place" by warning her of the dangers posed by the smooth-talking easterner Densmore. Like her namesake in a cautionary interior Salish story, Cogewea fails to heed those dangers, even as she hears differing versions – personal, community, historical – of the same story: white men's deception, betrayal, and abandonment of Native women. Quintasket's grand-niece, Jeannette Armstrong, honors how the novel "was following the rules and the format and the traditions of oral Okanagan literatures. I realized ... the story is organized and the references that she uses and the format that she uses really are very clearly situated in, and based on, a true Okanagan spirit." She goes on to note that in western traditions, "it is not seen as a great piece of literature, but in Salish literature, it's just outstanding; it just takes my breath away."[29] A celebrated First Nations language advocate, writer, and educator, Armstrong continues a lineage of Native women's writing and activism that crosses temporal and geopolitical borders.

When Cogewea hears a buffalo skull designate an Indian cowboy, Jim LaGrinder, as "*The Man!*" in "Indian tongue," what might seem an overbearing plot device emerges as a crucial sounding of Indigenous memory and knowledge.[30] More specifically, the speaking skull, like the grandmother's stories, serves as a living repository of intergenerational knowledge that can productively inform Cogewea's decision making, and most importantly, shift her script from one of diminishment, even death (Densmore) to one of futurity (Jim LaGrinder). In her essay "Encoded Knowledge: Memory and Objects in Contemporary Native American Art," Sherry Farrell Racette addresses how Indigenous-made objects both embody and elicit knowledge and narrative power. Refusing the frames still typically supplied by museum curation, Racette instead describes the potentiality of such objects: "inaction does not reduce meaning; rather objects are viewed for their potential for reanimation, but perhaps more importantly, for the history and memory of actions they hold within themselves. They remember. They remember us. They remember for us."[31] Whether basket or dress, blanket or beadwork, Native objects instigate what Racette calls "visual literacy."[32] In carrying and animating memory, these objects, she notes, "support[ed] oral text rather than replace[d] it; nudging memory, calling for a story."[33]

Contemporary artists such as Jaune Quick-to-See Smith highlight the ongoing generative influence of site-specific visual and nonalphabetic texts. In "The Story as Primary Source: Educating the Gaze" the artist Joe Feddersen (Okanagan) and poet Elizabeth Woody (Warm Springs/

Navajo), collaborators on mixed-media installations, describe petrographs as artworks that "serve the land and Indigenous history by providing a greater connection to the story of how we came to be, how we have learned to become human, and what prophetic visions we have inherited."[34] In her travel memoir, *Books and Islands in Ojibwe Country: Traveling in the Land of my Ancestors,* Louise Erdrich reads islands inscribed with petrographs, living texts of Ojibwe memory that also "refer to spiritual geography."[35] Although she does not always have the knowledge to understand the petrographs, Erdrich knows that "the rock paintings are alive."[36] By showing that the Ojibwe words for "book" and "rock painting" share the same root, *mazina,* Erdrich roots her own writing in a long-standing Ojibwe practice of textual production that includes birchbark scrolls. For the Ojibwe, she asserts, "Books are nothing all that new. People have probably been writing books in North America since at least 2000 B.C."[37] In asserting this expansive and continuing practice of Ojibwe textual production, Erdrich directs us to what Craig Womack calls the "vast, and vastly understudied, written tradition" in the Americas.[38] From birchbark scrolls to totem poles, from blankets to baskets, pictographic calendars to petrographs, Native nonalphabetic, visual languages and discursive systems have remained largely unmapped in histories of western American literatures. Such Indigenous mappings of place, history, and story dramatically reframe both the origin stories and the contemporary literary history of the West.

If we recognize, as Erdrich does, the vitality of Indigenous textual and visual traditions in Native literary history, we not only unsettle genealogies based on English alphabetic traditions, but also transgress generic categories. Chad Allen's formative work, demonstrated in both *Blood Narrative* and in *Trans-Indigenous: Methodologies for Global Native Literary Studies,* argues that "when we conceive written literatures within a more expansive, inclusive context of Indigenous arts, the alphabetic text becomes simply one option within a larger field of self-representation. Literary scholars ... ought to join writers, artists, and arts scholars to engage in Indigenous-centered conversations across the boundaries of traditional disciplines."[39] Allen's scholarship has repeatedly modeled new comparative Native literary methodologies through his attention to nonalphabetic and visual expressive forms and affiliated mnemonic discursive traditions. In *Blood Narrative,* for example, he shows how novels by James Welch (*Fools Crow*), Chief Dallas Eagle (*Winter Count*), and Leslie Silko (*Ceremony*) variously "appropriate and redeploy" pictographic systems such as winter counts and sand paintings to forward Indigenous historical memory.[40]

Doing Time

Jaune Quick-to-See Smith perceives the limitations of linear models of Native art history, asserting instead that "timelines should be flexible; they should have fluidity; they should not be locked in time or space."[41] Like the common rejection of the horizon line by contemporary Native landscape artists, nonuse of the time line rejects linear perspectives. Displacing the time lines of roadside histories and literary anthologies, LeAnne Howe proposes a framework, "tribalography," that honors collaboration across genre, time, and space. "Native stories, no matter what form they take, seem to pull all the elements together of the storyteller's tribe, meaning the people, the land, and multiple characters and all their manifestations and revelations and connect these in past, present, and future milieus (present and future milieus mean non-Indians)," she explains. "Tribalography comes from the Native propensity for bringing things together, for making consensus, and for symbiotically connecting one thing to another."[42]

Howe offers a powerful articulation of how Native writers engage in vital acts of restoring memory and restorying place. Such writers notably include Deborah Miranda, whose milestone California Indian memoir *Bad Indians* is a mosaic of collaborations: Poems, photographs, and family genealogies are juxtaposed with radical reframings of mission mythologies and demeaning newspaper and postcard representations of her ancestors. In Howe's novel *Miko Kings*, an old map of Indian Territory announces restorative efforts to reanimate forgotten histories from the era preceding statehood: "with the creation of Oklahoma, with the privatization of tribal lands, everything changes. Indians will be written out of Oklahoma's picture. And history."[43] By also making visible the Indigenous origins of that most American of pastimes – baseball – Howe, akin to Miranda and Smith, creates an alternative memory map that collages fiction, history, and theory. In stretching the frames of literary genre, Howe and Miranda underscore the need to stretch the bounds of what constitutes western American literature and its history. In demonstrating that activating Indigenous memory is a collaborative, intergenerational enterprise, they prompt us to animate other possibilities in relating western presents to western pasts and futures. What about the relationship between urban and Native histories in the West, as modeled by Coll Thrush's *Native Seattle*? Or the continuing relationship between hundreds of treaty documents and Native literary, arts, and political histories? It is time to extend the possibilities instigated by Native writers, artists, activists, and intellectuals in writing our regional literary histories.

Notes

1 Dean Rader offers a sustained reading of Smith's map-painting series and includes reproductions of many of them in *Engaged Resistance: American Indian Art, Literature, and Film from Alcatraz to the NMAI* (Austin: University of Texas Press, 2011), 49–71.

2 Jaune Quick-to-See Smith, *Postmodern Messenger*, Exhibition Catalogue, 2004, Smithsonian American Art Museum.

3 Deborah Miranda, *Indian Cartography* (Greenfield Center, NY: Greenfield Press, 1999), 76.

4 Jessica L. Horton, "A Shore without Horizon: Locating by Looking Anew," in *Shapeshifting: Transformations in Native American Art* (Salem, MA: Peabody Essex Museum, 2012), 151. The incorporated quote is from Gail Guthrie Valaskakis, *Indian Country: Essays on Contemporary Native Culture* (Waterloo, Canada: Wilfred Laurier Press, 2005), 103.

5 Jodi A. Byrd, *The Transit of Empire: Indigenous Critiques of Colonialism* (Minneapolis: University of Minnesota Press, 2011), xxx.

6 Jean M. O'Brien, *Firsting and Lasting: Writing Indians out of Existence in New England* (Minneapolis: University of Minnesota Press, 2010), xiii–iv.

7 Quoted in Louis Owens, *I Hear the Train: Reflections, Inventions, Refractions* (Norman: University of Oklahoma Press, 2001), 232.

8 Gerald Vizenor, "Western American Literature Association Achievement Award Lecture, October 20, 2005, Los Angeles, California," *Pembroke Magazine* 38 (2006): 98.

9 Deborah Doxtator, "Reconnecting the Past: An Indian Idea of History," in *Revisions*, ed. Joane Cardinal-Schubert (Banff, Canada: Walter Phillips Gallery, 1992), 26.

10 James H. Cox, *The Red Land to the South: American Indian Writers and Indigenous Mexico* (Minneapolis: University of Minnesota Press, 2012), 14.

11 Michael Nicoll Yahgulaanaas, "Artist's Talk." New York: American Museum of Natural History, November 22, 2014.

12 John Rollin Ridge, *Life and Adventures of Joaquin Murieta, Celebrated California Bandit* (1854; Norman: University of Oklahoma Press, 1977), 91.

13 John Rollin Ridge, *Sacramento Daily Bee*, July 21, 1857, p. 2.

14 Cari M. Carpenter, "Choking Off That Angel Mother: Sarah Winnemucca Hopkins's Strategic Humor," *SAIL* 26, no. 3 (Fall 2014): 1.

15 Carolyn Sorisio, quoted in Carpenter, "Choking Off That Angel Mother," 3.

16 Carpenter, "Choking Off That Angel Mother," 2.

17 Gerald McMaster, "Borderzones: The Injun-uity of Aesthetic Tricks," *Cultural Studies* 9, no. 1 (1995): 74.

18 Ned Blackhawk, "Remember the Sand Creek Massacre," *New York Times*, November 28, 2014, A31.

19 Simon Ortiz, e-mail: SAIL Discussion Group (ASAIL-Listserv), March 14, 2012, www.asail-l@listserv.uga.edu (accessed February 16, 2015).

20 Simon Ortiz, *From Sand Creek* (Tucson: University of Arizona Press, 1981), 9.

21 Ned Blackhawk, *Violence over the Land: Indians and Empires in the Early American West* (Cambridge, MA: Harvard University Press, 2008), 265.

22 S. Alice Callahan, *Wynema: A Child of the Forest* (1891; Lincoln: University of Nebraska Press, 1997), 92–3.

23 Diane Glancy. "Author Interview." C-SPAN, May 12, 2008, http://www.c-span.org/video/?282348-1/author-interview-diane-glancy (accessed February 13, 2015).

24 Sarah Winnemucca Hopkins, *Life Among the Piutes: Their Wrongs and Claims* (1883; Bishop, CA: Chalfant Press), 48.

25 Zitkala-Sa, *American Indian Stories* (1921; Lincoln: University of Nebraska Press, 2003), 7.

26 Robert Dale Parker credits this contemporary English translation to Dennis Johnson, Heidi Stark, and James Vukelich, *The Sound the Stars Make Rushing through the Sky: The Writings of Jane Johnston Schoolcraft*, ed. Robert Dale Parker (Philadelphia: University of Pennsylvania Press, 2007), 143.

27 Heid Erdrich, *National Monuments* (East Lansing: Michigan State University Press, 2008), 27.

28 Mishuana Goeman, *Mark My Words: Native Women Mapping Our Nations* (Minneapolis: University of Minnesota Press, 2013), 26, 41.

29 Prem Kumari Srivastava, "An Indian Encounter: A Conversation with Jeannette Armstrong," *Studies in Canadian Literature/Études en Littérature Canadienne* 37, no. 1 (2012), www.journals.hil.unb.ca (accessed March 2, 2015).

30 Mourning Dove, *Cogewea, The Half-Blood: A Depiction of the Great Montana Cattle Range.* (1927; Lincoln: University of Nebraska Press, 1981), 282.

31 Sherry Farrell Racette, "Encoded Knowledge: Memory and Objects in Contemporary Native American Art," in *Manifestations: New Native Art Criticism* (Santa Fe, NM: Museum of Contemporary Native Arts, 2012), 42.

32 Ibid., 41.

33 Ibid.

34 Joe Feddersen and Elizabeth Woody, "The Story as Primary Source: Educating the Gaze," *Native American Art in the Twentieth Century* 3rd ed., ed. W. Jackson Rushing (London: Routledge, 1999), 175.

35 Louise Erdrich, *Books and Islands in Ojibwe Country* (Washington, DC: National Geographic, 2003), 50.

36 Ibid., 50.

37 Ibid., 5.

38 Craig Womack, *Red on Red: Native American Literary Separatism* (Minneapolis: University of Minnesota Press, 1999), 2.

39 Chadwick Allen, *Trans-Indigenous: Methodologies for Global Native Literary Studies* (Minneapolis: University of Minnesota Press, 2012), xxii–xxiii.

40 Chadwick Allen, *Blood Narrative: Indigenous Identity in American Indian and Maori Literary and Activist Texts* (Durham, NC: Duke University Press, 2002), 170.

41 Jaune Quick-to-See Smith, "Keynote Address: Eiteljorg Fellowship for Native American Fine Art," Eiteljorg Museum, Indianapolis, November 10, 2007.

42 LeAnne Howe, "The Story of America: A Tribalography," in *Clearing a Path: Theorizing the Past in Native American Studies*, ed. Nancy Shoemaker (New York: Routledge, 2002), 42.

43 LeAnne Howe, *Miko Kings: An Indian Baseball Story* (San Francisco: Aunt Lute Press, 2007), 23.

CHAPTER 2

The Recovery Project and the Role of History in Chicano/a Literary Studies

José F. Aranda Jr.

In 1990 at virtually the same time Paul Lauter was finalizing what was then the most significant revision to the study of American literature, the *Heath Anthology of American Literature* – which was also a geographic remapping of literary history – and the New Western Historians were revisiting Frederick Jackson Turner's "Frontier Thesis" in general and Herbert Eugene Bolton's "Spanish Borderlands" in particular, an independent but quite complementary inquiry into the origins, legacies, histories, and politics of Hispanic literature in the United States was being launched. By all accounts, the Recovering the U.S. Hispanic Literary Heritage Project has been successful, if not wildly successful. With the mission to locate, preserve, evaluate, and publish materials written between the colonial period and 1960 and by individuals we would consider Hispanic, it has recovered and forwarded "letters, diaries, oral lore and popular culture by Cuban, Mexican, Puerto Rican, Spanish and other Hispanic residents of what has become the United States," including newspapers and periodicals.[1]

Over the last twenty-five years, the Recovery Project has created and promoted a national and international framework for reconstituting the *longue durée* of a "Hispanic" presence in what would become the United States of America. While the Project has always had a three-prong set of goals – archival preservation; publication of important, heretofore unavailable texts; and curricular reform from K–12 to university – one of the major consequences has also been a recovery and remapping of the settler colonialisms of North America. Through its publications, the Recovery Project has been able to rehistoricize and respatialize the imaginaries of what constitutes U.S literature, from Spanish North America to the beginning of the civil rights period (1492–1960), for a diverse set of Hispanic communities. This new historical and geographic literacy is readily apparent in the early publications of the Recovery Project.

Although other translations were available, the publication of *The Account: Álvar Nuñez Cabeza de Vaca's Relación* in 1993 by the recovery scholars Martin A. Favata and José B. Fernández was responding not only to critical attention to narratives of contact, but also to increased attention to the points of entry, journey, and exits of European conquistadors, missionaries, fortune seekers, and so on. Cabeza de Vaca's failed expedition begins in Cuba. With one mishap after another, he becomes stranded and captive in Texas by Natives and is reunited with Spanish compatriots only after years of hardship. His chronicle stands in dark contrast to narratives of exploration and conquest that will come to dominate folklore and history in North America. But if that chronicle typified the kind of contact zone understood by Mary Louise Pratt, other Recovery publications pointed to evolutions of the contact zone, with its potential as a space for a multiplicity of diverse cultural clashes and/or syntheses.[2] The evolving metropolis, as found in New York City, Philadelphia, New Orleans, San Antonio, Albuquerque, and San Francisco, among others, revealed itself as the ideal place to imagine the mutability and multiplicity of the contact zone.

This evolving contact zone is exemplified by the case of the Cuban exile Félix Varela, who in 1826 wrote *Jicoténcal*, the first historical novel published in Spanish in Philadelphia. Again in New York City, scholars have two examples of how Recovery publications problematize both the spatial and the temporal sense of Spanish North America. In 1858 José Elias Hernández edited a collection of proindependence poetry by Cuban exiles, *El Laúd de Desterrado* (1995); by the early twentieth century there were a whole new set of concerns emerging among different Hispanic communities; in 1914, the Colombian exile Alirio Díaz Guerra published *Lucas Guevara* (2001), the first novel in Spanish that represents the darker and more treacherous side of being an immigrant in the United States from Latin America.

Not surprisingly, contact zones diversify under the multiple colonial enterprises that visited what we generally consider the American West from the 1500s to 1848. Here the Recovery Project has much to contribute to western American literary history. These recovered texts all too often traverse literally and figuratively, for example, the frontiers of both Mexico and the United States. Depending on the historical period, the borderlands of these two evolving countries ebb and flow with an uncanny fluidity; even the territorial concepts of frontier versus *frontera* collide and struggle against each other. Such are the observations of Lorenzo de Zavala, ousted Mexican politico, as he records his travels through the United States in his 1834 narrative, *Journey to the United States of America* (2005). His journey is particularly interesting given the role he plays in the Texas War of Independence in 1836 as interim vice president of the Republic of Texas. Elsewhere we have a rare glimpse of the U.S. Civil War from the participation of a person of Mexican descent. In *A Life Crossing Borders: Memoir of a Mexican-American Confederate*, the Reverend Santiago Tafolla's life story provides a counterintuitive reminder that even Mexicans and Mexican Americans were drawn into the Civil War. In addition, his account as a Methodist minister serves as an early testimony about the role of Protestantism in the formation of the American West after 1848. The kind of border crossing experienced by Tafolla and others takes yet another turn as the West becomes the site of intense commercial interests from ranching and mining to agribusiness and railroad construction. The industrial need for labor becomes the economic engine that fuels unprecedented immigration from Mexico at the turn of the twentieth century and beyond. Novels such as Conrado Espinoza's *Under the Texas Sun* (1926, 2007) and Daniel Venegas's *The Adventures of Don Chipote* (1928, 2000) represent the harrowing experiences of Mexican immigrants seeking a better life in *el norte*. Their immigrants "cross over" at El Paso or Laredo, Texas, as day laborers for the railroad or as migrant field workers following the crops from Arizona to California. But unlike other U.S. novels depicting immigrant life, these novels advocate a return to Mexico because the American Dream is a myth and full of failure.

While publications of early Latina feminist texts like *The Rebel* (1920, 1994) by the Mexican revolutionary Leonor Villegas de Magnón have also significantly redrawn our perception of borders, be they political, historical, or our concepts such as gender and sexuality, perhaps no single recovered author has had such an influence on remapping the U.S. literary landscape as the nineteenth-century writer María Amparo Ruiz de Burton. Between *The Squatter and the Don* (1885, 1992), a novel about the corrupt railroad monopolists in California, and *Who Would Have Thought It?* (1872, 1995), a satirical novel bent on revealing the cultural and political hypocrisies of Manifest Destiny and the Civil War, and questioning the hegemony of the United States in the hemisphere, Ruiz de Burton's writing has helped to engender a whole new category of nineteenth-century scholarship. Whether her characters traverse the continent west to east, from California to Washington D.C., or north to south, from New England to the outskirts of Mexico City, by way of horse, wagon, steamship, or even transcontinental railroad, Ruiz de Burton's representation of the travels of people, who are much like herself, has given all critics great pause to imagine what other writers with such hemispheric reach are yet to be recovered.

The Chicano/a Movement's Usable Past
and the Limits of Aztlán

Because of such hemispheric reaches, the Recovery Project has been responsible for a historic paradigm shift in how critics understand Mexican American literary history. Yet in order to appreciate fully the cultural work that the Recovery Project has brought about in Chicano/a literary studies, we must ponder how such a large body of writing by diverse authors of Mexican descent in different locations from San Antonio to San Francisco and in different mediums could have been so forgotten, so quickly, by the time of the Chicana/o movement. Overwhelmingly, part of the answer lies in the situation that this body of literature was never incorporated into the canon of literary nationalism of the United States, nor for that matter of Mexico. As a consequence, neither were the histories and geographies embedded in the literature. Having said that, part of the answer also lies, I argue, in the role that a Chicana/o vision of history and geography played during the Chicano/a movement, and how a critique of colonialism was deeply involved in critiquing the efforts by previous generations of Mexican descent to deal with the Manifest Destiny that reterritorialized the Southwest and West after 1848. This is a power that nevertheless kept reshaping colonized relationships with every new capitalist development of those territories, including the conversion of the border into an economic and political failsafe for the vagaries of Anglo American commercial interests on the one side and periodic bouts of nativist paranoia on the other.

In what follows, I make the case that this broad critique of previous generations of Mexican American history and cultural production was perhaps unavoidable given the larger set of politics involved during the Chicano/a movement, but one that nonetheless forestalled a more complete engagement with a literary and intellectual archive that has been in process since 1848 and arguably well before that. Once reviewed, it becomes clearer why Chicano/a Studies in general, and literary studies in particular, up to now, have had so much to say about the relationship of Mexican Americans to postmodernity, but little to say about modernity and early Mexican American literature. Despite the literary and critical production of the movement, the argument I propose is that while literature and, more broadly speaking, cultural productions played a defining role in the establishment, maintenance, and evolution of the Chicano/a movement, it was actually a politically usable past and a preferred geographic imaginary that constituted the heart and backbone of the movement.

By the turn of the century in 2000, there was, I would argue, a deep consensus in Chicana/o literary studies, although from multiple perspectives and competing theoretical inclinations, that postmodernity and what we called Chicana and Chicano literature coincided with each other.[3] There were formal dimensions to consider; there were the counternationalist politics to acknowledge; there were debates and battles around sexism and homophobia; and there was Gloria Anzaldúa's *herida abierta* to remind us of the limits of academia when it comes to the possibilities of protest and activism. But we in the field had no doubt of the postmodernism of the period, nor of our texts' multivalent reflection of those same forces.

By contrast, when it came time to contemplate what preceded Chicano/a literature and its postmodernity, we had before us the Recovery texts to consider, everything from María Amparo Ruiz de Burton to María Cristina Mena to Daniel Venegas, and of course Américo Paredes and Jovita González. What we did not have in 2000, what we in Chicano/a Studies as a field struggled with, was a sense of their lack of connection to one another, and hence even more so to Chicano/a writers. When compared to the writers of the Chicano/a movement and their immediate successors, very little connected the writers of the premovement in the way that we had been accustomed when talking about Chicano/a writers. Even writers as different as Tomás Rivera and Cherríe Moraga were nonetheless hailed as fellow members because of the Chicano/a movement. This assessment was influenced by the fact that much of Chicano/a literary criticism was grounded in and about the movement and its immediate aftermath. Thus it was no accident, I would argue, that one could literally read Chicano and Chicana critics trying to assess recovered authors and texts in the early 1990s as if they were somehow a part of the movement. Words like "precursors," "proto-Chicanas," and "subalterns" were often deployed in an attempt to reach backward with the critical tools at hand in the early 1990s. As a result, I and other historicists soon pointed out the fallacies committed when treating someone such as Ruiz de Burton as a contemporary Chicana writer, or more broadly assuming that the politics and poetics of the Chicano/a movement could be easily and naturally traced backward in time.[4]

To do recovery work, scholars have had to accept what the historical record tells us about these writers and their works between 1848 and 1960. Unlike writers in typical national literary histories, the pre-Chicano/a movement writers did not consistently appear under the banner of American literature, or for that matter as part of a Mexican canon. As a consequence, these writers did not appear in either their own lifetime or with the generation before or after them as part of some emergent literary tradition. Ultimately, they were neither hailed as part of some nation-building imaginary Donald Pease might recognize, nor as party to some kind of national symbolic that Doris Sommer might identify as "foundational fiction."[5] Although one can readily find regional conversations between figures such as M. G. Vallejo and María Amparo Ruiz de Burton in California, on the one hand, or convergences between the literary and the scholarly in such writers such as Jovita González and Américo Paredes in Texas, neither these conversations nor convergences translated into anything typically recognized as a literary movement or literary influence. Although there are regional exceptions where the Spanish-reading press facilitated a variety of publications by immigrant groups from Mexico and Latin America in cities such as New York, Philadelphia, and Los Angeles, or communities such as Francisco Madero's exiled Mexican government in San Antonio (1910–1911), these moments did not outlast the historical specificities of their origins or their locale; they faded just enough to be forgotten by most by the early 1960s.[6]

As a result, the early Chicano critic Philip D. Ortego reached backward historically in order to describe what he saw flowering artistically in and around the various parts of the movement; to him, it made sense to hail the moment as a "Chicano Renaissance" (1971).[7] For Ortego, the term "renaissance" made sense in a double way: for him, the notion of "rebirth" was pre-Columbian and Indigenous, a true reawakening of artistic talents that had been forcibly held at bay by mainstream U.S. society; renaissance also made sense because he, like others, saw the connection to African American long-term efforts to pursue their communities' civil rights. By adopting the term, Ortego was making common cause with them as fellow communities of color in the United States, all of whom awoke in the 1960s to be part of the greater civil rights movement.

Yet, unlike the Harlem Renaissance and probably because the times and conditions for protest were so different, the Chicano Renaissance could not reach backward to go forward broadly enough. As a collective effort, it could only selectively retrieve a usable past. This usable past was itself an open-ended critique based not solely but largely on the concept that the Southwest of the United States was an "internal colony" and that its inhabitants of color, in this case Mexican American, were structurally oppressed in such a way that this system resembled other colonial situations globally. Rudy Acuña's *Occupied America* (1972) was at the forefront of advancing this concept, but it also coincided with a much broader popular analysis of the United States' imperial tendencies throughout its existence, but especially with regard to Manifest Destiny, the Mexican American War, and a culture of U.S. exceptionalism. Thus the activists, intellectuals, and artists of the movement adopted and adapted wherever possible a deep-seated critique of all things colonial, and these critiques emerged loudly and colorfully in the cultural, linguistic, and historical renderings about what the Chicano/a movement was about and who were Chicanas and Chicanos. Here I am thinking of a cluster of texts, such as Rodolfo "Corky" Gonzales's *I Am Joaquín* (1967), Luis Valdez's and Stan Steiner's anthology *Aztlán* (1972), Martha Cotera's *Diosa y Hembra: The History of Chicanas in the U.S.* (1976), and *Fan the Flames: Revolutionary Position on the Chicano National Question* (1976), written anonymously by a Chicano Marxist collective, the August Twenty-Ninth movement. But it was Alurista's "El Plan Espiritual de Aztlán" (1969) that captured the movement's unspoken need for a poetics of place; it was also part critique of U.S. imperialism, part manifesto for social change, and part rallying cry for the return of a Chicano/a homeland lost in the Mexican American War (1846–1848).

When Alurista presented "El Plan Espiritual de Aztlán" for the first time at the 1969 Chicano Liberation Youth Conference in Denver, Colorado, he declared in no uncertain terms that Chicanos and Chicanas have a place to call their own: "We are a Nation. We are a Union of free pueblos. We are Aztlán."[8] He articulated what activists had been struggling to name, a territorial space that was not already colonized or at least a naming of a political space that would cohere for the movement's desire for a decolonial sense of belonging. After Alurista, perhaps there was no one better at articulating the theory and praxis of Aztlán as the Chicano/a homeland than Luis Valdez, founder of *Teatro Campesino*. He popularized geographic coordinates for Aztlán that resonated with where the majority of people of Mexican descent traditionally lived in the United States: "Aztlán, in the Nahautl tongue of ancient Mexico, means 'the lands to the north.' Thus Aztlán refers to what is known as the southwestern states of this country."[9] In this vein, Aztlán became a spatial vehicle for not only reterritorializing the Southwest that was lost in 1848, but also a Southwest that was lost by its former Spanish/Mexican colonialists. By resurrecting the legendary homeland of the Aztecs, the movement activists were channeling politically the equivalent of a golden age for Chicanas and Chicanos, a pre-Columbian place and time where there was a balance between social and political life.

It is safe to say that the critique of colonialism during the Chicano/a movement was thorough and in many ways uncompromising, to a fault even, especially when the cultural nationalism inherent in the call for a return of the mythic homeland of Aztlán drowned out other pressing issues. The critique, while useful and strategic for presentist agendas, obliged everyone, but especially academics, to take a hard line with historical figures of Mexican descent who did not mirror the revolutionary ethos of the movement. Nowhere was this hard line more evident than in the way that Chicano/a scholars reiterated Carey McWilliams's analysis of the Anglo American co-opting and repackaging of a Spanish Mexican past into a commercially friendly "Spanish fantasy heritage" in California and the Southwest in general.[10] McWilliams's critique of this Anglo American conquest of Spanish Mexican culture influenced how Chicano/a scholars viewed individuals such as M. G. Vallejo, former governor and general of Alta California and a major player in California's early state history, or later Miguel Antonio Otero, first territorial governor of New Mexico. In *Fan the Flames*, individuals like Otero were part of a small group of "opportunists who sell their people out to the oppressor nation.... This class of feudal landlords became transformed into a comprador bourgeoisie, who acted as middlemen for the imperialists in selling the region's resources and the people's labor for super-exploitation."[11] Because of their overall conciliatory relations with Anglo power brokers, such post-1848 figures were viewed with disdain by the emerging new histories of Chicanos/as. They were the historical "sellouts." Overall the adoption of McWilliams's analysis led to a sophisticated guilt by association, on the one hand; on the other hand, there was also a more rigorous recognition of the colonial privileges that some elite members of premovement communities enjoyed before and after 1848 and the roles they played in the labor struggles that followed, from the hacienda to ranching, from farming to migrant picking of crops. Altogether, this colonial critique of the premovement period limited what and who could be resurrected for a usable past.

Elsewhere in literary criticism, the "fantasy heritage" thesis was also deeply implicated in the all-too-quick dismissal of premovement authors. Writers such as María Cristina Mena, a New York magazine writer of some repute in the early twentieth century, or Adelia "Nina" Otero Warren, who wrote at mid-twentieth century about her family's history, folklore, and culinary habits of her part of New Mexico, often found more support among Anglo readers. What these premovement writers lacked in the eyes of their Chicano/a critics was both an overall critique of Anglo society and any representation of a stoic but heroic "resistance" to their racial oppression as Mexican Americans. Anything less very often led to a writer's almost total erasure in the then newly constructed canon of Chicano literature. The "fantasy heritage" thesis had a disproportionate effect in isolating the premovement writers from consideration, not just in constructing a canon, but in the larger, more important metanarrative that was to underwrite Chicano literary history. These early Mexican American writers' occlusion from this metanarrative added a kind of backdoor credence to the popular notion that there was really nothing available prior to Américo Paredes's *With His Pistol in His Hand* (1958) or José Antonio Villareal's *Pocho* (1959).[12] This occlusion was all the more startling in retrospect given how a few critics, like, again Américo Paredes, or Luis Leal, or Cecil Robinson, or J. M. Espinosa, were aware of this more expansive history, a print history that in the case of New Mexico, for example, extended all the way back to the 1600s.

The political culture created by and around the Chicano/a movement fostered invariably, and to some degree unintentionally, a peculiar and uneven relationship to a premovement past. A broadly diffused and "selective" cultural memory served the movement in highly productive ways, but especially in focusing collective energies toward presentist ends. Thus, reviving and revising Mexican American history were deeply important to the Chicano/a movement, but its presentist agenda often precluded extracting from the same historical record matters, issues, peoples, and events that were not found germane to those agendas. In the hands of an activist such as Reyes Tijerina, the cultural nationalism inspired by the myth of Aztlán, coupled with a neo-Marxist critique of the Mexican American War, enabled his ability to garner popular support for the restoration of stolen land grants in New Mexico, such as "Tierra Amarilla." Time and time again, the urgent political needs of the moment – discrimination in the workplace, voting rights, housing rights, education, access to health care, women's rights, Vietnam, to name a few – could not make room for "quaint" Nuevo Hispano recipes, like Fabiola Cabeza de Baca's *The Good Life: New Mexican Traditions and Food* (1931) or a novel of manners set in the East Coast like Ruiz de Burton's *Who Would Have Thought It?*, and especially not Miguel Antonio Otero's nostalgic musings found in his 1936 memoir/biography, *The Real Billy the Kid*. What the times required and supported were the efforts of someone such as Luis Valdez and his Teatro Campesino or the door-to-door efforts of Gloria Velásquez and Lorna Dee Cervantes to sell their chapbooks in *la communidad*. Everything was about now, even at the cost of isolating the past from the present.

The Lincoln County War in New Mexico

What follows is a key example of a literary text that had to wait for the Chicano/a movement to succeed for a different renaissance to happen. The object here is to consider what the Chicano/a movement might have gained from a deep reading of Miguel Antonio Otero Jr.'s *The Real Billy the Kid* (1998, 1936).[13] In his attempt to rehabilitate the popular mythologies surrounding Billy the Kid in the 1930s, I argue, Otero invariably narrated a complex set of racial processes that existed after the Civil War, processes that were dramatically changing a sense of place and homeland for the Hispanos and Native peoples since the original Spanish colonizers in 1598. The Lincoln County War drew in every conceivable community at the time; this included not just Nuevo Mexicanos or Native peoples of the area, but also African American soldiers of the 9th Cavalry. Otero's text is an exemplary example of Mary Louise Pratt's notion of the contact zone, and as such, the text provides new ways to think about the emergent West of the nineteenth century and its embedded histories of multiraced communities. The mutability and multiplicity of the contact zone after the Mexican American War (1846–1848) and the U.S. Civil War (1861–1865) are on full display in the Lincoln County War.

In 1936, the former territorial governor of New Mexico and descendant of a powerful colonial family in the region Miguel Antonio Otero published a text that was both memoir and ethnography, but overtly a biography of the infamous outlaw, Billy the Kid. This curiously crafted text saw limited publication in its time, but subsequently in the cottage industry that surrounds Billy the Kid, it has become a mainstay of information for Kid scholars. Nonetheless, the text's Hispanic importance, like that of the author himself, languished in the margins of archival purgatory for decades. Fortunately, in 1998, the Recovery Project republished the Otero text. In his introduction, John-Michael Rivera makes two key arguments about Otero and his text. First, he resituates the importance of Otero to Chicano/a Studies. During the Chicano/a movement, Otero was routinely one of the historical figures much maligned as apologists for the U.S. takeover of the Mexican Southwest. Rivera argues that Otero, like other figures in the nineteenth century, was no simple vehicle for U.S. hegemony, but rather an astute politician for "Nuevo Mexicanos," who nonetheless believed in the democratic institutions of the United States. Second, in this complicated context, Rivera reads Otero's interest in Billy the Kid as a cultural project that allows him to critique U.S. colonialism, narrate the "real" Billy the Kid, and simultaneously contest a monolithic Anglo-European mythology about racial superiority in North America.[14]

My interest is not only to demonstrate Rivera's argument that Otero consciously makes use of the border figure that Billy the Kid cut historically across language, class, and nationalist sympathies, but specifically to call attention to the multiple race narratives that often exist in Recovery texts like Otero's. By 1936, although memory of the Lincoln County War, and the Santa Fé Ring, which made use of the law and lawlessness alike depending on the circumstance, was quickly fading, so too was the open-ended character of New Mexico's territorial period. Far more provocative in Otero's text are the narrative threads that weave a multiracial cast of characters – good guys versus bad guys, of course – some Anglo, some Nuevo Mexicano, some Native American, and some even African American at the height of the Lincoln County War. If in the territory west of New Mexico, Geronimo and his people were being persecuted by the U.S. and Mexican cavalry, here in New Mexico in the 1870s, moneyed interests were busy consolidating economic opportunities, where even gunmen like Billy the Kid had a role to play in the transformation of New Mexico into a territory suitable to join the union.

In hindsight, what is so interesting about this episode of vigilante hostilities is how it reveals the colonial mechanisms of power that were brought to bear on New Mexico in the decades after 1848. Not so unlike Ruiz de Burton's novel *The Squatter and the Don* (1885), which critiqued the willingness of monopolists to subvert democratic and legal institutions in the name of profit, Otero's rendering of the "real" Billy the Kid lifts the shroud of mythology off the Lincoln County War to expose how the continuing logic of Manifest Destiny undermined any pretense that the new Anglo regime was bettering New Mexico. Otero's text also makes clear how the continuing logic of Manifest Destiny over time blurred the line between colonizer and colonized under the nation-building project of the United States and its civic and financial institutions, and in the case of families like the Oteros, the post–Civil War politics of Manifest Destiny aggravated what was already submerged and complicated through hundreds of years of Catholicism and miscegenation by 1848. The elites of New Mexico owed their status and wealth in the region to their ancestors who colonized and oppressed the Indigenous peoples in the area since the Oñate Expedition in 1598. As perhaps a symbol of the political unconscious of this colonial legacy, Otero's text on Billy the Kid is virtually silent on the topic of colonial relations with Indigenous peoples.

By contrast, Otero's text is alert to the historical presence of African American cavalry at the nearby Fort Stanton. Their role in the Lincoln County War is yet another instance of how greed and avarice manipulated the racial groups in the area and in a complexity more recognizable in the late twentieth century. Nonetheless their participation is part of the historical record. Unlike the more celebrated "Gunfight at the O.K. Corral" in Arizona or even the distinctly regional "Massacre at Mussel Slough" in California, the events surrounding the "Battle of Lincoln," which was a siege of the Alexander McSween home in Lincoln, is less known despite the extent of the violence it wreaked on the locals. Over a four-day period, the town of Lincoln was divided by armed combatants. Holed up in the McSween home were Billy the Kid; a number of other Anglos, including wives; but also significantly quite a number of Nuevo Mexicanos. Opposing them was the Murphy, Dolen, and Riley group. A stalemate developed because the two sides were equally armed and provisioned. To break the stalemate, the Santa Fé Ring collaborators decided to call upon their ally Colonial Nathan A. M. Dudley and his troops, the 9th Cavalry, "a negro regiment," as one of Otero informants (George Coe) remembers, to pressure McSween further.

McSween took the presence of the cavalry as a hopeful sign that some kind of truce could be negotiated. Instead, the Murphy-Dolan-Riley faction took advantage of the confusion that the cavalry's entrance onto the scene caused and set fire to one of the back rooms of the McSween compound. According to Otero, Dolan himself set fire to the house, hoping to "burn them out like rats."[15] After the fire was set and shooting recommenced, "Colonel Dudley established his camp in the street between the McSween and Murphy stores, placing his cannon in a depression in the road between the opposing factions. He announced that he would turn his guns loose on the clan which fired the first shot over the heads of this troops. Yet though the firing went on the big guns remained silent."[16] In essence, Colonel Dudley gave the Murphy-Dolan-Riley faction the upper hand. In the end, the McSween home continued to burn into the night. Despite personal pleas from Mrs. McSween to Colonel Dudley, several defenders died, including McSween, but Billy the Kid and a handful of others managed to escape in a mad dash from the flames and the shooting and over the dead bodies of many comrades.

Although it is relatively easy to get lost in the revenge-filled plot of this part of Otero's text and be seduced to ask what happened to Billy the Kid next, I would instead return to that odd mental picture that Otero creates when he asks the reader to visualize the 9th Cavalry, its Gatling gun and cannon position between the McSween and Murphy stores, with the nearby McSween compound in flames. The geometric triangulation Otero draws among all the principal actors in this event also dovetails racially when readers unpack and identify the participants. There exist an Anglo dominant Murphy-Dolan-Riley faction on one side, the Anglo led McSween side that is overwhelmingly composed of Nuevo Mexicanos, and finally in the middle, the Anglo led 9th U.S. Cavalry, which is composed exclusively of African American soldiers, soldiers who were specifically commissioned to aid and abet the U.S. government policy of removal, containment, and eradication of Native peoples in the West, or in South Texas to deal with both Native peoples and Mexicans from south of the border. When viewed again, this scene of hostility at Lincoln straddles other narratives of hostility. It is an event just begging to be analyzed. I do not know of another historical instance when a rich confluence of racial narratives occurs in such a dizzying array of possibilities.

Later in the text, Otero offers his readers a second look, if you will, at the 9th Cavalry that amplifies and deepens why we might want to think of the Battle of Lincoln in racialized terms. After narrating the events that led to Billy the Kid's death at the hands of Pat Garrett, Otero decided to transcribe a series of interviews he had with "firsthand" informants and participants of the Lincoln County War still alive in the 1930s. One of them, George Coe, described an incident that threatened to undermine the town's relationship with the soldiers at Fort Stanton: "Murphy and his associates were not looking for honest men; they preferred men like themselves-with a lust for theft and murder. They always worked through men of this type and kept themselves in the background."[17] They had hired a man named Frank Freeman, who was originally from Alabama. One day, Freeman was having breakfast at a local restaurant when an African American soldier sat at his table to join him. Freeman had made it clear how deep his racism was against the 9th Cavalry soldiers. Without much fanfare, he shot the soldier in the forehead. Freeman fled quickly by horse. But " 'Freeman did not get out of the country while he had a chance, and in the end was captured by the negro soldiers, who lynched him without any sort of a trial.' "[18]

It has been difficult to corroborate this story about Frank Freeman and the 9th Cavalry, but I have no reason to suspect that it is not true. I have a hard time believing the U.S. Army has a record of the incident though. To record it would have forced the army to conduct an official investigation, as they did in fact with the Anglo officer Colonel Nathan A. M. Dudley in the aftermath of the Battle of Lincoln, but I do not think the

Freeman lynching would have been an incident that the army would have wanted explored given the already difficult race politics surrounding the employment of African American soldiers. Nevertheless, this incident is provocative in and of itself and demonstrates, I believe, the impact and significance of multiple race narratives found in Otero's biography of Billy the Kid.

Altogether, Otero's Lincoln County War points to the fact that more attention needs to be given to the intersections of raced communities in the United States. It is not the only recorded instance when African American soldiers played a role in the Hispanic Southwest. In fact, Otero's attention to the 9th Cavalry inadvertently reminds us that by the end of the nineteenth century during the Spanish American War of 1898, African American soldiers and Nuevo Mexicano volunteers, some of whom rode with Teddy Roosevelt's "Rough Riders," would join clearly on the same side in the United States' armed conflict with Spain. Less clear though is the idea, on the one hand, of Hispano fighting Hispano in a hemispheric colonial war, and, on the other, African American soldiers fighting Afro-mestizo Cubans when otherwise hemispheric racism against African descendants would have made them allies of one another.

Finally, although there are plenty of differences between the Chicano/a movement and the premovement period of the Mexican American literary archive, there are also deep overlaps. Each is compelling in its own terms, and while it might not be necessary for excellent critical work to be equally knowledgeable about each period, it is essential for the future of Chicano/a literary studies that these periods structure our understanding of the archive as a whole, guide our critical definitions of Mexican American literature, shape how we constitute canons and curricula, and most importantly inform our collective decisions about how to spend our institutional capital when we seek support for tenure-track lines, graduate students, program initiatives, and even how to do consciousness building within and without our own institutions. The goal should be not to argue that an archive exists, but rather to declare that the archive of Mexican America is now its own critical category because of its size, diversity, and complexity, and that it is completely integral to studies of the U.S. West. Attention to this literature as a critical category is vital not just as an intellectual project, but also because of its deep relation to the new demographics identifying Latino/a groups as the largest U.S. minority of the new century. These new demographics in turn point to emerging histories as well as new geographies. Within this greater social and political context, awareness of this expanded archive can only help to generate specific research questions and institutional agendas in ways that were unimaginable before the Recovery Project.

Notes

1 See Nicolas Kanellos, foreword to *Recovering the U.S. Hispanic Literary Heritage*, Vol. 1, eds. Ramón Gutiérrez and Genaro Padilla (Houston: Arte Público Press, 1993), 13.

2 See Mary Louise Pratt, *Imperial Eyes: Travel Writing and Transculturation* (New York: Routledge, 1992).

3 For a definition of postmodernism contemporaneous with the Chicano/a movement, see Ihab Hassan, "POSTmodernISM," in "Modernism and Postmodernism: Inquiries, Reflections, and Speculations," *New Literary History* 3, no. 1 (1971): 5–30.

4 See José F. Aranda Jr., "Contradictory Impulses: María Amparo Ruiz de Burton, Resistance Theory, and the Politics of Chicano/a Studies," *American Literature* 70, no. 3 (1998): 551–79.

5 See Donald Pease, *National Identities and Postnational Narratives* (Durham, NC: Duke University Press, 1994); and Doris Summers, *Foundational Fictions: The National Romances of Latin America* (Berkeley: University of California Press, 1993).

6 See Nicolás Kanellos and Helvetia Martell, *Hispanic Periodicals in the United States, Origins to 1960: A Brief History and Comprehensive Bibliography* (Houston: Arte Publico Press, 2000).

7 See Philip D. Ortego, "The Chicano Renaissance," *Social Casework* 52, no. 5 (1971): 294–307.

8 See Alurista, "El Plan Espiritual de Aztlán," in *Aztlán: An Anthology of Mexican American Literature*, ed. Luis Valdez and Stan Steiner (New York: Alfred A. Knopf, 1972), 402–6.

9 Ibid., 403.

10 See Carey McWilliams, *North from Mexico: The Spanish-Speaking People of the United States* (Philadelphia: J. B. Lippincott, 1949 [1948]).

11 See The August Twenty-Ninth Movement, in *Fan the Flames: Revolutionary Position on the Chicano National Question* (Los Angeles: ATM, 1976), 6.

12 Early attempts to describe the artistic, literary, and historiography side to the Chicano/a movement, though celebratory of the emergence of "Chicano" letters, inadvertently gave the impression it was only a recent phenomenon. See Gerald Haslam, "¡Por La Causa! Mexican-American Literature," *College English* 31, no. 7 (1970): 695–700, 705–9; Raymond J. Rodrigues, "A Few Directions in Chicano Literature," *English Journal* 62, no. 5 (1973): 724–9; Charles M. Tatum, "Contemporary Chicano Prose Fiction: A Chronicle of Misery," *Latin American Literary Review* 1, no. 2 (1973): 7–17; and Ralph C. Guzmán, "Chicano Control of Chicano History: A Review of Selected Literature," *California Historical Quarterly* 52, no. 2 (1973): 170–5.

13 See Miguel Antonio Otero Jr., *The Real Billy the Kid*, introduction by John-Michael Rivera (Houston: Arte Público Press, 1998).

14 Rivera, introduction to Otero, *The Real Billy the Kid*, xi.

15 Otero, *The Real Billy the Kid*, 54.

16 Ibid., 55.

17 Ibid., 102.

18 Ibid., 103.

PART II

Making a Region

CHAPTER 3

Domestic Frontiers
Settler Narratives by European American Women Writers
Nicole Tonkovich

Traditionally scholars who write about the women who settled the American West have organized their work geographically, focusing on area or region, territory or state. While effective, such an approach presumes regions, territories, and states to be self-evident categories that produce unique place-based subjectivities. Here I will focus not on the places of women's writing, but on how discourses of home, family, and domesticity underwrite the spatializing projects of settler colonialism. Under such an approach, the tenuous nature of *Western* as signifying "trans-Mississippi" becomes apparent, and the repeated phrase "first white woman" points our attention to earlier moments that demonstrate gender's importance to state-making processes.[1]

Settler colonists occupy and develop places already inhabited; whether they remain or depart, their settlements ensure the area's possession by a non-indigenous polity. As Ashley R. Sanders observes, such "colonists ... articulated two contradictory desires – one for autonomous settler government [and] the other for metropolitan resources and military [protection] and support." In asserting their autonomy, colonists often craft collective identities (Jayhawks, Sooners, Texans) that distinguish them from indigenes, metropolitan sponsors, and/or supervising polities. Often they relate this new identity to their shared place-based experiences of settlement, which quickly become mythologized.[2] Through this lens, narratives of independent emigrants, impoverished but virtuous squatters, and gentle tamers whose courage founded a nation become part of a larger project of state consolidation. Thus literary historical undertakings and even primary written sources are discursive means of creating and transmitting domestic frontier identities.

Here I will consider how texts by and about women document the means by which polities acquire land, direct its settlement, and govern the resulting nascent political units. Large portions of the present-day continental United States were purchased from Indigenous sellers or ceded through diplomatic negotiation. Other areas became U.S. properties through acts of war, by treaty, and/or by annexation. Incentives to settlement included legal initiatives such as the Northwest Ordinance, which transmuted royal land grants into federal properties that could be sold to immigrants, consolidated as territories, and eventually added to the nation as states. Capital investments underwrote settlement of these lands. Lewis and Clark, Zebulon Pike, and others led federally sponsored expeditions to explore routes for commerce and evaluate the land's potential to support settlers. Federally funded and federally protected trails and roads, canals and steamship lines, railroad and postal routes followed, transporting settlers to emergent territories, soon to be states, and sending their taxable resources of gold, silver, minerals, timber, and furs to metropolitan centers. Such early expansionist activity depended on women's status as property, whose defense justified frontier violence. Since landownership has historically been a prerequisite to the elective franchise for white men, the discourse of sexual threat, so common to captivity narratives, points to women's value as reproducers of birthright citizens. Moreover, family structures (often interracial) spurred trade and structured diplomacy in the West.[3]

To attend only to texts written *by* women yields a foreshortened view of gender's importance to narratives sometimes omitted from accounts of the earliest moments of westward expansion, such as *A Narrative of the Life of Mrs. Mary Jemison*.[4] In the early 1740s, Thomas Jemison settled on land occupied by Native peoples who had already been driven into the Susquehanna Valley by colonial ventures. Jemison did not "[purchase] land" in Pennsylvania. He was, "like many other Irish settlers, a squatter, as there are no deeds, grants, or patents for him" on file.[5]

Jemison's daughter, Mary, was taken captive by the Shawnee in 1758, twice married Seneca husbands, and mothered a large family of mixed-race children. Her captivity demonstrates women's value to intercultural and economic exchange as bearers of racialized identities and potential citizens. Popularly known as "the White Woman of the Genessee," Jemison identified neither as white nor as Seneca. An act of the New York legislature "naturaliz[ed her] and [gave] her title" to a land grant along the Genessee River.[6] She subsequently was defrauded of most of that property by an unscrupulous white man claiming to be her cousin. A second expropriation happened in 1823 as Jemison told her story to James Seaver, who, in Michelle Burnham's words, "took" her story and adapted it to his own investigations of "American national history, and ... the military acts of conquest on which the nation was secured." Her story thus exemplifies the "tricky rhetorical practices" of history making and expropriation of Natives that characterize settler colonialism.[7]

With the Proclamation of 1763, the British Crown attempted to contain westward migration. However, since frontier land speculation was "engaged in [by] most colonial elites," including Thomas Jefferson and George Washington (a surveyor by trade), the edict only impelled the American colonists toward revolution as land companies, aided by frontier guides such as Daniel Boone, continued to open rich lands west of the Appalachian crest.[8] Celebrating Boone's part in transforming Kentucky from wilderness to state, his biographer Joel Filson recounts the family's removal to Boonsborough, giving Boone these words: "We arrived safe without any other difficulties..., my wife and daughter being the first white women that ever stood on the banks of Kentucky river."[9]

After the Peace of Paris of 1783, the cash-poor United States used land to pay its soldiers and sold ceded lands as a means of revenue, heedless of the Native inhabitants of those lands. Congress sought to control illegal squatters in these areas, to discourage land speculation, and "to survey, claim, and develop [these] land[s] for individual farms and for larger communities" in two landmark laws.[10] The Land Ordinance of 1785 stipulated that public lands be surveyed, their potential value inventoried, and deeds of ownership recorded. This ordinance also budgeted taxes to support public schools for the offspring of white settlers. The Northwest Ordinance of 1787 provided the blueprint by which the territories became states. To accumulate the five thousand men required to warrant a territorial legislature, and then to swell the population to the sixty thousand inhabitants necessary for statehood, the ordinances presumed that heteronormative families would settle permanently in the territories and (re) produce citizens.

Caroline Kirkland's *A New Home, Who'll Follow?* emblematizes these early processes of westward expansion, spurred by wildcat land speculation.[11] Five years after Seaver interviewed Mary Jemison, Caroline and William Kirkland established a "School for Boys" in Geneva, New York, seventy-five miles east of the Jemison property.[12] They later moved to the frontier settlement of Pinckney, Michigan, where William Kirkland and others like him became not Jeffersonian yeoman farmers, clearing land and irrigating it with the sweat of their brows, but speculators, who saw the land as a commodity.

Likely the Kirklands emigrated via the newly constructed Erie Canal, which transported settlers westward even as it carried agricultural produce and books such as James Hall's *Legends of the West* from the Ohio

River Valley to the Atlantic seaboard. In Cincinnati, Hall and other transplanted New Englanders, including members of the Beecher family, vaunted westward emigration. Lyman Beecher, certain that "the moral destiny of our nation … turns on the character of the West," worried that "the competition now is for that of preoccupancy in the education of the rising generation, in which Catholics and infidels have got the start of us."[13] His 1835 *Plea for the West*, advocating missionary work and agrarian colonization, inspired Marcus Whitman, among others.[14] His eldest daughter, Catharine, considered education to be an efficient mode of colonizing. Her *True Remedy for the Wrongs of Women* advocated training white Protestant women as schoolteachers and civilizing influences on illiterate western settlers.[15]

Beecher's schoolteachers headed to locations bordering the Upper Mississippi and Missouri Rivers, where white squatters had begun to settle on lands long cultivated by Natives. Fraudulent treaties drove indigenes such as the Sauks from their farms and towns and relocated them on lands farther west. Native resistance to such policies of removal caused a series of wars east of the Mississippi, where protecting "defenceless [white] inhabitants" of the southern frontiers justified retaliatory vengeance, ultimately opened more lands for settlement, expanded the cotton empire, abetted the rise of slavery, and added new states to the nation.[16] *An Authentic Narrative of the Seminole War; and of the Escape of Mrs. Mary Godfrey and Her Four Female Children* links removal policies in Illinois with those in the Southeast: "At the termination of [the Black Hawk War] of 1833, … it was then the opinion of many, that neither they or any of their red brethren would be found so soon manifesting … a disposition to *disturb the repose of the white inhabitants* of any of our frontier settlements."[17] Godfrey's story, like Jemison's, is told by a white male narrator as part of an eyewitness account of outrages perpetrated by Seminole warriors, who "plundered, destroyed and laid waste every thing of value that came in their way" and who were doubly ferocious because they harbored fugitive slaves. The brave Mr. Godfrey, "drafted and compelled to leave his family … for the purpose of endeavoring to check the enemy in their murderous career," left his wife and daughters, one an infant, defenseless in his absence.[18]

The narrative's outcome exposes the racial fault lines underlying the Seminole Wars. Under Indian attack the Godfrey women flee into a nearby swamp, where the baby's whimpers betray them to "a straggling black, who had enlisted in the cause of the enemy." This "humane African," who "had two children who were held in bondage by the whites," obtained food and blankets for them, then fled with them to safety.[19] The *Narrative* offers no further information about Godfrey or her rescuer, but his presence reminds us that the "repose" of at least some settlers in the Southeast depended on the labor of enslaved black men, women, and children.

Hordes of hardscrabble settlers in search of livelihood were drawn to the land ceded by treaty after the Seminole Wars. Many were recruited by land speculators such as Jane McManus Storm[s] Cazneau, an ardent proponent of expansion, a journalist, and a war correspondent. In the early 1830s, she and others of her family, encouraged by Aaron Burr, speculated in Texas lands.[20] Later, as a correspondent for the *United States Magazine and Democratic Review*, she wrote the infamous editorial "Annexation," declaring, "Texas is now ours," and coining the phrase "Manifest Destiny."[21]

In 1849, Storm(s), who had converted to Catholicism and learned to speak fluent Spanish, married William L. Cazneau, a soldier, diplomat, entrepreneur, and developer. The couple moved to Eagle Pass, Texas, where they hoped to grow rich by mining.[22] Under the pseudonym "Cora Montgomery," she published *Eagle Pass*, an immigrant's guide to Texas.[23] Written during some of the most violent racial conflicts of her era, the book maps her fascinating, if incoherent, position on race, labor, and expansion. She considered slave labor necessary for Southwest agriculture, yet she vehemently opposed debt peonage. Eagle Pass's proximity to Coahuila, Mexico, the colony of Seminole maroons led by Wild Cat and John Horse, led Cazneau to recognize, as well, the possibilities of cross-racial affiliative alliances.

As Cazneau knew, federally subsidized roads, trails, railways, and water routes that facilitated long-distance trade were crucial to incorporating the vast new U.S. possessions. In "Annexation," she had advocated a transcontinental railroad following a southern route connecting "our fast-settling Pacific region with that of the Mississippi valley."[24] The (il) logical outcomes of such advocacy can be seen in María Amparo Ruiz de Burton's 1885 novel *The Squatter and the Don*. Set in Southern California after the Treaty of Guadalupe Hidalgo, the novel parses the interconnectedness of land, race, and greed. It shows that although the treaty had made Californios nominal citizens, the government's "settled purpose" was "to drive the natives to poverty, and crowd them out of existence."[25] She exposes federal support of Leland Stanford and Collis Huntington, principals of the Central Pacific Railroad, who prevented the construction of a southern rail line. She shows how federal courts supported white squatters' dispossession of Californio landowners. The words of

Mercedes Alamar, the don's youngest daughter, encapsulate the gendered sentiment that grounds the novel: "We, *the natives* of California, the Spano-Americans, were, at the close of the war with Mexico, left in the lap of the American nation, or, rather, huddled at her feet like motherless, helpless children. Congress *thought* we might as well be kicked and cuffed as treated kindly."[26]

Long before the transcontinental railroad, commerce proceeded apace along the Santa Fe Trail, long a route followed by invading colonial forces. Caravans of merchants, "the avant garde of economic colonialism," exchanged cattle, hides, tallow, and silver for items of domestic use.[27] By 1846, when the pregnant eighteen-year-old Susan Shelby Magoffin set forth on the trail with her trader husband, their company shared the road with U.S. soldiers headed south to invade Mexico. Magoffin, the descendant of early settlers in Tennessee and Kentucky, wrote of her journey in *Travels in Mexico, Commencing June, 1846: El diario de Doña Susanita Magoffin.*

Like the "as told to" narratives of Jemison and Godfrey, *Travels in Mexico* has been textually colonized by editors eager to establish Magoffin as the "first American white woman ever to go over the rude trail of the Santa Fe traders."[28] Such claims of primacy, of course, overlook Magoffin's Mexican sister-in-law, Doña María Gertrudis Valdez de Beremende, who, though Mexican by blood, was a U.S. citizen under the provisions of the Treaty of Guadalupe Hidalgo. Lamar describes the book as a "trail journal, a Mexican war account, and an insight into the political as well as economic role of the American borderlands merchant."[29] He might have noted the book's "insight into" the importance of merchants' wives like Magoffin, who socialized with trading partners, "learned Spanish, helped clerk in her husband's store, and even assumed the role of train leader in her husband's absence."[30]

Magoffin knew that home is a contingent concept. The tent she lived in en route was a mobile home; her pregnant body housed a potential American citizen. Her presence, like that of the Boone women, guaranteed a future civility. Yet, as Virginia Scharff has noted, the "avalanche of annotation" provided by Sheila Drumm, Magoffin's first editor, "directs the reader's attention away from" the diarist in the service of "invented traditions [of] genealogy and military history."[31] In a notable act of whitewashing, Drumm changed Magoffin's title to *Down the Santa Fe Trail into Mexico: The Diary of Susan Shelby Magoffin, 1846–47.*

Unlike the lands of the Southwest, which became U.S. possessions after the U.S. war with Mexico, those of the Pacific Northwest were acquired by less bellicose maneuvers. The southern border of Oregon remained in dispute until 1846, when the United States negotiated a generous concession with Great Britain that set it at the 49th parallel. The success of the agreement stemmed in large part from federal legislation designed to increase the area's population. In 1841 the Distribution-Preemption Act had legitimized preexisting squatter claims and invited new settlers, many of them impoverished by the financial panics of 1837 and 1841, to take 160-acre homesteads. This series of events demonstrates that if western lands were settled by brave pioneers seeking independent freeholds, their actions often responded to federal incentive.

Protestant missionaries preceded the onslaught of Oregon settlers, seeking to offset what they perceived as a dangerous Catholic dominance among Northwest Natives. Narcissa Whitman and Eliza Spalding now hold a place of honor as "first white women" – in this case, the first to cross the Continental Divide, although other women, white or otherwise, had either been born there or arrived in the Northwest by sea.[32] Discourses of family permeated both primary and secondary accounts of the missionaries' cross-racial relations in Oregon Territory. During his first trip to the Northwest in 1834–5, Marcus Whitman had, for example, "*adopted* two Nez Percé sons to guide him back."[33] Surely the act involved relations Laura Wexler has termed "tender violence."[34] Narcissa Whitman's letters to her family report that her Cayuse neighbors considered her first child, Alice Clarissa, to be "a Cayuse te-mi (Cayuse girl), because she was born on Cayuse wai-tis (Caysue land).... It makes them very much pleased to think she is going to speak their language."[35] Such observations show citizenship's dependence on bloodlines, language, and/or location. After the baby's arrival, wrote Whitman, "It being impossible for me to obtain permanent help here, husband wrote to V.[ancouver] for an orphan girl. Dr. McLoughlin send [*sic*] us one by express."[36] Her comment testifies to the economic value even of orphan girls (likely of mixed race) in frontier settlements. Like other necessary commodities, they could be ordered up and shipped "by express" to needy white settlers.

After Alice accidentally drowned, her devastated parents adopted "two little girls ... both of them natives of the Rocky Mountains and poor little outcasts," the daughters of James Bridger and Joe Meek.[37] That the Native mothers of these children are not named bears out Hyde's observation that such "linkages ... were business – and family – as usual in the century before 1850."[38] When the Whitman mission was destroyed in 1847, Mary Anne Bridger and Helen Meek were among the casualties, yet their deaths were obscured by the subsequent "smoke and mirrors of propaganda ... and chauvinism" that made Narcissa Whitman a martyr whose death hastened Oregon's admission to the union in 1848.[39]

Two documents written by Marcus Whitman highlight the ties binding federal sponsorship of colonizing efforts, missionizing, emigrants' consequent demands for protection, and Plains Indian warfare. Well-sited and federally funded and -manned forts along emigrant routes, he argued, would allow the "government ... [to superintend] the savages that endanger this line of travel," while resident customs officers could regulate the "contraband trade from Mexico."[40] As Clyde Milner has observed, "In effect, the trail west to Oregon and California became a site for government aid to private travelers."[41] Such way stations housed not only troops and inspectors, but their wives and families, laundresses, cooks, and sex workers, many of whom left written records of their lives. For example, Elizabeth Bacon Custer penned three memoirs that sketch domestic life within such enclaves.[42] Not incidentally, Custer's books also did much to recuperate the posthumous reputation of her husband.

Following a route parallel to the Oregon Trail, another group of emigrants maintained a river's breadth between them and other westward travelers. Like the Whitmans and Spaldings, members of the Church of Jesus Christ of Latter-day Saints dreamed of building a religious utopia in the West. Unlike them, they fled from towns they had built, persecuted by border ruffians who could not tolerate Joseph Smith's visions of a kingdom of the Saints in Illinois and Missouri. Hyde's *Empires, Nations, and Families* presents an incisive analysis of how Mormons "disrupted Anglo-American assumptions about how settlement should occur and who should benefit from it."[43]

Accounts written by these diverse women emigrants have been recovered in ambitious collections.[44] As David M. Wrobel has written, such "pioneer reminiscences are thoroughly unreliable as objective gauges of 'past reality' (itself a slippery phenomenon) because they were produced for very definite purposes."[45] Writers of primary sources often had larger promotional agendas in view; those who have subsequently edited collections of their work have frequently bowdlerized the primary sources, emplotting them as histories of sacrifice and progress, culminating in the founding of cities, states, and the continental nation. For example, many works by women were part of journalistic promotions of California as a paradise of health and wealth, *Overland Monthly*, *Land of Sunshine*, and Ferdinand Ewer's early *The Pioneer: A California Monthly Magazine* among them. Ewer published a series of twenty-three letters written from mining camps by the pseudonymous "Dame Shirley" (Louise Amelia

Knapp Smith Clapp[e]), who called herself "the only petticoated astonishment [in Indian Bar]," a reputation invisibly modified by "white."[46] As
Susan Lee Johnson has so carefully established, there were many wearers
of petticoats – some of them men, and many of them Natives, Chinese,
Mexican, Peruvian – in the mines.[47] Letters, fictional or factual, of course,
furthered the domestication of the West. Carried by federally subsidized
stage routes, by pony express, and by railroad, they connected family
members with their distant relatives. When published in eastern magazines they spawned literary movements of regionalism and local color.

Other women's narratives became part of celebratory anniversary publications. Sarah Eleanor Bayliss Royce wrote her 1850 memoir *Across the
Plains* at the request of her son, Josiah Royce Jr., who was then preparing a
history of California designed to "help the reader towards an understanding of two things: namely, the modern American State of California, and
our national character as displayed in that land."[48] *Across the Plains* covers about thirty-five years in the life of this educated genteel woman who
taught school in San Francisco and in mining camps as her husband failed
at making a fortune.[49] In 1932 Royce's memoir was published as *A Frontier
Lady: Recollections of the Gold Rush and Early California*, edited by Ralph
Henry Gabriel, who omitted "five sections of Royce's manuscript and
[shaped] her continuous writing ... into [titled] chapters."[50] Royce's Gold
Rush era accounts draw our attention to the vast variety of women in San
Francisco, many of whom supported themselves by selling services that
married men had taken for granted. Michelle E. Jolly presents a nuanced
history of such women: nuns, cooks, laundresses, prostitutes, and board-
inghouse keepers such as the abolitionist Mary Ellen Pleasants, who
passed for white and extended the Underground Railroad to California.[51]

Not every woman who immigrated to California followed the Overland
Trail. Jesse Benton Fremont and Mary Jane Megquier, among many others, embarked via steamship from the East Coast, portaged over a rough
trail in Panama, and sailed north to the gold fields.[52] Such travelers saw
Panama's putatively backward state as a preview of what awaited them
in San Francisco. As Jake D. Mattox has demonstrated, these emigrants,
privileged by their gender, race, and social class, assumed U.S. dominance
of the route and nurtured ideological expectations for the future conquest
or annexation of Panama.[53]

Westward migration was closely related to volatile issues of national
concern, particularly slavery. Oregon's admission as a free state set into
motion a series of political maneuvers centered on Kansas. Proponents of
abolition flocked to settle in the territory, where a vote of citizens was to

determine the new state's status. Sara Tappan Lawrence Robinson, a member of the New England Emigrant Aid Company and wife of the free-soil Kansas territorial governor Charles Robinson, published her diary, titled *Kansas: Its Interior and Exterior Life*, in 1856. Robinson's preface invokes the by-now-standard domestic violations accompanying acts of war, "the outrages hourly committed upon peacable [*sic*] and unarmed men, ... the devastation of burning homes."[54] The diary memorializes abolitionist settler-martyrs and encourages others to emulate them. Robinson writes, "there is many a person fresh from all the elegancies, the refinements clustering about a home in our eastern cities. The most I have met bear these hardships cheerfully, and hopefully looking to the hour when Kansas shall come into the glorious sisterhood of states, herself untrammeled by the dark rule of slavery."[55]

Two pieces of legislation in 1862 "bolstered loyalty to the Union" and ensured that patterns of western settlement would follow a "northern and Midwestern pattern."[56] The Pacific Railway Act authorized a northerly route for the first transcontinental railroad, and the Homestead Act opened even more so-called public lands, drawing settlers to the West, where they would "erect an effective barrier against the extension of slavery."[57] By limiting the size of individual plots, the law prevented the establishment of large plantations in the West. Family stability was at the cornerstone of its provisions, for through this legislation "Congress ... acknowledged that the [white heteronormative] family was the only agency to be entrusted with the task of settling the land."[58]

Postbellum fictions published about Great Plains settlement demonstrate how this complex history continues to be reemplotted. For newly emancipated blacks, Pauline Hopkins's *Winona: A Tale of Negro Life in the South and Southwest* contributed to the canonization of John Brown.[59] First published serially in *Colored American Magazine*, this sensational novella traces the intertwined fortunes of Native and black protagonists in antebellum Kansas, where they aid and are aided by Brown and his followers. After the Civil War, formerly enslaved people emigrated not only to northern cities, but to the West, where they were eligible to take homesteads. Some, calling themselves Exodusters, gathered in small agrarian communities in the Plains states. As did Hopkins, Toni Morrison traces the palimpsestic genealogies of this land in *Paradise*, the final novel in her trilogy of "rememory."[60] Centered on a group of diverse women sheltering in a former convent outside Ruby, Oklahoma, the novel's complex plot entices contemporary readers to reconstruct this land's racially intertwined histories. In 1935, Laura Ingalls Wilder's immensely popular *Little House on the Prairie* instructed children in the ideologies of heroic independent homesteading, free of the interference of federal government.[61] Recent scholars, however, have reminded us that Charles Ingalls was one of a flood of squatters occupying lands supposedly reserved for Native tribes.[62]

Alarmed at the violence accompanying antebellum western expansion, white women gathered in reform associations to seek solutions for the so-called Indian problem. They planned to rescue Natives from such exploitation by erasing their tribal identities and reconfiguring them as (potential) white citizens. Three texts written by women involved in Indian reform provide a culminating demonstration of how gender, domesticity, and education furthered late-nineteenth-century federal policies of state making and consolidation.

Groups such as the Women's National Indian Association, the Indian Rights Association, and the Friends of the Indian designed programs to educate Native people in "the rights and privileges ... the duties and responsibilities involved in American citizenship."[63] Teachers, home missionaries, and field matrons settled on Indian reservations, intent on whitening their charges, resiting them into small wood-frame houses, and reclothing them in vested suits and corseted dresses. *In the Land of the Grasshopper Song* is the memoir of two field matrons on the Hoopa Valley Indian Reservation in the early twentieth century. Even at this late date they claimed to be "the only white women" "in the sixty-mile stretch between Happy Camp and Orleans."[64] Elaine Goodale, the so-called *Sister to the Sioux*, traveled from New England to Hampton Normal and Agricultural Institute for African American Education, where she taught in the Indian Department. She then became a teacher on the Great Sioux Reservation, recounting her experiences in letters to eastern newspapers and reform periodicals. Her memoirs include an account of the Ghost Dance and the Wounded Knee massacre, as she helped her future husband, the Sioux physician Charles Eastman, care for the survivors.[65]

I close this essay by advocating attention to genres less apparently literary, for in the nineteenth century, theorizing done in the nascent human sciences fed ideologies of the inevitability of white civilization. Louis Henry Morgan's ideas about developmental anthropology, which posited that cultures progress through stages of savagery, barbarism, and civilization, undergirded federal policies designed to speed the process. Chief among these was the Dawes General Allotment Act of 1887, which opened Indian reservations to white enterprise by deeding homestead-size lands within them to individual Native owners, leaving the balance, often as

much as 90 percent of the total land, available for white development.
The allotment act encapsulates the themes I have developed here, marrying ideologies of individual landownership, capitalist competition, representative democracy, education, and citizenly incorporation in a piece
of legislation in which white women reformers had a major voice and in
whose application women served as agents.

The broad influence of Alice C. Fletcher, the first white woman to
practice participant-observer ethnology, illustrates the potent combination of science, federal policy, and the feminine personal. Fletcher's ethnographic monographs buttressed her authority as a spokeswoman for
Indian reform; as well, she herself engaged in bringing about the transformations she advocated. As she allotted the Nez Perce Reservation, her
epistolary reports from the field were read aloud to reformers gathered
at Lake Mohonk and published in reform newspapers. To broader popular audiences, she furnished a white woman's perspective on Native life.
Her best known writings can be found in *Century* magazine, where, in
the same issues that contained Mark Twain's *Pudd'n'head Wilson,* she published a series of "Personal Studies of [Plains] Indian Life" that skillfully
married domestication, scholarship, and colonial incorporation in titles
and subtitles such as "Home Life among the Indians: Records of Personal
Experience."[66] Fletcher's photographer-companion, E. Jane Gay, documented the pair's field experiences in her memoir, *Choup-nit-ki: With the
Nez Perce.*[67] Written two decades after the allotment closed, this collection
of letters from the field, illustrated with hundreds of Gay's black-and-white
photographs, purports to present an on-the-ground account of how allotment succeeded in transforming the Nez Perces into statesmen, bureau-
crats, and farmers.

Gay's recollections are grounded in the assumption that the West was
destined to be domesticated by white settlers. Closing *Choup-nit-ki* with a
retrospective "writer's note," she presents a set of "double pictures," comparative sketches of conditions on the Nez Perce Reservation in 1889 and
in 1904. She recalled that in 1889 she and Fletcher could "ride, unarmed
and unguarded, all over the Nez Perce country," while in 1904, "the white
man has entered the land, with pick-axe and plough and pistols."[68] She
includes photographs of small towns with their grain elevators and local
newspapers, named for the principals in the allotting enterprise. Such
details, meant to serve as a measure of Fletcher's success, effectively summarize the processes I have enumerated here: Western lands have been
acquired by means of war, purchase, federal edict, and/or naturalization
of Indigenous owners. Women aided in these processes, as properties to

be defended, as martyrs to the lands' inevitable civilization, as exemplars of domestic ideals, but also as theorists and agents of state policy, and as producers of the white (and whitened) citizens of those states.

Notes

1 My approach is similar to that of Brigitte Georgi-Findlay, who emphasizes women's part in "the development of a national narrative associated with the American West" in *The Frontiers of Women's Writing: Women's Narratives and the Rhetoric of Westward Expansion* (Tucson: University of Arizona Press, 1996), xi. Rather than characterize these writers as resistant or complicit, I focus on the gendered underpinnings of state initiatives.

2 Ashley R. Sanders, "What Is Settler Colonialism?" *Colonialism through the Veil*, http://colonialismthroughtheveil.wordpress.com/2012/09/07/what-is-settler -colonialism/#_ftn7 (accessed March 23, 2014).

3 See Anne F. Hyde, *Empires, Nations, and Families: A History of the North American West, 1800–1860* (Lincoln: University of Nebraska Press, 2011), 5.

4 James E. Seaver, *A Narrative of the Life of Mrs. Mary Jemison, 1824*, ed. June Namias (Norman: University of Oklahoma Press, 1992).

5 "Mary Jemison, Part II," "Message Boards>Surnames>Jemison>Mary Jemison," *Ancestry.com*, boards.ancestry.com/surnames.jemison/211/mb.ashx (accessed May 15, 2014).

6 June Namais, *White Captives: Gender and Ethnicity on the American Frontier* (Chapel Hill: University of North Carolina Press, 1993), 149, 185.

7 Michelle Burnham, "'However Extravagant the Pretension': Bivocalism and US Nation-Building in *A Narrative of the Life of Mrs. Mary Jemison*," *Nineteenth-Century Contexts* 23, no. 3 (2001): 327.

8 Colin G. Calloway, *The Scratch of a Pen: 1763 and the Transformation of North America* (New York: Oxford University Press, 2006), 55.

9 John Filson, *The Discovery, Settlement, and Present State of Kentucky* (London: J. Debrett, Opposite Burlington House, 1793), 39.

10 William F. Deverell and Anne F. Hyde, introduction to "Chapter Seven: The Creation of the American Republic: Incorporating the West," in *The West in the History of the Nation: A Reader*, Vol. 1. *To 1877*, ed. William F. Deverell and Anne F. Hyde (Boston: Bedford, 2000), 130.

11 Caroline M. Kirkland, *A New Home, Who'll Follow? or, Glimpses of Western Life*, 1839, ed. Sandra A. Zagarell (New Brunswick, NJ: Rutgers University Press, 1996).

12 Bill Treichler, "The Kirkland's School in Geneva," *Crooked Lake Review*, Feb. 1990, http://www.crookedlakereview.com/articles/1_33/23feb1990/23treichler .html (accessed May 16, 2014).

13 Lyman Beecher, *Autobiography, Correspondence, Etc., of Lyman Beecher*, Part 4, ed. Charles Beecher (New York, 1865), 224.

14 Lyman Beecher, *A Plea for the West* (Cincinnati, 1835).

15 Catharine Esther Beecher, *The True Remedy for the Wrongs of Woman: With a History of an Enterprise Having That for Its Object* (Boston, 1851).

16 *An Authentic Narrative of the Seminole War; and of the Miraculous Escape of Mrs. Mary Godfrey, and Her Four Female Children*, 1836, in *Women's Indian Captivity Narratives*, ed. Kathryn Zabelle Derounian-Stodola (New York: Penguin, 1998), 217.

17 Ibid., emphasis mine.

18 Ibid., 219, 221. Derounian-Stodola argues that "whether … Godfrey existed in the historical record is irrelevant and currently unknown," in the introduction to *An Authentic Narrative*, 215.

19 *Authentic Narrative*, 222, 223.

20 Megan Jenison Griffin, "Jane McManus Storm Cazneau, 1807–1875," *Legacy* 27, no. 2 (2010): 419.

21 "Annexation," *United States Magazine and Democratic Review* 16 (July–August 1845): 5. Cazneau's biographer has analyzed the style of the unsigned editorial, correlated it with Cazneau's other writings, and confidently attributed it to her. See Linda S. Hudson, *Mistress of Manifest Destiny: A Biography of Jane McManus Storm Cazneau, 1807–1878* (Austin: Texas State Historical Association, 2001), 60–2.

22 Hudson, *Mistress*, 25.

23 Cora Montgomery [Jane McManus Storm(s) Cazneau], *Eagle Pass; or, Life on the Border* (New York, 1852).

24 "Annexation," 8.

25 María Amparo Ruiz de Burton, *The Squatter and the Don*, ed. Rosaura Sánchez and Beatrice Pita (1885; Houston: Arte Público, 1993), 146.

26 Ibid., 174.

27 Georgi-Findlay, *Frontiers of Women's Writing*, 93.

28 Howard R. Lamar, "Foreword," to Susan Shelby Magoffin, *Down the Santa Fe Trail and into Mexico: The Diary of Susan Shelby Magoffin, 1846–1847*, 1926, ed. Stella M. Drumm (New Haven, CT: Yale University Press, 1962), ix.

29 Ibid., xxx.

30 Deborah J. Lawrence, "Susan Shelby Magoffin: A Wandering Princess on the Santa Fe Trail," in *Writing the Trail: Five Women's Frontier Narratives* (Iowa City: University of Iowa Press, 2006), 10.

31 Virginia Scharff, "The Hearth of Darkness: Susan Magoffin on Suspect Terrain," in *Twenty Thousand Roads: Women, Movement, and the West* (Berkeley: University of California Press, 2003), 38, 39.

32 Cameron Addis, "The Whitman Massacre: Religion and Manifest Destiny on the Columbia Plateau, 1809–1858," *Journal of the Early Republic* 25, no. 2 (2005): 232n18.

33 Ibid., emphasis mine.

34 Laura Wexler, *Tender Violence: Domestic Visions in an Age of U. S. Imperialism* (Chapel Hill: University of North Carolina Press, 2000).

35 Narcissa Whitman, "Letters Written by Mrs. Whitman from Oregon to Her Relatives in New York," *Transactions of the Nineteenth Annual Reunion of the Oregon Pioneer Association for 1891* (Portland, 1893), 91, 107.

36 Ibid., 92.

37 Ibid., 153.

38 Hyde, *Empires*, 5.

39 Addis, "Whitman Massacre," 224.

40 [Marcus Whitman], "Dr. Whitman's Bill and His Letter to the Secretary of War," *Transactions of the Nineteenth Annual Reunion of the Oregon Pioneer Association for 1891* (Portland, 1893), 73.

41 Clyde Milner, "Federal Support of Explorers and Emigrants," *Major Problems in the History of the American West*, ed. Clyde Milner, Anne M. Butler, and David Rich Lewis, 2nd ed. (Boston: Houghton, 1997), 115. See also John D. Unruh, "The Federal Government's Aid to Overland Emigrants," in Milner, Butler, and Lewis, *Major Problems*, 142–54.

42 Elizabeth Bacon Custer, *"Boots and Saddles"; or, Life in Dakota with General Custer* (New York: Harper and Brothers, 1885); *Tenting on the Plains; or, General Custer in Kansas and Texas* (New York: C. L. Webster and Co., 1889); and *Following the Guidon* (New York: Harper and Brothers, 1890).

43 Hyde, *Empires*, 358.

44 See, for example, Kenneth L. Holmes, ed., *Covered Wagon Women: Diaries and Letters from the Western Trails, 1940–1890*, 10 vols. (Glendale: Clark, 1983-).

45 David M. Wrobel, *Promised Lands: Promotion, Memory, and the Creation of the American West* (Lawrence: University Press of Kansas, 2002), 4.

46 Louise Amelia Knapp Smith Clapp[e], *The Shirley Letters from the California Mines, 1851–1852*, ed. Marlene Smith-Baranzini (Berkeley, CA: Heyday, 1998), 52. This edition was published in connection with the California sesquicentennial celebration.

47 Susan Lee Johnson, *Roaring Camp: The Social World of the California Gold Rush* (New York: Norton, 2000).

48 Sarah Royce, *Across the Plains: Sarah Royce's Western Narrative*, ed. Jennifer Dawes Adkison (Tucson: University of Arizona Press, 2009); Josiah Royce, *California, from the Conquest in 1846 to the Second Vigilance Committee in San Francisco: A Study of American Character* (Boston: Houghton, 1886), 1.

49 Similar texts were produced during other "rushes": in Pike's Peak, Colorado (1858–61); in the Black Hills (1874–77); in northwest Idaho (1863); in Nevada (1859); and in Alaska (1896–9).

50 Royce, *Across the Plains*, 9.

51 Michelle E. Jolly, "Inventing the City: Gender and the Politics of Everyday Life in Gold-Rush San Francisco, 1848–1869," PhD dissertation, University of California, San Diego, 1998.

52 Jesse Benton Fremont, *A Year of American Travel: Narrative of Personal Experience* (New York, 1878); Mary Jane Megquier, *Apron Full of Gold: The Letters of Mary Jane Megquier from San Francisco, 1849–1856*, ed. Robert Glass Cleland (San Marino: Huntington Library, 1949).

53 Jake D. Mattox, "Alternate Imperialisms in the Age of Manifest Destiny," PhD dissertation, University of California, San Diego, 2007.

54 Sara T[appan] L[awrence] Robinson, *Kansas; Its Interior and Exterior, Including a Full View of Its Settlement, Political History, Social Life, Climate, Soil, Productions, Scenery, Etc.* (Boston: Crosby, Nichols and Company, 1856), iii.

55 Ibid., 58.

56 Deverell and Hyde, *The West in the History of the Nation*, 294.

57 Eric Foner, *Free Soil, Free Labor, Free Men: The Ideology of the Republican Party before the Civil War* (New York: Oxford University Press, 1970), 236.

58 Lillian Schlissel, Vicki L. Ruiz, and Janice Monk, introduction to *Western Women: Their Land, Their Lives*, ed. Lillian Schlissel, Vicki L. Ruiz, and Janice Monk (Albuquerque: University of New Mexico Press, 1988), 4.

59 Pauline Hopkins, Winona: A Tale of Negro Life in the South and Southwest, 1902–1903, in *The Magazine Novels of Pauline Hopkins* (New York: Oxford University Press, 1988).

60 Toni Morrison, *Paradise* (New York: Knopf, 1997).

61 Laura Ingalls Wilder, *Little House on the Prairie* (New York: Harper, 1935).

62 Penny T. Linsenmayer, "Kansas Settlers on the Osage Diminished Reserve," *Kansas History* 24 (2001): 168–85.

63 Thomas Jefferson Morgan, "Instructions to Indian Agents in Regard to Inculcation of Patriotism in Indian Schools," in *Forty-ninth Annual Report of the Commissioner of Indian Affairs to the Secretary of the Interior, 1890* (Washington, DC, 1890), clxvii.

64 Mary Ellicott Arnold and Mabel Reed, *In the Land of the Grasshopper Song: Two Women in the Klamath River Indian Country in 1908–09* (1957; Lincoln: University of Nebraska Press, 1980), 9.

65 Elaine Goodale Eastman, *Sister to the Sioux: The Memoirs of Elaine Goodale Eastman, 1885–1891*, ed. Kay Graber, 2nd ed. (1978; Lincoln: University of Nebraska Press, 2004).

66 Alice C. Fletcher, "Home Life among the Indians: Records of Personal Experience," *Century* 54, no. 2 (1897): 252–63.

67 E. Jane Gay, *Choup-nit-ki: With the Nez Perces. Jane Gay Dodge Papers, 1861–1951*. Schlesinger Library, Radcliffe Institute, Harvard University, Cambridge, MA, http://pds.lib.harvard.edu/pds/view/3463914?n=1&imagesize=1200&jp2Res=.25&printThumbnails=no.

68 Ibid., 445.

CHAPTER 4

Labor and the Land
Narratives of Trading, Mining, and Ranching
Nathaniel Lewis

In *Ranch Life and the Hunting-Trail* (1888), Theodore Roosevelt reflected on the West's transitional moment, as the wild past retreated before what he calls "the white advance throughout all our Western land."[1] He presents three types – the trapper, the miner, and the cowboy – "the forerunners" of civilization's march. To Roosevelt, all three were heroic, alienated from an industrializing world, and doomed. "The trapper and the miner were the pioneers of the mountains, as the hunter and the cowboy have been the pioneers of the plains," writes Roosevelt; "they are all of the same type, these sinewy men of the border, fearless and self-reliant, who are ever driven restlessly onward through the wilderness by the half-formed desires that make their eyes haggard and eager."[2] Yet their time is limited as they slip into the remote pockets of both place and memory: "The old race of Rocky Mountain hunters and trappers, of reckless, dauntless Indian fighters, is now fast dying out. Yet here and there these restless wanderers of the untrodden wilderness still linger, in wooded fastnesses so inaccessible that the miners have not yet explored them, in mountain valleys so far off that no ranchman has yet driven his herds thither."[3] Roosevelt imagines this hunter and trapper not only "dying out" but already *buried,* deep within the western landscape. The cowboy, too, "brave, hospitable, hardy, and adventurous," is on his way out: "he prepares the way for the civilization from before whose face he must himself disappear."[4] It is the cowboy's job to prepare the trail that in turn becomes the landscaped mark of his absence.

Although, as Wallace Stegner reminds us, "the fur trade, the gold rushes, [and] the open range cattle industry ... lasted hardly longer than the blink of an eye,"[5] few western legacies are more enduring to the American West's popular and scholarly story than trading, mining, and ranching, and few western types are more enduring than the trapper, the miner, and the cowboy. What connects the three types? What links the narratives of trapping, mining, and ranching? Part of the answer can be found in a set of cultural codes (about masculinity, race, labor, wilderness, and so on) that continue to resonate in the twenty-first century. There is nothing simple or benign about these codes, and breaking them is time-honored work. For as long as we have had a recognizable western literature, critics and commentators have vilified and demythologized the kind of unrealistic, historically corrupting constructions that Roosevelt and others so successfully deployed.

For example, an *Overland Monthly* review of Alfred Henry Lewis's *Wolfville* (1897), which became a standard for the cowboy novel until Owen Wister's *The Virginian* (1902), complained that the book would appeal to eastern readers, but "Western readers will not be so apt to like it, finding it wofully [*sic*] exaggerated," its language being that which "an Eastern man imagines that a cowboy should use [rather] than anything real."[6] Wister's own celebrated book likewise came under attack for its romanticized, eastern imagination. Indeed, the corrective criticisms of the iconic cowboy in popular culture were established by 1888, the year of Roosevelt's *Ranch Life*, when Edward Aveling and Eleanor Marx Aveling included a decidedly antiromantic chapter, "The Cowboys," in *The Working-Class Movement in America*. "The cowboys of the West have been this long time objects of interest," they write, "but there is one aspect under which this class of men seem little known ... that is, in their capacity as proletarians." It is their status within the volatile world of *labor* that matters, they argue, not their popularity with "the spectators at 'shows' in which [the cowboy] has been exhibited on both sides of the Atlantic," for the cowboy is "as much at the mercy of the capitalist as a New or Old England cotton-operative," and the cowboy's "supposed 'freedom' is no more a reality than his."[7]

When we read Roosevelt's *Ranch Life*, Lewis's *Wolfville*, or Wister's *Virginian* against reality or, as some might prefer, *as* reality, we make the West – its history, its cultures, its landscapes – the primary referent of the region's literature. This essay considers how a number of nineteenth-century western American authors, in representing labor and the land, created strategies of referentiality that not only promoted a kind of marketplace authority but also effectively induced a kind of reading history, which is to say induced both a history of reading and a tendency to read for history. Given the thousands of nineteenth-century narratives devoted to labor and the land, and given the impressive scholarly treatment of these narratives over the last seventy-five years or so, this essay does not attempt to survey the literature of trading, mining, and ranching, let alone recognize the differences in labor practices or literary genres. Nor do I consider the ways in which western American writers implicitly promoted imperialist ideologies set within a troubled political economy, or consider how their narratives have shaped our contemporary notions of labor, land, and region. Rather, I am interested in how writers, thinking through the relationships among work, place, and history, reimagined the labor of *writing*, and consequently how this strategy has shaped our practices of *reading*. That is, this essay argues that any attempt to write a literary history of the period is always already shaped by the ways in which these authors imagined both literature and history.

The idea of *literary history* is profoundly vexed in western American literary studies, as the terms "literary" and "history" simultaneously seem to define and undo, create and critique each other. To understand the complex relationship between the terms, to understand the challenge of writing western U.S. literary history, we might well consider labor and the land, work and place, in nineteenth-century western writing. And we might begin with Roosevelt's observation that those dying-out western hunters and trappers, quietly slipping into the past, still linger in inaccessible woods and valleys – and we might then wonder about the passage's logical dilemma: How could Roosevelt know of their fragile existence in such remote places if the miner and ranchman cannot find them? How did *Roosevelt* root them out? The answer, of course, is that he put them there.

Losing Ground

Why is it that, in western American literary studies, the systems of analysis are inevitably situated in a certain "political economy" of historicity? In western studies, it is always the past that is at issue – the past and its forces, their utility and their docility, their distribution and their spectrality. If, as Foucault argued, the body is involved in a political field, so too is the notion of western history, including western literary history, and bound up in its economic uses; it is largely as a force of production that the past is invested with relations of power and domination. On the other hand, its constitution as labor power is possible only if it is caught up in a system of subjection. The past becomes a useful force only if it is both a productive narrative and a subjected one.

What is curious and perhaps uniquely western is that both scholarly and creative practices have shared this project of simultaneously inventing and interpreting the past. Wallace Stegner identified this desire in both historians and creative writers when, commenting on the novelist A. B. Guthrie Jr. and the historian Bernard DeVoto, he remarked that they "share a characteristic western impulse: they are intent on creating a past, firming up a ground on which the present can stand and by which it can be comprehended."[8] Here the term "creating" implies the possibility that both writers and scholars invent a past drawn from whole cloth, while "firming up a ground" suggests that the past has its place and only needs some memory work, akin to repairing an aging foundation. The two gerunds qualify and challenge each other, and the semantic doubleness produces an instructive ambiguity in the last phrase, for the "it" is grammatically uncertain and can reasonably be understood to refer to the present, the past, or the unstable, vulnerable ground. The sentence, affirming the possibility of comprehension, gives way under the shifts of metaphor ("firming up a ground") and the ambiguities of "the present."

What makes nineteenth-century western literature so enthralling is our ability to witness exactly this simultaneous creation and unsettling of a regional past. If the nineteenth-century American West and especially the antebellum West is "not yet a symbolically coherent or geopolitically recognizable region of the United States,"[9] then we can witness western authors working to find their place in the unfolding story of U.S. literature, moving toward a marketable identity for western writing. Their strategy was typically to anticipate the inevitable settlement of the West and yet to see this settlement as erasing something quintessentially western. This conceit is writ large in many of the century's major meditations on the West: in Lewis and Clark's *Journals*; Cooper's Leatherstocking Tales; Francis Parkman's *Oregon Trail* ("great changes are at hand in that region," and soon "its danger and its charm will have disappeared together"); Bryant's "The Prairies"; Thoreau's "Walking"; and Roosevelt's *Ranch Life*. This disappearing West is typically read as a nostalgia bound up in romantic constructions of wilderness and masculinity, fueled by anxieties over the acceleration of modernity. The notion of the disappearing West, though, was not all nostalgia. Some mourned the declining wildness of times past; others expressed relief that quieter times were arriving. In both cases, writers emphasized two themes: They insisted that the "great changes" signaled the loss of specific kinds of labor; and they implied that this loss could not only be recorded but even be replaced by their writing. That is, they worked the backward glance – their rooting of historicity – as a strategy for their own marketable authority.

In *Astoria* (1836), for example, Washington Irving deployed a fantasy of feudal Britain in describing Fort William and the fur trade. He describes the fort as containing a Council Hall and banqueting chamber, "decorated with Indian arms and accouterments and the trophies of the Fur trade."

Business meetings, or "grave and weighty councils," were, Irving says, "alternated by huge feasts and revels like some of the old feasts described in highland castles." Irving offers an apology for "dwelling too long, perhaps, upon these individual pictures," but explains his motivation: "It is one object of our task ... to present scenes of the rough life of the wilderness, and we are tempted to fix these few memorials of a transient state of things fast passing into oblivion; – for the feudal state of Fort William is at an end."[10] Irving here aligns the North American fur trade with a fanciful Anglo-Saxon history straight out of Scott, implying the loss of a heroic age of frontier capitalism. His "memorials" suggest an abandonment achieved by a double remoteness: the archaic quality of the "rough life in the wilderness" and the silent, deserted present. What remains for Irving is the writer's "task."

Through at least the 1860s, writers often turned to a more recent past, usually experienced by the author and implicitly just missed by the reader. For example, the notion of labor implied not only working in the gold fields but getting there as well. Such a past could be personal travails: In his dedication to *Life on the Plains and Among the Diggings* (1853), Alonzo Delano expresses both pride and relief that "the dangers are passed," "whether toiling through the deep sands of the barren desert, suffering from hunger and thirst; or weary and way-worn climbing stupendous heights of the Siérras."[11] In his account published only four years after he joined the gold rush in April of 1849, Delano looks back on the early days of mining and, at the end of his narrative, forward to the arrival of statehood and civil government.

But Eliza Farnham, in her lively *California, In-Doors and Out* (1856), hits the most familiar note, apologizing to her readers "if there appears to be discrepancies between the early and later pages," for "in many respects, there have been such changes in the things and aspects sought to be described, as half a century would not produce in many older countries."[12] Like Delano, she is enthusiastic about the region's economic future, for "America is young and strong."[13] "The period of wild enthusiasms and insane hopes has passed over California," she writes, expressing her approval that recent arrivals "entertain other considerations than those of the mineral wealth of the country." She concludes that "business will become better regulated, and labor more settled, as the population takes on a quieter character."[14] At the very moment that Farnham recognizes a shift in the concept of manual labor in California from the "wild enthusiasms" of mining to a "quieter character" of farming, dime novels and westerns are starting to advertise the opposite: the Wild West.

The gold rush produced its own recognizable doubled-up history, with early commentators emphasizing their own experiences in the changing world followed by a "second generation" – Bret Harte, Mark Twain, Ambrose Bierce, Joaquin Miller, and others – who, in Michael Kowalewski's words, "transformed the event into mythic history."[15] For all the vitality of their playful, often acerbic stories, these writers manipulated both the received history of the region (as Kowalewski suggests) and the market for their writing. The fact that they deployed obvious exaggerations and humor masked their focused attention to the power of inscribed historicity. Twain had fun with his comic speculations in *Roughing It* (1872), but his comments on the passing of history play as both a parody of earlier laments and something darker about the absolute disappearance of the past. At the end of a sparkling, expansive account of a once-thriving mining town – "labor, laughter, music, dancing, swearing, fighting, shooting, stabbing ... *everything* that delights and adorns existence" – Twain concludes: "and *now* nothing is left of it all but a lifeless, homeless solitude. The men are gone, the houses have vanished, even the *name* of the place is forgotten. In no other land, in modern times, have towns so absolutely died and disappeared, as in the old mining regions of California."[16] As the chapter unfolds, Twain continues to expand on this absence, pondering the fate of the miners, "all gone, or nearly all – victims devoted upon the altar of the golden calf – the noblest holocaust that ever wafted its sacrificial incense heavenward."[17] Twain takes the notion of the California Inferno, as the gold rush was sometimes called, and names it a holocaust, what amounts to epic (or biblical) self-immolation.

A less solemn play of memory, history, religion, and writing can be found in the 1932 publication of Sarah Royce's *A Frontier Lady: Recollections of the Gold Rush and Early California*. The text itself, written in the 1880s, is an appealing but unexceptional account of Royce's Gold Rush experiences with her husband and young daughter. "On the last day of April, 1849 we began our journey to California. Our out-fit consisted of a covered wagon, well loaded with provisions," she writes, explaining that they were "guided only by the light of Fremont's *Travels*, and the suggestions, often conflicting, of the many who ... were setting out for the 'Golden Gate.'"[18] Front-loading two signifiers – *1849, California* – that ground so many narratives of the time, Royce's book begins by recalling the moment of departure: all eyes west. They take with them both the stock material belongings (covered wagon, provisions) and a swirl of regional narratives already widely circulating. Royce describes how they "conquered the desert"[19] and then, facing "perils," crossed the Sierra Nevada. "On the 24th of October at evening we reached what in our Guide Book was called 'Pleasant Valley Gold Mines,'" Royce writes, and "that night, we slept, for the first time in several months, without the fear of Indians, or the dread of perils."[20]

As compelling as the story itself is, Royce's book is of particular interest for its complex textuality and publication history. Royce was the mother of the Harvard philosopher Josiah Royce, who, when working on his *California: A Study of American Character* (1886), one of the first serious academic histories of the West, asked his mother to "thread together and shape, as a continuous narrative, for his pleasure and instruction, her old 'Pilgrimage Diary.'"[21] She did so, apparently not intending publication, weaving passages from her diary into the "continuous narrative." Almost half a century later, the narrative was edited by Ralph Henry Gabriel, a Yale history professor. Sarah Royce's voice never speaks for itself; Gabriel's chief interest is in Josiah Royce, and in his introduction Gabriel explains that he "cannot, at times, escape the feeling that she is not merely narrating but is arguing with her philosopher son."[22] To convey this intertextual dialogue, Gabriel begins each chapter with "a comment by [Josiah] Royce upon the type of life experience which is most conspicuously illustrated in the section."[23] The 1932 text of Sarah Royce's narrative is thus a heteroglot affair, her 1880s narrative frequently interrupted by her own 1849 diary, Gabriel's editorial apparatus, and snippets of Josiah Royce's own writings.

Gabriel's introduction is titled "Concerning the Manuscript of Sarah Royce," yet it seems remarkably uninterested in the manuscript and only obliquely interested in Sarah Royce. It begins: "Josiah Royce was a young lecturer in philosophy ... when he was asked to prepare a history of the early American period in the state of California. The task was a congenial one for Royce had been born in a mining camp in the shadow of the Sierras.... Royce's parents, moreover, were Forty-niners who had jolted overland across the continent in a covered wagon."[24] Gabriel's opening move subverts our reading of Sarah Royce's narrative, for we are encouraged to read her words primarily in the context of her celebrated son's words, specifically in the context of his academic history of California. Gabriel's tautological prose authenticates each text by reference to the other: Sarah Royce's narrative is compelling because it was commissioned by a Harvard professor for a major work of western history, and Josiah Royce's book is trustworthy because the author ("born in a mining camp") could "collect" from the source. The work of mining has become the work of writing.

From its early nineteenth century start, then, western American literature was retrospective. Irving published *Astoria,* his attempt to "fix these few memorials" to the lost world of the western fur trade, in the same year that Emerson complained in *Nature* that American writers were building sepulchers. For western writers, though, there was pride in claiming that early authors beheld the West and nature face to face, while future generations would have to read the West through their eyes. Generally speaking, the claim is that the true West exists only in a past that would slip into oblivion if not for the writer's (heroic) efforts; often, that the writer was a witness, on the ground, though that ground no longer exists and that writer is no longer in that place or in that time; and frequently that the writing itself is elegiac. In *Ranch Life,* Roosevelt typically laments that "the great free ranches … must pass away before the onward march of our people; and we who have felt the charm of the life … will not only regret its passing for our own sakes, but must also feel real sorrow that those who come after us are not to see, as we have seen, what is perhaps the pleasantest, healthiest, and most exciting phase of American existence."[25]

In surprising ways, though, in creating this tone of loss, nineteenth-century western writers looked to a marketable future rather than a historical past. We do not have to doubt their sincerity or even veracity to recognize a successful writerly strategy. Of the many effects of this strategy, a few stand out as legacies of the region's writing. First, in asserting that the West's "wild enthusiasms" were gone, writers cleared some authorial space for themselves in an increasingly crowded market by establishing their primacy. Roosevelt's "sorrow" that his future readers would never see what he has seen may be "real," but it also establishes his narrative authority based on his witness of history.

Second, writers wove together (or conflated) concepts of wildness and wilderness, linking together the West's natural landscapes with the region's popularity as "the Wild West." Though this point is beyond the scope of this essay, we can at least acknowledge the expanding role of the creative *writer* as the figure whose labors will record that wild West before it slips into the past. Hubert Howe Bancroft, who created his own publishing industry centered on western history, remarks in *California Inter Pocula* (1888) that the "flush times" in California were "so full of oddities, and crudities, and strange developments" that they "cannot be vividly portrayed without a tolerably free use of words," though, he adds, not a "free use of the imagination." In a passage with Emersonian echoes, Bancroft proclaims that "the true artist who, with the hand of the master drawing from life, places before the observer the all-glowing facts, unbesmeared by artificial and deceptive coloring, has yet to appear."[26] (In his preface Bancroft avers that his own study will be "historical rather than fantastical, with no effort toward effect," a claim belied by the very next sentence, the first chapter's opening: "Drunk! aye, drunk with avarice! Behold the picture; California in her cups!")[27] In short, according to Bancroft, it falls to poets to record, if not legislate, the region's extraordinary past.

Third, and more complexly, authors explored the ways in which a constructed historicity could function within a literary marketplace. The power of their works, they suggested, lay in dramatic and accurate representations of a region already changing, in many ways becoming less itself with the passing of time, an emphasis that obscured their own writerly inventions and machinations. The question of whether the represented past was historically true was both displaced and centered, veiled by the exaggerations of popular entertainments, dependably unreliable as the century wore on. It subsequently became the business of twentieth-century literary scholarship to expose the mythologizing impulses of some western literature while upholding the cultural or historical justness of other western literature – moves that, while necessary when done in the name of historical veracity or social justice, nevertheless were limited by the epistemological value system of historicity itself.

Thus the paradise lost of western literature – the recent vanishing past of regional wholeness and beauty and wildness that we will never see – is not so interesting as a questionable historical reality and only slightly more interesting as the site of nostalgia. Instead of seeing nineteenth-century western writing as longing for a lost world of authentic westness, we can instead see these writers as inventing that lost world – or, rather, inventing the notion of western lostness itself: inventing an always already of absence. I mean *always already* in Derrida's sense of "a radical past ... that can never be fully reactivated or awakened to presence," one that "effaces itself and is from the outset in retreat," and yet "nonetheless leaves a mark, a signature that is retraced in the very thing from which it is withdrawn."[28] (Recall Roosevelt's notion that the cowboy "prepares the way for the civilization from before whose face he must himself disappear.") When antebellum western writers constructed that always already, that radical past forever in retreat, they were essentially leaving their mark and signature, retraced in the canon of western writing and enduring primarily as an absence. In this sense "creating a past" and "firming up a ground" turn out to be the same thing, for the memory work of ground firming amounts to planting a ground cover, a cultivated, faux rewilding of western literature.

If, as many writers implied, the geographical U.S. West became less western with each passing moment, then the *literary* West became at the same time more western, at least in the sense that it developed into a robust presence among the absences and ruins of the barely settled region. In many ways, contrary to its origin myth, western literature was "post-western" from its immaculate conception. As obsessively devoted to real place and real history as western literature purports to be, the complicated truth is that by its literature's own devices there never was a West to be represented, celebrated, or mourned. In the beginning was the word, and before Sarah Royce set out in a covered wagon for California in 1849, she was reading Fremont, studying her guide, and attending to the stories in circulation.

Gaining Ground

For some tourists and journalists intent on going back to the future, the recent drought in the American West has had an unexpected upside. "California Drought Launches New Gold Rush," declared *National Geographic* in August 2014, one of many newspaper and magazine accounts of this new old story.[29] As water levels in many rivers drop to unprecedented lows, new pockets of gold have been exposed. "Modern-day prospectors are heading to the hills," a Southern California Public Radio program reported, "a silver, or rather gold, lining of sorts" to the drought.[30] Most of these prospectors, hobbyists and vacationers, seem to enjoy the old-fashioned method of placer mining, dressing in period costumes. Further, in some places dropping reservoir or lake levels have exposed the detritus of human settlement, submerged under water for a century or more. Folsom Lake, for example, a California reservoir, made the news when its dropping waters revealed the remains of Gold Rush buildings and mining artifacts. As the waters recede on a human-made lake, the recession likely caused by human-created climate change, we "discover" the ruins of earlier human settlements, settlements such as mining towns that are themselves emblematic of an attitude toward region and land that was always acquisitive and ephemeral.

Such stories are as uncomfortably emblematic. What is hidden in the hills, beyond the valleys, and under the waters are the stories and characters that writers both buried and unearthed there. As nineteenth-century western authors created that always already of a radical past of loss and absence, a past simultaneously retreating and impending, they rethought the work of writing. To repeat, the idea of regional loss became writerly gain, licensing them to extract from the land (or from the representation of the land) their own material. Ralph Waldo Emerson, for example, recognized that the West provided lucrative natural resources for the writer's designs and doings, as he did by working his own mining metaphor in "The American Scholar": "Authors we have, in numbers, who have written out their vein, and who, moved by a commendable prudence, sail for Greece or Palestine, follow the trapper into the prairie ... to replenish their merchantable stock."[31] In *The Conduct of Life* (1860), a book infused with reflections on California and the West, Emerson reflected on men with a "surcharge of arterial blood" who are "made for war, for the sea, for mining, hunting, and clearing."[32] Yet, harshly critical of the rush for gold as he was, seeing it as "a scramble of needy adventurers," Emerson concluded on a wryly optimistic note: "Nature watches over all, and turns this malfaisance [*sic*] to good. California gets peopled and subdued, – civilized in this immoral way, – and, on this fiction, a real prosperity is rooted and grown."[33] Emerson's dizzying language upends the moralizing tone of frontier discourse ("civilized in this immoral way"), turning to a surprising conclusion: The ground for California's "real prosperity" is "fiction." The pivotal pun, "rooted," means both planted deeply and, antithetically, dug up, rummaged. "Rooted" also means "had as an origin"; thus "a real prosperity," what we might call an acceleration of the California real, is settled on, and unsettled by, fiction.

Henry David Thoreau doubled down on Emerson's disapproval of the Gold Rush – "the greatest disgrace on mankind," Thoreau called it – and on Emerson's deployment of mining's metaphors. In a startling 1852 *Journal* passage, Thoreau recognizes the mercantile fever of the "recent rush to California" as contributing to the extreme exploitation of labor: "of what significance the philosophy, or poetry, or religion of a world that will rush to the lottery of California gold-digging on the receipt of the first news, to live by luck, to get the means of commanding the labor of others less lucky, i.e. of slaveholding, without contributing any value to society?" His outrage is directed not only at those who "get their living by the lottery of gold-digging," but more broadly at a culture that celebrates and profits from such feral greed and exploitation, such "rottenness": "the hog that *roots* his own living, and so makes manure, would be ashamed of such company." Strong language: In contrasting the hog's digging (making his living) with the diggings in the gold field, Thoreau not only makes a point about value and labor, but he also uses an outrageous metaphor to reclaim philosophy, poetry, and religion: "Did God direct us so to get our living, digging where we never planted?"[34]

Naturally, Thoreau's answer is to do his own planting and rooting, using the power of metaphor to reimagine mining (the extraction of natural resources) as positing (putting in place). In the celebrated conclusion to *Walden*'s second chapter, Thoreau develops metaphors baroque in design and shape-shifting folds: "Let us settle ourselves, and work and wedge our feet downward through the mud and slush of opinion … till we come to a hard bottom and rocks in place, which we can call *reality*." Having reached the solid ground of this metaphor, "a place where you might found a wall or a state," he suggests one might plant "not a Nilometer, but a Realometer, that future ages might know how deep a freshet of shams and appearances had gathered from time to time." He concludes the chapter with a series of lightning moves:

> The intellect is a cleaver; it discerns and rifts its way into the secret of things. I do not wish to be any more busy with my hands than is necessary. My head is hands and feet. I feel all my best faculties concentrated in it. My instinct tells me that my head is an organ for burrowing, as some creatures use their snout and fore paws, and with it I would mine and burrow my way through these hills. I think that the richest vein is somewhere hereabouts; so by the divining rod and thin rising vapors I judge; and here I will begin to mine.[35]

Creating an almost impenetrable wall (or a state) of words, Thoreau himself becomes the *Journal*'s hog, rooting his living. The body (head, hands, feet, snout, forepaws, vein) dissected and abstracted by the intellect's cleaver, Thoreau begins to *mine*: to dig and to *claim*.

Emerson and Thoreau were hardly alone in reworking the metaphor of mining. As the nineteenth century unfolded, writers east and west increasingly saw mining and ranching as fodder for their imaginations (and valuable metal for their pockets). This process is visible even at the level of the sentence, as when Prentice Mulford wrote of his two mining partners that "rich mines of mental wealth might have been hidden in their brains, but such treasure was at that time buried in unfathomable depths."[36] The last third of the century, however, saw an explosion of popular writing about the West, and a more self-conscious literary movement, the San Francisco circle of Harte, Twain, Mulford, Ambrose Bierce, and others. It is worth noting that these authors had cusp experiences in the West, arriving after the initial Gold Rush yet in place to witness and participate in mining activities. Harte went west in 1853, Mulford in 1856, Twain in 1861, and Bierce in 1866. (In 1849, Twain had watched a number of young men emigrate to California from Hannibal, Missouri.) The result is an imbrication of literary ambition, subversive humor, and

subtle wistfulness – wistfulness that they were second-generation witnesses. Harte especially placed his most successful stories in the recent
past, often just a few years before his own arrival in California. (Though
written in the late 1860s, "The Luck of Roaring Camp" and "The Outcasts
of Poker Flat" are both set in 1850.) By the late 1870s, the literary West was
well established as a territory for "local color," humor pieces, and, increasingly, memoirs of earlier adventures. And by the 1890s, when magazines
such as *Harper's*, *Atlantic*, and *Scribner's* were publishing the likes of Owen
Wister and Frederic Remington, expectations were clear: Though the style
was realism and the market current, the gaze was backward, into a gilded
past. That is, while writers continued to encode historicity as the subtext
for their prose, it became harder to tell whether the writer or the market
was driving the literary machine.

It is not surprising that writers deployed mining as extended metaphor,
and it is not news that western writers turned increasingly to fiction in
the century's second half to represent mining and ranching. Nor do I suggest that there is nothing outside the text. The labor of regional writing takes on its own loaded meaning when, for example, we think of the
"fiction factories" that produced dime novel westerns;[37] and the regional
writing of labor needs to be understood in the context of the exploitation of Chinese mine workers during the Gold Rush, the Canadian River
cowboy strike of 1883, the brutal Colorado coal mining "wars" of the first
decade of the twentieth century, and the general rise (and suppression) of
organized labor over this period. Equally to the point, we can trace many
twenty-first-century environmental catastrophes back through the ecological myopia of nineteenth-century land-use practices and their sentimental
representations in regional writing. The exploitation of Native Americans
within the radical redistribution of resources in an already-global trade
economy; the arrogant destruction of waterways and riparian environments in the "fevered" rush for gold, "nature ... forced out of her legal
ways," as Eliza Farnham describes it;[38] the landscape of California "torn
and guttered and disfigured by the avaricious spoilers," in Twain's words;[39]
the extermination of bison and the plundering of western grasslands and
prairies – that these sorrows have been celebrated as romantic episodes in
the nation's wild oat-sowing youth is a source of lasting shame that casts a
pall over the study of nineteenth-century western literature.

Yet our impulse to plant a Realometer in a terra firma of western literature is unsettled by the textual strategies of its authors; the ground is
not solid, no matter how much "firming up" (recalling Stegner's metaphor) historians and novelists attempt, or perhaps exactly because of that

firming up. What is the relationship between the word and the world, between the literary and history? We might recall that when Derrida suggested that *il n'y a pas de hors-texte*, he hardly meant that the world consisted only of wordplay. "It is totally false to suggest that deconstruction is a suspension of reference," he later remarked. "Deconstruction is always deeply concerned with the *other* of language. I never cease to be surprised by critics who see my work as a declaration that there is nothing beyond language, that we are imprisoned in language; it is, in fact, saying the exact opposite. The critique of logocentrism is above all else the search for the *other* and the *other of language."* So perhaps we become Searchers for this "other" that, Derrida suggests, "is beyond language and which summons language."[40] In the end, the West in western literature is not the referent of the writing but rather the retreating, summoning "other," and if it is the object of our searching then we must traverse the territory created by our own mapping. In "The Problem of the Popular," Stephen Tatum argues that the new western historians, critical of popular western fantasies that they see as denying the reality of the regional past, miss the play of imaginative *desire*. "Denial for the New Western historians," Tatum writes, "is a matter of not seeing the real itself and not understanding the truths about reality because of the persuasive power of wishes and dreams, which is to say precisely because between humans and an external reality there always exists desire."[41]

Desire *is* the story, not only of the narratives of labor but equally of our own interpretive strategies, and desire is never self-contained for it is always pointing toward some longed-for other. Even to name the other (fur, gold, territory; wealth, lust, power; nature, West, nation) is not to satisfy that desire but to feed it. Think of Trina in Frank Norris's *McTeague* (1899), lying on her bed, surrounded by gold coins, "burying her face in them with long sighs of unspeakable delight"[42] – a perverted re-presentation of mining fever. Or recall her husband, the dentist McTeague, who, after murdering Trina and becoming both a cowboy and a miner, finds himself stranded in Death Valley on his way to Gold Mountain. Instead of Roosevelt's doomed frontier types who are driven by "half-formed desires that make their eyes haggard and eager," Norris gives us McTeague, "stupidly looking around him" as he confronts the "vast, interminable" landscape of the desert.[43] In a sense, by reaching "the measureless leagues of Death Valley," McTeague has arrived at the always already, this "vast, interminable" space corresponding to Irving's "oblivion" and Twain's "lifeless, homeless solitude." It has no meaning for McTeague, except perhaps as the terminus of both text and desire.

Norris's novel closes out the century, offering a cruel parody of western desire and labor that both creates and critiques expectations for western literature. In this sense it reinscribes the region's fascination with its own coding of historicity within the context of labor practices and landscape deformations. This is in part to say that by the end of the nineteenth century, western writers worked within a market both financially lucrative and aesthetically limiting. Bret Harte was not the only western writer to be "trapped in a cycle of self-parody by the demands of the literary market," as Gary Scharnhorst has written.[44] The trap, though, was largely of the writers' own making. By composing a literary landscape determined and defined by a radical past retreating before the advance of those who would name or wish it, writers designed their own working environment and shaped their own reception.

In many ways those who would write western American literary history in the twenty-first century are trapped as well, though perhaps not infelicitously so. Our labor practices – scholarly, institutional, sometimes competitive, covertly creative – follow the trail established nearly two centuries ago. To read western literature is to be isolated not only from the past (and all its duplicitous pretendings) but from present acts of reading as well. To read western U.S. literature is to be displaced – a marvelous effect, thrilling and wild. Thus in seeking to unlock the gate to the always already absent West, which is to say to secure the referent in the region's literature and to *fix* it, we design narratives that speak in professional tones of our own fevered desires. We become participants in the shared project of western literature, creating and critiquing an imagined past even as we attempt to open new routes and new Wests. As Eliza Farnham wrote of the drive for gold, "the earth ... is being searched and researched, washed and rewashed, one year after another."[45] We become miners making claims about an elusive West, golden or tarnished, seeking a usable past that explains our compromised present. This is good work, in any sense of that phrase, but we should be mindful that in our digging up we are also firming up, and we can find only what we have rooted.

Notes

1 Theodore Roosevelt, *Ranch Life and the Hunting-Trail* (New York: Century, 1888), 81.
2 Ibid., 172.
3 Ibid., 81.
4 Ibid., 100.

5 Wallace Stegner, *The American West as Living Space* (Ann Arbor: University of Michigan Press, 1987), 69.

6 Review of *Wolfville, Overland Monthly*, January 1898, 90. *Wolfville* is formally a collection of sketches, though unified by characters and thus loosely shaped as a novel.

7 Edward Aveling and Eleanor Marx Aveling, *The Working-Class Movement in America* (London: Swan, Sonnenschein, Lowrey, 1888), 154–5.

8 Wallace Stegner, foreword to A. B. Guthrie's *The Big Sky* (Boston: Houghton Mifflin, 2002), xi.

9 Stephanie LeMenager, *Manifest and Other Destinies: Territorial Fictions of the Nineteenth-Century United States* (Lincoln: University of Nebraska Press, 2004), 6.

10 Washington Irving, *Astoria* (New York: Library of America, 2004), 193.

11 Alonzo Delano, *Life on the Plains and among the Diggings* (1854; New York: Arno Press, 1973), iii.

12 Eliza Farnham, *California, In-Doors and Out* (New York: Dix, Edwards & Co, 1856), iii.

13 Ibid., 331.

14 Ibid., 506.

15 Michael Kowalewski, introduction to *Gold Rush: A Literary Exploration* (Berkeley, CA: Heydey Books, 1997), xxiv.

16 Mark Twain, Roughing It, in *The Innocents Abroad and Roughing It*, ed. Guy Cardwell (New York: Library of America, 1984), 839.

17 Ibid., 840.

18 Sarah Royce, *A Frontier Lady: Recollections of the Gold Rush and Early California*, ed. Ralph Henry Gabriel (New Haven, CT: Yale University Press, 1932), 3.

19 Ibid., 57.

20 Ibid., 74.

21 Ibid., iii.

22 Ibid., xi.

23 Ibid., xiv.

24 Ibid, vii.

25 Roosevelt, *Ranch Life*, 24.

26 Hubert Howe Bancroft, California Inter Pocula in *The Works of Hubert Howe Bancroft*, Vol. xxxv (San Francisco: History Company, 1888), v.

27 Ibid., 1.

28 Rodolph Gasché, introduction to *Readings in Interpretation: Holderlin, Hegel, Heidegger*, by Andrzej Warminski (Minneapolis: University of Minnesota Press, 1987), xi.

29 Brian Clark Howard, "California Drought Launches New Gold Rush," *National Geographic*, August 14, 2014, http://news.nationalgeographic .com/news/2014/08/140814-california-drought-gold-rush-water-climate -mining-panning/ (accessed January 15, 2015).

30 "Take Two," Southern California Public Radio, January 28, 2014, http://www .scpr.org/programs/take-two/2014/01/28/35743/california-drought-sends -gold-miners-to-the-hills/ (accessed January 15, 2015).

31 Ralph Waldo Emerson, "The American Scholar," in *Essays and Lectures*, ed. Joel Porte (New York: Library of America, 1983), 61.

32 Emerson, *The Conduct of Life*, in *Essays and Lectures*, 979.

33 Ibid., 1084.

34 Henry David Thoreau, *Journal* III (Cambridge: Riverside, 1906), 265–7.

35 Henry David Thoreau, *Walden* (1854; Princeton, NJ: Princeton University Press, 1971), 97–8.

36 Prentice Mulford, *Prentice Mulford's California Sketches*, ed. Franklin Walker (San Francisco: The Book Club of California, 1935), 29.

37 See Christine Bold's *Selling the Wild West: Popular Western Fiction, 1860–1960* (Bloomington: Indiana University Press, 1987) and *The Frontier Club: Popular Westerns and Cultural Power, 1880–1924* (New York: Oxford University Press, 2013).

38 Farnham, *California*, 343

39 Twain, *Roughing It*, 839.

40 Jacques Derrida, interview in *Debates in Contemporary Continental Philosophy*, ed. Richard Kearney (New York: Fordham University Press, 2004), 154. ,

41 Stephen Tatum, "The Problem of the 'Popular' in the New Western History," in *The New Western History: The Territory Ahead*, ed. Forrest G. Robinson (Tucson: University of Arizona Press, 1997), 156.

42 Frank Norris, McTeague, in *Novels and Essays*, ed. Donald Pizer (New York: Library of America, 1986), 514.

43 Ibid., 572.

44 Gary Scharnhorst, *Bret Harte: Opening the American Literary West* (Norman: University of Oklahoma Press, 2000), 112.

45 Farnham, *California*, 343.

CHAPTER 5

Nature Writing and the American West

Sarah Jaquette Ray

Nature writing about the American West is a kind of discourse that not only describes but also constructs the landscape of the West. Rather than seeing the American West as a static, given space, any investigation of the region must begin with the notion that the West is continually reconstituted as a space of the frontier, of vast wilderness, of freedom, of rugged individualism, of the destiny of American expansion, through discourses about it. In particular, the genre of the nature essay has played a major role in constituting the West, both as a material place and as a set of symbols in the American mind, to use Roderick Nash's term.[1] The nature essay as exemplified by Ralph Waldo Emerson's "Nature" and "Self-Reliance" is a tradition that weaves together forms of travel narrative, philosophy, landscape description, environmental reporting, reflections on field notes, outdoor writing, natural and local history, autobiography and diary, prose fiction, and other genres. Its modes are primarily the sublime and pastoral, which it deploys to define the West as a retreat from tradition and urbanization and a place where American national nature is born, and thus a landscape of transcendence. The nature essay promises this of the western landscape, which, as Krista Comer writes, "comes into representation by and large as symbol of a fixed and specific place."[2]

Further, western landscapes studies "masquerade as 'the natural,'" as Comer argues.[3] This is in large part because of the tradition of the nature essay about and from the American West. As the landscape par excellence of the wild – epitomized by Thoreau when he wrote that "the West of which I speak is another name for the Wild"[4] – the West both inspired and was constructed by the genre of the nature essay that was gaining popularity just as the West was "being won." The emergence of the nature essay as a protoenvironmentalist discourse helped justify the creation of national parks and other forms of public lands in the American West during the nineteenth and into the twentieth century. "In what is often called 'nature writing,'" Elliott West writes, "the western country usually has been seen as a dwindling reserve of 'nature,' which is defined in an introduction to a highly regarded collection of writing as 'everything that exists on this planet (or elsewhere) that was not made by man' and all things in which humans have no part."[5] The end of the "land of plenty," marked by the close of the frontier, turned nature writing from a celebration of American uniqueness to a politics of preservation. Thus, the expansion of the U.S. empire (as Amy Kaplan has called it) into the West during the same period underwrote the proliferation of much of that nature writing.[6]

The nature essay in particular, to the extent that it is written in/about/ from the American West, must be closely scrutinized for the exclusionary and colonial work it has done and continues to do. As new western historians, critical postwestern theorists, and some environmental justice ecocritics argue, the nature essay in the nineteenth century provides a lens through which to examine major *social* concerns of the era – Darwinian natural selection, transcendentalism, Manifest Destiny and the close of the frontier, territorial expansion abroad, segregation and the Civil War, the creation of the U.S.-Mexico border, increased immigration, the Gold Rush, and changing economic relationships, to name a few.

The fact that the nature essay has its roots in natural history hides its cultural work all the more. Passing sometimes as mere innocent description of the natural world, it deflects attention from the highly political dimensions of its subject. As John Elder and Robert Finch explain in the introduction to their anthology *The Norton Book of Nature Writing*, "nature writers are the children of Linnaeus."[7] Carl Linnaeus (1707–78) created the current, dominant system of taxonomy of all living things. Just as critics of Linnaeus's taxonomizing natural history form[8] have argued, the genre of the nature essay too has a reputation of being at times self-consciously apolitical, erasing human history, and satisfying the existential desires of a privileged leisure class. On their path to self-awareness, writers figuratively capture nature, containing and pressing it between their pages.[9] Worse, nature essays about the American West tie this rugged individualistic genre to the national project of Manifest Destiny, authorizing expansion and conquest in the name of nature. Exemplary of the colonizing work of the Linnaeus-influenced, natural history nature essay form is Thomas Jefferson's *Notes on the State of Virginia* (1785), which catalogs aspects of the natural landscape as America's resources, alongside Native American bodies in the landscape that become, like rivers, seaports, mountains, and climate, a resource base for the American economy. The contemporary author Jamaica Kincaid's "In History" is a nature essay that beautifully critiques that colonizing work by using the same aesthetic and literary form to challenge how Linnaeus and the natural history genre served to justify the conquest of land and the enslavement of Africans.[10]

I provide these two examples to illustrate the oppressive work that the nature essay does through its seemingly innocuous cataloging of nature as well as how one writer has challenged how the genre naturalizes colonial projects. Paul Outka writes, "the interweaving of natural beauty and trauma in African-American texts from [the early twentieth century] is clearly conversant with, and critical of, both the sublime and the pastoral modes, intervening on the naturalizing processes of racial identity formation."[11] The nature essay in particular aided in conquest in that it erased the ongoing relationship with nature that people of color maintained for centuries, an argument Priscilla Ybarra has made in detail.[12] As Jeffrey Myers writes of Zitkala-Sa, who wrote concurrently with Muir, such writing "speaks directly to the absence of nonwhite perspectives in the ecocentric position of Muir and offers a more fully ecological stance in its place."[13]

Furthermore, mainstream nature writing of this era reinforced the imperative of the natural history tradition of St. John de Crevecoeur, Thomas Jefferson, and William Bartram, whose works were expressly produced for the purpose of defining American identity. Concerned with articulating how nature was the source of a uniquely American character, what Perry Miller famously dubbed "nature's nation,"[14] nature writers of the mid-nineteenth century used writing about nature as a way to define America. As I describe in *The Ecological Other*, policies of social control (dispossession, immigration, Jim Crow, and eugenics in the twentieth century, for example) were intimately tied to policies of wilderness establishment; they emerged from the same ethos of purifying the body politic of nature's nation.[15] If wilderness became, as Bruce Braun has argued, America's "purification machine,"[16] writing about nature to protect it helped to serve that agenda, whether it did so self-consciously (from George Perkins Marsh in the mid-nineteenth century to Theodore Roosevelt in the Progressive Era to Edward Abbey in the mid-twentieth century) or not, as with the vast majority of other canonized nature writers.

Rachel Stein argues that the mythos of the founding of America through the close of the frontier at the turn of the twentieth century "grounds its operations through recourse to the natural."[17] The nature essay, then, illuminates ways that (Euro-) American identity was naturalized as a homogeneous "imagined community."[18] It is through representations of nature that we can understand how these imperial operations worked. So, rather than approach the nature essay as an apolitical genre, or as an aestheticized form of natural history, this essay suggests that the nature essay articulates imperial anxieties about affronts to the Euro-American social order, and that a critical approach to notions of the American West taken for granted in the canonized genre reveals the untenability of the genre itself (as it has been canonized, at least). As does wilderness itself, the nature essay "says more about the making of a Euro-American self than it does about any geographical landscape."[19]

Writing by marginalized authors suggests another way to deconstruct and expand the genre of nature writing. What happens when we consider Frederick Douglass, Zitkala-Sa, Ruiz de Burton, or Sui Sin Far as nature writers?[20] Scholarship such as Jeffrey Myers's *Converging Stories: Race, Ecology, and Environmental Justice in American Literature*, Paul Outka's *Race and Nature from Transcendentalism to the Harlem Renaissance*, Camille Dungy's *Black Nature: Four Centuries of African-American Nature Writing*, and Priscilla Ybarra's forthcoming *Brown and Green: Mexican-American Environmental Writing* are illustrative of the increased scholarly attention to writers outside the canon who not only addressed nature in their work, but often contested the very same ideological "recourses to the natural" occurring in dominant nature writing and American frontier mythology. Moreover, they challenged the very definition of nature underpinning the genre of nature writing, offering definitions that may at first elude the traditional nature writer.

John Elder and Robert Finch write that "nature writing in prose has achieved a unique fullness and continuity within the Anglo-American context."[21] Such a solipsistic definition of nature writing as the nature essay, as just coincidentally arising in an Anglo-American context, is exemplary of the exclusionary work that canonizing experts do in defining the genre. The exclusion of non-Anglo-American writers from the canon of nature writing only serves to reinforce the argument that nature writing is as much about human relations as it is about nature. The popularity of the sublime mode at this time, in western American literature in particular, occurred as a direct response to racial tensions in the east. The nineteenth-century nature essay suggests that a binary between what is human and what is natural cannot be as easily disentangled as the genre's detractors assume. It also reinforces the exclusions that the traditional nature writing form helped figuratively achieve in the spirit of expanding American territory. Removing native tribes from their lands in order to create empty wilderness, as well documented by William Cronon, Mark Spence, Carolyn Merchant, and Karl Jacoby, for instance, shows that the nature essay, along with promotional materials and government surveys, among other texts, wrote the way west.

It is important to trouble both the terms "nature writing" and "American West." When we trouble the definition of *nature writing*, we see that a certain style of nature writing emerges out of "the American West," from the canonical works by Owen Wister and Willa Cather to John Muir and Mary Austin. As nature writing, works such as Muir's *Mountains of California* and *My First Summer in the Sierra* and Austin's *The Land of Little Rain* are positioned as recording truths about the western landscape, oftentimes for the eastern reader, who might dismiss the possibility that anything is worth preserving in the West. With the aim of detailing concrete, specific truths about the beauty and value of the landscape that holds the potential to create a distinctly American nation, these texts exemplify the genre's ability to hide its expansionist interests. Muir's *Travels in Alaska*, Walt Whitman's *Leaves of Grass*, Aldo Leopold's *Sand County Almanac*, and Edward Abbey's *Desert Solitaire* are examples of the anti-Indigenous, racist tradition of the nature essay genre. As Jake Kosek has outlined extensively, these nature writers saw wilderness as a space where they could purify their white selves; their writings "flowed directly from the perceived need to differentiate and protect the 'pure' from the 'polluted'."[22]

If we challenge the region, as postwestern studies does, recognizing that the accepted view of its boundaries only serves to exclude as much as it includes certain voices, we can see that these boundaries are not at all arbitrary; they emerge from a particular politics and historical moment. They are socially constructed, and nature writing helps to construct them. Furthermore, what counted as the "West" in the nineteenth to early twentieth centuries was in flux. Borders were being established; territorial expansion was in process; land was being appropriated. Just as accepting the genre of nature writing in one particular way is exclusionary, accepting a static notion of the West at this time serves to erase this colonial history. How do we even talk about *an* American West during this time? How do we account for its dynamism, much less its contested boundaries by different groups?

If we assume that the relationship between the terms in the title are, in contrast, about nature writing producing the mythical idea of the "the West," more nature writing can be included in the genre. Henry David Thoreau's "Walking" – written in the East about going West – is exemplary. Nature writing emerging out of the East that romanticized going west – even if that geographical West was a moving target – preceded territorial expansion with literary "razing," as Mary Pat Brady calls it.[23] That is, the nature essay about the American West in the nineteenth century figured the West as empty yet full of resources, destined for conquest, and, often, like a woman waiting to be taken or rescued from Native Americans.[24] Considerations of the genre of nature writing *about* the American West suggest that the nature essay helped to produce the West in both mind and matter. As Elliot West contends, "The two basic narratives that compose the western – that of imposing an outside order and that of escape into prehistory – have been carried into the country and acted out upon it. The result has been a kind of narrative colonialism, but in this case outlanders have not extracted valuable resources" – however, I would argue they did that too. "Instead," he continues, "they have exploited the West by using it as a blank screen where they can project and pursue their fantasies."[25]

Several scholars have addressed how the West was written as empty as a process of conceiving it as such, thereby justifying erasing communities existing there or using that space. Mary Pat Brady's *Extinct Lands, Temporal Geographies: Chicana Literature and the Urgency of Space* is exemplary; likewise David Teague's *The Southwest in American Literature and Art* focuses on the Southwest in particular and explains how cultural texts represented the Southwest as barren as a way to justify occupation. Even the title of the introductory anthology on nature writing, *Constructing Nature: Readings from the American Experience*,[26] suggests that writing constructed American nature; nature does not exist prior to discourse. The importance of literature and literary form to underwriting policies of material dispossession cannot be overstated and suggests an analysis of how nature writing wrote the American West. As we can see, the title of this essay and its inclusion in a literary history suggest a deceptively simple task that obscures the complexity of this period's "legacy of conquest," as Patricia Nelson Limerick has described it,[27] as well as contested definitions of both the region of the West and the genre of nature writing.

Nature Writing

Depending on how we define nature writing, its era of emergence shifts. Michael Branch argues that if we consider the natural history and exploration narratives that influenced Darwin and Thoreau, a long tradition of *early* American nature writing exists. If, however, our definition of nature writing is that it be "written in a personal voice," "presented in the form of the nonfiction essay," "pastoral or Romantic in its philosophical assumptions," "modern or even ecological in its sensibility," and "in service to an implicit or explicit preservationist agenda,"[28] then it could arguably begin with Thoreau, as Lawrence Buell and many contemporary ecocritics might have it.[29] Branch thus argues that the genre of nature writing should encompass literary and nonliterary rhetorical forms, "including the scientific report, religious tract, captivity narrative, slave narrative, letter, and diary."[30] In Branch's assessment, expanding the genre of nature writing beyond the nature essay means expanding its founding myths. This means including more nonfiction forms besides the essay. Branch illustrates the importance of form and chronology to defining the genre; these limitations say more about contemporary politics than they do about nature. Branch's sense of the parameters of the genre (which Branch's *Reading the Roots* seeks to expand) testifies to its accepted definition. Dominant conceptions of the genre of nature writing also define it as distinct from the natural history essay and travel writing.

Similarly, Daniel Philippon's work, while challenging the dichotomy between the genres of natural history and nature writing, attests to the widely accepted distinction between them. Natural history is understood as a record of life in a place at a time, while nature writing scrutinizes cultural activities transforming the landscape and often considers ethical dimensions of that transformation. Philippon argues that Thoreau's *Journey West* blurs these distinctions, however, and outlines how Thoreau's style of cataloging is a "poetry of acknowledgement." By listing nothing but the name of an organism, Philippon continues, Thoreau "invites us to consider the mystery of its complexity, which we cannot capture in words."[31] Thomas Lyon's *This Incomparable Lande: A Guide to American Nature Writing*, defines "the literature of nature" as having three dimensions to it: "natural history information, personal responses to nature, and philosophical interpretation of nature." Field guides may only intend to "convey information," while if these facts "then give rise to some sort of meaning or interpretation," then we have "the basic conditions for the natural history essay." As the author's role "loom[s] a bit larger," on Lyon's "spectrum," we begin to have various forms of nature writing, some of which use the pastoral retreat from society as a trope, and others that draw more heavily on the travelogue or ramble form.[32] Environmental writing, ecocritics tend to agree, does not emerge until the modern ecology movement, in the early twentieth century.

Much has been said about the extent to which nature essayists such as Thoreau, Austin, and Muir were committed to issues of social justice, but the genre of the nature essay has for the most part been a genre invested in whiteness and American empire. The nature essay extends natural history and travel writing, forms that have their own roots in imperial expansion, erasure of native populations, and appropriation of natural resources.[33] Even Mary Austin's modernist appreciation for Native American ways of being in the land has been resoundingly critiqued as primitivist – projecting onto Native peoples the ecological vision of harmony that she valorizes, at the cost of recognizing the trauma of dispossession and how that attenuated Native land relations. So, primitivist nature writers paradoxically bemoaned the loss of Native people and their ecological ethic as they celebrated the forging of America's unique character in wilderness. Depending on an emptied landscape for the kinds of transcendental experience in nature so favored by the romantic nature writers, and constructing nature as an imagined space away from the chaos of urbanization, immigration, and cross-cultural contact, nature writing has typically been a genre of exclusion, primitivism, and nativism. Outka writes, "the West provided a place where whiteness could imagine its formation outside of the long terrible history of the black/white racial binary that had been so central to the definition of both whiteness and the American landscape back east."[34]

Nature-Writing the American West

It would be a mistake to assume the topic of this entry means "nature writing *about* the American West." The preposition "about" suggests a static view of landscape as backdrop to be described, as if it exists a priori to discourse. One of the reasons these two concepts – nature writing and American West – seem to go together so well is that they developed in tandem. This is not coincidental, as Thoreau's "Walking" demonstrates. The nature essay, as defined by Buell and in the definitions by Branch and Lyon, became popular alongside the so-called end of the frontier, which was declared in Frederick Jackson Turner's famous 1893 speech. Thoreau's "Walking" marks an important historical shift, in this sense. If for Thoreau the West is another word for the wild, and in wildness is the preservation of the world, the loss of the wild wrought by industrialization could only be achieved by further expansion west. As that West diminishes between Thoreau's writing and the close of the frontier – the second half of the nineteenth century – the nature essay gained its value as documenting a diminishing nature. As Bridget Keegan and James McKusick write, in their anthology, *Literature and Nature: Four Centuries of Nature Writing*, "The extension of the American frontier throughout the century, and the devastating divisions of the American Civil War at mid-century, contributed to stereotypical polarizations within American culture between the civilized, citified East and the wild Wild West." In terms of the nature essay, they continue, "the geographic growth of the United States westward was undeniably the most essential development."[35] What about westward expansion precipitated the growth of what we now call nature writing?

The special imaginary of "the West" operates as a trope to signify unknown and threatening territory and has little relation to the geographical West. On the one hand, the nature essay gained its momentum because of a popular expansionist spirit. On the other hand, it also filled the role of warning against unfettered development. This paradox is built into the frontier myth. Analogous to James O'Connor's Marxian theory of the second contradiction of capitalism, in which the very resources needed to support capitalism are used up by a therefore inevitably self-destroying capitalist system,[36] the West that was needed to forge the American character also needed to be conquered or contained in order to produce that character. Mainstream nature writing in this century reflects this conflict. Sometimes glorifying exploration of the West and sometimes bemoaning the introduction of the "machine in the garden," as Leo Marx frames it,[37] nature writing both upheld and critiqued the mythology that an encounter with nature forged the ideal, "rugged individualist" American. Since this drama played out in the landscape becoming known as the West, it is not surprising that so much nature writing produced in the nineteenth century addressed the West in some way. Nature writing like the nature essay may have articulated the experience of the "westward course of empire," but also, in the latter half of the century, especially in the writings of Muir, it conveyed the vulnerability of the landscape and its inhabitants. If nature writing's purpose, then, was to value a diminishing nature (the source of national character), then it became particularly important as the frontier was closing. People still read Muir and Austin in this nostalgic vein; they ostensibly described the West before it was developed. Twentieth-century nature writers such as Abbey and Terry Tempest Williams echo this tradition. The West remains a metonym for the frontier, and nature writing about the West evidence that an ideal American character still has a chance. The promise of regeneration is to be found in the West.

The sublime and the pastoral modes, emerging in force during the nineteenth century, helped create the landscape of the American West and contributed to the genre's self-selection as Anglo-American. Donald

Worster's definition of the nature essay, with its roots in Gilbert White's natural history, is that it is characterized by a theme of a "lost pastoral haven, for a home in an inhospitable and threatening world."[38] This mode narrows the genre's appeal to writers for whom this nostalgia and desire are constructed as appealing. All of these qualities of the nature essay – the emphasis on nonfiction, the emphasis on the alienation of work, the anti-urban emphasis, the pastoral retreat from society, the sublime aesthetic – arguably contribute to the genre's self-selection as Anglo-American. To anthologize nature writing by defining it this way is conveniently to select out other ways of portraying or engaging environmental concerns.

Two corrections to this problem have emerged in the critical scholarship. One draws attention to nonwhite and female writers who addressed similar concerns in similar ways. Ecocritical works including Barbara Cook and Alex Hunt's *Women Writing Nature: A Feminist View;* Karen Kilcup's *Fallen Forests: Emotion, Embodiment, and Ethics in American Women's Environmental Writing;* and Lorraine Anderson and Thomas Edwards's *At Home on This Earth: Two Centuries of US Women's Nature Writing;* Anderson's *Sisters of the Earth: Women's Prose and Poetry about Nature;* Karla Armbruster and Kathleen Wallace's *Beyond Nature Writing;* and Alison Deming and Lauret Savoy's *The Colors of Nature: Culture, Identity, and the Natural World* demonstrate the growth of interest in this field. Adding chairs to the table of nature writing is only one possible solution to the exclusion of women and communities who were written and driven out of the West during the nineteenth century.

The second major revision to the field has been to challenge the roots and assumptions of the genre itself as invested in whiteness and emerging from a tradition of excluding certain groups to preserve a particular kind of nature for the elite. This preserving occurs, as I argued previously, in both literary genre and public policy. Some reasons for the exclusion of African American literature are "a narrow conception of 'nature-writing' as a nonfiction form," as Jeffrey Myers explains. He goes on to note that the problem also involves "a reluctance to think of urban space as 'natural' space; a subordination of environmental justice issues to concerns over wildlife and wilderness preservation; and the extremely vexed but nonetheless intimate history that African Americans have had with the land with respect to slavery, Jim Crow-era racial violence and internal migration to northern cities."[39]

Some of the work that is best achieving this is in the fields of critical regional and postwestern studies, which show that the West itself is as exclusionary a geography as the genre of nature writing is a literary form. This perspective "works against a narrowly conceived regionalism, one that restricts western cultures of the past and present to some predetermined entity with static borders and boundaries."[40] Postwestern studies is "indigenist, anti-imperialist, and antiracist" in its cultural geographies.[41] Redefining the West from the perspectives of various groups that have been there, have claims to the space, are moving through there, and have definitions of the space that contradict the frontier myth shows that there is no one American West, and that the role the West serves in America's narrative about itself simply was and is not true, or certainly not the only truth.

Writing about the West could be called "regional" in geographic and literary critical terms. Regional writing articulates social knowledge from a vantage of "the local." Many western writers have, as Krista Comer writes, "participate[d] in and profit[ed] from a culture that hypercommodifies and fetishizes the local and primitive."[42] Mary Austin's work exemplifies this move, despite Austin's outward stance against profiting from her West. Contemporary geographical thinking, influenced by postmodernism and the robust critiques of geopolitical purposes to which regionalism and the reactionary retreat to the local have been put, can be helpful in recasting nineteenth-century nature writing in terms of its investment in racial and gendered conceptions of space. Illustrative of this kind of recasting of space as dynamic are Doreen Massey's theory of a "global sense of place";[43] Krista Comer's *Landscapes of the New West;* Paul Gilroy's *The Black Atlantic;* Ursula Heise's *Sense of Place, Sense of Planet;* and Neil Campbell's *The Rhizomatic West.* Drawing on diaspora and postmodern theories, these works suggest that movement tells a more just story about identity and place than stasis, that the local is embedded in rather than protected from the global, that history is spatialized rather than space's being determined by things that happen in it, and that identity is not territorially essentialized. Conventional views of the West as a static region gloss over "very complex relations and contacts that actually existed in the various spaces of the West, as well as the multiple ways in which the West spilled out beyond its immediate geographical boundaries, becoming a global, transnational phenomenon."[44] In contrast, as Massey argues, any region such as the West must be conceived as networked, connected to other spaces and times, layered with meanings, and an "intercultural contact zone," as Stephen Tatum characterizes it. As he explains, "places or region[s] need to be regarded not only as geopolitical and geological territories or physical landscapes, but also as sites produced by the circulation of peoples, of technologies and commodities, and of cultural artifacts, including of course images, stories, and myths."[45]

If we approach nature writing and the American West from these perspectives, as well as from the perspective described earlier that nature writing is about how nature works discursively as much as or more than it is about anything called "nature" itself, then what "counts" as nature writing shifts dramatically. What would nature writing look like if we included writing of those communities dispossessed of their land during the nineteenth century? And what if we saw twentieth-century writing of trauma as rooted in nineteenth-century discourses of nature, such as natural history and Darwinism, as the lingering effects of violence that earlier nature writing helped to naturalize? What we might consider "American," much less "western" was highly contested at that time. Not until the very end of the nineteenth century did a clear sense of American borders exist, and even today those borders are contested, as Gloria Anzaldúa's 1987 *Borderlands/La Frontera* illustrates so powerfully. Or, what if we examined writing about the western frontier through the lens of north-south strife and trauma, as Paul Outka does in *Race and Nature from Transcendentalism to the Harlem Renaissance*? If the frontier was a symbolic and spatial "safety valve" for the East's north-south battles over slavery, we must read together narratives of the sublime and trauma, Outka contends.

Environmental Writing: The Legacy of Nature Writing

Nature writing has been an especially important form in the history of the American West, where it has often been associated with the conservation and preservation movements, as well as figures such as Muir, Austin, Luther Standing Bear, Gary Snyder, Wallace Stegner, Ann Zwinger, Gretel Ehrlich, and Terry Tempest Williams. These authors use the form of nature writing to draw attention to the beauty and importance of nature in a world that ignores or commodifies it. Combining luminous forms of personal expression with environmental advocacy, writers began in the twentieth century to move from simply calling attention to the aesthetic qualities of nature to calling for its preservation, and debating the relative merits of conservation. Also, these writers were more likely to be suspicious of the links between nature and nation that so occupied nineteenth-century writers, witnessing as they did the rise of America's military-industrial complex and its attendant destabilization of the "America-as-nature reduction," to use Lawrence Buell's term.[46] While these authors are in tradition with the nineteenth-century nature essay in that they "defend the beauty of underappreciated topographies," maintain the "theme of solitary retreat to a remote spot of wilderness," and continue "the nineteenth century's interest in regionalism and celebration of America's diverse geography," they reflect a "growing awareness of the national and international significance of nature" and "the addition of incisive cultural criticism."[47] Gary Paul Nabhan is a good example of this expansive view of nature writing. Nabhan's western deserts are "the last place one would go to escape society," writes Elliott West. "Distinctions between 'nature' and 'cultural apparatus' make no sense.... Nabhan sees the desert as woven tight with exchanges among plants, spirits, rituals, stones, seeds, stories, experience, and sensations, ... and is crowded with memory and noisy with conversations among its parts, people included."[48]

Moreover, if we are truly to challenge the investment in whiteness that the form of nonfiction nature writing often reveals, then we ought to consider more seriously the value of various genres of fiction and mixed genres (such as Anzaldúa's *Borderlands/La Frontera* or Sesshu Foster's *Atomik Aztex*) to revealing truths about the relationship between nature and nation, about which early nature writing was so concerned. The very fact that nature writing has long been associated with the nonfiction form has excluded many voices; as Myers aptly reminds us, "the nonfiction nature-writing essay that has become the standard of the genre presupposes a degree of leisure, social status, and even safety that has been historically less available"[49] to writers of color in the United States.

Notes

1 Roderick Nash, *Wilderness and the American Mind* (New Haven, CT: Yale University Press, 2001).
2 Krista Comer, *Landscapes of the New West: Gender and Geography in Contemporary Women's Writing* (Chapel Hill: University of North Carolina Press, 1999), 15.
3 Ibid.
4 Henry David Thoreau, "Walking," in *Walden and Other Writings*, ed. Brooks Atkinson (New York: Random House, 1992).
5 Elliott West, *The Way to the West: Essays on the Central Plains* (Albuquerque: University of New Mexico Press, 1997), 156.
6 Amy Kaplan, "'Left Alone with America': The Absence of Empire in the Study of American Culture," in *Cultures of United States Imperialism*, ed. Amy Kaplan and Donald E. Pease (Durham, NC: Duke University Press, 1993), 3–21.
7 John Elder and Robert Finch, introduction to *The Norton Book of Nature Writing*, ed. John Elder and Robert Finch (New York: W.W. Norton, 1990), 21.

8 See, for example, David Spurr, *The Rhetoric of Empire: Colonial Discourse in Journalism, Travel Writing, and Imperial Administration* (Durham, NC: Duke University Press, 1993).

9 The distinction between nature writing and the genre of natural history is contested, and beyond the scope of this essay. The easy distinction, advanced by Lyon, is that nature writing is literary and aesthetic and foregrounds the author more than natural history. But taking into account the "nature fakers" debate of the nineteenth century, wherein natural history is objective truth about nature while nature writing is "fake," suggests this distinction is slippery. In this way, Christoph Irmscher refuses "to treat 'art' and 'science' as opposites," as it is "historically inaccurate anyway"; see his discussion in *The Poetics of Natural History: From John Bartram to William James* (New Brunswick, NJ: Rutgers University Press, 1999), 7. Therefore, although this entry is on "nature writing," much of what is discussed here applies to natural history as well. Following Mary Louise Pratt, Irmscher goes on to explain that both nature writing and natural history "were the willing, if slightly befuddled, accomplices of Western imperialism" (xxvi). This discussion forms much of the basis for my arguments here.

10 Jamaica Kincaid, "In History," in *The Colors of Nature: Culture, Identity, and the Natural World*, ed. Alison Hawthorne Deming and Lauret Savoy (Minneapolis: Milkweed, 2002), 18–27.

11 Paul Outka, *Race and Nature from Transcendentalism to the Harlem Renaissance* (New York: Palgrave Macmillan, 2008), 173.

12 Priscilla Ybarra, "Walden Pond in Aztlan? A Literary History of Chicana/o Environmental Writing since 1848," PhD dissertation, Rice University, 2002.

13 Jeffrey Myers, *Converging Stories: Race, Ecology, and Environmental Justice in American Literature* (Athens: University of Georgia Press, 2005), 22.

14 Perry Miller, *Nature's Nation* (Cambridge, MA: Belknap, 1967).

15 Sarah Jaquette Ray, *The Ecological Other: Environmental Exclusion in American Culture* (Tucson: University of Arizona Press, 2013), 15.

16 Bruce Braun, "'On the Raggedy Edge of Risk': Articulations of Race and Nature after Biology," in *Race, Nature, and the Politics of Difference*, ed. Donald Moore, Jake Kosek, and Anand Pandian (Durham, NC: Duke University Press, 2003), 175–203.

17 Rachel Stein, *Shifting the Ground: American Women Writers' Revisions of Nature, Gender, and Race* (Charlottesville: University of Virginia Press, 1997), 2.

18 Benedict Anderson, *Imagined Communities: Reflections on the Origin and Spread of Nationalism* (London: Verso, 2006).

19 Susan Kollin, *Nature's State: Imagining Alaska as the Last Frontier* (Chapel Hill: University of North Carolina Press, 2001), 21.

20 I want to thank Sarah D. Wald for provocatively reframing nature writing in terms of these particular writers (personal correspondence).

21 Elder and Finch, "Introduction," 22.

22 Jake Kosek, "Purity and Pollution: Racial Degradation and Environmental Anxieties," in *Liberation Ecologies: Environment, Development, and Social Movements*, ed. Richard Peet and Michael Watts (New York: Routledge, 2005), 137.

23 Mary Pat Brady, *Extinct Lands, Temporal Geographies: Chicana Literature and the Urgency of Space* (Durham, NC: Duke University Press, 2002), 13–48.

24 See Henry Nash Smith, *Virgin Land: The American West as Symbol and Myth* (Cambridge, MA: Harvard University Press, 1970).

25 West, *The Way to the West*, 165.

26 Richard Jenseth and Edward E. Lotto, eds., *Constructing Nature: Readings from the American Experience* (London: Longman, 1996).

27 Patricia Nelson Limerick, *The Legacy of Conquest: The Unbroken Past of the American West* (New York: W.W. Norton, 1987).

28 Michael P. Branch, introduction to *Reading the Roots: American Nature Writing before Walden*, ed. Michael P. Branch (Athens: University of Georgia Press, 2004), xvi.

29 Lawrence Buell's work is groundbreaking regarding this argument. See *The Environmental Imagination: Thoreau, Nature Writing, and the Formation of American Culture* (Cambridge, MA: Belknap, 1996).

30 Branch, "Introduction," xxv.

31 Daniel Philippon, "Thoreau's Notes on the *Journey West*: Nature Writing or Environmental History?" *ATQ: 19th Century American Literature and Culture* 18, no. 2 (2004): 111.

32 Thomas J. Lyon, *This Incomparable Land: A Guide to American Nature Writing* (Minneapolis: Milkweed, 2001), 20–23.

33 See Mary Louise Pratt, *Imperial Eyes: Travel Writing and Transculturation* (New York: Routledge, 2007) and Spurr.

34 Outka, *Race and Nature*, 153.

35 Bridget Keegan and James C. McKusick, *Literature and Nature: Four Centuries of Nature Writing* (Englewood Cliffs, NJ: Prentice Hall, 2001), 423.

36 James O'Connor, "On the Two Contradictions of Capitalism," *Capitalism Nature Socialism* 2, no. 3 (1991): 107–9.

37 Leo Marx, *The Machine in the Garden: Technology and the Pastoral Ideal in America* (Oxford: Oxford University Press, 2000).

38 Elder and Finch, "Introduction," 22.

39 Jeffrey Myers, "'Ready to Come Home': Teaching African American Literature as Environmental Literature," in *Teaching North American Environmental Literature*, ed. Laird Christensen, Mark C. Long, and Fred Waage (New York: MLA, 2008), 185.

40 Susan Kollin, "Introduction: Postwestern Studies, Dead or Alive," in *Postwestern Cultures: Literature, Theory, Space*, ed. Susan Kollin (Lincoln: University of Nebraska Press, 2007), xi.

41 Frieda Knobloch, quoted in Kollin, "Introduction," xiii.

42 Comer, *Landscapes of the New West*, 15.

43 Doreen Massey, "A Global Sense of Place," *Marxism Today* 38 (June 1991): 24–29.

44 Neil Campbell, *The Rhizomatic West: Representing the American West in a Transnational, Global, Media Age* (Lincoln: University of Nebraska Press, 2008), 7.

45 Stephen Tatum, quoted in Kollin, "Introduction," xiv.

46 Buell, *Environmental Imagination*, 15.

47 Annie Merrill Ingram, "United States Environmental Literature of the Twentieth Century and Beyond," in *Teaching North American Environmental Literature*, ed. Laird Christensen, Mark C. Long, and Fred Waage, 139–40.

48 West, *The Way to the West*, 156–7.

49 Myers, " 'Ready to Come Home'," 186.

CHAPTER 6

Tall Tales and Short Stories

Nicolas S. Witschi

Legend has it that during the height of the great silver mining rush, an unusually creative newspaper editor essentially invented a town out of nothing. For several years he maintained the joke by reportedly publishing a weekly paper that chronicled his town's entirely fictional economic, political, and social activities. Judging by the editorials, news items, and even advertising that the editor created, one would have thought that to the south of Carson City, Nevada, just across the California state line on the silver-rich eastern flanks of the Sierra Nevada mountains, lay a town of at least one thousand residents with enough grocery and clothing stores, not to mention saloons and banks and theaters, to meet the needs of an even greater population. Regional folklore also maintains that this endlessly inventive editor carried off the hoax at the behest of secretive speculators who wished to sell nonexistent shares in a nonexistent mine to investors in Britain. Finally, the legend states that the newspaperman known as "Lying Jim" Townsend not only served as the model for the speaker in Bret Harte's "Plain Language from Truthful James," but also was the original teller of a tale about a jumping frog that eventually found its way into Mark Twain's hands.

The known facts of James W. E. Townsend and his literary work are more mundane, though. For one, while his mendacity may actually have proven an inspiration to Harte, he was almost certainly not the originator of the jumping frog story. And the story of the town is also more legend than fact. In 1888, Townsend returned to the largely deserted town of Lundy, California, to resume the editorship of its moribund *Homer Mining Index*. Many of the advertising and mining patents he printed were simply borrowed from an earlier decade when both the town and the paper had been more prosperous. The core of the legend does, nevertheless, have some truth to it, for Townsend really did publish a fair number of entirely fictitious reports about what had transpired, such as a story about a somnambulist who returned every morning with his pockets mysteriously filled with gold ore ("Billy" had apparently discovered in his sleep a mine that had eluded everyone's notice in daylight). Of course, Townsend's assessments of mostly nonexistent mines did have an impact on stock value in the vicinity. And within a year, the ruse was exposed and the investment scheme became the subject of transatlantic litigation. Townsend stayed on at the paper for several years after the discovery, as Lundy did in fact still exist, it did have a small but steady population, and it did still occasionally experience a newsworthy event or two.[1]

Aside from its interest as a piece of regional folklore, the legend of "Lying Jim" Townsend's invented town points to something distinctive about the American West in the latter half of the nineteenth century: the high incidence of periodical-based hoaxes and humorous fiction. From the 1860s to the 1880s, when he was not working in Lundy, James Townsend reported for or contributed his editing, printing, and writing skills to newspapers across the region, in cities such as San Francisco, Sacramento, Carson City, and Virginia City, Nevada. Working alongside the likes of William Wright ("Dan De Quille"), Samuel Clemens ("Mark Twain"), Bret Harte, and many others, Townsend was part of a pioneering literary movement that perfected the use of hyperbole, non sequiturs, absurd or incongruous expressions, and ironic humor in the writing of local color or regional fiction. Of course, the mode commonly known as the tall tale is not unique to this period in U.S. literary history, particularly not in its connection to the so-called frontier. From the exploits of Davy Crockett and Mike Fink to the writings of such old Southwest humorists as George Washington Harris, Thomas Bangs Thorpe, and Augustus Baldwin Longstreet, exaggerated humor has long served the paired goals of communicating and mediating the shifting dynamics of power and economics in places where mostly European settlers were just beginning to establish industries and settlements.[2] However, in the wake of the California Gold Rush and particularly after the Civil War, in the American West such humor writing reached arguably its greatest levels of accomplishment and impact.

The tall tale–inspired fiction written by the likes of Bret Harte, Mark Twain, Stephen Crane, and many others was certainly instrumental in the creation of a region that could seem larger than life, that could in fact appear exceptional in its natural and social spaces. Indeed, the emergence in the eyes of late nineteenth-century readers of the American West as a distinctive location and idea was coeval with the development of regionalism in the literary marketplace. An interpretive consideration often made about local color or regionalist fiction as a whole is that the question of narrative value inheres in the position of the narrator. Which is to say, the question of whether a speaker is configured fundamentally as an insider or an outsider has affected the relative value of a narrative both in its day and in contemporary criticism.[3] The short fiction of the late-nineteenth-century American West, however, unmistakably demonstrates that narrators are always contingent, that they are always to some degree at odds with the narratives they narrate or the people and places they represent. One might even say that the full measure of the local color or regionalist short story in U.S. literary history may not be taken without full consideration of the tales that were spun in the Far West.

The rapid influx of people who possessed more than average levels of material goods, money, and, above all, education into the West soon after the discovery of gold in 1848 created what Franklin Walker called a "precocious frontier."[4] San Francisco newspapers such as the *Chronicle*, the *Daily Alta*, the *Morning Call*, the *Evening Bulletin*, and the *Mirror of the Times*, which was the first paper west of St. Louis published by and for African Americans, all arose to document the city's extraordinary growth. Meanwhile, early magazines such as the *Pioneer*, the *Hesperian*, the *Golden Era*, *Hutchings' Illustrated California Magazine*, and the *California Farmer and Journal of Useful Sciences*, to name but a few, also competed for the attentions of a literate and growing population that was intent on the next big strike. In this atmosphere, factual reportage was frequently printed side by side with greatly exaggerated or even entirely fabricated tales of prospects and success.[5] This pairing of genres was, in turn, expertly exploited by a generation of writers who seemed very much inclined to injecting a satirical tone into their newspaper work.

Among the writers who went west in search of gold was Alonzo Delano, who arrived in California in April 1849 in the company of a group of fellow townsmen from Ottawa, Illinois. Up to that point, Delano had sent several dozen dispatches about his overland journey back home to the Ottawa *Free Trader*, many of which he eventually combined with his more detailed overland diary and published as *Life on the Plains and among the Diggings* (1854). Soon after his arrival, though, Delano also began submitting, under the pseudonym "Old Block," humorous and satirical sketches to newspapers in Sacramento and San Francisco. Evincing a distinctly Hogarthian sensibility in his work as "Old Block," Delano employed a number of reflexive and self-deprecating literary techniques, among them the combining of sentimental and comic modes in the depiction of the hardships faced by miners. Of his time spent crossing the continent, he noted how his grueling "pleasure trip across the plains" had allowed him to develop a thorough familiarity with "hawks, crows, rats and other nutritious vegetables."[6] Most typically, Delano served up himself as his greatest target for satire, making equal fun of his propensity for hyperbole and his generously sized nose. His most frequently repeated representation, though, the effigy of a decrepit miner he had found propped against an abandoned cabin, would become a familiar Gold Rush trope: the old-seeming but in fact quite young fortune seeker who had wasted away to nothing because of his failure to find gold. "Old Block" was among the very first to render this image in print, and he did so with great sympathy.

Another writer who offered satirical impressions of life in the rapidly growing western regions was George Horatio Derby, who published under such names as "Squibob" and "John Phoenix." A lieutenant and engineer in the U.S. Army Topographic Corps, Derby traveled extensively throughout Oregon, California, and northern Mexico, primarily in the service of road building and water development projects. Between expeditions, though, he wrote essays, sketches, and brief little "squibs" that satirized local politics, elite society, and what he often took to be the military's pointless attempts at regional development, publishing them in a variety of periodicals in both San Diego and San Francisco. One notable account by "Professor Phoenix" lampooned the genre of the scientifically exhaustive railroad survey by reporting on the viability of a passenger line that would run between downtown San Francisco and Mission Dolores only three miles away. The numerous saloons that Phoenix passed along the way inevitably led him to conclude that the route was neither direct nor easily navigated without copious amounts of alcohol and weaponry. He also, while temporarily in charge of the San Diego *Herald*, managed to switch that weekly newspaper's editorial allegiance from the Democratic Party's gubernatorial candidate, named Bigler, to that of the Whig Party. Of course, the satirical treatment of Bigler, while infuriating to the paper's editor in chief, was so outrageously funny that voters were arguably more inclined to vote for him than they had been before Derby's lampooning of the entire electoral process.[7]

The finest collection of periodical mischief at this time, however, could be found to the east of California's gold fields, in the silver mines and boomtowns of western Nevada. It was here that "Lying Jim" Townsend published his best work, and it was in this region, too, that in 1876 another popular legend arose, about a hoax perpetrated by the residents of a town called Palisade. Tired of the constant wide-eyed questioning about the reputed wildness of the West from tourists passing through on the railroad, the people of Palisade began to stage mock gunfights, which

included blood obtained from a nearby slaughterhouse, at the train station. The heart of the joke, however, is that the performers never revealed
to their horrified audience that the violence had been staged. It was not
until after the train had departed that the bodies rose from the dust and
all repaired to the saloon to congratulate each other on another fine show.
Villainous blackguards being called out for having wronged an honest
woman, skulking Indians being tracked down with stolen goods in hand,
the roar of pistols and the ensuing smoke and bloody corpses strewn
about the platform – these are the now-familiar (and, of course, in some
measure offensive) clichés of the genre western, deployed by townspeople
who had relatively early in the Far West's history begun to recognize what
was expected of them by those not already residents of the region.[8] The
tall tale they spun evoked the blood-and-thunder conventions of the dime
novel westerns that would soon make a fortune for such writers as Ned
Buntline, launch the stage career of Buffalo Bill Cody, and thoroughly
define the otherwise nonliterary careers of such public figures as Wyatt
Earp and Calamity Jane.

More than a statement about a small community's theatrical creativity, though, the story of the Palisade hoax exemplifies the extent to which
the journalists of Nevada had by this time learned that truth and invention could go hand in hand in people's expectations of what was to be
found in the West. The core elements of the Palisade gunfights were alleg-
edly first reported in the Virginia City *Territorial Enterprise*, and it is not
entirely clear that the fake gunfights ever actually took place; no other
source has yet corroborated their occurrence, and it may in fact be the
case that the newspaper's account of the event is the real hoax. Indeed, the
involvement of the *Territorial Enterprise* is perhaps the most salient detail
in this legend, for it was in the pages of this newspaper that many of the
most important exaggerations, stretchers, tall tales, and western hoaxes of
the period were printed. More than just the paper of record for a mining
town, the *Territorial Enterprise* was the central organ for a group of writers
who have since become known as "the Sagebrush school."[9]

The names of the journalists who made up the Sagebrush school,
among them William Wright, Alf Doten, Sam Davis, Joe Goodman,
Rollin Daggett, and James Townsend, have received but scant attention in
accounts of western American literary history. And yet their influence was
tremendous. Collectively, they mastered the particular combinations of
irony, style, humor, moral outrage, and sentiment that would define the
western short story of the era. Wright, in particular, who wrote under the
nom de plume "Dan De Quille," published in the *Territorial Enterprise*

an almost endless stream of humorous sketches, "quaints," as he called them, on invented subjects as diverse as a group of rocks that mysteriously moved by themselves in the night (a hoax later imitated by Townsend); a suit of armor that would grow cooler as the sun heated it up, to the point that it froze to death a man who had made the mistake of wearing it in the desert; and the discovery in a mine of a corpse that had absorbed enough minerals from the water to become a solid "silver man."[10] This last piece of literary deception, in fact, was written as a direct response to a literary joke that had recently been published by another Sagebrush journalist, the one who would become the most famous of them all: Mark Twain.

Having traveled from Missouri to the Nevada Territory with his brother, Orion, in 1861, Samuel Clemens was quick to abandon an unsuccessful career as a speculator and miner. Instead, he drew upon his earlier apprenticeship as a *jour* printer to secure work as a journalist with the Virginia City *Territorial Enterprise*. Mentored by Wright/De Quille, Mark Twain, as he was soon identifying himself in print, contributed a number of significant bits of humor to the tally of sagebrush journalism.[11] His fake story about a "Petrified Man" was the hoax that De Quille modified and corrected with his own pseudoscientific explanation about the corpse's having in fact been turned not into rock but into silver. And Twain's entirely false report about a murderous rampage entitled "A Bloody Massacre near Carson" was circulated throughout the region as a sensational but presumably true news item.[12] According to Twain, his goal had been to trick several San Francisco newspapers into embarrassing themselves by inducing them to reprint a story about their own involvements in shady water distribution deals about which the assailant in Twain's story had become upset. And while the salient details of the "Massacre" hoax are rather crude and gory, the motivation behind the tale points to Twain's ultimate development as a moral writer, one more interested in drawing out complacency and puncturing corrupt pieties than in entertaining his readers.

In 1864, Mark Twain left Virginia City for San Francisco, where he briefly worked as a reporter for the *Call*. Not long after, though, he headed for the hills again, this time for the gold mining country around Angel's Camp, California. It was during this period in his career that Twain learned the tale of an inveterate gambler who had been bested in a wager over a frog. In less than a year, his written version of "Jim Smiley and His Jumping Frog" (1865) had been widely acclaimed by readers on the East Coast, and Twain was well on his way to becoming an international literary star. As an example of regionalist humor, the story that was soon retitled "The Celebrated Jumping Frog of Calaveras County" exhibited the signature mix of tall tale outlandishness, self-reflexivity, and a deadpan appeal to narrative plausibility that Twain had learned in his apprenticeship with Dan De Quille. Indeed, framed as a letter to Artemus Ward, the humorist and lecturer more properly known as Charles Farrar Browne, Twain's version explicitly announced its author as a member of the tradition that included such colleagues as Browne, Wright, Delano, and Derby. Moreover, Twain's innovative technique of employing a self-deprecating narrator who exhibits remarkably little awareness of the true significance of his own tale would prove useful some years later when he began to write *Adventures of Huckleberry Finn* (1885).

However, before fully turning to his boyhood home along the Mississippi River for story inspiration and locations, Twain effectively concluded his assessment of the Far West with *Roughing It* (1872), an episodic novel written in autobiographical form that thoroughly thematizes the literary mendacity of the time and place. As with the "Jumping Frog" tale, this book's narrator exists, at least at the start, in a naïve position, as what is often referred to as the "greenhorn" version of the Mark Twain persona, and he explores throughout *Roughing It* the merits and value of a great many stories and legends about the early days of the post–Civil War American West.[13] For instance, tall tales such as those that recount the fearsome deeds of gunfighters are largely punctured when Twain's traveler encounters a supremely gentlemanly Jack Slade, while others such as the reported chasing of a fellow traveler up a tree by a bison are treated with mirthful skepticism. Nonetheless, the stories that Twain encounters do have their value. One particularly humorous example traces the cross-country passage of an anecdote about the newspaper editor Horace Greeley's bruising ride to Placerville, California, in the care of the legendary stagecoach driver Hank Monk. The most salient element of this tale, namely, the absurdly identical, word-for-word version that Twain reports hearing on multiple occasions in multiple places while on his overland trek, actually testifies to the story's usefulness as something of an exchange commodity – people, including Twain, tell this tale as a way to gauge their passage across the plains and to establish their own presence within the greater narrative of westward travel. After this episode, Twain arrived in Nevada and proceeded alternately to report on the world of mining he had found and to test his narrator's gullibility and fallibility. Believing in the quick riches he might earn on the shores of Lake Tahoe, he succeeds not in staking a claim to a prime portion of real estate but instead accidentally burning a large swath of the forest to the ground. In the end, arguably only the writerly persona of Mark Twain emerges from the experience with any measure of stability or certainty, the rest of the West having been depicted as a region inimical to both material and narrative stability. Such are the lessons Twain learned in his work with the likes of Dan De Quille.

Another friend and mentor of Twain's, Bret Harte, also developed a distinctive approach to narrative value during his time in California, the first piece of evidence for which pertains to another hoax. In 1866, the state geologist and Harvard University professor Josiah Whitney proclaimed a skull found by some miners at the bottom of a shaft to be clear evidence of a prehistoric race of Californians who predated the known existence of humans on earth. Harte and many others, though, believed that the skull was nothing more than the remains of an unfortunate miner who had fallen to his death a few years earlier or whose bones had been deliberately reinterred in the hole for the sake of generating a sensation. In a mocking poem entitled "To the Pliocene Skull," the speaker asks directly of the skull for a clue to its provenance; it responds that his name was Bowers and that he'd simply fallen down a shaft and never recovered.[14] Harte clearly recognized the likelihood that a sensational-seeming story from the mines could be nothing more than a clever hoax, and his poem certainly acknowledged the culture of sensational and fraudulent claims that pervaded California in the 1860s. However, it also demonstrated Harte's interest in using literature to test narrative authority and truth, insofar as the dialogue between speaker and skull alternately invokes and relieves the silence imposed upon a speaker who has been falsely spoken for by others.

It was another poem by Harte, though, that even more fully revealed the distance that could exist among readers, narrators, and the stories they have in common. "Plain Language from Truthful James," which soon became more commonly known as "the Heathen Chinee," is a satire Harte published in September 1870 that dramatizes a Chinese card player's besting of a group of Irish swindlers at their own game. Harte employs one of the would-be swindlers as the eponymous speaker of the poem, and in turn "Truthful James" (whose name is almost certainly an allusion to "Lying Jim" Townsend) remains completely unaware of how his own prejudices regarding the Chinese have led to his not anticipating the possibility of being cheated. It is no doubt ironic that Harte's condemnation of anti-Chinese feeling among white miners was interpreted by many as a warning against what at the time was called the "yellow peril." As the history of the poem's reception suggests, "Plain Language from Truthful James" endured a very long and unfortunate career as a tool useful to those who favored race- and class-based policies against Chinese immigration and labor.[15] Harte, however, was more properly interested in satirically drawing attention to both racist attitudes themselves and the blindness to narrative clarity that characterizes prejudice, and thus his audience may not have fully appreciated their own complicity in the process.

As significant as his verse may be to the literary history of western approaches to truth and value, though, Harte's most consequential developments of narratorial points of view may be found in his fiction. In 1868, Harte was invited by the San Francisco publisher Anton Roman to serve as editor in chief of a new magazine that would do for the West what the *Atlantic Monthly* and *Harper's* had ostensibly done for the East. Called the *Overland Monthly*, Roman and Harte's new venture was explicitly designed to cultivate a refined literary milieu that would redefine the West as both genteel and sophisticated.[16] It represented the pinnacle of the periodical boom that had begun with the newspapers and magazines that had published the likes of Delano and Derby a decade earlier, and at least where Harte's fiction was concerned, it maintained the tradition of mixing satirical messages with earnest-seeming narrative forms. In its second issue, Harte published a particularly effective tale he had written about a mining camp full of coarse but earnestly heartwarming miners who find themselves beset by the needs of a newborn left motherless in their midst. "The Luck of Roaring Camp" (August 1868) recounts how the men's attempts at domestic reform, while initially appearing to succeed, amount to nothing as they are literally washed away in a torrential flood. This tale is in fact a subtle parody of the Nativity that satirizes the simple pieties of sentimental representations. For its effect it relies, in some measure, on the recognition that the narrator is not of the same class as the characters in the tale and thus does not share their earnest assumptions about successful reform.

A relatively quick series of comic mining country tales followed "The Luck" during the first eighteen months of the *Overland Monthly's* opening run. "The Outcasts of Poker Flat" (January 1869) crystallized in fiction both the figure of the golden-hearted prostitute and, in Oakhurst, the model of a fastidious and exceedingly honorable gambler. However, this tale also holds up to scrutiny the notion that a well-intentioned and hardy pioneer could, in all innocence, properly survive a winter in the wilderness. Other *Overland* stories such as "Miggles" (June 1869), "Tennessee's Partner" (October 1869), and "The Idyl of Red Gulch" (December 1869) presented, respectively, such literary types as the hellcat woman in buckskins who can outperform any man in the mountains; the crafty and grizzled 49er; and the schoolmarm from the East who symbolizes the arrival of civilization on the frontier. Throughout these tales, which were soon published together in the landmark collection *The Luck of Roaring Camp and Other Sketches* (1870), Harte's narrators maintain a genteel, sophisticated, and ultimately ironic distance from such dialect-speaking characters as Kentuck and Miggles. Harte's establishment of this distance serves both to heighten the humor of the stories and to emphasize the moral contrast that he lays at the centers of his satiric parables.

By the late 1870s and in no small measure because of the acclaim earned by Twain and Harte, western regionalist fiction was beginning to be published in periodicals throughout the nation. Mary Hallock Foote, for one, began in 1878 to publish short stories, sketches, and novels in the pages of magazines such as the *Atlantic Monthly* and the *Century*. While neither recognizable as tall tales nor generally satirical, Foote's fictions set in mining camps in regions such as California, Colorado, and Idaho nevertheless succeed as innovations along the lines established by her predecessors on the western slope, largely because of her plainly daring move to invest her narratives with women characters and women's points of view. To be sure, on several occasions Foote expressly positioned herself as the opposite of Bret Harte (a move that Mary Austin would echo several decades later, as well). Nevertheless, it bears noting that she, too, was a western writer who excelled at exploring the limits of narrational point of view. Meanwhile, a regional satirist more directly appreciative of Harte's influence was Edgar Wilson Nye, who called himself "Bill Nye" in part after a character mentioned in "Plain Language from Truthful James." Founder and editor in 1881 of the *Laramie Boomerang* newspaper (which he named after his mule), Nye used his regular column to poke fun at eastern misapprehensions about the West.[17] His success out west soon led to his assuming an editorial position with the *New York World*. He may have been partly inspired by Harte to take up the pen, but as his career developed as a comic lecturer on the national circuit, Nye in turn became something of a model for Twain.

The most caustic and in many ways most inspired practitioner of the self-reflexive tall tale in the West may in fact have been Harte and Twain's friend Ambrose Bierce. For much of his career, Bierce lived and worked in San Francisco, honing his craft chiefly as a satirist but also as an innovator in short story form. In the late 1860s, he was "the Town Crier" for the *San Francisco News-Letter and California Advertiser*, a posting from which he endlessly excoriated the political and social hypocrisies of the city's elite, and later in his career he enjoyed similarly free reign when he took over the "Prattle" column of the more mainstream *San Francisco Examiner*. Throughout this period, Bierce published tall tales, short stories, and many more satires in various Oakland and San Francisco newspapers and in area magazines such as the *Argonaut* and the *Wasp*. His aphoristic *Devil's Dictionary* (originally published in 1906 as *The Cynic's Word Book*) remains one of the most cogently satirical treatments of linguistic double-talk yet produced. Though he never achieved the same level of popularity as his two more famous colleagues, Bierce was very much a part of the culture of humor and narrative value that had helped to define much of their work. His two most famous Civil War stories, for instance, "An Occurrence at Owl Creek Bridge" (July 13, 1890, San Francisco *Examiner*) and "Chickamauga" (January 20, 1889, San Francisco *Examiner*), each in its own ways stresses the inherent limits of narrative point of view. They largely do so through their treatment of deeply subjective states of mind – and, hence, of narrative – as if they were plainly objective.

By the turn of the century, a major strain of western short fiction was intently focused on questions of subjectivity and point of view. Jack London starkly contrasted the feeble efforts of men in search of wealth with the perduring strength of nature in his almost fablelike tales such as "All Gold Canyon" (November 1905, *Century*) and "To Build a Fire" (August 1908, *Century*). And Frank Norris employed the form of the tall tale in satirical fables such as "The Passing of Cock-Eye Blacklock," in which a dialect-speaking, moralizing narrator recounts the fatal events surrounding a dog that loves to play fetch and a lazy fisherman who decides to use dynamite instead of a baited hook.

The most comprehensively self-reflexive examination of the consequences of popular western narratives, however, may be found in the western stories of Stephen Crane, who clearly understood the connection between the tall tale and the western short story. Two of his finer pieces of fiction in particular, "The Bride Comes to Yellow Sky" (February 1898, *McClure's*) and "The Blue Hotel" (November 26 and December 3, 1898, *Collier's Weekly*), take up the question of how the American West has come to exist as a larger-than-life space in which raw passions govern men's moods and firearms are never far from reach.[18] In the former story, Crane lampooned the convention of the "high noon"–style confrontational shoot-out. A Texas lawman returns to his small town a married man, and the revelation of his change of status so confounds and discourages his longtime nemesis that all prospects for further gunfights seem once and for all obliterated. And in "The Blue Hotel," a group of overnight lodgers at a railroad hotel in Nebraska are drawn into increasingly confrontational stances with each other because of the drunken paranoia of a character who assumes that in the rough-and-tumble West, he will inevitably be murdered. Ironically, his impressions of the West, learned from dime novels and the general tenor of tall tale–inspired western fiction, prove prophetic, for he indeed angers an honorable and fastidious gambler to the point of becoming his inevitable victim. In both instances, Crane diagnosed the by-now-conventional legends of great deeds and exaggerated doings that had come to define the West as simultaneously antiquated and indelible.

Thus, the western tall tale, which had first germinated in a culture of material instability and narrative hoaxes, has through Crane become the primary subject of the western short story. To be sure, over the course of the twentieth century the western short story evolves in multiple ways and through multiple points of view. But the lasting power of the myth of the Wild West, first laid out with tongues firmly planted in cheeks by writers such as Derby, Delano, and Twain, is never far from the heart of even the most serious western American literary expression.

Notes

1 Lawrence I. Berkove and Michael Kowalewski, "The Literature of the Mining Camps" in *Updating the Literary West*, ed. Thomas J. Lyon et al. (Fort Worth: Texas Christian University Press, 1997), 111; Richard A. Dwyer and Richard E. Lingenfelter, *Lying on the Eastern Slope: James Townsend's Comic Journalism on the Mining Frontier* (Miami: University Presses of Florida: Florida International University Press, 1984), 3–4, 38–70, 107–19.

2 James H. Justus, *Fetching the Old Southwest: Humorous Writing from Longstreet to Twain* (Columbia: University of Missouri Press, 2004): 4–9, 280–1, 337.

3 See especially Judith Fetterley and Marjorie Pryse, *Writing out of Place: Regionalism, Women, and American Literary Culture* (Champaign: University of Illinois Press, 2005); Stephanie Foote, *Regional Fictions: Culture and Identity in Nineteenth-Century American Literature* (Madison: University of Wisconsin Press, 2001); Richard Brodhead, *Culture of Letters: Scenes of Reading and Writing in Nineteenth-Century America* (Chicago: University of Chicago Press, 1993).

4 Franklin D. Walker, *San Francisco's Literary Frontier* (1939; Seattle: University of Washington Press, 1969), 3–16.

5 Stephen Fender, *Plotting the Golden West: American Literature and the Rhetoric of the California Trail* (Cambridge: Cambridge University Press, 1981): 105–28. For an extensive sampling of Gold Rush news, see Peter Browning, ed., *To the Golden Shore: America Goes to California – 1849* (Lafayette, CA: Great West Books, 1995).

6 Alonzo Delano, *Alonzo Delano's Pen-Knife Sketches; or, Chips of the Old Block*, ed. George Ezra Dane (1853; San Francisco: The Grabhorn Press, 1934), 30.

7 Walker, *San Francisco's Literary Frontier*, 43–4.

8 Nicolas S. Witschi, "'With Powder Smoke and Profanity': Genre Conventions, Regional Identity, and the Palisade Gunfight Hoax," in *Regionalism and the Humanities*, ed. Timothy R. Mahoney and Wendy Katz (Lincoln: University of Nebraska Press, 2009), 127–44.

9 Ella Sterling Cummins, *The Story of the Files: A Review of Californian Writers and Literature* (1893; San Leandro, CA: Yosemite Collections, 1982), 102–18. For a fuller analysis and a thorough collection of texts, see Lawrence I. Berkove, ed., *The Sagebrush Anthology: Literature from the Silver Age of the Old West* (Columbia: University of Missouri Press, 2006), 1–6.

10 Lawrence I. Berkove, ed., *The Fighting Horse of the Stanislaus: Stories and Essays by Dan De Quille* (Iowa City: University of Iowa Press, 1990), 3–19.

11 Richard A. Dwyer and Richard E. Lingenfelter, *Dan De Quille, The Washoe Giant: A Biography and Anthology* (Reno: University Nevada Press, 1990), 16–22; Berkove, *The Sagebrush Anthology*, 8.

12 "The Petrified Man" first appeared in the *Territorial Enterprise* on October 2, 1862, and "A Bloody Massacre near Carson" was first published in this same paper on October 28, 1863. Both are reprinted in Mark Twain, *Early Tales and Sketches: Volume 1 (1851–1864)*, ed. Edgar Marquess Branch and Robert H. Hirst (Berkeley: University of California Press, 1979), 159, 324–6.

13 See Henry B. Wonham, *Mark Twain and the Art of the Tall Tale* (New York: Oxford University Press, 1993), 89–111.

14 The Pliocene Age lasted roughly from 5.3 million to 2.5 million years ago. The current assumption about the artifact more commonly known as the Calaveras Skull, which is still housed at Harvard University, is that it is no more than one thousand years old, a Native American skull that had been found in a mine and then replanted as a joke to embarrass Whitney; R. E. Taylor, Louis A. Payen, and Peter J. Slota Jr., "The Age of the Calaveras Skull: Dating the 'Piltdown Man' of the New World," *American Antiquity* 57, no. 2 (1992): 269–75.

15 Gary Scharnhorst, "'Ways That Are Dark': Appropriations of Bret Harte's 'Plain Language from Truthful James,'" *Nineteenth-Century Literature* 51 (1996): 377–99.

16 See Stephen J. Mexal, *Reading for Liberalism: The Overland Monthly and the Writing of the American West* (Lincoln: University of Nebraska Press, 2013), 14–16.

17 David B. Kesterson, *Bill Nye* (Boston: Twayne, 1981), 29–50. See also Bill Nye, *Bill Nye and Boomerang; or, the Tale of a Meek-Eyed Mule, and Some Other Literary Gems* (1894; St. Clair Shores, MI: Scholarly Press, 1971).

18 Stephen Crane, *The Western Writings of Stephen Crane*, ed. Frank Bergon (New York: New American Library, 1979), 86–123.

CHAPTER 7

The Popular Western

Daniel Worden

The western genre is named after a geographic location – the American West – but despite its misleading geographic specificity, the western is a global genre. A genre that emerges in the nineteenth century, the western has persisted and changed throughout the twentieth and twenty-first centuries. Indeed, while the popular western originates in prose fiction, the genre is remarkable for its adaptability. A major category of popular and classic American literature, the western has also thrived in theater, film, television, radio, comic books, video games, music, and visual art, both in the United States and beyond. The versatility of the western can also be tracked in the variants of the genre that have sprung up over the decades. For example, one of the top-grossing western films of all time is a parody of the genre, Mel Brooks's *Blazing Saddles* (1974),[1] and western tropes have been parodied, satirized, subverted, magnified, and adapted in a variety of ways, from Joss Whedon's sci-fi western TV series *Firefly* (2002) and Rockstar Games's combination of the western and the zombie narrative in *Red Dead Redemption: Undead Nightmare* (2010) to Ishmael Reed's rapacious, postmodern western novel *Yellow Back Radio Broke-Down* (1969) and Kelly Reichardt's open-ended, meditative western film *Meek's Cutoff* (2010). The popular western is a generic formula, but one that has been rendered in multiple aesthetic and social modes.

The western consists of a cluster of recognizable tropes: the shootout, the open landscape of the American frontier, the clash between rustlers and ranchers, the noble outlaw, the madam with a heart of gold, the saloon brawl, the vanishing Indian, the innocent homesteader, the tenderfoot, and so on. The genre's elements often coalesce into a story of good versus evil, the white hat versus the black hat, though the actual historical, geographic, and political coordinates of "good" and "evil" vary widely in the popular western. For example, as Christine Bold has argued, some of the most celebrated westerns in the early twentieth century heroized cowboys and mercenaries who murdered innocent homesteaders and farmhands during the 1892 Johnson County War in Wyoming. Most notably, Owen Wister's *The Virginian* (1902) is part of a tradition of western genre writing that served the interests of "a cultural elite violently protecting its privilege in the name of democracy."[2] About the same historical moment, Michael Cimino's western film *Heaven's Gate* (1980) represents immigrant homesteaders as being violently harassed, murdered, and intimidated by greedy, monopolistic elites from the East. Though often associated with male writers and masculine heroes, the western is also, as Victoria Lamont has shown in her reading of Frances McElrath's 1902 novel *The Rustler*, "produced through debate in which the place of women in the mythological West is a crucial point of contention and … this very debate has authorized female as well as male voices."[3] The western, then, is a genre with no singular politics, though it is rooted in a particular historical imaginary – the closing of the frontier, the tensions between the rule of law and individual freedom, the shift from the nomadic cowboy to the modern farmer and industrial worker – that often makes political and social tensions central.

As the next section will discuss, the western's origins themselves point to the political malleability of the genre, as it can, on the one hand, articulate populist, egalitarian ideals, and, on the other, shore up class, gender, and racial hierarchies. This essay's second section analyzes how a best-selling western, Zane Grey's *Riders of the Purple Sage* (1912), articulates a secular mythology, while the third delves into the different political meanings of the popular western. The essay concludes with a survey of the western today, a global genre still central to art, literature, and culture.

The Western, the Detective Story, and the Origins of Popular Genres

The major works that led to the formation of the popular western were James Fenimore Cooper's *Leatherstocking Tales* (1823–41), a group of five novels featuring the frontiersman hero Natty Bumppo. *The Leatherstocking Tales* would serve as a template for the western genre, especially in its juxtaposition of romance, adventure, and heroic individualism in the frontier wilderness. Notably, the detective story and the western emerge around the same time. The final novel in James Fenimore Cooper's *Leatherstocking Tales*, *The Deerslayer* (1841), was published the same year as the first of Edgar Allan Poe's Auguste Dupin mystery stories, "Murders in the Rue Morgue." In his Dupin stories, including "The Mystery of Marie Roget" (1842) and "The Purloined Letter" (1844), Poe used a genius detective, whose powers of deduction solve what appear to be unsolvable crimes. If the iconic hero of the detective story is a canny logician and reader of people, then the western hero is an icon of truth and physical stature. Yet, the two genres, the western and the detective story, intermingle from their origins to our contemporary moment. As Jacques Derrida claimed, genre is an inextricable quality of any text: "a text cannot belong to no genre, it cannot be without or less a genre."⁴ Moreover, all genres intermingle, so the genre of the popular western is inherently imbricated, influential on, and adapting to other genre forms, not only the detective story, but also science fiction and the romance.

Emerging together in the nineteenth century, the western and the detective story most typically represent two different worlds. The western is often set in a historical wilderness or frontier, imagined as being just on the verge of being civilized. Cooper's novels are set in upstate New York in the eighteenth century, and most twentieth-century westerns are set in western territories between 1865 and 1890, after the Civil War, and on the verge of the "closing of the frontier" in 1893. As Robert Warshow remarked in a 1954 essay on western film, "Where the Westerner lives it is always 1870 – not the real 1870, either, or the real West – and he is killed or goes away when his position becomes problematical."⁵ Contrary to the western's open spaces, the detective story typically takes place in urban spaces, the labyrinthine and confounding underworlds generated by modernity – Poe's detective stories are set in Paris. While they seem disparate – the western deals with the frontier past, the detective story with the urban present – the two genres often intersect, as they both represent tensions among the law, individual freedom, and violence against others. As discussed later in this section, classic detective fiction often draws on western tropes and settings, while western fiction often incorporates elements of the detective story.

The iconic characteristic of the western, along with a frontier setting, is the western hero – a frontiersman, cowboy, bandit, or sheriff whose core qualities are evident in Cooper's novels. In *The Deerslayer*, Cooper describes Natty Bumppo's physical appearance and moral constitution:

> In stature, he stood about six feet in his moccasins, but his frame was comparatively light and slender, showing muscles, however, that promised unusual agility, if not unusual strength. His face would have had little to recommend it except youth, were it not for an expression that seldom failed to win upon those who had leisure to examine it, and to yield the feeling of confidence it created. This expression was simply that of guileless truth, sustained by an earnestness of purpose, and a sincerity of feeling, that rendered it remarkable.⁶

Elements of Cooper's frontier hero persist throughout the western genre, and even in gritty, more contemporary westerns, the weathered and jaded western hero serves as moral center to the narrative.

In the late nineteenth and early twentieth centuries, westerns as well as detective stories thrived in the dime novels. Dime novels, the first popular literature in the United States, were read widely and marketed to the working class, adolescents, and even the middle class.[7] As Michael Denning has argued, dime novel westerns reflect industrial capitalism and working-class politics, though those concerns are displaced through the genre conventions of the western: "The acts of Deadwood Dick, Jesse James and the other dime novel outlaws – the Younger brothers, the Dalton Boys, and Joaquin Murieta – were both sufficiently distant from and implicated in the battles of labor and capital to offer a figure of those battles, a figure of vengeance and heroism."[8] One of the most notable dime novel heroes, Deadwood Dick, appeared in a number of novels originally published by Beadle & Adams and reprinted in the *Deadwood Dick Library* later in the nineteenth century by the Arthur Westbrook Company. One Deadwood Dick dime novel, Edward L. Wheeler's *Deadwood Dick's Doom; or, Calamity Jane's Last Adventure* (1881), is set in a mining camp named Death Notch that has been built on stolen Apache land. The bandit hero first appears in the dime novel's second chapter. A "paleface," Caroll Carner, tries to force himself on Siska, "at a glance an Indian, but lighter complexioned than the average of her nation, betraying a mixture of white blood in her veins," and Deadwood Dick intervenes by punching Caroll Carner in the face and knocking him to the ground.[9] Deadwood Dick then introduces himself, making it clear that his identity is bound up in print culture: " 'A cuss from Custer – a bulldog from Bozeman – a diabolical devil from Deadwood,' Dick replied, dryly. 'I don't carry any visiting cards as I generally have a sheriff or marshal after me who carries them and posts 'em up in every convenient place, viz. – Five Hundred Dollars reward for the capture of the notorious outlaw, Deadwood Dick, dead or alive.' "[10] Later in the dime novel, interrupting the auction of a woman to the highest bidder, all of the debased male residents of Death Notch are killed by the Apache: "Like a hurricane of wrath the warriors under the lead of Dancing Plume swept down in pursuit of the late residents of Death Notch, and shot down and scalped them without mercy."[11] Protector of women, enemy of corrupt capitalism, and supporter of Indigenous land rights, Deadwood Dick is a western version of a working-class hero, an almost supernatural agent of social justice and equality.

Institutionalizing the historical coincidence of the western and the detective story, dime novels often combined the two genres. Stories in the

Old Sleuth Library (1885–1905) were set in the West, and detectives often appear as major and minor characters in the western stories popular in Beadle's Half Dime Library (1877–1905). These stories often combine the modern rationality of the detective story – the idea that scientific principles can unmask superstition and deceit – with the allure of the frontier and wilderness so popular in the western genre, a form much more overtly centered on passion, romance, and action. As Daryl Jones has remarked, dime novels often represent conflict in a way that emphasizes the workings of power in the industrial age, and by the 1880s, the dime novel "allegorizes the role of individual strength and virtue in maintaining personal freedoms and eradicating from existing society all forms of injustice and immortality which impede society's progress." As he goes on to explain, "The villains are wealthy capitalists who exploit the common man; bankers who thrive on others' adversity and who appropriate personal fortunes; politicians who make a mockery of the democratic process; lawyers who manipulate the law for personal gain."[12] The frontier is mapped, processed, and demystified in these stories, understood as less a primitive outpost, distant from civilization, than another type of modern locale, one that is corrupt in the same ways as the urban centers in which the dime novels were typically written and published, and where detective stories were often set.

The dime novel's cross-pollination of the western and the detective story, as well as the romance and early science fiction, would continue in pulp magazines such as, most famously, *Black Mask,* which published westerns and hard-boiled detective stories alongside one another. A number of pulp magazines, such as *Western Story Magazine* and *Wild West Weekly,* were devoted to western stories.[13] Often, as is the case with Dashiell Hammett's *Red Harvest* (1927), first titled *Poisonville* when serialized in *Black Mask*, hard-boiled detective stories were set in the American West, too. A vast number of western writers were published in pulp magazines, including Max Brand, Zane Grey, and Paul S. Powers, but scholarship on pulp magazines has largely focused on the detective and science fiction genres.[14] This coincidence of the western with other genres also popular in pulp magazines persists today, in, for example, the television series *Justified* and *Longmire*, both of which are based on detective stories that feature a cowboy hero, as well as the popular mystery novels of Tony Hillerman, set in the American Southwest and featuring Detectives Jim Chee and Joe Leaphorn of the Navajo Tribal Police.[15]

Indeed, Sir Arthur Conan Doyle's first Sherlock Holmes story, *A Study in Scarlet* (1887), contains a lengthy flashback sequence set in the Utah territory in 1847. In the story, Holmes is asked to solve a murder, whose motives are eventually traced back to the American West, involving vengeance for a young woman kidnapped by Mormons. Even in this first appearance of Sherlock Holmes, a character who would become the icon of urbane rationality, the American West looms in the background. The Utah section of *A Study in Scarlet* begins:

> In the central portion of the great North American Continent there lies an arid and repulsive desert, which for many a long year served as a barrier against the advance of civilisation. From the Sierra Nevada to Nebraska, and from the Yellowstone River in the north to the Colorado upon the south, is a region of desolation and silence. Nor is Nature always in one mood throughout this grim district. It comprises snow-capped and lofty mountains, and dark and gloomy valleys. There are swift-flowing rivers which dash through jagged cañons; and there are enormous plains, which in winter are white with snow, and in summer are grey with the saline alkali dust. They all preserve, however, the common characteristics of barrenness, inhospitality, and misery.[16]

Doyle's account of the western landscape as barren and uninhabited was all-too common in the late nineteenth century, along with representations of Native Americans as savages.

These representative traditions would continue in the pulps and in the paperback western novels of, for example, Dorothy M. Johnson, Elmer Kelton, Louis L'Amour, and Elmore Leonard. In L'Amour's novel *Hondo* (1952), the western hero Hondo Lane helps to secure Arizona against the Apache, with whom he does battle at the novel's conclusion. After killing Silva, an Apache chief, Hondo has a vision of what he has made possible, "a long meadow fresh with new-cut hay, a house where smoke would soon again rise from the chimney, and where shadows would gather in the darkness under the trees, quiet shadows. And beside him a woman held in her arms a sleeping child ... a woman who would be there with him, in that house, before that hearth."[17] In *Hondo* and many other westerns, Native Americans are represented as ultimately incompatible with American domestic life, and thus are figured as savage others to the often even more violent western hero. Whether set in a barren wilderness or a land filled with savages, the western genre in the early to mid-twentieth century dramatizes the processes of colonization and conquest, often in ways that reinforce the ideologies of American imperialism.

As within dime novels and pulp magazines, the western would also flourish in American film. The first western film is Edwin S. Porter's *The Great Train Robbery* (1903), a silent film that was followed by innumerous western films and, later, television shows. The French film critic André Bazin would describe the western as the "American film par excellence," noting that "the western was born of an encounter between a mythology and a means of expression."[18] This results, in Bazin's analysis, in "the ethics of the epic and even of tragedy. The western is in the epic category because of the superhuman level of its heroes and the legendary magnitude of their feats of valor. Billy the Kid is as invulnerable as Achilles and his revolver is infallible. The cowboy is a knight-at-arms."[19] This epic heroism is complicated and made distinct by the tragic imposition of law over the individualist courage of the cowboy hero, resulting in, for example, the outlaw or bandit status embraced by popular western heroes such as Deadwood Dick. Perhaps most pointedly dramatized in George Stevens's film *Shane* (1953), the cowboy hero must recede at the end of the western, after making the West safe for domestication. The western, for Bazin, turns this narrative of frontier settlement into a founding American myth about the heroism of imperial conquest, the Edenic value of the American wilderness, and the regenerative qualities of violence. Through film, the western and this American mythology would have a global reach.

The Western as Secular Myth

Following Bazin, one way to view the popular western is as a secular mythology, a set of inherently liberal, secular tropes that figure the subject's relationship to the world in modernity. As Charles Taylor argues, modernity produces a secular subjectivity: "Modernity is secular, not in the frequent, rather loose sense of the word, where it designates the absence of religion, but rather in the fact that religion occupies a different place, compatible with the sense that all social action takes place in profane time."[20] While Henry Nash Smith argued that popular westerns could not adequately address modernity, because the dichotomy between nature and civilization "imposed on Westerners the stigma of social, ethical, and cultural inferiority," the western actually grapples with modernity rather explicitly, and the popular western of the late nineteenth and twentieth centuries was determined by its modern context.[21] In the early twentieth-century United States, one particular conflict between religion and the state would provide the backdrop for one of the best-selling western novels of all time. Reflecting a controversy of the day, both *McClure's* and *Cosmopolitan* published serialized essays on the Mormon church, polygamy, and the church's imperial and monopolistic ambitions in 1911 and 1912. This wave of anti-Mormon sentiment also appears in Zane Grey's *Riders of the Purple Sage* (1912), which sold more than a million copies within a year of its publication. Scholarly treatments of this novel tend to focus on its representation of western masculinity and the novel's use of polygamy as a foil for naturalized monogamy.[22] The novel's interest in the politics of marriage and atypical romance is in no small part informed by Zane Grey's open marriage, which has been documented in Thomas H. Pauly's recent biography.[23] When scholars have discussed anti-Mormon sentiment, in this novel and in other texts, the focus tends to be on the racialization and orientalization of Mormonism in the U.S. popular press. As William Handley writes, "the reification of Mormon religious difference into ethnic status involved, for much of the latter half of the nineteenth century and even into the twentieth, a confused amalgamation of non-white stereotypes."[24] This certainly happens in *Riders of the Purple Sage*. As Lassiter, the gun-slinging hero of the novel, remarks, Mormons have a "dark set look thet makes them strange an' different to me."[25] While race is clearly a way of figuring the villain as "dark," the reason that *Riders of the Purple Sage* remains a popular text in American culture has less relation to the particular valences of anti-Mormonism in the 1910s than it has to the novel's articulation of a markedly secular understanding of human subjects and their relation to nature and society.

Riders of the Purple Sage is an exemplary western. The narrative has two major plot arcs. The first involves a Mormon woman named Jane Withersteen, who has inherited a sizable ranch from her father and is threatened with an arranged marriage to Tull, a villainous Mormon polygamist. Lassiter, a typical western hero and renowned "Mormon-killer," rides onto Jane's property and helps her fend off the Mormons. The two enter into a tentative romance, driven by Jane's desire to cure Lassiter of his violent ways and Lassiter's desire to disillusion Jane about her Mormon faith. The second narrative arc involves Jane's ranch hand, Venters, who flees Jane's ranch after being threatened by Tull, Jane's Mormon suitor. Venters is involved in his own romance with a rustler known as the "Masked Rider," who turns out to be a young woman named Bess. The novel concludes with Venters and Bess leaving for the East, Lassiter killing the Mormon bishop, and then escaping along with Jane and an adopted child named Fay to a remote, Edenic valley.

Jane's religious crisis occupies much of the novel, and she ultimately moves through doubt to embrace a "new revelation of self."[26] In a scene that refers to the biblical story of Sodom and Gomorrah, Jane agrees to leave Cottonwoods with Lassiter, after Lassiter has killed the Mormon bishop Dyer. Jane's embrace of her new life results in a surprisingly passionate appreciation of the Utah landscape: "Her doom had fallen upon her, but, instead of finding life no longer worth living she found it doubly significant, full of sweetness as the western breeze, beautiful and unknown as the sage-slope stretching its purple sunset shadows before her."[27] This moment of "sweetness" is then complicated when Lassiter engages in a gunfight. Jane meditates on violence and becomes indifferent to the world: "On sea, on land, everywhere – shooting, stabbing, cursing, clashing, fighting men! Greed, power, oppression, fanaticism, love, hate, revenge, justice, freedom – for these, men killed one another … she thought and wondered and did not care."[28] Immediately after this dour moment, Jane and Lassiter travel up to the Edenic valley and create an avalanche, killing their Mormon pursuers and trapping themselves – and little Fay – in "Surprise Valley." The narrative resolves Jane and Lassiter's opposed impulses of religious feeling and violent action through nature.

The novel creates a primitive human family, and their willful seclusion in "Surprise Valley" represents the regeneration of life on the frontier, a life that is "better, cleaner for the ways of men like Lassiter!"[29] The affirmation of the monogamous couple at the end of the novel fits into gender and sexuality norms, and the inclusion of little Fay places not just the couple but the family at the center of the social imaginary. Complicating this retreat to origins, though, are Fay's status as an orphan as well as Jane and Lassiter's heretofore unarticulated love for one another. Instead of a natural family, Jane, Lassiter, and Fay are joined together through altruism. In this sense, while Jane's emerging secularism is modeled on religion, the family itself is modeled on liberalism.

In his account of western films, Robert Pippin argues that westerns often ask "how legal order (of a particular form, the form of liberal democratic capitalism) is possible, under what conditions it can be formed and command allegiance, how the bourgeois virtues, especially the domestic virtues, *can be said to get a psychological grip in an environment where the heroic and martial virtues are so important.*"[30] In *Riders of the Purple Sage*, this psychological grip occurs through love, which is not determined by shared affiliations but develops between strangers. The novel does not naturalize the monogamous couple and the family, but instead dramatizes their construction, through conversion, channeling emotion outside religious affiliation, kinship, and willful privatization. Secularization entails this retreat to the family unit, as other forms of belonging – such as religious community – are subordinated to a modern notion of civil society.

Riders of the Purple Sage also articulates this secular mythology through descriptions of the landscape. After Venters discovers Surprise Valley, his relationship to the landscape changes:

> Above, through a V-shaped cleft in the dark rim of the cliff, shone the lustrous stars that had been his lonely accusers for a long, long year. To-night they were different. He studied them. Larger, whiter, more radiant they seemed; but that was not the difference he meant. Gradually it came to him that the distinction was not one he saw, but one he felt. In this he divined as much of the baffling change as he thought would be revealed to him then. And as he lay there, with the singing of the cliff-winds in his ears, the white stars above the dark, bold vent, the difference which he felt was that he was not alone.[31]

In this description of the landscape, Grey posits passionate secularism as a discipline of the self, a mode of self-discovery that does not entail the rejection of religious practice but instead the expansion and reworking of religious practice into a mode of involvement with not just other people but the world itself, a kind of transcendentalism outfitted for the age of American imperialism and industrialization. In its incessant repetitions of spiritual uncertainty, tentative conversions, and polarized affect, *Riders of the Purple Sage* articulates secularism as a mode of subjectivity derived from both the landscape and individual self-determination. In this novel, and in many of the popular westerns that would follow it, the American West allows for the cultivation of individualism as well as the establishment of an egalitarian social imaginary, often in violent reaction to exertions of tyrannical power.

The Politics of the Western

One of the central critical debates about the western genre relates to its politics. Some critics view the western as a conservative genre, one that naturalizes racial and gender hierarchies, while others find in the western allegories of class conflict and egalitarian politics. For example, Stanley Corkin reads classic western films as dramatizing cold war politics; Richard Slotkin finds in the western a consolidation of both Theodore Roosevelt's vision of American imperialism at the turn of the twentieth century and militarization during the Vietnam War; Walter Benn Michaels finds in Zane Grey's *The Vanishing American* (1925) the emergence of racial nativism in America; and, Jane Tompkins dwells on the ubiquity of traditional gender roles and violence in the western.[32] More contemporary westerns, though, have been read as subversive and progressive. Patrick McGee argues that western films often offer up ways of imagining resistance to capitalism, while Sara Spurgeon finds in contemporary, literary westerns the articulation of a hybrid, multicultural social imaginary.[33] Splitting the difference, Forrest G. Robinson has argued that the western genre is, in fact, constructed around binary oppositions, allowing readers to "have it both ways," to imagine the western narrative as conservative or progressive, conformist or subversive.[34]

While *Riders of the Purple Sage* makes clear how the western functions as a secular mythology, a liberal vision of social equality and natural harmony that nonetheless erases the Native American presence in the American West and instills a gender hierarchy, a western story like Owen Wister's *The Virginian* dramatizes the transition in the American West from the nomadic age of the cowboy to the settled, industrial West figured through the railroad. *The Virginian* concludes with the cowboy becoming a family man and a businessman allied with coal and railroad interests. This triumphalist vision of settlement and industry, though, is coupled in *The Virginian* with a melancholic attachment to the nomadic life of the now-obsolete cowboy. As a historical narrative, the western often dramatizes the passing of the frontier, and multiple political meanings and implications follow from that historical imagination, meanings and implications bound up in nationalism, class, gender, and race. A genre that often privileges white heroes against "dark" villains, the western has also been used to depict more complicated understandings of race and class, in texts such as the autobiography of the black cowboy Nat Love, *The Life and Adventures of Nat Love* (1907), in which Love claims to have been the real-life model for the dime novel hero Deadwood Dick, or in the *corrido* tradition, an example of which, the story of Gregorio Cortez Lima, is documented in Américo Paredes's *"With His Pistol in His Hand": A Border Ballad and Its Hero* (1958).

While *The Virginian* finds in the passing of the wild frontier the arrival of a legitimate social order, other western stories focus on the violence and exploitation necessitated by this transition. In Walter Van Tilburg Clark's *The Ox-Bow Incident* (1940), for example, a lynching is central. In *The Virginian*, lynching is a sign of the cowboy hero's maturity and acceptance of civilization; the Virginian lynches his friend Steve for cattle rustling, thus proving the Virginian's commitment to upholding law, especially property rights. In *The Ox-Bow Incident*, lynching marks the exploitative, unjust violence of western masculinity. Mistakenly believing that he has captured three rustlers, the former Confederate soldier Tetley convinces a mob to lynch the innocent men. One member of the lynch mob tries to convince the men not to go through with the lynching, but the dictates of western manhood triumph: "Most of the men had made up their minds, or felt that the rest had and that their own sympathy was reprehensible and should be concealed."[35] Unwilling to appear sympathetic and thus risk seeming feminine, the lynch mob kills three innocent men. What *The Ox-Bow Incident* makes clear are the ways in which violence in the Western often shores up racial and social hierarchies, and how the nobility and moral code of the western hero can blind us to the realities of violence.

Staging an even more extensive representation of gender, race, and class in the West, the television series *Deadwood* (2004–6) makes explicit how racial and gender hierarchies persist in the West and the western, from anti-semitism and brutal violence against Native Americans, to the exploitation of Chinese laborers and the Victorian norms restricting genteel white women's behavior. But, along with this, *Deadwood* represents the mobility and fluidity of these racial, gender, and class hierarchies in the West as well, as the frontier town allows people to forge alliances and act in ways that subvert and even ignore restrictive social norms. Moreover, *Deadwood* makes clear that the racial, gender, and class hierarchies that traveled to the West, and that are basic tropes used in the western genre, are inextricably connected to economic development. Reading politics in the western is a way of analyzing the forms that capitalism would take in the American West, as settler colonialism developed and produced a vision of the West as free and other to the processes of capitalism that, in fact, saturate both the West and the western.

The Persistence of the Western

While the western genre emerges in the United States, it is by no means limited by national borders. Indeed, many of the most intriguing western narratives have emerged from other places. Set in Australia, John Hillcoat's film *The Proposition* (2005) and Peter Carey's novel *True History of the Kelly Gang* (2000) use the specificity of Australian colonization to tell bandit stories. In film, especially, the genre has long been global, most notably in the Italian "spaghetti westerns" of Sergio Leone, many of which were inspired by the samurai films of the Japanese filmmaker Akira Kurosawa. The Japanese film *Sukiyaki Western Django* (2007), directed by Takashi Miike, makes these connections of the American western, the Japanese samurai movie, and the Italian "spaghetti western" explicit. In comics, Hergé's *Tintin in America* (1932) places the French comics character in the American West, parodying the western's depiction of Native Americans, and the long-running Franco-Belgian comics series *Blueberry*, created by Jean-Michel Charlier and Jean "Moebius" Giraud in 1963, centers on a cowboy hero.

In our contemporary moment, genre mash ups often include the western – in science fiction films such as James Gunn's *The Guardians of the Galaxy* (2014), western tropes are evident, and even more explicitly in Jon Favreau's *Cowboys & Aliens* (2011), based on a 2006 graphic novel. In contemporary literature, the western persists in historical novels like Jonathan Evison's *West of Here* (2011) and Patrick deWitt's *The Sisters Brothers* (2011); in subversions of the genre such as Sherman Alexie's *Flight* (2007) and Philipp Meyer's *The Son* (2013); in genre novels like Robert Olmstead's *Far Bright Star* (2009); and in more experimental forms, such as Larry McMurtry's *The Last Kind Words Saloon* (2014). McMurtry's novel distills a famous setting and cast of characters for the western – Tombstone, Arizona, and Wyatt Earp, Doc Holliday, Johnny Ringo, and others – into a kind of existential narrative, in which celebrity image, capitalist development, and human frailty become subjects of discussion, rather than the easy moral calculus of the traditional western formula.

While western films such as Gore Verbinski's *The Lone Ranger* (2013) continue to be produced, and western novels continue to be published, perhaps the most understudied yet most vibrant medium in which the western thrives today is in comics. Western comics have been around as long as the modern medium of comics, in series such as EC Comics's *Gunfighter* (1948–50); Marvel Comics's *Rawhide Kid*, written by Stan Lee and penciled by Jack Kirby in 1960; and DC Comics's *Jonah Hex*, created by John Albano and Tony DeZuniga in 1972. In the past two decades, there have been a number of notable western comics, from Chris Blain's madcap French-language *Gus & His Gang* (2008) and the supernatural western *The Sixth Gun* (2010–present) by Cullen Bunn and Brian Hurtt; to the retelling of the Lewis and Clark expedition *Manifest Destiny* (2013–present) by Chris Dingess and Matthew Roberts; and the archetypal, mystical *Pretty Deadly* (2014) by Kelly Sue DeConnick and Emma Rios. In comics today, the western has become a genre of renewed interest, and this makes sense given the tensions about nationalism, militarization, and violence that figure centrally in our contemporary moment. A genre that has proven to be elastic enough to accommodate any number of political and social tensions, while also retaining key tropes and genre conceits that provide familiar pleasures and narrative rhythms, the western informs the stories we tell ourselves about nearly everything, from nation and nature, to gender and guns.

Notes

1 John H. Lenihan, "Westbound: Feature Films in the American West," in *Wanted Dead or Alive: The American West in Popular Culture*, ed. Richard Aquila (Urbana: University of Illinois Press, 1996), 130.

2 Christine Bold, *The Frontier Club: Popular Westerns and Cultural Power, 1880–1924* (New York: Oxford University Press, 2013), 1.

3 Victoria Lamont, "History, Gender, and the Origins of the 'Classic' Western," in *Reading* The Virginian *in the New West*, ed. Melody Graulich and Stephen Tatum (Lincoln: University of Nebraska Press, 2003), 153.

4 Jacques Derrida, "The Law of Genre," trans. Avital Ronell, *Critical Inquiry* 7, no. 1 (Autumn 1980): 65.

5 Robert Warshow, *The Immediate Experience: Movies, Comics, Theater and Other Aspects of Popular Culture* (Cambridge, MA: Harvard University Press, 2001), 111.

6 James Fenimore Cooper, *The Deerslayer* (1841; New York: Penguin, 1987), 20–1.

7 For examples of dime novel westerns, see Bill Brown, ed., *Reading the West: An Anthology of Dime Novel Westerns* (Boston: Bedford/St. Martin's, 1997) and J. Randolph Cox, ed., *Dashing Diamond Dick and Other Classic Dime Novels* (New York: Penguin, 2007). For online, digitized collections of dime novels, see *Dime Novels and Penny Dreadfuls*, Stanford University, http://web.stanford.edu/dept/SUL/library/prod//depts/dp/pennies/home.html and *Dime Novels and Popular Literature*, Villanova University, http://digital.library.villanova.edu/Collection/vudl:24093 (accessed March 16, 2015).

8 Michael Denning, *Mechanic Accents: Dime Novels and Working-Class Culture in America* (New York: Verso, 1998), 166.

9 Edward L. Wheeler's *Deadwood Dick's Doom* originally appeared in *Beadle's Half-Dime Library* 205 (June 28, 1881). References here are to the reprint edition; see Edward L. Wheeler, *Deadwood Dick's Doom*, in *The Deadwood Dick Library* 3, no. 39 (March 15, 1898), 4.

10 Ibid., 5.

11 Ibid., 28.

12 Daryl Jones, *The Dime Novel Western* (Bowling Green, OH: Bowling Green University Popular Press, 1978), 154–5.

13 For a digital archive of pulp magazines, see *The Pulp Magazines Project*, http://www.pulpmags.org/ (accessed March 16, 2015); and for a history of pulp magazines and popular fiction in the early twentieth century, see David M. Earle, *Re-Covering Modernism: Pulps, Paperbacks, and the Prejudice of Form* (Burlington, VT: Ashgate, 2009).

14 For example, see Erin A. Smith, *Hard-Boiled: Working Class Readers and Pulp Magazines* (Philadelphia: Temple University Press, 2000) and Michael Ashley, *The Time Machines: The Story of the Science Fiction Pulp Magazines from the Beginning to 1950* (Liverpool: Liverpool University Press, 2000).

15 For the introduction to Raylan Givens, the hero of *Justified*, see Elmore Leonard's *Pronto* (1993); Walt Longmire of *Longmire* first appears in Craig

Johnson's *The Cold Dish* (2004); the first Joe Leaphorn mystery novel is Tony Hillerman's *The Blessing Way* (1970); Jim Chee appears in Tony Hillerman's *People of Darkness* (1980).

16 Arthur Conan Doyle, *A Study in Scarlet* (New York: Modern Library, 2003), 65.

17 Louis L'Amour, *Hondo* (1952; New York: Bantam, 1997), 179.

18 André Bazin, "The Western, or the American Film *par Excellence*," in *What Is Cinema?* Vol. 2, trans. Hugh Gray (Berkeley: University of California Press, 1971), 142.

19 Ibid., 147.

20 Charles Taylor, *Modern Social Imaginaries* (Durham, NC: Duke University Press, 2004), 194.

21 Henry Nash Smith, *Virgin Land: The American West as Symbol and Myth* (Cambridge, MA: Harvard University Press, 1950), 260.

22 See Lee Clark Mitchell, *Westerns: Making the Man in Fiction and Film* (Chicago: University of Chicago Press, 1996).

23 See Thomas H. Pauly, *Zane Grey: His Life, His Adventures, His Women* (Urbana: University of Illinois Press, 2005).

24 William R. Handley, *Marriage, Violence, and the Nation in the American Literary West* (New York: Cambridge University Press, 2002), 106.

25 Zane Grey, *Riders of the Purple Sage* (1912; New York: Modern Library, 2002), 58.

26 Ibid., 59.

27 Ibid., 239.

28 Ibid., 265.

29 Ibid., 264.

30 Robert B. Pippin, *Hollywood Westerns and American Myth: The Importance of Howard Hawks and John Ford for Political Philosophy* (New Haven, CT: Yale University Press, 2010), 20, emphasis in original.

31 Grey, 89.

32 See Stanley Corkin, *Cowboys as Cold Warriors: The Western and U.S. History* (Philadelphia: Temple University Press, 2004); Walter Benn Michaels, *Our America: Nativism, Modernism, and Pluralism* (Durham, NC: Duke University Press, 1997); Richard Slotkin, *The Fatal Environment: The Myth of the Frontier in the Age of Industrialization* (New York: Atheneum, 1985) and *Gunfighter Nation: The Myth of the Frontier in Twentieth-Century America* (New York: Atheneum, 1992); and Jane Tompkins, *West of Everything: The Inner Life of Westerns* (New York: Oxford University Press, 1992).

33 Patrick McGee, *From Shane to Kill Bill: Rethinking the Western* (Malden, MA: Blackwell, 2007) and Sara Spurgeon, *Exploding the Western: Myths of Empire on the Postmodern Frontier* (College Station, TX: Texas A&M University Press, 2005).

34 Forrest G. Robinson, *Having It Both Ways: Self-Subversion in Western Popular Classics* (Albuquerque: University of New Mexico Press, 1993).

35 Walter Van Tilburg Clark, *The Ox-Bow Incident* (1940; New York: Signet, 1968), 178.

PART III

Geographies of the Literary West

Literature of the Great Plains
Nature, Culture, and Community

Susan Naramore Maher

Late in Wright Morris's spare, hard-edged novel *Plains Song: For Female Voices* (1980), Sharon Rose Atkins leaves her comfortable New England life to visit her former home on the Nebraska plains. In a car driven by a blunt talking niece, Sharon leaves the city of Lincoln and watches as the countryside blurs by. Along the way, her niece Caroline peppers her with "brash" questions and opinions about family history, female independence, and domestic oppression.[1] Heat and sun overcome Caroline's forays with soporific effect, lulling Sharon into reverie. "The wires dipped and rose," Morris tells us; "the poles and trees flickered past, and in the fabric of fancy, like a patterned design, she sensed something both lost and something gained."[2] Sharon's family had homesteaded in this rolling country, and Caroline with her car full of children conceivably represents the leading edge of future life on this landscape, something gained. Yet when Caroline pulls off the road and takes her aunt to a place of "tall weeds ... tree stumps torn out by their roots ... [and] deep pits," Sharon looks over an unrecognizable plot, a yard that resembles "craters left by bombs."[3] She wonders, "Why had they stopped?"[4] Surveying the farmscape of her childhood, Sharon draws a blank. Nothing remains – no houses, no barns, no gardens, no windbreaks. "'Nobody wanted it,' Caroline explains. 'There was nothing worth saving.'"[5] The past, tangibly, irrevocably, is lost, and Sharon realizes this wasted battlefield is where her life began.

Morris economically captures, in this scene, a central collision point in Great Plains literature: the slippage between past and future marked in present spaces. Traces of violence, conquest, and unrealized desire lie buried like tectonic plates, surface erasure tracing something more menacing beneath. *Plains Song* connects to the longer literary tradition of Great Plains writing, borne out of a vexed history of contact, national expansion, and settlement. Across regions, centuries, cultures, genres, and traditions, Great Plains writers in the last two centuries have reckoned with

ephemerality and loss, displacement and escape, the hope of new beginnings and the collapse of dreams.

Without the history of forcible removal of Indigenous tribes and the
wholesale slaughter of bison, the Atkins family could never have staked
their claim near the town of Battle Creek, Nebraska. In John T. Price's
assessment, "no other American biome has suffered such an enormous
loss of life with so little protest."[6] This bitter history lies unspoken in the
text, one of the many silences that define Morris's examination of settlement and its aftermath. From the first military surveys and entrepreneurial ventures out onto the plains to settler colonialism, European and then
American groups explored, exploited, and claimed the vast area called
the Great Plains.[7] Narratives of triumphalism and ascendancy, of God's
will and Manifest Destiny trumpeted through the first century of a Great
Plains literary oeuvre. By the time Morris penned his late novel, the tim-
bre of this region's writing had lost its brassy sounds of fanfare. Muted
themes, darker, more somber, and conciliatory, took over.

The *Encyclopedia of the Great Plains* maps the physical dimensions of
this varied, diverse landscape, from central Texas and eastern New Mexico
up to the Dakotas, eastern Wyoming, and most of Montana. Other
maps include all of East Texas and western Iowa and Minnesota. Natural
boundaries – the Missouri River, the Rocky Mountains – help define the
fluid outlines of this space, an area that exceeds 970,000 square miles.[8] For
the first visitors, understanding the grasslands biome was a considerable
challenge, "something completely new to European and Euro-American
experience," in Candace Savage's assessment.[9] Encounters with the plains
revealed "a vast, dynamic ecosystem, a kind of tawny, slowly evolving
organism that, in a climate of constant change, had sustained itself ever
since the retreat of the glaciers thousands of years before."[10] Indigenous
tribes who settled and roamed the Great Plains knew this landscape intimately, over millennia of adaptation and use. Deep cultural memories
preserved and exchanged through stories present a wholly different experience from that of Europeans, late dwellers on the plains.

As Linda Hogan (Chickasaw) lyrically muses in her essay "The
Feathers," in the collection *Dwellings*, "there is a still place, a gap
between worlds, spoken by the tribal knowings of thousands of years."[11]
Such "sacred reason" passed forward through story and ceremony continues to find voice in Great Plains Native literature.[12] In contrast,
having broken from their own ancestral lands, European-descended
migrants, with little cultural or scientific understanding of this ecosystem, projected a tabula rasa onto the landscape, a blank screen

writ large with possibility, lust for possession, and political ambition. Detachment from and erasure of the past, origins, and familial practices factored into the first settlement era writings from the plains. At the same time, separation from ties and beginnings also led to a magnification of cultural biases, a glorification of one's own God, one's own beliefs and political leanings. Underappreciating or wholly dismissing Indigenous knowledge of place, facing a vast landscape that defied easy grasp, many writers followed the practice of the earliest Europeans on the plains and turned to familiar patterns of storytelling, myth making, and legend to lay larger claim to the land.[13] Later settlers, the people Wright Morris portrays in *Plains Song,* clung to their own preconceptions. "The homesteaders," William Least Heat-Moon explains in his masterwork *PrairyErth*, "brought with them a notion corroborated by their Christianity that this hugely open spread was a kind of failed forest that needed only the hand of civilized man to redeem it from its appalling waste."[14] As a consequence, "[rather] than learning what the prairie could provide and then changing their ways to harmonize with a land new to them, the settlers began trying to remake it into the East."[15] Environmental challenges propel much Great Plains literature, where the land looms large. In the last century of writings, authors across genres wrestle with climatic and topographical realities, and the best of them, in Robert Thacker's estimation, embrace the role of imaginative inhabitant.[16]

Between itinerancy and deep anchoring, movement and dwelling, this complex literary tradition unfolds. Neil Campbell has suggested that western American literature should be read "more as fluid graffiti" than as a freeze frame of myths.[17] Despite a central focus on settlement, he argues, movement, travel, and resistance to place provide counternarratives. Roots and routes interplay, tangle, and contest.[18] Diane Quantic notes that "Great Plains writers share a conviction that one must first come to terms with this vast stretch of space that leaves no place to hide from the physical emptiness or psychological horrors that trick one with mirages of water or ghosts from the past."[19] Struggle to comprehend, embrace, or love this challenging landscape connects the writings of the earliest European explorers with those of modern authors. To stay or go, endure or reject, adapt to or destroy: These are among the salient themes of Great Plains literature. "The coming of the frontier brought a terrific unsettling," the historian Elliott West explains.[20] Writers from this region of North America, Native and non-Native alike, have reckoned with this "contested" history ever since.[21]

Settlement and Its Aftermath

How one conceives of the plains may or may not bear any relation to the physical experience of living on the plains. "Part of the perceived environment," West argues, "does not exist in fact."[22] The most memorable of settlement and "postpioneering" literature creatively struggles with competing perceptions of the Great Plains as biome and lived place.[23] For many authors and their characters – Willa Cather and Jim Burden, for instance – departing the Great Plains becomes an act of survival.[24] Within plains literature runs a gamut of character types: visitors, tourists, failed settlers, committed dwellers, the dispossessed, and escapees. The tragic always lurks under the surface. In novels such as Willa Cather's *O Pioneers!* (1913) and *My Ántonia* (1918), Dorothy Scarborough's *The Wind* (1925), and O. E. Rølvaag's *Giants in the Earth* (1927); or life writings such as Mari Sandoz's *Old Jules* (1935) and Wallace Stegner's *Wolf Willow* (1962) – texts by authors who experienced homesteading firsthand – the land proves a formidable adversary, and even the strongest willed personalities like Rølvaag's Per Hansa face defeat and death.

Willa Cather has left an enduring, unparalleled body of work, with the plains landscape, in Thacker's assessment, "her paramount subject."[25] Her plains novels capture the transition from homesteading to "the definitive experiences and ideological movements of twentieth-century life – migration and immigration, nostalgia, Progressivism, the emergence of a fully fledged culture of consumption."[26] In weighing the march of this history, Cather balances a decided ambivalence. *O Pioneers!* interweaves competing narratives of pioneer successes and failures. The novel's part one, "The Wild," gives way to part two, "The Neighboring Fields" as Cather shifts sixteen years in quick succession. Homesteading parents succumb to challenges that orphaned children surmount.

In Alexandra Bergson's triumph over the dry land farming of the Divide, Cather traces the ascendant spirit of much pioneer literature. Yet Alexandra's brothers are unimaginative conformists, and their type in much of Cather's plains fiction people the growing towns, rein in and homogenize the diverse energies and cosmopolitan perspectives of the first settlers. Others, like Alexandra's younger brother, Emil, and best friend, Carl Lindstrum, cannot find sufficiency in the landscape and become restless and untethered. In resistance to the massive sod busting transforming the Divide stands Old Ivar, a man more attuned to the animal and natural worlds than he is to his own kind. "He preferred the cleanness and tidiness of the wild sod," Cather explains, and no guns are permitted on his land.[27] Old Ivar's biophilia presages plains environmental writing later in the twentieth century.[28]

Across Cather's plains oeuvre, a fateful causality exists between settlement and destruction as individuals contend with the landscape and their own communities. The heroine of Cather's greatest plains narrative, *My Ántonia*, Ántonia Shimerda, finds equanimity as a middle-aged farm wife and mother outside the fictional town of Black Hawk. She embraces this life in spite of childhood trauma. Her father had been unable to adapt to the challenges of homesteading, and in the family's first winter in Nebraska, he had committed suicide. In contrast, her peers Jim Burden, Lena Lingard, and Tiny Soderball all leave Nebraska and their homesteading past behind to succeed in bigger cities. Even with Jim Burden's return to Black Hawk in middle age, the reader discerns an emotional divide. While Jim embraces the adaptive energy of Ántonia's family out in the countryside, he detests the changes he perceives in town. "My day in Black Hawk was disappointing," he relates.[29] The rural landscape anchors his memories, but even Ántonia's world is ultimately ephemeral.

Cather's next plains novels present a wholly different take on the aftermath of settlement. The tragic fate of Claude Wheeler in Cather's Pulitzer Prize–winning novel *One of Ours* (1923) stands in opposition to Ántonia's fecundity and resiliency. A cog in his father's industrial farming operation, Claude longs to escape the narrow life his parents have mapped for him. Trapped in a loveless, sterile marriage and confined to extracting from the land, Claude throws himself into war fever to end a meaningless existence. He becomes a sacrifice on the killing fields of France. In the same year, Captain Forrester in *A Lost Lady* (1923) has participated in an epic venture across the plains to complete the transcontinental railroad, but his wife, Marian, suffers a psychic immolation in the home he has built in Sweet Water. This novel begins with a disturbing and sadistic maiming, Ivy Peters's cruel blinding of a woodpecker, a heinous action that suggests the underlying violence attendant on domestication, whether taming the land or America's manhood. The juxtaposition of Captain Forrester and Ivy Peters – two of Marian's several lovers in this novel – destabilizes the presentation of settlement history that Cather offers her readers.

Cather's shadow looms large across a century of Great Plains writing. Her complex narratives affirm, yet complicate the history of settlement on the plains. By the time she published *Obscure Destinies* (1932), among the most elegant suites of short fiction in American letters, Cather had clarified her response to the passing of an era and the emergence of modernity, with its leveling effects, aggressive materialism, and political divisions.

In the 1930s, the depression and Dust Bowl descended like twin biblical plagues, one economic and one environmental, upon the plains. From the turmoil of poverty and dust emerged two great studies of working-class endurance and social injustice: John Steinbeck's *The Grapes of Wrath* (1937) and Tillie Olsen's *Yonnondio: From the Thirties* (1974).[30] Both novels follow displaced families through episodes of cruelty, itinerancy, and surprising grace among compatriots. Additionally, Steinbeck and Olsen weave in folk, legend, and ballad materials to elevate their struggling protagonists. The plains environment makes the longed-for home, the desire for roots, elusive and haunting. Impersonal human institutions – banks, schools, law enforcement, businesses – behave in inhumane ways in these two works, adding crushing pressures to poor people struggling to survive.

Rose Wilder Lane, only child of Laura Ingalls Wilder, spun her parents' experience homesteading in the Dakotas into the novel *Free Land* (1938). The Beaton family, like Steinbeck's Joads and Olsen's Holbrooks, labor away in hope and prayer while wealthy landowners, "the big bonanza farmers, rich men able to buy thousands of acres from the government ... were doing more."[31] Writers younger than Cather, experiencing unprecedented collapse and environmental disaster, dissect the social and political landscapes that deny their protagonists dignity and purpose. At the same time, Steinbeck, Olsen, and Lane honor the character of farmers and working people, magnifying their role in America's story, and memorialize the struggle and renewal of plains people. Jeremiah Boles, a farmer in *Free Land*, could be speaking for all of them when he declares, "a man's got to have his belief to hold onto. We got to have something to sustain us, something to steer by."[32]

American popular culture during the first half of the twentieth century contributed its own version of the plains. Starting with Theodore Roosevelt's personal and historical narratives of ranching life and *The Winning of the West* (1894) and Owen Wister's enduring novel *The Virginian: A Horseman of the Plains* (1902); through Laura Ingalls Wilder's Little House series (1932–43); and Broadway hits like Rodgers and Hammerstein's Pulitzer Prize–winning musical *Oklahoma!* (1943), the Great Plains take on mythic resonance, a central site in the building of America. Such popular works project epic or sagalike qualities onto settlement stories, and forces that menace the integrity of family or community – Trampas in *The Virginian*, Native people in Wilder, Jud Fry in *Oklahoma!* – are marginalized or defeated. As the landscape of much western American literature, the Great Plains are the quintessential mythic frontier, the staging ground of Manifest Destiny and American exceptionalism. As later twentieth-century wars in Korea and Vietnam battered American confidence, popular writers across genres joined serious writers such as Frederick Manfred, Lois Phillips Hudson, Larry McMurtry, and Wright Morris in reanalyzing received stories and myths. McMurtry's beautiful and spare novel *The Last Picture Show* (1966) depicts the imminent collapse of a fictional town, Thalia, Texas. What remains of the mythic West in Thalia, if it ever existed, is shabby, emasculated, and on its last legs. The young men and women stuck in this town long for escape and something romantic, yet the little that could yield heroics or transformation, football and sex, disappoint. Also typical is Thomas Berger's picaresque novel *Little Big Man* (1969), which deconstructs and eviscerates any mythologizing of the West, any notion of settlement and civilization marching toward a progressive taming of plains spaces.

Plains Native writers, most prominently Louise Erdrich (Turtle Mountain Ojibwe), through an intertwined series of novels starting with *Love Medicine* (1984), have critiqued settlement and colonization through the perspective of North America's First People. Erdrich's novel *Tracks* (1988) asserts the tradition of social justice fiction from the plains and examines across interconnected families and stories the devastating effects of dispossession, racism, and warfare on the plains. Concentrated on the years 1912 to 1924, *Tracks* moves back and forth in time as the Nanapush, Morrissey, Lamartine, Kashpaw, Puyat, and Pillager families negotiate a twentieth-century world of reservations, federal control, boarding schools, and modern industrial war. Pestilence, suicide, World War I, and negation of Native identity weaken the ancient bonds of clan and tribe. To choose life as farmers or business owners, the life of settlers and the drumbeat of modernism, competes with old ways of existence: trapping, hunting, fishing, ricing, and gathering. Erdrich's characters complete a spectrum of choices: protecting the old ways, on one end; repudiating Native identity altogether, on the other end; or seeking a middle ground, as Nanapush does, between Native and non-Native practices. The world of the Anishinaabe has become destabilized by settler colonialism, and finding a track or tracks forward confounds characters in this book and others in Erdrich's ongoing fictional saga. Her most recent work has included the experience of immigrants settling the Near West of Minnesota and North Dakota. At this point in the twenty-first century, Erdrich became arguably the greatest novelist from the plains since Willa Cather.

In such questioning, ambivalence, and advocacy, one discerns again Cather's complicated influence across generations of writers from the plains. When she died in 1947, a new playwright was arising from Independence, Kansas: William Inge. Three of his greatest plays, *Picnic* (1953), *Bus Stop* (1954), and *The Dark at the Top of the Stairs* (1958), critique western American myths, as small towns and cities on the plains join the march of modernism. Hal Carter's arrival in *Picnic* immediately unsettles what Inge describes as "a typical small Midwestern town, including a grain elevator, a railway station, a great silo and a church steeple, all blessed from above by a high sky of innocent blue."[33] Wearing a T-shirt, jeans, and cowboy boots, Hal projects a restless, sexual energy that rattles the complacent surface of small town conformity. This diminished world of socials, gossip, and unexceptional goodness cages a man like Hal. He cannot fit in. Inge's treatment of Hal's disruptive, hypersexualized masculinity reveals the skewed gender dimensions of western American myth and popular culture. The prescribed roles that women and men are forced to play in the settled landscape strip them of agency and inhibit the life energy of individuals and communities. In *Bus Stop*, the ticky-tacky world of Cherie, a nightclub singer, and Bo Decker, a rodeo cowboy, stands in stark contrast to the little Kansas town in which they are snowbound. Taking refuge in a diner with their fellow bus mates, these two struggle in a complex, disturbing sexual dance. Bo approaches Cherie as if she were a heifer he must rope and return to his Montana ranch. Against the masculine backdrop of the expansive plains and its aggregate of cowboys, cavalry, and gunmen, Cherie's plaintive call for protection and autonomy falls muffled and unheard. Men and women in Inge's plays cannot find peace, and the mythos of settlement and agricultural domestication unravels in the wake of the modern, industrialized landscape.

Rubin Flood's situation in *The Dark at the Top of the Stairs* is particularly emblematic. All the men around him are running to emerging opportunities and industries: automobiles and the oil and gas boom of the 1920s in the Kansas-Oklahoma borderlands. Rubin, on the other hand, remains tied to a dying operation, selling harness. His son and daughter, Sonny and Reenie, struggle against the rigid social norms of their town, and his wife, Cora, silently suffers the humiliations of her husband's infidelities and fecklessness. Inge picks up on the social discord of Cather's *A Lost Lady* and adds layers of Freudian complexity and a queering gaze, what scholar Jeff Johnson calls "gendermandering."[34] The punctured, overworked landscape of boom and bust – the essence of an extractive economy – reveals something of the harassed, exhausted, and sexually, emotionally confused people in Inge's plays. At play's end, Cora and Rubin ascend the stairs of their home into the dark of their bedroom. Whether they find redemption or brief respite is up in the air. Inge's indictment of modern small town culture on the plains, however, is clear and trenchant.

While Inge may not enjoy the cachet of his peers Tennessee Williams and Arthur Miller, his was an important voice in the American theater scene of the 1950s. Horton Foote, whose career trajectory took off while Inge's declined in the 1960s, is popularly recognized for his great screenplays for such memorable films as *To Kill a Mockingbird* (1962), *Tender Mercies* (1983), and *The Trip to Bountiful* (1985). His theatrical masterpiece, *The Orphans' Home Cycle* (2009–10), recreates family history in Wharton, Texas.[35] Horace Robedaux, Foote's central protagonist, first appears in the play *Roots in a Parched Ground* as a child and matures to marriage and parenthood in the later plays *Courtship*, *Valentine's Day*, and *The Death of Papa*; in following Horace's difficult childhood and young adulthood, Foote traces the years 1902–28.[36] *The Orphans' Home Cycle* covers considerable familial ground while also uncovering the tragic aftermath of slavery, the troubled sexual politics of early twentieth-century American domestic life, and the challenges to a small town's livelihood from the growth of a large American city, Houston. Laurin Porter asserts that "identity for Foote lies in family, community, and the legacy of the past."[37] Like Inge in *The Dark at the Top of the Stairs*, Foote revisits the transitional history to modernism that so riveted Willa Cather. Indeed, Foote's attentiveness to family and communal relationships, his subtle detection of emotional tectonics, mirrors Cather's keen ability to gauge the smallest emotional temblor in her intergenerational short story "Old Mrs. Harris" in *Obscure Destinies*. Foote's characters lead obscure lives, as most of us do, but their stories reveal deep love, the binding ties of place, and powerful acts of sacrifice and forgiveness. While acknowledging the difficulties of sustaining kinship to others and to land, Foote celebrates human persistence in the face of grinding change. *The Orphans' Home Cycle*, then, is exactly the kind of "postpioneering prairie" literature that Robert Thacker defines in *The Great Prairie Fact and Literary Imagination*. "Like Cather herself," he posits, "many native-born writers have fled the prairies only to return ... to their 'home pasture.'"[38]

Nature

The Great Plains biome, since World War II, has become a central focus in plains nature and environmental literature. Writers increasingly appreciate that, if knowledge of place is not extended, culture and community exist tenuously on the plains. The Kiowa writer N. Scott Momaday speaks to this truth when he advocates a kind of dissolving or yielding to "a particular landscape ... to look at it from as many different angles as [one] can, to wonder about it, to dwell upon it."[39] As the historian Dan Flores characterizes it, "through analyzing deep time in a single place" communities learn resiliency.[40] A deep time view leads to this conclusion: "Disturbance is the natural state, and adjustment to it is ongoing and fundamental."[41] Nonfiction writers from the Great Plains, many of them deep dwellers and imaginative inhabitants, have contributed to a vital, growing body of literature that aims to widen our understanding of the natural history of place. This expanding oeuvre connects to biological, anthropological, and geological science as well as to Indigenous knowledge of Great Plains spaces gained through generations of cartographic, celestial, and storytelling practices.

A renaissance of plains nonfiction writing began in the final decade of the twentieth century. Ian Frazier published a best-selling collection of essays entitled, simply, *Great Plains* (1989), and the rush was on. In quick succession, William Least Heat-Moon's *PrairyErth: (a deep map)* (1991), Anne Matthews's *Where the Buffalo Roam: The Storm over the Revolutionary Plan to Restore America's Great Plains* (1992), Kathleen Norris's *Dakota: A Spiritual Geography* (1993), John Janovy Jr.'s *Dunwoody Pond: Reflections on the High Plains Wetlands and the Cultivation of Naturalists* (1994), Richard Manning's *Grassland: The History, Biology, Politics, and Promise of the American Prairie* (1995), Jonathan Raban's *Bad Land* (1996), and Dan O'Brien's *Buffalo for the Broken Heart: Restoring Life to a Black Hills Ranch* (2001) appeared. The rancher, poet, and nonfiction essay writer Linda Hasselstrom contributed a series of significant essays on the High Plains starting in 1987 with *Going over East*, and the Kansas-born writer Julene Bair published *One Degree West* (2001) and *The Ogallala Road: A Memoir of Love and Reckoning* (2014). In informative, beautifully limned essays, Matt White added an important volume on the southern plains, *Prairie Time: A Blackland Portrait* (2006). Such a plethora of publications suggests an upwelling of interest in the interior of North America and a desire to revisit the environmental impact of the Homestead Acts of 1862 through 1916.[42]

The great achievement of this era of plains nonfiction writing remains William Least Heat-Moon's *PrairyErth*, a 622-page deep map of Chase County, Kansas. Lawrence Buell regards this text as a cartographical journey that "unmoors" the readers from received history. "Chase County, Kansas," he puts forth, "was carved out during the nineteenth century according to Jefferson's grid. *PrairyErth* follows the same grid in seeking to invent a way of thinking about county landscape, culture, and history that will express both the durability and the arbitrariness of this legacy."[43]

Heat-Moon attacks and tests Jefferson's construct head on in his opening pages. "Since the National Survey of 1785," he explains, "seventy percent of America lies under such a grid, a system of coordinates that has allowed wildness to be subdued."[44] Breaking the landscape down, as the historian Donald Worster describes, started with townships six square miles: "A single township contained, after completion of a map, thirty-six uniform sections of 640 acres each; the sections could be further broken down into half-sections, quarter-sections, or quarter-of-a-quarter sections."[45] Heat-Moon sections his narrative into quadrangles in an attempt to contain the many stories of place. Yet from *PrairyErth*'s first pages, this organization fails to define Chase County. Each quadrangle elicits hidden stories, traces of deeper time, "invisible landscapes" that defy mapping.[46] In Saffordville, Kansas, he discovers a ghost highway, "the last exposed piece of the original concrete, however broken, of what was once U.S. 50 South in or touching Chase."[47] Ghost trails, building foundations, railroad grades, and other palimpsests haunt Heat-Moon's pages, complicating any straightforward telling of this county in the Flint Hills. As Heat-Moon discerns, Chase County contains vestiges of an ancient grasslands landscape, too, a biome that still holds power despite the grid's perceived omnipresence. The fact that settlement remains are often as difficult to find as centuries-old Indigenous artifacts bespeaks the forces of erasure constantly at work in the plains natural world. Modern people struggle to maintain toeholds in Chase County. In the 1980s, when Heat-Moon was visiting and revisiting the county, Kansas faced a tough economy and a farm crisis, and the small towns suffered and shrank as a result. Things blow away in Chase County, and at one point Heat-Moon humorously imagines, "maybe *I'm* the wraith here, a temporary ghost."[48]

Starting each section of his narrative map, Heat-Moon offers up a "commonplace book." Excerpts from plains poets, early visitors, environmentalists, journalists, and scientists, among others, help orient Heat-Moon's text. These many voices add to the sense that time's passage is both linear and cyclical, that any landscape iterates many histories. Walking the many sections of Chase County, Heat-Moon pushes the envelope of storytelling. When he encounters gaps, unconformities, or slippages in the storied land, he invites readers to engage in the construction of place, in "participatory cartography."[49] Heat-Moon's inventive, challenging narrative process has inspired a generation of deep map writing from the Great Plains, an environmental genre that has proved enduring and dynamic.[50]

Little remains of the vast, incredibly varied grasslands of the Great Plains. Protecting the fragments of tall and short grass prairies, preserving the watershed that feeds life, and questioning extractive industries that have generated boom or bust cycles motivate much contemporary plains nature writing. These current authors continue the critique begun a century ago in Willa Cather's plains fiction. In the twenty-first century, Old Ivar from *O Pioneers!* seems prescient. As territories of the American West opened up for settlement, the clean, wild sod that Old Ivar loved so deeply succumbed quickly to the steel plow. The ancient grasslands' passing has haunted Great Plains writing ever since. To advocate the restoration of that magnificent biome energizes many plains writers seeking environmental as well as social justice. The poet and essayist Kathleen Norris reminds us that spiritual restitution also matters. Instilling connection to and love of place – what the geographer Yi-Fu Tuan has famously called topophilia – was never a motivation in designing the Jeffersonian grid.[51] In *Dakota: A Spiritual Geography*, Norris strives to reinhabit not just her grandmother's home set in the town of Norris's childhood memories; she also seeks sacral grounding in the landscape of western South Dakota. Books like hers speak to a more practiced, adaptive, and respectful settlement, one that attends to the original inhabitants' knowledge and experience of place. As a result, nonfiction writing from the plains is increasingly bioregional in its focus and advocacy, one of the turns that postpioneering narrative has taken. An urgent recognition now spurs on this body of work: As the land goes, so go the communities. "The Great Plains grasslands are old," Candace Savage writes, "older than memory. For visitants like us, this ancient land offers a grounding in continuance."[52] But only, today's Great Plains writers warn, if we listen.

Writers from the Great Plains have contributed significantly to American letters. In the century since Willa Cather's first great plains novel, *O Pioneers!*, this region has produced such luminaries as Katherine Anne Porter, Evan S. Connell, James Welch, Lois Hudson, Larry Woiwode, Jane Smiley, and Ron Hansen. Three of the nation's most influential children's writers, Laura Ingalls Wilder, L. Frank Baum, and S. E. Hinton, received considerable inspiration from their experience living on the plains. Important African American writers, including Oscar Micheaux, Malcolm X, Gwendolyn Brooks, and Langston Hughes, spent formative years on the plains. Ted Kooser, a recent United States poet laureate, joins a distinguished group of poets who were born or spent time on the plains: John Neihardt, Weldon Kees, John Barryman, William Stafford, Carter Revard, and Joy Harjo, among others. Prominent nonfiction writers from Walter Prescott Webb and Woody Guthrie to Loren Eiseley and Linda Hasselstrom claim allegiance to this vast, environmentally significant ecosystem. Many plains writers produce luminous work across disciplines: N. Scott Momaday, Louise Erdrich, and William Kloefkorn among the very best. Literary production has not slowed on the Great Plains, and in the late twentieth and early twenty-first centuries textual creativity extends to cinematic expressions such as Terrence Malick's *Badlands* (1973), *Days of Heaven* (1978), and *The Tree of Life* (2011) or Alexander Payne's noteworthy films *Election* (1999), *About Schmidt* (2002), and *Nebraska* (2013). This grand territory of the interior of North America has given root to a unique, thriving literary culture, one that has coalesced around "the broad concepts of land, society, myth, and reality." Crossing genres, extending into American popular culture, delving deep into time, and reaching across diverse cultures, Great Plains authors have been and remain artistically inventive and influential contributors to western American literature.[33]

Notes

1 Wright Morris, *Plains Song: For Female Voices* (1980; Lincoln: University of Nebraska Press, 2000), 196.
2 Ibid., 197.
3 Ibid., 199–200.
4 Ibid., 200.
5 Ibid.
6 John T. Price, *Not Just Any Land: A Personal and Literary Journey into the American Grasslands* (Lincoln: University of Nebraska Press, 2004), 9.
7 See Margaret D. Jacobs, *White Mother to a Dark Race: Settler Colonialism, Maternalism, and the Removal of Indigenous Children in the American West and Australia, 1880–1940* (Lincoln: University of Nebraska Press, 2009), for a compelling analysis of settler colonialism.
8 The geographer David J. Wishart provides an overview and maps of "The Great Plains Region," in *The Encyclopedia of the Great Plains*, ed. David J. Wishart (Lincoln: University of Nebraska Press, 2004), xiii–xviii.
9 Candace Savage, *Prairie: A Natural History* (Vancouver: Greystone Books, 2011), 2. Savage's perspective is shared by two other essential scholars of the Great Plains literary tradition: Robert Thacker, *The Great Prairie Fact and Literary Imagination* (Albuquerque: University of New Mexico Press, 1989) and Diane Dufva Quantic, *The Nature of the Place: A Study of Great Plains Fiction* (Lincoln: University of Nebraska Press, 1995).
10 Savage, *Prairie*, 2.
11 Linda Hogan, "The Feathers," in *Dwellings: A Spiritual History of the Living World* (New York: Simon & Schuster, 1995), 20.

12 Hogan, "Feathers," 19.

13 An excellent example of cultural dissonance and the difficulty of reading the Great Plains landscape is analyzed in Daryl W. Palmer, "Coronado
   and Aesop: Fable and Violence on the Sixteenth-Century Plains," *Great
   Plains Quarterly* 29, no. 2 (2009): 129–40. Palmer asserts, "Coronado and
   his European comrades had been inspired by a mix of legend, literature,
   and rumor" (130). Exploring a vast, unknown landscape, these men sought
   explanation in such "scripted" stories. As Palmer states, "personal and professional biases emerge as the writers attempt to explain New World experiences
   through Old World frames of reference" (130).

14 William Least Heat-Moon, *PrairyErth: (a deep map)* (Boston: Houghton
   Mifflin, 1991), 55–6.

15 Heat-Moon, *PrairyErth*, 56.

16 See part 3 of Thacker's *The Great Plains Fact and Literary Imagination*. He
   states that "inhabiting the prairie was quite a different matter altogether from
   settling it" (187). The landscape's capacity to inspire imagination, adaptation,
   and persistence has proved essential in keeping communities and the literary
   tradition alive. As Thacker concludes, "[this] process of imaginative adaptation to the prairie is ongoing, probably never ending; it can be seen wherever
   one looks in prairie writing" (224).

17 Neil Campbell, *The Rhizomatic West: Representing the American West in a
   Transnational, Global, Media Age* (Lincoln: University of Nebraska Press,
   2008), 5.

18 Campbell's use of metaphor is particularly rich. His study, as he declares, "is
   transmotional 'route work' following connections, trails, traces, pathways, and
   echoes, peeling back layers of a complex, unending palimpsest" (*Rhizomatic
   West*, 37). On the Great Plains, "route work" aligns with "root work," and the
   rhizome becomes a biome-specific concept.

19 Quantic, Nature of the Place, 14.

20 Elliott West, *The Contested Plains: Indians, Goldseekers, and the Rush to
   Colorado* (Lawrence: University Press of Kansas, 1998), xxiii.

21 This is Elliot West's conceptualization in his study *The Contested Plains: Indians,
   Goldseekers, and the Rush to Colorado*. "The contest between Indians and whites,"
   he concludes in his epilogue, "is usually described as a power struggle. It was,
   but the struggle had many more shadings than it seemed" (331). In sum, West
   tells us, "two cultures acted out two compelling visions in a land that could only
   support one. The inspired struggle – of both peoples to enliven their dreams, of
   each to deny the other – was one of the great American stories" (336).

22 Ibid., xix.

23 Thacker, *Great Plains Fact*, 187. Thacker analyzes "prairie born," "postpioneering," and "inhabitant" writers in his final chapter, "A Complex of
   Possibilities."

24 I refer to Cather's great novel, *My Ántonia* (1918).

25 Thacker, *Great Plains Fact*, 146.

26 Richard H. Millington, "Willa Cather's American Modernism," in *The Cambridge Companion to Willa Cather*, ed. Marilee Lindemann (Cambridge: Cambridge University Press, 2005), 52.

27 Willa Cather, *O Pioneers!* (1913, New York: W. W. Norton, 2008), 23.

28 Biophilia is Edward O. Wilson's concept; see *Biophilia: The Human Bond with Other Species* (Cambridge, MA: Harvard University Press, 1984).

29 Willa Cather, *My Ántonia*, ed. Joseph R. Urgo (Toronto: Broadview Press, 2003), 242.

30 Part of Olsen's part one appeared in *Partisan Review* in the spring of 1934. See Linda Ray Pratt's introduction to *Yonnondio: From the Thirties* (Lincoln: University of Nebraska Press, 2004).

31 Rose Wilder Lane, *Free Land* (Lincoln: University of Nebraska Press, 1989), 210.

32 Ibid., 258.

33 William Inge, *Picnic*, in *Four Plays* (New York: Grove Press, 1979), 75.

34 Jeff Johnson, *William Inge and the Subversion of Gender* (Jefferson, NC: McFarland, 2005), 64.

35 Maps of the Great Plains vary, as the geographer David J. Wishart notes in his introductory comments to *The Encyclopedia of the Great Plains* (xiii–xviii). While the Center for Great Plains Studies in Lincoln, Nebraska, does not include Wharton, Texas, on its map of the southern Great Plains, the U.S. Bureau of Reclamation and other agencies do.

36 The plays in the cycle are *Roots in a Parched Ground* (1902–1903); *Convicts* (1904); *Lily Dale* (1910); *The Widow Clare* (1912); *Courtship* (1915); *Valentine's Day* (1917); *1918* (1987); *Cousins* (1925); and *The Death of Papa* (1928). In Foote's plays, the town of Wharton, Texas, is the fictional version of Harrison, Texas.

37 Laurin Porter, *Orphans' Home: The Voice and Vision of Horton Foote* (Baton Rouge: Louisiana State University Press, 2003), 4.

38 Thacker, *Great Plains Fact*, 190.

39 N. Scott Momaday, *The Way to Rainy Mountain*, illustrations by Al Momaday (Albuquerque: University of New Mexico Press, 1969), 83.

40 Dan Flores, *The Natural West: Environmental History in the Great Plains and Rocky Mountains* (Norman: University of Oklahoma Press, 2001), 101.

41 Ibid.

42 The original Homestead Act of 1862 was amended by the Southern Homestead Act of 1866, the Timber Culture Act of 1873, the Kincaid Amendment of 1904, the Enlarged Homestead Act of 1909, and the Stock-Raising Homestead Act of 1916.

43 Lawrence Buell, *The Environmental Imagination: Thoreau, Nature Writing, and the Formation of American Culture* (Cambridge, MA: Belknap Press of Harvard University Press, 1995), 273.

44 Heat-Moon, *PrairyErth*, 15.

45 Donald Worster, *A River Running West: The Life of John Wesley Powell* (Oxford: Oxford University Press, 2001), 40–1.

46 See Kent Ryden, *Mapping the Invisible Landscape: Folklore, Writing, and the Sense of Place* (Iowa City: University of Iowa Press, 1993).

47 Heat-Moon, *PrairyErth*, 46.

48 Ibid., 310.

49 O. Alan Weltzien, "A Topographical Map of Words: Parables of Cartography in William Least Heat-Moon's *PrairyErth*," *Great Plains Quarterly* 19, no. 2 (1999): 120.

50 See Susan Naramore Maher, *Deep Map Country: Literary Cartography of the Great Plains* (Lincoln: University of Nebraska Press, 2014).

51 Yi-Fu Tuan, *Topophilia: A Study of Environmental Perception, Attitudes, and Values* (New York: Columbia University Press, 1974). Tuan provides this definition of topophilia, a word he made famous in this study: "*Topophilia* is the affective bond between people and place or setting" (4).

52 Savage, *Prairie*, x.

53 Quantic, *Nature of the Place*, xx.

CHAPTER 9

Southwest Literary Borderlands

Audrey Goodman

The literary history of the region designated by the Spaniards as the northern borderlands, by residents of Mexico as *la frontera*, by the Mexican Texan folklorist and novelist Américo Paredes as Greater Mexico, and by residents of the United States as the Southwest might be said to begin with the Indigenous stories that recount the origins of the land and its people. One such story, told by the Diné poet Luci Tapahonso, describes the creation of her homeland by the Holy People: "When they created this world, Blanca Peak, the sacred mountain in the east, was decorated with a rainbow beam and adorned with white shell and morning light." Mount Hesperus, in the north, "was fastened to the earth with a rainbow beam and adorned with black jet to represent peace and harmony." She explains that cyclical restoration occurs each night when "Mount Hesperus urges us to rest. She is our renewal, our rejuvenation. She exists because of the rainbow beam. We exist because of the rainbow beam."[1] Tapahonso's story maps the sacred places and borders of Diné Tah (Navajo Country) as it transmits knowledge of how to live properly and cultivate the awareness of beauty in this land. It confirms a central feature of all stories of this region: attention to what the Laguna writer Paula Gunn Allen calls the "ongoing relationship, or conversation, among the human, the plant and animal, the land, and supernaturals, each perceived as members of the same geospiritual community."[2] It also suggests how broad the notion of "story" can be. As the Laguna novelist Leslie Silko notes in her memoir *The Turquoise Ledge,* for her people a story can refer to "historical accounts, village gossip, sacred migration stories, hummah-ha stories that included Coyote and the other animals and supernatural beings, deer hunting stories, even car wreck stories."[3] Linking deep spiritual and natural histories with contemporary experience, such varieties of storytelling can be found throughout oral and written accounts of the southwestern borderlands.

Other literary histories of the borderlands begin with the violent establishment of the U.S.-Mexico border in 1848 and trace the cultural and political effects of the land's U.S. conquest. These histories focus on the Texas-Mexico border, where Mexican citizens suddenly found themselves outsiders, *los mexicanos de afuera*, and writers later struggled to define the identities of Mexicans nominally integrated into the United States but dominated economically, socially, and culturally by Anglo-Americans. While the seminal historical analysis of this border region is David Montejano's *Anglos and Mexicans in the Making of Texas, 1836–1986*, the foundational fiction that imagines the negotiation and consolidation of the region's conflicted groups is *Caballero* by Jovita González and Eve Raleigh, a romance novel set during the Mexican-American War, written in English in the 1930s and 1940s, and published in 1996, edited by José Limón and María Cotera. The temporal gaps between the setting, the creation, and the publication of this novel reveal a great deal about the position of Mexican Americans in this region; as Limón argues, the resolution that *Caballero* imagined would not have been possible earlier because the "national consolidation" of Mexicans in Texas "kept being postponed."[4] Along with the folklore and fiction also written in English in this period by Paredes, Gonzáles's work demonstrates a complex regionalist engagement with the class, cultural, and racial conflicts particular to Mexican American South Texas.

For Chicano and Chicana artists and critics in the late twentieth century, the legacy of the U.S.-Mexico border has inspired wider-ranging theoretical explorations of hybrid identities, new languages, and global affiliations, providing a symbolic site for articulating the anticolonial epistemology Walter Mignolo calls "border thinking." Gloria Anzaldúa's *Borderlands/La Frontera* (1987) boldly invented the concept and language of "the new *mestiza*," creating a discursive space for Indigenous and Latina women inhabiting an occupied homeland. Her explorations of ways to think outside the history of European and Anglo domination exemplify the ways that writers in this region have imagined compelling alternatives to racism and coloniality.[5] However, the literary history of this land, its many borders, and its people may be too layered and complex to fit a single paradigm, even one that does the important work of interrogating relations between local articulations and global politics. Even within a single cultural tradition or historically bounded period, Southwest borderlands literature alternately reveals, resists, and reimagines the acts of violence, national rivalries, dislocations, and ecological damage that accompanied and facilitated the region's Spanish and Anglo conquests. As Limón cautions, "a hurried globalizing reading of this complex regional experience does not reveal the full outcomes of a regionalist engagement with the global."[6]

This essay offers several approaches to reading the late nineteenth- and twentieth-century literatures of the Southwest borderlands written in English and published in the United States. First I introduce two contemporary literary modes for telling stories of the region's Indigenous people and their environment, Native American poetry and ethnobotany, focusing on the work of two Sonoran borderlands writers, the Tohono O'odham poet Ofelia Zepeda and the Lebanese American naturalist Gary Paul Nabhan. Zepeda engages strategies of bilingualism and hyperlocalism to define individual and tribal identities, while Nabhan models practices of ecological and cultural restoration. Then I turn to the borderlands' colonial and imperial origins, examining accounts of its histories of conquest, the significance of the Treaty of Guadalupe Hidalgo, and the romantic stories of encounter with the land and its ancient past as told by Anglo writers at the beginning of the twentieth century. The essay's last sections examine how Mexican American and Chicano/a writers redefined the borderlands of South Texas, focusing on the examples set by Paredes beginning in the 1940s and Anzaldúa in the 1980s, border intellectuals who crossed many disciplinary, generic, and linguistic lines. Finally, I indicate some of the ways that this transnational poetics has led recent writers to stage the return of dead voices, spirits, and bodies in magical borderlands novels, an evolving mode that provides distinct literary solutions to the challenge of locating oneself in territory whose boundaries continue to be drawn, contested, and revised.

Indigenous Borderlands: The Poetics and Politics of Restoration

In "Redefining Home," Ofelia Zepeda declares home to be "both the spaces inside and outside the building," since the word "*Ki:* in O'odham means both 'house' and 'home.'" This poem from *Where Clouds Are Formed* (2008) enumerates the physical elements that sustain the speaker's connections with her ancestors, her tribal history, and her land: the aromas of "dry dust" and "green brush on the roof, in the walls," the smooth texture of the mud walls, and "the rough ribs from cactus and ocotillo, / the branches of cottonwood and posts from cedar and pine." For Zepeda, "Home is a place that has the right feel, / the right smell, / the right sense of coolness when you touch the walls."[7] Such an assertion of cultural survival and alignment with the natural environment and traditional ways of life represents a hard-won declaration of O'odham culture and language in territory that had been inhabited for at least hundreds of years before being claimed, divided, and renamed by cycles of Spanish, Mexican, and Anglo conquest. The stories Zepeda tells about her local places – whether a nearby irrigation ditch, her own kitchen, or the sacred Baboquivari Peak – create her home, linking her with what David Moore characterizes as "the broader cultures of the land on which frontiers have been imagined and overlaid, so often with tragic consequences" while resisting the cultural destruction that historically accompanied the border's divisions.[8] Language also promotes survival for Zepeda. The author of the original written O'odham grammar and founder of the American Indian Language Development Institute, Zepeda writes in both her first language and English, as well as in the "language of the land." Each poem chooses the language appropriate to the occasion or the words necessary to activate the power of memory: In "Proclamation," for instance, it is the original name for Tucson, "Cuk Son," that offers "the true story of this place / recalls people walking / deserts all their lives and / continuing today, if only / in their dreams."[9] By integrating the desert's Indigenous languages into a bilingual poetics, Zepeda regrounds southwestern literature through located Indigenous knowledge.

Another strong model for writing the Sonoran borderlands is the collaborative book *Desert Legends* by the ethnobotanist Gary Paul Nabhan and the photographer Mark Klett, which calls for renewed engagement with the desert's many senses of place. Nabhan encourages his readers "to listen, live, and work like natives of our particular homeland, and to pass that work on to the next generation."[10] He notes the ancient natural origins of the region, explaining that desert plants took root more than eighty-five hundred years ago; meanwhile, he discovers the arrowheads, knives shaped to trim mescal leaves, and rock-pile shrines that attest to its ancient cultural life. To integrate the land's natural and cultural environments, Nabhan and Klett read the desert closely and assemble a collection of stories from its Mexican, Anglo, Yaqui, O'odham, and Seri inhabitants. Nabhan further explores how the border itself tends to distort perception. He recounts a vision he had while working in a bean field at the border of the Tohono O'odham reservation: He looked out at the buttes and mesas of the Atascosas and Baboquivaris and saw "mirror images of Sonoran landforms piled up upon one another. They created hourglasses out of pyramidal buttes, and anvils out of flat-topped mesas."[11] Suddenly they dropped out of view, leading Nabhan to realize he "had been seeing most everything on the other side in a wildly distorted way," with each image becoming a mirage by the simple act of looking across a political boundary.[12] Resolving to create a new interpretive map, Nabhan presents in the book occasional, unconventional guides to the desert, organizing his chapters around experiences like transporting cacti, recovering trash, meeting a *curandera,* following a pilgrimage trail, witnessing a thunderstorm, or hunting for agave, all of which play with questions of perspective and versions of natural and cultural history. Through personal memories, collective narratives, and photographic images, the text forges a network of continuities across the border's artificial boundary and thus "restories" the desert borderlands.

Cultural Conquests and Desert Aesthetics in the Anglo Southwest

The Sonoran desert may be viewed as part of a larger bioregion defined by the intersection of arid lands (the Chihuahuan, Sonoran, and Mojave Deserts, as well as the Great Basin) and by two sets of mountains (in the north, by the Sangre de Cristo, San Juan, and Jemez Mountains; in the southwest, by the extension of the Sierra Madre mountains and Mogollon Rim).[13] However, the political and cultural territory of this region has been crisscrossed for centuries, divided by nationality, race, class, and language. From a geopolitical perspective, the inhabitants of what is now northwestern Mexico and the southwestern United States – termed "border people" by the historian Oscar Martínez – have always lived far from the centers of colonial and national power;[14] as a result, they learned strategies of physical and cultural survival, constantly negotiated their identities through experiences of contact and conflict, and developed independence from the dominant cultures of both nations, thus creating a border culture that Anzaldúa would famously characterize as a "third country."[15] The best source for borderlands history is still Edward Spicer's major study of the overlapping Spanish, English, and American conquests of North America, *Cycles of Conquest* (1962), which identifies the common process of invasion, resistance, and redrawing of cultural frontiers that linked cycles of conquest over a long period and analyzes the diversity of cultural responses to successive invasions. Spicer's unparalleled account of coloniality in the borderlands delineates the geopolitical patterns that shaped the locations of its major contact zones, providing regional scholars with an essential foundation for reading the region's literary texts as local responses to broader cultural and historical processes. Patricia Limerick's *The Legacy of Conquest* (1987) extends and expands Spicer's account of the southwestern borderlands to all of the United States, giving extra emphasis to the period leading up to and following the 1848 signing of the Treaty of

Guadalupe Hidalgo. When the treaty transferred roughly half of the land then under Mexican control in Texas, New Mexico, Arizona, Nevada, Utah, Wyoming, Colorado, and California to U.S. ownership, all inhabitants of the newly designated U.S. territory suddenly found themselves citizens of the United States in name, while often facing discrimination by Anglos in fact.[16]

Border control remained a contentious issue for years, as people on both sides fought over rights to pursue Apaches and other raiders, disputed over compensation for economic losses, and left matters of justice in the hands of the Texas Rangers. The complex tribal and national conflicts of this postwar period have generated an extensive body of Anglo literature, including Cormac McCarthy's *Blood Meridian* (1985) and Larry McMurtry's *Lonesome Dove* (1985), novels that reimagine the violence of the period with a mixture of horror and regret. When reciprocal crossing pacts and newly established reservations began to control some of the sources of border trouble, both nations used the territory to satisfy their extravagant economic ambitions and to project utopian desires through new frontier narratives that promised individual and social regeneration. The silver, copper, and gold deposits found in New Mexico, Arizona, Chihuahua, and Sonora led to corporate investment in mines and established the extractive economy that would dominate this and other regions in the modern U.S. West. Newly expanded farms and ranches depended on the labor of Hispanos, Mexicans, and Asian immigrants even as they threatened local economies and social organizations. Between 1880 and 1920 Anglo investors, settlers, and artists took full advantage of these new routes of access. For a diverse group of journalists, anthropologists, novelists, poets, painters, and photographers that included Charles Lummis, Frank Cushing, Timothy O'Sullivan, Ben Wittick, Zane Grey, Mabel Dodge Luhan, D. H. Lawrence, Willa Cather, Marsden Hartley, Ansel Adams, and Georgia O'Keeffe, the desert borderlands seemed to reveal the nation's precontact and colonial histories, provide space for imaginative projection, and offer models of authentic culture. In relation to Europe and the eastern United States, the land was still "waiting to be made into landscape," in the words of Cather's fictional Bishop Latour, the vigorous yet meditative hero at the center of her major southwestern novel, *Death Comes for the Archbishop*, and Anglo artists were eager to create them.[17] The eccentric, indefatigable, and prolific Charles Lummis saw the entire region as unparalleled opportunity, for it lay far beyond the boundaries of the New England and midwestern worlds he and his readers knew well. Lured west with the promise of a job as city editor at the *Los Angeles Times* and a ready audience for his adventures, Lummis capitalized on both. He set out from Ohio on foot and published his weekly reports first in the paper and then as *A Tramp across the Continent* (1892) before producing many more regional sketches and guides for tourists. Inspired by the pioneering scientific studies of the anthropologists Adolph Bandelier and Jesse Fewkes and intoxicated by the environment, Lummis fashioned himself a new kind of regional writer: an outsider who claimed authority on the basis of firsthand observation, but one who also freely took license to edit and romanticize history, as well as to enhance the region's natural and cultural attractions through hyperbolic description. Lummis's Southwest was full of "wonders," "picturesque" scenes, and "romantic" people, his prose punctuated with illustrations, photographs, and exclamation marks. His experience of living at Isleta Pueblo in the late 1880s, trying to learn Tiwa language and folklore, taking photographs, and transcribing pueblo stories, provided him with rich sources of information and led him to test various modes of cultural translation that anticipated later experiments with ethnopoetics. As a result of the combined effects of his own showmanship, his many publications, his association with Theodore Roosevelt and Porfirio Díaz, and his influence on Hollywood films, Lummis may have been Anglo imperialism's most influential regional agent.

The popular image promoted by Lummis combined exotic and prehistoric elements of the desert landscape with domesticated versions of its Indigenous cultures, thus offering an antimodern and utopian Southwest to readers in California and the East. Like Lummis, the popular novelist Zane Grey successfully managed the ideological contradictions of masculinity and modernity through creating romances that reconciled eastern newcomers with an earlier generation of settlers and rejected feminized domestic spaces for rugged and idealized representations of the southwestern landscape. Grey typically set his best-selling romances in the period of the greatest border conflict, either at the northern edges of the territories of Arizona or New Mexico or along the U.S-Mexico border, yet his narratives were structured around moments of uncontested encounter with pristine land. Grey's mythic southwestern spaces provided both escape and protection, as in the conclusion to his most famous novel, *Riders of the Purple Sage* (1912). Finally triumphant in capturing a masked rider from his cattle-rustling enemy, the hero Venters climbs a steep cliff and into a valley inhabited long ago, discovering "a glade that surpassed, in beauty and adaptability for a wild home, any place he had ever seen" – and discovering the masked rider to be a beautiful young woman named

Bess.[18] Venters expresses no ambivalence about his "invasion"; he "felt sure that he was the only white man who had ever walked under the shadow of the wonderful stone bridge, down into that wonderful valley with its circle of caves and its terraced rings of silver spruce and aspens."[19] As he and Bess develop their own romance in Surprise Valley, he feels that he "had come, in a way, to be a cliff-dweller himself."[20] This assertion of shared identity with the valley's original inhabitants sets the stage for the novel's dramatic finale, which sends a second couple, the Mormon rancher Jane Withersteen and the leather-clad outlaw Lassiter, rushing through the valley's only entrance. At the end, Lassiter pushes the massive boulder Venters named "Hanging Rock" off the cliff to seal the entrance and kill the vicious Mormon elders who have oppressed Jane and other Mormon women for too long. Readers close the book with the image of the two couples, alone in a magically fertile valley, ready to begin a new, ideal life together.

While Grey's crude symbolic transformations clearly served the needs of his romance plots, skilled modernist writers such as Cather and Mary Austin created more nuanced and ambivalent landscapes for spiritual and cultural engagement. Although raised primarily in Nebraska and known best for the novels that intertwine myths of migration in the Great Plains, Cather used her encounters with the southwestern desert beginning in 1912 to shape her practice of fiction and to convey to her readers their own complicity in the region's ongoing Anglo-European conquest. In her sketches of Panther Canyon in *The Song of the Lark* (1915) and of Blue Mesa in *The Professor's House* (1925), Cather represents abandoned dwellings as sites of imaginary access to the region's ancient history, artifacts like pottery shards and bones as physical conduits to Indigenous ways of life, and the desert air as a source of inexplicable happiness. In *Death Comes for the Archbishop* (1927), however, the history of the land keeps returning to challenge the protagonist's Anglo-European imperial perspective. The archbishop's narrative spans the establishment of the border in 1848, when New Mexico seemed like wilderness to his European eyes, to the emancipation of slaves following the Civil War, the Long Walk of the Navajo, and the continuation of Indian Wars. The novel narrates diverse encounters with the landscape and these critical events in territorial history through the protagonist's evolving consciousness, revealing both the limited knowledge produced through any single encounter and the cumulative effect of a lifetime's acculturation. Organized as discontinuous books modeled on the frescoes of Puvis de Chavannes and designed to resist the romance of conventional regional fiction, *Death Comes for the Archbishop* repeatedly tests the ability of the novel form to articulate the southwestern borderland's cultural and historical complexity as it reveals the distortions created through the archbishop's imperial eyes.

In one key scene, Archbishop Latour conducts a mass at Ácoma pueblo and feels as if he were addressing "antediluvian creatures."[21] Beginning to question both the need for Ácoma's great church and his own faith, he spends the night alone on the mesa, feeling "homesickness for his own kind, his own epoch, for European man and his glorious history of desire and dreams."[22] This deeply unsettling experience of alienation from European culture prepares him to apprehend anew the "brightness" at the edges of his familiar world as well as the extent of the region's Native history and customs: the significance of the Pueblo Revolt in 1680, the power of the ceremonial fire at Pecos and the cave called Stone Lips, and the refuge provided by a Navajo hogan that sheltered him "in the heart of a world made of dusty earth and moving air."[23] Although the novel concludes with the construction of a massive cathedral in Santa Fe, it also records its protagonist's intermittent awareness of his colonial perspective and privilege. Latour realizes that whereas "it was the white man's way to assert himself in any landscape, to change it, make it over a little," the Native manner was "to vanish into the landscape, not to stand out against it."[24] As the archbishop's death is officially announced, the tolling of the new cathedral's bell functions unofficially to unite the region's Mexican, Anglo, and Pueblo cultures. By dissolving the novel's material referents and concluding with the evocation of a reverberating sound and a common prayer, Cather refines her fictional consolidation of the region's diverse perspectives on the legacies of conquest while sustaining an uneasy sense that such imaginary harmony represents merely the protagonist's – and the reader's – desire for resolution.

As southwestern writing from this period imbued the knowledge derived from local and historical research with longings for personal and cultural fulfillment, it introduced new strategies for representing natural and social landscapes. Two important examples of this modernist aesthetics are Mary Austin's essays and stories of "lost borders" and Cleofas Jaramillo's *Romance of a Little Village Girl* (1955). Austin renamed the Mojave "the land of little rain" at the turn of the twentieth century, and she challenged her readers to abandon the lines drawn on their colonial maps and allow their contact with the earth, Indigenous species, and the region's first settlers to shape their understanding and transform their use of language. At the same time, Austin's sketches, stories, and novels about the desert attest to the opportunities and constraints faced by Anglo writers of this generation: Even as they claimed the accuracy and authenticity of their position, they recognized their responsibility to indicate the limits of their knowledge. Such an ethics of place would come to link these writers with environmental activists of the late twentieth century, such as Edward Abbey, Terry Tempest Williams, Ellen Meloy, and Rebecca Solnit. Jaramillo responded to the shifting social landscape of northern New Mexico by writing her own life as a nostalgic romance, publishing a cookbook and collection of family stories, and founding La Sociedad Folklórica in Santa Fe. Caught between a *nuevomexicana* generation struggling to manage material and social losses and an emerging Chicana sensibility that sought to remake communal identity on different terms, Jaramillo has frequently been dismissed for her nostalgia and complicity with colonial representations of the region's aristocratic "Spanish" heritage. However, her texts also provide active resistance to the loss of her land and culture. Because Jaramillo could keep neither the property she had inherited nor her family intact, she exerted fierce control over their representation in her own writing, especially in *Romance of a Little Village Girl,* which narrates family history through detailed renderings of the author's native Arroyo Hondo valley near Taos and the circular narrative structure of the village story. Complementing her brother, Reyes Martinez's, work as a field writer for the New Mexico WPA, Jaramillo also produced important documents regarding Spanish rituals and food traditions, anticipating a variety of studies of women's culture and society in New Mexico that continue to explore the dynamics of rural life, class, and gender in the Upper Rio Grande Valley.[25]

Greater Mexico's Border Ballads and *Mestiza* Poetics

While the borderlands acquired an Anglo-American literary, artistic, and commercial identity as the Southwest in the early twentieth century, the region remained dominated land for Mexican Americans. Mary Louise Pratt's definition of a contact zone as "social spaces where cultures meet, clash, and grapple with each other, often in contexts of highly asymmetrical relations of power" is especially relevant to the social spaces and discourses of the border in South Texas, where González, Paredes, and Anzaldúa, among others, explored the consequences of racial hierarchies and social injustice.[26] Through the powerful elaborations of these writers and their critics, the southwestern contact zone that emerged in the mid- and late twentieth century was simultaneously literal – located in the lands and bodies of people living in South Texas and elsewhere along the border – and figurative – an imaginary, mobile, multivalent space of encounter, resistance, and self-definition.

Paredes designated these borderlands "Greater Mexico," recognizing the fundamental continuities between Mexico and Texas, and his writing was essential to the exploration of vernacular culture and the recovery of transnational historical memory in the Lower Rio Grande Valley and beyond. His work effectively redefined the Mexican-American borderlands by rejecting a romantic notion of the cultural legacy of Old Spain in favor of what Héctor Calderón calls "a historically determined geopolitical zone of military, cultural, and linguistic conflict."[27] Bridging Anglo and Mexico worlds himself, Paredes moved as a child between Brownsville, Texas, and the rural area around his brother's ranch in Tamaulipas, Mexico, where he began to listen to folk music and collect material. His seminal text, *With a Pistol in His Hand*, recounts the history and cultural meaning of the border ballad or *corrido*, the popular local adaptation of the Spanish *romance*, and reveals Mexican American border culture to be caught between two worlds and between modernity's uneven temporalities. Drawing on his firsthand experiences in a community where the voices of common people had little public force or legal power, Paredes recreated in writing the specific place (the isolated "green, fertile belt" of the Lower Rio Grande, a tightly knit, patriarchal community settled by Indian outlaws, Spanish colonial families, Mexican outsiders, and American pioneers) where legends and songs about Gregorio Cortez (the man turned mythic outlaw who had come to embody Mexican resistance to the Texas Rangers and the rich Anglos) were performed again and again: "They still sing of him – in the cantinas and the country stores, in the ranches when men gather at night to talk in the cool dark, sitting in a circle, smoking and listening to the old songs and tales of other days."[28] Paredes exemplified the versatility and interdisciplinarity of the modern borderlands writer while presenting a coherent perspective on ongoing antagonisms in the region. The subtlety of his cultural analysis of the *corrido* and other forms of folklore extended to his poetry, *Between Two Worlds*; his story collection, *The Hammon and the Beans*; and the novel *George Washington Gómez*, all of which were conceived and drafted between the 1930s and 1950s, although published much later. Even when recounting rage and grief – as in the narrative of *George Washington Gómez*, in which the Mexican American protagonist assimilates into a middle-class Anglo-American society that refuses to acknowledge the rights of his people – Paredes's writing exhibited masterful linguistic and aesthetic control in its analysis of intractable political problems. While his work derives its power from its location in the Lower Rio Grande Valley and the writing's direct eloquence, his career continues to generate debate about the global applications of U.S.-Mexico borderlands experience.[29]

Another major reconfiguration of the literary and cultural significance of South Texas was Gloria Anzaldúa's *Borderlands/La Frontera*. Rather than seek to manage cultural and political conflict through assimilation or modernist narrative, this anticolonial and postmodern text confronts the historical fact of U.S. occupation; celebrates the author's mixed Indian, Mexican, and Anglo heritage; and unleashes her "wild tongue." Significantly, Anzaldúa opens and concludes her sequence of essays by declaring, "This land was Mexican once / was Indian always / and is. / And will be again."[30] Readers of this text such as Krista Comer have observed that it "is all about lost land, that is, stolen land – and with it, stolen identity and history."[31] Indeed, Anzaldúa never fully relinquishes either the land's physical presence or her effort to replace it with alternate notions of a more just and multiracial home. From the imagined recovery of the mythical Aztec homeland, Aztlán, within the territory of the contemporary U.S. Southwest to the *mestiza* woman's claim to universal citizenship on the basis of being "every woman's sister or potential lover," *Borderlands/La Frontera* continuously struggles to articulate a new country and a new Chicana poetics.[32] "To survive in the borderlands" means living with the knowledge of dispossession and oppression, accepting ambivalence, and envisioning an alternate future, the book's best-known poem insists. It also means wielding the power of language. Anzaldúa offers many vivid and violent figures for the border itself: "this thin edge of / barbwire," a "steel curtain," "a frontline, a war zone," and, most famously, "*una herida abierta* where the Third World grates against the first and bleeds."[33] Her forgiving and capacious "third country" takes in the "prohibited and the forbidden," those people rejected from both societies: "the squint-eyed, the perverse, the queer, the troublesome, the mongrel, the mulato, the half-breed, the half dead."[34] This is "not a comfortable territory to live in, this place of contradictions," Anzaldúa admits, but her invented country offers the rewards of an awakened consciousness and a place for her to speak freely in Chicano Spanish, the vagrant dialect of her "wild tongue." "I am my language," Anzaldúa declares, and this "language is a homeland closer than the Southwest."[35]

Magical Borderlands Fictions

Contemporary writers from the U.S. Southwest continue to explore the formal possibilities for telling its stories and to pursue the implications of wild tongues, multidimensional borders, and hemispheric histories. One major work that juxtaposes a diverse array of texts, narrative perspectives, and scales of time is Silko's *Almanac of the Dead* (1992). The novel begins with a five-hundred-year map that extends in every direction and shows all its stories to converge in Tucson. Whereas her earlier novel *Ceremony* narrates the spiritual reawakening of its mixed-race protagonist, Tayo, through proper contact with Laguna land and ceremonial practices, in *Almanac* Silko distinguishes between one Laguna character's circular homecoming, a return that reactivates both tribal and pantribal knowledge, and the unpredictable trajectories of other characters, which may lead to violence, self-destruction, revolution, or new consciousness. Silko has identified the novel's origin in a roll of film containing "odd, unrelated subjects," and the novel tests how these subjects connect through plots that use chance encounters, family relations, career pursuits, and common experiences of grief to reveal reality to be relative and the deep structure of coloniality to distort all vision in and of the Americas. In one scene, a Mayan revolutionary named Tacho, co-leader of a pantribal army, acquires possession of "an opal the size of a macaw egg," wrapped in red string and white feathers, protected by twelve coca leaves and nourished with grains of cornmeal; like the recovered almanac in the process of being transcribed throughout the novel, in the right hands this found object can wield visionary power and reveal a "Fifth World." Looking into its surface, Tacho sees "the coastline of the Pacific all the way from Chile to Alaska" and prophetic scenes of destruction in Mexico City.[36] In a pattern typical of this grand and disturbing novel, a material and magical object, one in transit across many borders and shifting shape as it moves, mediates a character's vision of the world and opens new routes for border thinking. Proceeding by networks and circles, like a three-dimensional web, the novel reveals how the process of representation itself discovers global linkages as it alternately exposes and conceals historical and other truths in this transcontinental border zone.

To see how borderlands writers are currently working to align the literatures of the U.S. borderlands and Latin America, we might look to *The Hummingbird's Daughter* by Luis Urrea (2006) and *Caramelo* by Sandra Cisneros (2003), two ambitious novels that reverse trajectories of migration, speak multiple dialects and literary languages, and posit the instability of rational or historical knowledge as the condition for gaining access to new spiritual or cultural identities. Like other great Latin American fiction, both novels orchestrate the epic reach of a family over many generations and conjure the magical reality of everyday life through the power of a rebellious narrative voice and the reappearance of dead relatives as irreverent spirits. In *The Hummingbird's Daughter*, Urrea draws on the facts and legends of his distant cousin Teresa Urrea, the illegitimate *mestiza* daughter of a Tehueco Indian woman and white hacienda owner who becomes a visionary healer popularly known in Sinaloa and Sonora as La Santa de Cabora. The novel confirms and amplifies Teresa's power through linking her to Aztec mythology; it also supplements the real and violent narratives of the Mexican Revolution with the alternative real and visionary narratives of Teresa's initiation into practices of Indigenous healing and faith.

In *Caramelo*, Cisneros delights in the extravagance of Chicano Spanish, American pop culture, and storytelling itself, creating a narrator named Celaya (Lala) Reyes, who recounts her family's many crossings of the border – for vacations in Acapulco, family visits in Mexico City, and necessary escapes from Texas – in exuberant, unromantic detail. Whereas the family's new life in San Antonio strands them "halfway between here and there, in the middle of nowhere," on the other side everything "switches to another language" and intensifies: "Sweets sweeter, colors brighter, the bitter more bitter."[37] Like many immigrant families, the Reyes struggle to assimilate better than their Mexican relatives but find themselves still watching telenovelas, listening to Mexican music, and cooking *barbacoa taquitas,* still "Mexican on both sides."[38] Lala names herself a "Cuentista – Busybody, Ogler, Liar/Gossip/Troublemaker, Big-Mouth – in Other Words, Storyteller," and Cisneros endorses her fast-talking heroine by supplementing each snapshotlike chapter with song lyrics, footnotes, and historical chronologies. *Caramelo* thus fractures the form of the borderlands novel to multiply its possibilities for articulating new transcultural and transnational affiliations. The novel's alternate title, "Puro Cuento," means either "only stories" or "untruthful tales." Often comic and celebratory, occasionally tragic, and always ambivalent in its vision of the impact of history on the land and its people, this novel, too, actively reimagines the Southwest borderlands as an ongoing collective conversation. In the end, it is through telling, revising, inventing, and listening to such stories, however fantastic or untruthful, that the region's literary life continues to thrive.

Notes

1 See Luci Tapahonso, "Ode to the Land: The Diné Perspective," in *The Multicultural Southwest: A Reader*, ed. A. Gabriel Meléndez, M. Jane Young, Patricia Moore, and Patrick Pynes (Tucson: University of Arizona Press, 2001), 98.

2 Paula Gunn Allen, preface to *Writing the Southwest, rev. ed.*, ed. David King Dunaway and Sara L. Spurgeon (Albuquerque: University of New Mexico Press, 2003), xviii.

3 Leslie Marmon Silko, *The Turquoise Ledge* (New York: Viking Books, 2010), 27–8.

4 José E. Limón, "Mexicans, Foundational Fictions, and the United States: *Caballero*, a Late Border Romance," in *The Places of History: Regionalism Revisited in Latin America* (Durham, NC: Duke University Press, 1999), 238.

5 For critical studies that pursue the national, transnational, and gendered implications of this borderlands poetics, see Walter Mignolo, *The Darker Side of Western Modernity: Global Futures, Decolonial Options (Latin America Otherwise)* (Durham, NC: Duke University Press, 2011); José David Saldívar, *Border Matters: Remapping American Cultural Studies* (Berkeley: University of California Press, 1997) and *Trans-Americanity* (Durham, NC: Duke University Press, 2011); Sonia Saldívar-Hull, *Feminism on the Border: Chicana Gender Politics and Literature* (Berkeley: University of California Press, 2000); and Debra Castillo and María Socorro Tabuenca Córdoba, *Border Women: Writing from La Frontera* (Minneapolis: University of Minnesota Press, 2002).

6 José E. Limón, "Border Literary Histories, Globalization, and Critical Regionalism," *American Literary History* 20, no. 1–2 (2008): 166.

7 Ofelia Zepeda, *Where Clouds Are Formed* (Tucson: University of Arizona Press, 2008), 67.

8 David L. Moore, *That Dream Shall Have a Name: Native Americans Rewriting America* (Lincoln: University of Nebraska Press, 2013), 26.

9 Zepeda, *Where Clouds Are Formed*, 43.

10 Gary Paul Nabhan and Mark Klett, *Desert Legends: Re-Storying the Sonoran Borderlands* (New York: Henry Holt, 1994), 193.

11 Ibid., 19.

12 Ibid.

13 For precise discussions of the geographical borders of the Southwest, see D. W. Meinig, *Southwest: Three Peoples in Geographical Change, 1600–1970* (New York: Oxford University Press, 1971) and Tom Lynch, introduction to *Xerophilia* (Lubbock: Texas Tech University Press, 2008).

14 See Oscar J. Martínez, *Border People* (Tucson: University of Arizona Press, 1994).

15 Gloria Anzaldúa, *Borderlands/La Frontera: The New Mestiza* (San Francisco: Spinsters/Aunt Lute, 1987), 25.

16 Recent scholarship – such as James Brooks, *Captives and Cousins: Slavery, Kinship, and Community in the Southwest Borderlands* (Chapel Hill: University of North Carolina Press, 2002); Samuel Truett and Elliot Young's edited volume, *Continental Crossroads: Remapping U.S.-Mexico Borderlands History* (Durham, NC: Duke University Press, 2004); and Robert Irwin, *Captives, Bandits, Heroines, and Saints: Cultural Icons of Mexico's Northwest Borderlands* (Minneapolis: University of Minnesota Press, 2007) – reveals some of the ways that disputes over the location, effectiveness, and cultural significance of the border continued, primarily as a result of aggressive imperialist plans by the United States, competition for land and resources among many border groups, and the turmoil of the Mexican Revolution.

17 Willa Cather, *Death Comes for the Archbishop* (1927; New York: Vintage Books, 1990), 95.

18 Zane Grey, *Riders of the Purple Sage* (1912; New York: Penguin Books, 1990), 93.

19 Ibid., 97.

20 Ibid.

21 Cather, *Death Comes*, 100.

22 Ibid., 103.

23 Ibid., 229.

24 Ibid., 233.

25 See, for example, *Women of New Mexico: Depression Era Images*, ed. Marta Weigle (Santa Fe: Ancient City Press, 1993) and *Expressing New Mexico: Nuevomexicano Creativity, Ritual, and Memory*, ed. Philip B. Gonzales (Tucson: University of Arizona Press, 2007).

26 Mary Louise Pratt, "Arts of the Contact Zone," *Profession* 91 (1991): 34.

27 Héctor Calderón, *Narratives of Greater Mexico: Essays on Chicano Literary History, Genre, and Borders* (Austin: University of Texas Press, 2005), 22.

28 Américo Paredes, *"With a Pistol in His Hand": A Border Ballad and Its Hero* (Austin: University of Texas Press, 1970), 33.

29 Paredes's body of work has generated extensive scholarship, from Hector Calderón, *Narratives of Greater Mexico: Essays on Chicano Literary History, Genre, and Borders* (Austin: University of Texas Press, 2005) to Ramon Saldívar, *The Borderlands of Culture: Américo Paredes and the Transnational Imaginary* (Durham, NC: Duke University Press, 2006); and José Limón, *Américo Paredes: Culture and Critique* (Austin: University of Texas Press, 2013).

30 Anzaldúa, *Borderlands/La Frontera*, 25, 113.

31 See Krista Comer, *Landscapes of the New West: Gender and Geography in Contemporary Women's Writing* (Chapel Hill: University of North Carolina Press, 1999), 219; Saldívar-Hull, *Feminism on the Border*; Castillo, introduction to *Border Women*; and Priscilla Ybarra, "Borderlands as Bioregion: Jovita González, Gloria Anzaldúa, and the Twentieth-Century Ecological Revolution in the Rio Grande Valley," *MELUS* 34, no. 2 (2009): 175–89.

32 Anzaldúa, *Borderlands*, 102.

33 Ibid., 24–5.

34 Ibid., 25.
35 Ibid., 81, 77.
36 Leslie Marmon Silko, *Almanac of the Dead* (New York: Penguin Books, 1991), 480–1.
37 Sandra Cisneros, *Caramelo* (New York: Alfred A. Knopf, 2003), 17.
38 Ibid., 351.

CHAPTER 10

Imagining the Rocky Mountain Region

Nancy S. Cook

From the early 1970s to the mid-1980s, music listeners around the world enjoyed a Rocky Mountain high due to the success not only of John Denver, but also of the myriad bands that recorded or mixed at the Caribou Ranch in Nederland, Colorado. Built by the music producer James Guercio, the studio made music from 1971 to 1985 that sold more than 100 million albums. While the recording studio closed after a fire in the mid-1980s, Caribou Ranch remained legendary in the development of popular music. Isolated, offering opportunities for musicians to experience "nature," it also provided a retreat from both the distractions of urban recording in London, New York, or Los Angeles and a place to dodge rigid union rules. As a "destination" studio, it attracted bands and artists across a spectrum of tastes, with a list like a Who's Who of 1970s and 1980s rock and pop stardom – the Beach Boys, Michael Jackson, Chicago, Earth, Wind and Fire, Rod Stewart, Frank Zappa, Jeff Beck, Supertramp, Carole King, Yes, John Lennon, and U2. Elton John recorded three albums there, naming *Caribou* after the studio. No doubt the location with recreational possibilities – horseback riding, snowmobiling, fly-fishing – its remoteness, and the acoustics of altitude were influential, even though the music is never considered "western."[1] Alas, Frank Zappa did not record his "Montana" there; nor did Caribou Ranch foster his dreams of becoming a "Dental Floss tycoon," for that anthem was released before he worked there.[2]

I begin here because the story of Caribou Ranch offers several parallels with stories of the literary history of the Rocky Mountain West. The producer Jim Guercio lights out for the territories, as it were, imagining a retreat from urban modernity. According to news articles published when Caribou Ranch was offered for sale, Guercio was searching for an escape from unionization in the music industry in New York and L.A. So like many a Euro-American in the nineteenth century, Guercio hoped that heading west would offer him financial rewards without stringent regulation, and he envisaged a more authentic life there. He imagined a natural playground to keep artists both distracted from urban desires and inspired by a carefully groomed "wilderness" experience. And, as elsewhere in the interior West, Caribou Ranch offers a version of a "boom and bust" story. By the mid-1980s, "destination" studios appeared worldwide and the competition threatened Guercio's business model. While the studio business went bust, Guercio managed to ride a real estate "boom," selling off various parcels and making a tidy profit by the time he sold the remaining acreage and buildings in 2014 for $32.5 million.[3] And certainly, the music created there was place-based, for the Rocky Mountain air at eighty-six hundred feet, thin, dry, affected voices and instruments alike.

Going back to albums as diverse as Earth, Wind and Fire's *That's the Way of the World* or Elton John's *Captain Fantastic and the Brown Dirt Cowboy*, can one discern the effect of place on the music? Can one isolate the variables – a day's successful fly-fishing expedition, shortness of breath, increased effects of alcohol, clear, dark skies, no sushi delivery – and locate them in the music? Can we hear Colorado or the Rocky Mountain West in any of this music? In all of it? This is also the task of the literary critic or historian who attempts to characterize more than two centuries of literary production across several states. Are there coherences? To what might we reliably attribute differences? Can we look back and recognize a flowering that is as finite as the beginning and end of a recording studio? Can we hear some sort of natural and/or cultural music running through a wide range of texts? How might one go about listening in? What tools might one use? Rubrics? Which texts? Why do we expect relationships between writer and place to be coherent, apparent to us, but not expect the same from artists in other media? The answer, in part, lies in the history of literary histories of the American West.

While strong scholarship about literary traditions in/of the American West appeared from the early twentieth century into the 1950s, with the founding of the Western Literature Association and the peer-reviewed journal *Western American Literature* in 1965, a discipline was established.[4] In the early years there were debates about where the West was, but the anxiety concerned respect, national audience, and erasing the curse of "regional" writer while keeping the concept of region. Much like a government survey team, scholars of western American literature carved out a space in the canon and defined it regionally, always already in competition with New England and the South.

The frustration of scholars studying literature of the West shows itself as late as 1987, in the preface to *A Literary History of the American West*. The critic Max Westbrook quickly moved on from old and continuing battles for legitimacy and onto a much more expansive vision of a multicultural West within a range of representational traditions. He addressed the difficulties of finding definitions, "in terms of geography, themes, subject matter, residence of the authors,"[5] or, most vexing, "a distinctively western style."[6] Opening up the canon, and the conversation, *A Literary History of the American West* remains a useful reference work while it reveals how much the discipline has changed in a little more than twenty-five years. Since 1987, most literary histories have rejected the single-author essay, instead subdividing the West into a number of regions, identities, or themes, recognizing that the western part of the nation is too diverse in culture, history, and environment to make sweeping generalizations.

But what is *this* region? The Rocky Mountain West is a loose baggy monster, full of more contradictions and differences than commonality, at least in the twenty-first century. The very notion of the "Rocky Mountain region" is a term that changes meaning and location over time and across points of view. In use since the 1820s, and reflecting a largely eastern perspective, it has shifted according to need to include at various times Arizona (!), northern or all of New Mexico, Colorado, Utah, Wyoming, Idaho, and Montana.[7] Many of these states are claimed as part of the Northwest, the Far West, the Southwest, the Great Plains, or the Great Basin. Occasionally, they have been reduced to Montana, Wyoming, and Colorado, or some combination that includes part of a state but not all of it. The Rocky Mountain West includes overlapping territories marked by aridity or moisture, altitude, and weather that can be abrupt, volatile, big. The Rocky Mountain West, then, is a matter of perspective. Generally, from Idaho and Utah to Montana, Wyoming, and Colorado, it is the place of both failed and working mines, denuded forests, shuttered mills, and continuing timber harvests, marginal ways, failed homesteads, suburban sprawl, and high altitude (Montana has the lowest average elevation at thirty-four hundred feet). It is generally arid with only pockets of rainfall exceeding twenty inches per year. Politically, these are largely red states with little blue dots in them. Increasingly they are places where a large service sector makes comfortable habitats for the rich. We might find new ways to link portions of the Rocky Mountain West – by laws, for example: restrictive abortion laws, open carry, concealed carry for firearms, open container, speed limits, labor laws. How might regional infrastructures – laws, news media, politics, interstates – color the literature of the region?

About the Rockies: The idea of the Rocky Mountain West as we imagine it carries most meaning when looked at from the East. From the

East, one encounters the Front – in Colorado it is the Front Range while in northern Montana it's the Rocky Mountain front or just the Front. It's an abrupt angularity that stops people in their tracks. But from the West, the Rocky Mountain region is not nearly so clear. On the northern border of the United States, a series of foothills, small mountains, and river valleys give way to the mountain ranges along the Continental Divide. Topography upsets expected flows. If one lives in Pagosa Springs, Colorado, Santa Fe is more likely the cultural hub than Denver. If one lives in Coeur d'Alene, Idaho, Spokane or Seattle is more an economic hub than Boise. Missoulians think Seattle or Portland rather than Salt Lake City or Denver.

It remains a region that favors movement and transience, a place of boom and bust. It is still a place where some people attempt to stay in the home of their ancestors. A sense of belatedness pervades. And one-upmanship. Many a conversation in the Rocky Mountain West begins with "my family has been here for three generations." Often, these utterances are made in the company of people whose families have been here for at least thirty generations. Newcomers can easily forget that the land was not empty when "discovered," but on my campus there are photographs of teepees where university buildings now stand. Many of the people in the Rocky Mountain West arrive from somewhere else and establish a home place, often at someone else's expense. Nevertheless, in Rocky Mountain West literature the rancher and the farmer continue to represent an old guard, a group of people placed on the land (by divine right?) under some kind of threat from new(er)comers.

Since the late nineteenth century the Rocky Mountains have produced transient, gulag, and oasis cultures. In terms of literature, unless an author is signed by a major trade press in New York, with a book tour to promote the work, the audience will be largely local. Missoula has two independent bookstores with the works of my neighbors and international writers, but not the writers from Colorado, Utah, Idaho, or Wyoming (unless they took their degrees at my university). Writing communities cluster around universities, but the change in economics for public universities has changed the conversation and the culture. At my university the visiting writer from Boulder or Boise is now a rarity. Subregion has become less meaningful, and even state literature rarely unites a citizenry already marketed into narrow demographics. We are in the age of microregions, much like microclimates.

The present collection, along with well-regarded literary and cultural histories such as *A Literary History of the American West* (1987), *Updating the Literary West* (1997), and *A Companion to the Literature and Culture of the American West* (2011), are organized according to different rubrics; each combines a geographical structure (Southwest, Northwest, Far West, Rocky Mountains) with a thematic or topical structure (genre, gender, ethnicity, critical "trends"). One problem with this is that the traditional themes and movements have been unalterably changed by the newly emerging critical concerns. So in each case, one organizing principal troubles, perhaps undercuts, the other. What I propose here, under the heading "Imagining the Rocky Mountains," is to borrow from another discipline and offer not a literary survey of the terrain over time, but an overlay, a verbal version of the mapping system developed by Ian McHarg and now known mostly as GIS (Geographic Information System). Such an overlay asks readers to reject linear conception and instead keep several rubrics, strands, and divergences in mind as they coexist. For at least twenty-five years, scholars of western American literature have understood that the literary productions and legacies of a region cannot be responsibly codified as a straightforward march of "history" and that any history requires a mix of organizing principles. What we sometimes forget is that these varied sections might best be read interactively, fully in conversation not only with each other, but with the scholarship produced by the contributors themselves, as well as other scholars in the field. My survey, then, will overlay rather than weave the following rubrics into an idiosyncratic rendering of a history of the literary terrain here called "the Rocky Mountain region."

First, we need to consider critical perspectives for they offer frameworks that critique and question every inclusion and omission in this chapter. When I think of the scholarly work of colleagues between these covers, I am stopped in my tracks by their trenchant critiques of the unstated assumptions that accompany so many surveys. Imagine them, then, as readers over our shoulders, asking us to read these chapters through the lenses afforded by their work. This literary history supplements rather than negates the histories that are already out there, and beginning with the criticism, we can better recognize critical positionings and assumptions. With an array of critical lenses, the myriad literary anthologies of western writing ought to be more useful, too.

Second, when thinking historically, it is important to remember the limitations of the time line, which leaves texts behind in the march forward, concealing influences and conversations among texts over time. For example, the legacies of Lewis and Clark can be seen across the state of Montana, both in the way they reinscribed perceptions and places, as well as in rhetorics of discovery that continue to inform writing about the natural world and the humans who occupied the territories "discovered." The rhetorical moves present in texts by Isabella Bird, Elinore Pruitt Stewart, and Nannie Alderson have analogues in the numerous late twentieth- and early twenty-first-century memoirs by tenderfeet who metamorphose into tough ranch women. I resist historical narrative here because there are so many good ones already available. For the northern Rockies, with an emphasis on Montana, one need only move from the section on the Rocky Mountains in *A Literary History of the American West* (1987), to *Updating the Literary West* (1997), followed by Alan Weltzien's essay in *A Companion to the Literature and Culture of the American West* (2011). Weltzien's chapter has the advantage of broader and more integrated coverage, for the editor, Nicolas Witschi, abandoned the author-centric organizational structure, as has the editor of this volume, Susan Kollin. Other forms of organization allow for putting both writers and texts in conversation.

Furthermore, the geography and physical challenges Euro-Americans faced in a region of extreme weather, steep topography, high elevation, aridity, and few straight paths continue to influence settlement patterns, cross-region travel, and economic development. In the twenty-first century, it might be more useful to think of the region as a series of microclimates, or a series of nodes – universities, good bookstores, a concentration of writers and readers – that radiate outward until they hit a barrier, such as a mountain range, no cell coverage, or a snow-closed interstate. Consider verbal overlays similar to the maps in the *Atlas of the New West* (1997). Or we might literally overlay literary culture onto the maps in that atlas. Start, let's say, with the map of "The Cultured West" and add a keyboard for homes of writers.[8] Would the accumulation of keyboards be in inverse proportion to Land Rovers on the map "Consuming in the New West"?[9] How about a correlation between brew pubs and writers' residences?

Geographically, the region, or subset, might be defined by the preceding descriptors, or by the Continental Divide, or by its geopolitical alliances. The Continental Divide loomed large in the nineteenth century. It figured differently as "the Backbone of the World" for Indigenous peoples. While overland travel writing of the nineteenth century featured the physical and psychological hardships of crossings, with the mountains themselves a kind of "hump" to be gotten over, writers in the twenty-first century revisit and recontextualize past discourses to address contemporary environmental and political issues. For example, the "rapid response" book, *The Heart of the Monster*, by Rick Bass and David James Duncan, began as a protest against Exxon Mobil's efforts "to convert 1100 miles of riverways and scenic byways into a 'High and Wide industrial corridor' that will connect the Tar Sands to the industrial nations of the Pacific Rim."[10] When citizens of Idaho and Montana heard that Big Oil wanted to transport equipment bound for Alberta's Tar Sands via cargo trucks more than two hundred feet long and "seven times heavier than the 80,000 pound loads the roads were designed to support," they imagined what such "Big Loads" might do as they cross from the Northwest to the plains, through a national "Wild and Scenic Corridor" where Highway 12 runs along the Lochsa and Selway Rivers.[11] Locals understand the trepidation of tourists who see the "Curves Next 65 Miles" sign, as well as the value of the corridor for recreation and transportation. The book project began with local outrage, but it developed into urgent advocacy that both hones in on the local and connects outward to the global. In doing so, the authors and researchers create alternative (and subversive) histories as they imagine ways, in Duncan's words, "to keep hearts – including my own – awake to some of the inviolable sources of balance, creative action, and inspiration."[12] Here, I am careful to use the word "imagined," as Nathaniel Lewis's *Unsettling the Literary West* whispers in my ear, encouraging me to think in terms that do not privilege a simplistic realism, a contrast between Old and New Wests, or to claim authenticity on behalf of Bass and Duncan. From Krista Comer, Neil Campbell, Susan Kollin, and others, I am mindful, as are Duncan and Bass, that often what seems most local is entangled within a web of global reach.

Fourth, we might think about the bioregions that comprise the Rocky Mountain region. Thinking ecocritically allows us to read early representations from north to south or west to east for shared flora, fauna, weather, foodways, modes of travel, or cultural adaptions specific to the Rockies. We might read narratives of exploration in conversation for what they show us about macro- and microregions, changes in populations, behavior, or scarcities and abundances. We might think about twentieth- and twenty-first-century writers whose range has included both southern edges and northern boundaries, looking for commonalities and differences. For example, what biota are present in both the southwestern writing of Craig Childs and his work on critters closer to his home in Colorado? Does Doug Peacock's voice, rhetorical repertoire, or observation style change between the southern Rockies and the "Grizzly Hilton" in the northern Rockies as he tracks bears the length of the mountain chain? Or we might look at David Quammen's natural history and science writing in terms of his local habitat in southwestern Montana or read his fiction through an ecocritical lens, where we might find a similar attentiveness to the natural world. Because it is often read as a Hemingwayesque "knockoff," what might we see in his story "Walking Out," if we attended to the biota, the microclimates, and the watershed?[13] What if we read James Galvin's *The Meadow* ecocritically, in conversation with John McPhee's *Rising from the Plains* or Alexandra Fuller's *The Legend of Colton H. Bryant*?

Thematic readings might link texts through shared experiences, issues, and identities. One could imagine a thematics of style, for example, one that would link stylistic innovations in D'Arcy McNickle's *Wind from an Enemy Sky* (1977); James Welch's *Winter in the Blood* (1974), *Fools Crow* (1986), *Killing Custer* (1994); and Debra Magpie Earling's *Perma Red* (2002) for the way each uses style as a means to reveal multiple epistemologies in play for any representation of Native life, especially post contact. Older stories of life in mining or timber camps, railroad work or ranching might be put into conversation with newer work from the oil patch or processing plant. We might adapt Stephanie LeMenager's distinctions between "easy oil" and "tough oil" for thinking through a history of "resource" exploitation in the Rocky Mountains, with its cultures of mining, timber, and "energy" industries. What might Denis Johnson's haunting *Train Dreams* have to say to booster accounts of railroad booms in Wyoming or Montana? What would a literary history of military presence in the Rocky Mountain region look like? We could borrow Simon Ortiz from another chapter and put his powerful work on the Sand Creek massacre in conversation with the work of Elizabeth Bacon Custer, Terry Tempest Williams, Rick DeMarinis's "Under the Wheat," Kristin Iversen's *Full Body Burden*, Richard Ford's "Great Falls," James Welch's *Killing Custer*, and so on.

A concatenation of conversations that foreground cultural similarities and differences across time and geographies might disrupt common assumptions about simple binaries such as urban versus rural. Denver has a body of crime fiction appropriate for a large metropolitan area. Does Boise? How might they differ? And how do urban crime novels differ from rural ones? What if we read the crime fiction of the Montana writers James Crumley, Jon A. Jackson, or James Lee Burke alongside the Denver fiction of Manuel Ramos, John Dunning, or Jeffrey DeShell? Or the Montana writers in conversation with their own work set outside Montana?

Perhaps the most vexing and controversial sheet in the overlay is the aesthetic one, and its evaluative cousin, taste. One can see two trends at work for the past several decades in western American studies. One moves in the direction of the encyclopedic, as if by unearthing every possible pamphlet, magazine, textual fragment, and book that is set in the West or by a "west-erner," an argument can be made by sheer volume for the importance of the region in forming national character or creating literary forms, or for representative samples in the canon of American letters. Aesthetically many of these reclaimed texts might not fit any frame for universal and timeless value, but they fit, singly or in aggregate, an aesthetic of the time, or as Nathaniel Lewis discusses in *Unsettling the Literary West*, their "authentic-ity." The other trend moves toward universal and timeless value, but often the arbiters of that value are not the western anthologists or the literary critics, but rather the eastern "establishment" that traditionally awards national prizes and compiles important canon-making anthologies. In *A Literary History of the American West*, essays point out which authors have won national literary prizes. For example, the chapter on Vardis Fisher documents his 1939 Harper Prize in fiction[14] and that "future scholars may find that … he compares not unfavorably with William Faulkner."[15] Note the hesitancy in this comparative evaluation. While Fisher merited his own chapter in *LHAW*, and Wallace Stegner proclaimed that " 'any serious study of the literature of the American West … will have to include Vardis Fisher,' "[16] a quick perusal of Amazon.com shows no recent reprintings by any major press. Kindle has one title, but for teachers who want to add Fisher to a syllabus, the pickings are slim.

Writing a literary survey of a place one knows can be tricky, especially in the outback oases of the Rocky Mountain West. In Missoula, where I live, one can't, in Mark Twain's words, "swing a dead cat" without hitting a writer. The shelves of local bookstores, independent and corporate, offer a bankrupting array of new books each season. And my colleagues, friends, bookstore owners – all could use a little boost from a reference work that, well, references them. While working on this essay I asked many writ-ers, bookstore staff, and other readers who they thought were our region's important writers. Taste enters in, certainly, but also in a small city other factors weigh in the evaluation of our region's literature. One friend dis-missed an authorial fresh face because he refused an invitation to our fair city. Another friend touted new novels by two of Missoula's carpenters who have MFAs. Indeed, Missoulians were tickled to find that Barnes and Noble's fall 2014 "Discover Great New Writers Selections" included those two carpenters.[17] This is not as unusual as it might seem, for Missoula not only boasts a few dozen writers of national, even international renown, but also an economy where an MFA in creative writing gets you a day job (or two) to make rent. The writers who make substantial money from writing tend to live out of town in large log homes and generally do not mingle with the local literati. All this is to say that if you ask a local about regional writing you are likely to get an often-sophisticated evaluation of the quality of the work, but almost always there is another motive for the oral "blurb." Were I to list all the writers I know who are producing interesting work that is at least partially set in our region, regardless of the length, I would leave out someone great, probably a former student or a dear friend. To concentrate on my hometown would slight those other oases, towns or cities with a strong creative writing program, several resident writers, and/or a good independent bookstore – Laramie, Ft. Collins, Boise, Moscow, Boulder, Bozeman, Salt Lake, Provo, and Denver.

Besides a tendency to value authenticity over creative imagination, there are other impediments to a Rocky Mountain avant-garde. For all the production of fiction, nonfiction, and poetry, writers here continue to write under the weight of a legacy of manly, realist fiction. Young women writers here continue to look and hope for an *écriture féminine* in the Wild West.

How then to discuss a literature of this big, broad region? We can reshuffle the deck, make new maps, new overlays. For example, because of the fine feminist literary criticism that began to appear in the 1960s, contemporary scholars and students can consult criticism that discusses nineteenth- and early twentieth-century women's narratives and writers such as Isabella Bird, Elinore Pruitt Stewart, Nannie Alderson, and B. M. Bower. But a glance at such authors' publication histories suggests nearly continuous interest in their stories since the first publication. The Englishwoman Isabella Bird's *A Lady's Life in the Rocky Mountains*, first published in London in 1879, has been translated into French, German, Italian, Chinese, and Japanese and has been nearly continuously in print in some edition through the nineteenth century, with editions in several decades of the twentieth century. We can situate her narrative within many different kinds of publishing histories, including the Victorian gentlewoman traveler, or we can compare her prose with that of John C. Fremont, noting the differing needs for self-aggrandizement. We can set her renderings of the wild Rockies within the framework of the domestic, as Cathryn Halverson has done, and find that men in the West are homemakers, too.

First published as letters in *Atlantic Monthly* in 1913 and 1914, and in book form by Houghton Mifflin in 1914, Elinore Pruitt Stewart's *Letters of a Woman Homesteader* was reprinted in the 1940s, the 1960s, the 1980s, 1990s, 2000s with new editions in 2012. Adapted for the screen as 1979's *Heartland* (with Annick Smith as executive producer and William Kittredge as cowriter), Stewart's story of homesteading in Wyoming has remained compelling for over one hundred years. Alderson's account of ranching in southeastern Montana as told to the historian Helena Huntington Smith was first published in 1942, with editions appearing in the 1960s, the 1970s, 1990s, and 2013. B. M. Bower was a successful popular writer whose series of novels about a ranch in Montana allowed her to leave that ranching life and a husband suspected to be abusive and recreate a much more stylish life in California. Montana, the scene of a difficult life, was reimagined by Bower into a profitable happy-go-lucky fantasy of a robust life on a ranch in Montana. Victoria Lamont's work on Bower restores complexity to this successful and overlooked author.[18]

While Alderson and her husband moved to Montana hoping to get rich quick with open range cattle ranching and then return to "civiliza-tion," Bower translates experience into profit through her popular novels. In each of these cases women placed themselves within a speculative mar-ketplace, hoping to turn their experiences into cash. For Bird, Stewart, and Bower, their representations of a life in the Rockies fashioned stories from experience, but it was their creative imaginations – eliding issues, suppressing details, making stories out of daily life – that earned them money and solid, enduring reputations as pioneers on the page. Unlike many works by women writers of the West, the publication history does not suggest a rediscovery solely attributed to the rise of feminist literary criticism in classrooms. What new stories might their texts tell us if we put them in conversation not only with other women writers of the West, but with other kinds of stories and discourses – the texts of botanizing women, of entrepreneurs such as Oscar Micheaux, or adventurers such as Roosevelt and what Christine Bold has called "the frontier club," elite white men of eastern privilege on the loose in the West.[19]

Using different maps, we might find additional ways of characterizing the work of William Kittredge, arguably the spokesman for an "antimy-thological" move in contemporary western letters. Kittredge has influ-enced the field through short fiction, essays, his mentoring of creative writers at the University of Montana's creative writing program, as well as work as an editor and anthologizer, most famously as coeditor of *The Last Best Place: A Montana Anthology* (1988), the massive anthology that began the trend in other western states. Often positioned as one of the "manly" writers, Kittredge has become the western writer everyone quotes but few actually write about. His work rewrites the Old West, describes and cri-tiques a transitional period between Old and New West ideologies, *and* stylistically challenges the default realism of so much western American writing. Occasionally he has repositioned his writing and moved into the "hypermythological," making a counterintuitive move to the actual, as he does in the short story "Phantom Silver." In it, Kittredge appropriates the Lone Ranger, placing him firmly within history and gifting him with dark family secrets. Kittredge narrates the story with surety of mythmaking voice, confident and declarative. But he unsettles his readers, in part by taking the masked man into the twentieth century and old age.

Kittredge transitions the Lone Ranger and Tonto within both space and time, taking them to the West Coast and showing the Lone Ranger trying to enforce the mythic in a modern West. Near the end, the narrative shifts tenses, leaving the past tense, moving between present and future as modernity asserts itself in a world unintelligible to the Lone Ranger. In this final section, Kittredge evokes the twentieth century, with its wars and environmental catastrophes that make the mythic West seem small. The story ends with a hazy daydream, back to incest with his sister in the thicket by the Brazos while Comanches kill their parents. Modernity cannot conquer the endurance of the shameful, but insistent dream of pleasure and power, as Kittredge blends the scene into one of explicitly *white* power, in the masked man's refusal to live in historical time, instead savoring both a dirty fantasy and an idealized West. This is how myth works: durable, resistant to history and the actual. Since the late 1960s, Kittredge has exhorted westerners to "find a new story to inhabit" while showing us why it is so difficult to do.

Among the Montana writers often cataloged with the "manly" male writers Thomas McGuane established himself as a prize-winning author with East Coast and European credibility early in his career, and he has managed to write about his adopted home state since the early 1970s while maintaining his literary stature outside the region. For decades McGuane has skewered the most entrenched platitudes of the rural West, puncturing rural pieties such as the way ranchers use "neighbor" as a verb, which he does in the story "Vicious Circle." He offers sharp and funny characterizations of small town small-mindedness, rich carpetbaggers, and some of the best renderings of sport and of manual work in contemporary letters. We might better see how McGuane writes about manual labor if we put those texts in conversation with the great elegy for manual labor, James Galvin's *The Meadow*.

The strong prose stylists who negotiate between myth and history continue to be exporters of western images and ideologies beyond U.S. borders. Among the most popular American literary authors in France, Jim Harrison, particularly *Legends of the Fall* (1979), has inspired dozens of graduate theses and dissertations at French universities. Using critical studies of the global West, we might productively interrogate what makes the French idolize Harrison's West, but not that of William Kittredge, Judy Blunt, or Mary Clearman Blew.

Contemporary critical approaches can put once important, but long neglected texts back into play, as Krista Comer does with A. B. Guthrie Jr.'s 1949 novel *The Way West* in her essay "New West, Urban and Suburban Spaces, Postwest."[20] Guthrie's most famous novel, *The Big Sky*, lamented the loss of innocence and freedom that accompanied settlement. Most critics use it to look backward, to reconsider Guthrie's rendering of an almost pristine natural world, but Comer connects the neglected *The Way West* with more recent history, the second half of the twentieth century and the explosion of urban development, and takes us into the twenty-first century. Such rereadings are crucial for the relevance of a western literary canon.

The western writing of Annie Proulx has garnered significant critical attention, with dozens of articles on the story "Brokeback Mountain" in particular. With the publication of William Handley's edited collection *The Brokeback Book*, we have a series of smart essays that richly contextualize both story and film. The standard comparative move is to place the story in conversation with precursor texts about gay men in the West, but there are many opportunities to place Proulx's western work, particularly stories of dysfunctional, even murderous parents, spouses, families, into conversations about the family and emotional and sexual expression in the West. What might her work look like in conversation with the books of Janet Campbell Hale, Judy Blunt, Mary Clearman Blew, Grace Stone Coates, Thomas Savage, or Kim Zupan? How might the sexualities she represents converse with those in books by Mary MacLane, Tom Spanbauer, Emily Danforth, or writers of lesbian romance novels such as Penny Hayes? How might our readings of Proulx alter if we look at her place writing in *Red Desert: History of a Place* and put it in conversation with McPhee, Galvin, or Bass and Duncan?

In addition to earlier literary histories, anthologies, and critical studies, where does one find the new voices of the Rocky Mountain region? The answer isn't simple, for most journals, anthologies, book reviews might mention that a book is set in the West, but fail to locate it specifically. Regional bookstores, especially independent ones, stock local and regional writers and promote them. The faculty and students in university creative writing programs sometimes write about where they are, and sometimes where they are from, and the West keeps producing new writers. Various organizations award prizes every year for the best of their region or the West. One can find new titles from the annual lists of the Pen Center USA West Literary Awards, Western Writers of America Spur Awards, the WILLA Awards, the Western Heritage Awards, the LA Times Prizes, the High Plains Book Award, and the Mountains and Plains Booksellers Best of the West Awards. Don't forget genre fiction. Another way to ground the region as literary territory is to understand Rocky Mountain Westness as a set of reading practices. Such a set of practices offers tools for orienting ourselves in a literary landscape; for bringing the issues, themes, critical questions to bear on the local; to find a literary-critical equivalent of hearing Nederland, Colorado, in a trumpet note, a piano chord, or a singer's voice. It might be, to borrow from SueEllen Campbell's book title, *Bringing the Mountain Home.*

Notes

1 See "Caribou Ranch," *Wikipedia*, en.wickipedia.org/wiki/Caribou_Ranch, and Alison Wallace, "Caribou Ranch Property, Historic Recording Studio near Nederland up for Sale," *Daily Camera* [Boulder, CO], July 22, 2013, http://www.dailycamera.com/business/ci_23707032/caribou-ranch-historic-recording-studio-near-nederland-up wallace (accessed December 10, 2014).

2 "Montana," *Wikipedia*, en.wikipedia.org/wiki/Montana_(Frank_Zappa_song) (accessed December 10, 2014).

3 This information is from Wallace, "Caribou Ranch property," and Alison Wallace, "Caribou Ranch: Music Central Part of Nederland Property's Future, Owners Say," *Daily Camera* [Boulder, CO], http://www.dailycamera.com/boulder-business/ci_23790361/caribou-ranch-music-central-part-nederland-propertys-future (accessed December 10, 2014).

4 Sabine Barcatta, "The Western Literature Association," *Western Literature Association*, http://www.westernlit.org (accessed December 10, 2014).

5 Max Westbrook, preface to *A Literary History of the American West*, xvii.

6 Ibid., xviii.

7 E-mail correspondence with Professor Derek Everett, Department of History, Metropolitan State University of Denver, October 24, 2014.

8 *Atlas of the New West: Portrait of a Changing Region*, ed. William E. Riebsame (New York: W. W. Norton, 1997), 113.

9 Ibid., 116.

10 David James Duncan, preface to Rick Bass and David James Duncan, *The Heart of the Monster: Why the Pacific Northwest and Northern Rockies Must Not Become an ExxonMobil Conduit to the Alberta Tar Sands* (Missoula, MT: All against the Haul, 2010), 9.

11 Ibid., 11.

12 Ibid., 15.

13 David Quammen, "Walking Out," in *Blood Line: Stories of Fathers and Sons* (St. Paul, MN: Graywolf Press, 1988), 1–41.

14 Louie W. Atteberry, "Vardis Fisher," in *A Literary History of the American West*, ed. J. Golden Taylor and Thomas J. Lyon (Fort Worth: Texas Christian University Press, 1987), 865.

15 Ibid., 881.

16 Wallace Stegner, "Born a Square – the Westerner's Dilemma," *Atlantic* 213 (January 1964), 46–50, quoted in Atteberry, "Vardis Fisher," 862.

17 "Discover Great New Writers Award," Barnes and Noble, www.barnesandnoble .com (accessed December 10, 2014).

18 Victoria Lamont has published extensively on B. M. Bower and currently is at work on a biography.

19 For a good history and overview of feminist criticism within western American studies, see Victoria Lamont, "Big Books Wanted: Women and Western American Literature in the Twenty-First Century," *Legacy* 31, no. 2 (2014): 311–26.

20 Krista Comer, "New West, Urban and Suburban Spaces, Postwest," in *A Companion to the Literature and Culture of the American West*, ed. Nicolas S. Witschi (Chichester, UK: Wiley-Blackwell, 2011), 244–60.

CHAPTER II

Writing the Pacific Northwest

Stephanie LeMenager

One of the Pacific Northwest's famous sons, the poet and essayist Gary Snyder, writes eloquently of bioregionalism, a form of political organization that eschews the "arbitrary" territorial boundaries of nation-states to redefine community around ecological features such as watersheds, the distribution of specific plants, or the range of migratory animals.[1] Snyder's bioregional emphases mirror geopolitical imaginaries long-standing in the Pacific Northwest, from Native American cultures linked to salmon spawning systems to the proposed nation of Cascadia, a northwestern country defined most recently by its capacity for energy independence due to its geothermal and hydrological resources. Before this post-oil Cascadia, there was *Ecotopia* (1975), a book by Ernest Callenbach and an eponymous nation that figures as a self-sustaining country of foresters, gatherers, and gender-bending counterculturalists. And before Ecotopia, there was Jefferson State, a proposed fifty-first state of the union comprising portions of northern California and southern Oregon and bearing the flag of the "double cross" – literally, two crosses – to express the region's abandonment by state governments who care little for rural constituencies. When John Muir wrote of the Puget Sound in *Picturesque California* (1888–90), he noted the difficulty of conceiving the Northwest in terms that are social, rather than ecological: "The edges [of Seattle and Tacoma] run back for miles into the woods which hide a good many of the houses and the stakes which mark the lots; so that, without being as yet very large towns, they seem to fade away into the distance."[2] Muir's defense of Washington State as not "a dim, nebulous expanse of woods," but rather "near to all the world and its possessions" is lost in literary histories that seize upon his plea to set aside a park to preserve Oregon's rainforest.[3]

The persistence of the Pacific Northwest as an ecological rather than social or political imaginary has been eloquently documented by the Canadian writer Laurie Ricou, whose books *Salal: Listening for the Northwest Understory* (2007) and *The Arbutus/Madrone Files: Reading the Pacific Northwest* (2002) rigorously map the cultures of the Pacific Northwest across the U.S.-Canada border by distribution of species, levels of rainfall, and geologic features such as the Kuroshio or North Pacific ocean current. A year into "contemplating the possibility of British Columbia as a coherent 'region,'" Ricou writes, "I realized that the focus had to be on a region figured by ocean currents and species distribution. Of course, I was influenced, largely unawares, by cultural and economic forces which have emerged ... as a 'Cascadian initiative.'"[4] Ricou's reflections on the Pacific Northwest include global economic imperatives, transnational labor migrations, settler colonialism, and other aspects of social history that complicate any notion of region predicated upon the geologic time of ocean or climate. In an era of global climate change when the Pacific Northwest suffers record drought, heat, and wildfire, a sense of region attuned to geologic time grows more volatile and insecure.

Yet the identification of the Pacific Northwest with the nonhuman lives and systems known under the sign of "ecology" remains formative and transformative, in terms of encouraging experimentation with sustainable modes of agriculture and urbanism celebrated by design projects like the award-winning architect Christopher Alexander's *The Oregon Experiment* (1975) and lampooned by the television series *Portlandia* (2011–), where chicken dinners have names and personal histories. The Pacific Northwest's sometimes-unsought ecological identities have encouraged innovation – and a national forgetting. Literatures of the region often write it off as either a depressed resource colony ("towns all hamstrung by geographic economies," as Ken Kesey notes) or a countercultural project.[5] Both representational strategies conceive the Pacific Northwest as largely outside history.

A Place Out of Time, and in It

Water, as in rain, rivers, and ocean, defines a unique regional pride *and* participates in the diminishment of the human as a primary actor in literatures of the Pacific Northwest – or the "Pacific Northwet," in the words of a popular bumpersticker. "The rain pervades the temperament of the people," the poet Tess Gallagher writes of her hometown of Port Angeles, Washington, in the essay "My Father's Love Letters" (1986). "The people don't mind getting wet. Galoshes, umbrellas – there isn't a market for them here. The people walk in the rain as within some spirit they wish not to offend with resistance."[6] What Gallagher identifies as an "allegiance" among the "faithful rain," "the trees," and "the people" creates a temperament of "meditativeness" that can tend toward alcoholism and despair, the situations of Gallagher's father and mother, or, in Gallagher's case, toward a forging of voice from those "dumb years," making poetry from taciturnity and blanketing weather. Gallagher's lover, Raymond Carver, finished out his career with her in Port Angeles, as a primary creator of literary minimalism, which in its economy of words and focus on material details gives voice to an enduring and taciturn western working class.

Writing past the silences of her childhood, Gallagher imagines youthful ecstasy and self-abandonment to rain:

> I'm still a boy under my breast spots.
> I can drink anywhere. The rain. My
> skin shattering. Up suddenly, needing
> to gulp, turning with my tongue, my arms out
> running, running in the hard, cold plenitude
> of all those who reach earth by falling.[7]

To reach earth by falling – a transcendence of individualism, egocentrism, even humanism – this is a long-standing dream that the Pacific Northwest has been called upon to host.

Perhaps no single book expresses the dream of the Pacific Northwest as a site of the "liberating" diminishment of the human in the face of geologic time more explicitly than Jack Kerouac's *Dharma Bums* (1957). Here Kerouac and Japhy Ryder, a scantily disguised Gary Snyder, stake their claim to being Bodhisattva by hiking into the Sierras of California and into the high Cascades, where Kerouac spent sixty-three days as a fire lookout at Desolation Peak in northern Washington. Japhy, the ultimate "dharma bum," offers a description of his childhood in Oregon as preparation for his embrace of Buddhist teachings. "When I was a little kid in Oregon I didn't feel that I was an American at all," Japhy tells Ray, the Kerouac figure.[8] Japhy identifies Oregon with "Indians" and the Wild West, setting the stage for his own transcendence of midcentury American conformism. The actual Gary Snyder would write simply of his childhood, "The woods were more of a home than home."[9] Snyder-cum-Kerouac elaborates: "With all that suburban ideal and sex repression and general dreary newspaper gray censorship of all our real human values but and when I discovered Buddhism and all I suddenly felt that I had lived in a previous lifetime innumerable ages ago and now because of faults and sins in that lifetime I was being degraded to a more grievous domain of existence."[10] Japhy adds, "That's why I was always sympathetic to freedom movements, too, like anarchism in the Northwest, the oldtime heroes of the Everett Massacre and all."[11] This passing reference to a key moment in Northwest labor history, when in 1916 some five to twelve I.W.W. protesters and two militiamen were killed in Everett, Washington, offers an unusually explicit historical reference.

The shingle workers of Everett, a coastal town opposite Whidbey Island, seem far from Japhy's and Ray's emulation of the Chinese monk and poet Hanshan, from their self-imposed solitariness. Labor history and even labor in any ordinary sense of material fabrication have little relation to the spiritual practice of hoboing, hiking, and meditation that define Beat experience in *Dharma Bums*. Yet Snyder has written extensively of his labors in the logging industry, and the Oregon-based Kesey, a countercultural descendent of the Beats, frames his sprawling second novel *Sometimes a Great Notion* (1964) as a labor story focused on the strike-busting Stamper family's conflicts with a local union and with the imposing Northwest rainforest. The most compelling moments in *Notion* depict the skill of loggers as a deep interrelationship with nonhuman life and force. "But the trees continued to fall, gasping long sighs and ka-whumping against the spongy earth. To be trimmed and bucked into logs. To be coaxed and cajoled downhill into the river with unflagging regularity. In spite of all nature could do to stop it."[12] Kesey's *Notion* marks the decadent end phase of frontierist triumphalism in the Pacific Northwest tradition associated with H. L. Davis's regional novel *Honey in the Horn* (1935), a paean to skilled rural labor in the region, from sheepherding to logging.

With less interest in mastery, the Canadian poet Daphne Marlatt presents, in *Steveston* (1974), a portrait of the British Columbia salmon-canning town at the mouth of the Fraser River. *Steveston* evokes the potent hold of woods and sea upon the bodies of ordinary laborers. The Canadian Japanese, First Nations, and Irish Canadians tied to the rhythms of the Fraser live much as do Kesey's Oregonians, but within a crafted context of humility. Marlatt writes of "sun. / a sea men sink their lives into, continue, dazzlingly undeciphered, / unread days, dazed with the simple continuance of water pour, of wind, of small / stores turning their annual credit ledgers."[13] In a different kind of homage to skill as an abiding relationship between human and other, Richard Hugo would thank the ecologies of the Pacific Northwest for honing his poetic craft. "Why did I go to the [Duwamish] River to find poems?" Hugo asks, recalling himself as a young man. "Once I imagined myself along the river, my language got hard and direct."[14]

When Gary Snyder remembers the working men with whom he shared the labor of chokersetting and skidding (attaching logs to cables and dragging them) in the late fifties, he describes their easy intimacy with the living forest. "A black bear kept breaking into the crummy truck to get the lunches until someone shot him and the whole camp ate him for dinner. There was no rancor about the bear, and no sense of conquest about the logging work."[15] Snyder interlaces his logging memoir with poetry nurtured by the work – skill becomes another means of being outside time, in a Zen-like, concentrated present.

> Ray Wells, a big Nisqually, and I
> each set a choker
> On the butt-logs of two big Larch
> in a thornapple thicket and a swamp.

Only with the corporatization of the logging industry does Snyder declaim an American environmental movement that he still tries to keep down-to-earth and working-class, tied to forest conservation rather than the more elusive Beat discontent Kerouac offers up as early ecological consciousness. "We are all endangered yokels," Snyder contends in the last decade of the twentieth century, amid a keen controversy over the fate of the spotted owl.[16]

Rethinking History, Nuancing Refusal

The first significant literatures by Pacific Northwestern Nisei speak of a desire for recognition within the national imaginary, against the affinity for geologic time over social history evident in some bioregionalist writing. John Okada's novel *No-No Boy* (1957) and Monica Sone's memoir *Nisei Daughter* (1953) are both set in Seattle, but they take on national and even global questions of integration and the affects of citizenship in the fraught political climate of the cold war. Okada pursues the problem of what might be the "natural [sociopolitical] feelings" of a Japanese American man circa 1946 – a man who has suffered two years in an internment camp and two more in federal prison because he answered no to both questions on the so-called loyalty questionnaire that was administered to male internees in 1943.[17] Saying no to service in the U.S. Armed Forces and no to unqualified allegiance and willingness to defend the United States brands Ichiro Yamada as a "no-no boy," enemy of the U.S. state, and target for social exclusion by other Nisei. Ichiro returns to Seattle and his family, who have resettled there, without a sense of who he is or what his life might become.

Although technically "he was still a citizen," Ichiro feels as if "he ... had stopped living two years ago" – when he refused to enlist.[18] The "shaken faith of an American interned in an American concentration camp" haunts Ichiro and, with terrible irony, it also haunts his Nisei neighbors who joined the segregated and much decorated 442nd Infantry Regiment.[19] Even those Nisei who defended the United States find themselves "still Japs."[20] One of the most painful moments in *No-No Boy* occurs when Ichiro meets a group of young African American men on Seattle's Jackson Street. As they shout taunts about "Tok-i-yo" boys, Ichiro directs unvoiced racial epithets back at them. His "terrifying hate" of these differently disenfranchised young men originates, he realizes, in the same place where his empathy for them "abides."[21] Ichiro suffers from an excess of social feeling that cannot attach anywhere. He can only choose to be not *not* American.

In some respects Okada's novel could take place in any U.S. city, but its Pacific Northwestern setting recalls a history of West Coast Asian settlement that created large and vibrant but also recognizable and vulnerable Asian American communities. The cooperation of the U.S. Census Bureau helped facilitate Franklin Roosevelt's Executive Order 9066, by which approximately 120,000 persons of Japanese heritage were forced to leave their lives and homes on the West Coast for internment at inland "relocation centers" now considered concentration camps. Sone's recollection of Seattle in *Nisei Daughter* stresses the multiethnic, raucous culture of Seattle's "Skidrow" as an alternative site of loyalty and virtual citizenship for her immigrant family. Like a regional historian, she delights in tracing the origin of the term "Skidrow" to the paths along which timber workers skidded logs in the Old Northwest. Her identification with a regional working class that includes Italians, Irish, Germans, and Swedes seems to save her from some of the heady questions of national belonging that haunt Okada's antihero. Reflecting on her parents' choice to send her to a Japanese-language finishing school, Sone writes: "I was too much a child of Skidrow."[22] Street smarts, slang, the willingness to fight "like a boy," and a network of working-class allies allow Sone to achieve a comic voice, even when she writes of the chilling commonplaces of Evacuation Day.

With other Japanese Americans, Sone's family, the Itois, were "labeled" and driven to Camp Harmony, a racetrack-fairground in Pullyup, Washington, where they lived for months in a barely renovated stable. Finally, they were transferred to the Minidoka war relocation center in southwestern Idaho, where they suffered extreme winters and blazing summers without appropriate clothing or ventilation. When U.S. Army personnel show up at Minidoka to recruit for the Nisei combat unit, Sone ironizes their invitation to give Nisei men "a chance to stand up and express yourselves."[23] She reflects, "We had become adjusted to our peripheral existence" in the camp, considering later in the memoir that the years dedicated to weathering the extreme seasons dispelled any illusions about the U.S. government as a "paternal organization."[24] The bicultural individualism she embraces grows out of her family's creative making of a world from desolate camp conditions. Hers is not a turn from history, but the recognition that cultivating a rich privacy might be a more successful strategy for survival than "expressing oneself" on the national stage. In a sense the literary form she chooses, memoir, makes that point – while also creating for her a self-selected public.

Ursula Le Guin's science fiction short story "Vaster than Empires and More Slow" (1972) returns to a consideration of geologic time, but within a critique of U.S. social conditions during the era of the Vietnam War. Le Guin offers a countercultural sequel to Kerouac's *Dharma Bums*. For most of her writing life Le Guin has been based in Portland, Oregon, and while she writes largely of improbable worlds, these places out of ordinary time and space sometimes resemble images, or dreams, of the Pacific Northwest. "Vaster than Empires" alongside Le Guin's *Always Coming Home* (1985), set in a remote northern California; Callenbach's *Ecotopia;* the bioregionalist essays of Gary Snyder; and the generative dystopias of the Seattle-based science fiction writer Octavia Butler imagine designs for more just modes of living, scenarios that in some small respects, at least, have been realized. The localized settlements connected through information technology in *Always Coming Home* predict community designs by peak-oil activists and permaculturalists who have supported Cascadian secession, while the ecofeminist subculture of *Ecotopia* came to ground in southern Oregon in the late 1960s and early 1970s as a cluster of radical feminist communes.

In Le Guin's "Vaster," an Extreme Survey crew of future humanlike scientists explores a distant planet, World 4470, which is governed by the chemically communicative root networks of verdant grasses and trees. Magisterial and terrifying, the green world of 4470 gestures toward the northern rainforests of Le Guin's adopted home. "Great boles stood well apart, almost regularly, almost alike; they were soft-skinned, some appearing smooth and others spongy, gray or greenish-brown or brown, twined with cablelike creepers and festooned with epiphytes."[25] Most of LeGuin's crew experiences the green planet as a threat to "rationality," to human exceptionalism. One dies of fear, but another, the crew's hyperempathic "sensor," Mr. Osden, chooses to remain on World 4470 as a colonist. Reflecting on his choice, the crew's captain imagines that "he had given up his self to the alien, an unreserved surrender.... He had learned the love of the Other."[26] In so doing, Osden joins a host of regional antiheroes pursuing alternatives to (post)industrial modernity, from the memoirist Cheryl Strayed in *Wild* (2012), to the eccentric Sylvie in Marilynne Robinson's *Housekeeping* (1980), to the purportedly "deaf and dumb" Chief Bromden in Ken Kesey's most well-known novel, *One Flew over the Cuckoo's Nest* (1962).

In *Cuckoo's Nest*, Bromden alone escapes the Oregon mental hospital that Kesey imagines as a synecdoche for the midcentury United States – a place where no one laughs and where men are lobotomized or virtually castrated by repressive maternal figures like Kesey's now-infamous nurse, "Mother Ratched."[27] The con man McMurphy (played by Jack Nicholson in the film adaptation of the novel) commandeers the novel's plot. But if McMurphy drives the novel's action, it is Chief Bromden, a "Columbia Indian" suffering posttraumatic stress disorder after World War II, who offers the capacity for reflection. Bromden's first-person narration is absent from Milos Forman's (1975) film adaptation – and given its importance to the novel, Kesey's objections to the omission, to the point of refusing even to watch the film, are understandable. Bromden recognizes better than the reactive McMurphy that the overbearing nurse is a mere symptom of a culture where surveillance, the medicalization of sexuality, and even imagination are normative forms of state-sanctioned discipline.

The regionalism of *Cuckoo's Nest* figures in its historicization of Bromden's insights about the national insanity. A betrayal of Northwest Native land and fishing rights figures as the primal scene of his education about the workings of "the Combine," or hegemonic power, which is the kind of power that elicits consent, power that shows itself, for instance, in the fact that most of the patients in *Cuckoo's Nest* chose to commit themselves to the hospital. While Bromden's Combine finds analogues in figures of mid-century normative power like Allen Ginsberg's Moloch in *Howl*, it also is specifically identifiable with the building of a hydroelectric dam on Native land near a historic salmon run. The run suggests Celilo Falls, the ancient fishing site drowned by the opening of the Dalles Dam near Portland in 1957. Remembering his Native father's harassment, beating, and humiliation by government-employed thugs and even tribe members eager for government checks, Bromden recalls, "He said, What can you pay for the way a man lives? He said, What can you pay for what a man is? They didn't understand. Not even the tribe."[28] Bromden's persistent hallucinations figure the mental hospital itself as "the inside of a tremendous dam" in whose bowels "people get cut up by robot workers."[29]

At the end of *Cuckoo's Nest,* the Pacific Northwest's violent history of Native American land theft and broken or compromised treaties involving fishing rights cannot be erased, but Bromden allows himself to revisit this past in hopes of making something better from it, an improvisational future. He returns to the Columbia Gorge. By creating Bromden, not McMurphy, as the sole survivor of his plot and therefore not the "Vanishing American" he is purported to be early in the novel, Kesey creates a more original invitation to imagining the Pacific Northwest than he might have done.

The humility and surrender of ego sought by Gallagher, Le Guin, or Kerouac could just as easily turn to humiliation, and humiliation to hatred in the face of "giant boles," desolate mountain peaks, and, in Kesey's words, an inexpressibly *"volatile* feeling about the new country."[30] We see traces of regional humiliation and rage in Kesey's McMurphy, in Hank and Lee Stamper of *Sometimes a Great Notion,* and in a much earlier literature of regional settlement. Surveys of Pacific Northwest writing often begin with Captain James Cook's cynical musings, circa 1778, on the Indigenous communities of the Nootka Sound in what is now Victoria. In the twentieth century, the Dakota/Lakota scholar Vine Deloria Jr.'s history of the Pacific Northwest, *Indians of the Pacific Northwest* (1977), notes that Cook's voyage probably triggered the first smallpox event of 1782 in Puget Sound. Ten years after Cook, Captain George Vancouver challenged Cook's poor characterization of the Northwestern tribes, and the journals of Lewis and Clark are noteworthy in their specificity and relative openness to Native cultures. Yet exploration literatures of the Pacific Northwest evince the discomfort and compensatory superiority often manifested by European travelers out to "discover" imperial plunder.

The Pacific Northwest made its Euro-American "discoverers" especially out of humor, for some of the same reasons that later writers sought the region as an escape from history and self-centeredness. A tone of resentment shadows the naming of Pacific Northwestern places by Europeans – from Cape Foulweather in central Oregon, attributed to Captain Cook, to Cape Disappointment in southern Washington, dually attributed to the Lewis and Clark Expedition, who were understandably disappointed not to find a supply ship waiting for them at the mouth of the Columbia, and to the fur trader John Meares, who in 1788 seems to have missed the Columbia altogether. When Lewis and Clark write of their stay at Fort

Clatsop, near the mouth of the Columbia, they make note of continual rain, rotting food, soaked blankets, and leather clothes disintegrating in the rain, which threatens to wear away their every mark of humanness. Practically speaking, the damp caused economic disaster, as Lewis notes on January 6, 1806. "This day I overhalled our merchandize and dryed it by the fire, found it all damp; we have not been able to keep anything dry for many days together since we arrived in this neighbourhood."[31] Supplies and trade goods significantly reduced, the party barely maintains its equanimity.

Later settlers to the Northwest would be thrown more completely into despair, humiliation, even death. Narcissa Whitman's sojourn as a missionary with her husband, Dr. Marcus Whitman, at Walla Walla, Washington, is marked in her letters by anxious self-doubt. The Whitmans' troubled tenure ended in violent conflict. Fourteen people, including the Whitmans, died in an event now known as the Whitman Massacre that, in turn, triggered the protracted Cayuse war of 1847–55, which initiated an unresolved era of treaty making. "It is the Kaiuses [sic] that cause all the trouble," Mrs. Whitman frets, identifying the group whom history holds responsible for her death. Yet she is equally disturbed by the encroachment of Catholic missionaries. The Whitmans settled in the Pacific Northwest near the beginning of a wave of missionaries to the region, many inspired by a delegation of Flathead and Nez Perces who went east, to St. Louis, to ask after the whites' Holy Book. As Deloria notes, this fateful journey sparked missionary in-migration to an Indigenous region that had been relatively unmolested by whites. "There had been nearly one hundred thousand Indians in the Pacific Coastal regions in 1800, but by the 1840s fewer than half that number were left," Deloria writes. "Their absence, of course, left miles and miles of land unoccupied."[32]

The early 1840s saw the turning of the Pacific Northwest toward the settlers who blazed the Oregon Trail – and afterward the fate of the region once so unknown by Europeans as to be imagined by Jonathan Swift as the mythical land of gigantism, Brobdingnag, would become territory of the United States. In the years 1854 and 1855, most Pacific Northwest tribes signed treaties with either Governor Isaac Stevens in Washington or General Joel Palmer in the Oregon Territory, losing rights in their traditional lands but securing some fishing rights that have – ever since – met with violent opposition from non-Natives. Yet nearly eighty years after Narcissa Whitman's death, in the 1920s, another woman settler, Betty McDonald, saw Washington's Olympic Peninsula as if it were still Indian Country, and Washington as if it were the end of the world. McDonald's memoir *The Egg and I* (1945), about her life with her first husband on a chicken farm in the Chimicum Valley, spawned a series of successful Hollywood films and two lawsuits by plaintiffs offended either by her stereotyping of Native Americans or of Washington as a land of yokels – the fictional "Ma and Pa Kettle" came into being as McDonald's Chimicum neighbors. The fundamental problem of hewing a living – and point of view – from a land characterized by massive and encompassing nonhuman force could close the imagination in crabbed defensiveness.

The condition of being engulfed in water, mountains, and trees has distinct meanings for Native writers with many thousand years' connection to the Pacific Northwest. Chief Seattle, leader of the Duwamish and Suquamish tribes, made a famous speech to Isaac Stevens in 1854 that, if its transcription by a white physician is unreliable, nonetheless remains compelling. To know the liveliness of place you must share in it, Seattle suggests, intermingling your substance. "Even the rocks that seem to lie dumb as they swelter in the sun along the silent seashore in solemn grandeur thrill with memories of past events connected with the fate of my people," Seattle said – or something like that.[33] Rather than an empty space inviting the projection of anxious settlers, Deloria reminds us that "the Puget Sound area was one of the most heavily populated areas north of Mexico City before the coming of the white man" and "completely suburbanized during the summer," when families returned to their hereditary fishing stations.[34] Native identities were so tied to the river systems that fed and transported them that they called one another by the names of these systems – "the suffix 'amish', which is found in many of the tribal names," for instance, Duwamish, indicates that these are the people of this river system. Such integration of persons and rivers produces an entirely different resonance in Indigenous place-names – an interspecies social context of belonging.[35] Deloria adds that "winter, though dreary and very rainy, was the time for the most important religious ceremonies," namely, the first-salmon ceremony that is observed at the beginning of the salmon runs in spring.[36]

Postmodern Native authors such as the Spokane/Coeur d'Alene poet and fiction writer Sherman Alexie remind us – in what Alexie wittily calls his "fancydancing," or hybridized literary performance for non-Native and Native readers – that Indians have a unique stake in the regional gloom. "Every Little Hurricane," the first short story in Alexie's arguably best collection, *The Lone Ranger and Tonto Fistfight in Heaven* (1993), riffs on the long-standing Pacific Northwest theme of rain, too much of it. "Some people liked the rain. But Victor hated it."[37] Victor, a primary protagonist in the volume, sees "weather" as an expressive form for the powerful feelings of his immediate family, neighbors, and cousins. Weather speaks unsayable things about childhood poverty, racialized trauma, the hate between brothers, husbands, wives – and their abiding love. Victor's father's descent into drink is as violent and beautiful as a storm, "maybe … like lightening tearing an old tree into halves."[38] Rain falls as "promises" and "treaties," sudden and inconstant, unresolved.

Alexie writes after the famous 1974 legal victory for Washington tribes known as the *Boldt* decision, which affirmed tribal treaty rights to co-manage salmon fisheries with the state. But he also writes in the shadow of ongoing regional violence against Native fishermen by whites and, more ominously, in the shadow of the massive dam-building projects of the mid-twentieth century, which – as we heard from Kesey's Bromden – forever impaired regional salmon runs. "Has anybody ever said that dam-building is an act of war against Indians?" Alexie asks in the poem "Sonnet, without Salmon" (2011). Water is a medium for Victor's dreams and fears. "For years, Victor feared that he was going to drown while it was raining, so that even when he thrashed through the lake and opened his mouth to scream, he would taste even more water falling from the sky."[39] This drowning also takes the form of "fluids swallowing him," namely, "whiskey, vodka, tequila" – rain becoming alcohol that floats him free of his relationships to this world, from family and from the connections to tribe and place available in traditional story.

In his dream of drowning into earth, Victor suggests, if unwittingly, the famous Haida story of Salmon Boy – a story Alexie has elsewhere subjected to gentle mockery. In the Haida version, a hungry boy who refuses to eat fish given him by his mother swims out into the river and drowns, taken into the heart of water by the salmon people, who subtly school him in respect for their kind. Eventually the boy reenters his tribal community, caught by his father (or mother) and restored to human form, as a shaman and healer. In "Salmon Boy" (1999), the Washington-based poet David Wagoner takes this parable of maturation and socialization into a community of human and animal people as a spur to imagine the perceptual affordances of a salmon's body, what it senses as it returns upstream.

> But the Post of Heaven shook, and the rain fell
> Like pieces of Moon, and the Salmon People swam,
> Tasting sweet, saltless wind under water,
> Opening their mouths again to the river's mouth,
> And Salmon Boy followed, full-bellied, not afraid.

Exuberant, "he flew among them," until his father speared him. "He lay on the riverbank with his eyes open, / Saying nothing while his father emptied his belly." Far from death per se, this ending finds Salmon Boy in a new relationship to life, "full of sun," becoming the gift of sustenance he once failed to acknowledge as a child.[40] For the Anglo poet Wagoner, the fate of becoming food rivals, or is analogous to, becoming shaman.

The transcendence in immanence that Wagoner implies reads more starkly than the conclusion of Alexie's poignant buddy narrative about Victor and his counterpart throughout *The Lone Ranger and Tonto,* the quirky storyteller Thomas-Builds-the-Fire. In "This Is What It Means to Say Phoenix, Arizona," which would be remade as the award-winning film *Smoke Signals* (1998), Victor gives half of his dead father's ashes to Thomas after the two have taken a road trip from the Spokane reservation to Arizona to take his father home. Pleased with this unorthodox gift, Thomas tells the following story, "I'm going to travel to Spokane Falls one last time and toss these ashes into the water. And your father will rise like a salmon, leap over the bridge, over me, and find his way home.... His teeth will shine like silver.... He will rise, Victor, he will rise."[41] Acknowledging that he, too, had planned to throw his father's ashes into the falls, Victor notes that the action might be more like "cleaning the attic" than transubstantiation.[42] Alexie's humor – which has garnered sharp criticism from the Native critic Louis Owens as a shirking of moral responsibility and as entertainment for non-Native readers – often works by juxtaposing a sacred topic with deflating pragmatism. Yet Victor's choice of the falls as the place to scatter his father's ashes implies that he, too, wishes to express something about the man. The Spokane falls are an ancient salmon fishing site, a locus of dreams and visions.

Alexie is interested in the palimpsestlike quality of time, in the material instantiation of multiple time frames – the deep time of tribal and ecological consciousness, the historian's time, the capricious time of day and night dreams, the rhythmic present time of dance – within everyday actions. If histories of dispossession haunt Alexie's present, that present also holds the millennialist temporality of Ghost Dance. Alexie writes in the poem "Powwow at the End of the World":

> I am told by many of you that I must forgive and so I shall
> after an Indian woman puts her shoulder to the Grand Coulee Dam
> and topples it. I am told by many of you that I must forgive
> and so I shall after the floodwaters burst each successive dam
> downriver from the Grand Coulee.

And so on, until the salmon swim through the mouth of the Columbia, and through the mouth of the Spokane River, where they will call "all the lost Indians home" and teach how to pray, how to laugh for hours, and "give us reason to dance."[43] The poem calls up this future to make it so.

The Pacific Northwest is a region whose history is especially deep, etched in thousands-year-old pictographs on the walls of riverside caves, carried forward from traditional Indigenous story into the postmodern novel, writing itself with dendritic certainty in the prehistoric ferns and giant boles of northern rainforests. The regional figure of Sasquatch, fleeing always just ahead of her pursuers through the dark woods, suggests a species being allied to the human but just a little off course – an almost-human agent, sacred in her elusiveness, indicative of the humbling failure of *Homo sapiens* fully to come out on top. If any single region of the North American West invites a reconsideration of both geologic and human force, a recalibration of the weight of history and climate, it is the Pacific Northwest. That makes it an especially interesting place to think with.

Notes

1 Gary Snyder, "The Place, the Region, and the Commons," in *The Practice of the Wild* (San Francisco: North Point, 1990), 25–47.
2 John Muir, *Picturesque California*, excerpted in *Northwest Passages: A Literary Anthology of the Pacific Northwest*, ed. Bruce Barcott (Seattle: Sasquatch Books, 1994), 100.
3 Ibid.
4 Laurie Ricou, *The Arbutus/Madrone Files: Reading the Pacific Northwest* (Corvallis: Oregon State University Press, 2002), 6.
5 Ken Kesey, *Sometimes a Great Notion* (1964; New York: Penguin, 2006), 49.
6 Tess Gallagher, "My Father's Love Letters," in *The Truth about the Territory: Contemporary Nonfiction from the Northwest*, ed. Rich Ives (Seattle: Owl Creek Press, 1987), 409.
7 Gallagher, "Sudden Journey," in Ives, *The Truth about the Territory*, 409.
8 Jack Kerouac, *Road Novels 1957–1960*, ed. Douglas Brinkley (New York: Literary Classics of the United States, 2007), 301.
9 Gary Snyder, "Ancient Forests of the Far West," in *The Practice of the Wild* (San Francisco: North Point, 1990), 125.
10 Kerouac, *Road Novels*, 302.
11 Ibid.
12 Kesey, *Notion*, 567.
13 Daphne Marlatt and Robert Minden, *Steveston* (Edmonton: Longspoon Press, 1984), 86.
14 Richard Hugo, *The Real West Marginal Way: A Poet's Autobiography* (New York: W. W. Norton, 1986), 12.

15 Snyder, "Ancient Forests of the Far West," 125.
16 Ibid.
17 John Okada, *No-No Boy* (Seattle: University of Washington Press, 1977), 212.
18 Ibid., 51, 64.
19 Ibid., 121.
20 Ibid., 163.
21 Ibid., 5–6.
22 Monica Sone, *Nisei Daughter* (Boston: Little, Brown, 1953), 28.
23 Ibid., 199.
24 Ibid., 198, 237.
25 Ursula LeGuin, "Vaster than Empires and More Slow," in *The Wind's Twelve Quarters* (New York: Harper & Row, 1975), 161.
26 Ibid., 177.
27 Ken Kesey, *One Flew over the Cuckoo's Nest*, ed. John Clark Pratt (New York: Penguin, 1996), 58.
28 Ibid., 208–9.
29 Ibid., 83, 87.
30 Kesey, *Notion*, 22.
31 The excerpt from Meriwether Lewis is from *The Journals of Lewis and Clark*, ed. Bernard DeVoto (Boston: Houghton Mifflin, 1981), 302.
32 Vine Deloria Jr., *Indians of the Pacific Northwest: From the Coming of the White Man to the Present Day* (Golden, CO: Fulcrum, 2012), 32.
33 Chief Seattle, "Chief Seattle's 1854 Speech," in *Northwest Passages*, 73.
34 Deloria, *Indians*, 5–6.
35 Ibid., 5.
36 Ibid., 6.
37 Sherman Alexie, *The Lone Ranger and Tonto Fistfight in Heaven* (New York: HarperPerennial, 1994), 6.
38 Ibid.
39 Ibid., 7.
40 David Wagoner, "Salmon Boy," in *Traveling Light: Collected and New Poems* (Urbana: University of Illinois Press, 1999), 124.
41 Ibid., 74.
42 Ibid., 75.
43 Sherman Alexie, "The Powwow at the End of the World," in *The Summer of Black Widows* (Brooklyn: Hanging Loose Press, 1996), 98.

CHAPTER 12

The Far North
Literatures of Alaska and Canada
Ernestine Hayes

At the age of forty, after a twenty-five year absence, I returned to my home in Alaska. Not long after, I joined an Alaska Native cast entertaining visitors in a summer theater. The old stories we performed reminded me of my Tlingit grandmother's lessons delivered in a loving, scolding voice so many years before. At the theater, I took my turn drumming, narrating, and acting out the accounts of our history, including the story of "The Woman Who Married a Bear."

In the final act, the woman realizes that even though she has witnessed the death of her bear-husband, removed the bearskin from her back, and returned to her village, she can no longer be fully human. Onstage, I circled the skin in the air behind my body, where it fell on my shoulders and transformed me. I walked in the slow manner of a bear, bending to place one leg deliberately forward, then one arm, then the next and the next in confident steps. After a few moments, I raised up in a shudder, moving my hide-covered head back and forth as though smelling the air, and dropped heavily back to the floor, swaying and raising my shoulders into a telltale brown bear hump. In that moment, the woman and I both became the bear.

Within the genre of interspecies marriage, stories of men and women who marry bears commonly appear in oral traditions of Arctic and Subarctic cultures and have been transferred to written accounts, in both the original languages for which writing systems have been developed and the English language. Generally, stories of human-ursus intimate interaction begin with the bear presenting itself to the human, often in response to violation of a cultural behavior code, for example, the utterance of an insult that, like all spoken words, can be heard by the distant bear. This testament to the power of spoken words is illustrated in the groundbreaking classic *Haa Shuká, Our Ancestors,* a comprehensive collection of oral narratives edited by the Tlingit poet and scholar Nora Marks Dauenhauer and her husband, Richard Dauenhauer. In this work, oral histories are written in Tlingit and in English on facing pages. The story is told of a young woman who utters an insult that sets the literary drama in motion. As Dauenhauer explains: "According to Tlingit oral tradition, animals of any kind can hear. . . . Regardless of the precise words used, the important message is that the girl violates taboo by insulting the bear. . . . Serious wrongs may be committed by lack of self control and failure to control our thoughts and speech."[1] The young woman encounters the bear in his human guise. Unable to resist his appealing human form, she falls in love and willingly leaves with him, gives birth to his children, and herself becomes a bear. She accompanies her bear husband into the unknown, shadowed world, where reality and perception differ from that in the human world but are no less authentic.

Nonhuman beings involved in interspecies marriages most often approach their prospective spouse in human form. The person at the center of the story perceives the being as human and falls in love. This common narrative prelude leads to the story's essential conflict of loyalty and betrayal. It also establishes the similarity of appearance that symbolizes and reinforces the cultural truth that all creatures enjoy an equal claim to life. Thus, in any interaction with a nonhuman being, members of the culture recognize the inherent kinship present in all things. This fundamental truth is conveyed in the literary tradition of virtually every northern culture, epitomized by oral and written accounts of interspecies marriage.[2] Such narrative histories encourage the listener/scholar to contemplate an enduring human question of identity: Does the robe with which I cover myself conceal or reveal my true nature? That question, as is true for all human issues addressed in great literature, is left to individual resolution.

Almost every popular historical source describes the long record of Native use and occupation that took place before European contact as "prehistory." Indigenous groups, however, possess histories of thousands of years of occupancy and exodus, relocation and settlement, and exploration and discovery, embedded throughout the generations in lawful process, artistic declarations, symbolic regalia, and oral tradition at least as accurately as and in many cases more accurately than the European system of writing that was used for many years after contact to remove rights and appropriate lands. Before contact, Indigenous cultures possessed vigorous legal systems, effective educational systems, efficient health systems, elaborate social orders, sophisticated kinship systems, complex languages, and profitable trade systems – every social institution needed for a culture to flourish for thousands of years.

Because of the eradication of those systems and institutions, we are left with written records that begin with European exploration. Accounts that privilege Western history begin with Bering's 1741 voyage eastward from Siberia and Cook's 1778 search for the Northwest Passage. However, it behooves us to learn about literatures of the Far North from a less Eurocentric perspective. Generally, cultures of the region that political boundaries now separate into Alaska and western Canada reflect landmass formations that in Alaska can typically be described as composing five divisions, broadly including cultural border regions: the temperate rainforest now called Southeast Alaska, homeland of Tlingit, Haida, Tsimshian, and Eyak peoples; the treeless, windy Aleutian Islands, homeland of Sugpiaq (Alutiiq), Unangan, and Koniag; the rivered boreal forests of Interior Alaska and western Canada, homeland of Athabascan groups, among them Ahtna, Koyukon, Gwich'in, and a number of other Dené nations; the alluvial plains and islands of the Western Coast, homeland of Yup'ik and Cupik; and the sparsely vegetated Arctic Slope, homeland of St. Lawrence Island Yup'ik, Iñupiaq, and Inuit nations. This complex diversity exists as intricately throughout the land that is now western Canada, a vast area that includes the provinces of British Columbia, Alberta, Yukon, and Northwest Territories. From all areas in these regions spring cultures that interact and identify with the enveloping, living landscape. Since time immemorial, that relationship has been celebrated and defended by the people whose history, identity, and survival are irrevocably joined to the land.

The cultures and social systems of the areas now known as the Far North were sophisticated and complex long before European contact, and they have persisted in that complexity and sophistication through relentless colonial pressures. Literatures of the Far North, rooted in oral tradition, exemplify this enduring richness and complexity. Narrative context, social relation, and ancestral legitimacy establish a cultural preface with audiences, who must participate during and after the performance is concluded, after the pages are turned, after the book is closed. As the writer, translator, and Yup'ik scholar Elsie Mather explains in "There Are No More Words to the Story," narratives are not meant to be questioned, but rather to prompt the listener to a state of wonder and engagement.[3] As with written literature, oral literature performs critical functions in all societies and in all cultures; one such essential concern of any literature is the strengthening of human connection to place with a concurrent affirmation of worldview. Instruction and entertainment are part of the process but are not its explicit purpose. This literary purpose manifests clearly within the geographical divisions noted previously.

The classic narratives of marriage between humans and other living beings, which frequently commemorate a conjugal joining that produces human offspring, illustrate the indestructible union of identity and place. A list of these events, memorialized in oral and written literatures, includes archetypal marriage to bears by both men and women as well as marriages to other living creatures, for example, fox, octopus, and whale, and marriage to heavenly bodies such as stars. Many of these accounts examine the consequences of the physical and ritual intimacy implied in marriage narratives: the conflict of loyalty, the tragedy of betrayal, the transformation of essence and spirit that is symbolized in the act of covering oneself with new skin. Embedded in these interspecies marriage narratives is the recognition of the animate possession of spirit, which itself leads to acknowledgment of the inherent equality of beings, a crucial theme that is present in all Arctic and Subarctic literatures that arise from Indigenous tradition.[4]

These inherent, embedded, and intuitive themes reveal themselves to audiences and readers in the oral and written literatures of the Far North. These literatures express the essential certainty of the reciprocal human relation to nonhuman beings, to place, and to one another. Other elements also emerge: respect for the power of spoken words, recognition of the intrinsic equality of all beings in the living world, perception of nonlinear time, acknowledgment of profound transformation in the human experience, reliance on metaphor, affirmation of community, confidence in the enduring quality and value of oral tradition, and, more recently, examination of the colonial experience, with a marked emphasis on separation as loss. In every narrative, the act of returning – whether physical, spiritual, or both – is the central and most propitious resolution. Amid these critical themes, the concept of place remains the primary element of individual and social identity and cannot be separated from the literatures produced by the people and cultures of the vast homelands so recently designated Alaska and Canada. As is true for human societies throughout history, Indigenous nations in these regions are formed in response to environmental characteristics, and those locational features of place continue to shape fundamental attributes of cultural and literary identity. Landscape does not reflect cultural expression that takes place upon it: Culture, language, and literature emerge from and manifest the land.[5]

Thus, a fundamental component of the Indigenous worldview of Arctic and Subarctic cultures of the Far North is the ubiquity of spirit in all things, made plain in these interspecies marriage narratives. In the

Indigenous view, these creatures are capable of being "people." In northern literature, this capability is understood, and its knowledge embedded in worldview. Unlike literature rooted in Western tradition, this quality of living existence is accepted in northern literatures without question and needs no explanation.

Interspecies marriage narratives commonly illustrate another fundamental component of worldview: that of transformation. In exemplary works of Indigenous literature, transformation is most often symbolized in the aspect of a garment that can be put on and removed at will by the nonhuman being, who removes the animal-like robe when entering the home and restores the garment before reentering the outside world. This change in appearance, signifying the change in one's nature, also occurs in the human counterpart. However, the phenomenon may not be immediately evident to the human experiencing the transformation. Nevertheless, the human being eventually becomes aware of the ability to "put on" and "take off" the outward symbol of transformed identity and often puts on a human identity when attempting to rejoin the human community, as is the constant desire.

A critical feature of Indigenous worldview that occurs in these stories is the concept of time not as a linear experience, but as an experience more akin to an ever-shifting ocean. In some narrative accounts of interspecies encounters, what may seem like a day to the story's protagonist is perceived as many days or even months by the protagonist's human relatives. Behavior that appears to humans to be bears catching and eating fish in short bursts of time is actually those beings putting up food for the winter, as humans do. In the time it takes the woman to step over a log when in her bear incarnation, a whole day has gone by in the human world where she so recently lived. This perception of the ever-changing fluidity of time reinforces the Indigenous experience: eat when hungry, rest when tired, wait as long as required to celebrate, to mourn, to endure. The cultural truth that symmetry and balance transcend inconstant human perceptions of shifting time is affirmed.[6]

Worldview and philosophy, progression of and relation to time, enspiritedness and metaphor – all are clear aspects of written literatures that manifest strong ties to oral tradition. Omnipresent human themes of love, betrayal, transformation, and sacrifice are central to the oral tradition and continue as significant refrains in the written northern literature of the twentieth and twenty-first centuries. Integrating recent history into timeless themes, aspects of postcontact life and the effects of colonialism now appear in contemporary Indigenous literatures of the Far North.

Characteristics of modern literature of the North exhibit an unsurprising direct link to oral tradition and the traits associated with that most human practice. The separation of Indigenous written literature from oral tradition cannot be accomplished: The appearance of traditional stories within contemporary text occurs so commonly as to be a convention of Indigenous writing. A deep, substantive, meaningful relationship exists, evidenced by the presence of characteristics of the oral tradition inseparable from the experience, thought, and writing of the North. Embedded knowledge, an unbreakable connection to place, and an unromantic recognition of postcontact history cannot be removed from the northern experience and cannot be severed from its literature, whether oral or written, traditional or contemporary, Indigenous or settler.

A significant bridge between oral and written literatures is shaped by non-Indigenous writers who provide excellent translations of important work in the Indigenous oral tradition. In the nineteenth and early twentieth centuries, translations from Indigenous languages into the English language concentrated on vocabulary studies, while translations from English into Indigenous languages primarily featured religious hymns and biblical myths. In the mid-twentieth century, more scholars began to recognize the elegance and intricacies of Indigenous expression, and translations focused on life stories and histories by virtue of their own merit. Notable among this group of scholars is the anthropologist Federica De Laguna, who described Tlingit life ways and culture in the ethnographic work *Under Mount St. Elias: History and Culture of the Yakutat Tlingit*. Also notable is the work of the anthropologist Catherine McClellan, whose works include the insightful ethnographic study "The Girl Who Married the Bear" and the three-volume *My Old People's Stories: A Legacy for Yukon First Nations*, edited by the Canadian scholar Julie Cruikshank. Cruikshank's works, which include *Life Lived Like a Story: Life Stories of Three Yukon Native Elders* and *Do Glaciers Listen? Local Knowledge, Colonial Encounters and Social Imagination*, reveal her deep respect for and understanding of oral history and Indigenous knowledge.

Deep respect is evident in the literature of those who arrived relatively late in northern lands and in the works of their literary descendants. In an interview with Mercedes O'Leary a little more than a year before his death, the essayist Alaska Poet Laureate John Haines acknowledged the commitment to older cultures that accompanies a true love of the land where he lived for decades. Referencing "that firm ground of our human heritage," Haines explained, "as I have mentioned in some of my writing, there is a need to turn away from this all-too common reference to the 'Frontier.' This has long been a cherished American illusion, and more so for Alaskans with that repeated auto license tag: 'The Last Frontier.'" Haines goes on to argue that "we need to put that away in a museum box, so to speak, and begin, as writers and citizens, to face this life as we have made it, whether willingly or not, and which includes that older displaced life and culture that once belonged to the Native people of this place we call Alaska." Finally, he concludes by noting, "I think that as writers and poets we need to reconnect with that older life and cultures, some of which still remains alive in parts of this planet Earth."[7]

An undeniable relationship between writer and land also resonates in the work of the essayist Sherry Simpson, author of *The Way Winter Comes*, *The Accidental Explorer*, and *Dominion of Bears*. Simpson writes about the land she loves as intimately as any who were born in the Far North. Belief in the equal claim to life rings through the words of such writers as the essayist and poet Eva Saulitis, author of *Leaving Resurrection* and *Into Great Silence*, works that examine her own northern life and her relationship with killer whales. Writer Laureate Nancy Lord puts years of commercial salmon fishing on the page in memoir, fiction, and environmental writing. As with all northern literatures, this sense of a lived place well loved permeates the voice of the memoirist and poet Alaska Writer Laureate Peggy Shumaker and 2014–2016 Alaska Writer Laureate Frank Soos. The fiction writers Eowyn Ivey and Seth Kantner infuse their writing with a lyrical awareness of northern place. In the works of the award-winning writers Don Reardon (*The Raven's Gift*) and Richard Nelson (*Ordinary Wolves*) is seen the regard for the land and its people that characterizes all northern literatures.

A list of Canadian writers would be as multifaceted and broad as the land itself. Among the notable writers of this region are Robert Service (*Songs of a Sourdough*), Joy Kogawa (*The Splintered Moon*), Michael Ondaatje (*The Collected Works of Billy the Kid*), and Guy Vanderhaeghe (*The Englishman's Boy*). These Canadian writers, their Indigenous counterparts, and many more have been acclaimed for their literary excellence. The literature produced by these writers gives shape to the transformations that were experienced, for better and worse, in the Far North during the last few generations.

During the twentieth century, great change occurred in Alaska and Canada as colonial practices introduced new languages, new values, new political systems, new education systems, and other challenges that threatened centuries-old Indigenous foundations to their core. While making every effort to hold on to traditional histories and oral literature, Indigenous people adapted to written methods of communication. In 1959, Paul Green wrote *I Am Eskimo, Aknik My Name*, and in 1962, Howard Rock, an Iñupiat artist, became the first editor of the *Tundra Times*, a northern newspaper that was nominated for a Pulitzer Prize in 1975.

Traditional culture bearers, cognizant of the need to preserve old ways with the use of new tools, researched, interviewed, and committed to writing the stories that had held the generations together for many lifetimes. These scholars also wrote of traditional worldviews, subsistence practices, and ways of knowing. Among these cherished intellectual authorities are Angayuqaq Oscar Kawagley, the Yup'ik anthropologist who in 1995 wrote the acclaimed *A Yupiaq Worldview: a Pathway to Ecology and Spirit*. Other scholars whose tireless work demonstrates their commitment to protecting the languages, histories, worldviews, and traditional narratives of northern cultures include Annie Blue, Yup'ik history keeper, whose stories were transcribed, translated, and published by the University of Alaska Press as *Cungauyaraam Qulirai: Annie Blue's Stories;* Walter Johnson, Dana'ina, whose accounts of life on Iliamna Lake were published by the Alaska Native Language Center as *Sukdu Nel Nuhtghelnek: I'll Tell You A Story;* Sydney Huntington, Athabascan storyteller and knowledge keeper, whose stories were told in *Shadows on the Koyukuk: An Alaska Native's Life along the River,* published by Alaska Northwest Books. In addition, the work of Nora Dauenhauer, Alaska writer laureate from 2012 to 2014 and a Tlingit scholar and poet, appears in the groundbreaking three-volume series Classics of Tlingit Oral Literature, published by Sealaska Heritage Foundation and University of Washington Press. Dauenhauer also wrote *Life Woven with Song,* a multigenre book of poetry, prose, and drama published by the University of Arizona Press.

Northern peoples have continued to experience dramatic cultural, social, and personal changes, all of which are reflected in contemporary literature. People of the northern regions have adapted to cultural and social changes that have sometimes been unwelcome and sometimes even perilous. Although gains and losses have been great beyond measure, northern peoples persist in the expression of their essential identity, however changed. People of the northern regions take up newly sharpened carving tools to fashion ancient designs, cover regalia with store-bought buttons and cotton thread, and type on keyboards the old and new stories that describe who they are, who they have become, and who they will be. A particularly expressive illustration of the incorporation of post-contact experience into literary form occurs in a poem titled "Piksinñaq," written

by the Iñupiaq writer Elizabeth "Sister" Goodwin, describing her grandmother's first experience with popcorn:

> Aana sat hunched over
> with her eyes squinched shut
> she grasped onto neat rows
> of willow branches
> waiting for the popcorn
> to make her bounce around[8]

An important example of the weight placed on northern literatures
by the colonial experience is seen in the work of Mary TallMountain, an
Athabascan poet born in the village of Nulato in 1918 who was adopted
and taken away from her culture. The themes of loss and trauma are
repeated in her influential works of poetry, as is the unbreakable bond to
the land that was her original home. TallMountain lived in San Francisco's
Tenderloin District, and although she visited Alaska as an adult, she never
returned to make her home again in the North. But her works reveal that
the land never left her. In one of her most admired poems from her collection *The Light on the Tent Wall*, titled "The Last Wolf," TallMountain
articulates the pain and futility of displacement:

> I heard his baying echoes
> down the steep smashed warrens
> of Montgomery Street and past
> the few ruby-crowned highrises
> left standing
> their lighted elevators useless[9]

The Tlingit poet Robert Davis (Hoffman) echoes the themes of the
colonized and attempts to reconcile history with postcontact experience
in his brilliant love song to the land, "Saginaw Bay: I Keep Going Back":

> Listen, I'm trying to say something –
> always our stories have lived through paintings,
> always our stories have stayed alive through retelling.
> You wonder why sometimes you can't reach me?
> I keep going back.
> I keep trying to see my life against all this history.[10]

As these poems illustrate, Indigenous people of the North have experienced drastic cultural, social, and personal changes, challenges that
have persisted into the twenty-first century. In the years following the
mid-twentieth century, Indigenous people became adept at expressing
themselves with modern tools, modern material, and modern idiom.

Thus, the blending of old ways and new ways, cultural practices that have gone on since time immemorial, have continued.

The contemporary Athabascan writer Velma Wallis gained fame with the publication of her first book, *Two Old Women* (1994), which became a worldwide best seller, and her subsequent books have enjoyed comparable reception. A storyteller in the finest tradition, Wallis has made a contribution to writing of the North beyond measure. Before the late twentieth century, it had long been an accepted colonial practice to perceive colonized people as studied rather than scholar, subject rather than actor, student rather than professor. Indigenous voices have long been hushed when editors have chosen to publish literature about Indigenous people rather than by Indigenous writers. Yet audiences recognize that the stories of the Far North can be compelling and eloquent when told by artists and thinkers, whether Indigenous or settler. In northern climes, the reliance on others so essential to physical survival cannot be excluded from the portrait of place that emerges in the written word.

The concept of community is fundamental to an understanding of northern literature. Alienation is tragedy; reconnection is triumph. In an interconnected world, what can be more tragic than separation? In the relatively few years since colonialism exerted authority over northern lifeways and appropriated northern lands – in some regions no more than 150 years – narratives that speak of separation permeate the oral and written literatures of Indigenous traditions. Examples of separation include children forcibly sent to boarding schools, where they were separated from families and cultures; adults pressured to migrate to urban areas, where they were separated from their languages and their histories; elders who were cut from the community by tuberculosis, smallpox, and alcoholism, their knowledge and experience disappearing with them. Themes of loss and separation, longing for reconnection to land, to community, to health, construct significant motifs of the North, and these same human themes are evident in the writings of those authors who have come to love and be loved by the same land that has sustained and inspired artists since time immemorial.

Artists such as the Siberian Yup'ik sculptor and poet Susie Silook ("Uncle Good Intentions") defy Western-based labels and show that layers of artistic expression are made deep and meaningful by diversity. In the work of the Iñupiaq and Inuit poet Dg Nanouk Okpik can be seen traces of oral tradition as well as echoes of the Western tradition. These literary artists are joined by many others whose work is on the horizon, including the poet, playwright, game developer, and storyteller Ishmael Angaluuk

Hope (*Strong Man, The Courtesans of Flounder Hill*), who carries on the tradition of his Iñupiaq mother, the poet Elizabeth Sister Goodwin, and his writer/activist Tlingit father, Andrew Hope III, and the King Island Inuit/Iñupiaq poet Joan Kane, whose award-winning works (*Cormorant Hunter's Wife, Hyperboreal*) have received deserving recognition for their exceptional blend of lyricism and landscape. These recognized northern writers and those others whose literary expressions are approaching the Western canon defiant, gifted, and headlong, carrying with them the excellence and truth of their written words, illuminate the bright path toward our inevitable tomorrow.

Among contemporary artists leading the way into the northern literary future are the Cree playwright and novelist Tomson Highway and multi-talented cross-genre artists such as the poet and sculptor Michael Nicoll Yahgulanaas ("Haida Manga") and the Stó:lō Nation member Lee Maracle (*Bent Box, Celia's Song*). These artists are forging the way toward recognition of a literary world where truth cannot be categorized. Northern writers and culture bearers shape new paths, where colonial contact occurred genera-tions before, and marriages to octopi, stars, and bears are often portrayed or taught as no more than myth. The meaning and messages carried by the oral and written traditions in Indigenous history are offered to readers and listeners without restriction. Thomas King reminds us that what we do with these lessons is, in the truest tradition, our individual responsibility. In *The Truth about Stories*, King tells us, "Don't say in the years to come that you would have lived your life differently if only you had heard this story. You've heard it now."[11] Meaning and substance live on, and the unbreakable con-nection between contemporary literature and oral tradition persists.

The living land and its many aspects exist as immediate, precise, and unmistakable metaphorical conduits to human knowledge and survival. Cloaked in narratives that are meant to be revisited again and again as understanding deepens and experience broadens, embedded lessons sum-mon images of living beings, giving birth to subtle spiritual interpreta-tions and practical life applications. From our human perspective, the land itself provides instruction, knowledge, and wisdom and occupies a primary role like that of a human mother: to provide comfort and sus-tenance, and to present a steadfast metaphorical pattern upon which to lay the understanding of life. As we change the land, we ourselves are changed: Our history is transformed and we transform our future. We are at the same time born from and married to the bear and to the stars, just as we are born from and married to the land. As is true for all writ-ten literatures, today's northern literature is born from and is married to the oral traditions from which all literature emerges and continues in an unbroken voice to tell the stories of shared human history. That shared history has joined ancient and modern voices; in "Spread My Ashes on Khaa Tú Kaxhsakee Heen," the poet Ishmael Angaluuk Hope speaks for all northern writers:

> I want to keep an unbroken line of storytellers,
> Orators, weavers, beaders, carvers, and Elders.
> I want to dance at large ceremonies,
> Where all my ancestors gather
> And give speeches about returning our love,
> Again and again, to our descendants.[12]

The literary dialogue of northern traditions has expanded but has also maintained its rootedness in identity with the land. Traditional values, humor, and recognition of shared experiences emerge in the written voice – perhaps not consciously, but simply because literary expressions cannot help but reflect worldview – rooted in place and connected to all, giving voice to the truth that everything is alive. The dialogue and the relationship it examines continue.

As I explained in my memoir, *Blonde Indian,*

> Who our land belongs to, or if land can even be owned, is a question for politicians and philosophers. But we belong to the land.... When as you conduct your life, you chance to see an eagle or a wolf or a bear, remember that it, too, is conducting its life, and it sees you as well. As does a tree. And the forest itself. The very land sees you. When you see this and feel this and know this, you will want to hug the land. You will want to embrace it. And when that happens, you can be sure the land feels the same way about you.[13]

At the end of the summer theater performance, the Woman Who Married a Bear, now more bear than human, walks into the forest with her bear-children. With one last look, she reminds us that we are all married to the bear and we are married to the stars. She tells us that the land that sustains and nourishes us is irrevocably present in northern literatures: traditional and contemporary, Indigenous and settler, poetry and fiction. In that lesson revealed by northern literatures, we, too, are transformed.

Notes

1 Nora Marks Dauenhauer and Richard Dauenhauer, notes to *Haa Shuká, Our Ancestors: Tlingit Oral Narratives*, ed. Nora Marks Dauenhauer and Richard Dauenhauer (Seattle: University of Washington Press, 1987), 374.

2 For further discussion, see Brian Thom, "The Anthropology of Northwest Coast Oral Traditions," *Arctic Anthropology* 40, no. 1 (2003): 1–28; Georgina Loucks, "The Girl and the Bear Facts: A Cross-Cultural Comparison," *Canadian Journal of Native Studies* 2 (1985): 218–39.

3 Elsie Mather, "There Are No More Words to the Story," *Journal of Oral Tradition* 13, no. 1 (1998): 233, 239.

4 See David Abram, *The Spell of the Sensuous, Perception and Language in a More-Than-Human World* (New York: Vintage Books, 1990); Tim Ingold, "Rethinking the Animate, Reanimating Thought," *Ethos* 71, no. 1 (March 2006): 9–20.

5 I discuss this concept at greater length in my autobiography, *Blonde Indian: An Alaska Native Memoir* (Tucson: University of Arizona Press, 2006).

6 See Thomas Thornton, *Being and Place among the Tlingit* (Seattle: University of Washington Press, 2007); Erica Hill, "The Non-Empirical Past, Enculturated Landscapes and Other-than-Human Persons in Southwest Alaska," *Arctic Anthropology*, 49, no. 2 (2012): 41–57; and D. Monteith, C. Connor, G. Streveler, and W. Howell, "Geology and Oral History – Complementary Views of a Former Glacier Bay Landscape," in *Proceedings of the Fourth Glacier Bay Science Symposium*, ed. J. F. Piatt and S. M. Gende (Washington, DC: U.S. Geological Survey Scientific Investigations Report, 2007), 50–3.

7 Mercedes O'Leary, "An Interview with John Haines," *Great River Review* 51 (Fall/Winter 2009): 96.

8 Elizabeth Sister Goodwin Hope, "Piksinñaq," *Alaska Quarterly Review: Alaska Native Writers, Storytellers & Orators* 17, no. 3 (Spring/Summer 1999): 197.

9 Mary TallMountain, "The Last Wolf," in *Light on a Tent Wall* (Los Angeles: University of California Press, 1990), 80.

10 Robert H. Davis, "Saginaw Bay: I Keep Going Back," *Alaska Quarterly Review: Alaska Native Writers, Storytellers & Orators* 17, no. 3/4 (Spring/Summer 1999): 165.

11 Thomas King, *The Truth about Stories: A Native Narrative* (Toronto: House of Anansi, 2003), 119.

12 Ishmael Angaluuk Hope, "Spread My Ashes on Khaa Tú Kaxhsakee Heen," in *Courtesans of Flounder Hill* (Berkeley, CA: Ishmael Reed, 2014), 56–57.

13 Hayes, *Blonde Indian*, ix, 173.

CHAPTER 13

The Problem of the Critical in Global Wests

Krista Comer

From James Fenimore Cooper's frontier novels to Gloria Anzaldúa's *Borderlands/La Frontera* (1987), so much of western American literature involves fraught borders and global contest. The ascendance of transnational paradigms in Americanist literary studies over the last two decades has fueled remappings of the literary West, calling attention to a thematics of colonial/national spillover and border travel, and claiming on behalf of them a critical perspective that opens the regional West, beyond its Turnerian limits, to the world. The work of Neil Campbell is exemplary in this regard, conceiving "westness as part of a larger system of discourse beyond the national imaginary, pointing in many directions at once."[1] But before transnational critique overhauled interpretive priorities and literary politics, what critics used to call classic popular and literary texts also showed strong inclinations toward a thematics of movement, of fluidities of borders, and a profound interest in the global – as examples, again Cooper, through dime novels, to Owen Wister's *The Virginian* (1902), Willa Cather, Mary Austin, Stephen Crane, Zane Gray, A. B. Guthrie's *The Way West* (1950), Edna Ferber, and Wallace Stegner.

The point is that one need not go, for a sense of the global or border crossing, to writers of the contemporary period whose literary works mix and interrogate the cultural geographies of the U.S. West, Asia, Canada, the Caribbean, Mexico, Brazil, Argentina, or Indian Country. For a sense of the global, one could as easily go to case studies in American exceptionalism overlaid onto settler colonial travel, like the one offered in *The Way West*, or like Stegner's claim for the West as a geography of hope, the landscape against which national character was forged.[2] Suggesting this is not to argue that classics carry out unambivalently their settler/border dwellings. Stegner's *Wolf Willow* (1962) is a journey of memory, history, fiction, and memoir, which chronicles a boyhood spent, in part, on the contested plains of the Saskatchewan/Montana region. To know where he is from as a way to know who he is (Stegner famously tells readers), he gathers a contentious history of the parties who battle over this place and, in doing so, evidences thorny questions about settler occupation as well as about nationalisms divided along American/Canadian lines. Edna Ferber's *Giant* (1952) situates a white woman's ethical reckonings with conquest/settlement unevenly against her constant fights against what she calls the "purdah" of the gender order on the legendary (fictionalized) King Ranch. In the second half of this essay I will analyze this novel in depth. Of course, Native American writings come in and out as classic texts of the literary West. The title and closing scenes of D'Arcy McNickle's *The Surrounded* (1936) alert readers to the mutual implication of Indigenous and western American globalities. Told via the embattled return of a half-Salish protagonist to the Flathead Nation in northwestern Montana, *The Surrounded* is a text, like *Wolf Willow,* concerned with cultural memory, history, and knowing place in order to know self. The problem of *The Surrounded* is not establishing a historical past, as it is for *Wolf Willow,* but surviving settler incursion upon extant knowledge, writing a history of the now, imagining a future.

What we are talking about then in discussions of the transnational turn are *not* the contests over borders or colonial/national zones of the global, which figure everywhere in U.S. West literary history and must be understood as its conditions of possibility. What we are talking about is the *politics* of movements across borders and in critical theory. The literary West is not itself "parochial" in the sense of being inward-gazing and obtuse to history (even if criticism can be parochial, or anyway, subject to the conditions of the moment in which it is conceived). It is a literature obsessed by borders and power and the violence of colonial desire.[3] It is a global literature in the sense that it is structured and attains cultural meaning by global forces: settler colonialism, colonial patriarchies that impose gender structures everywhere they go, all set into motion and given geosocial political logic by the concept of "Americanity." Anibal Quijano and Immanuel Wallerstein establish Americanity as the constitutive act of capitalist modernity, arguing that in the Américas, in the long sixteenth century, we witness the birthing of the capitalist world economy, the first modern world system.[4] Quijano, as well as Walter Mignolo, develop the term "coloniality of power" to name and grapple with the entangled systems of hierarchical social ordering, knowledge, and culture, installed, and persisting, in New World contexts.[5] The shorthand implication for theorizing transnational issues of place and politics: The concept of Americanity links "western American" to the (global) coloniality of power.

Unexceptional Wests and Critical Regionalism

The prominence of transnational critique in U.S. West Studies suggests its importance for conceptualizing "global Wests." Transnationalism as a field imaginary of American and western American literary study has seen itself as, and hoped to instigate, a critical knowledge project able to intervene upon American cultural imperialism.[6] Transnational thought has opened interpretation of the literary archive onto new global networks of texts, writers, literary trends, marketplaces, communities, in and beyond the English-speaking world. It has opened critics to histories of peoples and their movements, to travel and its problems, to migrating cultures and languages, to all manner of flora and fauna on the move, mixing together in contact zones occupied by civilizations on the ground. Transnationalism as the reigning model of Americanist literary analysis is, in this light, not so much about the fact of moving across space, but about an interpretive critical location, a politics concerning movement.

Readers may notice a slippage happening here already between "transnationalism" and "the global." Invoking one term seems to invoke another, and terms such as "hemispheric" and "postnational" are waiting in the wings. They should not be understood, however, as synonymous. All of them conceptualize different globalities and critical locations. Since little has been written on "global Wests" to date, some of the query at present must be a kind of sorting: What does it mean? Is it a descriptive term, a concept, a method? How does it map or is it mapped by this body of works called western American literature? What does it *do* or allow that would constitute its critical perspective(s)? What might a global Wests theorization learn from critiques of the transnational turn emerging more strongly in American Studies all the time?

"Global Wests" as a concept arises from different parts of the world and disciplinary locations and needs to be cobbled together from efforts in "comparative global Wests," "global pop Wests," and various international conferences on transatlantic or transnational or Latin American/U.S. Wests. To be sure, scholars of western American literature have addressed, implicitly, a global West, offering glimpses into its theorization.[7] But explicit theorizations are rare. In the context of his work on the U.S. West as a system of transnational westness, Campbell posits a "global West" as a "new architecture of area studies."[8] Building on Appadurai's sense of geography as "processual" rather than a discrete or static category, Campbell highlights place as "extroverted"; in effect, the outside is a privileged critical architecture that moves globalist theoretical innovation forward. Susan

Kollin also offers explicit engagement in her essay "The Global West: Temporality, Spatial Politics, and Literary Production."⁹ Evidencing her own postnational inclinations, Kollin synthesizes critical remappings of western spaces created by scholars and writers of the borderlands and Asian America and balances them against spatialities of Indigenous surviv-ance. Among her contributions is reading the global through a regional reassessment that allows critics to perceive global West circuits. If Kollin consolidates thinking about regional critique, the Stanford "Comparative Wests" collaborative historical research project thinks global Wests via the intersections of shared settler colonial spaces across the U.S. West, west-ern Canada, western Australia, western South America, and the Pacific Islands.¹⁰ What this substantive project offers to an emerging theoriza-tion of global Wests is its emphasis on the tensions among spaces settled, incorporated, and saturated by nationalist exceptionalisms, but never fully controlled by the nation-state. Border zones of intense contradiction such as these reveal the meeting up places between a global West and a global South and provide explanatory power for the extreme properties of com-bustion found in texts such as Cormac McCarthy's *Blood Meridian* (1985).

A few symposia also have made stabs at global West thinking. Loosely affiliated with the Stanford Comparative Wests project, "Global Pop Wests" was held in 2014 in Perth, Western Australia. Designed around the triangulation of the western United States, western Australia, and western China (where a vital "western-themed" literature exists), it argued gener-ally, with some dissent, in favor of pop Wests as migrating locations, not static hemispheric or conceptual structures.¹¹ In 2014, the University of Basque Country held its Third International Conference on the Literary West, posing the question, A Territory without Borders? Generally, the answer seemed affirmative, again, with dissent.¹² In 2011, at Rice University, I hosted "The American West/ Américas Seminar" as a project of the Américas Research Center and its Local/Global West Research Unit. Drawing together scholars of U.S. West, Chicano/a, Native American, and Latin American Studies, we asked what we could learn from each other about spatial concepts like "U.S. West," "the Global South," and "Latin America." Mindful of calls upon American Studies scholars to take care about a "hemispheric gaze," what would support comparativism or collaboration?¹³ Could the developing body of thought around the con-cept of critical regionalism serve to frame these concerns? Mignolo shows coloniality as the "darker side" of Western modernity; modernity and coloniality must be understood as a hinged power matrix that always reas-serts Europe as the world's center. "Delinking" from Eurocentric magnetic pull is a key step toward decolonial futures.[14] One take-away direction for critics of the U.S. West was to put theories of critical regionalism explicitly in conversation with notions of the coloniality of power and take seriously the need to decolonize knowledge production.

Transnational analyses have sometimes moved in the direction of decolonized knowledge, but recent critiques point to limits. In stock-taking moves on behalf of a field he helped to define, John Carlos Rowe delivered a series of lectures in 2014 entitled "The End of Transnationalism," wondering whether transnational models have exhausted their utility. Can they respond sufficiently to the " 'global' and 'planetary' scope of the U.S. state," he asks; are there "models of human mobility and affiliation" that are not suited to transnational interpretive domains?[15] Responding to charges by Robyn Weigman of the implication of transnational models in imperial knowledge production, Rowe questions whether American Studies intellectuals overreached on claims for a critical cultural politics.[16] In a related work of American Studies self-interrogation by Russ Castronovo and Susan Gillman, *States of Emergency,* the postcolonial critic Srinivas Aravamudan asks, Why hasn't a critical internationalism, rather than transnationalism, ascended to the fore of American Studies as the field's central problematic? Is the transnational turn another version of U.S. unilateralism in the world, a kind of new, neoliberal gaze?[17]

Such cautions seem especially relevant to attempts at thinking global Wests. I have written elsewhere about the double reference of West as a zone of national exceptionalism as well as West as the center of colonial powers, the dividing line between civilization and the rest of world, suggesting the degree to which the keyword "West" always signals dominant national and global genealogies.[18] The criticality of global Wests as an emerging problematic cannot thus be taken for granted. Recent work by Alex Young on the shared "smoothening" spatial logics of both settler and Deleuzian rhizomatic spreading also points to the problem of the critical in global Wests.[19] In spite of interventionist transnational theorizing, the dominant world meanings and popularized discourse of "global Wests" remain deeply uncritical. What then are we to do?

Part of the answer lies in exploring what is gained by attending more carefully to the word "global" preceding the word "wests." From a global perspective, what does western American literature look like? What are its contours, political effects, poetics? If we begin from the premise of settler colonialism and the lessons offered by the coloniality of power, which highlight the urgencies and legacies of First Nations, and (as I will address shortly) attend to decolonial feminisms, then several broad statements can be made about western American literature. One, it is part and parcel of other literatures, other settler colonial enterprises in the world. Its Euro-American exceptionalism (and Manifest Destiny) is less exceptional when compared to the rise of other literary nationalisms in Europe and its colonies. The frontiers figured in western American literature have their counterparts wherever modernity and coloniality structure space and social life; that means the gamut of socioeconomic and ecological relations bear resemblance to one another precisely because, as Quijano and Wallerstein teach us, modernity/coloniality is the first world system. To perceive the unexceptionalism of western American literature is crucial to practicing decolonial strategies and addressing the problem of the critical in global Wests.

In this context I would argue in favor of critical regionalism as a way to strategize about decolonial practice and develop methods that enact Mignolo's sense of "local" histories positioned to expose global designs.[20] Critical regionalism is a way of diagnosing the new configurations of meaning, time, and space occasioned by global restructuring and new technologies – it is a political/cultural imagination and a mode of embodiment whose keywords and ethical domains are under construction. It thinks toward issues of place, bodies in place, and knowledges derived via textuality and discourse, as well as from place as a critical location, an orientation, and material structure. Given the "'new geographies of power' associated with globalization," critical regionalism enacts what Stephen Tatum sees as the need for "new interpretive strategies for being in a world where various, disjunctive flows increasingly overdetermine and shape lives and the imagination of those living in specific places."[21]

The question for a big framing device such as "global Wests" is how to get in and out of it. Critical regionalism crosses borders and moves transnationally, and Campbell's work with the term demonstrates western American culture produced through its outsides, making the weight of national/colonial spatial grids collapse upon their own folds and multiplicities. Routing westness over transnational cultural circuits through the conceptual apparatus of the Deleuzian rhizome, emergent border discourses of critical regions frustrate retreats from zones of global outsides.[22] But if transnationalism has taught us how global Wests overrun boundaries, critics grapple still with the fact of immobilities, uneven development, frictions. Who moves when, under what conditions, which notions of place travel, which theories and texts and bodies travel? What would it mean to theorize the idea that some sites, for instance, tribal lands in the United States and women's bodies all over the world, are at pains to establish themselves as bounded, boundaried?[23] Crossing those boundaries is not by definition a liberation act or occasion for celebration; it may inflict harm, dispossess competing sovereignties. Critical regionalism is poised to speak to these problems not so much as a theory of transnational travel but as a problematic of critical global study attuned to big picture analyses that contend also with the deep local. A critical regionalism in this guise assumes global Wests are observable through strategic locals.

Recent resituatings of critical regionalism point critics away from its origins in Kenneth Frampton's architectural theory and toward it as a geopolitical concept. In *Other Asias* (2007) and *Who Sings the Nation-State?* (2011), Gayatri Spivak focuses on the economic restructuring of Asia to formulate critical regionalism as a problematic able to counter the "easy postnationalism" of globalization, rewrite "postcoloniality into globality," and foster, through citizen engagement, broad democratic renewal.[24] Critical regionalism names political imaginations that go "under and over" nationalisms while retaining "the abstract structure of something like a state," which serves the role of "an ally" for redistribution of resources.[25] As does Spivak, the border theorist and anthropologist/critic José Limón embraces critical regionalism as a critique of what he sees, in global literary studies, as an overestimation of postnationalism and underestimation of contemporary state power.[26] Limón's commitments to deep local place as well as to the global as it operates in border poetics moves him to caution critics not to sacrifice the specificity of U.S./Mexico border locations in quests to read the global through them. Christina van Houten understands critical regionalism as a feminist cultural movement that critiques postmodern aestheticism and attends to "the persistence of geographical history in contemporary [feminist] thought."[27] Tracing genealogies of spatial thinking in feminist theory, van Houten links materialist feminism, antiracist activism, and ecological Marxism to offer feminist critical regionalism as "an alternative map to neoliberal capitalism, one in which the local concerns of feminist politics are read in relation to global power relations."[28]

Writing broadly about materialist feminism, Mary Ellen Campbell and A. L. McCready note a new significance to place as a vector of power and site of feminist theory and politics. Not only does place usefully situate scholarship and those producing it in global/local tensions, but it forces analysis of the situatedness of production and social reproduction, which always rest upon historical relations to land and place.[29] An increasing consciousness about settler colonialism as well as impacts on environment of capitalist exploitation clarifies further the urgency of matters of land

and place. Campbell and McCready issue a general call on transnational, antiracist materialist feminisms to reterritorialize and decolonize these arenas of social relation and of knowledge.

That critical regionalism and its awareness of place as a broker of power should find common cause with settler colonial theory and materialist feminism is no accident. Patrick Wolfe famously argues that settler spatial operations are not initial historical "events" or one-time cultural contacts, but structures that adapt.[30] Global struggles over settler geographies are not therefore historically "done" or somehow finished but continuing into the present. Perhaps nowhere do we see this ongoing struggle more clearly than in the social life of subaltern women. The philosopher María Lugones coins the term "colonial/modern gender system" to theorize a structure through which European colonialism introduced "many genders and gender itself as a colonial concept and mode of organization of relations of production, property relations, of cosmologies and ways of knowing."[31] A feminist theory of the coloniality of power will historicize gender as a colonial/modern category in order to show that critiques of patriarchy must contend simultaneously with "mechanisms by which heterosexuality, capitalism, and racial classification" produce colonial/modern gendered subjects.[32] In other words, decolonial feminisms of global Wests will be tuned to the ways that the colonial/modern gender system renews itself in the present.

Revisiting *Giant*: Coloniality and the Limits of Civil Rights Agendas

How might scholars apply a critical regional strategy to a global Wests analysis of western American literature? I pursue this question through Edna Ferber's very rich novel *Giant* (1952).[33] This is a text that, on its own terms, productively figures many global Wests problems raised previously as well one through which other texts move. Some of them move directly – of course the cinematic version of *Giant* (1956) directed by George Stevens and featuring Elizabeth Taylor, Rock Hudson, James Dean, and Mercedes McCambridge, but also *Scene from the Movie Giant* (1995), a collection of poems by Tino Villanueva, who remembers himself as a Mexican American boy watching the film, frozen with fear, in a dark South Texas movie theater. The film reveals to him his own racial wounding, and that before seeing it, he had lived largely unaware. Lots of texts move indirectly and suggest the larger Spanish/Native borderlands literary trajectory in which *Giant* is entangled – from Cabeza de

Vaca's *La Relación* (1528), through Yellow Bird's *Joaquin Murieta* (1854), to González's *Caballero* (written 1930s, published 1996), Paredes's *With His Pistol in His Hand* (1958), and including more recently, McCarthy's Border Trilogy, the work of Sandra Cisneros, Gayl Jones's *Mosquito* (1999), Ruben Martinez's *Crossing Over* (2001), and Ire'ne Lara Silva's *Flesh to Bone* (2014). The list could be extended.

As a text very interested in issues of Mexican dispossession and labor exploitation, *Giant* also provides a site through which to consider the lessons of settler colonial thought for critical race theory. Patrick Wolfe's work is again helpful in this regard. Wolfe is not interested in Wests or global Wests per se, but in comparative racial regimes and the implications, for critical race theory, of settler society demands for both labor and land. The installation of settler racial regimes enslaves, on the one hand, some people as forced laborers, maintaining their inferior status through social segregation and exclusion, while, on the other hand, it expropriates land and conducts genocidal warfare against Indigenous people and subsumes any who survive via assimilation.[34] Clarifying the complex legacies of settler racial regimes for contemporary thinking about race and decolonial knowledge is a major contribution of settler colonial thought to a global Wests problematic. Increasingly, Indigenous political strategies and theories of refusal and sovereignty disentangle themselves from U.S. minority claims for recognition, inclusion, citizenship.[35] That is, the legacies of U.S. civil rights movements, which understood "minorities" to have some similar relation to the state and notions of inclusion, is undergoing radical revision. A text like *Giant* helps us to see what is at stake.

Giant opens and closes with a statement that hangs over all of its long middle. The protagonist, Leslie Benedict, says to her husband, Jordan, the patriarch of the fictionalized King Ranch: "You see. It's caught up with you. It's caught up with us. It always does."[36] It is early in the book. There has been a fight; their adult son has instigated and lost it; and the father is about to step in. Leslie whispers these words of conscience to her husband and the narrator shades them by telling the reader she speaks as though "continuing a conversation." In the epic tale that follows, readers enter and exit this conversation, implicating us too in its ethical dilemmas. What is the "it" in "It's caught up with you?" Who is the "us?"

In a global Wests context, the "it" is related to the everyday coloniality of power that capital T "Texas" represents to Leslie. Importantly, Ferber constructs Leslie as a greenhorn from Virginia, a New Woman heroine and protofeminist *Virginian*. If she is new to the West, she is still a southerner, hardly an innocent in terms of racial hauntings and histories. It is this history traveling with her from South to the West that makes her so productive as an outsider witness.[37] As she learns, so do readers. The first time we see Jordan Benedict we learn, through Leslie, that he is "ruler of an empire."[38] Jordan talks of Texas not as a man talks about his state but "as if it were a different country . . . that just happens to be in the middle of the United States."[39] Some of the big ranchers, Leslie tells her sister, call their spreads "my country," and, like kings, they name them after the family. For them Texas is "the most American country in the United States."[40] As a geopolitical entity, Texas falls somewhere between a state, country, kingdom, and empire and is saturated with multiple competing exceptionalist claims. Leslie is swept off her feet by the grandeur of these tales in history books, by their supposed novelty. "It's so fascinating. It's another world, it sounds so big and new and different. I love it. The cactus and the cowboys and the Alamo and the sky and the horses and the Mexicans and the freedom. It's really America, isn't it. I'm – I'm in love with it."[41] Of course she also means she is in love with *him*, Jordan Benedict.

This quasi-declaration of love is at powerful odds with a speech Leslie has delivered barely a moment earlier, and the pull between these political poles stages the tale's ethical tensions. "We really stole Texas, didn't we? I mean. Away from Mexico."[42] For saying this, Jordan Benedict reflects, a man might be killed in Texas. He barely trusts himself to respond, and asks whether Leslie might be joking. "I'm not joking, Mr. Benedict," she tells him. "It's right there in the history books. This Mr. Austin moved down there with two or three hundred families from the East. . . . The Mexicans were polite and said they could settle and homestead if they wanted to, under the rule of Mexico. And the next thing you know they're claiming they want to free themselves from Mexico and they fight and take it."[43] There is a kind of society girl's naiveté in the terms and tone through which this scolding of Jordan Benedict is conceived – protesting the manners of settlers who fail to respect hospitable hosts. But Leslie also perceptively communicates to the reader a sense of the relative legitimacy of land claims. "The Spanish explorers, and the French, that was different," she asserts; "there was nobody around and they were tramping and riding across the hot desert in all those iron clothes. . . . Still they didn't actually grab the land away from anyone. . . . Of course there were the Indians, but perhaps they didn't count."[44] If Leslie's declaration is half-cheeky, it identifies nonetheless the Mexican government as itself a settler colonial enterprise, made legitimate only through the displacement of Indigenous peoples whose claims do not count.

The problem of Native elimination in *Giant* is restaged as a battle between two settler colonial states, the United States and Mexico. Ferber's social realism now goes forward with Leslie as the voice of conscience who prosecutes Anglos' expropriation of Spanish land grant territories and exposes ranchers' exploitation of the undocumented workers in transit across their lands, as well as the workers permanently housed on those lands. Leslie calls to readers' attention the abhorrent camps in which workers live, their paltry wages, the coyote middlemen, the absence of medical or educational resources or political representation. She establishes the degree to which the Texas cowboy is a copy of the Mexican vaquero. She reports the explicit maneuvering of a handful of Texas ranchers who fix votes, redraw districting lines, manipulate tax laws, and, through it all, rule state politics. Their control intensifies as the cattle ranching economies of Texas transition into the global economies of oil extraction and its exponentially greater riches. Her husband is at the helm of the transition.

Over the twenty years that *Giant* spans, Leslie intervenes upon empire with projects that support workers' medical relief, wages, housing, education, and political representation. The fight on behalf of Others requires of her a fight against intense male domination. The text charts a cumulative outrage to be told that politics is "men's stuff," that she is "not well" when she refuses to be silent.[45] This battle is continual. On occasion, the gender order of Texas is likened to "a kind of purdah," meaning gender segregated.[46] Women are sent off to bed when conversations turn serious. She describes herself as veiled, a "Moslem woman in riding clothes," when she is instructed to cover her nose and mouth during a dust storm.[47] As a pregnant woman, she refuses to "huddle in the harem" or stay indoors in "her condition."[48] In a context of critical regional global Wests, Ferber's use of the figure of the Muslim woman to illustrate Texas patriarchal power suggests links between oil rich regions of the world and global capitalist support of patriarchal authority. There is no invocation of the idea that Western world gender norms can rescue Muslim women.

Let me return to the moment of Native erasure and replacement to suggest a number of points made more accessible by a critical regional reading of global Wests.[49] First, the removal of Indigenous people allows or makes possible Ferber's critiques about gender and race that the novel foregrounds. The dispossession of Native America on behalf of a civil rights agenda demonstrates the limits or the hold of colonial thinking exerted both on Ferber and on *Giant,* and the deep collusion between one settler colonial form (here Mexico) and another (Texas/

United States).⁵⁰ To advance this case of Mexican Americans alone is to reinforce indirectly the logic of settler colonialities. The emphasis on global designs and deep local histories that Mignolo counsels can alert critical regional projects to inquire after what is still missing in this local: Texas slavery is missing, for instance, and as Chicano critics have pointed out, so too is the organizing history of Mexican Americans on their own behalf through forums such as LULAC (League of United Latin American Citizens).

The final scene of crisis of the book allows us to raise again the ethical question of "it" catching up with "us." Leslie enters a roadside diner to placate her hungry mixed-race grandson, Polo. With them are Juana, the Mexican American mother of Polo, who is Leslie's daughter-in-law, and Leslie's own daughter, Luz. The proprietor points to a sign that says "No Mexicans Served" and tells them to leave. In the film *Giant* this scene is reordered and stripped of its feminist content. In the novel, however, it is the scene of Leslie's reckoning with self and with what it means to be a political ally to Mexicans, not their savior or spokesperson, but one who is targeted with racism by association and does not employ race or class privilege to escape, because Leslie herself now is mistaken for a "cholo."

The proprietor tells her, as one would tell a dog, "Git! You and your greasers."⁵¹ Leslie's body suddenly is subject to the white gaze, the proprietor saying to his waitress, "that old one [Leslie] was [a Mexican], black hair and sallow; you can't fool me."⁵² Instead of invoking her husband's name and power, Leslie tells her outraged blonde daughter, "We know this has been going on for years and years. It's always happened to other people. Now it's happened to us."⁵³ The diner scene sets up the closing scene of this novel, staged in the bedroom of Jordan and Leslie. We see Jordan, the great patriarch, revealing, "Things are getting away from me. Kind of slipping from under me, like a loose saddle. I swear to God I sometimes feel like a failure. Bick Benedict a failure."⁵⁴ This pondering about the possibility of a Bick Benedict, the ruler of an empire, becoming a failure, is not reassured at novel's close. Leslie instead spreads the damning net wider, saying the legacy of Texas bigotry itself guarantees failure. She locates "real success" on some future threshold where Mexicans and Americans intermix.⁵⁵

While keeping in mind the limits of the civil rights agenda of this text, preconditioned as it is on Indigenous removal, Ferber's analysis of Texas social life and her reflections on race and gender are nothing short of extraordinary in 1952.⁵⁶ No wonder Texas readers of the time were so outraged, to the point of threatening Ferber's life, reminding the public she was "a Jew" and should be "burned at the stake," or "lynched."[57] No wonder, perhaps, that the film director, George Stevens, changed that pivotal scene for the movie *Giant,* so that it is Bick Benedict battling it out in the diner with the proprietor, Sarge, the "Yellow Rose of Texas" playing as musical support. The film's ending too is tamed, as Leslie gushes over Bick's heroic fight and rescues his sense of failure. We see more clearly now that Stevens excised the more radical elements of the narrative, its decolonial feminist gestures, opting instead to reinscribe this moment of conflict and conscience as a contest between different forms of class-inflected patriarchy. Stevens also distances the film from the willingness of the novel to represent Leslie's whiteness as itself a fluid and malleable category. Who could have imagined the idea of Elizabeth Taylor mistaken for an "old sallow Mexican"? If the novel was nearly universally hated in Texas, the movie version of it was extremely popular.[58] Indeed it is the movie version of the tale that has traveled far and wide, evacuated of its sharpest feminist content and its most serious ethical and racial reckonings. This fact returns us to the earlier discussion of the problem of the critical in global Wests and of which texts travel, to remind critics how slippery global Wests is as a critical frame.

What conclusions follow? One is that critics attending to global Wests will need to take care with moments in which the criticality of a global Wests problematic hangs in the balance. Decolonial gestures are fragile, subject to displacement, marginalization. Critical regional emphases can aid us in keeping them in sight. In the novel's final chapters, immediately preceding the diner scene, a discussion about space and place between Leslie and her daughter, Luz, rings with local history/global designs thinking. Leslie and Luz are driving to another ranch a couple of hours away from home and remarking upon what they see through the car window. They are leaving behind a cast of incredible characters gathering at "the Big House" – the lodging space for guests of the Benedict ranch. These guests are arriving in advance of a party to be hosted in a few days by the new oil king, Jett Rink. Luz asks her mother who the visitors are. Her mother's response gives a sense of scale to the Benedict ranch as a circuit of global Wests. "Uh, let's see," Leslie begins, "a king and queen ... and a swarm of other people.... There's a prize fighter and a Russian dancer and a South American Ambassador. And a movie queen who has bought a ranch in California and wants to stock it [with cattle from the Benedict ranch]."[59]

They leave their own ranch, continue driving, and this journey occasions another, a journey of memories of this road over the twenty or so years they have driven it. A good-natured intergenerational quarrel takes place about Leslie's astonishment at the rapidity of change. Her daughter complains, "If you weren't so stubborn about letting me take you up in the little plane … you'd see the world."[60] Leslie's response suggests an alternative way of seeing. "You and [your brother] Jordy don't really see the world. You've learned your geography from planes. You think the world is little blocks and squares with bugs wriggling over them."[61] Leslie would have Luz notice instead what is in front of her – as Leslie will do herself shortly in her confrontation with Sarge and his control of the racial geography of the diner. "I don't think you ever really see anything from the angle of the ground. What with horses and planes and cars you never set foot on earth."[62] Ferber's critical regionalism falls within these spatial scales – among the global view afforded by planes, the local view of the person on foot, and the local-intermediate sense of travel by car or horse. But even while Ferber gives us, for the whole of the novel, a historical reach that foregrounds global designs, it is on the terrain of the local that she makes her interventions – without the specificity of that local site, there is not a critical global; the critical local is where bodies are in place, where they fight.

Notes

1 Neil Campbell, *The Rhizomatic West: Representing the American West in a Transnational, Global, Media Age* (Lincoln: University of Nebraska Press, 2008), 41.

2 Wallace Stegner, "Coda: The Wilderness Letter," in *The Sound of Mountain Water* (New York: Doubleday, 1969), 145–56.

3 Many scholars make related points. For discussion of colonial desire and its counternarratives, see Stephen Tatum, "Topographies of Transition in Western American Literature," *Western American Literature* 32, no. 4 (Winter 1998): 310–52. On the contest over nineteenth-century borders by contending colonial powers, see Stephanie LeMenager, *Manifest and Other Destinies: Territorial Fictions of the Nineteenth-Century United States* (Lincoln: University of Nebraska Press, 2008). On issues of crossings and "microfrontiers" of western American literature, and its location in global literatures of colonization and the age of imperialism, see Alex Hunt, "Postcolonial West," in *A Companion to the Literature and Culture of the American West*, ed. Nicolas S. Witschi (Chichester, UK: Wiley-Blackwell, 2011), 229–43, 231.

4 Anibal Quijano and Immanuel Wallerstein, "Americanity as a Concept, or the Américas in the Modern World-System," *International Social Science Journal* 29 (1992): 549–57.

5 Anibal Quijano, "Coloniality of Power, Eurocentrism, and Latin America," *Nepantla: Views from the South* 1, no. 3 (2000): 533–80; and Walter Mignolo,

"The Geopolitics of Knowledge and the Colonial Difference," *South Atlantic Quarterly* 101, no. 1 (Winter 2002): 57–96. For excellent explications of the coloniality of power in relation to literatures of Greater Mexico, see José David Saldívar, *Trans-Americanity: Subaltern Modernities, Global Coloniality, and the Cultures of Greater Mexico* (Durham, NC: Duke University Press, 2012).

6 The term "field imaginary" refers to the political unconscious of disciplines and is drawn from Donald E. Pease, "New Americanists: Revisionist Interpretations into the Canon," *Boundary 2* 17, no. 1 (spring 1990) 1–37.

7 See note 3 as well as Zeese Papanikolas, "Cowboys and Gauchos," in *Reading The Virginian in the New West*, ed. Melody Graulich and Stephen Tatum (Lincoln: University of Nebraska Press, 2003), 175–97. My work with the local/global subculture of surfing also thinks through global Wests; see Krista Comer, *Surfer Girls in the New World Order* (Durham, NC: Duke University Press, 2010). Also see Claudia Sadowski-Smith, *Border Fictions: Globalization, Empire, and the Writing at the Boundaries of the United States* (Charlottesville: University of Virginia Press, 2008); and Tom Lynch, "'Nothing but Land': Women's Narratives, Gardens, and the Settler-Colonial Imaginary in the US West and Australian Outback," *Western American Literature* 48, no. 4 (Winter 2014): 375–99.

8 Campbell, *Rhizomatic West*, 37.

9 Susan Kollin, "The Global West: Temporality, Spatial Politics, and Literary Production," in *A Companion to the Literature and Culture of the American West*, ed. Nicolas S. Witschi (Chichester, UK: Wiley-Blackwell, 2011), 514–27. Also see Kollin's *Captivating Westerns: The Middle East in the American West* (Lincoln: Nebraska, 2015).

10 For a description of the project, see http://comparativewests.stanford.edu and the special issue on "Comparative Wests" of the journal *Occasion*, http://arcade.stanford.edu/occasion_issue/volume-5 (accessed January 15, 2015).

11 For a statement of purpose and abstracts of presenters, including my own "Critical Regionalism, Global Wests, and Thinking Otherwise," http://popwest.org/ (accessed January 2, 2015).

12 For statement of purpose, see http://rewestresearchinggroup.blogspot.com/ (accessed December 17, 2014).

13 For an excellent overview, including trenchant challenges to Hemispheric Studies, see Ralph Bauer, "Hemispheric Studies," *PMLA* 124, no. 1 (2009): 234–50.

14 Walter D. Mignolo, *The Darker Side of Western Modernity: Global Futures, Decolonial Options* (Durham, NC: Duke University Press, 2011).

15 For recent developments in transnational thought, see the discussion at http://www.theasa.net/project_eas_online/page/project_eas_online_eas_featured_article (accessed December 27, 2014).

16 See Robyn Weigman, *Object Lessons* (Durham, NC: Duke University Press, 2012). Weigman analyzes the political hopes underwriting identity fields and their objects of study (her examples are nation in American Studies, women

in Women's Studies, and raced subjects in Ethnic Studies). Weigman finds that turns to the transnational, though spurred by anti-imperial social justice efforts, have masked U.S. intellectuals' implications in the imperial reach of transnational projects.

17 Srinivas Aravamudan, "Rogue States and Emergent Disciplines," in *States of Emergency: The Object of American Studies*, ed. Russ Castronovo and Susan Gillman (Chapel Hill: University of North Carolina Press, 2009), 17–35.

18 Krista Comer, "West," in *Keywords for American Cultural Studies*, 2nd ed., ed. Bruce Burgett and Glenn Hendler (New York: New York University Press, 2014), http://hdl.handle.net/2333.1/cfxpnxro (accessed January 5, 2015).

19 Alex Trimble Young, "Settler Sovereignty and the Rhizomatic West, or, The Significance of the Frontier in Postwestern Studies," *Western American Literature* 48, nos. 1 and 2 (spring and summer 2013): 115–40.

20 Walter D. Mignolo, *Local Histories/Global Designs: Coloniality, Subaltern Knowledge, and Border Thinking* (Princeton, NJ: Princeton University Press, 2000).

21 Stephen Tatum, "Spectrality and the Postregional Interface," in *Postwestern Cultures: Literature, Theory, Space*, ed. Susan Kollin (Lincoln: University of Nebraska Press), 3–29.

22 Campbell, *The Rhizomatic West*, 41–74. For extended discussion of *The Rhizomatic West*, see Krista Comer, "Exceptionalisms, Other Wests, Critical Regionalism," *American Literary History* 23, no. 1 (2011): 159–73.

23 Spivak distinguishes "borders" as sites of circulating global power flows from "frontiers" as sites that mark uncrossabilities. In particular, she notes, "the female body ... is a borderline. All bodies, in fact, are borderlines.... In the simplest possible sense, the female body is seen as permeable. It is seen as permeable in perhaps the most basic gesture of violence"; see Spivak, *Readings* (Calcutta: Seagull Books, 2014), 26.

24 Gayatri Spivak, *Other Asias* (Malden, MA: Wiley-Blackwell 2007), 1, 131.

25 Judith Butler with Gayatri Spivak, *Who Sings the Nation State? Language, Politics, Belonging* (London: Seagull Books, 2007): 94.

26 José Limón, "Border Literary Histories, Globalization, and Critical Regionalism," *American Literary History* 20, nos. 1 and 2 (2008): 160–82.

27 Christina Van Houten, "bell hooks, Critical Regionalism, and the Politics of Ecological Returns," *Materialist Feminisms against Neoliberalism*, ed. Mary Ellen Campbell and A. L. McCready, *Politics and Culture* (2014), http://politicsandculture.org/?s=critical+regionalism&searchsubmit (January 3, 2015).

28 Ibid.

29 Mary Ellen Campbell and A. L. McCready, "Introduction," in *Materialist Feminisms against Neoliberalism, Politics and Culture*.

30 Patrick Wolfe, *Settler Colonialism and the Transformation of Anthropology: The Politics and Poetics of an Ethnographic Event* (New York: Cassel, 1999), 163.

31 María Lugones, "Heterosexualism and the Colonial/Modern Gender System," *Hypatia* 22, no. 1 (2007): 186.

32 Ibid., 187.

33 Edna Ferber, *Giant* (New York: Perennial Classics, 2000).

34 Wolfe has written widely on this topic. For an accessible introduction, see "Comparing Colonial and Racial Regimes," podcast of a lecture delivered at the American University in Beirut, https://www.youtube.com/watch?v=xwj5bcLG8ic (accessed January 4, 2015).

35 For instance, see J. Kēhaulani Kauanui, "Colonialism in Equality: Hawaiian Sovereignty and the Question of U.S. Civil Rights," *South Atlantic Quarterly* 107, no. 4 (2008): 635–50.

36 Ferber, *Giant*, 51.

37 Limón puts the mutual histories of the U.S. South and Greater Mexico on maps of cultural theory and draws attention to the critical relation of Leslie to her southern heritage and its implications for her critique of anti-Mexican racism in the film *Giant*. See José Limón, *American Encounters: Greater Mexico, the United States, and the Erotics of Culture* (New York: Beacon Press, 1999), 119–24.

38 Ferber, *Giant*, 18.

39 Ibid., 72.

40 Ibid., 31.

41 Ibid., 75.

42 Ibid., 74.

43 Ibid., 75.

44 Ibid.

45 Ibid., 278.

46 Ibid., 170.

47 Ibid., 178.

48 Ibid., 241.

49 On the logic of elimination and replacement see Patrick Wolfe, "Settler Colonialism and the Elimination of the Native," *Journal of Genocide Research* 8, no. 4 (2006), 387–409.

50 On the notion of the collusion and collision of settler colonialities and effects on Mexican Americans after 1848, see José F. Aranda Jr., "Recovering Modernity in Early Mexican American Literature" in *Latino Studies and Nineteenth-Century America: Archives and Legacies*, ed. Rodrigo Lazo & Jesse Alemán (forthcoming from New York University Press).

51 Ibid., 394.

52 Ibid., 395.

53 Ibid., 396.

54 Ibid., 401.

55 Ibid., 402.

56 In this reading of the film's radicalism, I am in agreement with Limón, who, in *American Encounters*, debates the case of its radicalism with the critic Rafael Perez Torres (119–24). My emphasis departs from theirs in that I read the final film scene against that of the novel, to emphasize questions of gender and feminism, which intersect those of race.

57 For a deep history and critical consideration of Ferber's work, see J. E. Smyth, *Edna Ferber's Hollywood: American Fictions of Gender, Race, and History* (Austin: University of Texas Press, 2010); for a discussion of popular reception, see especially pp. 197, 199, and 200.

58 Ibid, 217–18.

59 Ferber, *Giant*, 388.

60 Ibid., 391.

61 Ibid.

62 Ibid.

PART IV

The Twentieth Century and Beyond
Literary Movements and Critical Perspectives

CHAPTER 14

Early Cinematic Westerns

Christine Bold

What first made westerns cinematic? If we start with the transition from print to film at the turn of the twentieth century, the first answer is "Indians" and the second, shoot-outs.[1] A different starting point would deliver another answer – most obviously, a focus on visual arts would lead to landscape, which is central to many major studies of westerns. How we get from one medium to the other also affects visibility and meaning. Here, I treat live performance as the lynchpin. In parts one and two, I follow Native presences from print to performance to movies, then, in part three, trace the emergence of the man-to-man shoot-out by the same route. These partially reconstructed origin stories revise the look of the genre in several senses.

From a Lakota Gaze to "Indian and Western" Films

On September 24, 1894, Thomas Edison took some Lakota performers from Buffalo Bill's Wild West (currently playing in Ambrose Park, Brooklyn) to his Black Maria studio in West Orange, New Jersey, where they were filmed dancing, drumming, and chanting. This was the first time that Native performers had appeared before a moving camera, in this case the Kinetograph. Among the shorts shot that day is the mesmerizing fifteen-second *Buffalo Dance*.[2] As Last Horse, Parts His Hair, and Hair Coat dance – bobbing, strutting, and weaving rhythmically in front of two drummers – one of them barely takes his eyes off the camera, turning and twisting to keep his gaze unbroken and, at one point, brandishing his stick directly at the lens. There are several ways to read this "provocative visual address."[3] Perhaps the dancer was simply going through the motions taught in Buffalo Bill's Wild West, by which Native performers mimicked "dangerous antagonists" for audience titillation.[4] Perhaps he was reveling in the "harnessing of visibility," the "exhibitionist confrontation" that Tom Gunning reads as the unique power of the first moving pictures, with actors recurrently looking at the camera and soliciting spectators' attention.[5] Perhaps he shook his stick defiantly at the federal forces that had forbidden first the Lakota, later Indigenous peoples more generally, to dance; perhaps he communicated a message comprehensible only to Indigenous spectators. Or perhaps he was "laughing at the camera," in the manner identified by the Seneca film scholar Michelle Raheja of another Indigenous performer, the Inuit actor Allakariallak, in the 1922 film, *Nanook of the North*. Raheja calls this a tactic of "visual sovereignty," confronting "the spectator with the often absurd assumptions that circulate around visual representations of Native Americans, while also flagging their involvement and, to some degree, complicity in these often disempowering structures of cinematic dominance and stereotype."[6] Whatever is coded in this Lakota gaze, it would certainly produce an intense and intimate experience for the Kinetoscope spectator standing with eyes pressed into the viewing lens inches away from the action.

This powerful, precinematic gaze is paradigmatic of the shift in Native presence from popular print object to filmic subject, mediated through commercialized live performance. From the middle of the nineteenth century, the largest print circulation of Indian images occurred in dime-novel wilderness adventures, out of which full-blown westerns developed. Although the formulaic action depends on various "Others" against whom the white hunter (later, cowboy) tests his manhood and wins his girl – comic African Americans, degenerate Mexicans, inscrutable Asians – above all stereotypes of "Indianness" fuel the plotline, the narrative tension, and the cultural affirmation of the American nation. Drawing on a long history of Indigenous caricaturing, they range from the sacrificial "Indian princess" to the "noble savage" to hordes of "howling devils"; the first Beadle's Dime Novel in 1860, *Malaeska, The Indian Wife of the White Hunter*, incorporated all three, all in the perpetual process of vanishing. Bill Cody imported this emphasis wholesale into Buffalo Bill's Wild West from 1883, when he created "the dime-novel western come to life," what Richard Slotkin judges "the most important commercial vehicle for the fabrication and transmission of the Myth of the Frontier" in the late nineteenth century.[7] While the show featured bronco riding cowboys, Mexican vaqueros, a transnational range of horsemen, women sharpshooters, and a few African American war veterans, its popularity depended overwhelmingly on Native performers. Garbed in versions of Plains Indian regalia, performing "war dances" and attacks on stagecoaches and settlers' cabins, these figures came to personify the Wild West on a global scale, with Buffalo Bill's North American and European tours leading to an international proliferation of Wild West shows well into the twentieth century.

There has been considerable scholarly analysis of the fine line walked by Indigenous performers in Wild West shows, as in international expositions and other commercial venues.[8] For some Native performers, Buffalo Bill's Wild West was the only alternative to imprisonment or to starvation conditions on reservations; for others, the rigors of international touring turned out to be a death sentence. On the one hand was the humiliation of "playing Indian."[9] On the other hand, on these transnational circuits, Native peoples devised forms of trans-Indigenous community and strategies for sustaining traditional ways within commercial conventions – what the Anishinaabe theorist Gerald Vizenor terms "survivance."[10] Particularly persuasive arguments have been made about dance as a site for survivance in the face of governmental and commercial regimes, as federal antidance prohibitions in the United States and Canada bore down on reservations at the same moment as the opportunity to dance in Buffalo Bill's Wild West arose. While the commercial staging of Indigenous dance, under the control of white entrepreneurs, was construed as containment, Indigenous performers embedded ceremony and celebration within commercial forms and used dance as a tool to resist and shape governmental policy. On- and off-stage, on- and off-reservation, according to Jacqueline Shea Murphy, they created "spaces in which to continue, and choose to experience honor for, their way of life."[11] John Troutman limns these struggles for cultural survival as "battles over power, executed through dance" – including, presumably, through the one filmed by Edison as *Buffalo Dance*.[12]

This finely balanced power dynamic – between containment and agency – was the legacy inherited by the silent film industry and continued in the training of precinematic and cinematic technologies on Native performers. As film moved from Kinetoscope parlors to vaudeville houses to nickelodeons to movie palaces, the dominant fascination with Indianness thrived. The "salvage ethnography" of actualités and the narrative plots of feature-length movies alike continued to draw on precinematic Indian stereotypes, but they also depended on Native talent. The director Thomas Ince, for example, made a deal with the Miller Brothers' 101 Ranch Real Wild West Show to supply large numbers of Native performers for the New York Motion Picture Company's Bison 101 films. When French and Italian companies threatened to win the U.S. film market, the western's link to Indigeneity became key to "Americanizing" the movie industry: Scott Simmon argues that "the figure of the Indian, even

more than the landscape, seems to have provided the initial terms for this
international industrial dispute."[13] "Indian and western" and "Indian and
cowboy" pictures, as they were known, not only retook the American market; they became major cultural exports to Europe. The Dakota historian
Philip Deloria says, "a surprising number of Indian people carved out lives
around the practice of representation, making the shift from Wild West
to film, from nineteenth century to twentieth, from South Dakota and
Oklahoma to Hollywood and New York"; he estimates that several hundred "Hollywood Indians" made a living.[14] The Essanay movie company's Indian-head trademark demonstrates the strong association between
Native peoples and early film.

Sometimes Indigenous filmmakers converted this popular fascination
with Indianness into cinematic control. From about 1909, for example, the
Ho-Chunk actor Lillian St. Cyr, stage name Princess Red Wing, and her
husband, James Young Deer (the Nanticoke actor, director, and producer
who came to identify as Ho-Chunk), exerted considerable influence. In
the international movie trade war, they were hired away from NYMPC
by the French company Pathé to run its West Coast branch.[15] Young Deer
produced and directed more than sixty Indian and western films, Red
Wing became "North America's first female silent movie star,"[16] and for
several years their work went energetically against the stereotypical grain.
They broke the mold on stereotypes of sacrificial Indian princess, "savage"
warrior, and vanishing race. Their films challenge myths of miscegenation, assimilation, racism, and "the Western-genre focus on Indian death
by emphasizing Native and mixed-race family ties."[17] Although, around
1913, this power couple began to lose their revisionist influence, other
Native figures continued to make critical contributions as actors, screen-
writers, directors, and directors' advisers. One all-Native film, *Daughter of
the Dawn*, was produced in 1920, and another, *The Silent Enemy*, in 1930;
James Cruze, most famous for directing the epic blockbuster *The Covered
Wagon* (1923), identified as Ute; Edwin Carewe, Chickasaw, directed over
fifty titles including *Ramona* (1928); his brothers, Finis and Wallace Fox,
were western screenwriter and director, respectively; and so on.[18] From
1911, Native spokespeople resisted the practice of allotting star Indian roles
to non-Native actors with public protests and, from 1926, Indigenous
labor organizations.[19]

With the rise of sound and the consolidation of the Hollywood studio system, whiteness served increasingly "as the color of versatility."[20]
While the representation of Indians – as variously savage, sexualized, vic-
timized, and sacrificial – remained a central plank of the genre, Native

performers were increasingly relegated to the uncredited margins, and trade journals began referring to "westerns" *tout court*.[21] Nevertheless, Indigenous-centered film scholarship insists on an unbroken continuum between the earliest films and now. Joanna Hearne explores how westerns emerged in dialogue with Native filmmaking into the sound era and beyond. Raheja elaborates her compelling concept of visual sovereignty to show the deep reciprocity across generation, tribe, and Nation by which early filmic efforts at "Native-centered articulations of self-representation and autonomy" initiate and are completed by contemporary Indigenous filmmaking.[22] One example of this dynamic is the highly acclaimed *Smoke Signals* (1998), directed by Chris Eyre (Cheyenne/Arapaho) and written by Sherman Alexie (Spokane/Coeur d'Alene), which continues "to find purpose in western tropes," in Susan Bernardin's nice phrasing, by "repurposing them."[23] Similarly, the Native band National Braid recoded Victor Schertzinger's silent film *Redskin* (1929) with their own musical accompaniment in 2002 and 2003. This work and these arguments, to speak somewhat metaphorically, insist that the Lakota dancer's gaze from 1894 has been caught and returned in recurrent cycles of Indigenous cinematic creativity.

Seeing Mohawk in *The Great Train Robbery*

Almost a decade later, another confrontational gaze, in another Edison production, is more often taken to herald the beginning of cinematic westerns. It occurs at the opening or closing – depending on the exhibitor's preference – of Edwin S. Porter's *The Great Train Robbery* (1903), when the vaudevillian Justus D. Barnes points the gaping hole of his revolver straight at the spectator and shoots. This eleven-minute film – whose plot follows a train robbery, violent attack, pursuit of outlaws, and final gun battle – is often identified as the first narrative western movie, sometimes with the wry observation that this first western includes no Indians. This is true, however, only on the representational level. When reconnected to the stageplay from which it was adapted and the live-performance venues in which it was first commonly exhibited, the film points to how Indigenous performers also structurally supported cinematic Westerns.

In parsing the power of this silent film, Gunning has sought to liberate "the cinema of attraction" from "the hegemony of narrative films." He identifies much of the film's impact in its nonlinear attractions arising from early cinema's "vital relation to vaudeville."[24] Vaudeville (and, overseas, Varieté) was globally popular from the 1880s, and the public projection of moving pictures began in these venues, as one-reel numbers sandwiched within live variety programs. Henry Jenkins has probed how "the vaudeville aesthetic," with its "emphasis upon performance, affective immediacy and atomistic spectacle," informed early filmmaking.[25] In *The Great Train Robbery*, quintessentially vaudevillian components include the melodramatic acting style, the digressive dance scene (a "lively quadrille" in a barroom), the action sequences on horseback (as the daredevil outlaws gallop through the forest), and the famous final address to the audience.[26]

A goodly proportion of those attractions in this cinema of attraction was provided by a Mohawk troupe, the Deer family – a buried presence that Patricia Galperin has recovered, working with the Deer archive. Georgette Deer performs in "three discrete dances" in the barroom sequence, prominent with "her soon to be a trademarked, rakish wide-awake hat" and her "hip-length hair."[27] Her husband, James Deer; his brother, John; and father, Chief Running Deer, also appear, most likely in the scenes in which riders variously shoot, leap, and fall from horseback. One of them may have substituted for "Broncho Billy" Anderson, who was emerging as the western's first male star but kept falling off his horse. These Indigenous presences are doubly disappeared, excluded from the credits, as were most Native performers in movies under non-Native control and dressed in settler and outlaw costumes.

Pulling this archival thread from the iconic first western leads to another wide-ranging, transnational network of live performance, occluded in the scholarly record by the near-automatic association of Indigenous performers in this period with Wild West shows.[28] Indigenous entertainers on vaudeville-Varieté circuits took to early cinema techniques of modernity that lent structural support to its circulation and popularity. The Deer family, at once a long-standing and a very modern entertainment troupe, are representative of this larger presence. By 1903, three generations of Deers had been traveling global circuits, moving flexibly back and forth among entertainment forms (medicine shows, Wild West shows, circus, music hall, melodrama, opera, as well as vaudeville, Varieté, and film), while remaining deeply connected to the Akwesasne and Kahnawake communities crossing the United States–Canada border. In contrast to the Lakota and other Wild West performers who toured as government dependents under impresarios' direct control, the Deers exercised considerable independence. They toured their own Wild West show and Indian Village ("Red Men Welcome") internationally, copyrighted their act as "Champion Indian Trick Riders of the World," and entered into labor relations with contractual agency, announcing in the *New York Clipper*: "We are always prepared to negotiate with responsible managers throughout the country."[29]

Part of their routine made play with racial switching. Georgette, for example, used their sketch *Daniel Boone, Indians of the Past*, to repeat a change in her legal identity. At first, as the English popular actor Georgette Osborne, she played Susie Boone, a white woman. When she married James Deer, whom she met in the show, she surrendered her British citizenship, became Native under the Indian Acts of the United States and Canada, and immediately became the Indian wife on-stage too, brandishing her tomahawk over the white woman she had just played.[30] The family's Wild West costumes combined the expected Plains Indian regalia (made with Mohawk beading skills) with traditional Mohawk pieces.[31] The young daughter, Esther, stage name Princess White Deer, moved among riding as a warrior, soloing in what they labeled a "war dance," and singing the maidenly "Pocahontas" song. This cultural mélange ended with the troupe doing the Cake Walk – the popular African American dance of the period.

Around 1896 several members of the family took this performative dexterity and wit to Scott Marble's stage play, *The Great Train Robbery*. They may have played the seven "Indian" parts – mostly hostiles attacking the dance in which Georgette later participated on film – and contributed to the second act's ever-changing "cast of speciality variety performers."[32] Only Chief Running Deer seems to have been credited, but Indian figures were a staple feature of the play's publicity.[33] Porter's filmic adaptation removed the Indians but retained the Indigenous talent. Via this history of live performance, we can see the Deers vanishing into the cinematic fabric, not just as individual Mohawk performers but as representatives of a larger history of trans-Indigenous, transnational, cosmopolitan modernity. A direct parallel can be made with other members of their nation in the early twentieth century – the Mohawk ironworkers – who built the iron scaffolding of iconic U.S. buildings, the Empire State Building included. Both cases point to formative Indigenous contributions that vanished into the deep structure of industrial culture.

I cannot hazard how many Indigenous presences hide in plain sight in the earliest westerns. A famous example is Will Rogers, who shared billing with the Deers in the South African leg of Texas Jack's Wild West Show, used vaudeville to switch from "the Cherokee Kid" to "King of the

Lasso" to "Cowboy Philosopher," and thereby entered a string of western films.[34] Another is the Abenaki actor Elijah Tahamont, stage name Chief Dark Cloud, who also toured his family on vaudeville and lecture circuits before entering film. So popular was he with D. W. Griffith that the director persuaded him to hide his long hair under a cap to play a white general in *The Birth of a Nation* (1915).[35]

For Indigenous women, whose bodies increasingly bore the brunt of racist representation as Hollywood's grip on westerns tightened,[36] vaudeville could be used for an enabling dialogue with film. Take the young Princess White Deer. When, just before the First World War, she went solo in European Varieté, then big-time New York vaudeville, she devised an act that spoke back to the "war" and "scalp" dances imported into western films from Wild West shows. The typically filmic function of the war dance is characterized by Alison Griffiths with reference to D. W. Griffith's violent *Elderbush Gulch* (1913): It "becomes the ready visual metaphor for Indian barbarity in general and provides audiences with a frame of reference for viewing scenes of native life."[37] Esther Deer's vaudeville-Varieté act offered those audiences a different frame of reference. Choreographing an act in which she "war-danced" like a man and sang like a woman, in increasingly skimpy outfits and parodic Plains Indian regalia, she set female beauty, aesthetic inventiveness, and dance virtuosity against filmic conventions of "Indian barbarity." Another vaudevillian, the Penobscot performer Molly Spotted Elk, served as one of the "off-screen supplements" on which early film relied to cover projection changeovers – for example, in the screening of George B. Seitz's *The Last Frontier* (1926).[38] While, on-screen, Custer's troops charged "upon the savage redskins" (including the uncredited Yakima actor Nipo T. Strongheart), in the auditorium, Molly Spotted Elk, a chorus girl in "The Round Up" and an "Indian Princess" in her dance solo, embodied Indianness differently.[39] Her challenge to stereotypes went on-screen when she participated in the all-Native cast performing precontact skills and modes of survival in *The Silent Enemy*. Native supplementation also became routine beyond the auditorium. In 1924, Northern Arapaho publicized *The Covered Wagon* in London, England.[40] In Brooklyn, a decade later, the Guna and Rappahannock "showbiz" family of Monique Mojica (herself a contemporary theater and film actor, playing, among other roles, Grandma-Builds-the-Fire in *Smoke Signals*) "rode on floats and ballyhooed to drum customers into the movie houses to see the latest John Wayne western."[41] In the 1940s, Saorevo (a Navajo living in Westerwald) drummed up German crowds for William Wellman's *Buffalo Bill: Der weisse Indianer,* in which, again, all the credited Indian parts are played by non-Natives.

Even when elbowed out of the credits and off the screen, Native performers contributed to shaping the formation of American spectatorship. Miriam Hansen has analyzed how, at the turn of the twentieth century, "'proper' relations among viewer, projector, and screen, the peculiar dimensions of cinematic space, were part of a cultural practice that had to be learned." In vaudeville and Varieté houses, live presences on- and off-stage helped audiences to make sense of the filmic experience and their own "collective presence."[42] Alison Fields, in tracing the movements of performers like the Deer family, has made a similar, Indigenous-specific case: "As Native performers traveled circuits of western spectacle and negotiated space within each performance venue, they contributed to turn-of-the-century practices of looking."[43] In this way, too, Native performers were fundamental to the impact of cinematic westerns.

Armando Prats has plumbed the tropes and devices by which westerns continue to absent Indigenous presence, even when Indigenous actors are on-screen.[44] One tactic is to funnel access to Indigenous characters through the consciousness of a white hero: Think Robert Redford in Sydney Pollack's *Jeremiah Johnson* (1972) or Kevin Costner in his *Dances with Wolves* (1990). Another is for the non-Native hero to displace Indigenous actors to a display of their own vanishing, from Richard Dix in George Seitz's *Vanishing American* (1925) to Daniel Day-Lewis in Michael Mann's *Last of the Mohicans* (1992). Even the double-edged opportunity for Indigenous actors to "play Indian" becomes usurped: See the movement from the Mohawk actor Jay Silverheels playing Tonto throughout the 1950s to Johnny Depp taking the role in Gore Verbinski's *The Lone Ranger* (2013). Of course, these racialized overlayings are neither binary nor simple in their power relations, as the Yiddish-speaking Indian chief in Mel Brooks's *Blazing Saddles* (1974) hilariously reminds us. In John Ford's early epic, *The Iron Horse* (1924), Chinese former railroad workers doubled as Indians; the Chickasaw director Horace Carewe groomed the Mexican Dolores Del Rio as the Indian Ramona; and in *The Great Train Robbery* a Mohawk trick rider may have "played white" by standing in for the Jewish "Broncho Billy" (Max Aronson).[45] Recovering some early material conditions of this perpetual race switching suggests another legacy. When westerns go cinematic, they bury and rely on an Indigenous support structure in their casting, exhibition, and promotion – that is, their negotiation with modernity.

Shoot-Outs and White Enclaves

Fast forward another decade to another origin point, in which the gaze is directed elsewhere again. This is Cecil B. DeMille's *The Virginian* (1914), in which, for the first time on film, Owen Wister's cowboy hero, the Virginian, and his rustler villain, Trampas, get in each other's sights and shoot it out. In focusing on the shoot-out, the film also visibly deflects the stereotyped Indian gaze. The moment points forward to a long-term structuring principle of cinematic westerns and backward, through print and live performance, to the ideological baggage it carries with it.

The print source for the 1914 film is Wister's best-selling novel of 1902, often said to have created the modern western. *The Virginian* emerged from, and owed much of its success to, an elite of eastern gentlemen with considerable cultural, financial, and political influence – elsewhere I have dubbed them "the frontier club."[46] The novel codifies their aristocratic values in the laconic cowboy hero, his gentrified violence, conquest of the pacificist eastern schoolma'am, homosocial company, and fealty to big ranchers. The most concentrated choreography of class, race, and gender privilege occurs in the novel's climactic showdown. On the Virginian's wedding day, he steps out of a hotel room, away from Molly, his sobbing bride, and into the main street at sunset, cautiously walking and watching, while the villain stalks him. The shot takes the hero by surprise: "A wind seemed to blow his sleeve off his arm, and he replied to it, and saw Trampas pitch forward. He saw Trampas raise his arm from the ground and fall again, and lie there this time, still.... 'I expect that's all,' he said aloud."[47] With two shots the hero kills the villain, maintains his public reputation, secures his financial future, and wins his wife.

Ritualized mano-a-mano violence reaches back to chivalric duels that appealed to frontier clubmen as part of their Anglo-saxon heritage. More immediately, Wister owed the pacing, suspense, and racialized power dynamics of the shoot-out to the Boone and Crockett Club, the group of gentlemen hunters at the center of the larger frontier club network. Under the editorship of Theodore Roosevelt and George Bird Grinnell, the club refined a hunting tale that codified the rituals of "honorable killing." These consisted of a stalk and showdown between superior specimens, so that "a vigorous, masterful people" went up against "the master of the herd."[48] Boone-and-Crockett hunting tales repeatedly clear women as well as Jewish, Mexican, and Native presences from the hunting trail so that anglo-saxon gentlemen hunters can go in quest of the purest big game. In this ritual, the American West was recreated as a network of white enclaves reserved for superior species, animal and human, fringed and threatened by degenerate species – a vivid manifestation of the clubmen's ideology.

In *The Virginian*, Wister translated this "sportsman's code" into "the code of the West." The novel similarly clears the pure space of Wyoming, caricaturing a range of "inferior races" and reducing Indians to near-invisibility, so that, in the final showdown, only white men qualify to bear the gun. Wister handles the racial equation delicately: While the Virginian, a southerner gone west, carries the weight of white manhood, Trampas has a tinge of the non-anglo in his Hispanic name (which denotes "treason") and his "slim black eyebrows, slim black mustache, and a black shirt tied with a white handkerchief."[49] He is white enough to qualify for manly combat, but his suppressed racialization suggests a larger erasure with his death. In 1903 Wister and the theater impresario Kirke La Shelle adapted the novel for stage, expunging Indian presence entirely and expanding the shoot-out to the point that, in Richard Hutson's words, the entire "melodramatic narrative structure" foregrounds "the polarized opposition of the Virginian versus Trampas."[50] The fine race line continued in Dustin Farnum (later, William S. Hart) as the clean-cut hero in white hat and cowboy gear playing against Frank Campeau as the villain in black, sometimes in a vaguely vaquero outfit.

When Cecil B. DeMille first "picturized" *The Virginian* as a feature-length film, he retained the popular Dustin Farnum and cast a mustached William Elmer as Trampas. (Winifred Kingston, who had just starred as the English lady for whom the Native woman sacrifices herself in DeMille's *The Squaw Man*, played Molly.) In many respects, the film follows Wister's text closely, but it reverses the stage play's erasure of Indian figures by creating scenes far beyond the novel's hint of Indian threat. Presumably DeMille was playing to the popularity of Indian and western films of the era, adding an Indian encampment, some stunt riding by befeathered warriors, and a couple of spectacular death dives as the Virginian guns down his sneaky assailants. These additions also make visible the deflection of the Indian gaze. In the Indian encampment, as the warriors feather up in pursuit of the Virginian, a Native woman abruptly strikes a stock pose, shading her eyes to peer off into the distance. However it came about, the gesture reads as a demonstration of the misdirected, irrelevant gaze. Meaningful gaze is reserved for the melodramatic love scenes between Anglo hero and heroine and for the shoot-out.

Five more films of *The Virginian* appeared over the next century, as well as a loosely adapted, long-running television series. Indian figures disappeared from the next three iterations of the film,[51] reappearing with the casting of Gary Farmer (Haudenosaunee) and Billy Merasty (Cree) in the television movie of 2000 directed by and starring Bill Pullman and again with the uncredited "Shoshone" in the Canadian straight-to-video version of 2014 directed by Thomas Makowski. Much of these actors' dramatic function remains focused, however, on their falling spectacularly off their horses. In contrast, the shoot-out has become more climactic and virtuosic. From 1923 to 2000, the camera lingers increasingly over the Virginian and Trampas as they become locked in an increasingly "balletic exchange of stares" and increasingly extended stalk sequence.[52] The parodic apex is reached in the most recent version, in which the shoot-out involves the Virginian, Trampas, Judge Henry, Molly, and even a Wister surrogate, Owen Walton, in an intricate dance of fast draws.

"The inevitable showdown," first codified by Wister by way of the Boone and Crockett Club, has structured an entire lineage of westerns.[53] It was used early by Griffith in *Under Burning Skies* (1912) and John Ford in his first feature-length western, *Straight Shooting* (1917), and is reiterated endlessly in "classic scenes," such as John Wayne stalking the streets of Lordsburg in Ford's *Stagecoach* (1939), Gary Cooper abandoning his bride for the shoot-out as the clock ticks down in Fred Zinnemann's *High Noon* (1952), and Alan Ladd facing down Jack Palance in the saloon in George Stevens's *Shane* (1953). Even when the shoot-out takes an ideological 180-degree turn (from, say, the Virginian protecting big ranchers to Shane defeating them), even when the intercession of spaghetti and black westerns changes its racial coding to include Mexican and African American gunfighters, even when the extraterrestrial enters the scene, as in Jon Favreau's *Cowboys and Aliens* (2011), the structural legacy of heroic individualism remains intact.

Among other effects, the shoot-out decisively changes the climactic gaze from the direct address of the Lakota dancer in *Buffalo Dance* and the shootist in *The Great Train Robbery* – the "gun vision" that forces spectators to look back.[54] The suspenseful cross-cutting and shot-reverse-shot choreography of the showdown gaze carve out space for gentlemen who have the racial right to bear the gun. This updating of the quintessential frontier club operation through cinematic technology links white male westerners in a racialized bond and relegates others – including Indigenous others – to the sidelines or off the screen altogether.

Conclusion

The most influential scholars of western movies have tended to position the early period as a kind of false start, divided from the genre's "golden age" – typically dated from around 1939 to the early 1970s, with a hiatus during World War II and intermittent revivals more recently.[55] Reattaching the genre to its beginnings changes that story. Scholars of early cinema (Hearne and Simmon included) argue that early westerns have greater political sophistication and creative range than later "classic" westerns. In a much-reprinted essay in genre criticism, Tag Gallagher reverses notions of "linear evolution": "so popular were westerns during narrative cinema's formative years (1903–1911) that it may well be that, rather than the cinema having invented the western, it was the western, already long existent in popular culture, that invented the cinema."[56] When Indigenous filmmakers and critics trace an unbroken continuum, they make the genre mean differently again: Native artists use cinematic westerns as resources for survivance and visual sovereignty, while Native audiences treat them as home movies in which they recognize their relatives, uncredited "extras" transformed into stars of their show.[57] Centering early westerns makes the genre less about possessive individualism, binary opposition, or regeneration through violence (as famously argued by Will Wright, John Cawelti, and Richard Slotkin, respectively) and more about the perpetual entanglement with Indigeneity and the ways in which, in hiding this history, westerns mask their modernity.[58]

These perspectives return us to the stakes in the history of the western's cinematic gaze. The consolidation of feature-filmmaking, around 1913, has been identified both as the moment when narrative cinema elbowed out the cinema of attraction and when Red Wing and Young Deer lost their power as movie makers. The connection lies in the cinematic reprogramming of spectacle and gaze, reoriented – again to speak somewhat metaphorically – from a Lakota dancer to an Anglo gunfighter. Whatever else it signifies, the shoot-out is also literally about land claims, as representatives of competing claimants (big ranchers, small farmers, sheepherders, rustlers, and cattle kings) variously beat each other to the draw. So we arrive at the western landscape after all, in the most material of terms. To be locked out of the shoot-out's gaze is to be removed from the claim to land. But Indigenous performers have persistently gazed back, as two final images from the period 1906–31 suggest.[59] In one, a Native performer with the 101 Ranch Real Wild West points his gun straight at the camera with an intense, half-mocking stare. In the other, a young Native boy with the show does the same, now with a big grin. Whether in conscious imitation of *The Great Train Robbery* or not, they target the camera with all the force of live performance, Indigenous power, spectatorial control, and cinematic potential which that gesture suggests.

Notes

1 I use "Indian" to refer to the stereotyped representation of Indigenous or Native peoples.

2 Library of Congress website, http://www.loc.gov/item/00694114/ (accessed December 1, 2014).

3 Alison Griffiths, *Wondrous Difference: Cinema, Anthropology, and Turn-of-the-Century Visual Culture* (New York: Columbia University Press, 2002), 175.

4 Philip J. Deloria, *Indians in Unexpected Places* (Lawrence: University Press of Kansas, 2004), 58.

5 Tom Gunning, "The Cinema of Attraction: Early Film, Its Spectator and the Avant-Garde," *Wide Angle* 8 (1986): 63, 66.

6 Michelle H. Raheja, *Reservation Reelism: Redfacing, Visual Sovereignty, and Representations of Native Americans in Film* (Lincoln: University of Nebraska Press, 2010), 193.

7 Robert V. Hine, *The American West: An Interpretive History*, 2nd ed. (Boston: Little, Brown, 1984), 293; Richard Slotkin, *Gunfighter Nation: The Myth of the Frontier in Twentieth-Century America* (New York: Atheneum, 1992), 87.

8 Among numerous publications, two focusing on Indigenous agency are L. G. Moses, *Wild West Shows and the Images of American Indians, 1883–1933* (Albuquerque: University of New Mexico Press, 1996); Linda Scarangella McNenly, *Native Performers in Wild West Shows: From Buffalo Bill to Euro Disney* (Norman: University of Oklahoma Press, 2012).

9 The phrase was coined by Rayna D. Green, "The Tribe Called Wannabee: Playing Indian in America and Europe," *Folklore* 9, no. 1 (1988): 30–55, and Philip Deloria, *Playing Indian* (New Haven, CT: Yale University Press, 1998).

10 Gerald Vizenor, *Manifest Manners: Narratives on Postindian Survivance* (1994; Lincoln: University of Nebraska Press, 1999).

11 Jacqueline Shea Murphy, *"The People Have Never Stopped Dancing": Native American Modern Dance Histories* (Minneapolis: University of Minnesota Press, 2007), 71.

12 John W. Troutman, *Indian Blues: American Indians and the Politics of Music, 1879–1934* (Norman: University of Oklahoma Press, 2009), 26.

13 Richard Abel, *Americanizing the Movies and "Movie-Mad" Audiences, 1910–1914* (Berkeley: University of California Press, 2006); Scott Simmon, *The Invention of the Western Film: A Cultural History of the Genre's First Half-Century* (Cambridge: Cambridge University Press, 2003), 9.

14 Deloria, *Indians*, 55, 78; see also Raheja, *Reservation*, 22–30.

15 Richard Abel, *The Red Rooster Scare: Making Cinema American, 1900–1910* (Berkeley: University of California Press, 1999), 165–6, 173–4.

16 Monique Mojica, "Stories from the Body: Blood Memory and Organic Texts," *Alt. Theatre: Cultural Diversity and the Stage* 4, no. 2–3 (2006): 16.

17 Joanna Hearne, *Native Recognition: Indigenous Cinema and the Western* (Albany: State University of New York Press, 2012), 52, 43–100; Deloria,

Indians, 94–103; Andrew Brodie Smith, *Shooting Cowboys and Indians: Silent Western Films, American Culture, and the Birth of Hollywood* (Boulder, CO: University Press of Colorado, 2003), 71–103.

18 See Angela Aleiss, *Making the White Man's Indian: Native Americans and Hollywood Movies* (Westport, CT: Praeger, 2005), 180n14; Raheja, *Reservation*, 248n43; Hearne, *Native*, 156–62.

19 Deloria, *Indians*, 91, 105; Lucy Maddox, "Politics, Performance and Indian Identity," *American Studies International* 40, no. 2 (June 2002): 30–1; Moses, *Wild*, 239.

20 Deloria, *Indians*, 107; see also Ralph E. Friar and Natasha Friar, *The Only Good Indian ... the Hollywood Gospel* (New York: Drama Book Specialists, 1972).

21 Simmon, *Invention*, 97.

22 Raheja, *Reservation*, 197.

23 Susan Bernardin, Introduction, *Indigenous Wests: Literary and Visual Aesthetics*, special issue, *Western American Literature* 49, no. 1 (spring 2014): 2.

24 Gunning, "Cinema," 63, 64, 66.

25 Henry Jenkins, *What Made Pistachio Nuts? Early Sound Comedy and the Vaudeville Aesthetic* (New York: Columbia University Press, 1992), 24. See also Robert C. Allen, "'A Decided Sensation': Cinema, Vaudeville, and Burlesque," in *On the Edge of Your Seat: Popular Theater and Film in Early Twentieth-Century American Art*, ed. Patricia McDonnell (New Haven, CT: Yale University Press, 2002), 61–89; and Robert C. Allen, *Vaudeville and Film, 1895–1915: A Study in Media Interaction* (New York: Arno, 1980).

26 Scott Marble [and Edwin S. Porter], *The Great Train Robbery (1903): Shooting Script* (Alexander Street Press, 2003), American Film Scripts Online, http:// solomon.afso.alexanderstreet.com.subzero.lib.uoguelph.ca/cgi-bin/asp/philo/ afso/documentidx.pl?work_code=FS000456 (accessed December 1, 2014).

27 David Mayer and Helen Mayer, "A 'Secondary Action' or Musical Highlight? Melodic Interludes in Early Film Melodrama Reconsidered," in *The Sounds of Early Cinema*, ed. Richard Abel and Rick Altman (Bloomington: Indiana University Press 2001), 227; Patricia O. Galperin, *In Search of Princess White Deer: The Biography of Esther Deer* (New York: Vantage Press, 2012), 55.

28 See Jace Weaver, *The Red Atlantic: American Indigenes and the Making of the Modern World, 1000–1927* (Chapel Hill: University of North Carolina Press, 2014); my in-progress research lists sixty (and counting) Indigenous perform-ers on vaudeville-Varieté circuits.

29 McNenly, *Native*, 127; Galperin, *Search*, 14, 53.

30 Galperin, *Search*, 43–5.

31 McNenly, *Native*, 134–5.

32 Galperin, *Search*, 25; David Mayer, *Stagestruck Filmmaker: D. W. Griffith and the American Theatre* (Iowa City: University of Iowa Press, 2009), 34.

33 Mayer and Mayer, "Secondary," 225.

34 Michael Moon, "A Long Foreground: Re-Materializing the History of Native American Relations to Mass Culture," in *Materializing Democracy: Toward*

a Revitalized Cultural Politics, ed. Russ Castronova and Dana D. Nelson (Durham, NC: Duke University Press, 2002), 272–3.

35 Kevin Brownlow, *The War, the West, and the Wilderness* (New York: Knopf, 1979), 332.

36 See S. Elizabeth Bird, "Savage Desires: The Gendered Construction of the American Indian in Popular Media," in *Selling the Indian: Commercializing and Appropriating American Indian Cultures*, ed. Carter Jones Meyer and Diana Royer (Tucson: University of Arizona Press, 2001), 62–98; Rayna D. Green, "The Pocahontas Perplex: The Image of Indian Women in American Culture," *Massachusetts Review* 16 (Autumn 1975): 698–714; M. Elise Marubbio, *Killing the Indian Maiden: Images of Native American Women in Film* (Lexington: University Press of Kentucky, 2006).

37 Alison Griffiths, "Playing at Being Indian: Spectatorship and the Early Western," *Journal of Popular Film and Television* 29, no. 3 (January 2001): 109.

38 Gunning, "Cinema," 65.

39 Bunny McBride, *Molly Spotted Elk: A Penobscot in Paris* (Norman: University of Oklahoma Press, 1995), 76–7.

40 Moses, *Wild*, 249.

41 Mojica, "Stories," 17–18.

42 Miriam Hansen, *Babel and Babylon: Spectatorship in American Silent Film* (Cambridge, MA: Harvard University Press, 1991), 25, 43.

43 Alison Fields, "Circuits of Spectacle: The Miller Brothers' 101 Ranch Real Wild West," *American Indian Quarterly* 36, no. 4 (Fall 2012): 463.

44 Armando José Prats, *Invisible Natives: Myth and Identity in the American Western* (Ithaca, NY: Cornell University Press, 2002).

45 Brownlow, *War*, 392; Hearne, *Native*, 161–3.

46 Christine Bold, *The Frontier Club: Popular Westerns and Cultural Power, 1880–1924* (New York: Oxford University Press, 2013).

47 Owen Wister, *The Virginian: A Horseman of the Plains* (New York: Macmillan, 1902), 480–1. See also Lee Clark Mitchell, *Westerns: Making the Man in Fiction and Film* (Chicago: University of Chicago Press, 1996), 102–3.

48 Theodore Roosevelt and George Bird Grinnell, eds., *American Big-Game Hunting: The Book of the Boone and Crockett Club* (New York: Forest and Stream Publishing Co., 1893), 14, 18.

49 Wister, *Virginian*, 167.

50 Owen Wister and Kirke La Shelle, *The Virginian: A Play in Four Acts*, introduction by N. Orwin Rush (Tallahassee, FL: n.p., 1958); Richard Hutson, "Early Film Versions of *The Virginian*," in *Reading The Virginian in the New West*, ed. Melody Graulich and Stephen Tatum (Lincoln: University of Nebraska Press, 2003), 129.

51 In 1923 (directed by Tom Forman), the 1929 talkie (Victor Fleming), and the 1946 color remake (Stuart Gilmore).

52 Mitchell, *Westerns*, 196.

53 Mary Lea Bandy and Kevin Stoehr, *Ride, Boldly Ride: The Evolution of the American Western* (Berkeley: University of California Press, 2012), 159.

54 Fields, "Circuits," 453–4.
55 For example, Edward Buscombe, *"Injuns!": Native Americans in the Movies* (London: Reaktion, 2006), 19–20.
56 Tag Gallagher, "Shoot-Out at the Genre Corral: Problems in the 'Evolution' of the Western," in *Film Genre Reader IV*, ed. Barry Keith Grant (Austin: University of Texas Press, 2012), 300.
57 For example, *Imagining Indians* (1992), by the Hopi filmmaker Victor Masayesva, retells Cecil B. DeMille's *The Plainsman* (1936) from the perspective of the Northern Cheyenne elder Charles Sooktis Sr., who "played Indian" in the movie and advised the star, Gary Cooper (hero of *The Virginian* and *High Noon*) (Hearne, *Native*, 191). Recent Indigenous resignifying of "classic westerns" includes LeAnne Howe, Harvey Markowitz, and Denise K. Cummings, ed., *Seeing Red – Hollywood's Pixeled Skins: American Indians and Film* (East Lansing: Michigan State University Press, 2013).
58 On more "hidden histories," see Janet Walker, ed., *Westerns: Films through History* (London: Routledge, 2001), 89–147.
59 Reproduced in Fields, "Circuits," 454, 453.

CHAPTER 15

The Environmental Novel of the American West

Dana Phillips

First a bald-faced proposition, and then a few broad observations, all of which will be refined in the sequel: *Any novel of the American West is likely to be "environmental" to some degree.* This likelihood is entailed by the geographical designation that serves to distinguish such a novel from other works of fiction. Otherwise the question of its character, as distinct from the general run of novels, might be moot. So one can argue that the novel of the American West tends to be "environmental" as a matter of literary and cultural necessity.

This necessity is illustrated by the history of the western as a perennially popular genre, one in which particular environments are referenced in titles and serve as settings for novelistic action, if only in a token and conventional fashion much of the time. Think of titles such as *Riders of the Purple Sage*, *The Sea of Grass*, *The Big Sky*, and *To the Far Blue Mountains*.[1] As if they were setting a stage, writers of genre westerns scatter sagebrush and prickly pear in the foreground like potted plants, prop cutouts of cattle and horses in the middle ground, hang turkey vultures and red-tailed hawks in the sky like paper moons, and pose characters before a lifelike scrim of distant, snowcapped mountains. This stage setting may be simplistic, but it is also surprisingly effective: Readers of westerns often develop a love of desert, prairie, and mountain landscapes without venturing into them other than on the page and come to regard such landscapes as quintessentially American – and as iconographic.

Nevertheless, that environment can be evoked in this perfunctory way, as splashes of local color, as mere backdrop, or as a matter of sheer coincidence, as the spot on the map where, thanks to the contrivances of plot, characters just happen to meet and interact; and that environment thus can be evoked without its becoming a shaping influence on a novel's composition and point of view, and without its posing a challenge to a reader's cozy assumptions about the course of U.S. national and environmental history; all this means that drawing a few distinctions is in order. The first distinction relates to what Timothy Luke has called "environing." Luke employs this rather awkward term because he recognizes that environments are never inert and passive, and therefore never really understandable, or even serviceable, as mere backdrops for human action, but always are engaged with actively by humans while being produced, at least in part, by human activity. At the same time, and continuously, environments shape humans both physically and mentally. According to Luke, an environment "must not be understood as the naturally given sphere of ecological processes which human powers try to keep under control, nor should it be viewed as a mysterious domain of obscure terrestrial events which human knowledge works to explain." He argues instead that it "emerges as a historical artifact that is openly constructed, not an occluded reality that is difficult to comprehend."[2] Luke traces the word "environment" back to its French roots, where it expresses not passivity but activity: where it means, "to environ." Hence "environing."

What really matters, then, or at least it does so in Luke's telling, is less ecological realities (be those what they may) than "discourses of environmentality," which shape "disciplinary environments where power/knowledge operate as ensembles of geo-power and eco-knowledge."[3] Luke probably overstates the forcefulness of "power/knowledge" and the effectiveness of the construction of environment as "a historical artifact" to be studied, as those influenced by Foucault are likely to do; and Luke definitely overlooks the fact that many scientists are perfectly well aware of the relativity and uncertainty of our knowledge of environment (it is something long since recognized, for example, by ecologists).[4] So if Luke intends to offer a critique of environmental science per se, as being overly positivist or whatever, his account has less bite than he imagines.

Yet the potential flexibility of the concept of environing – the deft fashion in which it can be used to put natural facts and ideologies of nature into fruitful relationship by making them seem less dichotomous than they otherwise would appear to be, and consequently awakening us to the unavailability of neutral ground when it comes to environment – makes it useful to the literary critic and historian, because it opens a window onto environmental matters that otherwise might remain closed by disciplinary limitations. That is, it gives literary critics and historians, who with the best will in the world can be only weakly empirical, a look-in on questions about environment that could be denied them on the grounds of, say, scientific realism. Such realism, to state the point once more in Luke's terms, tends to see nature as "occluded," and when science becomes embroiled in policy, also tends to designate environment as "a strong but sloppy force: it is anything out there, everything around us, something affecting us, nothing within us, but also a thing upon which we act."[5]

Bearing the strengths and weaknesses of Luke's analysis in mind – most importantly, the fact that it needs to be updated to take into account the recent and widespread acceptance of the notion of the Anthropocene, which suggests that environment is no longer seen by science as something "out there"[6] – we can sidestep the challenge that may (or may not) be posed by scientific realism by appealing directly to some fictional examples of environing. For on the revised account of environing being offered in this chapter, it should be clear that the novel of the American West also must be part of the process of shaping certain environmental realities (as opposed, say, to its merely "reflecting" them), since even mythical constructs can help determine real-world outcomes – recall the long careers of ideas like "the frontier" and "the wilderness" in American history and historiography alike.[7]

In Owen Wister's *The Virginian*, a novel first published in 1902 and long regarded as groundbreaking, even as definitive, the narrator, whose character echoes that of the author in obvious ways, finds himself transformed almost immediately upon his arrival in Wyoming Territory from the East. He is struck by the same things that will continue to strike narrators of novels set in the West up until the present day: by the quality of the high plains light and air, awash with sun and infused with the scent of sage; by the constant presence of pronghorn antelope and prairie dogs, which keep the narrator company while he daydreams in the high plains landscape just outside the town of Medicine Bow; and by other natural phenomena wholly new to him. Then, as he and the Virginian strike out cross-country, the narrator looks back at the town from five miles away and is surprised by the clairvoyance afforded by western views: "I looked back and there was Medicine Bow, seemingly a stone's throw behind us. It was a full half-hour before I looked back again, and there sure enough was always Medicine Bow. A size or two smaller, I will admit, but visible in every feature, like something seen through the wrong end of a field glass."[8] Scenes in Wister's novel like this one can be read as a recasting of experiences the writer had while on his first trip to the West in 1885. This was a summer-long vacation prescribed as a cure for a case of bad nerves Wister developed while working in a Boston bank. That Wister felt his western experiences to be as vitalizing as he did is, admittedly, an inverse measure of his psychological sensitivity at the time: He felt better in proportion to how much worse he felt before. Yet these experiences also can be read as touchstones of one important aspect of environing, its human dimension – with which novels are necessarily concerned.

Wister was first made aware of the difference of the American West from the East while passing over the Great Plains by train. On July 3, 1885, a day that began with breakfast in North Platte, Nebraska, Wister wrote in his journal: "The sky – there is none. It looks really like what it scientifically is – space. The air is delicious. As if it had never been in anyone's lungs before. I like this continual passing of green void, without any growing things higher than a tuft of grass."[9] Just five days later, and in language illustrating how the West tends to be seen as a region where brute realities can be encountered more directly than is possible elsewhere, Wister articulated the dramatic change of mind, mood, and appetite he was undergoing: "I'm beginning to be able to feel I'm something of an animal and not a stinking brain alone. Nailed up a strip of cloth over the crack of the big dugout door to keep the flies from the meat."[10] Apart from its careful qualification ("I'm beginning to be able to feel ") and Wister's disgust with his former self (here reduced to "a stinking brain"), the important aspect of this second journal entry – and this is a forma-tive paradox for all subsequent writing about the region – is that Wister found the western environment enlivening and transformative not despite but because of its insistent physicality and overwhelming presence. For the genteel Philadelphian, nailing the cloth over the crack in the door "to keep the flies from the meat" was like nailing the flag to the mast. Wister thereby declared himself a creature of the Wyoming environment, or in his own words "something of an animal." To put the point another way: After he had spent only a few days in Wyoming, Wister already had begun to be environed. And so had the American West, which would figure differently in American literature thanks to Wister's fiction, becoming – among other things – more literary, and therefore as much a wellspring of cultural as of natural resources.

The preceding paragraphs should not be taken to imply that where Frederick Jackson Turner once wrote "the frontier" and "wilderness," Henry Nash Smith later wrote "virgin land," and Roderick Nash more recently wrote "wilderness," we can now write "environment" and "envi-roning" while continuing to tell familiar stories about the West (as Wister, one of the great boosters of the region, certainly would have had us do).[11] Substituting more "theoretical" terms for the lay language used by earlier scholars does not enable an account of the environmental novel supple enough to cope with the recursive character of environments, environing, and – for that matter – fiction.

So another distinction needs to be drawn. If there are now a number of novels of the American West like Wister's, novels in which "environing" serves as a vitalizing factor, setting actions in motion and simultaneously posing a challenge to the consciousness of characters, both prompting and checking their desires, there are other novels of the American West in which the environment is indeed taken to be "out there," objectively and – if all goes well – perpetually, and whether the characters know it and like it, or not. These novels might be called *environmentalist*. (Certainly Wister's novel does not qualify as one of them: His cowboy hero winds up the owner of a coal mine. So much for the transparency of the western atmosphere!) In contrast to the former sort of novel, which to make a long word only slightly shorter I will call *environmental* (since I understand the distinction to be a weak but nonetheless an important one), the environmentalist novel of the American West, for all its literary sophistication, takes an approach to the landscape that is much closer to that taken by the genre western. This is a considerable irony.

Environmentalist Novels

In environmentalist novels, as in genre westerns, the Wild West is regarded as existing prior to and outside any attempts by human beings to tame it – to take its virginity, as it were – or even to understand it. All characters can do is respond to the still-primordial landscape as best they can, since it established the terms of engagement prehistorically (in the Pleistocene, say). And these are terms that give the environmentalist novel a streak of the same mysticism, which also travels by the name of romanticism, which reveals itself in occasional passages of the genre western.

We see this mysticism-cum-romanticism about the landscape and, inevitably, about its inhabitants, too, in occasional passages of Louis L'Amour's 1953 classic genre western *Hondo*, where it contrasts sharply with the author's affinity for the hard-boiled, the masculine, and the grimly pragmatic. When Hondo Lane is asked about the meaning of his now-dead Mescalero Apache wife's name – "Destarte" – he answers: "You can't say it except in Mescalero. It means Morning, but that isn't what it means, either." After this less than promising beginning, in which he already seems to be contradicting himself, Hondo explains why a precise definition of "Destarte" is elusive: "Indian words," he claims, "also mean the feel and the sound of the name." So among other things, including "Crack of Dawn," "Destarte" means "the first sound you hear of a brook curling over some rocks – some trout jumping and a beaver crooning. It means the sound a stallion makes when he whistles at some mares just as the first puff of wind kicks up at daybreak."[12] So if Hondo is correct about the subtleties of Mescalero, which appears to blend the denotative with the connotative and to fuse the spoken word with its meaning, he might have called his wife "environment," too, as that seems to be the option toward which his reflection on the meaning of "Destarte" is trending.

Yet Hondo's ideas about "Indian words," and their unique ability to capture phenomenological nuances and environmental relationships, are unlikely to pass muster with a field ecologist, a linguist, an analytic philosopher, a good translator, or a native speaker of Mescalero free of the prejudices of southwestern chauvinism.[13] Nevertheless, the fact that Hondo's imagination veers toward the erotic (and the poetic) as he explains the meaning of "Destarte," and that he evokes the jumping of trout, the crooning of a beaver, and the whistling of a stallion as it scents the pheromones of mares on a morning breeze is germane here: Environing is, in part, an erotic phenomenon, one that engages the appetites. That is as true for Hondo as it is for the hungry trout, the vocalizing beaver, and the horny stallion. It is equally true for readers of L'Amour's novel.

In the later fiction of Edward Abbey, we find upwellings of a similar merging of mysticism-cum-romanticism with an eroticism that, compared to L'Amour's, seems much cruder. (L'Amour's hard-boiled credentials were genuine, but he was as much the Barbara Cartland as he was the Dashiell Hammett of the Wild West; he wrote romance novels for sentimental gentlemen who fancied themselves tough guys.) This similarity is less surprising than it may seem, since Abbey began his career as a writer of genre westerns infused with environmentalist concerns. In *The Brave Cowboy* (first published in 1956), as the title character, Jack Burns, rides into a city readily identifiable as Albuquerque though it is never named as such, he watches the "Sangre Mountains" emerge from the shadows of early morning, and we are told that "the mountains loomed over the valley like a psychical presence." The narrator adds: "no man could ignore that presence; in an underground poker game, in the vaults of the First National Bank, ... in the heart of a sexual embrace, the emanations of mountain and sky imprinted some analogue of their nature on the evolution and shape of every soul."[14] Here, if environing can be said to have a happy ending, it also can be called deterministic: It imprints "some analogue" of itself on "every soul."

A comparably fatalistic meshing of the mystical, the romantic, and the erotic crops up in the descriptions of landscape that punctuate Abbey's *The*

Monkey-Wrench Gang. Many would consider this novel, first published in 1975, to be the ur-fiction of the contemporary environmental movement in the United States. In it, as elsewhere in his work, Abbey invests the southwestern landscape with absolute moral authority and treats it as prior to, apart from, and overriding any narrowly human concerns – except, of course, for the narrow concerns with pristine landscapes and wilderness shared by a few more enlightened, less compromised humans, especially the quartet whose monkey-wrenching acts of sabotage and hard-partying ways Abbey celebrates. This moral template and ethical justification of direct and destructive actions taken for the sake of environment does indeed make Abbey's novel paradigmatic – and leaves it open to criticism. In an early passage of *The Monkey Wrench Gang*, he writes: "Far beyond the dam, the reservoir, the river and the bridge, the town of Page, the highway, the Indians, the people and their leaders, stretches the rosy desert." But since this evocation of the desert may have the effect of making it seem attractive, Abbey adds: "No humans live in that pink wasteland.... Nothing grows out there but scattered clumps of blackbrush and cactus, with here and there a scrubby, twisted, anguished-looking juniper. And a little scurf pea, a little snakeweed. Nothing more."[15] That "the rosy desert" is home, with few exceptions, to no one and "nothing" makes it an ideal space for Abbey, one "far beyond" the reach and the powers of endurance of "the people and their leaders," even of "the Indians" indigenous to the region. Only civil engineers, aided by a monstrous technology, can penetrate and substantially alter this terrain by developing its "nothing" into something else.

The emptiness verging on nothingness of "the rosy desert" is more of a pop-philosophical idea in Abbey's fiction than it is a genuine reality of regional natural histories, which are richer than Abbey allows. (This richness is something of which he was aware, surely, but overlooked for rhetorical purposes.) The nothingness of arid lands enables Abbey to depict environmental problems as soluble by means of negation: the negation of civil engineering in particular instances of monkey-wrenching, and the negation of human civilization as a whole should monkey wrenching become a widely embraced practice. *The Monkey Wrench Gang* is a fantasy of escape not only from civilization, especially that latter-day form of civilization shaped by the hidebound morality of Middle America, but also from the demands of environmental crisis itself. In this novel, the desert landscape is imagined as a black hole in culture and nature, one capable of absorbing whatever destruction civil engineers – and their sworn enemies the monkey wrenchers – may devise.

Monkey wrenching is messy work, after all, and Abbey describes scenes of the devastation it wreaks with relish. For instance: "The train rose up from the rails, great balls of fire mushrooming under its belly.... loaded coal cars, completing their jump, came back down on the broken bridge. The girders gave, the bridge sank like molten plastic and one by one the coal cars – linked like sausages – trundled over the brink, disappearing into the roar the dust the chaos of the gorge."[16] But the coal train does not – cannot – simply "disappear," as Abbey suggests it does. It instead turns the gorge into a dump site, one likely to be toxic, given the kinds of material from which a modern-day train is made. Though in this novel we are repeatedly offered images of the power of the southwestern landscape to pull down mountains and carve out canyons, it seems unlikely that winds and flash floods will remove all traces of this wreckage, which will be more enduring than Anasazi potsherds, corncobs, and kivas. Geological time may not be the right time for environmentalism to set its watch by.

The most celebrated of Abbey's novels, *The Monkey-Wrench Gang*, is as much of a fantasy as *Hondo*. To make such an assertion is not to dismiss Abbey's novel entirely, since fantasy cannot be dealt with and dismissed, much less understood, so easily and in such simple terms. Fantasy traffics in the elemental and its logic is that of dreams, as is revealed by a passage describing a night George Hayduke, the outlaw figure at the center of the novel's action, spends in the mountains: "He slept well that night ... snug in his broad-shouldered mummy bag, his goosedown sack, light as a feather, warm as the womb.... He dreamt of home. Wherever that is. Of silken thighs. Wherever they may lead. Of a tree greener than thought in a canyon red as iron."[17] Only in a dream may a silken thigh lead to a "tree greener than thought in a canyon red as iron" (such a dream gives tree hugging a whole new meaning). Abbey seems to have taken a myth central to the environmental imagination, which has been captivated by "green thoughts" in the womblike enclosure of "a green shade" since the days of Andrew Marvell, and turned it into the sort of fantasy that drives action-adventure stories in which the hero gets the girl and saves the day, though in this novel the hero believes he is saving the Earth, too, and saving it one lovely and singular tree at a time. So in this instance, and in similar ones (the environmentalist novels of T. C. Boyle, which are brazenly imitative of Abbey's work when they are not merely journalistic, come to mind), the world "out there" and "far beyond" our reach proves to be too far out to be credible.[18]

The Environmental Novel

Environmental novels of the American West have less of an overt agenda than environmentalist ones do, yet one can say that they set out to close the credibility gap that opens in fictions like Abbey's. In environmental novels, an engagement with environment shapes more than the movements of plot and the portrayal and dialogue of characters; it is also fundamental to narration and the elaboration of a much more critical point of view. In short, in these novels environing is a matter of form as well as content.

If in the environmentalist novel environments remain "out there," "far beyond" the everyday routines of modern industrial society, in the environmental novel they are treated as fully integral to human lives – to all of them, not just those of a few monkey-wrenching environmentalists or hard-bitten loners with a taste for the backcountry. This does not mean that the characters in the environmental novel can be understood as if the local subsumed them wholly: It does not mean that they are pushovers when it comes to the environment in the places where they dwell. They are given more leeway than that. If they were not, the environmental novel also might be guilty of an unreflective determinism, and the environing it describes would be as rote as it generally is in Abbey's novels.

Perhaps the best way to grasp the function and flavor of environing in the environmental novel is again by way of example. Consider a short passage that illustrates how Tom McGuane understands the environing of the main character in *Nobody's Angel*. Patrick is a military veteran who has returned to his family's ranch outside Deadrock, the fictional Montana town in the Crazy Mountains where McGuane has set a number of his novels (the town's name is an ironic play on Livingston, where the author actually lives): "Patrick wondered seriously if this country had ever been meant to be lived in.... The Deadrock region was just exactly the dumb fucking dehumanized photogenic district that would require a bunch of American reformed Protestants to invent. His mood had begun to show."[19] Heterodox sentiments like Patrick's are a staple of McGuane's western novels, which taken together amount to a sustained critique of the boilerplate sublime that informs a lot of writing about the region's natural splendors. What McGuane understands better than a writer like Abbey is that environing is multidimensional: There are the "out there," and the "in here," and the various ways in which they meet and intertwine, or enter into conflict (and this is the more interesting, more telling possibility). McGuane also understands that environing is more than a matter of, say, the interactions of human consciousness with a landscap that, like it or not, is in many ways an objective reality: The boundary between the subjective and the objective is not so easily drawn – cannot, in fact, be drawn.

This does not mean that the relationship between landscape and mind-scape is, as the current jargon would have it, a liminal one. Environing is as concrete as any other material process a novel might describe, even if some of its outcomes do not take a definite shape (like a map used as a frontispiece, for instance), but instead assume the inchoate form of dis-satisfaction or a bad mood (as sometimes happens for Patrick in *Nobody's Angel*), or the more substantial form of an idea, which can be articulated. The environmental novel has more to offer than the disenchantment of environment alone, although its astringency is fundamental to its intel-lectual integrity (which might be said of all novels). Thus McGuane's habit of offering his reader offhand commentary on the challenges the western landscape poses to its inhabitants, such as this sardonic obser-vation from *Something to Be Desired*: "They drove into Deadrock. They were traveling light. The town crouched in front of the terrific mountains to the south, great wildly irregular peaks that seemed to say to the little town, Don't try anything."[20]

Yet McGuane is far from immune to the seductions of the West and the western; those seductions form a large part of what his novels are all about. Consider two passages from *Keep the Change*. In the first, the main character, Joe, is listening to Alvie, the irrigator who sometimes works for Joe on the ranch he is trying to restore, talk about the novels of Zane Grey. Alvie says, "I believe everything in them books. When them cow-boys are in the desert, I'm hot. When they're caught in a blizzard I send the old lady for another blanket. When they run out of food, I tear down to the kitchen to make a peanut butter sandwich." The narrator comments: "Even recalling these moments with his nose in Zane Grey caused rapturous transformation in Alvie, and the reality of a life directing muddy water downhill was made tolerable."[21] In the second passage, Joe is hitting a bucket of balls at a driving range with a woman he once slept with years before: "Ellen stood up on a kind of rubber mat and began fir-ing the balls out through the bug-filled flood of light, almost to the dark-ness beyond. At first Joe just watched her. There were gophers speeding around, running, stopping, looking, whistling, trying to fathom life on a driving range."[22] The two passages have much in common. In the first, Alvie makes sense of his own life by viewing it through a lens ground by Zane Grey. It hardly matters that this lens is imperfect, that to the eyes of a devoted reader like Alvie a peanut butter sandwich can substitute for cowboy beans and bacon, and an irrigator's life can partake of the bygone glories of the cattle drive. In the second passage, the gophers – Alvie's furry little counterparts – are likewise "trying to fathom life" in a western landscape that has been transformed by golfers (not every westerner is a rancher, after all), and touched with absurdity in the process. McGuane's novels are filled with tough customers, who seem to be another enduring feature of his western landscapes, where men (and women) like Alvie are as difficult to eradicate as prairie dogs and lead equally hardscrabble lives. For McGuane, the mythic western landscape, that "dumb fucking dehumanized photogenic district," figures as an irritant, and as a stimulant, which continues to plague, and to inspire, the inhabitants of the contemporary West he documents in his novels.

In environmental novels of the American West like McGuane's, the dynamic of irritation and stimulation – or in short, the environing – functions recursively, and environment is often portrayed as something humans can take only in relatively small doses, however much they fantasize about swallowing it whole. Jim Harrison's novels, in particular *Dalva* and *The Road Home* (both set on a farm in western Nebraska), deserve mention here; so do the novels of his Great Plains predecessors Willa Cather and John Steinbeck; and so does Cormac McCarthy's Border Trilogy. Novels such as these are as much comments on literary and popular fictions and myths of the West, and its landscapes, as they are narratives in their own right. The same can be said, albeit with qualifications, of such now-classic works of contemporary Native American fiction as Leslie Marmon Silko's *Ceremony*, James Welch's *Fools Crow*, and Louise Erdrich's *Tracks*. Even the genial novels of Barbara Kingsolver work to revise our understanding of western environmental fictions and western environments, in part by focusing on the struggles of women, but also by taking advantage of off-kilter, less than pristine, and underrepresented settings such as mixed-race working-class Tucson neighborhoods and the Cherokee reservation in Oklahoma. A similar strategy informs the work of the Chicana writer Ana Castillo, especially her novel *So Far from God*, set in a village near Albuquerque where human lives are intimate with the lives of animals but also are marred by chemical pollution in the workplace.[23]

What is most at issue in the environmental novel of the American West is the question of the region as "living space," to borrow a phrase from Wallace Stegner. A skeptical mood, and an ironic disposition, also might be borrowed from Stegner, whose credentials as a student and a spokesman for the West were impeccable. Stegner argues that what defines the West are "a general deficiency of water"; the lack of a vital agrarian tradition; the status of most of its residents as "displaced persons" – that is, settlers and refugees from elsewhere; tourism; a "heightened and romantic notion of itself"; and its spaciousness, which "continues to suggest unrestricted freedom, unlimited opportunity for testing and heroisms, a continuing need for self-reliance and physical competence."[24] Stegner suggests, in short, that the American West has been misread: In fact, it is not especially suitable as "living space."

This suggestion would have angered Edward Abbey (though he might have welcomed it as a reason for lone-wolf characters like him to continue their romance with the solitary desert). But it is a suggestion writers such as McGuane have taken to heart, and it accounts for the peculiar pathos of their work. In *Something to Be Desired*, the main character, Lucien, is a local boy made only somewhat good. A failed painter of landscapes, a failed member of the U.S. diplomatic corps, and a divorced father of one, he is now the newly rich developer of a resort centered around a hot spring and the would-be lover of an old flame, a Deadrock woman who in later life seems to have made a career out of killing her husbands and boyfriends. Lucien is not a man prone to enchantment, then. Nonetheless he is puzzled by the unimaginative response of the West's contemporary inhabitants to the living space in which they find themselves: "Lucien like so many had always felt the great echoes from the terminated history of the Indians – foot, dog and horse Indians. How could a country produce orators for thousands of years, then a hundred years of yep and nope?" Lucien suggests a provisional answer to this question: "Maybe the yeps and nopes represented shell-shock, a land forever strange.... Well, thought Lucien, it's not a bad spot for coyotes, schemers and venture capitalists."[25] If the environmental novel honors the hoodoo strangeness of the western landscape while questioning its sublimity, it is because such a novel recognizes that environing is not the same thing as, say, settlement, which often amounts to little more than occupation. At the same time, the environmental novel replaces the cast of characters that inform the environmentalist novel – brave cowboys, rugged river runners, and other outcasts – with a more plausible, more populous variety of western inhabitants, including coyotes, schemers, and venture capitalists. Their numbers are legion and they embrace a very different environmental ethos, yet they are as fully engaged in the complex dynamics of environing as are the most avid monkey wrenchers.

Notes

1 Zane Grey, *Riders of the Purple Sage* (1912; reprint, New York: Dover, 2002); Conrad Richter, *The Sea of Grass* (Athens: Ohio University Press, 1992); A. B. Guthrie Jr., *The Big Sky* (New York: Mariner, 2002); Louis L'Amour, *To the Far Blue Mountains* (New York: Bantam, 1984).

2 Timothy W. Luke, "On Environmentality: Geo-Power and Eco-Knowledge in the Discourses of Contemporary Environmentalism," *Cultural Critique* 31 (Autumn 1995): 67.

3 Ibid., 58.

4 See Dana Phillips, "Ecology Then and Now," in *The Truth of Ecology: Nature, Culture, and Literature in America* (New York: Oxford University Press, 2003), 42–82.

5 Luke, "On Environmentality," 64.

6 "Anthropocene" is the term used to mark the current geological era in recognition of the alteration of Earth's geography and climate by human activity. The Dutch atmospheric chemist Paul J. Crutzen was among the first to urge the change in nomenclature, though he did not coin the term himself.

7 For a sample of work that bookends the scholarly conversation on these topics, see Frederick Jackson Turner, "The Significance of the Frontier in American History," in *The Frontier in American History* (Tucson: University of Arizona Press, 1986), 1–38; Henry Nash Smith, *Virgin Land: The American West as Symbol and Myth* (Cambridge, MA: Harvard University Press, 1970); Roderick Nash, *Wilderness and the American Mind*, 3rd ed. (New Haven, CT: Yale University Press, 1983); Annette Kolodny, *The Lay of the Land: Metaphor as Experience and History in American Life and Letters* (Chapel Hill: University of North Carolina Press, 1984); Patricia Nelson Limerick, *The Legacy of Conquest: The Unbroken Past of the American West* (New York: Norton, 1987); and William Cronon, "The Trouble with Wilderness; or, Getting Back to the Wrong Nature," in *Uncommon Ground: Toward Reinventing Nature*, ed. William Cronon (New York: Norton, 1995), 69–90.

8 Owen Wister, *The Virginian* (1902; reprint, New York: Signet, 2002), 37.

9 Owen Wister, in *Owen Wister Out West: His Journals and Letters*, ed. Fanny Kemble Wister (Chicago: University of Chicago Press, 1958), 30.

10 Wister, in *Owen Wister Out West*, 32.

11 See note 7.

12 Louis L'Amour, *Hondo* (1953; reprint, New York: Bantam, 2011), 43.

13 A cursory search of the Internet reveals that "Destarte" is an uncommon proper name of uncertain origin; or, when it is not capitalized, a Portuguese adverb meaning "thus."

14 Edward Abbey, *The Brave Cowboy* (New York: Avon, 1992), 12–13.

15 Edward Abbey, *The Monkey Wrench Gang* (New York: Harper Perennial, 2006), 3–4.

16 Ibid., 203.

17 Ibid., 25.

18 See T. C. Boyle's novels, *A Friend of the Earth* (New York: Penguin, 2001) and *When the Killing's Done* (New York: Penguin, 2012).

19 Thomas McGuane, *Nobody's Angel* (New York: Vintage, 1982), 199.

20 Thomas McGuane, *Something to Be Desired* (New York: Random House, 1984), 12–13.

21 Thomas McGuane, *Keep the Change* (New York: Vintage, 1989), 93.

22 Ibid., 103.

23 See Jim Harrison, *Dalva* (New York: Washington Square Press, 1988) and *The Road Home* (New York: Atlantic Monthly, 1988); Willa Cather, *O Pioneers!* (New York: Houghton Mifflin, 1913) and *My Ántonia* (Boston: Houghton Mifflin, 1918); John Steinbeck, *The Grapes of Wrath* (New York: Viking, 1939); Cormac McCarthy, *All the Pretty Horses. Vol. 1. The Border Trilogy* (New York: Knopf, 1992), *The Crossing. Vol. 2. The Border Trilogy* (New York: Knopf, 1994), and *Cities of the Plain. Vol. 3. The Border Trilogy* (New York: Knopf, 1998); Leslie Marmon Silko, *Ceremony* (New York: Viking, 1977); James Welch, *Fools Crow* (New York: Viking, 1986); Louise Erdrich, *Tracks* (New York: Penguin Putnam, 1988); Barbara Kingsolver, *The Bean Trees* (New York: Harper, 1988), *Animal Dreams* (New York: Harper Perennial, 1990), and *Pigs in Heaven* (New York: Harper Perennial, 1994); Ana Castillo, *So Far from God* (New York: Norton, 1993).

24 Wallace Stegner, *The American West as Living Space* (Ann Arbor: University of Michigan Press, 1987), 6, 18, 21, 51, 68, 80.

25 Thomas McGuane, *Something to Be Desired* (New York: Random House, 1984), 122–3.

CHAPTER 16

Hard-Boiled Fiction and Noir Narratives

Lee Clark Mitchell

In the years following the First World War, a style of writing emerged that transformed expectations for a genre a little older than half a century: the detective or mystery novel. Hard-boiled fiction represented a newly terse, unsentimental fiction that displaced conventional narratives and customary styles, corresponding with the emergence of a tight-lipped aesthetic heralded by Hemingway and Dos Passos. Ever more graphic depictions of sex and violence would occur in shabby urban settings with a central figure given to unabashedly American turns of phrase. The slang-slinging, wisecracking gumshoe announced in his very self-presentation a rejection of traditional literary standards and established cultural values. What started out as cheap melodrama, written breathlessly words-per-minute, published by pulp magazines for a barely literate readership (people, as Mary McCarthy remarked, whose lips moved when they read), became transmuted into literary gold and cinematic masterpieces. Gradually, a set of sterile formulas and stock clichés grew into a genre that in multiple permutations would dominate the reading and viewing habits of the American middle class for nearly a century.

Hard-boiled narratives are not set exclusively in the American West or even in America itself, though the legacy of the western gunslinger adopting extralegal methods to right social wrongs is certainly discernable in the figure of a private investigator walking mean city streets. And earlier small-town confrontations between bullying outlaws and a craven citizenry are recognizable in hard-boiled narratives that simply shift the action to corrupt urban precincts. Now a solitary figure traverses his metropolitan setting in an automobile not on a horse, and more often than not finds himself (unlike his cowboy avatar) morally impugned by the world he traverses. That such a largely urban, largely compromised vision should have emerged in the 1920s comes as little surprise in the aftermath of a global war in which conventional ideals and language seemed inadequate to events. But the confluence of separate developments – of a publishing industry in transition, of notable writers able to transfigure tired materials, of a western landscape urbanized with unseemly speed, and of a literary shift to new modes of representation – all contributed to a hard-boiled vision that soon modulated into more sophisticated noir fictional modes. In short, "hard-boiled" was as much a stylistic development as a narrative one – as much a revolution in language as in plots that became a staple of American popular entertainment. And the author who first lent respectability to the genre was Dashiell Hammett, whose prose minimalism in the 1920s seems as much indebted to Hemingway as it was an influence upon him. In the 1930s, Raymond Chandler extended Hammett's innovations, moving the hard-boiled genre from San Francisco south to L.A. and transforming the P.I.'s patter into a self-conscious style. By the late 1940s, Ross Macdonald in turn reshaped the genre into a full-fledged noir mode as distinctive for its psychological nuance as its Angeleno setting. But however influential, they were only three of dozens of writers, many equally impressive. And because the scrutiny given to them as shapers of hard-boiled literature so often edges out others, the following reviews the larger field in an effort to provide a fuller understanding of a genre that continues to evolve.

Few genres can trace their origin to a single mass market magazine, which makes *Black Mask* significant as a pulp journal launched in 1920 just as popular dime novels were being squeezed out by costly postal regulations. Publishers turned to small-format magazines (seven by ten inches, 120 rough-edged pages, selling from a dime to a quarter), all made from paper produced with pulped wood at low cost. The cheap production encouraged coarse narrative strains, and in May 1923 the tough private eye emerged in the story "Three-Gun Terry" by Carroll John Daly. Soon after, Dashiell Hammett introduced his own operative, the anonymous figure who worked for the Continental Detective Agency's San Francisco office. Together, Daly and Hammett shaped a new brand of detective fiction that moved well beyond traditional crime fiction (Conan Doyle, Agatha Christie, Dorothy Sayers) in both its violent plots and its tight-lipped prose. Yet perhaps the most influential figure in fine-tuning this genre was Joseph T. Shaw, appointed editor of *Black Mask* in 1927, who had clear ideas about his kind of reader: "He is vigorous-minded ... hating unfairness, trickery, 'injustice ... responsive to the thrill of danger, the stirring exhilaration of clean, swift, hard action ... a man who ... knows the song of a bullet, the soft, slithering hiss of a swift-thrown knife, the feel of hard fists, the call of courage."[1]

Despite his melodramatic, even juvenile aspirations Shaw had a forceful impact on a range of writers eager to satisfy his vision. Hammett was in thrall, as was Chandler, who felt Shaw encouraged his best efforts, given his "great insight into writing."[2] Still, like other editors of the nearly two hundred mystery-detective pulp magazines that emerged between 1915 and 1950, Shaw fostered a slap-dash ideal of authorship. Paying one to five cents a word for stories authors submitted, he encouraged formidable efforts from writers who averaged from three thousand to five thousand words per day, sometimes considerably more. The very pressure to churn out narratives produced a version of automatic writing, while the plethora of stories in burgeoning pulp magazines ironically drove the pay per word lower, forcing writers to quit and leading to the decline of short story production. Writers soon turned full-time to novel production, which would become the most important development in the genre, continuing today.

Yet at the beginning, Carroll John Daly defined the contours of a popular urban myth, of a first-person (male) narrator in a largely masculine genre defying the untoward elements of city life, invoking slangy repartee and never standing down from confrontation. Daly realized the appeal of his stories for urban working-class readers had much to do with the dream vision of a hero physically poised but also cautious about the way the street worked. His private eyes always transgress the dull constraints of the law, setting the terms of vigilante justice that so often emerges in the hard-boiled genre. Moreover, Daly's piling up of corpses is matched only by his disdain for style, which he trumpeted as a moral virtue: "Punctuation ... I find a matter of editorial opinion ... paragraphing, well, I simply paragraph when I begin to see too many black lines one after the other ... about grammar. The answer is simple. I don't think anybody cares."[3] Yet this contempt for shaping his hard-boiled vision of life becomes itself part of that vision, as if a certain level of authenticity emerged from a lack of writerly care.

Hammett started with a similar premise but his early stories soon confirm a different conception as he shifts from stereotypical notions of heroism in the characterization of his dumpy Continental Op. Instead of unbuttoned descriptions of mayhem, he offers self-contained vignettes that unfold by means of calculated understatement. As Raymond Chandler wrote, "Hammett gave murder back to the kind of people that commit it for reasons, not just to provide a corpse; and with the means at hand, not with hand-wrought duelling pistols, curare, and tropical fish. He put these people down on paper as they are, and he made them talk and think in the language they customarily used for these purposes."[4] Hammett transformed the basic materials of violence, plotting, and characterization, in the process learning to speak a patois that seemed like the speech of the street. And his clear success inspired Paul Cain and Raoul Whitfield, both of whom moved the private eye's terrain to southern California, developing an ambivalence toward setting that continues to inform the genre today. Cain's only novel, *Fast One* (1932), originally written for *Black Mask*, offers a compelling mélange of figures caught up in a web of corruption, often sacrificing clear character development for bursts of visceral violence. As Irvin Faust observes, Cain "knows, or conveys that he knows – which is equally important in fiction – big city politics, crooked pols, snooping and doomed reporters and cops on the take, and on this mix hangs much of the helter-skelter, criss-crossing plot, if that is the word for so much interlocking action."[5] The regularity with which violence erupts evokes a random universe that is also at the heart of the genre, though Cain disorients the reader through moments of what has been called "delayed recognition," as if readers and characters were aligned in a paranoid worldview: "As readers, we cannot even feel sure that the narrator is trustworthy, since he is as likely as any other character to be guilty."[6]

Raoul Whitfield had already confirmed the importance of a southern California landscape in his vivid depiction of murder in one of the most iconic Angeleno sites, the Hollywood Bowl. His *Death in a Bowl* (1931) plays out a theme that persists from Chandler through Macdonald to Elmore Leonard, of the tinsel-town artificiality of life in an urban environment obsessed with looks, easy money, and the ephemeral pleasures of popular movies. The novel opens with the private investigator Ben Jardinn arriving at an orchestral premier, as a plane flies noisily over, the house lights suddenly dim, and the conductor is mysteriously shot dead. In the mutually suspicious relations that emerge, Jardinn cannot unravel who is guilty, including his secretary and his aide, confirming a world where everyone is suspect, families divided, allies duplicitous. Whitfield, even more than Chandler or Cain, establishes in the very confusions of his byzantine plot itself the intertwined motives and troubled psychologies that came to characterize a genre of mutual recriminations.

During this same period, other writers seized upon place as the signature shaper of plot, of distinctive western spaces as somehow aligned with a spare, straightforward style. Even Hammett's clamped-down, terse-lipped expression of personality became associated with investigators somehow identified with their habitat. Earl Derr Biggers took the most western of island plots, introducing Honolulu's Charlie Chan midway through *The House without a Key* (1925) in tones that established him as an iconic P.I. through a score of additional novels: "In those warm islands thin men were the rule, but here was a striking exception. He was very fat indeed, yet he walked with the light dainty step of a woman. His cheeks were as chubby as a baby's, his skin ivory tinted, his black hair close-cropped, his amber eyes slanting."[7] As Chan pursues clues, we find Biggers emulating Hammett's ear for idioms and spoken speech in the broken English that later would became politically incorrect, partly as a means of giving voice (and heroic self-restraint) to an otherwise marginal- ized group: " 'Begging most humble pardon,' he said, 'that are wrong atti- tude completely. Detective business made up of unsignificant trifles. One after other our clues go burst in our countenance.' "[8] Biggers, moreover, like Whitfield and Cain, would complicate plot as a means of question- ing the very terms of interpretation, forcing readers to align with Charlie Chan in restoring order to a murderous realm.

Perhaps the most distinctive author of hard-boiled possibilities, how- ever, was Horace McCoy, who transformed the brutal spontaneity of the genre into a style less easily construed. In his early story, "Frost Rides Alone" (1930), he perfects a staccato rhythm with a mildly predictable plot: "A pistol cracked, light blue and scarlet, and the bullet whistled by Frost's head. Pandemonium. Frost lashed out in the dark, heard a grunt, and lashed out again. Le Estrellita was an inferno. Tables and chairs rat- tled, glasses crashed."[9] But with his exceptional novel, *They Shoot Horses, Don't They?* (1935), he blended that disjointed paratactic style with the larger contours of Los Angeles as an empty space, a facade passing itself off as authentic. L.A. as fabled land of opportunity dissolves into what Lee Horsely describes as "the site of disappointment and failure, of disas- trous endings for rootless characters who arrive at a dead end of hopeless- ness."[10] A Malibu dance marathon centers a plot that depicts exhausted sexual energies, economic dismay, artistic fatigue, and finally fictional hope itself winding slowly down. McCoy, moreover, inventively altered the first-person voice into one of criminal self-admission: "*Nobody was ever any nicer to a girl than I was to Gloria, but there came the time when I shot and killed her. So you see being nice doesn't mean a thing.*"[11] The month (and the novel) that follows in the marathon dance contest results simply in a condemnation of life itself, as the narrator's partner announces in inducing him to kill her: "I'm finished. I think it's a lousy world and I'm finished. I'd be better off dead and so would everybody else.... Shoot me. It's the only way to get me out of my misery."[12] Perhaps no one better anticipates Nathanael West's vision of L.A. than McCoy in describing the mayhem that follows.

Shifting the hard-boiled school into a more sophisticated noir configuration was Chandler, in part simply by making Philip Marlowe an Angeleno, at once enamored and repeatedly disgusted by his hometown. Ever since his influential eight novels, fictional private eyes have been identified by their association with a distinctive urban locale, with specific mean streets, with a recognizable city environment sullied by its own peculiar forms of graft and corruption. More importantly, Chandler took the largely externalized character of Sam Spade and transformed him into a psychological figure, one who feels compassion for those he assists and whose acerbic responses to the often cretinous adversaries he confronts end by revealing a figure of wit, learning, and wry self-deprecation. As well, he took the action-packed plots of characters locked into unpredictable violence and transformed them through a self-conscious style into a more sophisticated mode. As Ross Macdonald claimed: "The Chandler-Marlowe prose is a highly charged blend of laconic wit and imagistic poetry set to breakneck rhythms. Its strong colloquial vein reaffirms the fact that the *Black Mask* revolution was a revolution in language as well as subject matter."[13] But Chandler's stylistic élan, in which as much occurs at the level of the sentence as of the represented action, has tended to shift attention from other, similarly gifted writers.

Frederick Nebel, for instance, churned out pulp fiction stories, yet on occasion, as with "Hell's Pay Check" (1931), produced intriguing narratives that mix local setting (in this case, Oregon), urban corruption, and police on the take, all in adamantine prose. James Cain likewise focused on southern California, mocking the American dream of starting anew. In two classic novels, *The Postman Always Rings Twice* (1934) and *Double Indemnity* (1936), he defines character as sheer desire that flames up and then struggles against its own demise, making it no coincidence that he also invented the figure of the femme fatale, the manipulative, often psychopathic figure who lures men to destruction for reasons rarely made clear. Even in "Pastorale" (1938), a story that revisits the theme of unquenched desire, Cain offers a first-person perspective that registers amazement at the brutality to which men are reduced by passion, and through its vernacular countrified voice suggests as well bemused contempt.

By the 1950s, Chandler's signature transformations had seemed to leave the field with nowhere to turn, and yet just then two writers emerged who would take the genre in different directions. Jim Thompson returned noir mysteries to hard-boiled crudity, offering up a smorgasbord of grifters, sociopaths, and abusively opportunistic figures. His triumph was *The Killer inside Me* (1952), a pulp fiction masterpiece that takes the first-person

mode perfected by Chandler and turns it inside out. Like his other novels, *Killer* presents a narrator who not only exposes his own psychopathic
antipathies, his sadomasochistic inclinations toward women, but does so
in a voice that itself defies his readers. As David Lehman states, "Besides
killing people, Lou Ford has devised a novel means of torturing people.
He corners somebody in conversation and clobbers him with clichés."[14]
Homicidal Sheriff Lou Ford cannot quite keep his story straight, lying
repeatedly in a strange blend of murderous rage that transforms setting
itself – the empty Okie–West Texas landscape where raw-boned figures are
transformed by Thompson's eviscerating narrative voice. As he observes of
elegant houses surrounded unexpectedly by oil fields:

> wells were drilled around 'em, right up to their doorsteps sometimes,
> and everything nearby became a mess of oil and sulphur water and red
> sun-baked drilling mud. The grease-black grass dies. The creeks and springs
> disappear. And then the oil is gone and houses stand black and abandoned,
> lost and lonely looking behind the pest growths of sunflowers and sage and
> Johnson grass.[15]

What had been for Chandler a setting of chintzy artificiality had become
for Thompson a nightmarish wasteland, where human depravity seemed
somehow a natural extension of ecological distress. Thompson is clearly
an heir to James Cain, whose warped heroes likewise confess to deeds they
may briefly regret, yet cannot help.

Dorothy Hughes likewise revels in psychopathology, lowering the bar
of hard-boiled psychology but raising its narrative possibilities in a more
sinuous manner. Her masterwork, *In a Lonely Place* (1947), presents a
serial murderer in the Los Angeles suburbs, though unlike Thompson she
leaves the reader in doubt about Dixon Steele's actual inclinations. Our
anxiety is intensified by our partial perspective, at once intimate, uncertain, sympathetic, yet tantalizingly incriminating. And the perspective is
enforced by a minimalist syntax, as if Steele's behavior were embodied
in the narrator's prose itself: "At Camden Drive he saw her. A girl, an
unknown girl, standing alone.... Dix pulled the buzzer cord but he was
too late ... he was smiling with his lips as he started back. His stride was
long his steps were quiet."[16] The effect in even this innocuous scene is to
sway the reader into sharing Steele's disjointed patterns of thought, making us guilty by proxy. Hughes shifted her locales throughout the West,
turning to drug running in El Paso and Ciudad Juárez in *The Candy Kid*
(1950), involving a complicated cross-border scheme that multiplies characters in a confusion of plot that is once again offset by a terse style that

seems a legacy from Hammett. In a scene as rain ends: "At four it was over. The gray of the sky became blue; a few white clouds, harmless as cotton, hung above the horizon."[17] In perhaps her most intriguing novel, *The Expendable Man* (1963), the crucial racial evidence determining the plot is withheld, allowing the reader only belatedly to understand the narrator's early anxiety and confirming Hughes's masterful shaping of perspective to produce a noirish effect.

Patricia Highsmith seems an unlikely hard-boiled writer, especially in ignoring the role of private investigators or the contours of mystery-novel construction. But her novels offer a macabre view of human relations every bit as disturbing as Thompson's or Hughes's. *Strangers on a Train* (1950) shifts among Metcalf, Texas to El Paso, Santa Fe, Mexico City, Haiti, and Great Neck, and through the very randomness of these settings underscores a haphazard rootlessness to characters. Bruno Anthony's accidental meeting of Guy Haines prompts his strange question "Ever felt like murdering somebody?" accompanied by "He thrust his smile solicitously half across the table."[18] And his suggestion of acting out criss-cross murders arouses in Guy a strange "impulse to tell Bruno everything, the stranger on the train who would listen, commiserate, and forget."[19] That doppelganger motif threads through the narrative, compounded by the violence lurking just beneath the surface of western life, or as Bruno telegrams Guy from Texas after murdering his wife: "All good wishes from the Golden West."[20] The rest of the novel is set in New York, as if Bruno's looming watchful presence only occurred in the East, compared with his active murderous life in the West. And by the end, Guy writes out the whole history of his growing affection: "As if Bruno were still alive, he wrote every detail he knew that might contribute to an understanding of him."[21] Like James Cain's novels, which invariably become confessions of personalities we never quite understand, it is as if Guy were writing the novel we are now reading, though with no greater insight into the psychological twinship it details.

The fourth of these midcentury novelists who intertwine western settings and inscrutable psychologies in a noir pattern is Dolores Hitchens, in a series of novels that range among genres. *Beat Back the Tide* (1954), among her best, depicts a man who purchases a house in California, not knowing a murder had occurred there years before, and is hired by the widow to find out the killer. The past looms mysteriously, not only of the former inhabitant but of the present owner, whose own experience lies buried: "So soon had the polite veneer cracked away, and so quickly had the hoodlum come out. In that flickering moment Glazer seemed to be back in the boxcar on the siding in El Paso; a man lay screaming on the floor, two others huddled away in a corner, and in Glazer's hands hung a bloody razor."[22] Glazer slowly grasps his hidden propensity for violence, even as the woman whose husband was murdered finds her past is mysterious, uncertain whether she killed her own husband. Glazer alone can set her free, though all the main characters seem to move in a haze of uncertainty.

More than any other writer, Ross Macdonald mastered the noir intersection of California terrain with the inescapability of past events and the psychopathology of everyday life. His private eye, Lew Archer, focuses a series of improbable narratives that weave together the bizarre yet banal details that seem significant only as looming possibilities. A current dilemma invariably twists back into the past, tugging the knot of disconnected figures into a crisis of recognition. And Macdonald nicely captures the ecological trauma to which Californians are exposing their land, while representing at the level of style itself the disorienting, syntactically disabling experience of life in the West. Chandler had wrenched apart discursive registers through a series of weird similes that embodied the dissociated sensibility of his P.I. Marlowe; Macdonald invokes analogies to a more deliberate thematic end, as in *The Chill*: "She was silent. Her face was like a colored picture straining in agony to come to life. Life glittered first in her eyes. A tear made a track down her cheek. I found myself standing beside her comforting her. Then her head was like an artificial dahlia on my shoulder."[23] The bizarre nature of the scene is established by the unnatural similes that evoke the woman's turgid anguish, flushing her features.

Two decades later, James Crumley shifted locale from southern California to the mountains of Montana and plains of Texas, with a more flamboyant pair of private eyes given to illicit drugs and alcohol. Milton Milodragovitch and C. W. Sughrue star in a series of novels in which (according to Crumley) "Milo's first impulse is to help you; Sughrue's is to shoot you in the foot."[24] But more than character or narrative coherence, it is regional setting that becomes a distinctive feature of the hard-boiled genre. Crumley maintains Macdonald's pattern of linking the land to the past, making Milodragovitch the heir of northern timberland that is itself a definition of his own troubled history, the son of two suicides trying to hold on to a legacy. This helps explain the prevalence of bars in Crumley's novel, the settings for one-sided brawls that repeatedly expose the inadequacy of frontier myths and cowboy codes. Yet even if Crumley continues the legacy of overly complicated plots in hard-boiled fiction, he adds a more sprightly, whimsical rhythm, as in the celebrated opening of *The*

Last Good Kiss: "When I finally caught up with Abraham Trahearne, he was drinking beer with an alcoholic bulldog named Fireball Roberts in a ramshackle joint just outside of Sonoma, California, drinking the heart right out of a fine spring afternoon."[25] The novel then persists in oddly affecting stylistic quirks, as a barmaid "slipped out of her daydreams and into a sleepy grin," or a rock singer appears without warning: "Ostrich skin makes a lovely boot leather – if you like leather that looks as if the animal had died of terminal acne – and it went well with Flowers' wine western-cut double-knit leisure suit, just as his suit matched the woman who followed him."[26] Yet just as often in Crumley's novels, the plot seems to spin out of control, as if the multiplying victims could not quite be explained by a style that draws admiring attention.

Much as Crumley was first inspired by Chandler's and Macdonald's writing, his own deft verbal turns have inspired in turn a generation of crime writers, including George Pelecanos, Dennis Lehane, and Craig McDonald. But Michael McGarrity may best follow this lead in combining plots that reveal the unmitigated endurance of the past with a southwestern landscape through which the Native American legacy regularly shimmers. Near the opening of *Tularosa* (1996), "Early-morning clouds, shreds of a heavy late-night rain-storm, masked the Ortiz Mountains. Wispy tendrils drifted over the foothills, turned into translucent streamers, and vanished in the sky. The cabin roof had leaked during the night.... The chair smelled like wet cat piss, and Kerney didn't own a cat."[27] McGarrity's main P.I., Kevin Kerney, is an ex-cop ruined by his erstwhile partner's drinking, drawn into a modern theft that repeats a nineteenth-century sacking of a wagon train by the Warms Springs Apache Victorio. In *Nothing But Trouble* (2005), Kerney finds that Arizona border smuggling is linked to earlier smuggled gems from Vietnam, as if the local habitat all but replicated the deeds themselves. "In the distance barrier mountains rolled skyward, promising relief from the heat of the day. It was raw country, where monsoon rains ran over the hard-baked soil and spilled into deep-cut arroyos, the sun cracked the earth into spider-like fissures, and harsh volcanic mountains stood, weathered and desolate, above the expanse of sand and scrub."[28] Bill Pronzini has produced some forty-two books in his Nameless Detective series, begun in 1971, which return the reader to San Francisco and Hammett's terse style, though the past looms once again as a wound in need of healing. And Robert Crais's fifteen novels, centering on Elvis Cole and has silent partner, Joe Pike, revive the genre of noir in the setting of Hollywood as a mixture of the trivial and the violent.

Among the most distinctively hard-boiled voices of recent years is that of James Ellroy, whose novels are set half a century ago, centering on the corruption in L.A.'s police department. His style is rapid-fire, revealing the influence of Mickey Spillane and James Cain, with a rudimentary syntax evoking scenes of vicious violence and senseless sexual behavior. *Black Dahlia* (1986) involves a rapist/murderer who cuts his victims in half, while *L.A. Confidential* (1990) extends the themes in a hard-boiled prose describing a double-crossing cop, Buzz Meeks, in "the San Berdoo" hills as he realizes he has been followed to a cheap motel. He kills those supposed to help him, then deceptively: "Meeks yelled, 'We got him!,' heard answering whoops, saw arms and legs coming out the window. He picked up the closest piece and let fly, full automatic: trapped targets, plaster chips exploding, dry wood igniting."[29] Ellroy offers a distinct throwback to pulp fiction rhythms, though he too delves into psychological explanations, with Bud White's violence depicted as the fruit of his mother's fatal beating by his father. The language is vulgar ("fucking your mother on roller skates takes a lot out of a kid"),[30] the descriptions of rape and murder are vivid, all in a staccato style that establishes facts, then forces the reader to work backward, inferring characters' importance to plot.

With less of a hard-boiled edge, Michael Connelly similarly focuses on the L.A. police, having been drawn to California by his love of Chandler's novels, actually renting a place in the High Tower Apartments where Marlowe had lived in order to begin his own series. The police detective Hieronymus Bosch has a taut relationship to his Angeleno surroundings, and an even more unsettling relationship to his own past. Bosch, who had served as a tunnel rat dismantling bombs in the Vietnam War, in his first appearance in *The Black Echo* (1992) experiences old fears come alive as he discovers murder victims in the L.A. tunnels: "Out of the blue and into the black is what they called going into a tunnel. Each one was a black echo. Nothing but death in there. But, still, they went."[31] A more tortured soul than his predecessors, Bosch is the son of a murdered prostitute, the product of youth shelters and institutional homes, who is regularly informed he is not part of the team. Connelly, however, slyly turns style back on itself by having Bosch in various novels listen to others, deducing motives in terms of odd verbal expressions: "Would he say 'My share has gone up,' or would he simply say, 'It's all mine'? Bosch's gut feeling was he would say the latter, unless there was still someone else sharing in the pot."[32] As well, Connelly extends Chandler's focus on setting itself, having Bosch observe of Hollywood that "sunsets did that here. Made you forget it was the smog that made their colors so brilliant, that behind every pretty picture there could be an ugly story."[33] Yet in a tantalizing inversion of Chandler, Connelly nudges us aslant his perspective, so that the reader is often aware before Bosch of what is likely to take place. Instead of following, we seem to precede him, as if the whole were told through the point of view of a telescope, focusing in on a Bosch who refuses to be known at all.

Connelly's grim view of the genre is transformed in Elmore Leonard's more facetiously self-conscious, more verbally playful vision. Known for his renditions of Detroit as much as of Miami Beach, Leonard is also the master of the tinsel-town landscape of Hollywood. As Vincent, the police hero, says to a colleague in *Glitz*, "Wonderful things can happen ... when you plant seeds of distrust in a garden of assholes" – to which the response is "Wait, I want to write that down."[34] This self-consciousness about their own conversation may seem ironic for an author whose ear for dialogue was legendary, registering Leonard's own persistent scrutiny of the genre he revives. For doubt about genre authenticity is everywhere in Leonard, expressed by the actress Karen in *Get Shorty* when she becomes convinced that the script she is reading for is unrealistic. And as one character tells another: "'Besides, making things grow is your life.' *Besides* – they used that word all the time in movies, but you hardly ever heard it in real life."[35] Writing and speaking convincingly become the self-evident exercise that earlier private investigators had assumed involved simply carrying a gun, with life now emulating movies rather than the other way around. Or as Karen muses after seeing Chili Palmer defend himself: "There was a scene like it in an Eastwood picture."[36] As *Get Shorty* ends, we are left with a claim that is at once the most artificial yet most authentic gesture of all: "Chili didn't say anything, giving it some more thought. Fuckin endings, man, they weren't as easy as they looked."[37] This riff on the difficulty of endings at the end of the novel alerts us to the way the novel has really ended in the middle, with the second half simply teasing us with alternative conclusions.

Self-consciousness about his own noir belatedness helps explain why Leonard's style eschews the figurative language that has been such a signature of noir since Chandler and Macdonald's inventive similes. He opts instead for gritty dialogue and understated scenes of violence that (unlike in Cain or Thompson) seem to distance us and the central character from his victims. In *Unknown Man #89*, an ex-con bent on vengeance "gave Bobby a load dead-center that pinned him against the dresser and gave Virgil time to pump and bust him again, the sound coming out in a hard heave *wham-wham* double-O explosion that Virgil figured, grinning about later, must have rocked some whores out of bed."[38] The present sound of the shotgun, conjoined with the recollection of its sonic effects, insulates us from the event itself in its self-consciously constructed sequence. Moreover, that Leonard eased out of urban descriptions that fascinated earlier writers, making his Hollywood seem little different from Miami Beach or even Detroit, suggests how far the genre of hard-boiled and noir has shifted. And the rhythms of Hammett's terse narratives, with spare descriptions of San Francisco and minimal evocations of Sam Spade's psychology, has – after decades of various permutations of the formula in terms of a forceful past, a shape-changing locale, a series of events that have determined psychological markers – now become once again the dominant mode. Still, the western propensity for straight talk and plot-driven narratives has contributed to a rise in all varieties of hard-boiled narratives, set in an increasing number of western locales. Private eyes determined to resolve injustice still haunt the psyches of readers caught in the grip of cultural dilemmas that offer no easy way out.

Notes

1 William F. Nolan, *The "Black Mask" Boys: Masters in the Hard-Boiled School of Detective Fiction* (New York: William Morrow, 1985), 28.

2 Ibid., 28.

3 Ibid., 39–40.

4 Raymond Chandler, "The Simple Art of Murder," in *Later Novels and Other Writings* (1944; New York: Library of America, 1995), 989.

5 Irvin Faust, afterward to *Fast One* by Paul Cain (1933; reprint, Carbondale: Southern Illinois University Press, 1978), 309.

6 Lee Horsley, *The Noir Thriller* (Basingstoke, UK: Palgrave, 2001), 42, 44.

7 Earl Derr Biggers, *The House without a Key* (New York: Grosset & Dunlap, 1925), 76.

8 Ibid., 207.

9 Nolan, *"Black Mask Boys,"* 39–40.

10 Horsley, *Noir Thriller*, 71.

11 Horace McCoy, *They Shoot Horses, Don't They?* (New York: Simon & Schuster, 1935), 51.

12 Ibid., 183.

13 Ross Macdonald, "The Writer as Detective Hero," in *Detective Fiction: A Collection of Critical Essays*, ed. Robin W. Winks (1973; Englewood Cliffs, NJ: Prentice-Hall, 1980), 183.

14 David Lehman, *The Perfect Murder: A Study in Detection* (New York: Free Press, 1989), 62.

15 Jim Thompson, *The Killer inside Me* (1952; reprint, New York: Vintage, 1991), 46.

16 Dorothy B. Hughes, *In a Lonely Place* (New York: Duell, Sloan and Pearce, 1947), 17–18.

17 Dorothy B. Hughes, *The Candy Kid* (New York: Duell, Sloan and Pearce, 1950), 149.

18 Patricia Highsmith, "Strangers on a Train," in *Patricia Highsmith: Selected Novels and Short Stories* (New York: W. W. Norton, 2011), 13.

19 Ibid., 19.

20 Ibid., 81.

21 Ibid., 224.

22 Dolores Hitchens, *Beat Back the Tide* (Garden City, NY: Doubleday, 1954), 103.

23 Ross Macdonald, *The Chill* (New York: Alfred A, Knopf, 1964), 197.

24 James Crumley, *Bordersnakes* (New York: Warner Books, 1996), 3.

25 James Crumley, *The Last Good Kiss* (New York: Random House, 1978), 3.

26 Ibid., 4, 89.

27 Michael McGarrity, *Tularosa* (New York: Norton, 1996), 9.

28 Michael McGarrity, *Nothing But Trouble* (New York: Dutton, 2005), 123.

29 James Ellroy, *L.A. Confidential* (New York: Warner Books, 1990), 5.

30 Ibid., 141.

31 Michael Connelly, *The Black Echo* (1992; reprint, New York: Grand Central, 2002), 76.

32 Ibid., 445.

33 Ibid., 73.

34 Elmore Leonard, *Glitz* (New York: Arbor House, 1985), 161.

35 Elmore Leonard, *Get Shorty* (1990; New York: Harper Collins 2011), 141.

36 Ibid., 216.

37 Ibid., 298.

38 Elmore Leonard, *Unknown Man No. 89* (New York: Delacorte, 1977), 97.

CHAPTER 17

The Beats and the American West

Robert Bennett

The Beat generation – a small literary coterie whose principal members include Jack Kerouac, Allen Ginsberg, and William Burroughs – is conventionally defined by its origins, or the shared spaces and experiences that initially drew the group together: a desire to write, aborted studies at Columbia University, Times Square's drug and hustler culture, some petty criminality, and occasional stints at local psychiatric hospitals.[1] Located thus, the Beat generation is routinely regarded as a prototype of post–World War II America's emergent counterculture.[2]

And yet this origin narrative often obscures as much as it reveals about the larger significance of Beat culture. For the Beat ethos relies less upon its singular genesis than on its multiple exoduses, or the Beats' constant taking to the road, their nonchalant (even eager) exchanging of roots for routes, and their copious unpredictable departures, far-flung voyages, and heterogeneous lines of flight – from Denver, San Francisco, and New Orleans to Mexico City, Tangiers, Prague, and beyond.[3] Consequently, the very term "Beat generation" is practically a misnomer, mistakenly reifying what is better understood as a Beat diaspora. After all, Beat culture was little more than embryonic and even largely made up of mere juvenilia, until *after* the Beats hit the road, headed west, and then anointed Neal Cassady, the "western kinsman of the son," as its primary muse, making the Beat movement not only a diasporic *movement* but one traveling in an explicitly westward direction.[4] The Beats may have been conceived in the East, but Beat culture was born, like Cassady himself, in a jalopy traveling west. For absent Cassady's explicitly western "wild yea-saying" it is not even clear that the Beat movement would have ever taken anything remotely resembling the form that it eventually did.[5] Cassady, his westernness, and the literal physical western journeys that he inspired – arguably more, even much more, than post–World War II New York City – was the prime mover and the sine qua non of Beat culture at large.[6]

Obviously, the Beats' travels, Cassady, and the American West have all inescapably formed part of the Beat story, and new feminist, multicultural, and transnational analyses have already extended our understanding of Beat culture's wider possibilities.[7] But while my own literary history of the Beats clearly shares broad sympathies with previous revisionist scholarship, my specific argument follows a somewhat different, regionalist or even postregionalist, direction, arguing à la James Clifford or Arjun Appadurai that Beat culture is best understood as a polynucleated diasporic community constantly in motion.[8] Moreover, the grand mythologies, landscapes, and personae of the American West not only set Beat culture in motion, but also gave it an initial direction, endowed it with an ethos and a mythology, established its mature voice, empowered its new visions and vistas, and provided it with its primary, indispensible muse. If nothing else, we gain a new perspective on the Beats when they are reconsidered as western American writers.[9] In addition, we develop a new perspective – a postregional, diasporic, outsider, Beat perspective – on the American West itself.

Nowhere is Beat culture's connection to the West more evident than when Sal Paradise, Kerouac's alter-ego narrator in *On the Road*, pauses mid-cross-country journey in Des Moines to sleep at a "gloomy old Plains inn of a hotel" where he has an extraordinary experience: "the one distinct moment in my life, the strangest moment of all, when I didn't know who I was – I was far away from home, haunted and tired with travel, in a cheap hotel room I'd never seen ... and I looked at the cracked high ceiling and really didn't know who I was for about fifteen strange seconds. I wasn't scared; I was just somebody else, some stranger, and my whole life was a haunted life, the life of a ghost."[10] More importantly, Paradise describes how this epiphany occurs "halfway across America, at the dividing line between the East of my youth and the West of my future, and maybe that's why it happened right there and then, that strange red afternoon."[11] While characters in American culture – from Huck Finn to Holden Caulfield – have routinely lit out for the western territories seeking transformations of one kind or another, few characters have ever made this western transformation as quickly or as easily as Paradise. For it is inside a mere "fifteen strange seconds" that Paradise transforms himself from easterner to westerner, reproducing in extreme miniature American culture's grand metanarrative of western transformation.[12]

Taken at face value Paradise's account appears facile, even ridiculous. Certainly geography changes us, even transforms us, but not just like that – all in a flash. Surely the transition to westernness must come at a price of travel, toil, and travail. But Kerouac's account offers only a far-cical reductio ad absurdum of Turner's grand themes of the West's vast, open landscape, of working this land and being shaped by its soil, and ultimately of forging a new rugged democratic western identity. For isn't *this* what it means to become western: that one has traveled the stations of Turner's cross and through this pilgrimage been transformed into an authentic westerner, stripped of the contaminating influences of cities and civilization. Is it really enough simply to be a westward moving traveler or even a mere tourist? Isn't westernness, like Irishness, something to be forged deep within the smithy of the soul? Moreover, by midcentury standards Paradise had barely even begun his westward journey and was yet even to see, let alone experience, what remained of the West's vast, open landscapes. A night in a cheap hotel in Des Moines is not what Turner meant, and yet for Kerouac it somehow sufficed.

But how and why? Could it be possible that Kerouac is actually offering us some new sense of the West? Paradise's West may not evoke grand Turnerian ideals, but might it not offer some new, more diminutive vision of the West and of westernness: perhaps one more closely resembling what Sara Spurgeon refers to as being "incidentally" western or what Stephen Colbert might even call Western-i-ness?[13] Clearly a product of his diasporic dislocation, Kerouac was one of the first writers to redefine a post-Turnerian New West with shallower, more frontierless roots but also with greater mobility and modernity.

For there is no question that Kerouac's novel is shaped fundamentally by its westward trajectory, its need to "go on the road," to "go west," and to follow its western hero, Dean Moriarty.[14] For as Kerouac explains, Paradise's entire journey is premised on a desire to escape the "stulti-fied," "negative," and "tired bookish" East, turning instead toward the West's "wild yea-saying overburst of American joy."[15] And while I focus on Kerouac's more obvious transmutation of Cassady into his protagonist Moriarty, certainly the "cocksman and Adonis of Denver" and his western ways had no less sway over Ginsberg, whose magnum opus, *Howl* (1956), which "journey[s] to Denver," concluded its third section, "I am with you in Rockland in my dreams you walk dripping from a sea-journey on the highway across America in tears to the door of my cottage in the Western night."[16]

But the "new horizon" of Kerouac's novel is decisively not Turner's open, wild, free frontier landscape with its rugged democratic individuals, but rather a Beat West, a beaten down, rundown, degraded, degenerate West, and yet both in spite of and because of its blightedness,

Kerouac, in the classic Beat tradition, sees this beaten down West as simultaneously beaten and beatific.[17] For if we analyze Kerouac's West carefully, every Turnerian experience of "zooming all night across Nebraska, Wyoming, and the Utah desert" or "rolling under the stars, generally the Western stars" is matched by another, or even two, experiences of an exhausted and disappearing West: a West that has been transformed into "cute suburban cottages, of one damn kind or another," a West now populated by "fat businessmen in boots and ten-gallon hats," and a West whose mining towns turned "ghost towns" have in turn turned into New Western playgrounds for "chichi tourists."[18] These are not Turner's vast, open spaces but their beaten down opposites. In fact, Kerouac describes the West not as a new frontier at all, but as the "end of America" itself, an explicitly frontierless region at continent's end where there simply is "no more land."[19] And consequently, instead of being peopled by rugged individuals, this frontierless Beat West, and above all its end-of-the-road California, is a "land of lonely and exiled and eccentric lovers who come like birds, and the land where everybody somehow looks like broken-down, handsome, decadent movie actors."[20] Or as Kerouac adds later, his West is a place where everybody "look[s] like a broken-down movie extra, a withered starlet; disenchanted stunt-men, midget auto-racers, poignant California Characters with their end-of-the-continent sadness, handsome, decadent, Casanova-ish men, puffy-eyed motel blondes, hustlers, pimps, whores, masseurs, bellhops – a lemon lot, and how's a man going to make a living with a gang like that?"[21] In California, in particular, the Beats found the epitome of their Beat New West: a West at the end of the frontier.

And yet for Kerouac these frontierless spaces and faces are the real West, or at least the real emerging postfrontier New West, a new diasporic or rhizomatic postregion uprooted and unmoored from any nostalgia for roots – or even for the soil they grow in. Moreover, it is within this West that Kerouac finds the Beat virtues of being simultaneously beaten down and beatific. What makes this Beat vision of the American West so powerful is precisely its rejection of any hint of Turnerian idealism; its clear-eyed perception of and analysis of the New frontierless (suburban, tourist, and even toxic) Wests that have replaced the Turnerian past – *and* its move-it-on-a-long aspiration to keep exploring new postwestern frontiers (first in Mexico and later elsewhere across the globe). For Kerouac, the American West is truly what Neil Campbell has defined as a rhizomatic West, one lacking in pristine nostalgic forms but abundant in new impure, globally mobile possibilities.[22] In fact, if the cultural logic of Kerouac's novel is correct, then the last place that you might find new frontiers anymore is in the American West itself.

Taken to its extreme, Kerouac's new vision of the West becomes outright apocalyptic, offering what Stephen Tatum describes as "Wovoka's neo-catastrophist epistemology," which replaces "Turner and his theory of progressive development" with a "more suggestive model for reinterpreting western American history."[23] Or as Kerouac's vision of Dean characterizes it, the West either is or is fast becoming a "burning shuddering frightful Angel ... approaching like a cloud, with enormous speed ... I saw his wings; I saw his old jalopy chariot with thousands of sparking flames shooting out from it; I saw the path it burned over the road ... destroying bridges, drying rivers.... Behind him charred ruins smoked."[24] Like Ginsberg "listening to the crack of doom on the hydrogen jukebox," these are of course cold war images of a very real threat of nuclear annihilation, but they also herald a new western ecocritical warning of resource depletion and environmental contamination, offering yet another example of how Beat culture helped articulate a bold, new vision and understanding of the American West itself: beaten down, frontierless, uprooted, and even apocalyptic.[25]

Finally, I mention only in passing that Kerouac's and the Beats' sense of the western frontier also turns global when Kerouac redirects his journey "no longer east-west, but magic *south*."[26] No longer privileging the American West as some singular, essential frontier of discovery, Kerouac and company would turn south toward Mexico while William Burroughs and Paul Bowles would end up in Tangiers with Ginsberg traveling to Morocco, India, Paris, Prague, and beyond. These writers' destinations, modes of travel, and worldviews might not have ever entirely freed themselves of vestigial traces of neo-Turnerian western romanticism, but the Beat travelers who refused to stop at America's western shores would completely redefine and globalize what it now means in American culture to light out for western territories and explore new frontiers that now extend in many directions. Reconceptualizing Beat culture as diasporic rather than generational only helps further emphasize how the Beats extended their western journeys in myriad directions toward numerous, postnational frontiers.

Now if we are talking about this post-Turnerian, post-west, then it is more believable that Kerouac could have intuited some new westernness in a cheap motel in Des Moines in a matter of seconds. In fact, how could he not, really? For ultimately Kerouac is not experiencing Turner's grand West but a new highly mobile, frontierless, transnational, and even apocalyptic Beat (beaten down/beatific) postwestern landscape for which a cheap motel in Des Moines is arguably as good an emblem as any other. More importantly, Beat literature helped create much of the cultural framework through which American culture at large has come to understand (or at times even perceive) the post–World War II American West as diasporic Beat writers have performed the cultural work of imagining and reimagining western narratives and spaces. After all, while the Beats may not have been the first artists to light out for the territories, they were among the first major American literary movements both to relocate itself en masse to the American West and simultaneously to emerge from the West Coast itself. Moreover, Beat culture, including its regional engagement with the American West, ultimately proved influential within American culture at large, so if we take Beat culture as a westward-moving and western-located literary movement (instead of an East Coast one), this might demonstrate western culture's own increasing national visibility with the Beats' westward diasporic migration representing one of the first significant examples of American culture's realignment in response to the post–World War II Sunbelt shift in American politics and demographics.

West Coast Beat Writers

In addition to moving west, becoming western, and engaging the West in art, the Beat generation can be understood as western because so many Beat writers were themselves westerners – either by birth or by relocation – thereby providing yet one more western dimension to Beat culture.[27] Lawrence Ferlinghetti and Gary Snyder are perhaps the two most recognizable Beats who made their careers primarily on the West Coast, but other Beats who can be considered West Coasters, in whole or in part, include Lew Welch, Kirby Doyle, Diane DiPrima, Philip Lamantia, Joanne Kyger, Robert Duncan, Michael McClure, Philip Whalen, Jack Spicer, and Robin Blaser. In fact, in terms of pure numbers there were arguably more West Coast than East Coast Beats, and California – San Francisco in particular – played as central a role in the development of Beat culture as New York City did. From Allen Ginsberg's famous reading of *Howl* at the Six Gallery to City Lights Books ongoing publication of Beat works, including *Howl* itself, San Francisco helped anchor the production of Beat culture throughout the Beat period. Moreover, the West Coast Beats can arguably be seen as having explored a wider variety of literary projects, ranging from Snyder's ecopoetry and Eastern mysticism to Diane DiPrima's psychedelic eroticism and Jack Spicer's eclectic mixture of deep image poetry, queer poetics, and a sense of the poet as essentially a medium for receiving intergalactic messages. They don't call it the Left Coast for nothing, and its diverse Beat poets explored a remarkably broad, not to mention eclectic, range of poetic visions. Moreover, given the continual, even incessant, interaction and cross-pollination between East and West Coasts, drawing rigid distinctions between the groups seems both futile and counterproductive, and certainly the West Coast Beats have earned the right to be considered peers with their unmoored East Coast counterparts.

Because Ferlinghetti and Snyder are already widely known, I want to discuss briefly the significance of one West Coast Beat poet who is only beginning to receive his due recognition through works such as Maria Damon's *The Dark End of the Street: Margins in American Vanguard Poetry* and *Postliterary America: From Bagel Shop Jazz to Micropoetics.*[28] Bob Kaufman, an African American and Jewish poet originally from New Orleans, was himself a transplant to San Francisco, but that is where he spent most of his career living the Beat lifestyle, often performing his poems spontaneously in coffee shops or even in the streets and occasionally finding himself in jail after doing provocative things like urinating on a police officer. He even took a decade-long vow of silence after the assassination of John F. Kennedy. "Bagel Shop Jazz" may not be Kaufman's best poem, but it is perhaps his most direct statement about the relationship between the East and West Coast Beats. Interjecting into Beat culture a far more sophisticated understanding of race and ethnicity than we find in Kerouac's blackface minstrelsy, Kaufman calls out Beats like Kerouac, in a gentle but pointed way, for being mere "Coffee-faced Ivy Leaguers" whose Ivy League privilege shaped their more brown than black understanding of the black culture that they exploited.[29] In addition, Kaufman criticizes those for whom being Beat is more of a fashion statement or cultural fad, describing them as "Shadow people, projected on coffee-shop walls" and "Mulberry-eyed girls in black stockings" who smell "vaguely of mint jelly and last night's bongo drummer."[30] In contrast, Kaufman describes his own less superficial and blacker understanding of Beat culture, which he has learned from less ethnically and class privileged parts of the city "during [his] long Grant Avenue night" or his "personal Harvard" on a "Fillmore district step."[31] And Kaufman's more powerful understanding of the racial and class complexities of Beat culture extends throughout almost every poem in his oeuvre, raising profound issues for our conceptualization of Beat culture: Is it not possible that the racial and class complexity of Kaufman's poetry might make it often not only better poetry, but also more Beat, than Kerouac's own writing? There are single poems by Kaufman that have far more to say about black history and the black experience – even as a basis for being Beat – than Kerouac's magnum opus, *On the Road*, with its faux jazzy I want to be the "happy, true-hearted, ecstatic Negroes of America," but I also want a "rich girl" to pull a "hundred-dollar bill out of her silk stocking" for me.[32] Compare that with Kaufman's "America, I forgive you … I forgive you / Nailing black Jesus to an imported cross," while "Every day your people get more and more / cars, televisions, sickness, death dreams."[33] And the kicker is "You must have been great / Alive."[34] Certainly, I cannot demonstrate the comparative and distinct abilities of Kerouac and Kaufman with only a handful of lines, but I do hope to demonstrate that it is not always clear that the East Coast Beats should be the principal Beats while the West Coast Beats play second fiddle. When it comes to constructing and reconstructing the Beat canon – East and West – there are an ever-increasing number of approaches, but both eastern and western Beats need to be read critically with an open mind that gives West Coast Beats a fair consideration and an equal share in defining what it means to be Beat in the first place.

The Beats' Western Progeny

The final way that we can think of the Beat generation as western is in terms of its influence on later generations of western American culture. Of course, the obvious way to do this would be to list such writers as Charles Bukowski, Ken Kesey, and Hunter S. Thompson as either precursors or heirs to, or at times even augmenters of, the Beats' counterculturalism, substance abuse, sexism, and existential nomadism – essentially a tradition that heads quickly toward the Haight-Ashbury hippie scene of the late 1960s or the tragic 1969 Rolling Stones concert at Altamont. What is more difficult to do is to construct an alternative, specifically western, legacy of the Beats that continues to evolve, critically analyzing and conceptually complicating oversimplified notions of Beat culture itself. And here Kaufman provides an excellent starting point – for Kaufman rejects, critically analyzes, and offers alternatives to Beat culture's often exoticized, if not outright fetishized, sense of cultural otherness. Even selecting something like Oscàr Zeta Acosta's work over Thompson's engages and complicates the naive racial identities that frequently plague Beat writing. Or we might even consider Jessica Hagedorn's *Gangster of Love* as a very different kind of multicultural, global second-generation Beat novel.

But the West Coast heir to the Beats that I want to mention quickly is Maxine Hong Kingston's *Tripmaster Monkey*, a novel about an Asian American Beat poet living in posthippie San Francisco. Hardly a Hunter S. Thompson knockoff, either in literary style or in lifestyle, Kingston still makes her novel's protagonist a Beat poet of Chinese ancestry named Wittman Ah Sing, a clever nod to the fact that the Beats' ultimate roots lie more in Walt Whitman than in recreational drug use. Similarly, she calls her novel a fake book, nodding again toward the Beats' love of jazz, only refiguring it more in terms of artistic improvisation than in the Beat generation's often unseemly black primitivism. Moreover, Kingston's Beat poet espouses a wide range of Beat values from refusing to work and being a strict pacifist to living diasporically with shallow roots and elevating the value of art and writing in daily life. But Kingston also insists, even demands, that the Beat tradition evolve, that it move past its narrow racial stereotypes, sexist macho posturing, and cultural narrow-mindedness. Consequently, her Beat hero directly addresses and criticizes – instead of excuses – the Beat generation's worst faults while augmenting its best qualities. Refuting Kerouac's primitivist racializing of Asian Americans as twinkling and little, Kingston's character instead declares that he will "refute 'little'" and "Gainsay 'twinkling.'" "A man does not twinkle. A man with balls is not little. As a matter of fact, Kerouac didn't get 'Chinese' right either. Big football player white all-American jock Kerouac. Jock Kerouac. I call into question your naming of me. I trust your sight no more."[35]

Like Kaufman, Kingston criticizes Kerouac for reducing people to their "race. And the wrong race at that," grabbing Kerouac instead "by the lapels of his lumberjack shirt. Pull[ing] him up on his toes" and challenging him mano a mano: "What do you know, Kerouac? What do you know? You don't know shit. I'm the American here. I'm the American walking here. Fuck Kerouac and his American road anyway. Et tu, Kerouac."[36] What could be more Beat than to tell off Kerouac, and yet Kingston also displays here a radically different sense of being Beat, pointing out the flaws in Kerouac's racial and cultural imaginary.

Certainly Kingston's novel belongs to the Beat tradition – portraying the beatnik lifestyle, exploring Beat poetics, inhabiting San Francisco, drawing heavily on Whitman, and loosely modeling its form after jazz – but it also makes the Beat tradition its own on its own terms, rejuvenating Beat culture in the process. In fact, I can think of few passages that ask as directly or as intelligently what it really means to be Beat, who has the right to determine that, and how might that Beat culture continue to evolve in new times and places. That Kingston, a West Coast Beat, is putting her esteemed eastern counterpart in his place only further demonstrates just how far west Beat culture has traveled.

Notes

1 Even my own *Deconstructing Post–WWII New York City: The Literature, Art, Jazz, and Architecture of an Emerging Global Capital* (New York: Routledge, 2002) largely situates the Beats within the context of post–World War II New York City, though my subsequent research increasingly reconceptualizes Beat culture in broader, more diasporic terms.

2 Examples of this can be found in Steven Watson, *The Birth of the Beat Generation: Visionaries, Rebels, and Hipsters* (New York: Pantheon, 1995) and Morris Dickstein, "On and Off the Road: The Outsider as Young Rebel," in *Beat Culture: The 1950s and Beyond* (Amsterdam: VU University Press, 1999), 31–48.

3 This movement outward, away from Beat origin myths and toward a broader, more mobile understanding of Beat culture, is excellently exemplified in A. Robert Lee, *Modern American Counter Writing: Beats, Outriders, and Ethnics* (New York: Routledge, 2010) and *The Transnational Beat Generation*, ed. Nancy M. Grace and Jennie Skerl (New York: Palgrave Macmillan, 2012).

4 Jack Kerouac, *On the Road* (Reprint; New York: Penguin, 2011), 7.

5 Ibid.

6 This westwardly diasporic perspective can be contrasted against the earlier perspective of something like Steve Wilson's "The Author as Spiritual Pilgrim," in *The Beat Generation: Critical Essays*, ed. Kostas Myrsiades (New York: Peter Lang, 2002), 77–91. Instead of taking the Beats' travels literally as a physical diaspora of movement, Wilson explores Kerouac's work primarily figuratively as either a "quest for spiritual enlightenment," a "search for a spiritual cure," or a discovery of the "essence of human existence" (78, 82, 83). Not surprisingly, Wilson makes little of the specifically westward direction of Kerouac's travels as well.

7 Recent examples of this can be found in *Women of the Beat Generation: The Writers, Artists, and Muses at the Heart of a Revolution*, ed. Brenda Knight (Berkeley: Conari, 1996); Joyce Johnson, *Minor Characters: A Beat Memoir* (New York: Penguin, 1999); Manuel Luis Martinez, *Countering the Counterculture: Reading Postwar American Dissent from Jack Kerouac to Tomás Rivera* (Madison: University of Wisconsin Press, 2003); and again in Lee (*Modern American Counter Writing*) as well as Grace and Skerl (*Transnational Beat Generation*).

8 See James Clifford, *Routes: Travel and Translation in the Late Twentieth Century* (Cambridge, MA: Harvard University Press, 1997) and Arjun Appadurai, *Modernity at Large: Cultural Dimensions of Globalization* (Minneapolis: University of Minnesota, 1996).

9 In "Beat and the San Francisco Renaissance," a chapter in Christopher Gair's *The Beat Generation: Beginner's Guides* (Oxford: Oneworld, 2008), the author

does contextualize the Beats' relocation to the American West, but he discusses Ginsberg's latest sexual partners as much as he does the larger influence
of the American West on Beat culture, which he explains no further than a
few quick references to how various West Coast Beat poets shared a "love
of nature" or were "concerned with rural scenes" (67, 71). Similarly, David
Sterritt, *The Beats: A Very Short Introduction* (Oxford: Oxford University
Press, 2013) accurately describes how the Beat movement became a "worldwide cultural revolution," traveling "far beyond the United States," but says
little about how this diasporic traveling substantively transformed the historical evolution of Beat culture itself (107).

10 Kerouac, *On the Road*, 14.

11 Ibid.

12 This metanarrative finds some of its classic expressions in Frederick Jackson
Turner, *The Significance of the Frontier in American History* (Reprint; Eastford,
CT: Martino Fine Books, 2014) and R. W. B. Lewis, *The American Adam*
(Chicago: University of Chicago Press, 1955).

13 See Sara Spurgeon, "Incidentally Western," Past President's Address, Western
American Literature Association Conference, Oakland, California. October
2013. Or consider "westerniness" as a variation on Stephen Colbert's squea-
mishly vacillating neologism "truthiness" as first used on the premier episode,
"Truthiness," of Comedy Central's *The Colbert Report*, October 17, 2005,
http://thecolbertreport.cc.com/episodes/jnv7om/october-17--2005---stone
-phillips (accessed January 15, 2015).

14 Kerouac, *On the Road*, 1.

15 Ibid., 7.

16 Allen Ginsberg, *Howl and Other Poems* (San Francisco: City Lights Books,
1959), 17, 26.

17 Kerouac, *On the Road*, 7.

18 Ibid., 22, 23, 15, 27, 46.

19 Ibid., 71.

20 Ibid., 157.

21 Ibid., 159.

22 Neil Campbell, *The Rhizomatic West: Representing the American West in a
Transnational, Global, Media Age* (Lincoln: University of Nebraska Press,
2008).

23 Stephen Tatum, "Postfrontier Horizons," *Modern Fiction Studies* 50, no. 2
(2004): 461.

24 Kerouac, *On the Road*, 247.

25 Ginsberg, *Howl and Other Poems*, 11.

26 Kerouac, *On the Road*, 253.

27 Michael Davidson's groundbreaking analysis of the West Coast Beats can be
found in *The San Francisco Renaissance: Poetics and Community at Mid-Century*
(Cambridge: Cambridge University Press, 1989).

28 See Maria Damon, *The Dark End of the Street: Margins in American Vanguard
Poetry* (Minneapolis: University of Minnesota Press, 1993) and *Postliterary*

America: From Bagel Shop Jazz to Micropoetries (Iowa City: University of Iowa Press, 2011

29 Bob Kaufman, *Cranial Guitar* (Minneapolis: Coffee House Press, 1996), 107.

30 Ibid.

31 Ibid.

32 Kerouac, *On the Road*, 170–1.

33 Kaufman, *Cranial Guitar*, 105.

34 Ibid.

35 Maxine Hong Kingston, *Tripmaster Monkey: His Fake Book* (New York: Vintage, 1990), 69–70.

36 Ibid., 70.

CHAPTER 18

Contested Wests
Indigenous Americans and the Literature of Sovereignty
John Gamber

In 1830 President Andrew Jackson signed into the law the Indian Relocation Act, "to provide for an exchange of lands with the Indians residing in any of the states or territories, and for their removal west of the river Mississippi."[1] The ever-shifting American West has been Indian Country within the settler psyche ever since. Native people dwell in the spaces west of the national collective self; as such, it seems natural to speak of the land as a contested space of sovereignty when viewed from an Indigenous perspective.[2] Yet what any settler colonial nation believes about the Indigenous people and peoples of the land it occupies – as well as how it defines them legally – should always be viewed skeptically. The United States' construction of the West as Indian Country has always served to justify its presence on the lands it paints to be its overt birthright. The lands of the American West had to be conquered by the denizens of the settled and civilized East Coast. The story of the conquest of those eastern lands thus is written out of the national history ("that was the doing of the French and British") or whitewashed as some happy cooperation (see Thanksgiving).

Just as Native people have been placed in the American West by the settler imaginary, they have also been relegated to the past. Whether temporally or physically, they are, in all cases, "over there," just over the (event) horizon, never "here." American Indians thus represent a spectral distance in time and space. Settler colonialism operates under what Patrick Wolfe calls the "logic of elimination," which "not only refers to the summary liquidation of Indigenous people, though it includes that," but also to the delegitimizing of Indigenous claims to place and identity.[3] Accordingly, the settler state asserts that all the real Indians are dead; what remain are withered relics or inauthentic, assimilated tragedies. Native American people, and with them, Native American Studies, must correct these imposed temporal distances. Native artists have developed a number of strategies for dealing with them, with many opting to draw links between past and present in their work, and to rectify literary history in the process. Within Native American literature, this demonstration of the past and present as inexorable often takes the form of narratives that move back and forth across spans of time: Leslie Marmon Silko's *Ceremony*, N. Scott Momaday's *The Way to Rainy Mountain*, Craig Womack's *Drowning in Fire*, LeAnne Howe's *Miko Kings*, and Louise Erdrich's *Tracks* all move back and forth between the past and present in order to demonstrate that the present only makes sense in relation to the past. What is more, these texts connect the present and past to demonstrate the ongoing presence of Native people, a tacit indication that they have never ceased to be and never ceded their place to settlers. Native literature, however, seldom overtly addresses the future and the ways that Native people can maintain and even bolster their sovereignties moving forward in time. Seldom, but not never. A few Native American authors have crafted works of speculative fiction, a movement that has been branded Indigenous futurism. This essay addresses two such works – Silko's *Almanac of the Dead* and Gerald Vizenor's *Bearheart: The Heirship Chronicles* – and argues that these works seek to define Native sovereignty in the contested spaces of the American West in the present and future, offering examples of what Indigenous sovereignty could, should, and, equally importantly, should not be. These texts, however, also connect their representations of the future to mythic pasts that serve to underscore Native sovereignties as simultaneously permanent and fluid – enduring across time, changing, but never eradicated. While I focus on these two novels of Native futurism, issues of sovereignty crop up throughout Native American literature, albeit in a host of differing forms.

Naturally, any attempt to summarize those forms will most certainly be fraught with overgeneralization and riddled with elisions. Nonetheless, within the prominent texts arising from the 1960s to the present we can identify countless examples. N. Scott Momaday's publications focus on Native continuity in the face of movement and ever-changing cultural contexts. *House Made of Dawn* (1968) represents Pueblo connections to place and the importance of physical presence within tribal space as a critical element in cultural maintenance and participation. Meanwhile, *The Way to Rainy Mountain* (1969) explores Kiowa movements, establishing tribal presence across a wide geographic range that includes their eventual nation established in Oklahoma in 1867. The other novels categorized as "homing plots" – which portray Native characters returning to their homelands to heal physically and/or psychically, including Leslie Marmon Silko's *Ceremony*, among many others – assert similar positions to that of

House Made of Dawn: Native people are most healthy among their community members and in their community's home space. Political claims of sovereignty are often present, if understated, and these texts generally assert a cultural sovereignty, a right and need for Native citizens to exist within their sovereign spaces.

The 1980s and 1990s give rise to what critics call mixedblood narratives, texts that focus on a hybridized Native positionality. These novels generally follow characters who are of mixed racial descent – usually Native and white – and often, though certainly not always, are away from their homelands attempting to navigate what the texts posit as a liminal personal space. Such novels fit into a spectrum of literature by authors of color at the time, experimenting with so-called hyphenated identities (Asian American, African American, etc). Such approaches tend to deemphasize the importance of citizenship and/or political recognition for racial politics. Nonetheless, they frequently allude to the importance of reclaiming the community that claims the Native person, a collective identity not bound by colonially-imposed racialization. Works including those by Louis Owens, Linda Hogan, and to some degree Louise Erdrich fit under this umbrella.[4] More recent Native American literature is difficult to categorize even broadly without the benefit of hindsight. Nonetheless, writings by LeAnne Howe, David Treuer, and Craig Womack tend to focus on tribally specific issues that emphasize issues of sovereignty, often quite directly, as in Howe's *Shell Shaker* and Womack's *Drowning in Fire*, or in more subtle ways like Treuer's *The Translation of Dr. Apelles*. Meanwhile, such prominent authors as Sherman Alexie or prolific writers as Stephen Graham Jones tend to take significantly less tribally specific approaches.

Silko's *Almanac* – published in 1991 to correspond with the quincentenary of Columbus's voyage – marks the author's foray into the epic, a sprawling text that details the overlapping lives of four primary characters, the identical twin sisters Zeta (a smuggler) and Lecha Cazador ("a well-known psychic who was returning home to Tucson after many years because she was dying of cancer") and two of their employees, Seese and Sterling, the latter an exile from Laguna Pueblo.[5] Much of the novel details the intersecting lives of these characters prior to and after their encountering one another in Arizona, where the sisters, entrusted with the eponymous almanac, work to decipher it. The almanac itself derives from a Maya codex to which pages and text have been added and subtracted as it has been passed down across generations and thousands of miles.[6] An array of characters populate Silko's text: Indigenous people from throughout North America, mafiosos, wealthy white supremacists, land developers, homeless men, Mexican power brokers, Latin American Marxists, and many others. Unlike *Bearheart, Almanac* takes place not after, but just on the cusp of the United States' collapse. Whether that collapse will happen in the near or distant future remains unknown, though the end of the "Great Experiment" does seem nigh.

The brewing action of *Almanac* arises as a pair of Mayan twins, Tacho and El Feo, walk northward from Chiapas, the southernmost state in Mexico. These twins lead a massive and growing "army" of mainly Indigenous people as they work through military, financial, and spiritual means to reclaim the lands of North America from colonial and corporate interests. How long this journey will take is unclear, but the text portrays it as an inevitable tide, akin to Marx's prophecy of a proletarian revolution, though devoid of Leninism's professional revolutionaries. This revolution, the novel insists, must grow organically, provided the primary and unwavering tenet remains that the land must be restored to Indigenous communities.[7]

Gerald Vizenor published *Bearheart* in 1990; it is actually a slightly revised version of his 1978 *Darkness in Saint Louis Bearheart* recast with a different framing device.[8] Set in the not-too-distant future, the novel follows Proude Cedarfair IV from his ancestral home in a Minnesota cedar forest (for which his great grandfather, the first Proude Cedarfair, was named) on a journey toward the Chacoan site of Pueblo Bonito, near Santa Fe, New Mexico. The U.S. government lies in a state somewhere between disarray and nonexistence, a condition brought about primarily by the exhaustion of petroleum reserves and by its inability or refusal to invest in alternative fuel sources. As such, the foundering United States claims one-half of all timber within its boundaries as emergency resources. Cedarfair refuses to allow the trees to be cut down and frightens off the federal agents who arrive to cut them. Nonetheless, a nearby tribal politician rounds up a goon squad, and Cedarfair has no choice but to flee in order to save his skin.

Cedarfair travels by river, by donated car, by foot, by liberated U.S. mail truck, and finally by rail, meeting up with an odd assortment of fellow pilgrims, including several dogs and crows, seeking out a "New world paradise in New Mexico."[9] As we will see, Vizenor puns on both pilgrims and "new world." The first reference plays with the foundational story of settler colonialism in the United States in the form of the Pilgrims and the first Thanksgiving. Native people were (and remain) displaced by these invaders, yet the United States glorifies them as brave but innocuous, and as welcomed by the Wampanoag whom they displaced. The second refers not to "the New World" with its Eurocentric connotations, but to an actually new world beyond our current terrestrial place. *Bearheart* does not term this paradise a nation, despite what I will demonstrate is a deep and abiding interest in the issues of Native national sovereignty at the text's outset. Along the way, almost all of the pilgrims die, while those who survive transform into bears and enter into another world, in an ending whose tone, as Alan Velie notes, "is happy, even triumphant."[10]

I begin with a discussion of *Almanac* to establish the way Silko's text emphasizes Indigenous mobility over broad spans of time, demonstrating international Indigenous connections that critics have yet to note.[11] The novel's denouement approaches as twin brothers, El Feo and Tacho – who speak to and travel with sacred macaws – walk northward from Mexico toward the border with the United States.[12] In a version of a Pueblo origin story, the people follow a pair of twin brothers into this world. Eventually, the community that walks with those twins reaches the site of its village. Some of the people (those who carry a brightly colored bird's egg) choose to stay, while others (who carry a dull colored bird's egg) choose to walk farther south. Ironically, when the eggs hatch, the monochrome crow emerges from the brightly colored egg, while the brightly colored macaw (or parrot in some versions) emerges from the dull one.[13] The people to the south, the Indigenous people who now populate Mexico and the regions in which macaws live, are the brothers, sisters, and cousins of Pueblo peoples who split off during this period. Macaws and parrots have decorated Pueblo art and been revered within Pueblo communities for centuries. Silko draws on specifically Pueblo traditions to demonstrate connections between Pueblo and erstwhile Pueblo Indigenous communities. The roots of her kinships date back to time immemorial, a similar mythic time to Vizenor's use of Pueblo stories, as we will see. *Almanac*, then, crafts an Indigenous internationalism of Native people from one nation creating new ones. To that end, La Escapía exclaims, in contrast to the claims of provincial tribalism from condescending white Marxists, "*We* are internationalists! *We* are not just tribal!... Tribal internationalists!"[14] However, while Silko's text overtly portrays characters calling for Native internationalism, her narrative in fact places that internationalism within a proto-Laguna origin.[15] Indigenous people within the Pueblo traditions that Silko builds upon have been connected throughout history; settler colonialism, however, benefits from severing those connections and fostering loyalty to the colonial nation over cross-tribal and international community.

Like *Bearheart*, *Almanac* demonstrates the importance of Indigenous physical as well as temporal mobilities that challenge all manner of borders in favor of connections among the mythic past, the present, and the future. Silko alludes to specific tribal origin narratives that assert Indigenous traditions and rights of movement predating the establishment of colonial federal borders. Silko's use of the Pueblo narrative describing a macaw-bearing ancestor migrating south does more than connect Laguna people within a matrix of Indigenous community (including those who dwell south of what would become the Mexico/United States border); it also reasserts and rearticulates the classic call-and-response rallying cry of Chicana/o activism: "We didn't cross the border. The border crossed us."[16] Calabasas, a Yaqui smuggler, proclaims, "We don't believe in boundaries. Borders. Nothing like that. We are here thousands of years before the first whites. We are here before maps or quit claims. We know where we belong on this earth. We have always moved freely. North-south. East-west."[17] He continues, "We pay no attention to what isn't real. Imaginary lines. Imaginary minutes and hours. Written law. We recognize none of that. And we carry a great many things back and forth. We don't see any border. We have been here and this has continued thousands of years. We don't stop. No one stops us."[18] Calabasas asserts a location of belonging, but rather than a bounded place, it has the form of a bioregionally defined territory (the Sonoran desert, in this case). Belonging includes a freedom of movement that is incommensurate with Westphalian rigid boundary making. Of course, borders create exclusions and binaries of belonging (inside/outside, native/foreign), as well as complexes of legality of bodies (citizen, resident alien, undocumented). The fixity of borders (and laws) likewise depends on a fixity of time, the temporal border between the past and the present, a temporal border made murky by Calabasas's use of the present tense in establishing Yaqui presence (he asserts, "We *are* here thousands of years before the first whites. We *are* here before maps or quit claims," rather than "we *were* here").[19] Borders also create crimes, in this case, smuggling. Calabasas demonstrates that Yaqui people have been moving objects, technologies, knowledge, religions, animals, plants, tools, and themselves since time immemorial. There was never any crime in that until European powers established their own spatially defined legalities and illegalities. The fixities of these definitions, the border imagined as rigid and real (or always pushing outward as is more appropriate of the United States' expansionist agenda), *create* crimes of these ongoing movements. They criminalize Indigenous bodies for doing what they have always done. Nonetheless, from a position that regards Indigenous sovereignty as legitimate, not only are the laws criminalizing border crossing illegitimate, but so are the nations themselves.[20]

Bearheart and *Almanac* insist on the sovereignty of the land itself, on the rights of the other than human to exist in space and place. But the specific qualities of the Cedar Nation mark it as distinct from many constructions of nationhood. The novel declares the circle of cedar trees sovereign in the third paragraph of the main novel (after the framing epistle). This front-end assertion of sovereignty in a text that largely predates current academic emphases on tribal nationhood and sovereignty stands out within Native American literature, particularly as Vizenor is often claimed by cosmopolitan critics as one of their own and as averse to Native nationalism. I have asserted elsewhere the shortcoming of such statements.[21] However, I contend that Vizenor's theorization of the unsustainability of place-based sovereignty means to create tribal sovereign possibilities.

Cedarfair explains the kinship between humans and their arboreal hosts in addressing their sovereignty to a government official. With his chest expanded he proclaims, "This is a sovereign nation.... These trees were the first to grow here, the first to speak of living on this earth.... These trees are sovereign. We are cedar and we are not your citizens.... We are the cedar and the guardians of the sacred directions into the fourth world.... Can you see and feel how we shun your indifference to our lives."[22] It is worth noting that the final line "Can you see and feel how we shun your indifference to our lives" does not end with a question mark, but with a period. The sovereignty of this space allows for this question to exist as a statement understood as inequivocable fact. Sovereignty, after all, cannot exist where it must be asked for; it cannot be granted; it can only be recognized.[23] The people of the cedar forest refuse to recognize claims of any other government, Native or non-Native, tribal, state, or federal over their land, their bodies, or their political existences. Cedarfair disavows citizenship to any of these political constituencies. What is more, he claims kinship to the other than human in a critical way. While many Indigenous communities recognize kinship to other than human creatures (such kinship lies at the root of totemic social structures – and these totemic relationships are often seen as utterly literal), Vizenor's Cedarfair goes further. The trees themselves are sovereign and the narrative first-person plural *are* the trees. He does not claim that these are *our* trees, nor that we are *of* the trees, but that we *are* the trees.

Knowing, as we do, that Cedarfair is removed from the Cedar Circus, the tribal homeland; that the trees are almost certain to be removed, living kin killed by invaders, what exactly happens to the cedar nation, its citizens, and its sovereignty? We have to reexamine the prior quotation to answer such questions. Cedarfair declares that the trees are "guardians of the sacred directions into the fourth world." The term "fourth world" carries overlapping meanings, both in terms of Indigenous people globally and in terms of migrations of Native people over spans of mythic time. The Secwepemc (also called Shuswap) chief George Manuel is often (albeit possibly erroneously) credited with coining the term "fourth world" to mean the Indigenous and landless populations of the world – distinct from the first and third worlds, in particular – in his 1978 book *The Fourth World: An Indian Reality*.[24] Since then, Indigenous groups have claimed the term – though this use ousts many of the non-Indigenous but landless communities Chief Manual originally included under the term's definitional umbrella (the Romani, for example). Beyond this more widely known use of "fourth world" lies a key mythic element of this novel.

The fourth world also refers, within a number of Native traditions, to other worlds in which we dwelled before the one we currently inhabit. Vizenor makes use of such stories, placing them within a syncretic ancestral Pueblo and Anishinaabe tradition with his pilgrims seeking out "*Wanaki* Pueblo Bonito, a place of peace in the village of the heard."[25] Pueblo origin stories (which include the twins of Silko's text) explain that the people emerged from the earth to the north of their current locations, mainly in New Mexico along the path of the Rio Grande.[26] They traveled south to reach the places they would eventually settle. However, prior to this emergence, there existed other worlds, deeper within the earth. In various iterations of these stories, the previous worlds were uninhabitable for differing reasons, though commonly because their darkness disallowed the growth of plants, especially corn.[27] Twins (in some instances females, as in Laguna and Acoma stories; in other males, as in those from Zuni) are reared beneath the earth, in many cases by Thought-Woman, who conjures the world into being by thinking or speaking it. The people move up into this, the fourth world.[28]

As a part of its Indigenous syncretism, *Bearheart*'s prelude also provides a version of the Anishinaabe origin and migration story that offers a mythic explanation of Native mobility as a long-standing Anishinaabe practice. It explains, "the earth turtles emerge from the great flood of the first world. In the second world the earth is alive in the magical voices and ceremonial words of birds and the healing energies of plants.... The third world turns evil with contempt for living and fear of death.... In the fourth world evil spirits are outwitted in the secret languages of animals and birds."[29] Vizenor's narrative offers a story of the people's relocation from various worlds, a sequencing that appears in countless Native histories. Vizenor's version emphasizes the world being corrupted, subjected to a fall from a golden age into an evil one. The great evil, though, lies not in mere death and destruction as in *Almanac*, but in contempt and fear. Vizenor measures these as negative emotions that stand in the way of the exercise of our imaginations, the very faculties we will use in the next world to outwit (though never completely defeat) the forces of evil.

In the Anishinaabe story, the people moved to the Great Lakes from the Atlantic Ocean and emerged into this world after a great flood that ended when earth was cast from beneath the waters onto the back of a great turtle (hence, the Americas as Turtle Island in many Native traditions). The people have moved not only from world to world, but all over this world. Similar stories of emergence into this world (earth diver tales, among others) abound in Native narratives. The movements within these stories can serve, Vizenor's text suggests, for a reimagination of indigeneity as something not exclusively place based.[30] While being Indigenous within the Americas in particular (this is significantly less true in Polynesia, for example) has come to be associated with a very specific location, Vizenor's text challenges such rigid notions.[31] Native people have always been on the move, these stories tell us. They have traveled across this world, but they have also moved between worlds. Native people can continue this move – transporting themselves wherever they need or choose to go, without losing their ties to place, and without forfeiting their indigeneity. When we consider how many Native communities and groups have been removed (forcibly or otherwise) from their ancestral lands, we understand how important such transportability is.

Vizenor, then, draws upon both Anishinaabe (the transformation into bears, the migration to the Great Lakes) and Pueblo (Chaco Canyon as emergence site) stories to explain and even encourage the movements of his pilgrims and their leader, Proude Cedarfair. The novel explains, "We are finished with the third world now"[32]; the time has come to travel to the world the people are prophesied to inhabit. Moreover, Vizenor moves out of his Anishinaabe nationalist mode, into an internationalist one. The conclusions of Vizenor's statement that we are finished with the third world are powerful. If the world of this text, a world that has not quite come to be but that rather resembles our own, is not the fourth world, then we are only passing through.[33] We are not meant to remain, and as such, we are not meant to form lingering physical bonds with place here. Bearheart explains, "Fourth Proude saw his cedar nation existing in the minds and hearts of the living, he did not feel he needed to prove the endurance of sovereignties."[34] Proude understands sovereignty to be a concept, one that begins with the mind and can present itself in countless forms and iterations. This is not to say that people should merely accede to forced changes of place. The Cedarfairs fight generation after generation for the land of which they are a part. *Bearheart* does not promote the blithe acceptance of displacement. It promotes the refusal to accept other people's disidentification of displaced Native people as Indigenous. The settler state may move Native people and, in so doing, attempt to eliminate Native people, but Native people need not accept such elimination. As Deloria reminds, "Although Indians surrendered the physical occupation and ownership of their ancestral lands, they did not abandon the spiritual possession that had been a part of them."[35] Instead, Native people can rearticulate their indigeneity, in this world and the next. In the face of displacement, Native people must go on.[36]

While the pragmatic utility of such spiritual connections to space might at first seem challenging to determine, they in fact emphasize the possibilities for Indigenous mobility. Cedarfair explains some of the potential in such mobility. The text tells us, "First Proude ... spoke with the trees. He became the cedar wood. 'We are the cedar,' he told his sons. 'We cannot leave ourselves.... We are the breath and voice of this woodland.'"[37] If the Cedarfairs are the cedar and cannot leave themselves, then dwelling in the location of the specific cedar trees from which they originate need not serve as the sole definition of their indigeneity. Native people take their Indigenous home with them wherever they travel and their indigeneity does not end when they leave. Such statements are critical in light of the prevalence of discourses regarding Native authenticity favoring reservation-based people despite the fact that the overwhelming majority of Native people (78 percent) do not live in their reservation communities.[38] If living on land recognized by the federal government as Native land marks a person or community as Indigenous, then most people who identify as Native are not. That being the case, we must rethink the idea that Indigenous people must be bound to a specific space. Inasmuch as this is true, Vizenor's text seeks to push the ways we frame sovereignty in terms of this mobility.

Bearheart perceives human relationships to space as primarily psychic; we form and maintain those bonds with our imagination. While the people of the cedar forest are displaced, they remain the people of the cedar forest. Moreover, the land is never truly lost to them. On multiple occasions Proude revisits the cedar wood in personal and social imaginative contexts. We see one example of this recurrent theme throughout the novel as follows: "Proude soared through his breath to the *migis* sandridge where he undressed and swam through the brume to the graves of his fathers in the water."[39] Proude visits his ancestors in his imagination, seeking their graves as a way of maintaining his connections in the face of relocation. If travel to ancestral homelands can be psychic and imaginative, then removal need not sever Indigenous ties to place.

While Vizenor challenges static notions of space and our relationships to it, Silko establishes a global permanence, but both maintain that Indigenous space exists in a variety of locations. As such, our relationships to space and place should always be in process. This is not to justify abuse or theft of space and place. Rather, Vizenor's text emphasizes that concepts of human ownership and anthropocentrism are simply faulty. Land is never stolen from people, because people do not own it. Land can be, however, abused – treated as an inferior thing rather than a sovereign entity in its own right. People can also be abused, removed from land they see as kin. For Silko, though, space takes on a fixity through the permanence of the earth itself and the inherent sacredness it possesses. *Almanac* contends, "land and water could never be desecrated; blasted open and polluted by man, but never desecrated. Man only desecrated himself in such acts.... Earth always was and would ever be sacred."[40] The earth in its entirety remains sacred within *Almanac*'s worldview, and no amount of human tampering with it can change that. Silko's text continues, "Mother Earth might be ravaged by the Destroyers, but she still loved the people."[41] The earth is both changed and permanent, but our relationship to it never truly alters.[42]

While Vizenor's text might view the possession of land ambivalently, Silko's absolutely exalts it. Characters repeat, again and again, that within the brewing pan-Indian movement, "nothing mattered but taking back tribal land."[43] This, the land, and Native ownership of it trump all other considerations. Within an Indigenous framework, the land, however, is more than mere possession. Land represents kin as well as relationships with countless species and spaces. Pueblo people often point to a single location, the *sipapu*, from which they emerged into this world.[44]

To that end, the presence of settlers on the aboriginal lands of the Americas in *Almanac* represents more than a trespass; it is casus belli, an act of war. Zeta asserts, "War had been declared the first day the Spaniards set foot on Native American soil, and the same war had been going on ever since: the war was for the continents called the Americas."[45] In this war, weapons have many forms. We learn, for example, that Lecha keeps "the notebooks and fragments of the old manuscript" in a "wooden ammunition box."[46] The almanac (and perhaps *Almanac*) itself is a weapon. However, many in the movement understand the need for more conventional weapons. "All that mattered was obtaining the weapons and supplies the people needed to retake the land."[47] Some characters insist that the retaking of Native land will happen in part through violence (or at least the threat of violence); others disagree, but all recognize that it will not occur through violence alone. At any rate, the return of Native land serves a broader purpose, and if violence is required, it is not without a good reason. *Almanac* rather optimistically opines, "With the return of Indian land would come the return of justice, followed by peace."[48] No justice is possible from governments that exist on stolen land. Everything about them is born of the ongoing crime that is the settler colonial state. Once the settler state falls, Native people will return to power. In Silko's imagination, this will lead invariably to justice. One can certainly doubt Silko's conclusions, which seem convenient, if not naive. Nonetheless, one can make a case that for justice to exist in any way in the Americas, the colonial legal structures, the originary injustice of modern nations, must be eradicated. Justice represents a square peg to colonialism's round hole – the two can be made to appear to fit, but only through the application of brute force over time.

Such is the contested nature of the West, of Indian Country, and of the Americas. A hope for a tomorrow that is distinct from the present cannot arise in repetitions of old patterns. Native nostalgia (be it cultural, spatial, or racial) is, like all nostalgia, a memory of a time that never was. Moreover, relying on colonial models of static, bounded, ethnic, or especially racialized nations is bound to replicate those colonial models. For Silko, Native communities must be tied to land above all else, but the boundaries between them should be deemphasized if not eliminated. For Vizenor, the new nation must be born in motion – and, perhaps there is also hope in a mythic time parallel to our own. Above all else, these texts reminds us that, as Patrick Wolfe demonstrates, invasion is a structure, not an event.[49] Native people and nations have been structured by that invasion – undoing it is impossible and restructuring it is not as simple as mere recognition. Native people, nations, and sovereignties continue to question the very legitimacy of the settler nation, its simple right to exist. These novels look toward a time when it does not and attempt to conceive a postcolonial America with indigeneity at its center, as its history, and as its future.

Notes

1 *Indian Removal Act*, 1830, chap. CXLVI, sec. 1, http://memory.loc.gov/cgi-bin/ampage?collId=llsl&fileName=004/llsl004.db&recNum=455 (accessed March 17, 2015).

2 We can consider the geographical locations of the sixteen states with no federally recognized Native nations as evidence of this national myth: Arkansas, Delaware, Georgia, Hawaii, Illinois, Kentucky, Maryland, Missouri, New Hampshire, New Jersey, Ohio, Pennsylvania, Tennessee, Vermont, Virginia, West Virginia.

3 Patrick Wolfe, "Settler Colonialism and the Elimination of the Native," *Journal of Genocide Research* 8, no. 4 (2006): 388.

4 It is worth noting that Erdrich's portrayal of human relationships to a specific forest in her novel *Tracks* demonstrates some interesting similarities to Vizenor's that I discuss later.

5 Leslie Marmon Silko, *Almanac of the Dead* (New York: Penguin, 1992), 21.

6 For more on the role of almanacs as a theme relating to Silko's epic, see Joni Adamson, *American Indian Literature, Environmental Justice, and Ecocriticism: The Middle Place* (Tucson: University of Arizona Press, 2001), and Mishuana Goeman, *Mark My Words: Native Women Mapping Our Nations* (Minneapolis: University of Minnesota Press, 2013); the latter contends, "the almanac, as a foundational colonial form of writing, is an originary document producing the myth of nations – myths that are foundational to abusive global economies" (183). Maya Codices are books written in Maya hieroglyph. While only three semicomplete codices remain (the Paris, Dresden, and Madrid Codices, named for the cities in which they are currently housed) hundreds, if not thousands, existed prior to European arrival. Spanish forces destroyed the rest.

7 As Adamson explains, Silko's epic actually presages the Zapatista Army of National Liberation in Chiapas, a predominantly Indigenous collectivity and movement dedicated to land reform in terms of environmental justice, Indigenous land claims and resource control, and the active opposition to neoliberal globalization in *American Indian Literature*, 128.

8 See Gerald Vizenor, *Bearheart: The Heirship Chronicles* (Minneapolis: University of Minnesota Press, 1990). *Bearheart* begins with a chapter titled "Letter to the Reader," a strangely Victorian invocation, allusion, and device. In some ways, Vizenor's move from poetry to the novel is akin to the shift in generic emphasis between the romantic and Victorian eras. Of course, this convention predates these eras, tracing back to the dawn of the novel in *Don Quixote* and continuing through perhaps its most famous U.S. iteration in *Uncle Tom's Cabin*. However, this epistolary frame exists only in this chapter, which Christopher Teuton asserts moves this later version of the novel from "political statement" to one that "highlights aesthetic issues"; see *Deep Waters: The Textual Continuum in American Indian Literature* (Lincoln: University of Nebraska Press, 2010), 105.

9 Vizenor, *Bearheart*, 97.

10 Alan Velie, "Vizenor: Post-Modern Fiction," in *Critical Perspectives on Native American Fiction*, ed. Richard F. Fleck (Pueblo, CO: Passeggiata, 1993), 70.

11 Rachel Adams points out that no one "has adequately explained why Silko ... would locate a significant portion of her novel in Mexico" and rightly offers a

critique of the border between the United States and Mexico as a focus of her international Indian coalition; see Adams, *Continental Divides: Remapping the Cultures of North America* (Chicago: University of Chicago Press, 2009), 50. I add to that the fact of the Pueblo origin connection between Native peoples.

12 As such, the role of so many figures from Pueblo stories begins to make sense. Lecha and Zeta are twin sisters, like the first Pueblo people, Uretsete and Naotsete. For more on these similarities, see Severin Fowles, *An Archaeology of Doings: Secularism and the Study of Pueblo Religion* (Albuquerque: SAR Press, 2013); and Hamilton A. Tyler, *Pueblo Gods and Myths* (Norman: University of Oklahoma Press), 1972.

13 Crow eggs have a dappled turquoise color, while macaw eggs are white or off-white.

14 Silko, *Almanac*, 516.

15 Scholars have offered a variety of other terms for La Escapía's formation: Consider Adams's "Indigenous transnationalism" in *Continental Divides*, 35; Shari Huhndorf's "Pan-Tribal Identity," in *Mapping the Americas: The Transnational Politics of Contemporary Native Culture* (Ithaca, NY: Cornell University Press, 2009), 157; and Elizabeth Cook-Lynn's "Fictionalized Pantribal Nationalism," in *Why I Can't Read Wallace Stegner and Other Essays: A Tribal Voice* (Madison: University of Wisconsin Press, 1996), 90. Like Adams's chapter, Huhndorf's monograph represents an important complication of nationalism with its focus on transnationalism. Nonetheless, as relates to this chapter in particular, Huhndorf's focus is on historical movements of Native people more than those of the future represented in these novels.

16 Adams similarly draws on this phrase in her analysis of *Almanac* in *Continental Divides*, 35.

17 Silko, *Almanac of the Dead*, 216.

18 Ibid.

19 Goeman asserts that within these settler nationalisms, "Borders, like Indians, become common sense," despite the fact that both are invented; see *Mark My Words*, 164.

20 From Calabasas's perspective, smuggling cannot be a crime, not only because of Indigenous rights of movement but also because of the illegitimacy of the United States itself. He wonders: "How could one steal if the government itself was the worst thief. . . . There was not, and there never had been, a legal government by Europeans anywhere in the Americas. Not by any definition, not even by the Europeans' own definitions and laws. Because no legal government could be established on stolen land" (*Almanac* 133). As I argue elsewhere, however, Europeans did indeed craft legal precedents to justify their presence in the Americas.

21 See John Gamber, "Wild Word Hunters: Tricky Language and Literary Allusion in Harold of Orange," in *Gerald Vizenor: Texts and Contexts*, ed. Deborah L. Madsen and A. Robert Lee (Albuquerque: University of New Mexico Press, 2010), 70.

22 Vizenor, *Bearheart*, 26.
23 Glen Coulthard demonstrates some of the shortcomings of the politics of recognition, especially in terms of attempts to "reconcile Indigenous claims to nationhood with Crown sovereignty via the accommodation of Indigenous identities in some form of renewed relationship with the Canadian state though this work carries over to settler states globally"; see "Subjects of Empire: Indigenous Peoples and the 'Politics of Recognition' in Canada," *Contemporary Political Theory* 6 (2007): 438.
24 The term was likely coined by the Tanzanian High Council secretary, Mbuto Milando, who used it during a conversation with Chief Manuel; see George Manuel, *The Fourth World: An Indian Reality* (Toronto: Collier-Macmillan, 1974), xvi.
25 Vizenor, *Bearheart*, 241. Wanaki connotes "Place of Peace" in Anishinaabemowin, the Anishinaabe language. Pueblo Bonito is an ancient, currently uninhabited Chacoan site.
26 Of the twenty-one pueblos, Laguna and Acoma are not located directly on the river, but lie within the same river valley and tributary complex, while Zuni lies about a hundred miles to the west. Ysleta del Sur is located on the river, but in El Paso, Texas.
27 As such, these narratives should not be confused with creation stories. The people exist prior to this world.
28 *Almanac* portrays this as the Fifth World, a model similar to those of Diné (Navajo) and Mexica (Aztec) cosmologies.
29 Vizenor, *Bearheart*, 5.
30 Of course the word "Indigenous" itself refers etymologically to the location of one's birth. In modern parlance it comes to mean the place of one's *people's* birth – as an Indigenous person of the White Earth Reservation such as Vizenor might be born anywhere and still be recognized (by the nation and by others) as Indigenous.
31 This outgroup association of indigeneity and singular locations has changed profoundly over time (from portrayals of them as nomadic and placeless people), largely dictated by colonial desires.
32 Vizenor, *Bearheart*, vii.
33 Vine Deloria Jr. echoes the ecological and spiritual ties that many Native people have understood, ones that predate European presence in the Americas. He explains, "When all resources are exhausted, there will be tremendous upheaval and a new heaven and earth will be created"; see *The Nations Within: The Past and Future of American Indian Sovereignty* (New York: Pantheon, 1984), 245.
34 Vizenor, *Bearheart*, 15.
35 Deloria, *Nations Within*, 233.
36 The land might, as *Almanac* asserts, be worth killing for, but in Vizenor's mind, it is not worth dying for, not because the dying is not valiant, but because it is unproductive.
37 Vizenor, *Bearheart*, 7.

38 2010 United States Census, http://www.census.gov/2010census/ (accessed March 17, 2015).

39 Vizenor, *Bearheart*, 143. The migis sandridge marks this as a sacred location, as the migis shells serve a key role in guiding the Anishinaabe to the Great Lakes. For more see Victor Barnouw, *Wisconsin Chippewa Myths and Tales and Their Relation to Chippewa Life* (Madison: University of Wisconsin Press, 1993); and Edward Benton-Banai, *The Mishomis Book: The Voice of the Ojibway* (Hayward, WI: Indian Country Communications, 1988).

40 Silko, *Almanac*, 625.

41 Ibid.

42 We note the gendered contrast in this instance as well, as land is polluted by a masculine representation of humanity, whereas the earth is understood as feminine.

43 Silko, *Almanac*, 517.

44 The differences between Pueblo and Anishinaabe origins may even come into play in these structures, as the community whose emergence place is remembered bears a much stronger tie to a specific *territory* than the community who is not.

45 Silko, *Almanac*, 133.

46 Ibid., 245.

47 Ibid., 513. This passage continues, "so Angelita had lied to all of them – the US, Cuba, Germany, and Japan. But to their African friends they were truthful. They didn't lie because Africans were tribal people who had taken back a continent from the Europeans" (513). Throughout *Almanac*, Silko reiterates the connection between African and American colonization, steadily repeating that, as Africans reclaimed their continent from Europeans, so shall Native Americans. Such a conflation, however, misses the critical differences between dependent and settler colonialisms. Native Americans constitute 2 percent of the people of the United States. The kinds of anticolonial movements that succeeded in Africa are simply less feasible in super-Sonoran America.

48 Silko, *Almanac*, 513.

49 Wolfe, "Settler Colonialism and the Elimination of the Native," 388.

CHAPTER 19

Asian American Writers and the Making of the Western U.S. Landscape

Jane Hseu

Since the mid-nineteenth century, when Asians began immigrating to the U.S. West in significant numbers, they have played an integral role in developing and shaping the region through such activities as mining, building the transcontinental railroad, farming, creating businesses and communities, and participating in transnational capital flows that connect Asia and the western states. While they have played a constitutive role in the region, Asian Americans have historically been marginalized and excluded from full political and cultural citizenship in the U.S. West and the nation through legal, political, and social means that target their racial and cultural difference. This marginalization and exclusion are exhibited in the relative invisibility of Asian Americans in prominent narratives of the U.S. West and their stereotyping in much U.S. western literature. As Hsuan Hsu asserts, "Although historically the largest concentration of Asian Americans has been in the western states, they have been written out of dominant narratives of the region. When they are represented, it is often through stereotypes such as the 'Heathen Chinee,' Charlie Chan, the 'Yellow Peril,' the model minority, or the laundrymen, prostitutes, and cooks that infuse western settings with 'local color.'"[1] Asian American writers address this contradictory situation – of being constitutive yet liminal – in literary works that invoke dominant narratives of the U.S. West about such topics as mobility, freedom, land, gender, and domesticity and that demonstrate the limitations of these western myths for Asian American subjects. Asian American literature also puts western literature in a global, hemispheric context by highlighting the relationship between the U.S. West and the Pacific Rim and the transpacific ties of urban and suburban spaces. This essay examines how selected Asian American literary works create and shape as well as affirm and critique discourses of the U.S. West.

Constriction and Mobility

Frederick Jackson Turner's 1893 frontier thesis locates the distinctive American character in westward movement across the continent.[2] As Sau-ling Wong observes, the frontier thesis links together several key American myths: "[It] regards the availability of free land – presupposing unconstrained mobility to take advantage of it – coupled with equality of opportunity, to be crucial determinants of American character and the source of American democracy."[3] For Asians in the United States, however, presumed basic American rights such as citizenship, the ability to own land, and freedom of mobility were limited from early on in their history in the nation. As Lisa Lowe points out in *Immigrant Acts*, in U.S. law and dominant discourses, after Asians began immigrating to the United States in significant numbers in the mid-nineteenth century, fears of the "yellow peril" racialized Asians as a group in contrast to the normative white male citizen.[4] The 1882 Chinese Exclusion Act was the first U.S. law to restrict the immigration of a specific group based on race or ethnicity. Subsequent exclusion acts targeting other Asian ethnicities, including Asian Indians, Koreans, Japanese, and Filipinos, were passed in the period from 1917 to 1934. These laws excluded Asian immigration except for a few protected categories and prevented Asian immigrants from becoming naturalized citizens. Furthermore, in stark contrast to the frontier promise of unlimited free land, the "Alien Land Laws ... prohibited Asian immigrants from owning land and other forms of property."[5] While repeal laws passed between 1943 and 1952 allowed Asian immigrants to become citizens, as Claire Kim argues, late twentieth-century racial discourses continue to characterize Asians as "immutably foreign and unassimilable with Whites on cultural and/or racial grounds in order to ostracize them from the body politic and civic membership."[6] Asian American literary texts engage these restrictive laws and discourses and emphasize the constriction of the western ideal of mobility.

Located in the San Francisco Bay, Angel Island was used as a detention and processing center for Chinese entering the U.S. mainland between 1910 and 1940. These migrants were members of the groups exempted from the 1882 Exclusion Act – "government officials, merchants, students, teachers, visitors" – or those "claiming U.S. citizenship" by birth in the country.[7] Because of deep suspicion of and racist attitudes toward the Chinese, they were subjected to lengthy, detailed, and frequently arbitrary interrogations by government officials before being allowed to land.

A migrant could be detained for months or years in the island barracks while waiting for his or her case to pass through bureaucratic channels, or be deported if he or she did not satisfactorily pass the interrogations.

Him Mark Lai, Genny Lim, and Judy Yung's volume *Island* collects 135 Chinese poems that migrants wrote or carved on the barrack walls. Most poems were unsigned by their authors and untitled. The poems reveal how Chinese experiences and literary representations depart from conventional images of the U.S. West: Rather than roaming freely in and communing with the natural landscape, poetic lines repeatedly represent nature as a restrictive prison. For instance, Poem 23 asserts that "this mountain wilderness is a prison," and Poem 25 maintains, "My body is detained in this building / I cannot fly from this grassy hill / And green waters block the hero."[8] Images of water and the ocean frequently occur in the poems; however, as do the "green waters," water is not associated with freedom of movement and travel, even after the long ocean voyage from China, but is another confining obstacle. The poem "Imprisonment in the Wooden Building," published in the *Chinese World* newspaper and collected in *Island*, narrates, "When I arrived in America, all I could do was gaze at the sea water in vain. / The ship docked at the wharf and I was transferred to the lonely Island."[9]

Carlos Bulosan's autobiographical[10] *America Is in the Heart* (1946) further addresses the contradiction between American ideals and the experiences of Asian American subjects. Part one of the book describes the narrator's family of peasant farmers in the Philippines in the early twentieth century. The family loses its land and living in the context of the system of absentee landlordism that had been maintained by the previous Spanish colonizers and, in the time of the narrative, under U.S. colonial rule, which existed in 1898–1942 and 1944–6. Compelled to migrate in 1930 to escape the poverty of the Philippines, upon arriving in the United States, Bulosan becomes a menial laborer who embarks on a constant journey of flight following seasonal labor patterns up and down the West Coast, from cannery work in Alaska to migrant farmwork and domestic labor in the Pacific Northwest, California, and the plains and other Southwest states. Because of discriminatory laws and attitudes that restrict Filipinos to ethnic ghettos, Bulosan also finds himself confined to these "islands," which he characterizes as degraded and animalistic spaces filled with gambling, violence, and prostitution. Therefore, his life of "flight from dawn to dawn"[11] trying to find work, returning often unwillingly to the Filipino areas, and running from police brutality and white vigilantes exhibits forced and constrained mobility rather than the freedom of mobility.

This forced mobility and the circumstances in which Bulosan finds himself in the book contradict and undercut his desire to believe in and promote the vision of America as the land of freedom, opportunity, and mobility. In the book's final chapter, he looks out the window of a bus he is taking to do cannery work in Portland, Oregon, and experiences an epiphany about the American land and values: "I glanced out of the window again to look at the broad land I had dreamed so much about, only to discover with astonishment that the American earth was like a huge heart unfolding warmly to receive me."[12] While Bulosan views the image of the open land and continent as a presence that welcomes the new immigrant with unbridled opportunity, the repetitive, circular motion of his experiences throughout the book questions and critiques the celebration of the American ideal.

Literary texts about Japanese American internment during World War II further demonstrate how racial and ethnic background limit citizenship rights and national belonging. Japanese Americans were interned on the basis of ethnicity during wartime hysteria and suspicion and not on the basis of any actual proven espionage for or collusion with Japan. Internment also exhibits how the U.S. West Coast was viewed as a vulnerable space in relation to Japanese Americans and their supposed ties across the Pacific. Thus, they were interned in camps farther into the interior and "heartland" of the United States. In his analysis of children's literature about the internment, John Streamas argues that most of the literary texts reproduce and affirm the U.S. government's use of frontier mythologies to justify internment.[13] Japanese Americans faced the contradictory situation in which they were interned within barbed wire fences with armed guards pointing their guns at them while the U.S. government literature characterized them as "pioneers" moving into new "frontiers" in the desert. Thus, the physical constriction of internment is juxtaposed with an ideology of expansiveness to attempt to counter the physical constriction and experience. Stephen Hong Sohn analyzes Julie Otsuka's novel *When the Emperor Was Divine* (2003) for the ways in which the narrator, on the train ride to the internment camp, uses visual symbols of the U.S. West, such as horses and desert landscapes, both to escape the constriction of internment and to delude herself about the constriction.[14]

Hisaye Yamamoto's short story "The Legend of Miss Sasagawara," published in 1950 shortly after the end of World War II, is also ambivalent about the ability, in this case, of poetry, art, and the mind to transcend, provide an escape from, and resist the internment experience. To the other internees in the Poston, Arizona, camp where the story is set, the thirty-nine-year-old spinster Miss Sasagawara is a bizarre, unconventional individual. Her unusual behavior makes her the gossip of the camp: She refuses to participate in the expected ways of camp life, for instance, eating in the mess hall, and the artistic activities with which she is associated, dancing and playing the guitar, contrast with the drab, utilitarian nature of the camp's everyday rhythms.

However, in the irrational world of the internment camp in which innocent citizens were incarcerated, Miss Sasagawara's seemingly unusual behavior may be more reasonable and appropriate than the other internees' adherence to normative behavior. Miss Sasagawara is sent away twice to a mental institution, once for surreptitiously observing an adolescent boy sleeping. Her attraction to the boy appears related at least in part to his masculine physicality and sexuality indicated by the "sports and western magazines" he reads and his "drawling voice."[15] Although the other internees consider Miss Sasagawara a social outcast, her confinement in the mental hospital bears much similarity to their being incarcerated in the camp behind barbed wire. In the face of the physical confinement of the camp, the mind and imagination become the spaces within which one may attempt to resist and transcend the physical limitations. The story's first-person narrator, a young woman who has been allowed to leave the camp to attend college on the East Coast, speaks of her higher education as allowing her to enter an intellectual frontier, as one "who had so newly had some contact with the recorded explorations into the virgin territory of the human mind."[16] The mind becomes the space of the frontier, as the language of the "virgin territory" resonates with Henry Nash Smith's characterization of the U.S. West as "virgin land" in his book published the same year as "Miss Sasagawara."[17]

At the end of the story, the narrator discovers Miss Sasagawara's published poem, which discusses the promise and difficulty of the mind transcending the body and everyday cares. The poet's biography is listed as "a Japanese American woman who is, at present, an evacuee from the West Coast making her home in a War Relocation center in Arizona."[18] While the mind and artistic imagination are presented as possible avenues to resist the colonizing, restrictive nature of the camps, being able to decolonize the mind when being physically imprisoned remains under question in the story.

Gender, Domesticity, Family

"The Legend of Miss Sasagawara" is also a narrative about domesticity and gender in the West in the internees' attempts to create a home in a desert prison and Miss Sasagawara's wayward sexual fascination with the western symbols of masculine physicality. Gender, domesticity, and family play important roles in shaping western myths and the ways in which these myths characterize Asian American subjects. The iconic western image of a lone cowboy on the plains is also dependent on fleeing constraining domestic spaces run by strict, matronly women. As Wong states, this is an undeniably male subject, a prime example of which is "Huck Finn lighting out for the territory, away from the domesticating, emasculating, 'sivilising' influences of women."[19] However, Asian American men were historically emasculated by laws that restricted the immigration of Asian women in order to limit the growth of the Asian American family, antimiscegenation laws that forbade marrying non-Asian women, and their domestic work as houseboys and restaurant and laundry workers. Thus, the emasculated portrayal of Asian American men contrasts with the hypermasculine image of the western cowboy. Elaine Kim draws attention to the differing representations of Chinese men and (white) cowboys: "Chinese are as much a part of American history and traditions as cowboys. Moreover, cowboys are thought of as manly and rugged; they are in stark contrast to the exotic stereotypes of Chinese as pigtailed heathens in silk gowns and slippers."[20]

Frank Chin's play *The Chickencoop Chinaman* (1972) attempts to critique and counter emasculated images of Chinese and Asian American men. To do so, Chin tries to create a heroic tradition for Asian American men based on Chinese as well as western myths. Chin promotes a typical masculine identity – strong, hard, tough, and resilient – for Asian American men by emphasizing the history of Chinese men building the railroad. Tam Lum, the protagonist of *Chickencoop Chinaman*, praises the mythical train called the Iron Moonhunter, combining Chinese and western myths in an image of strength and power. He represents Asian American masculinity in terms of potency and physical strength: "We built the fuckin railroad! Moved a whole Sierra Nevada over."[21] However, *Chickencoop Chinaman*'s vision of a virile Asian American masculine tradition contrasts with received mythologies of the U.S. West. While Tam fantasizes that the Lone Ranger is a "Chinaman," whose mask hides his "slanty eyes,"[22] the Lone Ranger makes his appearance in the play and dashes Tam's fantasy, affirming emasculating stereotypes of Asian American men: "China boys, you be legendary obeyers of the law, legendary humble, legendary passive."[23] Unlike the individualist cowboy figure in the lawless, unrestricted West, the Chinese men are beholden to the laws. The Lone Ranger thus symbolizes white masculinity from which

Asian American men are excluded. As Tam says, "The Lone Ranger ain't no Chinaman, children."[24]

The chapter "The Grandfather of the Sierra Nevada Mountains" in Maxine Hong Kingston's "(auto)biographical fiction"[25] *China Men* (1980) also explores the impact of laws restricting the immigration of Chinese women – laws that contributed to the emasculation of the Chinese male immigrants. Ah Goong, in helping build a bridge for the transcontinental railroad, is lowered in a basket into the valley between the mountains. The fear and terror of the experience spur his sexual desire, which results in climax: "Suddenly he stood up tall and squirted out into space. 'I am fucking the world,' he said. The world's vagina was big, big as the sky, big as a valley."[26] While male erection and ejaculation typically indicate potency, in this instance, Ah Goong's experience signifies the desire for masculine prowess, for spilling his seed in the world. However, as Ah Goong is also prevented by the U.S. laws from sending for his wife in China and creating offspring, the ejaculation into empty space also indicates his inability to perpetuate his family and genealogy. In contrast to the image of the western settler communing with the land, Ah Goong experiences nature as emptiness and absence, and the fertility of the land is inverted to fruitless desire. *China Men*, however, in its very writing of the marginalized stories of Chinese men in the United States, also inserts these figures into U.S. history, and, in a form and style that blend history with myth, draws attention to the ways in which we create and perpetuate these received histories and stories.

While *Chickencoop Chinaman* and *China Men* focus on the contributions of and challenges faced by Chinese men in the United States, Sui Sin Far's stories collected in *Mrs. Spring Fragrance and Other Writings* (1912) represent the small but significant number of Chinese women who were allowed into the United States before the 1940s. While such laws as the 1875 Page Law, which targeted the Chinese, restricted the immigration of Asian women, a large number of the Chinese women who entered the United States before 1875 were prostitutes who serviced the male laborers.[27] There were also high-profile Chinese women put on display as exotic curiosities such as Afong Moy. The perception of Chinese women as prostitutes or exotic spectacles led to the stereotyping of Asian American women as highly sexualized "lotus blossoms" or "dragon ladies."[28] Rather than perpetuate these stereotypes, Far's stories portray Chinese merchants' wives such as the Mrs. Spring Fragrance of the title story of her book, and Chinese women and children in Chinatown families. Many stories address the relationship between the Chinese and white communities and the conflicts and exchanges that occur between them. Far herself was the biracial daughter of a Chinese woman and white English father, and works such as "The Story of One White Woman Who Married a Chinese" depict biracial families in an era of miscegenation laws. As Amy Ling and Annette White-Parks state, "The stories give voice and protagonist roles to Chinese and Chinese North American women and children, thus breaking stereotypes of silence, invisibility, and 'bachelor societies' that have ignored small but present female populations."[29]

Bharati Mukherjee's novel *Jasmine* (1989) also examines the position of Asian women in relation to western myths of the frontier and mobility. The novel traces the journey of its protagonist, "J," from being a peasant girl in Punjab, India, to becoming an undocumented nanny and caregiver in New York and Iowa. Alternately known as Jyoti, Jasmine, Jase, and Jane throughout the novel, J assumes names and identities based on the various men to whom she is attached at different times. The novel explicitly uses the language of the frontier to indicate the promise and potential of new experiences and mobility for J. At the novel's end, J is about to set off on a new adventure with Taylor, a physics professor, to California, and the frontier myth is configured as entering the domestic space with which she is identified: "Adventure, risk, transformation: the frontier is pushing indoors through uncaulked windows."[30] However, as Matt Burkhart argues, the danger, suffering, tragedy, and lack of fulfillment that have plagued J in every new experience and identity she takes on undercut the seeming endless possibility that occurs with her new adventure with Taylor.[31] J's position as a Third World woman worker in the First World also hinders her attainment of the ideal of unlimited mobility as fulfillment as expressed on an aerogram sent to India: "CELEBRATE AMERICA, the American postal services commanded. TRAVEL ... THE PERFECT FREEDOM."[32]

Transpacific Currents

Asian American literary critics have made the argument that focusing on Asian American literature and the U.S. West necessitates putting the region in the context of "transnational elements, global flows, and colonial/postcolonial histories."[33] Burkhart draws the connection between the U.S. West as region with the spaces of the global West and global East. He deems *Jasmine* "a narrative of the New West, which, in this instance, can refer to an American West undergoing dramatic demographic changes or to the New Occident, in which diasporic movements from the so-called Third World are also causing substantial shifts in the cultural composition of occidental nations."[34] Thus, Asian American literature and the U.S. West should be situated in a global context wherein the U.S. West is linked to the broader imaginary geographies of "West" and "East," occident and orient. As Asia is the standard definition of the global "East," an examination of Asian American literature and the U.S. West as region repeatedly demonstrates how the U.S. West is connected to the global East through immigration; histories of U.S. colonization, imperialism, and military engagements in Asia; and transnational relationships between the U.S. West and Pacific Rim.

In terms of western U.S. spaces, Hawaii has a unique position in the U.S. regional and national imaginary and history. The state geographically farthest from the U.S. mainland in the Pacific Ocean, and the closest to the Asian continent, Hawaii is the westernmost state of the U.S. West. That state resulted from imperialist U.S. practices. In 1893, U.S. businessmen and military overthrew the government of the Kingdom of Hawaii, and Hawaii was annexed to the United States in 1900. Hawaii became a U.S. state in 1959, and, according to the 2010 U.S. Census, Asians make up the largest racial group of the state's population.[35] Besides its geographic proximity to Asia, the state's large Asian population is attributed to Asian laborers taken in to work the sugarcane plantations beginning in the 1850s. Literary texts such as Milton Murayama's novel *All I Asking For Is My Body* (1975), which presents the story of Japanese Americans in Hawaii around the time of World War II, discuss the laborers' experiences working on the plantations.

Lois-Ann Yamanaka's novel *Wild Meat and the Bully Burgers* (1996) is set in the 1970s in Hilo, Hawaii, yet the characters and social structures depicted in the novel still bear the legacy and stratification of the sugar plantation system, which declined in the mid-twentieth century. Haoles (whites) composed the majority of the plantation supervisory positions, and Asian immigrant laborers performed the backbreaking work in the fields.[36] As in *America Is in the Heart* and other western narratives, land is a central theme in the novel. The novel's first-person narrator, the burgeoning adolescent Lovey Nariyoshi, descends from a grandfather who immigrated from Japan to Hawaii to work in the sugarcane fields, and her father, Hubert, grew up working on the sugarcane plantation owned by the haole Rice family. When Hubert is blinded by an accident and hospitalized, Lovey journeys to take back soil from the plantation for him to remind him of what he considers "home" despite the difficult circumstances in which he grew up. When Lovey arrives at the plantation, a Hawaiian cowboy (*paniolo*) acting as security for the plantation owner, Mrs. Rice, denies her entrance: "The cowboy rides back ... and says, 'Sorry, man, but no can. Mrs. Rice said no ... so you best be turning around." Lovey, however, quickly and furtively grabs dirt from "the side of the road" of the plantation if not from the plantation and Hubert's childhood home proper.[37]

Like Carlos in *America Is in the Heart*, Lovey attempts to claim the U.S. western land as "home," in this instance, not just from a visual view from the bus window onto the land (as we saw with Bulosan), but in the gathering of the actual soil of the land itself. However, the cowboy's and haole plantation owner's preventing Lovey from even entering the land on which Hubert grew up and that he considers "home" shows the continuing legacy of racial and class disenfranchisement and stratification of Japanese and Asian Americans in Hawaii. Thus, the Japanese American immigrant family cannot fully claim Hawaii as "home."

While the Nariyoshi family's story is affected by the history of the migration of Asian labor to Hawaii, Theresa Hak Kyung Cha's experimental mixed genre work *DICTEE* (1982) traces the Korean diaspora's Pacific crossings and returns. *DICTEE* contains elements of autobiography, biography, history, and poetry and includes various media such as photographs, film stills, and diagrams. The Cha family's personal exilic and immigrant journey appears in the work: Cha's parents lived in exile in Manchuria, China, during the Japanese colonization of Korea from 1910 to 1945. Born in Pusan, South Korea, in 1951, Cha, at age eleven, immigrated with her family to Hawaii and then San Francisco.

In *DICTEE*, Cha's journey, as well as the migration of other members of the Korean diaspora, crosses the Pacific from Korea to the United States and returns across the Pacific. This journey is psychological in addition to physical, and memory allows the migrant to hold transpacific spaces together or superimpose them on one another. In writing about her return to Korea for the first time after eighteen years, Cha states: "Eighteen years later. Nothing has changed, we are at a standstill. I speak in another tongue now, a second tongue a foreign tongue. All this time we have been away. But nothing has changed. A stand still."[38] While this passage comments on the similarities of the Korean political situations across those eighteen years, another passage a few pages later in the section comments on the change that *has* occurred for Cha, but also the connection to the past: "I am here for the first time in eighteen years.... We left here in this memory still fresh, still new. I speak another tongue, a second tongue. This is how distant I am. From then. From that time. They take me back."[39] The repetition of similar words ("eighteen years") with contrasting commentary ("nothing has changed," "This is how distant I am.") highlights the conflation of space and time as well as the dislocations of the Korean exile and immigrant. These dislocations are also affected by multiple histories of colonization and imperialism. To recover histories and stories that have been subordinated by multiple colonizations, including the Japanese colonization of Korea, U.S. imperialism in Korea during the Korean War, and the racialization and gendering of the Korean female immigrant in the United States, there must be a process of "ALLER/RETOUR," translated from the French as "to go and to return," which is discussed in the chapter "ELITERE LYRIC POETRY." The Korean female immigrant must move back and forth between migrant spaces, and between past and present, to excavate these buried histories and voices.

Cities, Suburbs, Ethnoburbs

U.S. wars in Southeast Asia in the 1960s and 1970s also ushered in refugees and migrants to the U.S. West, a situation that is then represented in works of Southeast Asian American literature. Vietnamese Americans constitute the largest population of Southeast Asian refugees and immigrants and accordingly, have the most developed literary production. Vietnamese Americans are concentrated in California, with the largest number in "Little Saigon" in Orange County. Much of Vietnamese American literature concerning the U.S. West centers on the experience and aftereffects of the Vietnam War. Aimee Phan's book *We Should Never Meet* (2004) contains short stories whose setting moves back and forth between Saigon before the city's fall in 1975 and Little Saigon in California. Operation Babylift, the U.S. evacuation of thousands of Vietnamese children, many of them orphans or the children of U.S. servicemen, just before the fall of Saigon in 1975, connects the characters' stories, from their Vietnamese childhood to their young adulthood in Little Saigon.

Works such as *We Should Never Meet* depict western spaces not only as open spaces of desert and landscape, but also as highly urban and suburban environments. As Nicolas Witschi states, "In 1990, US census data demonstrated that 86 percent of the West's population could be found in an urbanized environment, in contrast to only 75 percent of the population east of the Mississippi River.... Since then, this trend has only increased.... The population of the American West continues to shift and diversify in not only urban but also suburban and rural settings."[40] A new development for Asian Americans in the West in terms of space and geography is the rise of the "ethnoburb," a suburb with a concentrated ethnic minority population. "Little Saigon," which straddles the Los Angeles suburbs of Westminster and Garden Grove, themselves part of the archetypical suburban atmosphere of Orange County, is one of the well-known Asian "ethnoburbs," which also include Monterey Park and cities in the San Gabriel Valley outside Los Angeles. Several scholarly books examine ethnoburbs of the greater Los Angeles area, also known as the "Southland," itself often configured as a widespread network of suburbs: Wei Li's *Ethnoburb: The New Ethnic Community in Urban America* focuses on the Chinese American San Gabriel Valley; Leland Saito's *Race and Politics: Asians, Latinos, and Whites in a Los Angeles Suburb* studies Monterey Park; and Karin Aguilar-San Juan's *Little Saigons: Staying Vietnamese in America* discusses Orange County as well as Boston.[41]

The title story "We Should Never Meet" presents the setting of Little Saigon as a degraded image of the idealized post–World War II suburb of wide lawns, single-family homes, and domestic bliss. The Operation Babylift children Kim and Vinh, now independent adults, live in a cramped apartment in which "three boys shared one room while Kim and Vinh got the other" in a neighborhood that "was shit, wedged between a string of consignment shops and liquor stores."[42] The store Mekong Gifts and Collectibles, where Kim befriends a female store owner in hopes of finding a substitute mother, is located in "a particularly depressing strip mall. A cheaply built two-story building painted a bland cream and streaked gray from pollution. It housed some of the typical Little Saigon businesses: hair salon, chiropractor's office, bakery, and minimart."[43] However, as the Vietnamese community grows and prospers in Little Saigon, the suburban landscape changes from decrepit strip malls to Orange County's famed massive and spectacular malls: "Little Saigon was changing, outgrowing the pagoda-style shopping centers and replacing them with spacious indoor, multilevel malls. The newest one that opened last month boasted four levels and a giant concrete Buddha squatting between two gleaming red pillars with a water fountain courtyard."[44] The description of the gleaming new mall also shows the cultural hybridization of the Southland ethnoburb, the conventional architecture of the mall mixed with the Vietnamese cultural symbols of the Buddha and red pillars for prosperity.

As noted previously, in contrast to the Old West image of deserts and open space, the New West is characterized by its urban and suburban environments. The archetypal city of the West is Los Angeles, where the open space of the western becomes the quintessential postmodern, decentered city. In terms of geography and transnational, hemispheric connections and movements, Los Angeles is also where the Asia-Pacific region meets Latin America in the most concentrated form. Karen Tei Yamashita's magical realist novel *Tropic of Orange* (1997) delves into the complexities of Los Angeles as a postmodern, global, transnational, and hemispheric city in which the Asia-Pacific and Latin America regions intersect, where the East/West and North/South axis meet. In the novel, Manzanar Murakami, an eccentric Japanese American homeless person named for the internment camp in which he was born, "conducts" traffic on an overpass overlooking the Harbor Freeway that runs through downtown Los Angeles. While conducting, he has something "like an out-of-body experience" that allows him to see the ways in which LA is connected to the Pacific Rim: he sees "the great Pacific stretching along its great rim, brimming over long coastal shores from one hemisphere to another." LA is also the meeting place of the global West and East: "this strange end and beginning: the very last point West, and after that it was all East." The Pacific Rim then connects with "the great land mass to the south, the southern continent and the central Americas."[45]

Being the point of concentrated intersection of East and West, North and South, LA is also the epicenter of the connections and movements of global capitalism. The powerful forces of global capitalism from above are represented in the novel in such examples as the multinational corporations flattening the world with their products, as we see in the American beers the mystical character Arcangel is offered in a small cantina in Mexico, along with Coca-Cola, Pepsi, and "a hamburger, Fritos, and catsup."[46] The dark underbelly of global capitalism is represented in the movement of drug trafficking from a shipment of tainted oranges from Latin America as well as organ trafficking. Global corporate capitalism also initiates the migration of poor laborers such as Bobby Ngu, a Chinese character from Singapore who migrates to the United States via Vietnam by pretending to be a war refugee. Bobby's family in Singapore owned a bicycle company but could not compete when a U.S. company opened in the city, forcing Bobby to migrate to the United States for work. Bobby's wife, Rafaela, is also a manual laborer in the global economy, an Afro-Mayan Mexican woman who was undocumented in the United States before Bobby marries her.

The novel's plot follows the path of a magical orange that travels from Mazatlán, Mexico, north to LA, carrying with it the latitude line of the Tropic of Cancer that runs through Mazatlán. The movement of the line symbolizes the movement of time and space in the interconnected channels of globalization. *Tropic of Orange* represents the struggles of globalization from above with globalization from below. In the final chapters, the symbolic Ultimate Wrestling Championship occurs in the aptly named Pacific Rim Auditorium; the match pitches the wrestler SUPERNAFTA against El Gran Mojado ("The Great Wetback"). The match results in the deaths of both SUPERNAFTA, who represents the powerful political and economic interests of the North American Free Trade Agreement passed in 1994, and El Gran Mojado, who represents those, like Bobby and Rafaela, who provide the manual and often oppressed labor for the greater powers of global capitalism. While the wrestling match does not end with any clear winner, the novel ends on a hopeful note with the reunion of Bobby and Rafaela – the characters themselves, along with their mixed race son Sol, suggestive of a meeting of the Asia-Pacific region and Latin America. Thus, the novel indicates optimism for the resistance and survival of global laborers from below such as Bobby and Rafaela.

Asian American literary texts represent the western U.S. landscape as a space associated with the desire for mobility in the face of constriction, a gendered place that impacts its subjects, and a rural, suburban, and urban setting with frequently inequitable global connections. Thus, Asian American writers emphasize how spatial discourses influence ethical issues of citizenship, belonging, and justice. The texts discussed in this chapter expose the contradictions of western myths in relation to Asian American subjects and indicate the possibility of resistance to and revision of these hegemonic narratives.

Notes

1 Hsuan L. Hsu, "Chronotopes of the Asian American West," in *A Companion to the Literature and Culture of the American West*, ed. Nicolas S. Witschi (Chichester, UK: Wiley-Blackwell, 2011), 145.

2 Frederick Jackson Turner, *The Frontier in American History* (New York: Holt, Rinehart, & Winston, 1962).

3 Sau-ling Cynthia Wong, *Reading Asian American Literature: From Necessity to Extravagance* (Princeton: NJ: Princeton University Press, 1993), 118.

4 Lisa Lowe, *Immigrant Acts: On Asian American Cultural Politics* (Durham, NC: Duke University Press, 1996), 11.

5 Ibid., 13.

6 Claire Jean Kim, "The Racial Triangulation of Asian Americans," *Politics and Society* 27 (1999): 107.

7 *Island: Poetry and History of Chinese Immigrants on Angel Island, 1910–1940*, ed. Him Mark Lai, Genny Lim, and Judy Yung (Seattle: University of Washington Press, 1980), 12.

8 Ibid., 60.

9 Ibid., 139.

10 As Carey McWilliams states, *America Is in the Heart* can be read not only as Bulosan's life story, but as the "collective life experience of thousands of Filipino immigrants" to the United States. Bulosan may not have personally experienced all the "brutalities and indecencies" described in the book, but "some Filipino was indeed the victim of each of these or similar incidents." Thus, *America* constitutes both an individual autobiography and a collective biography of the Filipino experience in the United States. Carey McWilliams, "Introduction" to *America Is in the Heart* by Carlos Bulosan (Seattle: University of Washington Press, 1973), vii.

11 Carlos Bulosan, *America Is in the Heart* (Seattle: University of Washington Press, 1973), 124.

12 Ibid., 10.

13 John Streamas, "Frontier Mythology, Children's Literature, and Japanese American Incarceration," in *Postwestern Cultures: Literature, Theory, Space*, ed. Susan Kollin (Lincoln: University of Nebraska Press, 2007), 173.

14 Stephen Hong Sohn, "These Desert Places: Tourism, the American West, and the Afterlife of Regionalism in Julie Otsuka's *When the Emperor Was Divine*," *Modern Fiction Studies* 55 (2009).

15 Hisaye Yamamoto, "The Legend of Miss Sasagawara," in *Seventeen Syllables and Other Stories* (Latham, NY: Kitchen Table, 1988), 31–32.

16 Ibid., 32.

17 Henry Nash Smith, *Virgin Land: The American West as Symbol and Myth* (Cambridge: Harvard University Press, 1950).

18 Yamamoto, "Legend," 32.

19 Wong, *Reading Asian American Literature*, 148.

20 Elaine H. Kim, *Asian American Literature: An Introduction to the Writings and Their Social Context* (Philadelphia: Temple University Press, 1982), 177.

21 Frank Chin, *The Chickencoop Chinaman and The Year of the Dragon: Two Plays* (Seattle: University of Washington Press, 1981), 53.

22 Ibid., 32.

23 Ibid., 37.

24 Ibid., 38.

25 Donald Goellnicht, "Tang Ao in America: Male Subject Positions in *China Men*," in *Reading the Literatures of Asian America*, ed. Shirley Geok-lin Lim and Amy Ling (Philadelphia: Temple University Press, 1992), 191.

26 Maxine Hong Kingston, *China Men* (New York: Vintage, 1989), 133.

27 Ronald Takaki, *Strangers from a Different Shore: A History of Asian Americans* (New York: Penguin, 1989), 41.

28 Amy Ling, *Between Worlds: Women Writers of Chinese Ancestry* (Elmsford, NY: Pergamon, 1990), 11.

29 Amy Ling and Annette White-Parks, "introduction" to *Mrs. Spring Fragrance and Other Writings*, ed. Ling and White-Parks (Urbana: University of Illinois Press, 1995), 6.

30 Bharati Mukherjee, *Jasmine* (New York: Fawcett Crest, 1991), 214.

31 Matt Burkhart, "Rewriting the West(ern): *Shane*, Jane, and Agricultural Change in Bharati Mukherjee's *Jasmine*," *Western American Literature* 43 (2008): 16.

32 Ibid., 75.

33 Sohn, "These Desert Places," 163.

34 Burkhart, "Rewriting the West(ern)," 5.

35 According to the 2010 U.S. Census, Asians constitute 37.7 percent of the population, whites 22.7 percent, Native Hawaiians and other Pacific Islanders 9.4 percent, Latinos 8.9 percent, and blacks 1.5 percent. http://factfinder .census.gov/faces/tableservices/jsf/pages/productview.xhtml?src=bkmk (accessed March 17, 2015).

36 Takaki, *Strangers*, 138.

37 Lois-Ann Yamanaka, *Wild Meat and the Bully Burgers* (New York: Picador, 1996), 305.

38 Theresa Hak Kyung Cha, *DICTEE* (Berkeley: Third Woman Press, 1995), 80.

39 Ibid., 85.

40 Nicolas S. Witschi, "Imagining the West," in *A Companion to the Literature and Culture of the American West*, 5–6.

41 Wei Li, *Ethnoburb: The New Ethnic Community in Urban America* (Honolulu: University of Hawaii Press, 2011); Leland T. Saito, *Race and Politics: Asian Americans, Latinos, and Whites in a Los Angeles Suburb* (Urbana: University of Illinois Press, 1998); Karin Aguilar-San Juan, *Little Saigons: Staying Vietnamese in America* (Minneapolis: University of Minnesota Press, 2009).

42 Aimee Phan, *We Should Never Meet: Stories* (New York: St. Martin's Press, 2004), 32–33.

43 Ibid., 29.

44 Ibid., 47.

45 Karen Tei Yamashita, *Tropic of Orange* (Minneapolis: Coffee House Press, 1997), 169–170.

46 Ibid., 131.

CHAPTER 20

African American Literature
Recasting Region through Race

Jonathan Munby

The West of the African American imagination and experience has played a subordinate role to the dominant "Great Migration" story, which unfolded along a South-North axis. Moreover, the racialized conventions associated with the frontier myth and western narratives have necessarily excluded African Americans. Crudely put, black folks have not belonged in the stereotypical story of the conquest of the West, in which whites fight Indians on the plains in a contest between the virtues of civilization and nature. African Americans feature in a different foundational national drama and space: the problem of slavery in the Deep South and the road to emancipation. Working both with and against such proscriptions, African American writers engaged with the West have created two allied legacies, one that is in conversation with the tropes of the rural or wild frontier and another that documents arrival on an urban frontier.

The Black Wild West

Despite its literary invisibility, the journey west was clearly part of the black American experience. Key black figures can be traced back to the 1520s and Estevanico, the Moroccan Berber slave and primary scout for the Spanish exploration of what is now the United States–Mexico borderland, including the mission to find the Seven Cities of Gold or "Cibola." Or York, William Clark's slave who participated fully in the Lewis and Clark expedition, as scout, hunter, and manual laborer, from St. Louis to the Pacific coast and back, 1804–6. And James Beckwourth, a mixed race ex-slave who journeyed west from St. Louis in the 1820s to trap fur and trade in the Rockies, discovering a pass over the Sierra Mountains and becoming an adopted Crow Indian with the name of Morning Sun.

Importantly, and unprecedented for a mountain man let alone a nonwhite one, Beckwourth published a full account of his life in 1856. *The Life and Adventures of James P. Beckwourth, Mountaineer, Scout, and*

Pioneer and Chief of the Crow Nation of Indians is a mix of fact, gross exaggeration, and hubris that, in complying with frontier literature conventions, compromised what we assume to be autobiography. That he would spin a larger-than-life yarn and sell it as a true story, however, was consistent with Beckwourth's status as an intrepid mountain man adventurer.[1] It is also important to consider this tendency to making oneself the hero of one's own story as intimately linked to the aspirations of a former slave. Self-realization out west for Beckwourth the former slave, whose father was his owner, needed declaiming through an autobiographical act of self-aggrandizement. This literary form of the black oral tradition of "toasting" would be shared with Nat Love.[2]

Love's 1907 autobiography bears a title that again discloses much about the terms of inclusion for a black American in the dominant Wild West narrative: *The Life and Adventures of Nat Love, Better Known in the Cattle Country as "Deadwood Dick"* – BY HIMSELF – *A True History of Slavery Days, Life on the Great Cattle Ranges and on the Plains of the "Wild and Woolly" West, Based on Facts, and Personal Experiences of the Author.* The emphasis is on firsthand experience and facts. Equally, the actualities of cattle country are framed in more mythical terms, as "Wild and Woolly." Love takes ownership of a moniker, "Deadwood Dick," the result of winning a rodeo competition on July 4, 1876, in the eponymous town in South Dakota. No doubt the name secured cultural capital with the success of the Deadwood Dick western dime novel series published a year later. Moreover, because a former slave such as Love had inherited his name from his white owner, Robert Love, this act of renaming had obvious significance. The open space of the frontier and the new identity Love adopts are set in relation, then, to a prehistory of slavery. Not surprisingly, the narrative that follows often casts the facts of his escapades in stereotypically romantic western terms.

The opening of the autobiography provides the most sustained attack on white racism. Love reflects on the ignominy of prejudice during his early years, having been born into slavery in Tennessee in 1854. Consequent on the ending of slavery and his heading west, the issue of race rarely appears. Probably this is in part related to Love's strategic separation of the South as a space of dependence and bondage and the West as one of independence and freedom. He abandons a disheartening world of tenant farming in Tennessee for Dodge City, Kansas, and life as a cowboy. The world of cattle drivers does not seem to discriminate. He notes that the outfit he wants to join has several "colored" cowhands.[3] Such a fact remains undeveloped, but it is clearly significant in terms of Love's portrayal of the West as somewhere someone black can achieve what is denied elsewhere. His riding and shooting skills earn him a reputation in herding cattle, hunting buffalo, and rodeo competition. He demonstrates courage and guile in enduring capture by Indians and surviving nature's more extreme conditions. He mixes with some of the West's more notorious outlaws (the James brothers and Billy the Kid) and meets iconic exploiters of frontier experience (Buffalo Bill and Kit Carson). Not only does this blend of tall tale and fact help an African American place himself in a rhetorical space that has marginalized black presence, but it positions the West as a region of particular opportunity and agency for a former slave. Out west, as he puts it, "mounted on my favorite horse, my long horsehide lariat near my hand, and my trusty guns in my belt ... I felt I could defy the world."[4]

Simply understood, Love and Beckwourth's heightened autobiographical mode constituted a way to correct black absence from the hegemonic record. Their writing takes the form of testimony whose authority, excesses and exaggerations aside, lay in the detailing of the facts of their derring-do on the frontier and in the rhetorical invocation that "I was there (and how!)." As such these early black authors represent the West as a place for relatively iconoclastic individuated black male ambition consistent with the patriarchal myth of the West as a space where American individualism could thrive.

It would take until the end of Reconstruction (1877) for "Westward Ho'!" to become a rallying call that appealed to those interested in a more ordinary life of settlement and community building. The first westward movement of African Americans was precipitated by the so-called Exodusters. In the wake of the withdrawal of federal troops from the South in 1877 and the return of racial oppression, a mix of push and pull factors precipitated an exodus of thousands of African Americans from the Deep South to the promised land west of the Mississippi – most notably to Kansas.[5] While the Exoduster movement was a very limited success, it symbolized a different understanding of what the West could represent to African Americans in comparison to that represented in the works of Beckwourth and Love. And we find the legacy of this more communal and less sensational image of frontier life embodied in works by Oscar Micheaux, Era Bell Thompson, and Pearl Cleage. For these writers, displacement west was hardly "Wild and Woolly." Rather it was a place of more mundane realities and modest ideals – of the struggle to be a successful homesteader, to settle, and the possibility to demonstrate self-reliance and resilience in the Dakotas and Kansas.

Micheaux's *The Conquest: Story of a Negro Pioneer* (1913) demonstrated its author's entrepreneurial acumen. For this homesteader's account of the prairie as a space of black self-realization and self-reliance was written in part to raise cash after a devastating drought. A devotee of Booker T. Washington, Micheaux celebrated the land out west as free of the constraints holding back the race elsewhere as long as one was prepared to work hard. Telling his own story of homesteading was intended to communicate the great Northwest's potential for racial uplift. He accumulates land and profits from independent agricultural husbandry. He confronts and survives adverse weather conditions. He is party to the economic and political machinations that characterized the building of frontier towns. And he lambasts members of his own race who fail to take up the chances this region offers to them. For Micheaux, staking a place in the otherwise white narrative of Manifest Destiny also involved the perpetuation of a negative view of Indians, who are represented as unwarranted spendthrift beneficiaries of government land allotment and an obstacle to "bona fide" settlers.[6] *The Conquest*, then, is an act of self-celebration linked to ideas of economic self-reliance and contradictory participation in the racialized narrative of nation building. The individual heroism evinced here is tied to the cultural myth of the West as a place in need of taming and civilizing. What he learned through homesteading was a way to hone his entrepreneurial skills. Faced with crop failure, he turned to writing, which he in turn adapted to film. *The Conquest* would be reworked as the basis for a second novel, *The Homesteader* (1917), and its film version (1918), marking the beginning of a career as the pioneer of independent black filmmaking.

By comparison, Era Bell Thompson's autobiography, *American Daughter* (1946), is far less boosterish and self-promoting. Thompson published her reflections on coming of age on the North Dakota plains late in life after she had moved to Chicago. She narrates a story contiguous with the best aspirations of the Exodusters, seeing the world from the point of view of a young girl growing into early adulthood mainly between 1914 and 1933, trying to comprehend the good and the bad of a remote rural life. While family values and religious unity are central to making the prairie home for a black community, distance from other African Americans and separation from origins in the South have an adverse effect. Thompson sees how her parents no longer have a church life. She dwells on how only a special occasion merited the gathering together of otherwise widely dispersed black families. Even as she loves the natural world, seeing God's benign presence in the vast landscape and the big skies, she cannot endure the isolation, desiring the sense of community that only a city life or a return to the South can offer.[7]

Contrastingly, some fifty years later, the playwright Pearl Cleage reclaimed the prairie as a site and model for collective black female empowerment. Her 1995 play, *Flyin' West*, focuses on a group of resilient black women who have migrated from the South to Kansas in the wake of the Homestead Act. In revisiting issues central to the Exoduster movement, *Flyin' West* sets up a tension between black women's steadfast commitment to building the new black community of Nicodemus, on one hand, and feckless misogynist black men and unscrupulous white speculators, on the other. Cleage's late twentieth-century dramatic reconstruction, in which black sisters outwit and kill patriarchal foes, adds a feminist perspective to Micheaux and Thompson's firsthand insights. *Flyin' West* works as a corrective to the masculine terms of settlement and the symbolic value of the West. It qualifies Micheaux's uplift or "race man" paradigm with its gendered conception of disempowerment and disenfranchisement, understood as "emasculation" to be overcome through the restoration of black manhood. And in dramatizing how landownership and self-sufficiency were so fiercely valued by black women on the prairie more than a century ago, Cleage's play also begs questions of the post–Los Angeles riots present of 1995.

If Beckwourth, Love, Micheaux, and Thompson sought ways to include themselves in the predominantly white story of westward movement and settlement, primarily through autobiographical articulation, Ishmael Reed took a pronouncedly different tact. In the racially assertive climate of the late 1960s, Reed published *Yellow Back Radio Broke-Down* (1968), an implicit rejection of attempts at inclusion and a fundamental critique of the white-racist tenets that underpin the western genre. The West of the dominant American imagination for Reed is something that needs symbolic reevaluation for the consequences of what it includes and excludes. To this end, he disconnects the myth of the West from its monotheistic Christian underpinnings and connects it to distinctly Afrocentric forces, especially polytheistic practices such as voodoo.

Stripped of its maverick black twists that render it satirical, *Yellow Back Radio Broke-Down* is a classic western revenge narrative. A circus troupe touring the frontier arrives in Yellow Back Radio. The town is almost deserted save for some children who claim they have driven out the corrupt adults. The adults, however, return and kill the children and most of the circus troupe. The key survivor is a skilled horseman who sets out to avenge these murders. With the help of a Native American chief, he manages to locate and overcome the source of evil in the region, a mega-lomaniac cattleman.

The novel features a range of stock western types and scenes. We have the "good outlaw" in the form of the main protagonist, a horseman called the Loop Garoo Kid, and his archnemesis, the "bad land-grabbing rancher," Drag Gibson. This good versus bad setup is typical of the western's dichotomous structure, which complicates the value oppositions it sets up by often putting the positive on the wrong side of the law. In Reed's case, however, this showdown scenario is further complicated by the fact that Loop is black and carries with him a set of associations and powers that are incongruent with the normative world of the western. Indeed these powers are derived from "foreign" African, Caribbean, and New Orleans roots. Loop Garoo's name (from the French *loup-garou*) translates as "werewolf" – and it is eventually revealed that he is Christ's forgotten black brother.

Loop arrives in the frontier town of Yellow Back Radio as part of a circus troupe in the company of Zozo Labrique, "charter member of the American Hoo-Doo Church" and *mambo* (female priest).[8] When Zozo is dying, she passes on a mad dog's tooth to Loop, which will give him "con-naissance" alongside the gris-gris, mojo, and *wangols* she has taught him as a *mambo*.[9] He will need these voodoo or black magic powers out west. As a black voodoo "horseman," Loop represents a spirit riding a human form. His magical powers will be needed to combat Drag Gibson, who turns out to be a zombie, a decomposing escapee from hell. With the help of a third major protagonist, Chief Showcase, a plainclothes, champagne-drinking Crow Indian and helicopter pilot, Loop is able to enervate Drag's power by cursing him with a retroactive itch and scaring him with a ghostly visit at his wedding.

The white world Loop encounters out west is portrayed as sexually decadent, a space of wanton desires linked to capitalist greed. Drag's ava-ricious attempt to own Yellow Back Radio goes hand in hand with his patrician and misogynist notion of wedlock. He kills wives who are frigid and mail-orders one for the sole purpose of siring an heir. Additionally, his sexuality is coded as perverse. In line with his first name, he sports makeup and dresses in a monogrammed silk robe and matador's outfit. He is seen to love only himself and his property. When readers are intro-duced to Drag, "embracing his property" is rendered as French kissing his prize horse.[10] Drag's mail-order bride, Mustache Sal, initially judged the way a horse is according to the quality of her teeth, is a black widow with designs on killing Drag and inheriting his fortune. Sal's manipulation of sex for money and favor is not simply a pragmatic choice. She is portrayed in graphic detail as a nymphomaniac with an insatiable sexual appetite, sleeping with the vast majority of Drag's men and Chief Showcase. While these excessive renditions of Drag and Sal's sexuality are open to criticism as homophobic and sexist, they are designed to reveal rather than conceal more candid truths that underpin the conventional western value system and the ideology it legitimates.

In the name of continually connecting the otherwise magic realist aspects of the novel to actual historical events, Reed lets a few real frontier figures, such as Lewis and Clark and John Wesley Harding, make cameo appearances, albeit to demystify them. Alongside the debunking of romantic sentiment associated with these white figures, Reed alludes to a couple of key but overlooked black western ones, including Estevanico and his search for the Seven Cities of Cibola and James Beckwourth. And it is the latter that provides a connection between *Yellow Back Radio Broke-Down*'s rhetorical excesses and the first black western writing. For even as Loop knows himself as an interloper in the world of the western as a myth, he is recognized by Chief Showcase as an incarnation of a real African American frontier pioneer, James Beckwourth.

Reed's rhetorical strategy here is metafictional. He includes an altercation between Loop and the leader of a gang of neo–socialist realist writers, Bo Shmo, over the function of fiction. Having been called too abstract, Loop defends his right to "write circuses": "No one says a novel has to be one thing. It can be anything it wants to be, a vaudeville show, the six o'clock news, the mumblings of wild men saddled by demons." Bo Shmo's riposte is that "all art must be for the end of liberating the masses. A landscape is only good when it shows the oppressor hanging from a tree."[11] From a black perspective, the image of a lynching as the aim of meaningful art is hardly copacetic. Reed's jab at the limits and cultural insensitivity of such aesthetic proscription is intertwined with his critique of other forms of orthodoxy, such as monotheism. Later Loop recites a voodoo *wangol* (incantation) in the name of his personal *Loa* (voodoo spirit), Judas, in which he asks that the spirits "please ... open up some of these prissy orthodox minds so that they will no longer call Black People's American experience 'corrupt' 'perverse' and 'decadent.'" Under the maxim "all experience is art," he asks that black popular music acts, Booker T. and the MGs, Etta James, Johnny Ace, and Bojangles, be seen "as just as beautiful as anything that happened anywhere else in the world."[12]

The novel is dominated by dialogue rather than description, consistent with Reed's mission to break down the conventions of the western as a mode of storytelling and open it up for African American articulation. The title of the novel pays homage to the popular dime novel (yellow back) influence on the West of the imagination. It also announces itself as an attempt to "break down" or develop that popular tradition through orality, as radio. The opening paragraph starts out like a western yarn but quickly morphs into a bad man "toast" most commonly associated with African American street poetry. The constant integration or interference of arcane African American terms and cadences derived from jive talk and soul slang is at odds with the western because of their doubled outsider status as both black and urban.

If *Yellow Back Radio Broke-Down* ultimately jettisons or abandons the western, despite nods to Estevanico and Beckwourth, this trace of black journeying, both real and conjured, from South to West, is more implicitly part of the revisionism at the heart of Percival Everett's western writing. In describing *God's Country* (1994), Everett has stated that he "was consciously writing a parody of that form ... I was looking to exploit the fact that there is a mythic West.... And how that mythology that was invented for the West is really the American story."[13] Negotiating a black relationship to that myth and examining its material consequences for African Americans are central to this and at least one other novel, *Wounded* (2005).

God's Country is set in 1871 and narrated firsthand by a bigoted white rancher, Curt Marder, who sets out to hunt down a gang of outlaws posing as Indians who burned down his home, shot his dog, and kidnapped his wife, Sadie. Marder contracts a black tracker, Bubba, to lead the search, promising to give him half of his homestead in return. These two are joined by a child, Jake, whose parents were killed by the gang and is also seeking revenge. The novel could be described as picaresque, or rather a satirical take on the picaresque, given the way our main white protagonist hardly has the wit or intelligence to survive the series of misadventures that befalls him.

The scenario, wittingly or not, evokes a range of classic western stories, both literary and cinematic. A story line in which a girl motivates a search for the killers of her parents echoes that of *True Grit* (1969), an iconic John Wayne film based on Charles Portis's popular 1968 novel. A further invocation of a classic western (again with Wayne) is *The Searchers* (1956), based on Alan Le May's 1954 novel, in which a white racist bigot sets off to save a white girl from Indian captor-contaminators. In *God's Country*, however, the captivity narrative's miscegenation trope is subject to reversal and parody. The searcher is a black man out to save the white damsel in distress. Moreover, the Indians who capture the white woman are whites in disguise, and their apparently helpless captive seems to have been quite happy to cooperate with her captors – it is intimated that she willingly services them sexually.[14] As the novel progresses, the search party itself loses sight of its mission. Marder seems increasingly less interested in finding Sadie; young Jake turns out to be a girl, whose main challenge becomes saving herself from prostitution; and Bubba becomes embroiled in trying to avenge Custer's massacre of his Indian friends.

Everett adopts a doubling device in pairing Marder and Bubba in a conjoined or joint venture. Linked by the promise of sharing property, Marder and Bubba embark on a flawed quest. For Marder has no intention of fulfilling his contract. He cannot conceive of a black person being a property owner. For Bubba, as a slave on the run seeking sanctuary in the West, owning a homestead is a compelling goal, even if it unsettles Marder's or the myth of the West's racist exclusion of African Americans. As readers we have the myth of the West regurgitated through Marder's idiotically sentimental first-person narration. He observes but barely comprehends what he sees. At one point he pronounces to Bubba and a white acquaintance, Tucker: "I love the West.... The West is far as I can see when I'm facing that way.... Why a white man can come out here with nothing and die with everything." To which Tucker retorts, "it's a stupid love you got ... the West don't love you back."[15]

While *God's Country* delivered its demythification of the West through satire and dark humor, *Wounded* (2005) adopted a more sobering naturalist mode.[16] A contemporary western, *Wounded* is narrated by a reclusive black Wyoming horse trainer, who is also a modern art–loving Berkeley alumnus, John Hunt, whose racial and cultural difference from others in the Far West is initially incidental to him. In this remote high plains landscape, a natural world presumably indifferent to race, the taciturn Hunt should be free to enjoy his solitude and freedom from bigotry. Hunt is a widower who shares his home with his ex-con uncle, Gus. Symptomatically, he is most comfortable in the company of horses rather than people. The relative isolation of Hunt's life is dramatically disturbed when a young gay man is found brutally murdered. Police attention falls on Hunt's ranchhand, Wallace, a dull-witted itinerant. Rather than helping Wallace protest his innocence, Hunt opts to keep a low profile to stave off any animosity toward him as one of the few black people in the area. The result is Hunt's complicity not only with the white racist prejudice he fears but also with the homophobic bigotry that led to the murder of a gay man and the suicide of the falsely accused Wallace.

Questions of individual responsibility become unavoidable, however, with the arrival of David, the gay son of a university friend. David goes missing and Hunt fears that he has been abducted by the rednecks who escaped prosecution for the first homophobic hate crime. In the search for David, Hunt is exposed to the quotidian prejudices about race and sexuality in this ranching community. Working independently of the untrustworthy law and with the help of Gus and a Native American, Elvis Monday, Hunt finds the neo-Nazi gang responsible for the abduction and fatal beating of David. Gus kills the thugs and Elvis covers up the incident. Everett's naturalist mediation of frontier experience allows for a more intimate and psychologically engaging portrait of how prejudice roams the West than his parodic work. Detailed attention to daily issues reveals the black ranch to be a compromised sanctuary in an environment capable of nurturing as much bigotry as anywhere else.

Alongside autobiography, parody, and naturalism, African American writers have worked within the framework of the historical novel. Most notably, David Anthony Durham's *Gabriel's Story* (2001) provides a dis-abusing historical corrective to the hubris of Beckwourth and Love's accounts of the West. In a manner redolent of Cormac McCarthy's histor-ically researched writing, Durham confronts the reader with an uncom-promising view of a violent frontier world. At Civil War's end, a young African American man abandons homesteading in Kansas for the dream of becoming a cowboy in Texas. The romanticized vision of a life in the saddle is shattered through a series of brutally violent experiences – includ-ing witnessing starving Native Americans on death marches and unwilling participation in the psychopathic killing sprees of an outlaw gang. Burned from these events and aware of his being a marked man by virtue of his race, Gabriel decides to return home alone. On the journey back he learns to appreciate the splendid isolation, solitude, and indifference the western landscape grants him.

While solitude and retreat are revered characteristics of black western writing, there is a competing interest in affiliations with other "others." The early generation of writer-pioneers adopted contradictory views of Native Americans. Beckwourth staged himself as belonging in the story of the West as a frontiersman through a doubled image of trapper and adopted Crow Indian. For Micheaux, as a homesteader and settler, shar-ing a white racist perspective on the redundancy of the Indian was a means to including himself in the story of that phase of nation building. By contrast, Reed and Everett, as members of the more recent post–civil rights generation, have reimagined the West as a space where black and

Native American interests conjoin in fighting white racism and the narrative supporting it.

The Urban Noir Frontier

While African American writers necessarily engaged with both the myth and the reality of the wild or rural western experience, the major black movement westward was to urban environments. Prior to World War II, black southerners migrated mainly to cities in the North such as Chicago, Detroit, and New York. The advent of the war, however, turned urban-industrial centers in California, especially Los Angeles, into significant migration destinations. Becoming a primary site for defense production with $11 billion in war contracts, Los Angeles needed a bigger labor force.[17] African Americans seized the opportunity, transforming the city's black community, which expanded from around 75,000 in 1940 to 215,000 in 1950 (reaching 931,000 in the 1990s).[18] The impact of resettlement in Los Angeles can be understood through the writing by members of the first wave of migrants, such as Arna Bontemps.

A prominent member of the Harlem Renaissance, Bontemps took a circuitous route to New York. He was born in Louisiana, and his family moved to Mudtown (a section of Watts) in Los Angeles in 1905, when he was three. As such, Bontemps was part of a less-traveled migratory path from the Deep South to the West Coast for African Americans in the early twentieth century. Although he was California educated, he headed to Harlem in the mid-1920s, as this was the primary haven for aspiring black artists and intellectuals. From the other side of the continent he would write his first novel, *God Sends Sunday* (1931). Significantly, Harlem was not the setting for this work. Rather, Bontemps provided an unsettling story of a Louisiana jockey, Little Augie, who triumphs on the Mississippi valley racing circuit and commits himself to the fast and loose "sporting life" of drinking, gambling, and womanizing. Losing his fortune in St. Louis (gateway to the West), he jumps a freight train as an itinerant to Los Angeles (the terminal of the West) and is last seen heading for Mexico. Little Augie, whose initials conflate the names of the place of his birth, the state of Louisiana, and his terminal destination, Los Angeles, was based on Bontemps's uncle Buddy, a conserver and purveyor of Deep South folkish culture and wit among the migrant Mudtown community.

Reflecting Bontemps's own dissatisfaction with Los Angeles as a new center for black cultural flowering, the novel sets up a tension between an unpredictable and deracinated future, figured in the profligacy of Augie's behavior and its tragic destiny, and the idea of a lost home, the Deep South. When the destitute Augie arrives in Watts, what he sees is in part nothing new. Mudtown's relative isolation from the rest of the city, as a rural outskirt and backwater, and its racially segregated character gave it an ambivalent meaning in terms of supporting a better life for its denizens: "Here, removed from the influences of white folks, they did not acquire the inhibitions of their city brothers. Mudtown was like a tiny section of the deep south literally transported."[19] In a later article, "Why I Returned" (1965), Bontemps rationalized his attachment to the South as the true home spiritually, culturally, and politically for African Americans, by affectionately quoting Buddy: "Folks talk a lot about California ... but I'd a heap rather be down home rather than here, if wasn't for the conditions."[20]

The relative separation and slow growth of the black community in Los Angeles would continue until the eve of World War II. The defense industry spurred a major migration of African Americans to jobs in mixed race workplaces. And one black migrant party to this experience was Chester Himes, who would document the harsh reality of his Los Angeles wartime work experience in two 1940s novels, *If He Hollers Let Him Go* (1945) and *Lonely Crusade* (1947).

If He Hollers Let Him Go covers four days in the life of a newly arrived black migrant worker from Ohio at the Atlas shipyard in Los Angeles. Bob Jones is given the position of leaderman, in charge of a mixed race crew. He experiences white racist resentment from those who hate working to a black person's orders. He discovers that his promotion is an act of racial tokenism, designed to placate dissent among other black workers. A white female worker, Madge, who outwardly despises him, is sexually attracted to him. To her pronouncement "I ain't gonna work for no nigger," Jones retorts, "screw you then, you cracker bitch."[21] He is demoted for his insult while Madge's racism remains unchecked. Himes gives us a vivid nightmarish portrayal of the psychological torment both blatant and institutional racism inflicts on his protagonist. Jones's rage and hurt become channeled into the desire to rape Madge. When he has the chance, however, she preempts his assault by crying out, "rape me," declaring her sexual attraction to him. He goes cold and refuses to oblige. The two are discovered by other workers, and Madge, protecting herself from any impression she might be interested in an interracial union, accuses Jones of attempted rape. The racist bias of the justice system means Jones knows his account will not be believed and he will face a prison sentence. He is saved from this fate by the shipyard owner, who

wants to suppress the case because it could incite race hate and violence
at the workplace. A compliant judge tells Jones that he must enlist in
the army and risk his life fighting for Uncle Sam instead. This catch-22
scenario provides an absurdist ending to a work of candid social realism.
Himes followed up *If He Hollers* with *Lonely Crusade*, a novel that dealt
with the way a black worker at a wartime airplane factory in Los Angeles
suffers psychologically when he becomes a pawn in the game of union
politics.[22]

Perhaps Himes's noirlike cynicism about the urban West as a place for
a better black future was confirmed by the catastrophic scale of the Watts
Riots (or Rebellion) in 1965. Johnie Scott, a member of the Watts Writers
Workshop that was initiated in the immediate aftermath of the devastation, however, wrestled with the problem of fleeing black Los Angeles
and questions of responsibility to the community. In his autobiographical
short story, "The Coming of the Hoodlum," he narrates the quandary of
a bright Watts student (Hoodlum), son of a Louisiana migrant, who has
a chance to go to Harvard. He can bear only a year away, however, feeling a deep sense of ivory tower isolation, alienation, and disconnection
from the culture that shaped him. As such, Scott's 1967 story seeks to
overcome the split between the South as roots and Watts as displacement.
He returns to Watts on the eve of the riots – but he now understands this
place as home.

In the work of fellow Watts denizen and Writers Workshop attendee,
Wanda Coleman, Los Angeles is a place of racism, poverty, and outcasts.
Her candid evocation of urban actualities reveals a city riven by socioeconomic, racial, and gender frontiers, its tropes sometimes constituting a merging of the Wild West and the street. In the short story "Friday
Night Shift at the Taco House Blues (Wah-Wah)" (1988), for example,
Coleman views the human traffic passing through the doors of a taco restaurant from the perspective of a street-wise African American woman.
Carol works front of house with a small team of black women serving
customers. The restaurant constitutes an updated western saloon, replete
with new versions of its borderland types: a Vietnam War vet (frontier soldier), illegal aliens (Mexican renegades), drug dealers (medicine peddlers),
gamblers, pimps, and whores. She witnesses a disturbingly violent macho
showdown between her potential date and the traumatized vet. Despite
the testosterone-fueled action, Coleman asserts an affirmative view of the
pragmatic and savvy capacity of black women – as shift workers, welfare
claimants, carers, lovers, and sex workers – in surviving this otherwise
hostile environment.[23]

Grappling with both the iniquitous reality and the misperceptions of this urban West only became harder after the Los Angeles riots in 1992. Anna Deveare Smith's one-person show, *Twilight Los Angeles, 1992* (1994), engaged the hyperbole associated with the outrage and violence consequent on the acquittal of the police officers involved in the beating of Rodney King. Using tape-recorded testimony from a variety of people, Smith took on different roles, giving voice to mourning Koreans, angry black and Chicano gang bangers, complacent whites, and indifferent cops. In doing so she tried to humanize and give expression to a desire for order against the grain of those who perpetuate the image of the urban West as wild and anarchic.

The major chronicler of the troubled emergence of Los Angeles as a new black roots culture as opposed to a dreamed destination is Walter Mosley. Mosley's first novel, *Devil in a Blue Dress* (1990), in many ways picks up where Chester Himes left off. In 1948 Los Angeles, a black war veteran and migrant from the western South (Houston area), Easy Rawlins, loses his defense plant job. Desperate to meet mortgage payments, Easy agrees to undertake some amateur sleuthing for a white man trying to locate a blond woman who has a love of African American jazz clubs. A detective story ensues that reveals not only whodunit but more importantly the migrant character of 1940s black Los Angeles. Mosley's intimate knowledge of both the place and time of the novel's action is partly based on his own father's story, first as a hopeful migrant to Los Angeles from Louisiana, and second as a disillusioned African American war veteran who returned to peacetime Los Angeles only to be treated as a second-class citizen.

In *Devil in a Blue Dress*, Mosley paints a contradictory picture of California as a black destination. Easy visits an illegal nightclub, Johns, on Central Avenue. There some of his "homefolks," a migrant jazz trio from Houston, are playing in front of fellow displaced southerners. Easy ruminates on the way the club offers a way to keep the dream of migration alive despite its disappointing truth, commenting that "California was like heaven for the southern Negro. People told stories of how you could eat fruit right off the trees and get enough work to retire in one day." He then qualifies this cliché, reflecting that "the truth wasn't the dream. Life was still hard in L.A. and if you worked every day you still found yourself on the bottom."[24]

Mosley's sensitivity to the broken promises of Los Angeles for its black population is necessarily attuned to regional belonging and difference. In 1948, black Los Angeles is permeated by the voices and idioms of the Deep

South that, on one hand, guarantee a sense of a home away from home but, on the other, might prove a barrier to communication and movement beyond the community. Significantly, Easy demonstrates a form of bilingualism in being at home both in southern vernacular and in Standard English. It is this dialect dexterity that allows him to traverse black and white worlds. This having been said, he finds himself often caught in limbo over the morality of his position and actions. It takes a visitor from the South to be decisive, especially in terms of violent resolution. His best and most dangerous friend, Mouse Alexander, arrives from Houston and can kill without compulsion. He appears as an avenging southern trickster spirit, indifferent to issues such as the law and moral conscience. Mouse's violence is condoned because of the way the legitimate world consistently fails African Americans in the noir city of Los Angeles.

While subsequent novels play out the history of black Los Angeles since World War II, it is significant that Mosley felt it was important to interrupt the chronological order of events by publishing a prequel, *Gone Fishin'* in 1997. Set in Houston and the bayou world of Pariah, Texas, in 1939, when Easy was nineteen, this novel provides a pre–Los Angeles background to Easy and Mouse's friendship. In doing so, it biographically connects and confirms the special relationship between the culture of the Deep South and postwar Los Angeles. The story is one of a murderous road trip into the swamplands. Here Easy comes of age as he witnesses Mouse's killing of a bad paternal figure and has sex with a voodoo *mambo*, Momma Jo, who teaches him love. By the end, Easy knows Houston cannot be enough for him. He takes a train north across the Texas desert landscape, in the company of a black couple heading to Los Angeles whose son has a job at the Arthur airplane factory. This glimpse of the future, of *Devil in a Blue Dress*, is followed by a jump cut that finds Easy in Paris at the end of the war, preparing to return to the United States.

While Mosley is not strictly a writer of westerns, his work illustrates the complexity of trying to make space for a black West. If the earliest black writers tried to muscle their way into the dominant myth, later writers have questioned the value of trying to do so, adopting a variety of aesthetic modes to make space not just for critique, but for an African American voice to be heard. Even as the iniquity of the white racist tenets of western mythology have been exposed, in making literary space for the black experience on the frontier, African American writers have produced a vital and rich reconceptualization of the region, both real and imagined.

Notes

1 Delmont R. Oswald, "Introduction," in James P. Beckwourth, *The Life and Adventures of James P. Beckwourth* (1856; reprint, Lincoln: University of Nebraska Press, 1972), xi.
2 See Blake Allmendinger, *Imagining the African American West* (Lincoln: University of Nebraska Press, 2005) for fuller treatment of Beckwourth.
3 Nat Love, *The Life and Adventures of Nat Love* (1907; reprint, Lincoln: University of Nebraska Press, 1995), 41.
4 Ibid., 70.
5 Nell Irvin Painter, *Exodusters: Black Migration to Kansas after Reconstruction* (New York: Norton, 1992).
6 Oscar Micheaux, *The Conquest* (1913; reprint, Lincoln: University of Nebraska Press, 1994), 130, 178, 184, 210.
7 See Michael K. Johnson, *Hoo-Doo Cowboys and Bronze Buckaroos: Conceptions of the African American West* (Jackson: University Press of Mississippi, 2014) for further coverage of Thompson and comparison with Micheaux.
8 Ishmael Reed, *Yellow Back Radio Broke-Down* (1968; reprint, London: Allison and Busby, 1995), 10.
9 Ibid., 26.
10 Ibid., 19.
11 Ibid., 36.
12 Ibid., 64.
13 Robert Birnbaum, "Author Interview: Percival Everett," *Identity Theory*, May 6, 2003 http://www.identitytheory.com/percival-everett/ (accessed March 17, 2015).
14 Percival Everett, *God's Country* (Boston: Beacon Press, 1994), 67.
15 Ibid., 44.
16 Rone Shavers, "Interview: Percival Everett by Rone Shavers," *Bomb Magazine* 88 (summer 2004) http://bombmagazine.org/article/2666/percival-everett (accessed March 17, 2015).
17 Josh Sides, *L.A. City Limits: African American Los Angeles from the Great Depression to the Present* (Berkeley: University of California Press, 2003), 37.
18 Philip J. Ethington, William H. Frey, and Dowell Myers, "The Racial Resegregation of Los Angeles County, 1940–2000," Race Contours 2000 Project, Public Research Report 2001–04. http://www.usc.edu/schools/price/research/popdynamics/pdf/2001_Ethington-Frey-Myers_Racial-Resegregation.pdf (accessed March 17, 2015); Sides, *L.A. City Limits*, 36–56.
19 Arna Bontemps, *God Sends Sunday* (1931; reprint, New York: Washington Square Press, 2005), 119.
20 Arna Bontemps, "Why I Returned," *Harper's Monthly* (April 1965), reprinted in *The African American West: A Century of Short Stories*, ed. Bruce A. Glasrud and Laurie Champion (Boulder: University Press of Colorado, 2000), 92.
21 Chester Himes, *If He Hollers Let Him Go* (1946; reprint, New York: Thunder's Mouth Press, 1986), 27.

22 See Brian Dolinar, *The Black Cultural Front: Black Artists and Writers of the Depression Generation* (Jackson: University Press of Mississippi, 2012), for more on Himes's 1940s writing.

23 See Krista Comer, "Revising Western Criticism through Wanda Coleman," *Western American Literature* 33, no. 4 (winter 1999): 357–83, for further coverage of Coleman.

24 Walter Mosley, *Devil in a Blue Dress* (New York: Pocket Books, 1991), 27.

CHAPTER 21

Hollywood Westerns
1930s to the Present

Andrew Patrick Nelson

From the late 1930s up until the 1960s, the western was one of the most popular movie genres in the United States, and westerns routinely ranked among the highest earning films in any given year. This period, often referred to as the genre's golden age, saw the release of celebrated westerns such as *Stagecoach* (John Ford, 1939), *Red River* (Howard Hawks, 1948), *High Noon* (Fred Zinnemann, 1952), *Shane* (George Stevens, 1953), *The Searchers* (John Ford, 1956), *Rio Bravo* (Howard Hawks, 1959), *The Magnificent Seven* (John Sturges, 1960), along with countless others. In the 1940s and 1950s, westerns consistently made up one-quarter of all films produced in the United States, roughly one hundred westerns a year. Even into the 1960s, moviegoers could reliably expect twenty new westerns annually. This was a time when overall film production levels in Hollywood were dropping, such that westerns still made up about 15 percent of movies playing in American cinemas.[1] Beginning in the late 1960s, however, after nearly thirty years of being one of Hollywood's most reliably popular products, the western experienced a precipitous decline. This fall was reflected in not only a dramatic decrease in the number of films being made, but also a more negative critical response to the genre by both critics and filmmakers. Production of westerns fell throughout the 1960s and 1970s, and by the 1980s the western had faded away as a popular genre. Despite a number of small revivals in the ensuing decades – most notably in the early and mid-1990s, after the releases of *Dances with Wolves* (Kevin Costner, 1990) and *Unforgiven* (Clint Eastwood, 1992) – this state of affairs remains largely unchanged. "The genre ... is more or less dead," proclaimed the critic Scott Eyman in 2014, "except when a powerful director or star gets an urge to make a vanity western."[2]

The narrative of the Hollywood western's rise and fall is as well known as it is lamented. It also raises a number of questions, which scholarship on the genre has spent more than a half-century debating. Where did the western originate in the first place? What made the western so popular with audiences in the mid-twentieth century? And how was a genre that once dominated our movie screens relegated to the sidelines of popular culture?

Brave cowboys, noble Indians, rowdy barrooms, majestic mountain ranges, and other people and places associated with the American West were cinematic staples from the medium's inception in the late nineteenth century. Yet historical events that transpired on the western frontier of America had been a source of inspiration and fascination for writers and artists since before the founding of the country.

We can trace the lineage of the western movie back to at least the late seventeenth and eighteenth centuries, when the first captivity narratives appeared in the American colonies. These stories of white settlers captured by American Indians were often based on fact and were sometimes written by the captives themselves after their rescue. A seminal early example is the story of Mary Rowlandson, a New England woman who, along with her three children, was held captive for eleven weeks by Narranganset Indians in 1675. Life on the American frontier was further sensationalized in the early nineteenth century by writers such as James Fenimore Cooper with his Leatherstocking Tales, a series of historical novels about the adventures of the frontiersman Natty Bumppo, a white raised by Mohican Indians (and inspired, in part, by the real-life frontiersman Daniel Boone).

In these and other works, we see that conventions associated with the western film of the twentieth century were established in literature long before a cowboy ever graced the silver screen. Captivity narratives pitting brave white men against the savage Indians who have kidnapped their women remained popular in literature until the late nineteenth century and feature in many well-known western films. *The Searchers*, for example, was inspired by the true story of Cynthia Ann Parker, who was kidnapped as a young girl by the Comanche from her West Texas settlement in 1836.[3] Cooper's Natty Bumppo is an early example of a character type the cultural historian Richard Slotkin has influentially termed "the man who knows Indians": the invariably white protagonist who, either by upbringing or by proving himself through trials, is "able to both think and fight like an Indian."[4] This character is a staple of classic western cinema – including *Fort Apache* (John Ford, 1948), *Broken Arrow* (Delmer Daves, 1950), and *The Searchers* – as well as later westerns such as *Little Big Man* (Arthur Penn, 1970) and *Dances with Wolves*. Readers will also recognize a futuristic variant of the "man who knows Indians" in the science fiction blockbuster *Avatar* (James Cameron, 2009), proving that this character, though removed from the western proper, is still very much present in contemporary popular culture.

In the second half of the nineteenth century, even more sensational and stirring tales of life in the American West began to appear in penny dreadfuls and dime novels: cheap storybooks offering fictionalized accounts of the lives of such contemporary frontier figures as Jesse James, Wyatt Earp, and "Buffalo" Bill Cody. Cody's famous traveling Wild West exhibition also enjoyed its greatest success in the United States in the last two decades of the nineteenth century, at the same time as the vogue for dime novels gripped the nation.

Although western exhibitions and dime novels remained popular into the 1900s, representations of the American West accrued greater respectability around the turn of the century through the publication of more "serious" novels about life on the frontier, as well as a growing appreciation for painting and sculpture depicting western scenes. Key figures in these respective areas were Owen Wister and Frederic Remington. Wister's 1902 novel *The Virginian: A Horseman of the Plains* is considered by many to be the first western novel, and it had a significant shaping influence on western literature and then cinema – especially the characterization of the western hero as stoic, righteous, and quick-witted. Immensely popular upon its release, *The Virginian* was viewed as offering a more authentic account of frontier life than that found in dime novels. Wister drew heavily upon his own experiences on ranching, hunting, and fishing trips in Wyoming and Montana between 1885 and 1900, and his novel is filled with minutiae of life in the West. In similar fashion, Remington began painting western scenes in the late 1880s after his own travels throughout the American West. Portraying in his work the moments of danger and conflict that came to define the archetypal romance of the American West, Remington's paintings captured the public's imagination at the time and influenced a generation of artists and, significantly, filmmakers. As the director John Ford explained of his 1948 Technicolor western *She Wore a Yellow Ribbon*, "I tried to copy the Remington style there – you can't copy him one hundred percent – but at least I tried to get in his color and movement, and I think I succeeded partly."[5]

American cinema's early and transitional periods, from the late 1880s to the mid-1910s, produced a number of successful and noteworthy films that contained cowboy imagery or frontier themes. Initially, many of these films were documentary or ethnographic in nature, capturing short performances by Indian bands, western show performers such as Annie Oakley, or rodeo competitions. By the early aughts narrative films

featuring lawmen, outlaws, and scenes from the "Old West" became popular. Throughout the teens and twenties, western movies were increasingly
associated with individual performers. William S. Hart rose to stardom
playing the "good badman" – the cowboy with the shady past who is
redeemed by love – while Tom Mix epitomized the noble western action
hero. Across dozens of films, Hart, Mix, and other actors offered viewers
slight variations of the same basic characters, establishing a model of performance that would be emulated by nearly every western star to follow.[6]

Some expensive western features were made in the 1920s – John Ford's
The Iron Horse (1924) among them – but the majority of those produced
during this period tended to be unpretentious, low-budget films that
catered to a largely rural and southern viewership. This would remain
the case into the 1930s, after cinema's transition to sound. In 1930, for
example, two big-budget prestige westerns, *The Big Trail* (Raoul Walsh)
starring John Wayne and *Billy the Kid* (King Vidor) starring Johnny Mack
Brown and Wallace Beery, were released, each in a nascent 70-mm wide-
screen format. Neither found favor with audiences, and the financial failure of these and other films prompted the Hollywood studios to shelve
the production of high-cost westerns until the end of the decade. Instead,
Hollywood focused on producing western B films. Running around sixty
minutes in length and often shot in a week or less, these low-cost, low-risk
films were designed to fill the second half of a cinema's double bill (a
depression era invention designed to attract patrons). The majority of B
films, westerns included, were produced either by minor studios such as
Columbia Pictures or by "poverty row" outfits including Republic and
Monogram.[7]

Although "B westerns" often display scant interest in the history of the
American West – many, in fact, have contemporary rather than historical
settings – they nonetheless evidence a firm belief that the assumed western ideals of fair play, honor, and justice are fundamentally American and
to be defended by the hero. This doctrine is particularly evident in the
films made by the most famous B western stars of time, William Boyd
and Gene Autry. Boyd played the character of the good cowboy Hopalong
Cassidy in more than sixty films in the late 1930s and 1940s, while Autry,
"The Singing Cowboy," made more than forty westerns in the 1930s and
early 1940s before he enlisted in the U.S. Army during World War II.[8] The
movie career of Roy Rogers, another signing cowboy, also began in the
late 1930s.[9]

Eventually, elements from these B movies and earlier western narratives coalesced in a remarkable series of A westerns released in 1939 and

1940 that formalized most if not all of the familiar character types, narratives, and other conventions that continue to shape western film to this
day. Titles include *Stagecoach*, *Jesse James* (Henry King, 1939), *Dodge City*
(Michael Curtiz, 1939), *Union Pacific* (Cecil B. DeMille, 1939), *Destry
Rides Again* (George Marshall, 1939), *The Westerner* (William Wyler, 1940),
and *The Return of Frank James* (Fritz Lang, 1940). In addition to boasting
famous directors and leading stars including Tyrone Power, Errol Flynn,
and Gary Cooper, each of these films takes place in the American West in
the late nineteenth century, and many dramatize events from American
history including the construction of the transcontinental railroad and the
lives of frontier legends such as Jesse James and Wyatt Earp.

What accounted for the sudden interest in the western in Hollywood?
Westerns were certainly popular throughout the 1920s and 1930s, but that
popularity entailed demographic and industrial qualifications such that
the genre was not seen as appropriate for ongoing A-level production. Just
forty-four A westerns were made in the 1930s of a total of more than a
thousand feature-length westerns.[10] Taking a chance on a single large-scale
western is one thing, but how to explain the appearance of more than a
dozen such films within the span of a few years?

A successful large-scale western had, in fact, been released earlier in
the decade: *The Plainsman* (Cecil B. DeMille, 1936), a highly fictionalized account of the adventures of Wild Bill Hickok, Calamity Jane, and
Buffalo Bill Cody. Yet *The Plainsman* was the product of a number of
trends shaping Hollywood moviemaking in the 1930s – trends that only
intensified as the decade wore on. One was an interest in films with a historical and/or literary pedigree. In addition to the westerns named earlier,
we see this in other hits of the late 1930s such as *The Adventures of Robin
Hood* (Michael Curtiz, 1938), *Gunga Din* (George Stevens, 1939), *Drums
along the Mohawk* (John Ford, 1939), and *Gone with the Wind* (Victor
Fleming, 1939). Another influence was Hollywood's attempt to cater to
female moviegoers. In the 1930s the studios believed that the majority
of their audience was women, an assumption that accounts not only for
the emergence of the "woman's film" – pictures like *Stella Dallas* (King
Vidor, 1937), *The Women* (George Cukor, 1939) and *Now, Voyager* (Michael
Curtiz, 1942), which featured female protagonists and explored "feminine" subject matter – but also for the rise of the western, a genre well
suited to showing off the talents of attractive male actors such as Power,
Flynn, Cooper, Henry Fonda, James Stewart, and John Wayne.

The western did not have a monopoly on historically themed adventure
movies featuring dashing male stars – we could just as easily point to the

many popular "swashbucklers" of the time such as *The Prisoner of Zenda* (John Cromwell, 1937) and *The Sea Hawk* (Michael Curtiz, 1940). Also, John Ford's *Stagecoach*, by far the most famous western of the 1939–40 cycle, is arguably the most anomalous. Though the film is set in the Old West, it concerns neither a famous personage nor a historical event. Wayne, who plays the Ringo Kid, was not a star; after his ill-fated turn in *The Big Trail* he spent a decade making B westerns. And the film's scenario – in which an assortment of strangers is united by dint of their confinement in a particular space – recalls *Grand Hotel* (Edmund Golding, 1932) more than any earlier western. (The film was even advertised as "a powerful story of 9 strange people.") Yet it was not the swashbuckler but the western – and especially the western of John Ford and John Wayne – that not only emerged as the fullest expression of Hollywood's masculine historical drama but by the 1950s represented, in the words of the French film critic André Bazin, "the American cinema par excellence."[11]

Though Bazin held that the western achieved classical perfection in 1939 (largely on the strength of *Stagecoach*), histories of the genre linger on the numerous outstanding films released in the two decades that immediately followed the Second World War. Many of these westerns were the product of sustained collaborations between directors and stars: Ford and Wayne, including the "cavalry trilogy" of *Fort Apache, She Wore a Yellow Ribbon* (1949), and *Rio Grande* (1950), as well as *The Searchers* and *The Man Who Shot Liberty Valance* (1962); Howard Hawks and Wayne, in *Red River, Rio Bravo,* and *El Dorado* (1964); Anthony Mann's five westerns with James Stewart, including *Winchester '73* (1950) and *The Naked Spur* (1953); and Budd Boetticher's seven westerns starring Randolph Scott, including *Seven Men from Now* (1956) and *The Tall T* (1958).

Outside these films, the two postwar westerns to receive the most critical attention are *High Noon* (Fred Zinnemann, 1952), about a marshal who leaves his wife on their wedding day to protect his town from an old villain, and *Shane* (George Stevens, 1953), about a mysterious gunfighter who protects a group of homesteaders from a ruthless cattle baron. *High Noon* is famous for its reflection of contemporary cultural concerns. The screenwriter Carl Foreman, who refused to "name names" before the House Un-American Activities Committee and would later be blacklisted by the film industry, intended the picture to be an allegory about the hunt for communists in Hollywood led by Senator Joseph McCarthy: The hero, Will Kane, finds himself alone and outnumbered, abandoned by those he thought were his friends. *Shane*, by contrast, is noted for timelessness. The western hero is distilled to his essence – a wandering, lonely man with a gun – while attention to costume and staging lends the proceedings an almost ceremonial air.

What explains the broad appeal of the western to American moviegoers of the postwar period, whose daily concerns were presumably far removed from those of their pioneer ancestors? Critics began to ask these questions seriously in the 1950s, and a half-century's worth of inquiry has yielded many possible answers. By far the most accepted explanation for the western's popularity centers on its social function – what the western *meant* to the people watching it so enthusiastically.

Jim Kitses, in his seminal 1969 monograph *Horizons West*, contends that at the heart of the western lies an overarching opposition: wilderness and civilization. This is a conflict that, in reality, cannot be easily reconciled, and by and large the historical march of civilization has meant the retreat of nature. This dialectic is significant to American culture because the United States was carved out of a mythic wilderness, with a westward moving frontier on which these opposed forces clashed on a daily basis – mixed feelings about which, Kitses argues, endured long after the frontier was closed.

Kitses was not the only scholar in the 1960s and 1970s to articulate similar ideas about the appeal of the western film. John G. Cawelti, Peter Wollen, and Will Wright also invoke the wilderness/civilization binary in their work, a reflection of both the enduring influence of the historian Frederick Jackson Turner's "frontier thesis" as well as the growing influence of structuralist analysis.[12] Among other things, structuralism provided a means of justifying the study of popular literature and culture by treating its artifacts as akin to the myths of earlier societies, which, as Claude Levi-Strauss influentially argued in the 1950s, provided imaginary resolutions to real questions, problems, and contradictions.

American history did not provide an amicable solution to the opposition between wilderness and civilization, but the Hollywood western did. At the center of the classic western film stands the mythical frontier hero – the Ringo Kid, Wyatt Earp, Will Kane, Shane, Ethan Edwards – who is neither fully integrated into society nor wholly a part of nature. This hero figuratively and often precariously straddles the symbolic divide between civilization and wilderness – between East and West, community and individual, progress and tradition – always embodying the best of each side, and thereby reconciling them in the American imaginary. The infatuation with the cowboy in American culture is thus understood as a reflection of society's ambivalence about the costs associated with progress and a valorization of a mythical character who embodies the "best of both worlds." The western hero's placement at the border of civilization and wilderness also marks him as a tragic figure, doomed to a life of endless wandering between two worlds. He can try, as Shane does, to turn in his pistol for a plow, but it won't take. Civilization has need of this hero; it needs his superior force to purge society of evil. Yet violence, though occasionally required to protect society, ultimately has no place within it. Thus the hero, who is inextricably linked with violence, must return to a mythic wilderness where he is equally alone.

The appeal of the structural approach to the western is apparent. Not only is it easily applied to a large number of films, but it also connects the rituals carried out time and again on-screen to the people watching them in a meaningful way. Beginning in the 1990s, however, film scholars such as Steve Neale and David Bordwell raised thoughtful objections to the premise that films straightforwardly reflect the social contexts of their production and consumption.[13] Both filmmaking and filmgoing are activities with a multiplicity of determinants. Is either act really an unconscious expression of the hopes and fears of an entire nation? Is it fair to reduce films released around the same time, even those of the same genre, to a single underlying structure or ideological position? Might different people not reasonably interpret the same film in different ways? For example, although Carl Foreman intended *High Noon* to be a liberal cold war allegory, some interpreted Marshal Kane's refusal to walk away from confrontation as an affirmation of America's mission in Korea. (Also, in 1994 the *National Review* magazine ranked the film as one of the "best conservative movies.")[14]

The rub, of course, is that these objections, usually articulated within the context of film historiography or theory, have seldom been applied to actual studies of the western, which happily continue to employ reflectionist methodologies. This is especially true in the work of scholars trained not in film studies but in literature or history, who, despite the influence of the new western history's move away from grand Turnerian narratives and toward emphases on the specific social, economic, and ecological features of the American frontier, continue to interpret popular representations of the West symptomatically.[15] Indeed, one of the advantages of the reflectionist explanation for the western's appeal is that it is also able to account for the genre's demise.

The western's numerical decline from the 1960s onward certainly indicates that attitudes toward the genre were changing. To many critics the western's unremitting celebration of the taming of the lawless frontier by brave Anglo Americans came across as not just clichéd but gravely backward, as, for example, scenes of deadly conflict on a new "frontier" in Southeast Asia played out on television screens in living rooms across the United States. At the same time, "revisionist" westerns such as *The Wild Bunch* (Sam Peckinpah, 1969), *McCabe & Mrs. Miller* (Robert Altman, 1971), *Doc* (Frank Perry, 1971), *The Culpepper Cattle Co.* (Dick Richards, 1972), *Dirty Little Billy* (Stan Dragoti, 1972), and *Buffalo Bill and the Indians, or Sitting Bull's History Lesson* (Robert Altman, 1976) began to echo these concerns by questioning, and in some cases forcefully rebuking, the ideology of cowboy heroism inherent in earlier westerns. *Little Big Man* and *Soldier Blue* (Ralph Nelson, 1970) drew parallels between the massacre of Vietnamese civilians by American soldiers at My Lai and the military massacres of American Indians at Washita River (1868) and Sand Creek (1864).

While we should question whether the average moviegoer of the time shared these films' ambivalence or antipathy – most revisionist westerns were in fact met with indifference at the box office – decreased production certainly signaled diminished interest in the western among mainstream audiences. Changing demographics are undoubtedly part of this story, as are changing production patterns. Starting after the Second World War and increasing steadily thereafter, the general American movie audience became younger and more interested in action, horror, and science fiction films – genres that would form the foundation of the Hollywood blockbuster of the late 1970s and 1980s. It bears noting, however, that westerns of a more conventional bent were produced throughout the 1960s and 1970s, most of them starring John Wayne – for example, *True Grit* (Henry Hathaway, 1969), *Big Jake* (George Sherman, 1971), *The Shootist* (Don Siegel, 1976) – and other aging screen icons including Burt Lancaster and Gregory Peck. Although critics frequently dismiss them as outmoded retreads of earlier westerns, these films often performed as well as if not better than contemporaneous revisionist efforts, and Wayne remained one of Hollywood's most popular and bankable actors up to his death in 1979. Clint Eastwood's westerns of the 1970s, including *High Plains Drifter* (Eastwood, 1973) and *The Outlaw Josey Wales* (Eastwood, 1976), can also be viewed as traditional: As Michael T. Marsden and Jack Nachbar observe, "Eastwood's Westerns develop a pattern of values that defends proper civilization as strongly as the oldest Westerns."[16]

Expectedly, the most common explanation for the genre's wane involves its social function. Westerns, it is claimed, became less relevant to our increasingly civilized, increasingly technological daily experiences, and thus the genre, as Richard Maltby writes, "ceased to function as a vehicle for American culture to tell itself the stories it needs to hear."[17] While the western's cultural relevance, or lack thereof, may well have contributed to its decline as a popular genre, so too did a confluence of other factors, including shifting demographics, modified production patterns and processes, changing tastes, and the failure to develop new stars. Thus, in the end, the traditional westerns of Wayne and Eastwood did little more than the socially conscious films of Robert Altman and Arthur Penn to sustain the western. Though it is often claimed that the critical and commercial failure of *Heaven's Gate* (Michael Cimino) in 1980 sounded the final death knell for the genre, in truth production of westerns had dipped into the low single digits years earlier.

The western did not die, however. As noted earlier, in the 1990s one successful film, *Dances with Wolves*, was followed by another, *Unforgiven*, which in turn led to a small resurgence of the big-screen western. Among this cycle of films were new interpretations of heroes such as Wyatt Earp (*Tombstone* [George Costamos, 1993] and *Wyatt Earp* [Lawrence Kasdan, 1994]) as well as westerns about groups the genre had marginalized in the past, including American Indians (*Dances with Wolves*, *Geronimo: An American Legend* [Walter Hill, 1993] and *Dead Man* [Jim Jarmusch, 1995]), blacks (*Posse* [Mario Van Peebles, 1993]), and women (*The Ballad of Little Jo* [Maggie Greenwald, 1993], *Bad Girls* [Jonathan Kaplan, 1995], and *The Quick and the Dead* [Sam Raimi, 1994]).

Criticism of this cycle of westerns often stresses connections with the revisionist films of the 1970s, particularly with respect to how these new movies addressed issues of race and gender. The renewed emphasis in the 1990s on the ideological aspects of the genre's mythology has been seen as a reflection of broader social changes in the United States, including an emphasis on multiculturalism.[18] But while the influence of these films' more nuanced and historically plausible portrayals of women and Indians is still felt in more recent works, the 1990s cycle of westerns ultimately proved to be just that: a cycle, short-lived and temporary, rather than a full-fledged revival. Several westerns were released to cinemas in the latter half of the decade, but these failed to renew interest in the genre among either producers or audiences.

Audiences in the 2000s onward could expect one, and sometimes two, new westerns in cinemas each year. The Coen Brothers have directed two of the most critically successful entries: the modern western *No Country for Old Men* (2007), adapted from the novel by Cormac McCarthy, and a remake of *True Grit* (2010). Other pictures that attained some measure of recognition include *Open Range* (Kevin Costner, 2004),

3:10 to Yuma (James Mangold, 2007), *The Assassination of Jesse James by the Coward Robert Ford* (Andrew Dominik, 2007), *Django Unchained* (Quentin Tarantino, 2012), and *The Homesman* (Tommy Lee Jones, 2014).

Film criticism has continued to explore how these new westerns "revise" the conventions – and, by extension, ideological positions – of the classic western. In contrast to the examinations of identity politics that characterize responses to the western of the 1990s, an emerging focus in analyses of the 2000s western is the ways in which the genre is seen to respond to the terrorist attacks of September 11, 2001, and the ensuing "war on terror" waged by the United States against Islamic militants.[19] This approach is, perhaps, to be expected, given the degree to which the Cold War and the Vietnam War have figured into analyses of the western in the 1950s and 1970s, respectively. Yet, whether because there are now fewer westerns, or because their appearances have been more diffuse and not concentrated into a distinct cycle, a clear picture of the relationship between the post-9/11 American zeitgeist and the western genre has yet to emerge. Though the western remains a story form that individual artists may draw upon to grapple with contemporary issues, we should seriously question whether the genre retains the same privileged relationship with the American subconscious that it is argued to have enjoyed in earlier decades.

If we allow that a genre "speaks" to the broader population under ideal conditions – when a hundred films are produced annually, as was the case with the western in the 1940s and 1950s – can the same case be credibly made when only one film is released per year? This question speaks to the challenge of explaining what the western means in the contemporary context.

It does not take a cynic to recognize, as Scott Eyman does, that many westerns are now made as awards bait. Brad Pitt's reasons for producing and starring in *The Assassination of Jesse James by the Coward Robert Ford* and the Coen Brothers' motivation for updating *True Grit* are obviously very different from their motivation when the star and filmmakers make the comedy *Burn after Reading* (2008). *Dances with Wolves* and *Unforgiven*, both of which won the Academy Award for Best Picture, were certainly influential in this regard. Including these films, four of the roughly forty westerns released since 1990 have been nominated for Best Picture, compared to only ten nominations and no wins for the more than *three thousand* westerns released between 1939 and 1989. Rather than characterizing it as simply an outlet for the vanities of major stars and directors, though, it is more accurate to say that the western has changed from a popular genre into a *prestige* genre.

It is certainly true that some recent westerns are the result of powerful directors like Quentin Tarantino or the Coen Brothers being in the enviable position of making any film they choose. Yet many have been labors of love for Hollywood stars, from Kevin Costner's nostalgic *Open Range* to Ed Harris's melancholic *Appaloosa* to Tommy Lee Jones's somber yet strange *The Homesman*. There have also been unconventional independent films, including Jim Jarmusch's *Dead Man* and Kelly Reichardt's *Meek's Cutoff* (2010). In all cases, though, the average western movie made today is not intended to attract large audiences and big box office. It is intended to appeal to a specialized audience and garner critical acclaim.

While the western film retains many of its traditional iconographic, narrative and thematic features – westerns today are still recognizably westerns – the genre is nevertheless governed by different forces. A prestige film intended for a serious intellectual audience can do certain things that a film intended for a popular audience cannot. This is, on balance, a good thing, because while fewer westerns may be produced today, they have not ceased to innovate.

Notes

1 For production figures for western films and television series, see the appendices in Edward Buscombe, ed., *The BFI Companion to the Western*, new ed. (London: Andre Deutsch/BFI, 1993), 426–8.

2 Scott Eyman, *John Wayne: The Life and the Legend* (New York: Simon & Shuster, 2014), 569.

3 *The Searchers* was adapted from Alan Le May's 1954 novel of the same name. The film and novel present a very different ending to the female captive's story. After twenty-four years among the Comanche, during which she became the wife of a warrior and the mother of a future chief, Cynthia Ann Parker was returned to the white world only to die in misery and obscurity. For more on Parker and her place in American culture, see Glenn Frankel, *The Searchers: The Making of an American Legend* (New York: Bloomsbury, 2013).

4 Richard Slotkin, *Gunfighter Nation* (Norman: University of Oklahoma Press, 2008), 16.

5 Quoted in Peter Bogdonovich, *John Ford* (London: Studio Vista, 1967), 87. For more on the influence of Remington on the western, see Edward Buscombe, "Painting the Legend: Frederic Remington and the Western," *Cinema Journal* 23, no. 4 (summer 1984): 12–27.

6 For a history of the silent western, see Andrew Brodie Smith, *Shooting Cowboys and Indians: Silent Western Films, American Culture, and the Birth of Hollywood* (Boulder: University Press of Colorado, 2004).

7 For a history of the western in the 1930s, see Peter Stanfield, *Hollywood, Westerns, and the 1930s: The Lost Trail* (Exeter: University of Exeter Press, 2001)

8 Gene Autry resumed his career after the war, starring in B westerns at Columbia Pictures until 1953 as well as on television, in *The Gene Autry Show*, from 1950 to 1955.

9 For a comprehensive account of the movie western's development up to the 1940s, see Scott Simmon, *The Invention of the Western Film: A Cultural History of the Genre's First Half Century* (New York: Cambridge University Press, 2003); for a study of the singing cowboy, see Peter Stanfield, *Horse Opera: The Strange History of the 1930s Singing Cowboy* (Chicago: University of Illinois Press, 2002).

10 Buscombe, *BFI Companion to the Western*, 428.

11 André Bazin, "The Western, or the American Film par Excellence," in *What Is Cinema?* vol. 2, trans. and ed. Hugh Gray (Berkeley: University of California Press, 2005), 140.

12 See John G. Cawelti, *The Six-Gun Mystique* (Bowling Green, OH: Bowling Green University Popular Press, 1971); Peter Wollen, *Signs and Meaning in the Cinema* (London: BFI, 1969); and Will Wright, *Sixguns and Society: A Structural Study of the Western* (Berkeley: University of California Press, 1975).

13 See Steve Neale, "'The Last Good Time We Ever Had?' Revising the Hollywood Renaissance," in *Contemporary American Cinema*, ed. Linda Ruth Williams and Michael Hammond (London: Open University Press, 2006) and David Bordwell, *Poetics of Cinema* (New York: Routledge, 2008).

14 "National Review's Best Conservative Movies," *National Review*, October 24, 1994: 53.

15 Ideas about the history of American expansion entailing civilization's triumph over wilderness (or "savagery") were espoused beginning in the late nineteenth century not only by Turner but also by Theodore Roosevelt in his four-volume history *The Winning of the West* (1889–96). These ideas received renewed attention after the publication of Henry Nash Smith's *Virgin Land: The American West as Symbol and Myth* in 1950. This suggests the possibility that the meanings detected, retrospectively, in western movies by cultural critics from the 1950s onward were in fact consciously inscribed by those films' makers. A comparable example would be the use of psychoanalysis to examine Hollywood films of the 1940s and 1950s that were patently influenced by the then-fashionable ideas of Sigmund Freud.

16 Michael T. Marsden and Jack Nachbar, "The Modern Popular Western: Radio, Television, Film and Print," in *A Literary History of the American West*, ed. J. Golden Taylor and Thomas Lyon (Fort Worth: Texas Christian University Press, 1987), 1271.

17 Richard Maltby, *Hollywood Cinema*, 2nd ed. (Malden, MA: Blackwell, 2003), 100.

18 See, for example, Jim Kitses, "Post-modernism and the Western," in *The Western Reader*, ed. Jim Kitses and Gregg Rickman (New York: Limelight Editions, 1996), 17.

19 See Steven McVeigh, *The American Western* (Edinburgh: Edinburgh University Press, 2007), especially pp. 219–20; Robert Westerfelhaus and Celeste Lacroix, "Waiting for the Barbarians: HBO's *Deadwood* as post-9/11 Ritual of Disquiet," *Southern Communication Journal* 74, no. 1 (2009): 18–39; *The Last Western: Deadwood and the End of American Empire*, ed. Paul Stasi and Jennifer Greiman (New York: Bloomsbury Academic, 2012); Steven McVeigh, *9/11 and the American Western: The Significance of the Frontier in the War on Terror* (New York: Bloomsbury Academic, 2015).

CHAPTER 22

Urban New Wests

Stephen Tatum

It should be clear by now that the truth about the place is elusive, and must be tracked with caution.[1]

Dark Space

In "John Wayne: A Love Story," an essay in her collection *Slouching Towards Bethlehem* (1968), Joan Didion describes a dinner party she and her husband attended, with John Wayne and his wife, Pilar, "in an expensive restaurant in Chapultepec Park," on one night during the last week of the filming of *The Sons of Katie Elder* in Mexico City. Didion frames this event by concisely summarizing the "number of ways" she had thought about Wayne's film persona since first seeing him as an eight-year-old girl in the summer of 1943 in *War of the Wildcats*. Twenty-two years later, in 1965, she first recollects how, after a few drinks over dinner, she had "lost the sense that the face across the table was in certain ways more familiar than my husband's." But then "something happened": "Suddenly the room seemed suffused with the dream, and I could not think why." This abrupt, unexpected transformation of "a nice evening, an evening anywhere" into a dreamscape that dates from her childhood past occurs as three men playing guitars appear at their table. At this interruption Wayne raises his glass "imperceptibly" toward Pilar and then orders more wine for the table – and "some red Bordeaux for the Duke." As the ensuing communion with wine proceeds, the musicians continue playing and eventually, Didion comments, "I realized what they were playing, what they had been playing all along: 'The Red River Valley' and the theme from *The High and the Mighty*. They did not quite get the beat right, but even now, I can hear them, in another country and a long time later, even as I tell you this."[2]

At the essay's outset Didion claims that the John Wayne film persona "determined forever the shape of certain of our dreams," dreams whose

utopian shape existed in stark contrast to that real-world shape of the tur-
bulent 1960s "characterized by venality and doubt and paralyzing ambiguities." His was a reel world "which may or may not have existed ever but
in any case existed no more"; his body was the "perfect mold" into which
film directors could pour "the inarticulate longings of a nation wondering
at just what pass the trail had been lost." Didion spatializes this "Eden lost"
as a pastoral enclave of domestic harmony imaged by a dialogue line the
Duke utters (a house built by hand "at the bend in the river where the cottonwoods grow"); by quoting lines from "Out Where the West Begins," a
1911 cowboy poem set to music; and by contrasting the Durango, Mexico,
location of the current film's exterior scenes with Mexico City. As is the
case with Bel Air, Beverly Hills, and Acapulco – other urban locales referenced in the essay – Mexico City signifies domestic consumerism and
the social scene of the film principals' wives, whereas Durango is coded
as "Man's Country. Out where the West begins." Nevertheless, in the
Churubusco studio's sound stage in Mexico City, "for just so long as the
picture lasted," this "world peculiar to men who like to make Westerns" –
this dream of a "man's country [that] was receding fast" – seemingly can
be sustained against mounting odds. For in the aftermath, the magical
resurgence of "the dream" during a farewell dinner in the secluded sanc-
tum of a Mexican restaurant recurs in the enclave space of Didion's study,
located literally and figuratively "in another country." Through its com-
pression of time and space and its equation of architectural and psychological spaces, Didion's retrospective memory transforms both the terrain
of her study and her imagination into an analogue of the movie theater,
the sound stage, and – at the last – the restaurant where the masculine
code of the West precariously resides.[3]

And yet: nested within this retrospective – and ultimately conflicted –
longing for "the dream" emblematized by the Duke's monumental presence and his screen promise to build a house "at the bend in the river
where the cottonwoods grow" exists the cowboy lament titled "The Red
River Valley." As if in counterpoint to the dream of constancy composed
by the outdoor spaces in "Out Where the West Begins," the lyric speaker
in "The Red River Valley" desires to stay the moment of a loved one's
departure ("do not hasten to bid me adieu"). However, even within the
present tense of the song and the presence of the lyric's intended auditor,
its speaker proceeds to imagine this pending farewell as a loss akin to that
of death. The river valley topography is not only going to be left behind,
but the cowboy's "bright eyes and smile" are also projected as a kind of
theft, a "taking the sunshine" with him, thus enshrouding both the valley

and the speaker's psyche in darkness. With the impending physical separation of the lovers paralleled by the speaker's abiding uncertainty as to whether remembrance will sustain a bleak future defined by both temporal and spatial distance, the song – like the overall tenor of the essays in *Slouching Towards Bethlehem* – composes a dark, haunted space of mourning *in advance of its actual cause*.

Didion initially confesses she "could not think why" the restaurant suddenly "seemed suffused with the dream." Although she realizes later that the song being played in the room was "The Red River Valley," that she does not reproduce or comment on its lyrics presents this allusion as an unsettling parallel to the "obscure anxiety" that she feels – and that necessitates her trip to Mexico in the first place – upon hearing the news of Wayne's lung cancer. As will be the case with the literature of new urban Wests in the wake of 1968, throughout Didion's essays appears a certain corporeal and cognitive dissonance and suspended agency. This dissonance is embodied by guitar players not quite getting the beat right, by Wayne's cancer, and by reports of bodies never recovered in the Mojave desert between Los Angeles and Las Vegas; by the built environment one sees in "the underside of Hollywood, south of Sunset Boulevard, a middle-class slum of 'model studios' and warehouses and two-family bungalows"; and by the melancholy realization of "how much of anyone's memory is no true memory at all but only the traces of someone else's memory." This suspended agency is embodied by her judgment that "California is a place in which a boom mentality and a sense of Chekhovian loss meet in uneasy suspension; in which the mind is troubled by some buried but ineradicable suspicion that things had better work here, because here, beneath that immense bleached sky, is where we run out of continent."[4] Thus, whether via an imagined projection of a lesser future ("The Red River Valley") or a retrospective memory that proceeds via fragmented, at times elliptical moments, the result in Didion's essays (and novels) is a somber nostalgia that forwards an affective sense of dread: any moment of fulfillment conjured up from the distant or immediate past that could be regarded as predicting a future moment of plenitude – this moment never happens.

Helpfully defining an emergent urban New West both historically and in terms of cultural production, Krista Comer claims "the signature text announcing the arrival of 1968 and the New West is Joan Didion's first collection of essays *Slouching Towards Bethlehem* (1968)." For Comer, the essay collection as a whole, and especially its title essay, dramatize "the postwar American Dream in total disarray"; its "center was not holding," "pressured from the inside by heroes gone mad (like John Wayne in the classic film *The Searchers*), by powerful women (like Didion), and by its own rebelling suburban youth (middle-class disillusioned hippies). It was pressured at its borders by those whom it excluded, displaced, and othered."⁵ For Comer, too, the new, more critical regionalism that emerged after 1968 "is born out of, and responds to, the emerging culture of postmodernism." From this perspective, Didion's motifs of corporeal and cognitive dissonance and suspended agency anticipate the need for new cognitive maps to navigate emergent postmodern space that Fredric Jameson locates, in his canonical 1984 essay on an emergent postmodernism, in the architecture of downtown Los Angeles' Hotel Bonaventura.⁶ From another perspective, all this disarray and dissonance marks a tension predominant in post-1970 new urban West literary and cultural production between, on the one hand, forces of territorialization or centralization and, on the other hand, forces of deterritorialization or dispersal – a tension, it should be added, that echoes the structural logic of globalization.⁷ To be sure, as Richard White observes, at the time of the 1970 census, "two different, but intertwined Wests had emerged: one mostly rural and largely powerless, and the other metropolitan and increasingly powerful."⁸ But as suggested by Didion's triangulation in *Slouching Towards Bethlehem* of California urban locales with not only Las Vegas, New York, and Hawaii, but also Mexico (Mexico City, Durango, Acapulco, Guaymas), literary and cultural production in the urban New West "is born out of, and responds to," not only postmodernism but also a globalizing world system's restructuring of the economic and social landscape into postfordist industrial metropolises and "world cities," spatial nodes in "multiple networks of economic, social, demographic, and information flows."⁹

Whether one focuses on earlier or more recent case studies of "new" urban western American literature, as Neil Campbell argues, any "new spatial cultural geohistory of the American West gathers the 'traces,' the artifacts, and the fragments in order to articulate, not a unified and totalizing story, but one in which many voices speak, many, often contradictory, histories are told, and many ideologies cross, coexist, and collide."¹⁰ Here in "John Wayne: A Love Story": such artifacts as a song or photograph or movie dialogue; elsewhere in the literature of the new urban West: a postcard, a painted mural, a church's stained glass windows; cemetery grave markers, a box of artifacts in a university anthropology building, animal taxidermy, a purported snuff movie. Campbell's contrast between a "unified and totalizing story" and one "in which many voices speak" articulates a narrative tension between concentration and dispersal characterizing the literature of newer urban Wests. And though contradictory histories with many different ideologies emerge in such new stories, taken together their representation of new urban Wests can be seen to share an investment in spectrality both as a theme (haunting absences in the present and being haunted by the past; the speculative flows of capital) and as image or trope (specters).[11] This narrative tension and thematic investment often result in 1) image clusters of interior and exterior dark spaces (basements, bathrooms, hotel corridors, alleys) that signify literal and metaphorical homelessness and in 2) both plot structures and represented built environments that typically compose uncanny architectures of vagabondage and abandonment. A dialectic of mobility/immobility organizes such narrative and spatial architectures, so that various characters' nomadism through and across unhomely urban and suburban thresholds functions both to magnify and to critique urban systems that are, at bottom, "socially and spatially polarized between high value-making groups and functions on the one hand and devalued social groups and downgraded spaces on the other."[12] What for Didion is a declension away from "the unified and totalizing story" of the American Dream organized by the Duke's body and voice, and imaged as "a house on the bend in the river where the cottonwoods grow" mutates, in Sherman Alexie's version of a John Wayne love story, "Dear John Wayne" (2000), into a retirement home on the Navajo reservation where a white anthropologist tapes an interview with a displaced 108-year old Spokane Indian woman who narrates her love affair with the Duke when she served as a youthful extra during the filming of *The Searchers*.[13]

Posturbanism/Postmetropolis

As Edward Soja has argued, the "geohistory" of urbanism from the mid-eighteenth century to the present "can be told through the increasingly globalized economic and cultural rhythms of capitalist development and the associated interplay of modernization and modernism."[14] His neologism "postmetropolis" connotes the particular form of the postmodern metropolis that emerged with the advent of "late capital," or a globalizing world system's ongoing restructuring of the economic, sociocultural, and political landscapes across the geographical scales of the local, regional, and national. As we can see, for example, with the transformations of the built environment of the Las Vegas Strip over the past four decades – from the commercial sprawl centered on the automobile studied by Robert Venturi in *Learning from Las Vegas* to the more recent "pedestrian promenade" – "the economic and cultural rhythms of capitalist development" arguably have weakened a sense of "the local," including its specific history.[15] A "network of monuments" – arches, columns, gates, and statues – that once composed "a complex mental map of significance by which the [traditional] city might be recognized as 'home' "[16] morphs in postmodernity, as Jean Baudrillard writes in *America*, into an "exaltation of mobile deserts and simulation": "No oases, no monuments; infinite panning shots over mineral landscapes and freeways. Everywhere: Los Angeles or Twenty-Nine Palms, Las Vegas or Borrego Springs."[17] Because of the dynamic interplay of what Soja calls "modernization and modernism," architectural "monuments" emerge in the form of freeway designs (Reyner Banham's "autotopia") and in corporate skyscrapers that exist – in novels like Chuck Palahniuk's *Fight Club* and Sherman Alexie's *Indian Killer* – in dialectical opposition to the subterranean spaces and closeted interiors of houses on the edge of urban industrial wastelands and freeway viaducts.[18] In an increasingly global architecture, the local or regional, if it appears at all, appears "as a trace souvenir of the old culture, a token at a remove" – thus, "the old city," in Anthony Vidler's words, "presents itself to the postmodernist as a *haunting absence,* not a haunting presence."[19]

These same "increasingly globalized economic and cultural rhythms of capitalist development" additionally have destabilized "the longstanding conceptual division between city and region," reconstituting the postmetropolis as "some variant on city-region, urban-region, or more broadly regional urbanism."[20] Here we can consider a moment in Douglas Coupland's novel *Generation X* (1991), when a central character – calling his roommates in Palm Springs from a telephone booth in Scotty's Junction, Nevada – tells a tale about a man suffering from "bomb anxiety," who searches for relief by traveling from southern Nevada to Alamagordo and Las Cruces, at one point stopping in southwestern Utah, "visiting the filming site of a John Wayne movie – the movie where more than half the people involved in its making died of cancer." Instead of providing relief, however, the man's trip on "the Nuclear Road" ends up retriggering his anxiety as he drives on I-10 outside Phoenix and passes a megashopping mall and "yuppie housing development."[21] This textual moment exemplifies the novel's overall critique of human alienation as a result of rampant consumerism and "history's" absorption by the spectacle (the trip is inaugurated by images: postcards and photographs; the cold war anxiety framed by the reference to John Wayne). Additionally, the motif of the road trip here and elsewhere in the novel registers the impact of what Stephanie LeMenager calls "petromodernity": a life "based in the cheap energy systems long made possible by petroleum" and materially evident in "the now ordinary U.S. landscape of highways, low-density suburbs, strip malls, fast food and gasoline service islands, and shopping centers ringed by parking lots or parking towers."²² In *Generation X*, a "regional urbanism" arises as the Palm Springs locale emerges as "a network of urban nodes nested together in a regionally defined system," one that links cities (here Phoenix, Los Angeles, Las Vegas), with suburbs and so-called "edge cities," with towns, the open spaces of agricultural production, federal and military lands, and desert wilderness areas.²³

In discussing the "blocks of neat little houses in tidy gardens" and the "dingbat" apartment complexes populating the "flat plains" of Los Angeles, the "heartland of the city's Id," Banham concludes – as if channeling Frederick Jackson Turner's frontier thesis – that in such structures "the plainsman's dream of urban homesteading can still be made real."²⁴ Yet as we can see in novels such as *Generation X, Fight Club,* and *Indian Killer,* petromodernity's networked merger of downtown center and with its industrial margins, its edge city commercial developments, and its outer suburban residential rings produces the new urban West as "a space of 'disjunctive inclusion': it *has to include* places whose existence is not part of its 'ideal-ego,' i.e., which are *disjoined* from its idealized image of itself."²⁵ In *Fight Club*, for example, Tyler Durden's rental house on Paper Street is neighbored by a closed machine shop, warehouses, and a paper mill, while Marla lives at the Regent Hotel, "nothing but brown bricks held together with sleaze ... so many people go there to die."²⁶ At another moment in *Generation X*, the central characters – all of whom confess to suffering crises associated with a failure of youth, "a failure of class and of sex and the future" – drive to West Palm Springs to "tell stories and to make our own lives worthwhile tales in the process." Their drive takes them past a mobile home park ("a modern ruin") and an abandoned Texaco gas station; their picnic eventually transpires at an empty street intersection on "a crumbling asphalt road being reclaimed by sage and creosote bushes," adjacent to the empty lots of a housing development abandoned after the "oil shock" created by the 1973–4 Arab oil embargo.²⁷

Such "disjoined spaces" resemble what the architect Rem Koolhaus terms "junkspace," or the leftover residue of modernist city space. Such "junkspace" is positioned in the literature of new urban Wests in relation to, on the one hand, the more "self-conscious architecture" associated with performing arts spaces, museum districts, and the megashopping mall or "festival marketplace"; and, on the other hand, to the "now ordinary" built environment of "petromodernity's" commercial and residential sprawl.²⁸ In the post–World War II cold war era mapping of new social relations in the urban West in Raymond Chandler's novels, Fredric Jameson has argued, the narrative shaping of Chandler's thematic content materializes through an expanded sense of "the office" (business offices, hotel lobbies, bedrooms and bathrooms, secluded outbuildings, porches) as a space not only of meeting but, predominantly, of *waiting*.[29] In the literature of the new urban West, by contrast, the psychological and geocultural map of social relations predominantly centers *on thresholds, zones or precincts of transition*, entrances that are in fact potential passages.[30] If we consider windows as built environment versions of the threshold, then we can better understand some of the distance traveled between the cold war era urban West and an emergent posturban sensibility by examining the motif of an observer looking from an interior space through a window outward onto the urban scene. In Chandler's 1953 novel *The Long Goodbye*, the detective Phillip Marlowe drives home to his house in the hills above Los Angeles after being grilled by police detectives. He mixes himself a drink and then sips it while listening to the traffic below him on Laurel Canyon Boulevard and looking at "the glare of the big angry city," his reflection on the people "out there in the night" proceeding in serial fashion through various forms of bodily and mental suffering only to conclude with a totalizing summary statement about a deeper truth about Los Angeles: this city "no worse than others, a city rich and vigorous and full of pride, a city lost and beaten and full of emptiness."[31]

A little more than three decades later, in Bret Easton Ellis's *Less Than Zero*, the novel's narrator, Clay, often is characterized through a pose of surveillance: looking out windows, looking up at billboards, looking across a table in a bar or restaurant, looking in mirrors. On one rainy night in Los Angeles, he describes lying awake on his bed, taking some Valium to counter the effects of cocaine. Unable to sleep, he turns off the television and the radio, and then stares out across the valley, looking "at the canvas of neon and fluorescent lights lying beneath the purple night sky," watching the clouds pass by, eventually returning to bed hoping "to remember how many days" he has been home. All this activity occurs in the wake of "three weird silent phone calls" and his earlier sighting of traffic signals below him on Sunset "short-circuited, so a yellow light will be flashing at an intersection and then a green one will blink on for a couple of seconds, followed by the yellow and then the red and green lights will start to shine at the same time." Unscrolling here in serial fashion prior to any totalizing judgment, comment, or adjudication of value, Clay's privileged point of view and movements in this interior private space betray a field of anxiety.

The particular colors he observes from the interface of rain clouds with the city's lights produce a "canvas" or simulacra; the "short-circuited" traffic lights outside the window parallel both the semiotic and communication breakdown inside his room (the phone calls, the dysfunctional media) and the contradictory signals the Valium and cocaine give his nervous system, increasing his anxiety. Flickering apparitions – these framed by a window functioning as both reflective and transparent surface – trigger this generalized field of anxiety, as if, in the manner of the uncanny, external alien presences have penetrated both the home and its human host. As a double of the unified subject's disappearance, the threshold space composed by the house's glass skin and the body's epidermis blurs the boundaries between inside/outside, the real/simulated, and waking/dreaming, effectively translating this subject's liminal status as a dead/undead subject into an elemental spatial insecurity. This spatial insecurity metastasizes into a hallucinogenic blurring of temporal scales when Clay later references a rumor, published in a local magazine, that people driving on Sierra Bonita Street "saw ghosts: apparitions of the Wild West": Indians on horseback, one throwing a tomahawk through an "open window," another invading an elderly couple's living room.[32] Thus Ellis's narrative and linguistic strategies double the novel's continuous tonal "sliding between states of terror, amusement, and sheer banality" with a parallel oscillation between spatial and temporal scales, its emergent paranoiac space, on the one hand, contrasting with Marlowe's arrival at some deeper truth about the city and, on the other, anticipating the Seattle psychometropolis of Alexie's 1996 *Indian Killer*.[33]

Vagabond Architecture

In the first published version of his linkage of postmodernist aesthetics with late capitalism, Fredric Jameson's critique of Los Angeles' Hotel Bonaventura stressed how this "postmodern hyperspace" transcends "the capacity of the individual human body to locate itself . . . and cognitively to map its position in a mappable external world."[34] Seven years later, in his 1991 critique of the architect Frank Gehry's Santa Monica, California, house, Jameson notes Gehry's use of "the cube" as a "novel spatial intervention" in redesigning the classic California bungalow aesthetic as a version of postmodern pastiche. However, regarding Gehry's innovative use of corrugated aluminum and chain link fencing, Jameson extrapolates from such materials the presence of a repressed "history." Such materials signify "the junk or Third World side of American life today," an image that calls to mind not only Koolhaus's concept of "junkspace," but also "the production of poverty and misery, people not only out of work but without a place to live, bag people, waste and industrial pollution, squalor, garbage, and obsolescent machinery."[35] Recognizing how the material and corporeal traces of the peripheral Third World occupy the very center of the First World's postmetropolis, Jameson's reading of the Santa Monica house highlights how "the return of the migrants, the minorities, the diasporic" and the homeless to the center of the contemporary postmetropolis establishes a "contentious *internal* liminality" and a recovery of history and material culture that will be explored in contemporary transnational, urban regional western American writing.[36]

Exploring how the increasing Latino immigrant presence reinvents contemporary U.S. cities, Mike Davis surveys how *maquila* industrialization, especially in Ciudad Juárez and Tijuana, has not only "elaborated complex cross-border divisions of labor within larger webs of international trade," but also led to the exploitation of female labor and the violence associated with the import-export trade of drugs and weapons across the border.[37] At one point in his book *Dreamland* (2010) Charles Bowden represents this "new geography" of the U.S. West and Southwest – one based less on the "lines" and "national boundaries" theorized by Turner's frontier thesis, and more on "forces and appetites and torrents of people" on the move in a globalizing world system – by portraying the nomadic journey of an unnamed woman who walks in the heat, dust, and noise of this border city, her transit across its dirt and paved streets from a *maquiladora* to a *mercado* to "an old table in a shack made of cardboard that sits in a dirt yard surrounded by pallets from loading docks." Bowden presents a spatial model of the self: Desires and needs ("appetites" and "hungers") are manifested via both physiological processes (wandering journeys) and material objects (a plastic bag full of foodstuff) embedded within the built environment and the centrifugal movements of the city's "new geography." Through the mediation of wooden pallets that are metonymically linked both to the walking woman's destination and to the nearby loading docks, Bowden embeds the local in the logistics of global production and transportation networks. From this perspective, those who are doomed to be "local" are subject to not only visible, but invisible everyday predations, threatened by the vast, seemingly instantaneous accumulation of wealth on display, both in the media spectacle and in the gleaming monuments of corporate capitalism's tourism and entertainment economy straddling the border. As a result of the seeming sorcery of the global market's invisible and shifting, its unequal spectral flows, whose transits produce the dead and the walking dead at the dark end of a street, "the city lives two lives. One looks like order. One feels like decay."[38]

So instead of Didion's dream of a house on a bend in the river where the cottonwoods grow, there is Bowden's portrayal of a drug cartel's rented condo for disposing of bodies, a "house of death" that now represents not only the "truth center of the city" – "And in other cities. And these houses seem to be multiplying" – but also our new "little house on the prairie and our little house on Elm Street."[39] Bowden's motif of nomadism – the female working poor crossing city thresholds, the uprooted immigrants massing to cross the border, the transnational circulation of commodities – establishes a new type of urban space: a vagabond architecture, where nomad spaces of becoming and heterogeneity intersect with the more established, demarcated and regulated space of urban realms.[40] Now both as a represented built environment and as a structural element of plotting and characterization that favors the mobile and nomadic, a motif of "vagabondage" can serve in certain contexts, on the one hand, as a critique of fixed monumentality: one that in new urban Wests we can witness in Banham's celebration of the freeway as "autotopia," or in the postmodern architectural hyperspace of the Hotel Bonaventura and L.A.'s Crocker Bank Center whose design – their glass skins and sleek, flowing metal exteriors; their exposed interiors with floating curtain walls; their airy, light-filled atriums – seemingly desires to erase the constraints posed by the earth's gravity, by history. But, on the other hand, such a critique of fixed, sedentary monumentality through nomadism also more often appears as a critique of late capitalist development, as a questioning of the triumphant mythology of western American history, and as an unearthing of buried or silenced histories and spectral voices. If the "territory" of real land and a so-called real you changes, says a character in Karen Tei Yamashita's *IHotel*, but the "map" of the territory and the one in your head stay the same, the resulting dissonance between the abstraction and the reality "causes one to be insane," to become a literal and metaphorical orphan – a person without an estate, to recall one connotation of the vagabond.[41]

Characterized as "a falling star, brief and homeless," the main character in Alexie's *Indian Killer*, the adopted John Smith, knows "he should carry a map because he was always getting lost," during his repetitive journeys to and from Seattle's downtown area, through its parks and across its bridges, and into the suburbs where his white adoptive parents live. At the construction site of "the last skyscraper in Seattle," Smith looks at the encompassing city's skyline and understands "the myth and lies of

its construction, the myths and lies of its architect." Later, in his increasingly paranoid state as he walks through downtown Seattle, he imagines
the Anglo-Saxon conquest of the West as white flames and white lights
progressively building dams, creating electricity that connects houses and
builds cities, these "animals with neon eyes" pushing back the darkness
as they "tear everything down and rebuild it in their image." Beneath
the Alaskan Way viaduct, the precinct of the homeless and urban Indian
population, he saves an old homeless Indian woman from being beaten
by some white racists. In the dialogue scene that follows, she tells him,
"I ain't homeless. I'm Duwamish Indian, and all this, the city, the water,
the mountains, it's all Duwamish land." Here the "myths and lies" of the
city's skyline appear as a return of the repressed, so to speak; the homeless native's woman's presence (here below a freeway overpass; in another
textual moment, a university's anthropology building's basement where
native artifacts are stored) effectively transposes the secure home into an
unhomely, haunted space. The clearing of so-called empty land appropriated for urbanism and the void spaces of the skyscraper's steel skeleton –
these "hollow spaces of capitalism," to use Ernst Bloch's phrasing – become
doubles of the spatial margins and dark recesses of the city's pathological
space of the nomad. "Every building was a tomb," John Smith realizes, as
he contemplates burying the body of his own double figure – the putative
mixed-blood Indian author Jack Wilson – in the last skyscraper in Seattle's
concrete foundation.[42]

Writing about emergent postnational spaces in Yamashita's *Tropic of
Orange,* Elisabeth Mermann-Jozwiak argues that the novel "intervenes
in the official production of Southern California" by rendering a "spatial archaeology" whose excavation of the city's neighborhoods "reveals
various layers – of past and present inhabitants of the city, of regulations that restricted access to certain areas, and of the distribution of
resources and development of infrastructures in those neighborhoods."[43]
As is the case for Alexie and Bowden, the trope of "spatial archaeology"
usefully describes these authors' intersection of organic, biological, and
nomadic bodies with the demarcated and regulated social spaces organized by power. In the literature of new urban Wests, the metaphor of
the palimpsest suggested by the image of the layering of history often is
grafted together with another spatial trope organized by surface-depth
logic: embedding and disembedding. "Embedding" describes a process by which certain material objects and architectural forms "embed"
the past in the present: for example, in *Indian Killer* the presence of
audiotapes of a native woman's voice secreted in boxes in a university

building's basement; in *Dreamland* Bowden's semiotic linkage of the red facial cosmetics for women from the time of Cortez's conquest of Mexico forward with a lipstick tube he finds among the discarded items left by illegal immigrants crossing the border. "Dissembedding" refers to the process accompanying modernization in which social relations become lifted out of their local contexts and resituated across indefinite spans of time and space. As places become thoroughly penetrated by "absent others" and shaped by social, economic, and political determinants quite distant from them, urban locales become increasingly *phantasmagoric*, haunted by the spectral traces of the past, as we see in these examples.[44]

Here we can consider how the hybrid narrative form, the polyvocality, and the plots in the ten novellas that comprise Yamashita's *IHotel*, for example, center on the vagabond flows of labor, capital, and aesthetic and political ideologies through various architectural nodal points – the IHotel, the Monkey Block, the Ferry Building, Angel Island, Alcatraz – that testify to San Francisco's historical development into a postregional and transnational "world city" from the moment at the turn of the twentieth century when Frank Norris's character McTeague sits in his dentist chair in his second story apartment on Polk Street and chronicles its street life. In the novella from *IHotel* titled "1975: Internationale Hotel," the principal character – a Russian émigré woman named Estelle Hama – journeys with her two sons to Coit Tower, a 210-foot-tall cylindrical structure atop Telegraph Hill, in order to commemorate the memory of their recently deceased Japanese husband and father, who had worked as a longshoreman and political organizer for the Communist Party. In 1934, he also was one of twenty-six artists commissioned by the WPA to paint the tower's interior frescoes with "images of powerful working people. The people involved in factories, on farmlands, on railroads, and in shipyards." The trajectory of their enclosed ascent of the tower's levels takes them past one fresco depicting a street scene outside the Monkey Building, where Estelle and her husband lived during the 1934 labor strikes. Their ascent ends when they reach the open-air viewing platform offering a 360° view of the city's landmarks, and as they view this "living mural" of the city Estelle points out the Transamerica pyramid building, "where the Monkey Building used to be," located near both Chinatown and the aging IHotel. Just as the Transamerica pyramid has displaced the Monkey Building, so too – as the focal point of the overarching novel's plot – a multinational corporation based in Hong Kong will take possession of the aging IHotel, home both to old Filipino and Chinese bachelors and to the offices of various hybrid political coalitions that cross social categories of race, class, and gender.[45]

"It should be clear by now that the truth about the place is elusive," Joan Didion suggests in "Notes from a Native Daughter," and "must be tracked with caution."[46] Whether looking at an old deserted carnival or at the old family house in Palm Springs, Clay's vagabondage in *Less Than Zero* repetitively wanders in body and mind across thresholds of the same, their signs no longer decipherable, "crossing nothing to go nowhere." As is the case with *Fight Club*, the temporality of sojourns in representative postmodern texts such as Ellis's novel is compressed or elided entirely: Characters seemingly never depart, travel, and arrive somewhere but rather are portrayed as having already arrived – at the restaurant, club, office, apartment, hotel room, or home; at the airport – in spaces whose interchangeability and ephemerality underline the characters' increasingly paranoid, fragmented, or split subjectivities and beleaguered memories. In contrast to Clay's notational inventory of what he sees while gazing from his bedroom window out at clouds covering the L.A. basin on a rainy night, the scenography from atop the Coit Tower in *IHotel* – as well as the pedestrian journey of the female working poor toward her cardboard shack in *Dreamland* and the plural sojourns of John Smith's body and mind in *Indian Killer* – illustrates a spatial archaeology whose dialectic of embedding and disembedding through the tactic of human vagabondage produces heterogeneous, nomadic spaces. From such spaces, the minority, the exilic, and the marginal restore to visibility the multiple, often contradictory and repressed truths of a place like the postmetropolitan, postregional, and transnational urban West, in the process critiquing what Ramón Saldívar has termed "the false historicity of the integrationist narrative that will drive the course of events through the mid-[20th] century."[47]

Notes

1 Joan Didion, "Notes from a Native Daughter," in *Slouching Towards Bethlehem* (1968; reprint, New York: Farrar, Straus & Giroux, 2008), 178.
2 Didion, "John Wayne: A Love Story," in *Slouching Towards Bethlehem*, 40–1.
3 Ibid., 30–1, 35–6, 40–1.
4 Didion, *Slouching Towards Bethlehem*, 66, 172, 177.
5 Krista Comer, "New West, Urban and Suburban Spaces, Postwest," in *A Companion to the Literature and Culture of the American West*, ed. Nicolas S. Witschi (Malden, MA: Wiley-Blackwell, 2011), 245.

6 Fredric Jameson, *Postmodernism, or the Cultural Logic of Late Capitalism* (Durham, NC: Duke University Press, 1991).

7 The cultural geographer Edward Soja: "what may be the most revealing window through which to understand the new global cultural economy and the new cultural politics of representation and identity that is so vital a part of it: the dynamic interplay between *deterritorialization* and *reterritorialization.*" See his *Postmetropolis: Critical Studies for Cities and Regions* (Malden, MA: Blackwell, 2000), 211–12.

8 See Krista Comer, *Landscapes of the New West: Gender and Geography in Contemporary Women's Writing* (Chapel Hill and London: University of North Carolina Press, 1999), 2; Richard White, *"It's Your Misfortune and None of My Own": A History of the American West* (Norman: University of Oklahoma Press, 1991), 541.

9 David Smith and Michael Timberlake, "Hierarchies of Dominance among World Cities: A Network Approach," in *Global Networks, Linked Cities*, ed. Saskia Sassen (New York and London: Routledge, 2002), 118.

10 Neil Campbell, *The Cultures of the American New West* (Chicago and London: Fitzroy Dearborn, 2000), 20.

11 See Stephen Tatum, "Spectrality and the Postregional Interface," in *Postwestern Cultures: Literature, Theory, Space*, ed. Susan Kollin (Lincoln: University of Nebraska Press, 2007), 3–29.

12 Manuel Castells, "The Informational City is a Dual City: Can It Be Reversed?" in *High Technology and Low-Income Communities*, ed. D. Schon, B. Sanyal, and W. Mitchell (Cambridge, MA: MIT Press, 1999), 27.

13 Sherman Alexie, "Dear John Wayne," in *The Toughest Indian in the World* (New York: Grove Press, 2000), 189–208.

14 Soja, *Postmetropolis*, 109.

15 See Robert Venturi, Denise Scott Brown, and Steven Izenour, *Learning from Las Vegas* (Cambridge, MA: MIT Press, 1972); Mark Taylor, "Ground Zero," in *Hiding* (Chicago: University of Chicago Press, 1997), 218–62.

16 Anthony Vidler, *The Architectural Uncanny* (Cambridge, MA: MIT Press, 1992), 177.

17 Jean Baudrillard, *America* (1986; reprint, London and New York: Verso, 2010), 133.

18 Reyner Banham, *Los Angeles: The Architecture of Four Ecologies* (1971; Berkeley: University of California Press, 2001), 195–204; Chuck Palahniuk, *Fight Club* (1996; reprint, New York: Norton, 2005); Sherman Alexie, *Indian Killer* (New York: Grove Press, 1996).

19 Hal Foster, "Designing a Second Modernity," in *The Political Unconscious of Architecture: Re-opening Jameson's Narrative*, ed. Nadir Lahiji (Burlington, VT: Ashgate, 2011), 108; Vidler, *Architectural Uncanny*, 183. Emphasis added.

20 Soja, *Postmetropolis*, 179.

21 Douglas Coupland, *Generation X: Tales for an Accelerated Culture* (New York: St. Martin's Press, 1991), 70.

22 Stephanie LeMenager, "The Aesthetics of Petroleum, after *Oil!*" *American Literary History* 24 (Spring 2012): 64.

23 Soja, *Postmetropolis*, 179.

24 Banham, *Los Angeles*, 143, 159.

25 Slavoj Žižek, "The Architectural Parallax," in *The Political Unconscious of Architecture*, 286. The term "disjunctive inclusion," as Žižek notes, is from Deleuze.

26 Palahniuk, *Fight Club*, 58.

27 Coupland, *Generation X*, 30, 10, 14, 16.

28 Rem Koolhaus, *Junkspace: For a Radical Rethinking of Urban Space* (Macerata: Quodlibet, 2006); Nan Ellin, *Postmodern Urbanism* (New York: Princeton Architectural Press, 1996), 84.

29 Fredric Jameson, "The Synoptic Chandler," in *Shades of Noir: A Reader*, ed. Joan Copjec (London and New York: Verso, 1993), 44.

30 Vidler, *Architectural Uncanny*, 184.

31 Raymond Chandler, *The Long Goodbye* (1953; reprint, New York: Vintage, 1992), 273. Jameson ("Synoptic" 44) describes a similar scene where Marlowe looks out his office window in Chandler's 1942 novel *The High Window*.

32 Bret Easton Ellis, *Less Than Zero* (New York: Vintage, 1988), 114–15, 206.

33 Vidler, *Architectural Uncanny*, 185. On "paranoiac space," see 223–5.

34 Fredric Jameson, "Postmodernism; or, the Cultural Logic of Late Capitalism," *New Left Review* 146 (July/August 1984): 85.

35 Jameson, *Postmodernism*, 127–8. Jameson traces the initial statement of this need for new cognitive maps to respond to the mutations in city space to Kevin Lynch's classic work *The Image of the City* (Cambridge, MA: MIT Press, 1960).

36 Homi K. Bhabha, "DissemiNation: Time, Narrative, and the Margins of the Modern Nation," in *Nation and Narration*, ed. Homi K. Bhabha (London and New York: Routledge, 1990), 300; 319–20.

37 Mike Davis, *Magical Urbanism: Latinos Reinvent the U.S. City* (London and New York: Verso, 2001), 31.

38 Charles Bowden and Alice Leora Briggs, *Dreamland: The Way Out of Juárez* (Austin: University of Texas Press, 2010), 138, 16.

39 Bowden and Briggs, *Dreamland*, 136, 152.

40 Vidler, *Architectural Uncanny*, 214.

41 Karen Tei Yamashita, *IHotel* (Minneapolis: Coffee House Press, 2010), 34.

42 Alexie, *Indian Killer*, 134, 252–2, 405. The Ernst Bloch quote is from Vidler, *Architectural Uncanny*, 13.

43 Elisabeth Mermann-Jozwiak, "Yamashita's Post-National Spaces: 'It All Comes Together in Los Angeles,'" *Canadian Review of American Studies* 41 (2011): 2. Also useful in this context, though her focus is more on Yamashita's novel *Tropic of Orange*, is Rachel Adams's "The Ends of America, The Ends of Postmodernism," *Twentieth Century Literature* 53 (2007): 248–72.

44 For a discussion of Anthony Gidden's conceptualization of embedding and dis-embedding, see Derek Gregory, *Geographical Imaginations* (Cambridge, MA:

Blackwell, 1994), 118–24. For the deterritorialization of place in global contexts, see Ursula Heise, "Local Rock and Global Plastic: World Ecology and the Experience of Place," *Comparative Literary Studies* 41 (2004): 133.

45 Yamashita, *IHotel*, 495, 402–3.

46 Didion, *Slouching Towards Bethlehem*, 178.

47 Ramón Saldívar, "The Second Elevation of the Novel: Race, Form and the Postrace Aesthetic in Contemporary Narrative," *Narrative* 21 (January 2013): 11.

CHAPTER 23

Queer Frontiers
Gender and Sexuality in the American West
David Agruss

Western American literature figures the western landscape as offering clarity about the individual and about "America." In this model, projects of self-discovery and national discovery and of self-definition and national definition merge and collude: To explore the West is to excavate the self, and to come to terms with the self amid the stark landscape of the West is to confront, and finally to understand truly, what it means to be American. But the paradox of the genre is that the space of self-discovery and self-reinvention, seemingly limitless under the endless sky and prairie, has stark boundaries. One's past inevitably catches up with one's present as soon as the landscape reveals intrusive signs of civilization: outposts, railroads, fences. Of course, the limits of the West reveal the limits of reinvention itself: The retired sheriff returns to duty reluctantly, the outlaw is exposed and made to answer for his previous misdeeds, the lone explorer returns to the settlement. Western American literature's investment in heterosexuality and heteronormative desire function similarly, butting up against their inevitable social and representational limits. The intense male homosociality of travel and exploration, of lonesome days on the range and all-night cattle drives, is heavily bounded by investments in heterosexuality and heteronormativity: the husband's relentless defense of the family homestead against attacks by Indians and drunken outlaws; the settlement school mistress's instructing children in reading and arithmetic and "civilization" amid the ever-encroaching wilds of the West; the male adventurer's, explorer's, or prospector's inevitable return to his waiting wife or his eventual, long-overdue marriage.

All of this changed with the publication of Annie Proulx's short story "Brokeback Mountain" in 1997[1] and Ang Lee's film adaptation in 2005.[2] The story and the film recount the lives of the ranch hands Jack Twist and Ennis del Mar over a twenty-year period. The two meet in 1963 as twenty-something summer sheepherders working on Brokeback Mountain in Wyoming. After a night of whisky drinking, Jack makes a sexual advance toward Ennis, who, although momentarily reluctant, quickly responds in kind, and the two embark on a sexual and emotional relationship that lasts through the summer and over the ensuing twenty years, during which both men marry women. Several times, Jack suggests to Ennis that they make a life together, buy a ranch, and settle down, but Ennis always refuses, first because he does not want to leave his wife, and later, after his divorce, because he wants to live near his children, but also because he remains haunted by the childhood memory of violence toward a man suspected of being gay.

The short story and the film help create a twenty-first-century western American literature in which homosociality is transformed into homosexuality despite their investments in standard tropes of western literature – wide-open landscapes that both transform and discipline individuals, the promise of self-discovery, the threats of the law and of vigilantism. Homosocial relationships, a fierce dedication to a certain kind of rugged masculinity, and the allure of self-discovery and promise of self-mastery – those hallmarks of traditional western literature and films – are cast in a radically new light both in contemporary literature and in the literature of previous eras. By showing how western American literature's and the western's generic investments in emotional austerity, personal struggle, and self-transformation dovetail with American narratives of gay struggle and sexual self-discovery, "Brokeback" (the short story) and especially *Brokeback* (the film) facilitated a wider cultural discussion of same-sex male desire, which in turn seemed to make western American literature newly relevant to discussions of masculinity, heterosexuality, homosociality, and gayness and to understandings of western American literature's larger role in enabling the cultural imagination of self-transformation and self-making even – and perhaps especially – in the post-Stonewall age of queer identities.

Lee Clark Mitchell's *Westerns: Making the Man in Fiction and Film* offers a helpful starting point for thinking about the ways the film *Brokeback Mountain* typifies the western and simultaneously reimagines and subverts the genre. Mitchell notes that "the Western relies on an assortment of visual props: colorful garb (from ten-gallon hats to high-heeled boots), photogenic terrain (high plains ranchland, desert Southwest), and a stock cast of characters (ranchers and farmers, sheriffs and desperados, boys in blue surrounded by red men in paint)."[3] *Brokeback Mountain* offers up nearly all these visual props in repeated shots throughout the film that linger on Ennis's and Jack's cowboy hats and boots, soar over breathtaking mountain landscapes and document the dusty roads of austere rural ranch towns, and feature the usual cast of ranchers, bar patrons, and rodeo men and women. In the place of an Indigenous threat, the film asserts another sort of threat, one not external and racial, but internal and sexual. For as the film progresses, the homosociality of the western reveals itself as homoeroticism and queer desire: Standard shots of tight jeans, beat-up cowboy boots, slow drags on cigarettes, and men languidly sizing one another up and down give way to Jack and Ennis engaging in passionate sex and a decades-long relationship that far surpasses in intensity their relationships with girlfriends and wives. Through a series of shifts and substitutions, *Brokeback* brings into relief a threat that has been hidden in plain sight all along in narratives of the West. Instead of the standard trope of the Indian who threatens white womanhood and, by extension, civilization itself, both of which must be safeguarded and saved by white men, in Lee's film same-sex male desire threatens womanhood (neither Ennis's wife, Alma, nor Jack's wife, Lureen, has any chance of winning her husband's affections, which lie elsewhere) and civilization more broadly in that it literalizes homosociality's homoeroticism, which must be violently disavowed if the western is to continue to produce masculine heterosexual men. In *Brokeback*, the sexual thus stands in for the racial, and the sexual thrill and threat of queerness supplant the thrill and threat of Indianness. Both the film and the story urge us to reflect on why male same-sex desire is not only so culturally threatening in the American West, but also so generically threatening in the western.

While the visual tropes of *Brokeback Mountain* both evoke and subvert the western, Mitchell explains that these familiar visual elements "are only so many unwoven raw strands. What actually brings them together into the narrative we recognize as a Western are a set of problems recurring in endless combination." Many of the "problems" that Mitchell identifies – progress, honor, law, justice, violence – are problems precisely because they name tensions and conflicts at the interface between private and public, self and other, the individual and the nation, human agency and the power of the state, all of which underwrite the western: "the problems of progress, envisioned as a passing of frontiers; the problem of honor, defined in a context of social expediency; the problem of law or justice, enacted in a conflict of vengeance and social control; the problem of violence, in acknowledging its value yet honoring occasions when it can be controlled." Crucially, however, according to Mitchell, it is gender and sexuality – specifically, male gender and sexuality – that both determine and are determined by these cultural and social problems explored in the western: "subsuming all," notes Mitchell, is "the problem of what it means to be a man, as aging victim of progress, embodiment of honor, champion of justice in an unjust world."[4]

Insofar as *Brokeback Mountain*'s narrative of male-male sexual and emotional desire in rural Wyoming during the pre-Stonewall period and early 1960s ticks all of Mitchell's boxes, Lee's film would seem to be a prime and unproblematic example of a western. After all, when Ennis and Jack first have sex on Brokeback Mountain, they indeed "pass … frontiers" – from heterosexual to gay, from homosocial to homosexual – and thus set in motion the progression of their queer relationship.

At the same time, this border crossing problematizes and troubles the teleological "progress" of a heteronormative life. During the course of the film, as Ennis and Jack pursue their relationship in sporadic and constrained ways, other standard tropes of the western emerge. As their wives slowly begin to intuit the sexual and romantic nature of Ennis and Jack's long-term relationship, Ennis and Jack's secret queerness threatens their heterosexual "honor" within the social context of homophobia. The problems of queer "law" and "justice," the specters of "vengeance and social control," and "the problem of violence" bookend Ennis's life: As a young boy he is taken by his father to see the murdered body of Earl, an older male neighbor rancher living with another male rancher and suspected of being gay, who was bludgeoned to death with a tire iron, his penis severed, left lying in an irrigation ditch. After learning of Jack's death, Ennis calls Jack's wife, Lureen, who explains unconvincingly to Ennis that Jack died when a car tire he was changing exploded. The viewer sees a montage in Ennis's mind in which Jack dies in a gay bashing, bludgeoned to death, like Earl, with a tire iron. Violence here has no value, however, as it normally does in the western, according to Mitchell. Instead it is only and utterly destructive.

Subtending all of *Brokeback*'s narrative, of course, is "the problem of what it means to be a man": Is Ennis, after Jack's death, an "aging victim of progress," stuck in the limbo of the early 1980s, at which point the glimmer of gay rights may have been on the horizon in urban centers but not in rural Wyoming? Is Ennis – divorced, lonely, and alone at the end of the film, with nothing but his memories of Jack – the "embodiment of [gay] honor" and "champion of [queer] justice in an unjust [homophobic] world"? Or was Ennis and Jack's love for each other both too early and too late, both premature and belated, for any sort of queer liberation? And, perhaps most provocatively, is Ennis and Jack's story the apotheosis of the western and its necessary, newly evolved, newly transformed, post-Stonewall, postqueer form? Or is their story the threatening antithesis of the western in that it literalizes, as homosexuality, the homosociality necessary to the western, revealing homoerotic disavowal as constitutive of heterosexuality itself?

It is not as if queerness – that is, gender and sexual nonnormativity – is absent in western American literature and in the western. Rather, these representations traditionally rely on suppression, invisibility, and ignorance in order to blend into the generic landscape as unremarkable and unremarked. Swaggering male homosociality is one of the staple ingredients of western American literature and the western. While homosociality is a hallmark of hypermasculinity and heterosexuality, it also gestures toward the specter of homoeroticism that seemingly lurks everywhere. Willa Cather's novels, for example, are filled with women who flout traditional gender roles. This female masculinity is often narratively figured as a sort of necessarily hardened frontier femininity, but it also hints at a masculinity wielded by women that might challenge and be independent of men and male masculinity.[5] Other, relatively oblique thematizations of gender and sexual nonnormativity include Owen Wister's *The Virginian* (1902), Jack Schaefer's *Shane* (1949), and the much earlier example of Bret Harte's short story "The Luck of Roaring Camp" (1868). Harte's story offers a prescient mid-nineteenth-century example of male homosociality and all-male parenting that hints at the possibility that men might make babies together and might love each other in a way as "natural" as husband and wife, father and mother. "Luck" is the name of a baby boy born to Cherokee Sal, the only woman in a struggling California gold prospecting community of Roaring Camp. Sal is described in the typical nineteenth-century language of racial and sexual abjection as "a coarse, and … very sinful woman," presumably because she is sexually intimate with many or even all of the miners.[6] "Dissolute, abandoned and irreclaimable," Sal dies shortly after giving birth, and the reluctant miners foster the child, uncomfortably at first and then with greater affection and emotional investment.[7] The miners' increasingly adept "mothering" skills at first call into question their fitness as masculine western heroes but end by affirming a western masculine self-sufficiency that valorizes all-male homosocial relations and that gestures toward a western frontier fantasy world in which men are free of women even in the realm of reproduction.

In addition to these more indirect tales of gender and sexual nonnormativity, there are more recent examples of western American fiction that focus explicitly on same-sex desire. Notable examples include Thomas Savage's novel *The Power of the Dog* (1967) – in which the imbricated relations among western male machismo, repressed gay desire, and brutal cruelty are explored – and Jane Rule's novel *Desert of the Heart* (1964), as well as Donna Deitch's film adaptation *Desert Hearts* (1985) – in which a female professor who travels to Reno, Nevada, for a divorce has a romantic relationship with a female casino dealer.[8] Emily M. Danforth's recent *The Miseducation of Cameron Post* (2012), a queer coming-of-age novel set in rural Montana, explores conservative Christianity, conversion therapy, and the cost of denying one's gay self.[9] History and literature collide, coalesce, and mutually transform one another in Moisés Kaufman's play *The Laramie Project* (2001), which explores brutal violence, homophobic hate, and finally compassion and redemption in its recounting of life in Laramie, Wyoming, in the year following Matthew Shepard's 1998 savage beating and murder.[10] Not all recent examples of western American fiction that engage homosociality engender explicit, let alone sympathetic, narratives of gay and lesbian lives, however. Cormac McCarthy's novel *Blood Meridian, or The Evening Redness in the West* (1985), for example, is a western – or an antiwestern[11] – that is steadfastly invested in male homosociality and homoeroticism interwoven into a narrative not of gayness but instead of brutal relentless violence in nineteenth-century Mexico and the American Southwest.[12] The narrative follows a marauding lawless character named simply "the kid," and later "the man," who over the course of decades participates in bloody slaughters of Americans and Mexicans, militiamen and natives, businessmen and frontiersmen. With references to rapes, bestiality, and prostitution throughout, finally merging at the novel's end with the suggestion of male-male sexual assault and murder, *Blood Meridian*, unlike Harte's "The Luck of Roaring Camp," can only understand male-male friendship and desire as a site of violence.[13]

While recent literary scholarship challenges traditional readings of these instances of gender and sexual nonnormativity that understand them as outliers, "Brokeback" and *Brokeback* go even further, revealing how even apparent "outliers" are actually central to and constitutive of the genre. Showing us the ways that gayness is so painfully difficult to express, enact, and even articulate, as a result of both the generic pressures of western American literature and the western, and the cultural pressures that forbid and foreclose the possibility of living gay lives, Proulx's story and Lee's film reveal how our previous readings of western American literature and westerns are incomplete to the degree that they fail to recognize queerness at the very heart of narratives of the American West.

A number of critics have offered rich analyses of Proulx's "Brokeback" and Lee's *Brokeback*. In addition to dozens of scholarly articles, there are two essay collections devoted to the story and the film, an issue of *Film*

Quarterly largely devoted to the film, and a special "*Brokeback Mountain* Dossier" in *GLQ: A Journal of Lesbian and Gay Studies.*[14] Leopold Lippert analyzes a mock movie trailer on YouTube entitled *Broke Trek: A Star Trek Brokeback Mountain Parody*, which imagines a film that combines *Brokeback Mountain* and the 1960s television drama *Star Trek: The Original Series*. Focusing on "tropes of time," "tropes of the nation," and "political imaginings of 'America,'" Lippert argues that "*Broke Trek* shows that the queering of national cowboy mythology goes hand in hand with a queering of futurity."[15] Matthew Bolton and D. A. Miller examine affect, identification, universality, and the relationship between the film's (heterosexual) viewers and its (homosexual) characters Jack and Ennis.[16] In an attempt to account for *Brokeback*'s immense appeal, Jack Halberstam notes that the film's popularity "cannot be explained simply in terms of the spectacular revelation of the previously implicit and buried erotic relations between men in the genre ... nor can it be explained away, as so many critics have done, by a quick nod to the universality of love." Instead, attention to "loneliness" and to "the homoeroticism of the genre in relation to ... guns, heroic and homoerotic masculinities, and women" reveals that "the Western has always been queer."[17]

In addition to criticism of *Brokeback*, recent criticism of western American literature has focused more broadly on masculinity, homoeroticism, and the American West. Chris Packard examines, for instance, queer interracial families in the works of James Fenimore Cooper, marriage in the works of Owen Wister, and men's clubs in the works of Mark Twain and others in order to argue that "the cowboy is queer; he is odd; he doesn't fit in; he resists community; he eschews lasting ties with women but embraces rock-solid bonds with same-sex partners; he practices same-sex desire."[18] Daniel Worden argues for the centrality of the American West to literary modernism. Through readings of late nineteenth-century dime novels as well as the works of Willa Cather, Ernest Hemingway, Nat Love, Theodore Roosevelt, John Steinbeck, and Owen Wister, Worden demonstrates how "cowboy masculinity" and male self-fashioning reveal "masculinity as both an aesthetic and social project," as a performative, rather than simply representational, practice that, "from the 1860s to the 1950s ... produce[s] new ways of thinking about gender, sexuality, the family, property, and public culture."[19]

Brokeback Mountain reveals how queerness is not simply thematic. The ways in which queer desire both propels the film's western narrative of struggle and self-discovery amid the arid western landscapes and threatens the hyperbolic heterosexual masculinity on which the western relies reveal the form's generic (over)investment in male erotics. Queer theory is thus valuable to literary history for thinking about the western, not because queer theory helps locate and recover previously overlooked gay themes or characters in particular westerns, but because queer theory makes visible to literary history the western's generic demands that have relied on the simultaneous evocation and erasure of homoeroticism. In this way, queer reading practices help us think more and differently about the western and about the production of masculinity and Americanness in western American literature. In *Brokeback*, queer reading practices help us see the temporal strategies on which the western relies in order to tell its teleological struggles of *bildung*: conflict, self-discovery, transformation.

In both the western more generally and *Brokeback*, temporality and sexuality are linked.[20] On the one hand, the temporal structure of *Brokeback Mountain* troubles the notion of linear, progressive time and gestures toward something other than the heteronormative arc of a life during which one falls in love, marries, and has children. On the other hand, narrative closure built on a structuring melancholia of a lost queer love object evokes Judith Butler's notion of "heterosexual melancholia": "the melancholy by which a masculine gender is formed from the refusal to grieve the masculine as a possibility of love.... The straight man *becomes* (mimes, cites, appropriates, assumes the status of) the man he 'never' loved and 'never' grieved.... It is in this sense, then, that what is most apparently performed as gender is the sign and symptom of a pervasive disavowal."[21] *Brokeback Mountain* has been received as a queer-liberatory and queer-celebratory film in that it renders visible and emotionally accessible the particularity of queer love and loss. At the same time, however, the film violently reproduces and reinscribes heteronormativity insofar as it generalizes and renders universal the particularity of queer desire, magically transforming the specificity of queer foreclosure into the universality of heterosexual subjectivity.

In mainstream westerns, narrative often unfolds as progressive, developmental, and teleological time, as standard and dependable as the good guys' wearing white hats and the bad guys' wearing black. Narratively, however, *Brokeback* seems to be composed of two stories: One is the story of Jack and Ennis working, falling in love with their wives, marrying, having children, and the other is the story of Jack and Ennis falling in love with each other. The former is progressive, developmental, successive, and cumulative, as one event leads in a more or less understandable way to the next. The latter is disjointed, nonprogressive, and noncumulative in the story it tells (or does not tell) and in the meanings it produces (or fails to produce). Put another way, the former is recognizable as narrative in the genre in which it participates, and the latter is not; it is something else.

A number of queer theorists – from Elizabeth Freeman, to Lee Edelman, to Halberstam, among others[22] – have recently made arguments about what they term "queer time" as "temporal drag" (Freeman's term) or as time with "no future" (Edelman's phrase). Tom Boellstorff points out that these notions of time, queer though they may be, still rely on a linear and heteronormative notion of time. Time may speed up or slow down, and may even be blocked from progressing into the future, but time still operates along a linear continuum. Boellstorff proposes thinking instead, not about queer time, but about what he calls "queer timing" and "coincidence."[23]

Brokeback indeed participates in this notion of queer timing. Its two interspersed narratives have two different and competing temporalities that, while co-incidental, do not follow identical logics of linear or cumulative temporality. One narrative, the heterosexual stories of Jack and Ennis and their wives and children, is structured according to *time,* and the other, the queer story of Jack and Ennis, is structured according to *timing.* While the stories of Jack and Ennis and their families are fairly straightforwardly narrative, the story of Jack and Ennis is remarkable for how it is structured by a certain nonnarrativeness: Events occur but do not progress; time unreels, but does not accumulate.

This is the case in particular in the flashbacks the film employs at two key moments. The first occurs when Jack and Ennis fight during what will be their last meeting. On a riverbank at the end of one of their infrequent camping trips, Ennis collapses to his knees in grief and humiliation, saying, "I honestly can't stand this anymore, Jack," and there is a flashback to their first summer together, in which Ennis walks up and embraces a sleepy Jack from behind, whispering and crooning in Jack's ear just as Ennis's mother used to do when Ennis was a boy. Later, when Ennis learns from Lureen that Jack is dead, Ennis experiences Jack's supposed gay-bashing death as a flashback. Unlike traditional flashbacks, however, which revisit moments that have already appeared in a film, neither of these flashbacks references prior scenes in this film. There is thus no original, temporally sequential moment to which the film later flashes back. Instead, both flashbacks show temporally anterior moments that exist nowhere earlier in the film, but only exist in the temporally unfurling narrative present. In this way, the flashbacks mark both nostalgia for the past, and loss in the filmic present of the historical narrative moment, a moment marked by nostalgia, but one that appears nowhere prior in the film. The flashbacks – one conjuring the aching tenderness of early love and the other conjecturing the violent erasure of Jack's and Ennis's desire and same-sex desire more generally – produce, in their romantic (heterosexual) idealization of epic love and loss, a sympathetic queerness in the heterosexual viewer such that the specificity of queer love and loss, the ostensible progressive subject matter of *Brokeback Mountain*, is routed through the universality of heterosexual mourning and melancholia.

While gayness plays an explicit narrative role in Proulx's story and Lee's film, queer desires, identities, disavowals, temporal logics, and generic tensions in these texts structure and alter western American literature more generally. For "Brokeback" and *Brokeback* move to the fore and offer the opportunity to read a set of structures and tropes that characterize western American literature and, as a result, urge us as readers to rethink our approaches to literary and film history by employing queer reading practices not just for texts with explicitly gay characters, but, most importantly, for texts that appear utterly normative and conventional in order better to understand how normativity and conventionality are themselves vigorously produced and reproduced precisely via queer erasure in the western.

Notes

1 Annie Proulx, "Brokeback Mountain," *New Yorker* (October 13, 1997), 74–85. "Brokeback Mountain" was republished, with the addition of an epilogue, in Annie Proulx, *Close Range: Wyoming Stories* (New York: Scribner, 1999), 251–83.
2 *Brokeback Mountain*. Dir. Ang Lee. Focus Features, 2006.
3 Lee Clark Mitchell, *Westerns: Making the Man in Fiction and Film* (Chicago: University of Chicago Press, 1996), 3.
4 Ibid.
5 For an examination of nineteenth- and twentieth-century female masculinity and the masculine woman as historical figure, see Judith Halberstam, *Female Masculinity* (Durham, NC: Duke University Press, 1998).
6 Bret Harte, "The Luck of Roaring Camp," *Overland Monthly* (August 1868), 183.
7 Ibid.
8 Thomas Savage, *The Power of the Dog* (Boston: Little, Brown, 1967); Jane Rule, *Desert of the Heart* (Toronto: Macmillan, 1964); *Desert Hearts*, Dir. Donna Deitch. The Samuel Goldwyn Company, 1985.
9 Emily M. Danforth, *The Miseducation of Cameron Post* (New York: Harper Collins, 2012).

10 Moisés Kaufman, *The Laramie Project* (New York: Vintage–Random House, 2001.)

11 Susan Kollin, "Genre and the Geographies of Violence: Cormac McCarthy and the Contemporary Western," *Contemporary Literature* 42, no. 3 (2001): 557–88.

12 Cormac McCarthy, *Blood Meridian, or the Evening Redness in the West* (New York: Random House, 1985).

13 Drawing a constitutive link between the western and violence, Mark Seltzer goes so far as to assert that "serial murder and its representations … have by now largely replaced the Western as the most popular genre-fiction of the body and of bodily violence in our culture. And recent splatterpunk Westerns, such as Cormac MacCarthy's [*sic*] novel *Blood Meridian* or films like Clint Eastwood's *The Unforgiven* or Jim Jarmusch's *Dead Man*, make the case that the Western was really about serial killing all along." See Seltzer, *Serial Killers: Death and Life in America's Wound Culture* (New York: Routledge, 1998), 1.

14 See *The Brokeback Book: From Story to Cultural Phenomenon*, ed. William R. Handley (Lincoln: University of Nebraska Press, 2011); *Reading Brokeback Mountain: Essays on the Story and the Film*, ed. Jim Stacy (Jefferson, NC: McFarland, 2007); "Special Feature on *Brokeback Mountain*," *Film Quarterly* 60, no. 3 (spring 2007): 20–67; and "*Brokeback Mountain* Dossier," *GLQ: A Journal of Lesbian and Gay Studies* 13, no. 1 (2007): 93–109.

15 Leopold Lippert, "Queering Cowboys, Queer Futurity: The Re/Construction of American Cowboy Masculinity," in *ConFiguring America: Iconic Figures, Visuality, and the American Identity*, ed. Klaus Rieser, Michael Fuchs, and Michael Phillips (Bristol, UK, and Chicago: Intellect, 2013), 135, 146.

16 Matthew Bolton, "The Ethics of Alterity: Adapting Queerness in *Brokeback Mountain*," in *Queer Love in Film and Television: Critical Essays*, ed. Pamela Demory and Christopher Pullen (New York: Palgrave Macmillan, 2013), 257–68; D. A. Miller, "On the Universality of *Brokeback*," *Film Quarterly* 60, no. 3 (spring 2007): 50–60.

17 Judith Halberstam, "Not So Lonesome Cowboys: The Queer Western," *The Brokeback Book*, 191, 201.

18 Chris Packard, *Queer Cowboys: And Other Erotic Male Friendships in Nineteenth-Century American Literature* (New York: Palgrave Macmillan, 2005), 3.

19 Daniel Worden, *Masculine Style: The American West and Literary Modernism* (New York: Palgrave Macmillan, 2011), 2, 16.

20 Temporality plays an important role as well in Gloria Anzaldúa's influential *Borderlands/La Frontera: The New Mestiza*. While Anzaldúa's text focuses on language, landscape, identity, and the U.S.-Mexican border, it also engages history – and thus temporality – in its interweaving of autobiography and the history of the peoples of Mexico. Gloria Anzaldúa, *Borderlands/La Frontera: The New Mestiza* (San Francisco: Aunt Lute Books, 1987).

21 Judith Butler, *Bodies That Matter: On the Discursive Limits of "Sex"* (New York: Routledge, 1993), 235–36.

22 See Elizabeth Freeman, "Packing History, Count(er)ing Generations," *New Literary History* 31, no. 4 (2000): 727–44; Lee Edelman, *No Future: Queer Theory and the Death Drive* (Durham, NC: Duke University Press, 2004); Judith Halberstam, *In a Queer Time and Place: Transgender Bodies, Subcultural Lives* (New York: New York University Press, 2005).

23 Tom Boellstorff, *A Coincidence of Desires: Anthropology, Queer Studies, Indonesia* (Durham, NC: Duke University Press, 2007).

CHAPTER 24

Postwestern Literature and Criticism

Neil Campbell

> I am of that culture and yet I am against that culture. I am of my
> time and yet out of my time. I drive fast down freeways but I have no
> belief that these roads lead to a future.[1]

In the late twentieth century, westerns entered a revisionist cycle whereby
mythic structures as well as generic codes and conventions were placed
under critical scrutiny. After World War II, the civil rights movement,
along with antiwar protests, a growing environmental awareness, and the
women's rights movement, created a culture that reevaluated the central
themes, conflicts, and characters of the genre. These new literary and cinematic westerns, now defined in a broader and more fluid way, extended,
revised, and challenged the national, regional, racial, and gender imaginaries typically encoded in the established genre to make space for new
narrative possibilities, thus ushering in what might be called the "postwestern." This essay explores some of the reasons for this postwestern turn
by examining its critical histories and its articulation across a range of literary examples.[2]

Sergio Fabbrini has written of "a general consensus that the 2008
financial crisis has been more than a physiological economic downturn,"
since it also called into question the political paradigm of a deregulated
economic system "hierarchically controlled by the United States." This
resulted in a world "much less western than in the past ... a post-western
world that now is shading the western power itself."[3] Key to this position were new structures of influence questioning U.S. hegemony under-
pinned by a national narrative of settlement, power, identity formation,
and development extending back historically and mythologically to
westward expansion. This shift relates to the subject of this essay, which
deals specifically with the post-western as a consequence of similar political, cultural, economic, and aesthetic challenges in the post-1945 period,
when the assumed centrality of the American West's regional attributes

that had constructed the creation myth of national identity were themselves under question. This supposed unanimity cohered around certain core values underlining American certainty and helping to shape an idea of "the people" as a unified and consensual group, which, in Gilles Deleuze's words, were "already there, real before being actual, ideal without being abstract."[4] This was expressed in classic western fiction and film by "addressing a people ... presupposed already there" populating its settlements and narratives with actions and attitudes that reinforced a specific ideological landscape.[5]

The regional West's ideological core was best summarized in Frederick Jackson Turner's essay "The Significance of the Frontier in American History" (1893), as exceptionalist, providential, heroic, and relentless, and it was from these "traits," he argued, that Americans have "taken their tone."[6] In "The Problem of the West" he added that "the West was another name for opportunity ... an open field, unchecked by restraints" in which capitalism flourished to empower "Western man" further as the flag bearer of "manifest destiny."[7] The post-western is an unswerving response to Turner's imperial assumptions and their consequential effects upon how the West was represented in much literature and film, and to borrow Fabbrini's metaphor, "shades" the western because it exists differently but always in productive relation to its earlier forms.

A major factor in the reassessment of the western post 1945 is a consequence of massive economic, social, political, and cultural changes, with the growth of urbanization, rural depopulation, increased military presence, and the consequent development of new centers of wealth and influence such as Los Angeles and Las Vegas. Notions of a region of sweeping, open landscapes, half-built towns, and rugged, lone horsemen needed to be rethought in the light of increasingly corporatized, urban, and suburban spaces with different cultural values. Edward Abbey's *Brave Cowboy* (1957), filmed as *Lonely Are the Brave* (1962), is an exemplary novel charting postwestern themes through its man out of time, Jack Burns, riding a horse in a time of Jeeps and superhighways, struggling to accept the fences interrupting his path and the borders dividing up his West. As the novel characterizes him, "Jack's been to too many Westerns. Too much Zane Grey."[8] For Burns nature is rooted in the past as an imagined space of hard riding freedom, with no family or community, finding solace purely in wilderness, but the "civilization" he confronts is marked by "a pair of tin cans riddled with bullet holes ... an empty sardine can dissolving in rust ... trails of jeeps and motor-cycles ... broken bottles and windblown Kleenex."[9] At the novel's end, the two worlds collide literally on the highway, when Burns and his horse are hit by a truck, leaving the reader with an apocalyptic commentary upon environmental decline and disaster, while what remains is the "great four lane highway ... steel, rubber ... the fury of men and women immured in engines." Abbey's final irony is that those inheritors of this post-West are themselves "immured" or walled in and imprisoned by their technology while Burns is dead but "all right," merging with the "near-silent world" of nature.[10] Ambiguously, the novel leaves us tinged with sadness at Burns's inevitable death within the context of this West as a modern, technological space, while representing him as a fading Marlboro Man, clinging on to a myth dream of a time that never really existed. This tension characterizes the shift toward the post-western with its questioning of unanimity and the emergence of alternative voices always complicating Burns's notion of the masculine, open range in the postwar West.

Abbey fictionalizes a postwestern landscape later named in 1973 by Philip French in relation to films that dealt with "the West today, and draw upon the western itself or more generally 'the cowboy cult'" to show how "characters are influenced by, or victims of, the cowboy cult," and in doing this, "intensify and play on the audience's feelings about, and knowledge of, western movies."[11] Alongside this concern for the aftermath of frontier myth, the possibility of "a postwestern history" emerged in Virginia Scharff's questioning "the stability of our most cherished historical categories of analysis" in order "to imagine history anew" and *both* recognize "the weight of the western frame" and treat it with skepticism, or, in her words, to be "alert, edgy and restless" to "burst the boundaries of region."[12] Scharff urged critics to move "outside" the "weight of the western frame" with its inherent and deep-rooted cultural myths and national identity markers, to see it differently and askew.

In the wake of this initial exploration, other critics continued to define and explore this postwestern turn (see Klein 1996; Knobloch 1996; Campbell 2008, 2013), which Stephen Tatum encapsulated as the "ongoing reorientation of the field imaginary of the literary West" into its "postfrontier" phase, when old ideas of assimilation and unambiguous lines of expansion were disrupted by viewing the region as "an intercultural contact zone."[13] Susan Kollin's collection *Postwestern Cultures* (2007) finally defined "postwestern" thought as "an emerging critical approach" linked specifically to the increasing awareness of critical regionalism laboring "against a narrowly conceived regionalism" demarcating the West as a "predetermined entity with static borders and boundaries."[14] She explains how the problem manifests itself as a "dominant national discourse" wherein

> the American West has been imagined and celebrated largely for its status
> as "pre" – for its position as a pre-lapsarian, pre-social, and pre-modern
> space ... so that like the very spaces of an idealized western geography ...
> literary and cultural scholarship about the region ... adopted a pre- or even
> anti-theoretical stance, as if regional studies could offer a similar retreat or
> refuge from a dehumanizing culture.[15]

Kollin's invocation of "post" provides a potent critical counterbalance, refusing to "know its place" within an established generic and cultural grid, making it instead a platform from which to examine and assess some of the reinventions of the western over the subsequent period.

In 2013 Krista Comer's "Introduction: Assessing the Postwestern" claimed the "postwestern ... [is] the cultural space and critical practice involving the crossings, flows, transnational circulations, of a regionalism not-bounded" and "coheres in a sense of place as mobile and in a subject who can move and who is disjoined from static or singular or phenomenological moorings."[16] As the examples in this chapter will demonstrate, the attention to mobility can be a limiting reading of postwestern texts, which in many cases "move" and "disjoin" from mythic concepts precisely to reengage then with places as intensely local while remaining aware of the context and complex relations with the world they exist within and to which they relate. In this sense the post-western can be attentive to its "phenomenological moorings" in place and its ties to the past, while also understanding its critical role in questioning the values that have often defined and limited the very region from which it originates. The Native American critic Gerald Vizenor, for example, explains his term "postindian" as "long past the colonial invention of the indian. We come after the invention, and we are the postindians ... [who] create a native presence, and that sense of presence is both *reversion and futurity*."[17] For Vizenor, despite Indigenous territorial claims, "stories of survivance are an active presence," suggesting that for him too "the post" indicates "reversion and futurity" through which "transmotion" does not drive one away from the local, rooted territory, but rather expands and deepens it with "creation stories, totemic visions, reincarnation, and sovenance ["presence in remembrance"] ... not a monotheistic, territorial sovereignty."[18] This "active presence" of regionality in the West is crucial to the post-westerns explored here since it signals the dialogical relationship as both "territorialized" *and* "deterritorialized," reversion and futurity, engaging with traces of the past, location, and genre while also moving them, affecting them, differing and deferring them through its critical, self-conscious commitment to creating different cultural political narratives.

The problematic prefix "post" is best explained by Stuart Hall as the "closure of a certain historical event or age" *and* a "going beyond ... commenting upon a certain intellectual movement" thereby, articulating "a shift or transition conceptualised as the reconfiguration of the field, rather than as the movement of linear transcendence between two mutually exclusive states."[19] Thus when used in "post-western" it should be seen as "a process of disengagement" from the system it is in tension with (the westerns of the past), *but*, and this is critical, in the full knowledge that it is "probably inescapable" from that system as well. Consequently post-westerns are constituted by dialogical, knotted relations whereby the present engages with the past, the "pre" with the "post," and so, Comer's description of "regionalism not-bounded" is now considered, following Hall, as regionalism *reconfigured*. Hence, the western and its "post-western" forms "never operated in a purely binary way," but always function *after, beyond,* and in *relations with* one another as an active presence of territorialization and deterritorialization.[20] Therefore, as I have expressed elsewhere, post-westerns are hauntings, shady "ghost-Westerns," drawing into the present and future the inescapable traces of the past from which they emerged to explore "western" themes in new contexts, casting fresh light on the regionalist ideologies that initiated the fabled West, becoming generic mutations, offering challenging interruptions, unsettling through "minor" language the dominant forms of established westerns.[21]

Suffice to say, one could claim many texts as postwestern in this chapter if only because they investigate the aftereffects of western myth played out in western spaces: those of William Eastlake, William Burroughs, Ishmael Reed, Larry McMurtry, Annie Proulx, Sherman Alexie, Leslie Marmon Silko, Marilynne Robinson, Bret Easton Ellis, and many others. I will, however, focus on four brief examples, John Williams, Cormac McCarthy, Willy Vlautin, and Karen Tei Yamashita, to give some sense of the scope of postwestern writing as it responds to both the importance of the West in the American imagination and its continued ideological and ideational reverberations.

Published in 1960 John Williams's *Butcher's Crossing* works within the archetypal framework of the classic western, perpetuating the dialogical narrative described previously both honoring the myths of the West and self-consciously reflecting upon them, drawing the reader into a critical, demythicizing perspective. A young Harvard man goes west to search for "the Wildness" and to "see as much of the country ... *to know it.*"²² Under the influence of Emerson's *Nature* and the belief that, as the novel's epigraph has it, "The knapsack of custom falls off his back with the first step he takes into these precincts," Will Andrews expects the West to release his potential and fulfill his dreams. But as the novel unveils while engaged in an ill-fated buffalo hunt, "the west was a vague country whose limits and extents were undefined," and his imagined country "seen in books, in magazines, when he was at home in Boston" cannot measure up to the pitiless, material landscape: "the thin black lines wavered upon the real grass before him, took on color, then faded."²³ The clearly defined "lines" of myth are now wavering and undefined in a region already in transition, with the railroad altering the geography and economy so that the buffalo hides so ruthlessly procured by his obsessive partner, Miller, become worthless as the town of Butcher's Crossing becomes ghostly and unrecognizable within the span of one year.

As the hunting adventure ends in death, loss, and disappointment in the unforgiving Colorado landscape, Andrews faces the stark truth of the West explained to him by the wise, but tainted entrepreneur McDonald: "You get born, and you nurse on lies, and you get weaned on lies, and you learn fancier lies in school.... When you're ready to die, it comes to you – that there's nothing, nothing but yourself and what you could have done. Only you ain't done it, because the lies told you there was something else."²⁴ He says, "You can't deal with this country as long as you're in it; it's too big, and empty, and it lets the lies come into you," and yet Andrews remains in the town, now "like a small ruin" waiting to disappear imminently in the boom and bust cycles of the West. Ironically, even as he rides off into the sunrise, as fulfilling the resolution of a Hollywood western, "he did not know where he was going."²⁵ As the second epigraph from Melville's *The Confidence Man* suggests, "poets send out their sick spirits to green pastures" only to be confronted by its harsh reality and be "made an idiot of," and this is the lesson of this proto-postwestern novel. Andrews's understanding of his "vanity" is tied to the lies and the dreams of the West, and the "nothingness" he feels is a terrible indictment of the yearning that created the region in the first place and that, ironically, persists, driving him "forward without hurry" at the novel's conclusion.²⁶

Cormac McCarthy's *Blood Meridian or the Evening Redness in the West*, and his "Border Trilogy," *All the Pretty Horses, The Crossing,* and *Cities of the Plain,* extend and deepen Williams's philosophical ruminations on westness. It is present in *Blood Meridian*'s terrifyingly excessive imperialist Judge Holden rewriting history through death and erasure alongside the bildungsroman of the "kid" moving west in search of a new life; or in *All the Pretty Horses'* reimagining of the epic trails of westerns across borders, yearning for the old times, full of romance yet tainted by horror. McCarthy traces a post-West "gone from the oil lamp and the horse and buggy to jet planes and the atomic bomb," with characters endlessly searching for meaningful values and narratives through which to restructure lives caught between the dreamed-of past and the inevitable present sense of disappointment and loss.[27] Yet the desire to stabilize history and identity in some imagined West is continually frustrated in McCarthy's novels, reminding us that like the landscape itself, identity changes, and the supposedly unwavering romance of the past is only illusion: "The candleflame and the image of the candleflame caught in a pierglass twisted and righted."[28] As his trilogy closes Billy Parham sleeps by the roadside, watching "the pale and naked concrete pillars of an east-west onramp ... curving away, clustered and rising without pediment like the ruins of some older order standing in the dusk," as if gazing upon the desired western "older order," now reduced to concrete ruins hovering liminally over the desert landscape, unfinished, and going nowhere.[29] This commingling of loss and beauty, dream and horror, is like the "framed photograph" at the conclusion of *Cities of the Plain*: "printed from a glass plate broken into five pieces" where "certain ancestors were puzzled back together in a study that *cohered with its own slightly skewed geometry*. Apportioning some *third* or separate meaning to each of the figures seated there."[30] As with this image, so with the trilogy, McCarthy's West has a "skewed geometry," a puzzle drawn from fragments creating a "third ... meaning" from the collision of people's dreams and lived experience, their real and imagined worlds. At its end, Billy's body has ironically become as marked as the landscapes he has crossed in search of coherence and purpose, as if constructing "a map enough for men to read ... to make a landscape. To make a world." However, no map can "make a world" because it is complex and multiple: "It looked like different things ... different perspectives one could take," and as much as we might desire some absolute bearing, it fails to deliver, since so much evades mapping.[31] Traditional maps are closed narratives, controlled and plotted, whereas in McCarthy's post-western "skewed geometry" there remain inconsistencies, gaps, and questions making it an "immappable world," "[w]here ... no narrative is possible." In this resides a vision of the post-western as a form confronting the aftereffects of myth, an unfinished, unfinishable story constantly awaiting new narratives and alternative mappings from which to construct and represent its future.[32]

McCarthy's *No Country for Old Men* (2005) grapples with such aftereffects through his man out of time, the western sheriff Ed Tom Bell, who, like Jack Burns, constantly comments and reflects upon the past as a means of trying to understand the heartless, inexplicable present. The order he imagines is the mythic past once again, an apparently controlled time of unanimity and consensus now under attack from drug wars, illegal immigration, youth crime, and baffling acts of random violence. In the spirit of the post-western, however, McCarthy reveals ironically a West without a redemptive past or regenerative violence, a region always already steeped in blood, secrets, and loss. In a key chapter Bell visits his uncle Ellis; their conversation ranges across family history, personal failings, memory, and illusions and yet builds, from these local details, an affective commentary on the West itself. "There aint no such thing as a bargain promise," Ellis says, indirectly referring to the expectations associated with the western landscape and the dream of settlement, and exemplified through his recollection of the brutal death of his own uncle, Mac, killed by Indians on his front porch. He provides a searing commentary on the "country": "How come people don't feel like this country has got a lot to answer for? They don't. You can say the country don't do nothing, but that don't mean much.... This country will kill you in a heartbeat and still people love it."[33] Understanding the weight of Ellis's story, Bell concludes the scene by saying, "I'm not the man of an older time they say I am. I wish I was. I'm a man of this time."[34] Of course, he struggles throughout the narrative to understand the present but can find little comfort in the past described by Ellis either and, in trying to balance both, is caught between understanding that "the dead have more claims on you than what you might want to admit" and "just ... try[ing] ... [to] figure out what might be headed your way."[35] Trying to "answer for" the West is a key driver of the post-western because its history, its assumptions, its mythic foundation stories, and its consequences are still resonating in people's lives today.

Willy Vlautin's *Northline* (2008) is postwestern precisely because it "answers for" the West through its attention to the affective regional landscape attaching to people in positive and negative ways. Set in Las Vegas and Reno, Nevada, *Northline* reveals an underclass struggling with precarious lives caught among low wage jobs, family crises, and personal trauma against the ever-present mythic promise and disappointments of the West. Vlautin's West is uncoupled from the optimism contained in its traditional myth of Manifest Destiny and from the supposed benefits of globalization and free markets, where lives splinter, collapse, and fall apart amid the supposed glamour and expectation of newer dreams of casino culture capitalism. As Mike Davis comments acidly of Las Vegas, where Vlautin's novel opens, it's "the terminus of western history, the end of the trail."[36]

Central to the novel is Allison Johnson, trying to make a life for herself against the backdrop of an abusive relationship and anxieties about her self-worth. In the opening chapter she is brutally sexually assaulted by her boyfriend, Jimmy Bodie, in the executive washroom of Circus Circus in Las Vegas. Immediately the carnival promise of Las Vegas is reversed, as this postmodern, tourist West reveals itself as another abusive arena of masculine power like a terrible haunting from the frontier past. Bodie's colonization of Allison's body through violent dominance and hypermasculinity is symptomatic of the aftereffects of westness played out uncannily in the lives of the present. His apartment frames his character, revealing "an American flag hanging by the door, and a lamp made from the fender of a 1946 Ford coupé," with books on "guns and self defense ... tattoos ... immigration, US history" and records by "Hank Williams, Johnny Cash, David Alan Coe [sic], Buck Owens, Chet Atkins. Hundreds of country and rockabilly records."[37] It is here he leaves Allison naked and handcuffed to the bed for ten hours, further asserting his patriarchal power, like the marking of her body with tattoos and bruises, defining Bodie's macho signature and his perverse attachment to a type of outlaw West identified with an essentially narrow and uncompromising version of masculinist regionalism. It remains a man's world defined through action and hierarchical power over women, nonwhites, and all forms of difference, and yet, as the novel shows, this is a world undergoing significant change. However, Bodie reacts to it with violence, as an old gunfighter might, displaying clear sympathies with the neo-Nazi World Church of the Creator and seeing Las Vegas as the epitome of America's racial decline: "It was a dump to begin with, then you add all the fucking new people. And the Mexicans come in like fog, cover everything, get in everywhere.... Pretty soon they're gonna ruin everything."[38]

Recalling the dream of "country" in Williams's *Butcher's Crossing*, Bodie's distorted vision aims to escape the threat of the borderlands and its "fog" of immigrants by moving to a mythical "North," fantasized as a renewed West, a static white frontier like Turner's, where nation is defined as masculinist, untrammeled, and free. In a letter to Allison, once she has escaped his physical controls, Bodie explains this fantasy as "A Northline. The farther north, the better. Away from everyone ... from all the weirdos and freaks and Mexicans and Niggers ... the farther North you go, the better it'll be. A place saner and normal. Simpler.

Maybe get a place out in the woods. Maybe Alaska."[39] The Northline is an essentialist vision of a *New* New West *without* immigration but with all the associated imagery of the mythic frontier space, "simpler" because it refuses, as in all mythology, to deal with the complications of history. Jimmy's "North" is an illusory space that abolishes human complexity and contradiction in favor of an essential, time-locked West; it is "saner and normal … [s]impler," with Allison as a powerless sexual partner and a new type of frontier child bearer.

Countering Bodie, Vlautin's postwestern novel restores complexity through Allison's story, full of intense emotion, local details, crises of survival, and the weird intricacies of what Kathleen Stewart calls "ordinary affects" giving "everyday life the quality of a continual motion of relations, scenes, contingencies, and emergences."[40] One scene that suggests Allison's tentative transition is the final chapter, where she meets her boyfriend, Dan Mahony, on the streets of Reno the day its oldest casino, Harold's Club, is to be pulled down. In this postwestern contact zone, past, present, and future collide; individual lives share public space; and actions proceed as possibilities, like "spreading lines of resonance and connection."[41]

Place becomes a site of memory and commemoration for Dan, who has lived in Reno all his life, and as he takes pictures at the scene, each click of the lens evokes an associated memory, mingled with his uncle's stories of the place's history, and their lived experience of it now, at this exquisite moment of transition. Dan's attachment to place and to the West is contrasted to Bodie's violent fear, because it translates into productive actions, memories, and affects that he subsequently passes on to Allison as they both "try […] to move back into the world."[42] "All the old places from that era are disappearing," he tells Allison; "nothing stays the same," only "strip malls" and corporate industrialized landscapes without rooted connections to specific place or time: "They don't have any sorta roots. Maybe chain places are the only roots people have anymore. Maybe roots are Kentucky Fried Chicken and Taco Bell and Wendys. And places like Wal-Mart and K-Mart." Her response to Dan's elegiac tribute to old Reno and to the demolition of the casinos is more pragmatic: "I guess people just need a place to live." Yet she instinctively understands his response to change, for it is a version of what she undergoes throughout the novel as "things get worse or different" in her own life, and yet she adapts, lives on, gets by, survives.[43]

Central to this scene is the mural at Harold's Club depicting westward expansion and proclaiming in red neon letters, "Dedicated in all humility to those who blazed the trail." This epitomizes the good life dream of Old West optimism, distorted by Bodie into his "Northline," but always for Dan "presence in remembrance," as Vizenor termed it earlier: an imaginative, relational space eliciting stories "about all the people in it," about the name of the "mountain man," "where the Indian lived," and "how many kids the lady in the wagon train had."[44] So within this collision of temporal and spatial memories, of Dan's past and Allison's recent trauma, something intense, new, and potentially generative emerges as they locate in each other's stories some fragile and possible hope for the present and future, "with fear and hope and uncertainty."[45] Within these ordinary and local "forms of attention and attachment," as Stewart calls them, their bodies connect uncertainly, tentatively, expressing a moment of intimacy unseen elsewhere in the novel.[46] This is no romantic or heroic western resolution; nor is it a fantasy of a "simpler" Northline, but rather a contingent and uncertain post-West "saturated with affect's lines of promise and threat."[47]

My final contrasting example is Karen Tei Yamashita's experimental *Tropic of Orange,* which reimagines the post-West as an urban borderland in which previously fixed lines stratifying and organizing space, dividing North and South, East and West are moving; pulling, for example, the Tropic of Cancer north and with it a new, usually excluded, population. The novel enacts a self-conscious intertextual stretching out from the West to the world, owing much to Latin American magical realists and to Thomas Pynchon, William Gibson, Mike Davis, Guillermo Gomez-Peña, and Gloria Anzaldúa. Using metaphors of export/import Yamashita suggests how the "approved" trade of global capital and the "illegal" traffic of people are becoming increasingly fuzzy, resulting in an imaginatively provocative remapping of the West, through Los Angeles, the region west, and its multiple relations with the world as a kind of a layered, compositional plane. As a novel of globality and regionality it speaks *from* the local pulsing details of life (like Stewart's "ordinary affects"), drawing on the affective, multiple experiences of diverse peoples across borders and frontiers to frame a web of transnational relations. Together, the novel's interlocking, expanding grid, set out in its "HyperContexts" of interlinked days, themes, and characters, forms an alternative atlas of affective performance, of the post-West as relational, alive, still-forming, rooted, shifting, and collapsing. Within it Yamashita explores uneven distributions of power, wealth, and control in cities, regions, and worlds, remapping the West through the subaltern nonwhite populations of the Americas, suggesting alternatives to the conventions of settler regionalism.

The postwestern aspects of the novel are best explored through one of its characters, the Japanese American Manzanar Murakami, who is "maybe ... schizoid, but maybe not" and yet, "No one was more at home in LA."[48] As a homeless former surgeon he now metaphorically makes "careful incisions through layers of living tissue," to conduct the symphony of traffic flowing and stuttering on the L.A. freeway: "The great flow of humanity [that] ran below and beyond his feet in every direction, pumping and pulsating, that blood connection, the great heartbeat of a great city ... an organic living entity ... a great writhing concrete dinosaur ... the greatest orchestra on earth."[49] What he senses and conducts is not a unanimous West, but one of untapped human potential, symbolized by these living lines adrift from notions of historic space, settlement, and tradition; shifting and writhing with global tensions and flows. However, these processes are not distanced from the people living in these western spaces, for they touch them as global warming, ecological change, toxic pollution, unemployment, border wars, immigration, and violence. "The complexity of human adventure over lines of transit" is revealed through Manzanar's emblematic schizoid vision and affective relations with the city materialized as another example of postwestern remapping. He comments, "There are maps and there are maps and there are maps," and yet he "could see all of them at once, filter some, pick them out like transparent windows and place them even delicately and consecutively in a complex grid of pattern, spatial discernment, body politic."[50] For Yamashita, these layers are not abstract for they are emblematic of a far richer West that "began within the very geology of the land," with rivers below "connected and divergent, shifting and swelling," coexisting with the "man-made grid of civil utilities."[51]

The postwestern refrains of regionality flow through Manzanar's alternative atlas like an urban palimpsest conjoining personal memories of internment and loss, and with it a whole vision of global/regional coloniality, into the freeway's symphony, and beyond that to the world.[52] As he suggests, "Encroaching on this vision was a larger one: the great Pacific stretching along its great rim, brimming over long coastal shores from one hemisphere to another"; from West to East, South to North, across continents, a postwestern culture where "human civilization covered everything in layers, generations of building upon building the residue, burial sites, and garbage that defined people after people for centuries."[53] In Manzanar's redistributed globality, it is the local layers that inform the structure, the little refrains that connect people, place, and time that relate to, and characterize, the greater refrains of worldly culture. Yamashita's layered urban symphony remaps an alternative deep grid of postwestern regionality that is about much more than geography, for it includes the active and affective relations of people, place, time, and history.

In these varieties of the post-western, from tentative revisionism to full-blown postmodern palimpsest, the unanimity of region and nation is under question, as are the values "supposed already there" that shape and reinforce limited conceptualizations of the West. Post-westerns, as Bowden's epigraph states, are "of that culture and yet ... against that culture ... of ... time and yet out of ... time," and yet viewed together they amount to a productive dissensus refusing to remain within the circle of mythic familiarity and proffering instead an alternative, dialogical, *active presence* of critical regionality, articulating in Deleuze's suggestive, but hopeful words "the invention of a people.... Not the myth of a past people, but the story-telling of the people to come."[54]

Notes

1 Charles Bowden, *Some of the Dead Are Still Breathing: Living in the Future* (Boston: Houghton Mifflin Harcourt, 2009), 242.
2 In my other writing on the subject, I use the term "post-Western." Throughout this chapter, however, I will refer to the "post-western" when writing about the genre and "postwestern" when using the term as an adjective, following Cambridge University Press conventions. Other writers use the spelling "postwestern"; where I am referring to their work I will use their original spelling.
3 Sergio Fabbrini, "After Globalization: Western Power in a Post-Western World," 2010 http://www.globalpolicyjournal.com/articles/global-governance/after-globalization-western-power-post-western-world (accessed December 13, 2014).
4 Gilles Deleuze, *Cinema 2: The Time-Image* (Reprint: London: Athlone Press, 2000), 216.
5 Ibid., 217
6 Frederick Jackson Turner, "The Significance of the Frontier in American History," in *Frontier and Section*, ed. Ray Allen Billington (Englewood Cliffs, NJ: Prentice-Hall, 1961), 61.
7 Turner, "The Problem of the West," in *Frontier and Section*, 69.
8 Edward Abbey, *The Brave Cowboy* (Reprint; London: Four Square, 1962), 75.
9 Ibid., 14.
10 Ibid., 224, 155.
11 Philip French, *Westerns* (London: Carcanet, 2005), 84, 85.
12 Virginia Scharff, "Mobility, Women, and the West," in *Over the Edge: Remapping the American West*, ed. Valerie Matsumoto and Blake Allmendinger (Berkeley: University of California Press, 1999), 167, 166.

13 Stephen Tatum, "Postfrontier Horizons," *Modern Fiction Studies* 50, no. 2 (2004): 460–68, 462.

14 Susan Kollin, "Introduction: Postwestern Cultures: Dead or Alive," in *Postwestern Cultures: Literature, Theory, Space*, ed. Susan Kollin (Lincoln: University of Nebraska Press, 2007), xi.

15 Ibid., xiii.

16 Krista Comer, "Introduction: Assessing the Postwestern," *Western American Literature* 48, no. 1–2 (Spring/Summer 2013), 3–15, 11.

17 Gerald Vizenor, *Postindian Conversations* (Lincoln: University of Nebraska Press, 1999), 84 (emphasis added).

18 Gerald Vizenor, *Fugitive Poses: Native American Indian Scenes of Absence and Presence* (Lincoln: University of Nebraska Press, 1998), 15.

19 Stuart Hall, "'When Was the Post-Colonial'? Thinking at the Limit," in *The Postcolonial Question*, ed. Iain Chambers and Lidia Curti (London: Routledge, 1996), 253.

20 Ibid., 253, 254, 246

21 Neil Campbell, *Post-Westerns: Cinema, Region, West* (Lincoln: University of Nebraska Press, 2013), 33–8.

22 John Williams, *Butcher's Crossing* (Reprint: London: Vintage, 2014), 18, 19 (emphasis added).

23 Ibid., 43, 80.

24 Ibid., 296

25 Ibid., 297, 325, 326.

26 Ibid., 326.

27 Cormac McCarthy, *Cities of the Plain* (London: Picador, 1998), 218.

28 Cormac McCarthy, *All the Pretty Horses* (Reprint; New York: Vintage, 1993), 3.

29 McCarthy, *Cities of the Plain*, 289.

30 Ibid., 290 (emphasis added).

31 Ibid., 291, 269.

32 Ibid., 288, 277.

33 Cormac McCarthy, *No Country for Old Men* (New York: Alfred A. Knopf, 2005), 267, 271.

34 Ibid., 279

35 Ibid., 124, 40.

36 Mike Davis, *Dead Cities* (New York: New Press, 2002), 86.

37 Willy Vlautin, *Northline* (London: Faber and Faber, 2008), 8.

38 Ibid,. 28.

39 Ibid., 98

40 Kathleen Stewart, *Ordinary Affects* (Durham, NC: Duke University Press, 2007), 2

41 Ibid., 4.

42 Vlautin, *Northline*, 166.

43 Ibid., 191.

44 Ibid., 191–2.

45 Ibid., 192.
46 Stewart, *Ordinary Affects*, 5.
47 Ibid., 5, 129.
48 Karen Tei Yamashita, *Tropic of Orange* (Minneapolis: Coffee House Press, 1997), 43, 36.
49 Ibid., 56, 35, 37.
50 Ibid., 56.
51 Ibid., 57.
52 Ibid., 57.
53 Ibid., 170
54 Deleuze, *Cinema 2*, 223.

Selected Bibliography

See the notes to individual chapters for a list of works cited in the volume. The following bibliography contains selected works related to the study of western American literature, including essay collections, monographs, and literary histories.

GENERAL WORKS

Bold, Christine. "Westerns." In *The Oxford History of Popular Print Culture, Volume 6: U.S. Popular Print Culture 1860–1920,* ed. Christine Bold, 317–36. Oxford: Oxford University Press, 2012.

The Frontier Club: Popular Westerns and Cultural Power, 1880–1924. New York: Oxford University Press, 2013.

Brown, Bill. "Reading the West: Cultural and Historical Background." In *Reading the West: An Anthology of Dime Novel Westerns,* ed. Bill Brown, 1–40. Boston: Bedford/St. Martin's, 1997.

Campbell, Neil. *The Cultures of the American New West.* Chicago and London: Fitzroy Dearborn, 2000.

Graulich, Melody, and Stephen Tatum, eds. *Reading The Virginian in the New West: Centennial Essays.* Lincoln: University of Nebraska Press, 2003.

Hamilton, Amy T., and Tom J. Hillard, eds. *Before the West Was West: Critical Essays on Pre-1800 Literature of the American Frontiers.* Lincoln: University of Nebraska Press, 2014.

Handley, William R. *Marriage, Violence, and the Nation in the American Literary West.* New York: Cambridge University Press, 2002.

Handley, William R., and Nathaniel Lewis, eds. *True West: Authenticity and the American West.* Lincoln: University of Nebraska Press, 2004.

Hunt, Alex, ed. *The Geographical Imagination of Annie Proulx: Rethinking Regionalism.* Lanham, MD: Lexington Books, 2009.

Karell, Linda K. *Writing Together/Writing Apart: Collaboration in Western American Literature.* Lincoln: University of Nebraska Press, 2002.

Kolodny, Annette. *In Search of First Contact: The Vikings of Viland, the Peoples of Dawnland, and the Anglo-American Anxiety of Discovery.* Durham, NC: Duke University Press, 2012.

"Letting Go Our Grand Obsessions: Notes toward a New Literary History of American Frontiers." *American Literature: A Journal of Literary History, Criticism, and Bibliography* 64, no. 1 (March 1992): 1–18.

LeMenager, Stephanie. *Manifest and Other Destinies: Territorial Fictions of the Nineteenth-Century United States.* Lincoln: University of Nebraska Press, 2005.

Lewis, Nathaniel. *Unsettling the Literary West: Authenticity and Authorship.* Lincoln: University of Nebraska Press, 2003.

Lewis, R. W. B. *The American Adam: Innocence, Tragedy, and Tradition in the Nineteenth Century.* Chicago: University of Chicago Press, 1955.

Papanikolas, Zeese. *American Silence.* Lincoln: University of Nebraska Press, 2007.

Trickster in the Land of Dreams. Lincoln: University of Nebraska Press, 1998.

Rio, David, and Øyunn Hestetun, eds. "Postfrontier Writing," Special Issue of *European Journal of American Studies* 6, no. 3 (2011). http://ejas.revue.org/9245.

Robinson, Forrest G. *Having It Both Ways: Self-Subversion in Western Popular Classics.* Albuquerque: University of New Mexico Press, 1993.

Robinson, Forrest G., ed. *The New Western History: The Territory Ahead.* Tucson: University of Arizona Press, 1998.

Saldívar, José David. *Border Matters: Remapping American Cultural Studies.* Berkeley: University of California Press, 1997.

Simonson, Martin, David Rio, and Amaia Ibarran, eds. *A Contested West: New Readings of Place in Western American Literature.* Madrid: Portal Editions, 2013.

Slotkin, Richard. *The Fatal Environment: The Myth of the Frontier in the Age of Industrialization, 1800–1890.* New York: Atheneum, 1985.

Gunfighter Nation: The Myth of the Frontier in Twentieth-Century America. Norman: University of Oklahoma Press, 1998.

Regeneration through Violence: The Mythology of the American Frontier, 1600–1860. New York: Harper Perennial, 1996.

Smith, Henry Nash. *Virgin Land: The American West as Symbol and Myth.* Cambridge, MA: Harvard University Press, 1950.

Spurgeon, Sara L., ed. *Cormac McCarthy:* All the Pretty Horses, No Country for Old Men, The Road. New York: Continuum, 2011.

Spurgeon, Sara L. *Exploding the Western: Myths of Empire of the Postmodern Frontier.* College Station, TX: Texas A&M University Press, 2005.

Steiner, Michael, ed. *Regionalists on the Left: Radical Voices from the American West.* Norman: University of Oklahoma Press, 2013.

Tatum, Stephen. *In the Remington Moment.* Lincoln: University of Nebraska Press, 2010.

Weltzien, O. Alan, ed. *The Norman Maclean Reader.* Chicago: University of Chicago Press, 2008.

Witschi, Nicolas S., ed. *A Companion to the Literature and Culture of the American West.* Chichester, UK: Wiley-Blackwell, 2011.

Witschi, Nicolas S. *Traces of Gold: California's Natural Resources and the Claim to Realism in Western American Literature.* Tuscaloosa: University of Alabama Press, 2001.

CRITICAL REGIONALISMS

Anzaldúa, Gloria. *Borderlands/La Frontera: The New Mestiza.* San Francisco: Aunt Lute, 1987.

Bailey, Caleb. "Creating a Coyote Cartography: Critical Regionalism at the Border." *European Journal of American Studies* 9, no. 3 (2014). http://ejas.revues.org/10368.

Campbell, Neil. *The Rhizomatic West: Representing the West in a Global, Media Age.* Lincoln: University of Nebraska Press, 2008.

Comer, Krista. "Exceptionalism, Other Wests, Critical Regionalism." *American Literary History* 23, no. 1 (Spring 2011): 159–73.

"New West, Urban and Suburban Spaces, Postwest." In *A Companion to the Literature and Culture of the American West,* ed. Nicolas S. Witschi. Chichester, UK: Wiley-Blackwell, 2011. 244–60.

Dainotto, Roberto. "'All the Regions Do Smilingly Revolt': The Literature of Place and Region." *Critical Inquiry* 22, no. 3 (Spring 1996): 486–505.

Hsu, Hsuan. "Literature and Regional Production." *American Literary History* 17, no. 1 (spring 2005): 36–69.

Kollin, Susan, ed. *Postwestern Cultures: Literature, Theory, Space.* Lincoln: University of Nebraska Press, 2007.

Limón, José. "Border Literary Histories, Globalization, and Critical Regionalism." *American Literary History* 20, no. 1–2 (Summer 2008): 160–82.

Martí, José. *Our America by José Martí: Writings on Latin America and the Struggle for Cuban Independence,* trans. Elinor Randall, ed. Philip S. Foner. New York: Monthly Review Press, 1977.

Saldívar, José David. *The Dialectics of Our America: Genealogy, Cultural Critique and Literary History.* Durham, NC: Duke University Press, 1991.

Tatum, Stephen. "Postfrontier Horizons." *Modern Fiction Studies* 50, no. 2 (2004): 460–8.

RACE, ETHNICITY, AND WESTERN AMERICAN LITERATURE

Allen, Chadwick. *Blood Narrative: Indigenous Identity in American Indian and Maori Literary and Activist Texts.* Durham, NC: Duke University Press, 2002.

Trans-Indigenous: Methodologies for a Global Literary Studies. Minneapolis: University of Minnesota Press, 2012.

Allmendinger, Blake. *Imagining the African American West.* Lincoln: University of Nebraska Press, 2005.

Aranda Jr., José. *When We Arrive: A New Literary History of Mexican America.* Tucson: University of Arizona Press, 2003.

Bernardin, Susan, ed. "Indigenous Wests: Literary and Visual Aesthetics," Special Issue of *Western American Literature* 49, no. 1 (Spring 2014).

Brady, Mary Pat. *Extinct Lands, Temporal Geographies: Chicana Literature and the Urgency of Space*. Durham, NC: Duke University Press, 2002.

Bruyneel, Kevin. *The Third Space of Sovereignty: The Postcolonial Politics of U.S.-Indigenous Relations*. Minneapolis: University of Minnesota Press, 2007.

Byrd, Jodi A. *The Transit of Empire: Indigenous Critiques of Colonialism*. Minneapolis: University of Minnesota Press, 2011.

Chuh, Kandice. *Imagine Otherwise: On Asian Americanist Critique*. Durham, NC: Duke University Press, 2003.

Chuh, Kandice, and Karen Shimawaka, eds. *Orientations: Mapping Studies in the Asian Diaspora*. Durham, NC: Duke University Press, 2001.

Herman, Matthew. *Politics and Aesthetics in Contemporary Native American Literature: Across Every Border*. New York: Routledge, 2010.

Hsu, Hsuan. "Chronotopes of the Asian American West." In *A Companion to the Literature and Cutlure of the American West*, ed. Nicolas S. Witschi, 145–60. Chichester, UK: Wiley-Blackwell, 2011.

Sitting in Darkness: Mark Twain's Asia and Comparative Racialization. New York: New York University Press, 2015.

Huhndorf, Shari M. *Mapping the Americas: The Transnational Politics of Contemporary Native Culture*. Ithaca, NY: Cornell University Press, 2009.

Irwin, Robert McKee. *Bandits, Captives, Heroines, and Saints: Cultural Icons of Mexico's Northwest Borderlands*. Minneapolis: University of Minnesota Press, 2007.

Johnson, Michael K. *Black Masculinity and the Frontier Myth in American Literature*. Norman: University of Oklahoma Press, 2002.

Hoo-Doo Cowboys and Bronze Buckaroos: Conceptions of the African American West. Jackson: University Press of Mississippi, 2014.

King, Thomas. *The Inconvenient Indian: A Curious Account of Native People in North America*. Minneapolis: University of Minnesota Press, 2013.

The Truth about Stories: A Native Narrative. Minneapolis: University of Minnesota Press, 2008.

Lee, Robert G. *Orientals: Asian Americans in Popular Culture*. Philadelphia: Temple University Press, 1999.

Lowe, Lisa. *Immigrant Acts: On Asian American Cultural Politics*. Durham, NC: Duke University Press, 1996.

Nanda, Aparajita, ed. *Black California: A Literary Anthology*. Berkeley, CA: Heyday, 2011.

Nguyen, Viet Thanh. *Race and Resistance: Literature and Politics in Asian America*. Oxford: Oxford University Press, 2002.

Saldívar, José David. *Trans-Americanity: Subaltern Modernities, Global Coloniality, and the Cultures of Greater Mexico*. Durham, NC: Duke University Press, 2012.

Saldívar, Ramón, ed. *The Borderlands of Culture: Américo Paredes and the Transnational Imaginary*. Durham, NC: Duke University Press, 2006.

Tonkovich, Nicole C. *The Allotment Plot: Alice C. Fletcher, E. Jane Gray, and Nez Perce Survivance.* Lincoln: University of Nebraska Press, 2012.

Vizenor, Gerald. *Manifest Manners: Narratives on Postindian Survivance.* 1994. Lincoln: University of Nebraska Press, 1999.

GENDER AND SEXUALITY

Bahm, Nina. *Women Writers of the American West, 1833–1927.* Urbana: University of Illinois Press, 2011.

Comer, Krista. *Landscapes of the New West: Gender and Geography in Contemporary Women's Writing.* Chapel Hill: University of North Carolina Press, 1999.

Surfer Girls in the New World Order. Durham, NC: Duke University Press, 2010.

"Taking Feminism and Regionalism to the Third Wave." In *A Companion to the Regional Literatures of America,* ed. Charles L. Crow, 111–28. Malden, MA: Blackwell, 2003.

Eng, David. *Racial Castration: Managing Masculinity in Asian America.* Durham, NC: Duke University Press, 2001.

Georgi-Findlay, Brigitte. *The Frontiers of Women's Writing: Women's Narratives and the Rhetoric of Westward Expansion.* Tucson: University of Arizona Press, 1996.

Halverson, Cathryn. *Maverick Autobiographies: Women Writers and the American West, 1900–1940.* Madison: University of Wisconsin Press, 2004.

Playing House in the American West: Western Women's Life Narratives, 1839–1987. Tuscaloosa: University of Alabama Press, 2013.

Handley, William R., ed. *The Brokeback Book: From Story to Cultural Phenomenon.* Lincoln: University of Nebraska Press, 2011.

Kolodny, Annette. *The Land before Her: Fantasy and Experience of the American Frontiers, 1630–1860.* Chapel Hill: University of North Carolina Press, 1984.

Lamont, Victoria. "Big Books Wanted: Women and Western American Literature in the Twenty-first Century." *Legacy: A Journal of American Women Writers* 31, no. 2 (2014): 311–26.

Lippert, Leopold. "Queering Cowboys, Queering Futurity: The Re/Construction of American Cowboy Masculinity." In *ConFiguring America: Iconic Figures, Visuality, and the American Identity,* ed. Klaus Rieser, Michael Fuchs, and Michael Phillips, 133–48. Bristol, UK, and Chicago: Intellect, 2013.

Mitchell, Lee Clark. *Westerns: Making the Man in Fiction and Film.* Chicago: University of Chicago Press, 1998.

Saldívar-Hull, Sonia. *Feminism on the Border: Chicana Gender Politics and Literature.* Berkeley: University of California Press, 2000.

Tatonetti, Lisa. *The Queerness of Native American Literature.* Minneapolis: University of Minnesota Press, 2014.

Worden, Daniel. *Masculine Style: The American West and Literary Modernism.* New York: Palgrave Macmillan, 2011.

Yates, Norris W. *Gender and Genre: An Introduction to Women Writers of Formula Westerns, 1900–1950.* Albuquerque: University of New Mexico Press, 1995.

MICROREGIONS OF THE AMERICAN WEST

Allmendinger, Blake. *A History of California Literature.* Cambridge: Cambridge University Press, 2015.

Bennett, Robert. "Tract Homes on the Range: The Surburbanization of the American West." *Western American Literature* 46, no. 3 (2011): 281–301.

Dunaway, David King, and Sara L. Spurgeon, eds. *Writing the Southwest.* Albuquerque: University of New Mexico Press, 2003.

Giles, Paul. "Metaregionalism: The Global Pacific Northwest." In *The Global Remapping of American Literature*, 242–54. Princeton, NJ: Princeton University Press, 2011.

Glotfelty. Cheryl, ed. *Literary Nevada: Writings from the Silver State.* Reno: University of Nevada Press, 2008.

Goodman, Audrey. *Lost Homelands: Ruin and Reconstruction in the 20th-Century Southwest.* Tucson: University of Arizona Press, 2010
   Translating Southwest Landscapes: The Making of an Anglo Literary Region. Tucson: University of Arizona Press, 2002.

Hafen, P. Jane, and Diane Quantic, eds. *A Great Plains Reader.* Lincoln: University of Nebraska, 2003.

Harrison, Brady, ed. *All Our Stories Are Here: Critical Perspectives on Montana Literature.* Lincoln: University of Nebraska Press, 2009.

Kollin, Susan. *Nature's State: Imagining Alaska as the Last Frontier.* Chapel Hill: University of North Carolina Press, 2001.

Maher, Susan Naramore. *Deep Map Country: Literary Cartography of the Great Plains.* Lincoln: University of Nebraska Press, 2014.

Ricou, Laurie. *The Arbutus/Madrone Files: Reading the Pacific Northwest.* Corvallis: Oregon State University Press, 2002.

Teague, David. *The Southwest in American Literature and Art: The Rise of a Desert Aesthetic* Tucson: University of Arizona Press, 1997.

Thacker, Robert. *The Great Prairie Fact and Literary Imagination.* Albuquerque: University of New Mexico Press, 1995.

Weltzien, O. Alan. "The Literary Northern Rockies as *The Last Best Place.*" In *A Companion to the Literature and Culture of the American West*, ed. Nicolas S. Witschi, 115–29. Chichester, UK.: Wiley-Blackwell, 2011.

WESTERN FILM AND TELEVISION

Bandy, Mary Lea, and Kevin Stoehr. *Ride, Boldly Ride: The Evolution of the American Western.* Foreword by Clint Eastwood. Berkeley: University of California Press, 2012.

Bold, Christine, and Victoria Lamont, eds. "Popular Westerns: New Scholarship," Special Issue of *Canadian Review of American Studies* 39, no. 2 (2009).

Buscombe, Edward. *'Injuns!': Native Americans in the Movies*: London: Reaktion, 2006.

Campbell, Neil. *Post-Westerns: Cinema, Region, West*. Lincoln: University of Nebraska Press, 2013.

Carter, Matthew. *Myth of the Western: New Perspectives on Hollywood's Frontier Narrative*. Edinburgh: Edinburgh University Press, 2014.

Cawelti, John. *The Six Gun Mystique Sequel*. Bowling Green, OH: Popular Press, 1999.

Corkin, Stanley. *Cowboys as Cold Warriors: The Western and U.S. History*. Philadelphia: Temple University Press, 2004.

Fisher, Austin. *Radical Frontiers in the Spaghetti Western: Politics, Violence and Popular Italian Cinema*. London: I. B. Tauris, 2014.

Frayling, Christopher. *Spaghetti Westerns: Cowboys and Europeans from Karl May to Sergio Leone*. London: I. B. Tauris, 2006.

French, Philip. *Westerns: Aspects of a Movie Genre*. Manchester: Carcanet Press, 2005.

Graulich, Melody, and Nicolas S. Witschi, eds. *Dirty Words in Deadwood: Literature and the Postwestern*. Lincoln: University of Nebraska Press, 2013.

Hearne, Joanna. *Native Recognition: Indigenous Cinema and the Western*. Albany: State University of New York Press, 2012.

Higgins, MaryEllen, Rita Keresztesi, and Dayna Oscherwitz, eds. *The Western in the Global South*. New York: Routledge, 2015.

Kites, Jim, and Gregg Rickman, Gregg, eds. *The Western Reader*. New York: Limelight Editions, 2004.

Kitses, Jim. *Horizons West: Directing the Western from John Ford to Clint Eastwood*. London: British Film Institute, 2004.

Howe, LeAnne, Harvey Markowitz, and Denise K. Cummings, eds. *Seeing Red: Hollywood's Pixeled Skins: American Indians and Film*. East Lansing: Michigan State University Press, 2013.

Kollin, Susan. *Captivating Westerns: The Middle East in the American West*. Lincoln: University of Nebraska Press, 2015.

Marrubio, M. Elise. *Killing the Indian Maiden: Images of Native American Women in Film*. Lexington: The University Press of Kentucky, 2006.

McGee, Patrick. *From Shane to Kill Bill: Rethinking the Western*. Malden, MA: Wiley-Blackwell, 2006.

McMahon, Jennifer L., and B. Steve Csaki, eds. *The Philosophy of the Western*. Lexington: University Press of Kentucky, 2010.

Nelson, Andrew Patrick, ed. *Contemporary Westerns: Film and Television since 1990*. London: Scarecrow Press, 2013.

Prats, Armando José. *Invisible Natives: Myth and Identity in the American Western*. Ithaca, NY: Cornell University Press, 2002.

Raheja, Michelle H. *Reservation Reelism: Redfacing, Visual Sovereignty, and Representations of Native Americans in Film*. Lincoln: University of Nebraska Press, 2011.

Simmon, Scott. *The Invention of the Western Film: A Cultural History of the Genre's First Half-Century*. Cambridge: Cambridge University Press, 2003.

Singer, Beverly. *Wiping the War Paint off the Lens: Native American Film and Video*. Minneapolis: University of Minnesota Press, 2001.

Tompkins, Jane. *West of Everything: The Inner Life of Westerns*. Oxford: Oxford University Press, 1993.

Walker, Janet, ed. *Westerns: Film through History*. New York: Routledge, 2001.

Wright, Will. *Sixguns and Society: A Structural Study of the Western*. Berkeley: University of California Press, 1977.

WESTERN NATURES AND ENVIRONMENTS

Beck, John. *Dirty Wars: Landscape, Power, and Waste in Western American Literature*. Lincoln: University of Nebraska Press, 2009.

Cella, Matthew J. C. *Bad Land Pastoralism in Great Plains Fiction*. Iowa City: University of Iowa Press, 2010.

Cronon, William. "The Trouble with Wilderness; or, Getting Back to the Wrong Nature." In *Uncommon Ground: Toward Reinventing Nature*, ed. William Cronon, 69–90. New York: Norton, 1995.

Davis, Mike. *City of Quartz: Excavating the Future in Los Angeles*. New York: Vintage, 1992.

Ecology of Fear: Los Angeles and the Imagination of Disaster. New York: Vintage, 1999.

Gamber, John Blair. *Positive Pollutions and Cultural Toxins: Waste and Contamination in Contemporary U.S. Ethnic Literatures*. Lincoln: University of Nebraska Press, 2012.

Harding, Wendy. *The Myth of Emptiness and the New American Literature of Place*. Iowa City: University of Iowa Press, 2014.

LeMenager, Stephanie. *Living Oil: Petroleum Culture in the American Century*. Oxford: Oxford University Press, 2014.

Lynch, Tom. *Xerophilia: Ecocritical Explorations in Southwestern Literature*. Lubbock: Texas Tech University Press, 2008.

Nash, Roderick. *Wilderness and the American Mind*, 3rd ed. New Haven, CT: Yale University Press, 1983.

Slovic, Scott, ed. *Getting Over the Color Green: Contemporary Environmental Literature of the Southwest*. Tucson: University of Arizona Press, 2001.

Solnit, Rebecca. *Savage Dreams: A Journey into the Hidden Wars of the American West*. 1994. Reprint; Berkeley: University of California Press, 2014.

Stegner, Wallace. *The American West as Living Space*. Ann Arbor: University of Michigan Press, 1987.

Index

Abbey, Edward, 84, 86, 90, 154, 247–9, 253, 375
About Schmidt (2002), 141
Accidental Explorer, The (Simpson), 198
Account, The (Cabeza de Vaca), 31, 212
Acosta, Oscar Zeta, 277
Across the Plains (Royce), 57
Acuña, Rodolfo F., 36
Adams, Ansel, 150
Adams, Rachel, 294n11, 295n16
Adamson, Joni, 294n6, 294n7
Adventures of Don Chipote, The (Venegas), 33
Adventures of Huckleberry Finn (Twain), 104
African American authors, 58, 140, 276, 314–28
African Americans, 40, 42, 43, 52–3, 91, 182
Agruss, David, 9
Aguilar-San Juan, Karin, 309
Alaska Native authors, 192–5, 203
Albano, John and Tony DeZuniga, 123
Alderson, Nannie T., 167, 171
Alexander, Christopher, 178
Alexie, Sherman, 123, 187, 189, 229, 349, 350,
    355–6, 378
All I Asking for Is My Body (Murayama), 306
All the Pretty Horses (McCarthy), 379
Allakariallak, 226
Allen, Chadwick, 10n1, 26
Allen, Paula Gunn, 145
Allmendinger, Blake, 329n2
Almanac of the Dead (Silko), 283, 284, 286–7
Alsultany, Evelyn Azeeza and Ella Habiba
    Shohat, 10n1
Altman, Robert, 339, 340
Alurista, 37
Always Coming Home (Le Guin), 183
America (Baudrillard), 350
America Is in the Heart (Bulosan), 300, 306
American Daughter (Thompson), 317
American Encounters (Limón), 221n37
American exceptionalism, 2, 37, 99, 135, 209,
    210, 375

American Indian authors, 15–30, 135, 145, 147–8,
    157, 169, 186–90, 192–204, 206, 252, 282–97
and comic books, 19
and Indigenous Futurism, 283
and Indigenous memory, 16, 18, 19, 25
and Lewis and Clark Expedition, 23
and mapping, 15, 17
and mixedblood narratives, 284
and tribalography, 27
American Indian Literature (Adamson), 294n6
American Indians, 52, 59, 77, 130, 185, 186, 215
in African American literature, 323
mounds and earthworks, 19
and pictographic systems, 26, 190
relation to white settler women, 50
resistance to settler colonialism, 52
and visual sovereignty, 226
"American Scholar, The" (Emerson), 75
Anderson, Lorraine and Thomas Edwards, 91
Angel Island, 299, 357
Anglos and Mexicans in the Making of Texas
    (Montejano), 146
Anthropocene, the, 244
Anzaldúa, Gloria, 10, 35, 93, 94, 146, 154, 156
Appadurai, Arjun, 207, 271
Appaloosa (2009), 342
Arab American authors, 3–4, 94, 147, 148–9
Arab Americans, 3
Aranda Jr., José F., 7
Arbutus/Madone Files, The (Ricou), 178
Armbruster, Karla and Kathleen Wallace, 91
Armstrong, Jeannette, 25
Aronson, Max, 233
Asian American authors, 181–3, 277, 278,
    298–311, 355, 356, 357, 378, 384, 385
*Assassination of Jesse James by the Coward Robert
    Ford, The* (2007), 341
Astoria (Irving), 68, 72
At Home on This Earth (Anderson), 91
Atlas of the New West (Riebsame), 167

Atomic Aztex (Foster), 94
Austin, Mary, 86, 89, 92, 107, 152, 153, 205
Authentic Narrative of the Seminole War
  (Godfrey), 52
authenticity, 154, 168, 170, 171, 258, 291
Autry, Gene, 334, 343n8
Avatar (2009), 332
Aveling, Edward and Eleanor Marx Aveling, 66
Aztlán, 37, 39, 156
Aztlán (Valdez and Steiner), 37

Bad Girls (1995), 340
Bad Indians (Miranda), 27
Bad Land (Raban), 138
Badlands (1973), 141
Bair, Julene, 138
Ballad of Little Jo, The (1993), 340
Bancroft, Hubert Howe, 72
Barryman, John, 140
Bartram, William, 84
Bass, Rick, 174
Bass, Rick and David James Duncan, 167
Baudrillard, Jean, 350
Bauer, Ralph, 219n13
Baum, L. Frank, 140
Bazin, André, 117, 336
Beadle's Half-Dime Library, 115
Bearheart (Vizenor), 283, 285, 288–92
Beat Back the Tide (Hitchens), 263
Beat Diaspora, the, 270, 274
Beat Generation, The (Gair), 279n9
Beats, the, 180, 270–9
Beats, The (Sterritt), 279n9
Beckwourth, James, 314, 320
Before the West Was West (Hamilton and
  Hillard), 6, 17
Bennett, Robert, 9
Bent Box (Maracle), 202
Berger, Thomas, 135
Bering, Vitus, 194
Berkove, Lawrence and Michael
  Kowalewski, 109
Bernardin, Susan, 7, 229
Between the Middle East and the Americas
  (Alsultany and Shohat), 10n1
Between Two Worlds (Paredes), 155
Beyond Nature Writing (Armbruster and
  Wallace), 91
BFI Companion to the Western, The (Buscombe),
  342n1
Bierce, Ambrose, 70, 76, 107
Big Jake (1971), 339
Big Sky, The (Guthrie), 242
Big Trail, The (1930), 334, 336
Billy the Kid (1930), 334

bioregionalism, 177, 181, 183
bioregions, 149, 168, 177
Bird, Isabella, 167, 171
Birth of a Nation, The (1915), 232
Black Atlantic, The (Gilroy), 92
Black Cultural Front, The (Dolinar), 330n22
Black Dahlia (Ellroy), 266
Black Echo, The (Connelly), 266
Black Mask, 257, 261
Black Nature, 85
Blackhawk, Ned, 21
Blain, Chris, 123
Blaser, Robin, 275
Blazing Saddles (1974), 111, 233
Blew, Mary Clearman, 174
Blonde Indian (Hayes), 203, 204n5
Blood Meridian (McCarthy), 150, 208, 367, 379
Blood Narrative (Allen), 26
Blood Run (Coke), 19
Blue, Annie, 199
Blueberry (Charlier and Giraud), 123
Blunt, Judy, 174
Boellstorff, Tom, 370
Boetticher, Budd, 336
Bogdonovich, Peter, 342n5
Bold, Christine, 6, 8, 111, 172
Bolton, Herbert Eugene, 31
Bolton, Matthew and D. A. Miller, 368
Bonnin, Gertrude, 23
Bontemps, Arna, 324–5
Books and Islands in Ojibwe Country
  (Erdrich), 26
Boone and Crockett Club, the, 234, 236
Boone, Daniel, 51, 332
border (U.S.-Canada), 178, 205
border (U.S.-Mexico), 32, 83, 93, 145, 146,
  147, 205, 208, 212, 287, 314, 354, 357, 382,
  384, 385
Border Fictions (Sadowski-Smith), 219n8
Border Trilogy (McCarthy), 213, 252, 379
borderlands studies, 1, 19, 31, 148, 149, 211
Borderlands/La Frontera (Anzaldúa), 10n1, 93,
  94, 156, 205
Bordwell, David, 338
Bowden, Charles, 354–5
Bower, B. M., 171, 172
Bowles, Paul, 274
Boyd, William, 334
Boyle, T. C., 249
Brady, Mary Pat, 87
Branch, Michael P., 7, 87
Brand, Max, 115
Braun, Bruce, 84
Brave Cowboy (Abbey), 375
Bridger, Mary Anne, 55

Bringing the Mountain Home (Campbell), 175
Brokeback Book, The (Handley), 174, 372n14
Brokeback Mountain (2005), 362, 363–71
"Brokeback Mountain" (Proulx), 174, 362, 367
Broken Arrow (1950), 332
Brooks, Gwendolyn, 140
Brooks, Mel, 111, 233
Brown and Green (Ybarra), 85
Bryant, William Cullen, 68
Buell, Lawrence, 88, 93, 138
Buffalo Bill (1944), 233
Buffalo Bill and the Indians (1976), 339
Buffalo Bill's Wild West show, 225, 226, 227, 333
Buffalo Dance (1894), 225, 227, 236
Buffalo for the Broken Heart (O'Brien), 138
Bukowski, Charles, 277
Bulosan, Carlos, 300
Bunn, Cullen and Brian Hurtt, 123
Burke, James Lee, 169
Burkhart, Matt, 305
Burnham, Michelle, 50
Burroughs, William, 270, 274, 378
Bus Stop (Inge), 136
Buscombe, Edward, 241n55, 342n1, 342n5
Butcher's Crossing (Williams), 378–9, 382
Butler, Judith, 369
Butler, Octavia, 183
B-Westerns, 334, 336
Byrd, Jodi A., 2, 16–17

Caballero (González and Raleigh), 146, 213
Cabeza de Vaca, Álvar Nuñez, 32, 212
Cabeza de Vaca, Fabiola, 39
Cain, James M., 259, 261, 262, 263, 266
Calderon, Hector, 155
California (Royce), 71
California Inter Pocula (Bancroft), 72
California, In-Doors and Out (Farnham), 69
Callahan, Alice S., 22–3
Callenbach, Ernest, 177, 183
Cameron, James, 332
Campbell, Mary Ellen and A. L. McReady, 211
Campbell, Neil, 10, 92, 131, 168, 205, 207, 210, 273, 348, 376
Campbell, SueEllen, 175
Canadian authors, 123, 180, 197, 198, 202
Candy Kid, The (Hughes), 262
capitalism, 69, 90, 114, 119, 121, 122, 206, 211, 212, 298, 310, 349, 353, 354, 356, 375, 382
Captivating Westerns (Kollin), 11n8, 219n9
captivity narratives, 50–1, 321, 332
Caramelo (Cisneros), 157
Carewe, Edwin, 228
Carewe, Horace, 233
Carey, Peter, 122

Caribou Ranch, 162–3
Carpenter, Cari, 21
Carver, Raymond, 179
Cascadia, 177
Cassady, Neal, 270
Castillo, Ana, 252
Castronovo, Russ and Susan Gillman, 209
Cather, Willa, 86, 132, 152–3, 205, 366, 368
cattle industry, 65, 215, 237, 252
Cawelti, John, 237, 337
Cazneau, Jane McManus Storm[s], 53
Celia's Song (Maracle), 202
Ceremony (Silko), 252, 283
Cervantes, Lorna Dee, 39
Cha, Theresa Hak Kyung, 307
Chandler, Raymond, 257, 259, 261–2, 265, 266, 267, 352
Changing is Not Vanishing (Parker), 19
Charlier, Jean-Michel and Jean Giraud, 123
Chicano/a authors, 31–45, 93, 94, 121, 145, 146, 147, 149, 153–8, 205, 213, 252, 384
Chicano/a movement, the, 34, 35, 37, 39, 40, 44
Chickencoop Chinaman, The (Chin), 303, 304
Chief Dallas Eagle, 26
Chief Dark Cloud, 232
Chief Running Deer, 231
Chief Seattle, 187
Childs, Craig, 168
Chill, The (Macdonald), 264
Chin, Frank, 303
China Men (Kingston), 304
Chinese American authors, 278, 303–5
Chinese Americans, 77, 105, 299–300, 303–4
Chinese Exclusion Act, the (1882), 299
Choup-nit-ki (Gay), 60
Cimino, Michael, 112
Cisneros, Sandra, 157, 213
Cities of the Plain (McCarthy), 379, 380
civil rights movement, the, 213, 216, 374
Clapp[e], Louise Amelia Knapp Smith, 57
Clark, Walter Van Tilburg, 121
Cleage, Pearl, 316, 318
Clifford, James, 271
climate change, 74, 178
Coates, Grace Stone, 174
Coen brothers, the, 340, 341, 342
Cogewea (Quintasket), 25
Coke, Allison Hedge, 19
Colbert, Stephen, 272
Cold War, the, 181, 352
Coleman, Wanda, 326
Collected Works of Billy the Kid, The (Ondaatje), 198
colonial adventure narratives, 6
coloniality, 5–6, 10, 146, 149, 157, 206, 208, 209, 212, 213, 385

Colors of Nature, The (Deming and Savoy), 91
Comer, Krista, 8, 82, 92, 168, 174, 219n8,
  220n18, 330n23, 347, 377
*Companion to the Literature and Culture of the
  American West, A* (Witschi), 166, 167,
  176n20, 218n3, 219n10
Conduct of Life, The (Emerson), 75
Connell, Evan S., 140
Connelly, Michael, 266–7
Conquest, The (Micheaux), 317
Constructing Nature (Jenseth and Lotto), 87
contact zones (Pratt), 32, 40, 154
Continental Divides (Adams), 294n11
Converging Stories (Myers), 85
Cook, Barbara and Alex Hunt, 91
Cook, James, 185, 194
Cook, Nancy S., 8
Cooper, Gary, 236, 335
Cooper, James Fenimore, 68, 112, 113, 205,
  332, 368
Corkin, Stanley, 120
Cormorant Hunter's Wife (Kane), 202
corrido, 121, 155
Costamos, George, 340
Costner, Kevin, 233, 331, 340
Cotera, María, 146
Cotera, Martha, 37
Coulthard, Glen, 296n23
counterculture, the, 178, 180, 183, 270, 277
Countering the Counterculture (Martinez), 279n7
Coupland, Douglas, 350–1
Courtesans of Flounder Hill, The (Hope), 202
Covered Wagon, The (1923), 228, 232
cowboys, 4, 65, 66, 73, 111, 115, 117, 121, 123, 136,
  251, 253, 303, 346, 368
Cowboys and Aliens (2011), 123, 236
"Cowboys and Gauchos" (Papanikolas), 219n8
Cox, James, 19
Crais, Robert, 265
Crane, Stephen, 99, 108, 205
Crevecoeur, St. John de, 84
critical regionalism, 1, 208, 210, 211, 218, 348,
  376, 386
Cronon, William, 85
Crossing Over (Martinez), 213
Crossing, The (McCarthy), 379
Cruikshank, Julie, 197
Crumley, James, 169, 264
Cruze, James, 228
Culpepper Cattle Co., The (1972), 339
Cultures of the American New West, The
  (Campbell), 359n10
Cungauyaraam Qulivai, 199
Curtiz, Michael, 335
Cushing, Frank, 150

Custer, Elizabeth Bacon, 56, 169
Cycles of Conquest (Spicer), 149

Dakota (Norris), 138, 140
Dalva (Harrison), 252
Daly, Carroll John, 257
Damon, Maria, 276
Dances with Wolves (1990), 233, 331, 332,
  340, 341
Danforth, Emily M., 174, 367
Dark at the Top of the Stairs, The (Inge), 136, 137
Dark End of the Street, The (Damon), 276
Darkness in Saint Louis Bearheart (Vizenor), 285
Darwin, Charles, 87
Dauenhauer, Nora Marks, 199
Dauenhauer, Nora Marks and Richard
  Dauenhauer, 192
Daughter of the Dawn (1920), 228
Daves, Delmer, 332
Davidson, Michael, 280n27
Davis, H. L., 180
Davis, Mike, 354, 382, 384
Davis, Robert, 200
Dawnland Voices (Senier), 17, 19
Day-Lewis, Daniel, 233
Days of Heaven (1978), 141
De Laguna, Federica, 197
De Quille, Dan, 102
Dead Man (1995), 340, 342
Deadwood (2004-2006), 122
Deadwood Dick Library, The (Beadle and
  Adams), 114
"Dear John Wayne" (Alexie), 349
Death Comes for the Archbishop (Cather), 150, 152
Death in a Bowl (Whitfield), 259
"Decolonial Reflections on Hemispheric
  Partitions" (Mignolo), 11n21
DeConnick, Kelly Sue and Emma Rios, 123
deep time, 138, 189
Deerslayer, The (Cooper), 112, 113
Deitch, Donna, 367
Del Rio, Dolores, 233
Delano, Alonzo, 69, 100
Deleuze, Gilles, 375, 386
Deloria Jr., Vine, 185, 186, 187, 291, 296n33
Deloria, Philip, 228, 238n9
DeMarinis, Rick, 169
DeMille, Cecil B., 234, 235, 335
Deming, Alison and Lauret Savoy, 91
Denning, Michael, 114
Denver, John, 162
Depp, Johnny, 233
Derrida, Jacques, 73, 78, 113
Desert Hearts (1985), 367
Desert Legends (Nabhan and Klett), 148

Desert Solitaire (Abbey), 86
DeShell, Jeffrey, 169
Destry Rides Again (1939), 335
Devil in a Blue Dress (Moseley), 327
DeVoto, Bernard, 67
deWitt, Patrick, 123
Dharma Bums (Kerouac), 179, 183
diaspora studies, 1, 92, 271
Díaz, Porfirio, 151
DICTEE (Cha), 307
Didion, Joan, 345–8, 355, 358
Dingess, Chris and Matthew Roberts, 123
Diosa y Hembra (Cotera), 37
DiPrima, Diane, 275
Dirty Little Billy (1972), 339
Dix, Richard, 233
Django Unchained (2012), 341
Do Glaciers Listen? (Cruikshank), 197
Doc (1971), 339
Dodge City (1939), 335
Dolinar, Brian, 330n22
Dominik, Andrew, 341
Dominion of Bears (Simpson), 198
Dos Passos, John, 256
Double Indemnity (Cain), 261
Douglass, Frederick, 85
Downing, Todd, 19
Doxtator, Deborah, 18
Doyle, Kirby, 275
Dragoti, Stan, 339
Dreamland (Bowden), 354, 357, 358
Drowning in Fire (Womack), 283, 284
Drumm, Sheila, 54
Dumas, Firoozeh, 1
Duncan, David James, 174
Duncan, Robert, 275
Dungy, Camille, 85
Dunning, John, 169
Dunwoody Pond (Janovy), 138
Durham, David Anthony, 323
Dwellings (Hogan), 130

Eagle Pass (Cazneau), 53
Earling, Debra Magpie, 169
Eastlake, William, 378
Eastman, Charles, 59
Eastwood, Clint, 331, 339
Eaton, Edith Maude (Sui Sin Far), 85, 304
ecocriticism, 91, 168, 169
ecocritics, 83, 88
Ecological Other, The (Ray), 84
Ecotopia (Callenbach), 177, 183
Edelman, Lee, 370
Edison, Thomas, 225
Egg and I, The (McDonald), 187

Eiseley, Loren, 141
El Dorado (1964), 336
El Laúd de Desterrado (Hernandez), 32
El Plan Espiritual de Aztlán (Alurista), 37
Elder, John and Robert Finch, 83
Elderbrush Gulch (1913), 232
Election (1999), 141
Ellis, Bret Easton, 352–3, 378
Ellroy, James, 266
Elsie's Business (Washburn), 23
Emerson, Ralph Waldo, 72, 75, 82, 379
Empires, Nationa, and Families (Hyde), 56
Encyclopedia of the Great Plains, The (Wishart), 130
Englishman's Boy, The (Vanderhaeghe), 198
environing, 243, 250, 252, 253
Erdrich, Heid, 24
Erdrich, Louise, 23, 26, 135, 141, 252, 283, 284
Espinosa, J. M., 39
Espinoza, Conrado, 33
Estevanico, 314, 320
Ethnoburb (Li), 309
Everett, Percival, 321–3
Evison, Jonathan, 123
Executive Order 9066, 182
Exodusters, 58, 316, 317
Expendable Man, The (Hughes), 263
Extinct Lands (Brady), 87
Eyman, Scott, 331, 341
Eyre, Chris, 229

Fabbrini, Sergio, 374
Fallen Forests (Kilcup), 91
Fan the Flames (The August Twenty-Ninth Movement), 37
Far Bright Star (Olmstead), 123
Farmer, Gary, 236
Farnham, Eliza, 69, 77, 79
Favata, Martin A. and José B. Fernández, 32
Favreau, Jon, 123, 236
Fedderson, Joe, 25
feminism, 1, 183, 209, 211, 271, 374
Feminism on the Border (Saldívar-Hull), 10n1
Ferber, Edna, 205, 212–18
Ferlinghetti, Lawrence, 275, 276
Fields, Alison, 233
Fight Club (Palahniuk), 350, 351, 358
Filipino/a American authors, 277, 300, 312n10
Filson, Joel, 51
Finch, John and Robert Finch, 85
Firefly (2002), 111
First Nations actors, 226
First Nations authors, 25, 197, 202, 209
Firsting and Lasting (O'Brien), 17
Fisher, Vardis, 170

Flesh to Bone (Silva), 213
Fletcher, Alice C., 60
Flight (Alexie), 123
Flores, Dan, 138
Flyin' West (Cleage), 318
Flynn, Errol, 335
Fools Crow (Welch), 169, 252
Foote, Horton, 137
Foote, Mary Hallock, 107
Ford, John, 233, 236, 331, 332, 333, 334, 335
Ford, Richard, 169
Foreman, Carl, 338
Fort Apache (1948), 332, 336
Foster, Sesshu, 94
Foucault, Michel, 67, 243
Fourth World, The (Manuel), 289
Fox, Finis and Wallace, 228
Frampton, Kenneth, 211
Frazier, Ian, 138
Free Land (Lane), 134
Freeman, Elizabeth, 370
Freitig, Florian and Kirsten A. Sandrock, 5
Fremont, Jesse Benton, 57
Fremont, John C., 171
French, Philip, 376
"Friday Night Shift at the Taco House Blues
      (Wah-Wah)" (Coleman), 326
From Sand Creek (Ortiz), 22
Frontier Club, The (Bold), 6, 172, 234
Frontier Lady, A (Royce), 70
"Frost Rides Alone" (McCoy), 260
Full Body Burden (Iversen), 169
Fuller, Alexandra, 169
Funny in Farsi (Dumas), 1
fur trade, 65, 68, 69, 72
Fus Fixico Letters, The (Posey), 20

Gabriel, Ralph Henry, 57, 71
Gabriel's Story (Durham), 323
Gair, Christopher, 279n9
Gallagher, Tag, 237
Gallagher, Tess, 178, 185
Galperin, Patricia, 230
Galvin, James, 169, 173, 174
Gamber, John, 9, 295n21
Gangster of Love (Hagedorn), 277
Gay, E. Jane, 60
Generation X (Coupland), 350–1
Geographical Imaginations (Gregory), 360n44
George Washington Gomez (Paredes), 155
Georgi-Findlay, Brigitte, 61n1
Gerby, George Horatio, 101
Geronimo (1993), 340
Get Shorty (Leonard), 267
Giant (1956), 212

Giant (Ferber), 212–18
Giants in the Earth (Rølvaag), 132
Gibson, William, 384
Gidden, Anthony, 360n44
Gilroy, Paul, 92
Ginsberg, Allen, 184, 270, 272, 274, 275
"Girl Who Married the Bear, The"
      (McClellan), 197
Glancy, Diane, 23
Glitz (Connelly), 267
"Global West, The" (Kollin), 208
globalization, 1, 3, 4–6, 77, 92, 146, 168, 174,
      178, 181, 205, 274, 298, 305, 310, 348, 354,
      384, 385
God Sends Sunday (Bontemps), 324
God's Country (Everett), 321–2
Goeman, Mishuana, 24, 294n6, 295n19
Going Over East (Hasselstrom), 138
Gold Rush, 57, 65, 69, 70, 75, 76, 77, 99, 101
Gomez-Peña, Guillermo, 384
Gone Fishin' (Moseley), 328
Gonzales, Rodolfo, 37
González, Jovita, 35, 36, 154, 213
González, Jovita and Eve Raleigh, 146
Good Life (Cabeza de Vaca, F.), 39
Goodale, Elaine, 59
Goodman, Audrey, 8
Goodwin, Elizabeth "Sister," 200, 202
Grace, Nancy M. and Jennie Skerl, 279n3
Grapes of Wrath, The (Steinbeck), 134
Grassland (Manning), 138
Graulich, Melody, 11n9
Graulich, Melody and Stephen Tatum, 219n8
Gray, Zane, 205
"Great Falls" (Ford), 169
Great Plains (Frazer), 138
Great Train Robbery, The (1903), 116, 229–30,
      233, 236, 237
Green, Paul, 199
Green, Rayna, 238n9
Greenwald, Maggie, 340
Gregory, Derek, 360n44
Grey, Zane, 112, 115, 118, 120, 150, 151–2, 251
Griffith, D. W., 232
Griffiths, Alison, 232
Grinnell, George Bird, 234
Guardians of the Galaxy, The (2014), 123
Guercio, James, 162
Guerra, Alirio Díaz, 32
Gunfighter, 123
Gunn, James, 123
Gunning, Tom, 225, 229
Gus and His Gang (Blain), 123
Guthrie, Jr., A. B., 67, 174, 205
Guthrie, Woody, 141

Haa Shuká, Our Ancestors (Dauenhauer and Dauenhauer), 192
Hagedorn, Jessica, 277
"Haida Manga" (Yahgulanaas), 19, 202
Haines, John, 197
Halaby, Laila, 3
Halberstam, Jack, 368, 370
Hall, James, 51
Hall, Janet Campbell, 174
Hall, Stuart, 378
Halverson, Cathryn, 171
Hamilton, Amy T. and Tom J. Hillard, 6–7, 17
Hammett, Dashiell, 115, 257, 258
Hammon and the Beans, The (Paredes), 155
Handley, William R., 118, 174, 372n14
Hansen, Miriam, 233
Hansen, Ron, 140
hard-boiled fiction, 256–68
Harjo, Joy, 140
Harris, Ed, 342
Harrison, Jim, 173, 252
Hart, William S., 334
Harte, Bret, 70, 76, 98, 99, 105, 107, 366, 367
Harte, William S., 235
Hartley, Marsden, 150
Hasselstrom, Linda, 138, 141
Hathaway, Henry, 339
Having It Both Ways (Robinson), 125n34
Hawks, Howard, 331, 336
Hayes, Ernestine, 8, 203
Hearne, Joanna, 229, 237
Heart of the Monster, The (Bass and Duncan), 167
Heartland (1979), 171
Heath Anthology of American Literature, The (Lauter et al.), 31
Heat-Moon, William Least, 131, 138–9
Heaven's Gate (1980), 112, 340
Heise, Ursula, 92, 360n44
"Hell's Pay Check" (Nebel), 261
Hemingway, Ernest, 256, 368
hemispheric studies, 156, 207, 219n13, 298
Hernández, José Elias, 32
heteronormativity, 362, 365, 369, 371
heterosexual melancholia, 369
heterosexuality, 212, 362, 363, 366
Higgins, MaryEllen, Rita Keresztesi, and Dayna Oscherwitz, 11n9
High Noon (1952), 236, 331, 336
High Plains Drifter (1973), 339
Highsmith, Patricia, 263
Highway, Tomson, 202
Hill, Walter, 340
Hillcoat, John, 122
Hillerman, Tony, 115

Himes, Chester, 325–6, 327
Hinton, S. E., 140
Hitchens, Dolores, 263
Hogan, Linda, 130, 284
Homesman, The (2014), 341, 342
Homestead Act, the (1862), 58
Homestead Acts (1862-1916), 138
Homesteader, The (1918), 317
Homesteader, The (Micheaux), 317
homophobia, 322–3, 365, 367
homosexuality, 363, 366
homosociality, 362, 363, 364, 365, 366, 367
Hondo (L'Amour), 116, 246–7
Honey in the Horn (Davis), 180
Hoo-Doo Cowboys and Bronze Buckaroos (Johnson), 329n7
Hope III, Andrew, 202
Hope, Ishmael Angaluuk, 202, 203
Hopkins, Pauline, 58
Horizons West (Kitses), 337
Horton, Jessica L., 16
House Made of Dawn (Momaday), 283
House Un-American Activities Committee, 336
Housekeeping (Robinson), 184
How to Read the American West (Wyckoff), 4
Howe, LeAnne, 19, 27, 283, 284
Howl (Ginsberg), 184, 272, 275
Hseu, Jane, 9
Hsu, Hsuan, 4, 298
Hudson, Lois Phillips, 135, 140
Hughes, Dorothy, 262
Hughes, Langston, 140
Hummingbird's Daughter, The (Urrea), 157
Hunt, Alex, 218n3
Huntington, Sydney, 199
Hutson, Richard, 235
Hyde, Anne, 55
Hyperboreal (Kane), 202

I am Eskimo, Aknik My Name (Green), 199
I am Joaquín (Gonzales), 37
If He Hollers Let Him Go (Himes), 325
IHotel (Yamashita), 355, 357, 358
Imagining the African American West (Allmendinger), 329n2
Immigrant Acts (Lowe), 10n1, 299
In a Lonely Place (Hughes), 262
In the Land of the Grasshopper Song (Ellicott and Reed), 59
Ince, Thomas, 227
Indian Cartography (Miranda), 16
Indian Country Today (Smith), 15
Indian Journal, 20
Indian Killer (Alexie), 350, 351, 353, 355–6, 358
Indian Map (Smith), 15

Indian Relocation Act, the (1830), 282
Indians of the Pacific Northwest (Deloria), 185
Ingalls, Charles, 59
Inge, William, 136–7
Injuns! (Buscombe), 241n55
internment camps, 181, 182, 301, 310, 385
Into Great Silence (Saulitis), 198
Iranian American authors, 1–2
Iranian Americans, 1
Irmscher, Christoph, 95n9
Iron Horse, The (1924), 233, 334
Irving, Washington, 68, 72
Ishi, 17–18
Ishi and the Wood Ducks (Vizenor), 18
Island (Lai, Lim, and Yung), 300
Iversen, Kristin, 169
Ivey, Eowyn, 198

Jackson, Andrew, 282
Jackson, Jon A., 169
Jacoby, Karl, 85
Jameson, Fredric, 348, 352, 353
Janovy Jr., John, 138
Japanese American authors, 181–3, 301–3, 306, 310, 355, 384–6
Jaramillo, Cleofas, 153, 154
Jarmusch, Jim, 340, 342
Jarrar, Randa, 3–4
Jasmine (Bharati), 305
Jefferson, Thomas, 83, 84
Jenkins, Henry, 230
Jeremiah Johnson (1972), 233
Jesse James (1939), 335
Jiconténcal (Varela), 32
Joaquin Murieta (Ridge), 213
John Ford (Bogdonovich), 342n5
"John Wayne" (Didion), 345–8
Johnson County War, 112
Johnson, Denis, 169
Johnson, Dorothy M., 116
Johnson, Michael K., 329n7
Johnson, Susan Lee, 57
Johnson, Walter, 199
Jolly, Michelle E., 57
Jonah Hex (Albano and DeZuniga), 123
Jones, Daryl, 115
Jones, Gayl, 213
Jones, Tommy Lee, 341, 342
Journals of Lewis and Clark, The, 68
Journey to the United States of America (Zavala), 32
Justice, Daniel, 18
Justified (2010), 115

Kane, Joan, 202
Kansas (Robinson), 58

Kantner, Seth, 198
Kaplan, Amy, 83
Kaplan, Jonathan, 340
Kasdan, Lawrence, 340
Kaufman, Bob, 276–7, 278
Kaufman, Moises, 367
Kawagley, Angayuqaq Oscar, 199
Keegan, Bridget and James McKusick, 89
Keep the Change (McGuane), 251
Kees, Weldon, 140
Kelton, Elmer, 116
Kerouac, Jack, 179, 181, 183, 185, 270, 271, 276, 278
Kesey, Ken, 178, 180, 184–5, 188, 277
Kilcup, Karen, 91
Killer Inside Me, The (Thompson), 261
Killing Custer (Welch), 169
Kim, Claire, 299
Kim, Elaine, 303
Kincaid, Jamaica, 83
King, Henry, 335
King, Thomas, 202
Kingsolver, Barbara, 252
Kingston, Maxine Hong, 278, 304
Kirkland, Caroline, 51
Kitses, Jim, 337
Kittredge, William, 172–3, 174
Klein, Kirwin Lee, 376
Kloefkorn, William, 141
Knight, Brenda, 279n7
Knobloch, Frieda, 96n41, 376
Kogawa, Joy, 198
Kollin, Susan, 11n8, 95, 96n40, 167, 168, 208, 372n11, 376–7
Koolhaus, Rem, 351, 354
Kooser, Ted, 140
Korean American authors, 307–8
Kosek, Jake, 86
Kowalewski, Michael, 70
Kroeber, Alfred, 18
Kurosawa, Akira, 122
Kyger, Joanne, 275

L.A. Confidential (Ellroy), 266
La Shelle, Kirke, 235
labor, 66, 69, 72, 77
Lady's Life in the Rocky Mountains, A (Bird), 171
Lamantia, Philip, 275
Lamont, Victoria, 112, 176, 176n18
L'Amour, Louis, 116, 246
Lancaster, Burt, 339
Land of Little Rain, The (Austin), 86
Landscapes of the New West (Comer), 92
Lane, Rose Wilder, 134
Laramie Project, The (Kaufman), 367

Last Best Place, The (Kittredge and Smith), 172
Last Frontier, The (1926), 232
Last Good Kiss, The (Crumley), 265
Last Kind Words Saloon, The (McMurtry), 123
Last of the Mohicans (1992), 233
Last Picture Show, The (McMurtry), 135
"Last Wolf, The" (TallMountain), 200
Laughing Without an Accent (Dumas), 1
Lauter, Paul, 31
Lawrence, D. H., 150
Le Guin, Ursula, 183–4, 185
Leal, Luis, 39
Learning from Las Vegas (Venturi), 349
"Leatherstocking Tales, The" (Cooper), 68,
   112, 332
Leaves of Grass (Whitman), 86
Leaving Resurrection (Saulitis), 198
Lee, A. Robert, 279n3
Lee, Ang, 362
Lee, Stan and Jack Kirby, 123
Legacy of Conquest, The (Limerick), 149
Legend of Colton H. Bryant, The (Fuller), 169
Legends of the Fall (Harrison), 173
"Legend of Miss Sasagawara, The"
   (Yamamoto), 301
Legends of the West (Hall), 51
Lehane, Dennis, 265
Lehman, David, 262
LeMay, Alan, 321
LeMenager, Stephanie, 8, 169, 218n3, 350
Leonard, Elmore, 116, 259, 267–8
Leone, Sergio, 122
Leopold, Aldo, 86
Less Than Zero (Ellis), 352, 358
Letters of a Woman Homesteader (Stewart), 171
Levi-Strauss, Claude, 337
Lewis and Clark Expedition, the, 50, 166, 185
Lewis, Alfred Henry, 66
Lewis, Nathaniel, 168, 170
Li, Wei, 309
Life Among the Piutes (Winnemucca), 21
Life and Adventures of James P. Beckwourth, The
   (Beckwourth), 315
Life and Adventures of Joaquin Murieta, The
   (Ridge), 20
Life and Adventures of Nat Love, The (Love),
   121, 315
Life Crossing Borders (Tafolla), 33
Life Lived Like a Story (Cruikshank), 197
Life on the Plains and Among the Diggings
   (Delano), 69, 100
Life Woven with Song (Dauenhauer), 199
Light on the Tent Wall, The (TallMountain), 200
Limerick, Patricia Nelson, 87, 149
Limón, José, 146, 211, 221n37, 221n56

Linnaeus, Carl, 83, 84
Literary History of the American West, A
   (Westbrook), 163, 165, 170
literary marketplace, 66–7, 73, 99
"Literature of Mining Camps, The" (Berkove
   and Kowalewski), 109n1
Literature and Nature (Keegan and
   McKusick), 89
Little Big Man (1970), 332, 339
Little Big Man (Berger), 135
Little House on the Prairie (Wilder), 59
Little Saigons (Aguilar-San Juan), 309
local color writing, 77, 99
"Local Rock and Global Plastic" (Heise),
   360n44
London, Jack, 108
Lone Ranger and Tonto Fistfight in Heaven, The
   (Alexie), 187, 189
Lone Ranger, The (2013), 123, 233
Lonely Are the Brave (1962), 375
Lonely Are the Brave (Abbey), 375–6
Lonely Crusade (Himes), 325, 326
Lonesome Dove (McMurtry), 150
Long Goodbye, The (Chandler), 352
Longmire (2012), 115
Lord, Nancy, 198
Lost Lady, A (Cather), 133, 136
Loucks, Georgina, 204
Love Medicine (Erdrich), 135
Love, Nat, 121, 315–16, 368
Lowe, Lisa, 10n1, 299
Lucas Guevara (Guerra), 32
Luck of Roaring Camp, The (Harte), 107
"Luck of Roaring Camp, The" (Harte), 77, 366, 367
Luhan, Mabel Dodge, 150
Luke, Timothy, 243
Lummis, Charles, 150
Lyman, Beecher, 52
Lynch, Tom, 219n8
Lyon, Thomas, 88

Macdonald, Ross, 257, 261, 264, 265, 267
MacLane, Mary, 174
magic realism, 147, 157–8, 310, 320, 384
Magnificent Seven, The (1960), 331
Magoffin, Susan Shelby, 54
Maher, Susan Naramore, 8
Makowski, Thomas, 236
Malaeska (Stephens), 226
Malcolm X, 140
Malick, Terrence, 141
Maltby, Richard, 339
Man Who Shot Liberty Valance, The (1962), 336
Manfred, Frederick, 135
Mangold, James, 341

Manifest and Other Destinies (LeMenager), 218n3
Manifest Destiny, 33, 34, 37, 41, 83, 130, 134, 210, 317, 375
Manifest Destiny (Dingess and Roberts), 123
Mann, Anthony, 336
Mann, Michael, 233
Manning, Richard, 138
Manuel, George, 289
Map of Home, A (Jarrar), 3
Maracle, Lee, 202
Mark My Words (Goeman), 24, 294n6
Marlatt, Daphne, 180
Marriage, Violence, and the Nation in the American Literary West (Handley), 125n24
Marsden, Michael T. and Jack Nachbar, 339
Marsh, George Perkins, 84
Marshall, George, 335
Martinez, Manuel Luis, 279n7
Martinez, Oscar, 149
Martinez, Ruben, 213
Marx, Leo, 90
masculinity, 68, 118, 121, 136, 151, 303, 363, 366, 368, 382
Massey, Doreen, 92
Mather, Elsie, 194
Matthews, Anne, 138
Mattox, Jake D., 57
McCabe and Mrs. Miller (1971), 339
McCarthy, Cormac, 150, 208, 213, 252, 323, 340, 367, 378, 379–81
McCarthy, Joseph, 336
McCarthy, Mary, 256
McClellan, Catherine, 197
McClure, Michael, 275
McCoy, Horace, 260
McDonald, Betty, 186
McDonald, Craig, 265
McElrath, Frances, 112
McGarrity, Michael, 265
McGee, Patrick, 120
McGuane, Thomas, 173, 250–2, 253
McHarg, Ian, 166
McMaster, Gerald, 21
McMurtry, Larry, 123, 135, 150, 378
McNickle, D'Arcy, 169, 206
McPhee, John, 169, 174
McTeague (Norris), 78, 357
McWilliams, Carey, 38, 312n10
Meadow, The (Galvin), 169, 173
Meek, Helen, 55
Meek's Cutoff (2010), 111, 342
Megquier, Mary Jane, 57
Meloy, Ellen, 154
Memory Map (Smith), 15
Mena, María Cristina, 35, 38

Merasty, Billy, 236
Merchant, Carolyn, 85
Mermann-Jozwiak, Elisabeth, 356
Mexican American War, 37, 39, 40
Meyer, Philipp, 123
Michaels, Walter Benn, 120
Micheaux, Oscar, 140, 172, 316–17, 323
Mignolo, Walter, 5–6, 10, 146, 206, 208, 210, 216
Miike, Takashi, 122
Miko Kings (Howe), 27, 283
Miller, Arthur, 137
Miller, Joaquin, 70
Miller, Perry, 84
Milner, Clyde, 56
mining, 77, 98–9
 as extended metaphor, 75, 77, 79
Minor Characters (Johnson), 279n7
Miranda, Deborah, 27
Miseducation of Cameron Post, The (Danforth), 367
Mitchell, Lee Clark, 9, 363, 364, 365
Mix, Tom, 334
"model minority," 298
Modern American Counter-Writing (Lee), 279n3
modernity, 6, 34, 68, 113, 117, 133, 151, 155, 162, 173, 184, 208, 210, 230, 231, 233, 237, 272
Mojica, Monique, 19, 232
Momaday, N. Scott, 19, 137, 141, 283
Monkey-Wrench Gang, The (Abbey), 248
Montejano, David, 146
Moore, David, 148
Moraga, Cherríe, 35
Morgan, Louis Henry, 59
Mormons, 56, 116, 117–19, 152
Morris, Wright, 129, 130, 131, 135
Morrison, Toni, 58
Mosley, Walter, 327–8
Mosquito (Jones), 213
Mountains of California (Muir), 86
Mrs. Spring Fragrance and Other Writings (Eaton/Sui Sin Far), 304
Muir, John, 86, 90, 177
Mukherjee, Bharati, 305
Mulford, Prentice, 76
Munby, Jonathan, 9
Murayama, Milton, 306
Murphy, Jacqueline Shea, 227
My Ántonia (Cather), 132, 133
"My Father's Love Letters" (Gallagher), 178
My First Summer in the Sierra (Muir), 86
My Old People's Stories (Cruikshank), 197
Myers, Jeffrey, 84, 85, 91, 94

Nabhan, Gary Paul, 94, 147
Nabhan, Gary Paul and Mark Klett, 148

Naked Spur, The (1953), 336
Nanook of the North (1922), 226
Narrative of the Life of Mrs. Mary Jemison
    (Seaver), 50
Nash, Roderick, 82, 245
National Geographic, 74
Nations Within, The (Deloria), 296n33
Native Seattle (Thrush), 27
natural history, 83–4, 88, 93, 168
    relation to African slave trade, 84
    relation to nature essay, 83, 89
Nature (Emerson), 379
nature essay, 82–5
    role in U.S. expansion, 82, 83, 89
nature writing, 82, 94, 140
    and racial exclusions, 83, 84, 85, 86, 89
    and the pastoral, 90
    and the sublime, 85, 90, 91
    treatment of urban space, 91
Nature's State (Kollin), 95n19
Neale, Steve, 338
Nebel, Frederick, 261
Nebraska (2013), 141
Neihardt, John, 140
Nelson, Andrew Patrick, 9
Nelson, Ralph, 339
Nelson, Richard, 198
neoliberalism, 209, 211, 294n7
"New Americanists" (Pease), 219n7
New Home, Who'll Follow, A (Kirkland), 51
New Western History, the, 78, 83, 338
Nisei, 181
Nisei Daughter (Sone), 181, 182
No Country for Old Men (2007), 340
No Country for Old Men (McCarthy), 381
Nobody's Angel (McGuane), 250
noir fiction, 261
No-No Boy (Okada), 181
Noodin, Margaret, 18
Norris, Frank, 78, 108, 357
Norris, Kathleen, 138, 140
Northline (Vlautin), 381–4
Norton Book of Nature Writing (Elder and
    Finch), 83
nostalgia, 68, 73, 90, 91, 132, 154, 293, 347
Notes from a Native Daughter (Didion), 358
Notes on the State of Virginia (Jefferson), 83
"'Nothing But Land'" (Lynch), 219n8
Nothing But Trouble (McGarrity), 265
Nye, Edward Wilson, 107

O Pioneers! (Cather), 132, 140
Oakley, Annie, 333
O'Brien, Dan, 138
O'Brien, Jean, 17

Obscure Destinies (Cather), 133, 137
Occupied America (Acuña), 36
O'Connor, James, 90
Ogallala Road, The (Bair), 138
Okada, John, 181–2
O'Keeffe, Georgia, 150
Oklahoma! (Rodgers and Hammerstein), 134
Okpik, Dg Nanouk, 201
Old Jules (Sandoz), 132
O'Leary, Mercedes, 197
Olmstead, Robert, 123
Olsen, Tillie, 134
On the Road (Kerouac), 271, 277
Once in a Promised Land (Halaby), 3
Ondaatje, Michael, 198
One Degree West (Bair), 138
One Flew Over the Cuckoo's Nest (1975), 184
One Flew Over the Cuckoo's Nest (Kesey), 184
One of Ours (Cather), 133
Open Range (2004), 340
Ordinary Affects (Stewart), 383
Ordinary Wolves (Nelson), 198
Oregon Experiment, The (Alexander), 178
Oregon Trail, the, 56
Oregon Trail, The (Parkman), 68
Orphans' Home Cycle, The (Foote), 137
Ortego, Philip D., 36
Ortiz, Simon, 21–2, 169
O'Sullivan, Timothy, 150
Otero, Miguel Antonio, 38, 39, 40–4
Other Asias (Spivak), 211
Otsuka, Julie, 301
Outback narratives, 6
"Outcasts of Poker Flat, The" (Harte), 77
Outka, Paul, 84, 85, 89, 93
Outlaw Josey Wales, The (1976), 339
Owens, Louis, 28, 189, 284
Ox-Bow Incident, The (Clark), 121

Pacific Rim, 1, 168, 298, 306, 310
Packard, Chris, 368
"Painting the Legend" (Buscombe), 342n5
Palahniuk, Chuck, 350
Palmer, Daryl W., 142n13
Papanikolas, Zeese, 219n8
Paradise (Morrison), 58
Paredes, Américo, 35, 36, 39, 121, 145, 147,
    154–6, 213
Parker, Robert Dale, 19, 24
Parkman, Francis, 68
"Pastorale" (Cain), 261
Pauley, Thomas H., 118
Payne, Alexander, 141
Peacock, Doug, 168
Pease, Donald, 36, 219n7

Peck, Gregory, 339
Peckinpah, Sam, 339
Pelecanos, George, 265
Penn, Arthur, 332, 340
Perma Red (Earling), 169
Perry, Frank, 339
petromodernity, 350, 351
Phan, Aimee, 308
Philippon, Daniel, 88
Phillips, Dana, 9
Picnic (Inge), 136
Picturesque California (Muir), 177
"Piksinñaq" (Goodwin), 199
Pippin, Robert, 119
plaasroman (African farm novel), 6
"Plain Language from Truthful James" (Harte), 98, 107
Plains Song (Morris), 129, 131
Plainsman, The (1936), 335
Playing Indian (Deloria), 238n9
Plea for the West (Beecher), 52
Pleasants, Mary Ellen, 57
Pocho (Villareal), 39
Poe, Edgar Allan, 112
Poetics of Natural History, The (Irmscher), 95n9
Pollack, Sydney, 233
Porter, Edwin S., 116, 229
Porter, Katherine Anne, 140
Portis, Charles, 321
Portlandia (2011), 178
Posey, Alexander, 20, 21
Posse (1993), 340
postcolonial studies, 4, 146, 209, 293, 305
"Postcolonial West" (Hunt), 218n3
"Postfrontier Horizons" (Tatum), 280n23, 386n13
postindian, the (Vizenor), 377
Postliterary America (Damon), 276
Postman Always Rings Twice, The (Cain), 261
Postmetropolis (Soja), 359n7
postmodernism, 9, 34, 45n3, 92, 156, 187, 190, 211, 309, 310, 348, 349, 353, 355, 358, 382, 386
Postwestern Cultures (Kollin), 11n8, 96n40, 220n21, 312n13, 359n11, 376, 387n14
post-western history, 376
post-western studies, 5, 74, 83, 86, 92, 274, 275, 376
post-westerns, 374–86
Post-Westerns (Campbell), 378
Power of the Dog, The (Savage), 366
Power, Tyrone, 335
Powers, Paul S., 115
"Powwow at the End of the World" (Alexie), 189
Prairie Time (White), 138
Prairies, The, 251

PrairyErth (Heat-Moon), 131, 138–9
Prats, Armando, 233
Pratt, Mary Louise, 32, 40, 154
Pretty Deadly (DeConnick and Rios), 123
Price, John T., 130
"Problem of the Popular, The" (Tatum), 12n26, 78
Professor's House, The (Cather), 152
Pronzini, Bill, 265
Proposition, The (2005), 122
Proulx, Annie, 174, 362, 378
Pullman, Bill, 236
Pynchon, Thomas, 384

Quammen, David, 168
Quantic, Diane, 131
queer desire, 364, 366
queer theory, 369, 370
queerness, 136, 156, 174, 276, 364, 366, 367, 369
    suppression of in Westerns, 366, 367
Quick and the Dead, The (1994), 340
Quijano, Anibal and Immanuel Wallerstein, 206, 210
Quintasket, Christine, 24–5

Raban, Jonathan, 138
Race and Nature from Transcendentalism to the Harlem Renaissance (Outka), 85, 93
Race and Politics (Saito), 309
Racette, Sherry Farrell, 25
Rader, Dean, 28n1
Raheja, Michelle, 226
Raimi, Sam, 340
Ramona (1928), 228
Ramos, Manuel, 169
Ranch Life and the Hunting-Trail (Roosevelt), 65, 68, 72
Raven's Gift, The (Reardon), 198
Rawhide Kid (Lee), 123
Ray, Sarah Jaquette, 8, 84
Reading Asian American Literature (Wong), 311n3
Reading the Roots (Branch), 88
Reading The Virginian in the New West (Graulich and Tatum), 219n8
Real Billy the Kid, The (Otero), 39, 40
Reardon, Don, 198
Rebel, The (Villegas de Magnon), 33
Recovery Project, The, 31, 32, 34, 40, 45
Red Dead Redemption (2010), 111
Red Desert (Proulx), 174
Red Harvest (Hammett), 115
Red Land to the South, The (Cox), 19
Red River (1948), 331, 336
Red Wing, Princess, 228, 237
Redford, Robert, 233

"Redefining Home" (Zepeda), 147
Redskin (1929), 229
Reed, Ishmael, 111, 318–21, 378
Reichardt, Kelly, 111, 342
Remington, Frederic, 77, 333
Return of Frank James, The (1940), 335
Revard, Carter, 140
"Revising Western Criticism through Wanda
    Coleman" (Comer), 330n23
Rhizomatic West, The (Campbell), 10n1, 92, 273
Richard, Dick, 339
Ricou, Laurie, 177
Riders of the Purple Sage (Grey), 112, 118, 121,
    151, 242
Ridge, John Rollin, 20, 21, 213
Rio Bravo (1959), 331
Rio Grande (1950), 336
Rio, David, 3
Rising From the Plains (McPhee), 169
Rivera, Tomás, 35
Road Home, The (Harrison), 252
Robinson, Cecil, 39
Robinson, Forrest G., 121
Robinson, Marilynne, 184, 378
Robinson, Sara Tappan Lawrence, 58
Rock, Howard, 199
Rogers, Roy, 334
Rogers, Will, 231
Rølvaag, O. E., 132
Romance of a Little Village Girl (Jaramillo), 153
Romero, Diego, 19
Roosevelt, Theodore, 5, 19, 44, 65, 66, 67,
    68, 72, 73, 84, 120, 134, 151, 172, 234,
    343n15, 368
Roughing It (Twain), 20, 70, 104
Round House, The (Erdrich), 23
Round, Phillip, 21
Rowe, John Carlos, 209
Rowlandson, Mary, 332
Royce, Josiah, 71
Royce, Sarah, 57, 70–1, 74
Ruiz de Burton, María Amparo, 33, 35, 36, 39,
    41, 53, 85
Rule, Jane, 367
Rustler, The (McElrath), 112

Sacajawea, 23
Sacramento Bee, 20
Sadowski-Smith, Claudia, 219n8
Sagebrush School, the, 102
"Saginaw Bay" (Davis), 200
Saito, Leland, 309
Salal (Ricou), 177
Saldívar, José David, 219n6
Saldívar, Ramón, 358

Saldívar-Hull, Sonia, 10n1
"Salmon Boy" (Wagoner), 188
San Francisco Renaissance, The (Davidson),
    280n27
Sand County Almanac (Leopold), 86
Sanders, Ashley R., 49
Sandoz, Mari, 132
Saorevo, 232
Saulitis, Eva, 198
Savage, Candace, 130, 140
Savage, Thomas, 174, 366
Scarborough, Dorothy, 132
Schaefer, Jack, 366
Scharff, Virginia, 54, 376
Scharnhorst, Gary, 79
Schertzinger, Victor, 229
Schoolcraft, Jane Johnston, 24
science fiction, 183
Scott, Randolf, 336
Sea of Grass, The (Richter), 242
Searchers, The (1956), 321, 331, 332, 336, 349
Seitz, George B., 232, 233
Seltzer, Mark, 372n13
Senier, Siobhan, 19
Sense of Place, Sense of Planet (Heise), 92
Service, Robert, 198
settler colonial studies, 1, 212, 213, 282
settler colonialism, 16, 31, 49, 51, 122, 130, 135,
    178, 205, 206, 208, 209, 213, 214, 215, 216,
    282, 285, 286, 293
"Settler Sovereignty" (Young), 220n19
Seven Men From Now (1956), 336
Shadows on the Koyukuk (Huntington), 199
Shane (1953), 117, 236, 331, 336
Shane (Schaefer), 366
Shaw, Joseph T., 257
She Wore a Yellow Ribbon (1949), 333, 336
Shell Shaker (Howe), 284
Shepard, Matthew, 367
Sherlock Holmes (Conan Doyle), 115
Sherman, George, 339
Shooting Cowboys and Indians (Smith), 342n6
Shootist, The (1976), 339
Shumaker, Peggy, 198
Siegel, Don, 339
*Significance of the Frontier in American History,
    The* (Turner), 280n12
Silko, Leslie Marmon, 18, 26, 145, 157, 252,
    286–7, 378
Silook, Susie, 201
Silva, Ire'ne Lara, 213
Silverheels, Jay, 233
Simmon, Scott, 227, 237
Simpson, Sherry, 198
Sisters Brothers, The (deWitt), 123

Sixth Gun, The (Bunn and Hurtt), 123
Slotkin, Richard, 120, 226, 237, 332
Slouching Toward Bethlehem (Didion), 345
Smiley, Jane, 140
Smith, Andrew Brodie, 342n6
Smith, Anna Deveare, 327
Smith, Helena Huntington, 172
Smith, Henry Nash, 117, 245, 302, 343n15
Smith, Jaune Quick-to-See, 15–16, 25, 27
Smoke Signals (1998), 189, 229, 232
Snyder, Gary, 177, 179, 181, 183, 275, 276
So Far from God (Castillo), 252
Sohn, Stephen Hong, 301
Soja, Edward, 349, 359n7
Soldier Blue (1970), 339
Solnit, Rebecca, 154
Something to Be Desired (McGuane), 253
Sometimes a Great Notion (Kesey), 180, 185
Sommer, Doris, 36
Son, The (Meyer), 123
Sone, Monica, 181, 182–3
Song of Hiawatha (Longfellow), 24
Song of the Lark, The (Cather), 152
Songs of a Sourdough (Service), 198
"Sonnet, without Salmon" (Alexie), 188
Soos, Frank, 198
South Asian American authors, 305
Southwest in American Literature and Art, The (Teague), 87
Spaghetti Westerns, 122, 236
Spalding, Eliza, 55
Spanbauer, Tom, 174
"Spectrality and the Postregional Interface" (Tatum), 220n21, 359n11
Spence, Mark, 85
Spicer, Edward, 149
Spicer, Jack, 275
Spillane, Mickey, 266
Spivak, Gayatri, 211
Spotted Elk, Molly, 232
"Spread My Ashes on Khaa Tu Kaxhsakee Heen" (Hope), 203
Spurgeon, Sara, 121, 272
Squatter and the Don, The (Ruiz de Burton), 33, 41, 53
St. Cyr, Lillian, 228
Stafford, William, 140
Stagecoach (1939), 236, 331, 335, 336
"State Painting" (Smith), 16
States of Emergency (Castronovo and Gillman), 209
Stegner, Wallace, 65, 67, 132, 170, 205, 252
Stein, Rachel, 84
Steinbeck, John, 134, 368
Sterritt, David, 279n9

Stevens, George, 117, 236, 331, 336
Steveston (Marlatt), 180
Stewart, Elinore Pruitt, 167, 171
Stewart, James, 336
Stewart, Kathleen, 383, 384
Stone Heart (Glancy), 23
"Story of One White Woman Who Married a Chinese, The" (Eaton/Sui Sin Far), 305
Straight Shooting (1917), 236
Strangers on a Train (Highsmith), 263
Strayed, Cheryl, 184
Streamas, John, 301
Strong Man (Hope), 202
Strongheart, Nipo T., 232
Sturges, John, 331
"Subjects of Empire" (Coulthard), 296n23
Sukdu Nel Nuhghelnek (Johnson), 199
Sukiyaki Western Django (2007), 122
Surfer Girls in the New World Order (Comer), 219n8
Surrounded, The (McNickle), 206
Swift, Jonathan, 186

Tafolla, Rev. Santiago, 33
Tall T, The (1958), 336
TallMountain, Mary, 200
Tapahonso, Luci, 145
Tar Sands, 168
Tarantino, Quentin, 341, 342
Tatum, Stephen, 9, 12n26, 78, 92, 210, 218n3, 274, 359n11, 376, 386n13
Taylor, Charles, 117
Teague, David, 87
Teatro Campesino, 37, 39
Tender Mercies (1983), 137
Thacker, Robert, 132, 137, 142n16
"There Are No More Words to the Story" (Mathers), 194
They Shoot Horses, Don't They (McCoy), 260
This Incomparable Lande (Lyon), 88
"This Is What It Means to Say Phoenix, Arizona" (Alexie), 189
Thom, Brian, 204
Thompson, Era Bell, 316, 317
Thompson, Hunter S., 277, 278
Thompson, Jim, 261
Thoreau, Henry David, 68, 75–6, 82, 86, 87, 88, 89
3:10 to Yuma (2007), 341
Thrush, Coll, 27
Tintin in America (Herge), 122
To the Far Blue Mountains (Lamour), 242
Tombstone (1993), 340
Tompkins, Jane, 120
Tonkovich, Nicole, 7

"Topographies of Transition in Western American Literature" (Tatum), 218n3
topophilia, 140
Townsend, James W. E., 98–9
Tracks (Erdrich), 135, 252, 283
Train Dreams (Johnson), 169
Tramp Across the Continent, A (Lummis), 151
Trans-Americanity (Saldívar), 219n6
Trans-Indigenous (Allen), 10n1, 26
Transit of Empire (Byrd), 2
Translation of Dr. Apelles, The (Treuer), 284
Transnational Beat Generation, The (Grace and Skerl), 279n3
transnational regionalism, 5
transnational studies, 3, 19, 92, 147, 155, 158, 205, 206, 209, 210, 212, 231, 271, 274, 305, 306, 310, 354, 355, 358, 377, 384
Travels in Alaska (Muir), 86
Treaty of Guadalupe Hidalgo, the, 53, 54, 147, 150
Tree of Life, The (2011), 141
Treuer, David, 284
Tribal Map (Smith), 15
Tribal Map II (Smith), 15
"Tribe Called Wannabe, The" (Green), 238n9
Trip to Bountiful, The (1985), 137
Tropic of Orange (Yamashita), 310, 356, 384–6
Troutman, John, 227
True Grit (1969), 321, 339
True Grit (2010), 340, 341
True History of the Kelly Gang (Carey), 122
True Remedy for the Wrongs of Women (Whitman, C.), 52
Truth About Stories, The (King), 202
Tuan, Yi-Fu, 140
Tularosa (McGarrity), 265
Tundra Times, 199
Turner, Frederick Jackson, 31, 89, 205, 245, 272, 273, 274, 299, 337, 338, 351, 354, 375, 382
Turquoise Ledge, The (Silko), 145
Twain, Mark, 20, 60, 70, 76, 77–8, 98–9, 103, 170, 368
Twilight Los Angeles, 1992 (Smith), 327
Two Old Women (Wallis), 201

U.S. empire, 5, 17, 37, 83, 116, 120, 151, 306, 308
"Uncle Good Intentions" (Silook), 201
Under Burning Skies (1912), 236
Under Mount St. Elias (De Laguna), 197
Under the Texas Sun (Espinoza), 33
"Under the Wheat" (DeMarinis), 169
Unforgiven (1992), 331, 340, 341
Union Pacific (1939), 335
Unknown Man #89 (Leonard), 267
Unsettling the Literary West (Lewis), 168, 170

Updating the Literary West (Lyon), 166
urban West, the, 169, 174, 178, 201, 256, 259, 261, 298, 308, 309, 311, 314, 324, 326, 327, 346, 347, 352, 375, 384, 385
Urrea, Luis, 157

Valaskakis, Gail Guthrie, 28n4
Valdez de Beremende, Doña María Gertrudis, 54
Valdez, Luis, 37
Valdez, Luis and Stan Steiner, 37
Vallejo, M. G., 36, 38
van Houten, Christina, 211
Van Peebles, Mario, 340
Vancouver, George, 185
Vanderhaeghe, Guy, 198
Vanishing American, The (1925), 233
Vanishing American, The (Grey), 120
vaquero, 215, 226, 235
Varela, Félix, 32
"Vaster than Empires and More Slow" (Le Guin), 183
vaudeville, 227, 229, 230, 231, 233, 320
Velásquez, Gloria, 39
Venegas, Daniel, 33, 35
Venturi, Robert, 349
Verbinski, Gore, 123, 233
"Vicious Circle" (McGuane), 173
Vidler, Anthony, 350
Vidor, King, 334
Vietnam War, 120, 183, 266, 308, 326
Vietnamese American authors, 308–9
Villanueva, Tino, 212
Villareal, José Antonio, 39
Villegas de Magnón, Leonor, 33
violence, 2, 20, 42, 50, 91, 93, 102, 113, 129, 133, 146, 150, 157, 188, 206, 234, 256, 258, 259, 261, 263, 266, 267, 293, 300, 326, 327, 328, 338, 354, 364, 367, 381, 382, 385
Violence Over the Land (Blackhawk), 22
Virgin Land (1950), 343n15
Virginian, The (1914), 234
Virginian, The (Wister), 66, 112, 121, 134, 205, 234, 244, 333, 366
film and television versions of, 235
Vizenor, Gerald, 23, 227, 285–6
Vlautin, Willy, 378, 381–4

Wagoner, David, 188
Wald, Sarah D., 95n20
Walden (Thoreau), 76
Walker, Franklin, 100
Walker, Janet, 241n58
"Walking" (Thoreau), 68, 86
"Walking Out" (Quammen), 169
Wallis, Velma, 201

Walsh, Raoul, 334
Warren, Adelia Otero, 38
Warshow, Robert, 113
Washburn, Frances, 23
Washington, Booker T., 317
Waterman, T. T., 18
Way to Rainy Mountain, The (Momaday), 283
Way West, The (Guthrie), 174, 205
Way Winter Comes, The (Simpson), 198
Wayne, John, 232, 236, 321, 334, 336, 339, 345, 347
We Should Never Meet (Phan), 308, 309
Webb, Walter Prescott, 141
Weigman, Robin, 209
Welch, James, 26, 140, 169, 252
Welch, Lew, 275
Weltzien, O. Alan, 167
"West" (Comer), 220n18
West of Here (Evison), 123
West, Elliot, 82, 87, 94, 131
West, Nathaniel, 260
Westbrook, Max, 164
Western American Literature (journal), 163
Western in the Global South, The (Higgins,
      Keresztesi, and Oscherwitz), 111n9
Western Literature Association, 163, 280n13
western tall tales, 102, 104, 107
Westerner, The (1940), 335
westerns
   codes and conventions of, 111, 242, 332, 337,
      363, 364
   relation to colonial matrix (Mignolo), 6
   relation to settler colonialism, 6
westerns (fiction and film), 111–23
westerns (fiction)
   African American authors, 318, 321
   American Indian authors, 24
   Australian tradition of, 122
   French tradition of, 122, 123
   in comics, 122, 123
   in dime novel tradition, 77, 114, 205, 226,
      315, 321
   in global contexts, 111, 122
   relation to the detective story, 113, 114, 115
westerns (film), 225–37, 331
   African American tradition of, 236
   after 9/11, 2, 341
   Australian tradition of, 122
   and the Cold War, 338, 341
   and the Deer family, 230
   in global contexts, 1, 122
   Indigenous filmmakers, 228, 233, 237, 241n57
   Italian tradition of, 122
   Japanese tradition of, 122
   relation to science fiction, 123
   restoring Native presence in, 225

   and singing cowboys, 334
   and the Vietnam War, 341
   and violence against gay men, 363, 365, 367
Westerns (Mitchell), 363
westerns (television series), 115, 122
Wexler, Laura, 55
Whalen, Philip, 275
Whedon, Joss, 111
Wheeler, Edward L., 114
When the Emperor Was Divine (Otsuka), 301
"When Was the Post-Colonial?" (Hall), 387n19
Where Clouds Are Formed (Zepeda), 147
Where the Buffalo Roam (Matthews), 138
white settler women, 49–61, 186
   beliefs about race and labor, 53
   contributions to local color movement, 57
   and politics of adoption, 55
   and politics of motherhood, 54
   promotional writings of, 56
   relation to Indian reform, 59
   and role of education in colonization, 52
   and state-making processes, 49
   and tender violence, 55
White, Gilbert, 91
White, Matt, 138
White, Richard, 348
Whitfield, Raoul, 259
Whitman, Catharine, 52
Whitman, Marcus, 52, 55, 56, 186
Whitman, Narcissa, 55, 56, 186
Whitman, Walt, 86, 278
Who Sings the Nation State? (Spivak), 211
Who Would Have Thought It? (Ruiz de
      Burton), 33, 39
"Why I Returned" (Bontemps), 325
Wild (Strayed), 184
Wild Bunch, The (1969), 339
Wild Meat and the Bully Burgers
      (Yamanaka), 306
"Wild Word Hunters" (Gamber), 295n21
Wilder, Laura Ingalls, 58, 134, 140
wilderness, 68, 72, 84, 85, 86, 117, 163
Williams, John, 378–9, 382
Williams, Tennessee, 137
Williams, Terry Tempest, 90, 154, 169
Winchester '73 (1950), 336
Wind from an Enemy Sky (McNickle), 169
Wind, The (Scarborough), 132
Winnemucca, Sarah, 21, 23–4
Winning of the West, The (Roosevelt), 134
Winona (Hopkins), 58
Winter in the Blood (Welch), 169
Wister, Owen, 66, 77, 86, 112, 121, 134, 205, 234,
      236, 244, 333, 366, 368
With His Pistol in His Hand (Paredes), 39, 121

"'With Powder Smoke and Profanity'"
  (Witschi), 110n8
Witschi, Nicolas S., 8, 110, 167, 308
Wittig, Ben, 150
Woiwode, Larry, 140
Wolf Willow (Stegner), 132, 205
Wolfe, Patrick, 212, 213, 282, 293
Wolfville (Lewis), 66
Wollen, Peter, 337
Womack, Craig, 18, 26, 283, 284
Women of the Beat Generation (Knight), 279n7
Women Writing Nature (Cook and Hunt), 91
Wong, Cynthia Sau-ling, 299, 303
Woody, Elizabeth, 25
Worden, Daniel, 8, 368
Working-Class Movement in America, The
  (Aveling and Aveling), 66
Worster, Donald, 91
Wounded (Everett), 322–3
Wright, Will, 237
Wright, William, 99, 337
Wrobel, David M., 56
Wyatt Earp (1994), 340

Wyckoff, William, 4
Wynema (Callahan), 22

Yahgulanaas, Michael Nicoll, 19, 202
Yamamoto, Hisaye, 301
Yamanaka, Lois-Ann, 306
Yamashita, Karen Tei, 310, 355, 356, 378, 384–6
Ybarra, Priscilla, 84, 85
Yellow Back Radio Broke-Down (Reed), 111, 318–21
"yellow peril," 105, 298, 299
Yonnondio (Olsen), 134
York, 314
Young Deer, James, 228, 237
Young, Alex, 209
Yupiaq Worldview, A (Kawagley), 199

Zappa, Frank, 162
Zavala, Lorenzo de, 32
Zepeda, Ofelia, 147–8
Zinneman, Fred, 236, 331, 336
Zitkala-Sa, 84, 85
Žižek, Slavoj, 360n25
Zupan, Kim, 174